Contents at a Glance

Ivor Horton's
Beginning ANSI C++:
The Complete Language,
Third Edition

IVOR HORTON

Apress™

Ivor Horton's Beginning ANSI C++: The Complete Language, Third Edition
Copyright ©2004 by Ivor Horton

ISBN (pbk): 1-59059-227-1

Printed and bound in the United States of America 10987654321

Technical Reviewer: Gabriel Dos Reis

Editorial Board: Steve Anglin, Dan Appleman, Gary Cornell, James Cox, Tony Davis, John Franklin, Chris Mills, Steven Rycroft, Dominic Shakeshaft, Julian Skinner, Martin Streicher, Jim Sumser, Karen Watterson, Gavin Wray, John Zukowski

Assistant Publisher and Project Manager: Grace Wong

Copy Manager: Nicole LeClerc

Copy Editor: Rebecca Rider

Production Manager: Kari Brooks

Production Editor: Janet Vail

Proofreader: Lori Bring

Compositor: Diana Van Winkle, Van Winkle Design

Cover Designer: Kurt Krames

Manufacturing Manager: Tom Debolski

Distributed to the book trade in the United States by Springer-Verlag New York, Inc., 175 Fifth Avenue, New York, NY, 10010 and outside the United States by Springer-Verlag GmbH & Co. KG, Tiergartenstr. 17, 69112 Heidelberg, Germany.

In the United States: phone 1-800-SPRINGER, email orders@springer-ny.com, or visit http://www.springer-ny.com. Outside the United States: fax +49 6221 345229, email orders@springer.de, or visit http://www.springer.de.

For information on translations, please contact Apress directly at 2560 Ninth Street, Suite 219, Berkeley, CA 94710. Phone 510-549-5930, fax 510-549-5939, email info@apress.com, or visit http://www.apress.com.

The source code for this book is available to readers at http://www.apress.com in the Downloads section.

Contents

Chapter 19 Input and Output Operations *863*

Chapter 20 Introducing the
Standard Template Library *939*

About the Author

Ivor Horton started out as a mathematician but after graduating, was lured into messing around with computers by a well-known manufacturer. He has spent many happy years programming occasionally useful applications in a variety of languages as well as teaching scientists and engineers to do likewise. He has extensive experience in applying computers to problems in engineering design and manufacturing operations. He is the author of a number of tutorial books on programming in C, C++, and Java. When not writing programming books or providing advice to others, he leads a life of leisure.

About the Author

Ivor Horton started out as a mathematician but after graduating was lured into business dealing with computers by a well-known manufacturer. He has spent many happy years programming occasionally useful applications in a variety of languages as well as teaching people how and designing to go hardware. He has extensive experience in applying computers to problems in engineering design and manufacturing operations. He is the author of a number of tutorial books on programming in C, C++, and Java. When not writing programming books or providing advice to others, he leads a life of leisure.

About the
Technical Reviewer

Gabriel Dos Reis graduated with a Ph.D in Mathematics as a differential geometer from École Normale Supérieure de Cachan and Université Paris VII (France). He is an active member of the ISO C++ standards committee and the C and C++ Experts Group of AFNOR (French national body for standards). Since 1996, he has been working on applications of C++ and generic programming in the area of scientific computations; in particular, he has been involved in international computational projects ranging from polynomial systems solving to computer-aided design. He is an active contributor and maintainer of the GNU C++ standard library and has served as release manager of the GNU Compiler Collection. He is a regularly invited speaker at worldwide C++ conferences.

Dr. Dos Reis' main research topics include computer science methods in differential geometry, scientific computations, generic programming, and programming tools and techniques. He can be reached at gdr@integrable-solutions.net.

Acknowledgments

I'D LIKE TO THANK Gary Cornell for being so enthusiastic about putting together this new edition and for his help in getting the whole thing started. I'd also like to thank all the people at Apress who worked so hard to convert my initial efforts into this finished product. Among those, I'd especially like to thank Nicole LeClerc and Rebecca Rider who managed to interpret so many of my obscurities and made the book more readable.

My heartfelt thanks also go to those readers of previous editions who took the trouble to point out my mistakes and areas that could be better explained. I also greatly appreciate all those who wrote or e-mailed just to say how much they enjoyed the book or how it helped them get started in programming.

Finally I'd like to thank my wife, Eve, who makes it all possible. She remains unfailingly cheerful and supportive, pandering to my every need, even in the face of my incessant grumblings about my self-imposed workload.

Introduction

WELCOME TO *Beginning ANSI C++: The Complete Language, Third Edition*. This is a tutorial guide to Standard C++. During the course of the book you'll cover all the fundamentals of syntax, grammar, object-oriented capability, and the principal features of the standard library. You'll soon gain enough programming know-how to write your own C++ applications.

Why C++?

C++ is arguably the most widely used programming language in existence. It's used in professional application development because of its immense flexibility, power, and efficiency. For high-performance code across a vast range of programming contexts, C++ is unrivalled.

It's also much more accessible than many people assume. With the right guidance, getting a grip on C++ is easier than you might imagine. By developing your C++ skills, you'll learn a language already used by millions, and you'll acquire a new tool in your programming toolbox that is likely to be more powerful than any of the others.

The Standard for C++

In 1998, the International Standard for C++, ISO/IEC 14882, was finally approved and adopted by the American National Standards Institute (ANSI) and the International Committee for Information Technology Standards (INCITS). This was the culmination of nine years of work by a joint ANSI/ISO committee whose objective was to establish a single definition of the C++ programming language that would be accepted worldwide. Although at the time of this writing the 1998 standard is still current, the work of improving the language is ongoing and may well result in further features being added to C++ in the future.

The 1998 standard for C++ provides a single blueprint for compiler writers to work from. The result is that today many, but unfortunately not all, C++ compilers conform closely to the standard. If you endeavor to use compilers that conform to the standard, you'll maximize the portability of your code, and in the future, you'll avoid being caught by the vagaries of non-standard language elements.

Of course, the standard for C++ has been defined so that it can be used as the reference frame for the development of compilers in any hardware or operating system context. Also, it has been defined with the intention of providing the possibility for maximizing performance in any development context. This means the compiler writer has considerable flexibility in many areas to accommodate differences in machine architecture. For instance, definitions relating to numerical data and arithmetic operations are defined so that the compiler writer can take full advantage of the individual characteristics of particular machines so that that they can optimize execution performance. The compiler writer also chooses the encoding for the characters that are used to define C++ programs. In this way, variations in the default character encoding in various operating systems can be accommodated. Without this kind of flexibility, the standard would impose constraints that might result in poor performance in particular computers, which is not a desirable trait for a general purpose programming language.

Within the book, I'll point out where you're likely to encounter significant potential variations between machines. However, I needed a practical working context to show output from the examples in the book. Therefore, I've executed all the examples on a PC with the Intel processor architecture.

Errata and Updates

I and the editorial staff at Apress have made every effort to make sure the text and code have no errors. However, to err is human, and because I can certainly claim to be that, at least after around 9:30 a.m., it's quite possible that a few of my errors are buried within the thousand or so pages that follow. If you want to check whether any of my mistakes have been discovered, I recommend that you go to this web page on the Apress website:

`http://www.apress.com/book/download.html`

If you select this book's title from the list on this page, not only will you be able to download the errata list and the code for all the examples in the book, you'll also be able to record any other mistakes that you find. The code download also contains the solutions to all of the exercises, but I recommend you don't look at them before you have tried extremely hard to complete them on your own.

Using the Book

To learn C++ with this book, you'll need an ANSI/ISO-compliant compiler and a text editor suitable for working with program code. Most compilers that come with professionally produced C++ development environments conform to the standard these days, but it's a good idea to check before you buy. Also, some of the freeware and open source C++ compilers that are available on the Internet are consistent with the C++ standard. You could combine one of these with a freeware program text editor to make an economical but workable learning context.

I've organized the material in this book to be read sequentially, so you should start at the beginning and keep going until you reach the end. However, no one ever learned programming by just reading a book. You'll only learn how to program in C++ by writing code, so make sure you key in all the examples—don't just copy them from the download files—and compile and execute the code that you've keyed in. This might seem tedious at times, but it's surprising how much just typing in C++ statements will help your understanding, especially when you may feel you're struggling with some of the ideas. If an example doesn't work, resist the temptation to go straight back to the book to see why. Try to figure out from your code what is wrong. This is good practice for what you'll have to do when you are writing C++ code for real.

Making your own mistakes is also a fundamental part of the learning process and the exercises should provide you with ample opportunity for that. The more mistakes you make, the greater the insight you'll have into what can and does go wrong. Make sure to complete all the exercises, and remember, don't look at the solutions until you're sure that you can't work it out yourself. Many of these exercises just involve a direct application of what's covered in a chapter—they're just practice, in other words—but some also require a bit of thought or maybe even inspiration.

I wish you every success with C++. Above all, enjoy it!

—Ivor Horton

CHAPTER 1

Basic Ideas

AT FIRST SIGHT, a connection between learning C++ programming and poultry would seem to be unlikely, but there is—it's the chicken-and-egg problem. Particularly in the early stages of understanding C++, you'll often have to make use of things in examples before you properly understand them. This chapter is intended to solve the chicken-and-egg problem by giving you an overview of the C++ language and how it hangs together, and by introducing a few of the working concepts for things that you'll be using before you have a chance to understand them in detail.

All the concepts that you'll read about here are covered in more detail in later chapters. Most of this information is just to set the scene before you get into the specifics of writing C++ programs. You'll see what a simple C++ program looks like, and then you'll pull it to pieces to get a rough idea of what the various bits do. You'll also look at the broad concepts of programming in C++ and how you create an executable program from the source code files you'll be writing.

Don't try to memorize all the information in this chapter. Concentrate on getting a feel for the ideas presented here. Everything mentioned in this chapter will come up again in later chapters. Here's an overview of what this chapter covers:

- What the features of C++ are that make it so popular

- What the elements of a basic C++ program are

- How to document your program source code

- How your source code becomes an executable program

- How object-oriented programming differs from procedural programming

Programming Languages

You're probably familiar with the basic ideas of programming and programming languages, but to make sure we're on common ground, let's do a quick survey of some of the terms you'll encounter as you progress through the book. You can also put C++ into perspective in relation to some of the other programming languages you'll have heard of.

There are lots of programming languages, each with its advantages and disadvantages, and its protagonists and detractors. Along with C++, other languages that you're likely to have come across include Java, BASIC (an acronym for **B**eginner's **A**ll-purpose **S**ymbolic **I**nstruction **C**ode), COBOL (an acronym for **C**ommon **B**usiness-**O**riented **L**anguage), FORTRAN (an acronym for **for**mula **tran**slator), Pascal (after Blaise Pascal, a French mathematician), and C (simply because it was a successor to a language called B). All of these are referred to collectively as **high-level languages**, because they're designed to make it easy for you to express what the computer is to do, and they aren't tied to a particular computer. Each source statement in a high-level language will typically map to several native machine instructions. A **low-level language** is one that is close to the native machine instructions and is usually referred to as an **assembler language**. A given assembler language will be specific to a particular hardware design, and typically one assembler instruction will map to one native machine instruction.

A Potted History

FORTRAN was the first high-level language to be developed, and the first FORTRAN compiler was written in the late 1950s. Even though FORTRAN has been around for over 40 years, it's still used today for scientific and engineering calculations although C++ and other languages have eroded much of its usage.

COBOL is a language exclusively for business data processing applications, and it's almost as old as FORTRAN. Although relatively little new code is written in COBOL, there is an immense amount of code that was written years ago that's still in use and still has to be maintained. Again, C++ has become the language of choice for many business data processing programs.

BASIC emerged in the 1970s when the idea of a personal computer was being conceived. Interestingly, the first product sold by Microsoft was a BASIC interpreter. The ease of use inherent in the language resulted in a rapid growth in its popularity that continues to this day.

Java was developed in the 1990s. Its original incarnation as a language called Oak was really intended for programming small consumer electronics devices. In 1995 Oak evolved into the Java language for embedding code in web pages and from there into what it is today. The primary reason for the success of Java is its portability. A Java program can run unchanged on any hardware platform that supports it. The syntax of the Java language has many characteristics that make it look similar to C++, but there are significant differences. Although Java gains over C++ on portability, it can't match C++ in execution performance.

C was developed in the early 1970s as a high-level language that could be used for low-level programming, such as implementing operating systems. Most of the Unix operating system is written in C.

C++ was developed by Bjarne Stroustrup in the early 1980s as an object-oriented language based on C. Hence the name, C++, which in C++ means C incremented. Because C++ is based on C, the two languages share a common subset of syntax and functionality, and all of the capabilities in C for low-level programming are retained in C++. However, C++ is a much richer and more versatile language than its ancestor. The vastly improved memory management features and the object-oriented capabilities of C++ means that C functionality represents a very small subset of C++. C++ is still unrivaled in scope, performance, and power. For this reason, the majority of high-performance applications and systems are still written in C++ today.

Interpreted vs. Compiled Program Execution

Whatever the programming language, the programs that you write are made up of separate **instructions** or **source statements** that describe the actions that you want the computer to carry out. These are referred to collectively as **source code** and are stored on disk in a **source file**. A single C++ program of any size will consist of several source files.

Programming languages are designed to make it relatively easy for you to describe the actions you want a computer to carry out compared with the form of program that a computer can actually execute. Your computer can only execute programs that consist of **machine instructions** (also called **machine code**), so it can't execute your program's source code directly. There are basically two ways in which a program written in one of the languages I mentioned previously can get executed and, for the most part, a particular language will use one or the other. Programs written in BASIC, for example, are often **interpreted**—that is, another program called an **interpreter** inspects the BASIC source code, figures out what it's supposed to do, and then causes that to be done. This is illustrated on the left side of Figure 1-1.

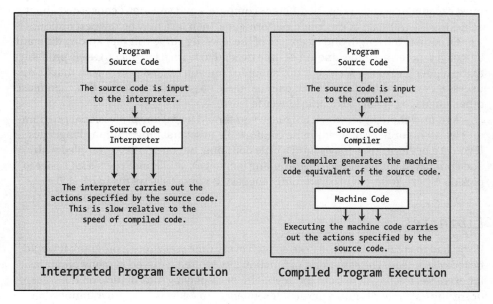

Figure 1-1. Interpreted and compiled program execution

C++, on the other hand, is usually a **compiled** language. Before you can execute your C++ program, it must be converted to machine language by another program called a **compiler**. The compiler inspects and analyzes the C++ program and generates the machine instructions that will produce the actions specified by the source code. Of course, in reality neither interpreting nor compiling is quite as simple as I've described them here, but in principle that's how they work.

With an interpreted language, execution is "indirect," by which I mean the intent of the source code needs to be determined each time a program is executed. For this reason, execution is much slower—sometimes of the order of 100 times slower—than the equivalent program in a compiled language. The upside is that you don't have to wait and compile a program before you run it. With an interpreted language, as soon as you've entered the code, you can execute the program immediately. A given language is usually *either* compiled *or* interpreted, and it's typically the design and intended use of the language that determines which. Having described BASIC as an interpreted language, I should point out that it isn't exclusively so; there are compilers for the BASIC language.

The question of which language is the "best" language sometimes comes up. The short answer is that there is no such thing as the "best" language—it depends on the context. Writing a program in BASIC is typically very rapid compared with most other languages, for instance, so if speed of development is important to you and obtaining the maximum execution performance isn't, then BASIC is an excellent choice. On the other hand, if your program requires the execution performance that C++ provides, or you need the capabilities in your application that are available in C++ but not in BASIC, then C++ is obviously what you would use. If your application really must execute on a wide range of different computers and you aren't concerned about achieving the ultimate in execution performance, then Java may be the best option.

Of course, the length and steepness of the learning curve will vary among different languages. In terms of the amount of time needed to learn a language, C++ is probably at the higher end of the scale, but this shouldn't put you off. It doesn't mean that C++ is necessarily more difficult. It does mean that there's a great deal more to C++ than most other languages, so it takes a little longer to learn.

As a final thought on which language you should learn, any professional programmer worth his or her salt needs to be comfortable in several programming languages. If you're a beginner, this may sound a little daunting, but once you've grappled with and conquered your first two programming languages, you'll find it gets a lot easier to pick up others. Your first programming language is almost always the hardest.

Libraries

If you had to create everything from scratch every time you wrote a program, it would be tedious indeed. The same kind of functionality is often required in many programs—for example, reading data from the keyboard, or displaying information on the screen, or sorting data records into a particular sequence. To address this, programming languages usually come supplied with considerable quantities of prewritten code that provides standard facilities such as these, so you don't have to write the code for them yourself every time.

Standard code that's available for you to use in any of your programs is kept in a **library**. The library that comes with a particular programming language is as important as the language itself, as the quality and scope of the library can have a significant effect on how long it takes you to complete a given programming task.

Why Is C++ Such a Great Language?

C++ enjoys extraordinary popularity across virtually all computing environments: personal computers, Unix workstations, and mainframe computers. This is all the more remarkable when you consider the degree to which history weighs against a new programming language, no matter how good it is. The inertia implicit in the number of programs written in previous languages inevitably slows the acceptance of a new language. Added to this, there's always a tendency among most professional programmers to stick with what they know and are expert and productive in, rather than jump in at the deep end with something new and unfamiliar, in which it will take time to develop fluency. Of course, the fact that C++ was built on C (which itself was the language of choice in many environments before the advent of C++) helped tremendously, but there's a great deal more to it than that. C++ provides you with a unique combination of advantages:

- C++ is effective across an incredible range of applications. You can apply C++ to just about anything, from word processing to scientific applications, and from operating system components to computer games.

- C++ can be used for programming down at the hardware level—for implementing device drivers, for instance.

- C++ combines the facility for efficient procedural programming that it inherits from C with a powerful object-oriented programming capability.

- C++ provides extensive facilities in its **standard library**.

- There are many commercial libraries supporting a wide range of operating system environments and specialized applications for C++.

You'll also find that just about any computer can be programmed in C++, so the language is pervasive across almost all computer platforms. This means that it is possible to transfer a program written in C++ from one machine to another with relatively limited effort. Of course, if this is truly going to be a straightforward process, you need to have in mind when you write the program that you intend to run it on a different machine.

The ANSI/ISO Standard for C++

The international standard for C++ is defined by the document ISO/IEC 14882, which is published by the American National Standards Institute (ANSI). You can get a copy of this standard if you wish, but remember, the standard is intended for use by compiler writers, not by students of the language. If that hasn't discouraged you, you can download a copy for a relatively reasonable fee from http://webstore.ansi.org/ansidocstore/default.asp.

Standardization of a language is fundamental when you want to transfer a program written for one type of computer to another. The establishment of a standard makes possible a consistent implementation of the language across a variety of machines. A full set of standard facilities across all conforming programming systems means that you'll always know exactly what you're going to get. The ANSI standard for C++ defines not only the language, but also the standard library. Using the ANSI standard for C++ makes the migration of applications between different machines easier and eases the problems of maintaining applications that run in more than one environment.

Another benefit of the ANSI standard for C++ is that it standardizes what you need to learn in order to program in C++ in any environment. The existence of the standard itself forces conformance over time, because it provides the only definitive reference for what a C++ compiler and library should provide. It removes the license to be "flexible" that compiler writers have had in the absence of an agreed standard, so when you buy a C++ compiler that conforms to the ANSI standard, you know what language and standard library capabilities you're going to get.

A Simple C++ Program

Let's take a look at a very simple C++ program and find out what its constituents are. You don't need to enter this code right now; it's just here so that you can get a feel for what goes into making up a program. I don't go into all the details at the moment either, as everything that appears here will be explored at length in later chapters. Figure 1-2 illustrates a simple C++ program.

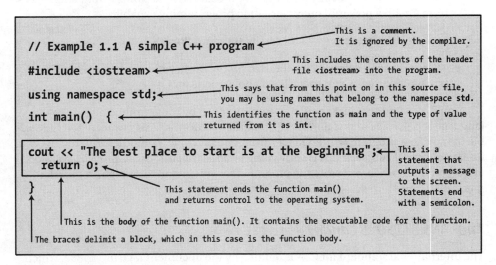

Figure 1-2. A simple C++ program

The program shown in Figure 1-2 displays the following message:

```
The best place to start is at the beginning
```

This isn't a very useful program, but it serves to demonstrate a few points. The program consists of a single function, main(). A **function** is a self-contained block of code that's referenced by a name, main in this case. There may be a lot of other code in a program, but *every* C++ application consists of at least the function main(). There can be only one function called main() within a program, and execution of a C++ program always starts with the first statement in main().

The first line of the function is

```
int main()
```

which identifies that this is the start of a function with the name main. The int at the beginning indicates that this function will return an integer value when it finishes executing. Because it's the function main(), the value will be received by the operating system that calls it in the first place.

This function main() contains two executable statements, each on a separate line:

```
cout << "The best place to start is at the beginning";
return 0;
```

These two statements are executed in sequence. In general, the statements in a function are always executed sequentially, unless there's a statement that specifically alters the sequence of execution. You'll see what sorts of statements can do that in Chapter 4.

In C++, input and output are preferably performed using **streams**. If you want to output something from a program, you put it into an output stream, and when you want something to be input, you get it from an input stream. A stream is thus an abstract representation of a source of data, or a data sink. When your program executes, each stream is tied to a specific device that is the source of data in the case of an input stream and the destination for data in the case of an output stream. The advantage of having an abstract representation of a source or sink for data is that the programming is the same regardless of what the stream actually represents. You can read data from a disk file in essentially the same way as you read from the keyboard, for instance. The standard output and input streams in C++ are called cout and cin, and by default they correspond to your computer's screen and keyboard, respectively.

The first line of code in main() outputs the character string "The best place to start is at the beginning" to your screen by placing it in the output stream, cout, using the **insertion operator,<<**. When we come to write programs that involve input, you'll see its partner, the **extraction operator**, >>.

A **header** contains code defining a set of standard facilities that you can include in a program source file when required. The facilities provided by the C++ standard library are stored in headers, but headers aren't exclusively for that. You'll create your own header files containing your own code. The name cout referred to in this program is defined in the header iostream. This is a standard header that provides the definitions necessary for you to use the standard input and output facilities in C++. If your program didn't include the following line:

```
#include <iostream>
```

then it wouldn't compile, because the <iostream> header contains the definition of cout, and without it the compiler can't know what cout is. This line is an example of what is called a **preprocessing directive**, which you'll investigate in depth later in the book. The effect of the #include is to insert the contents of the <iostream> header into your program source file at the point where the directive appears. This is done before your program is compiled.

 TIP *Note that there are no spaces between the angled brackets and the standard header name. With many compilers, spaces are significant between the two angled brackets, < and >; if you insert any spaces here, the program may not compile.*

The second and final statement in the body of the function name is

```
return 0;
```

This ends the program and returns control to your operating system. It also returns the value zero to the operating system. Other values can be returned to indicate different end conditions for the program and can be used by the operating system to determine if the program executed successfully. Typically, zero indicates a normal end to a program, and any nonzero value indicates an abnormal end. However, whether or not a nonzero return value can be acted upon will depend on the operating system concerned.

Names

Lots of things in a C++ program have **names** that are used to refer to them. Such names are also referred to as **identifiers**. There are five kinds of things that you'll give names to in your C++ programs:

- **Functions** are self-contained, named blocks of executable code. Chapter 8 goes into detail on how to define these.

- **Variables** are named areas in memory that you use to store items of data. You'll start with these in Chapter 2.

- **Types** are names for the *kinds* of data that you can store. The type int, for example, is used for integers (whole numbers). You'll see something on these in Chapter 2 and more in subsequent chapters, particularly Chapter 11.

- **Labels** provide a means of referring to a particular statement. These are rarely used, but you'll look at them in action in Chapter 4.

- **Namespaces** are a way of gathering a set of named items in your program under a single name. If that sounds confusing, don't worry—I'll say more about them shortly, and you'll look at them again in Chapter 10.

In C++, you can construct a name using the upper- and lowercase Latin letters *a* to *z* and *A* to *Z*, the underscore character (_), and the digits 0 to 9. The ANSI standard for C++ also permits Universal Character Set (UCS) characters to be included in a name for reasons I cover in a moment.

The ANSI standard allows names to be of any length, but typically a particular compiler will impose some sort of length limit. However, this is normally sufficiently large (several thousand characters) that it doesn't represent a serious constraint.

Whitespace is the term used in C++ to refer to spaces, vertical and horizontal tabs, and newline and form-feed characters. You must not put whitespace characters in the middle of a name. If you do, the single name won't be seen by the compiler as such; it will be seen as two or more names, and therefore it won't be processed correctly. Another restriction is that names may not begin with a digit.

Here are some examples of legal names:

```
value2   Mephistopheles   BettyMay   Earth_Weight   PI
```

Here are some names that aren't legal:

```
8Ball      Mary-Ann     Betty+May   Earth-Weight   2PI
```

 CAUTION *Note that names that contain a double underscore (_ _) or start with an underscore followed by an uppercase letter are reserved for use by the C++ standard library, so you shouldn't choose such names for use in your programs. Your compiler probably won't check for this, so you'll only find out that you have a conflicting name when things go wrong!*

Names Using Extended Character Sets

As mentioned in the previous section, the C++ standard permits UCS characters to be included in a name. You can write them in the form \Udddddddd or the form \udddd, where d is a hexadecimal digit in the UCS code for the character.

No one really expects anyone to include characters in names like this, though. Embedding \U followed by a bunch of hexadecimal digits in a name would hardly improve the readability of the code. The purpose of allowing UCS characters in a name is to allow compiler writers to accommodate names written in characters for national languages other than English, such as Greek, or Korean, or Russian, for instance.

The C++ standard allows a compiler to be implemented so that any characters can be used to specify a name. Any compiler that takes advantage of this must then translate the characters that aren't in the basic set to the standard representation for UCS characters noted previously, before the compilation of the code begins. In the source code someone may write the name Книга, which will be meaningful to a Russian programmer. Internally the compiler will convert this name to one of the two standardized representations of UCS characters before it compiles the code, perhaps as /u041A/u043D/u0438/ u0433/u0430. Indeed, regardless of the character set used to write names in the source, it will always end up as characters from the basic set that you saw initially, plus possibly UCS characters as \Udddddddd or as \udddd.

You must always use the basic set of characters *a* to *z*, *A* to *Z*, 0 to 9, and the underscore in a name as explicit characters. Using the UCS codes for these characters in a name is illegal. The reason for this is that the standard doesn't specify the encoding to be used for the basic set of characters, so this is left to the compiler. Consequently, if you were to specify any of the basic characters by its UCS code, it's possible it will be different from the encoding used by the compiler when the character is specified explicitly with the obvious chaotic result.

Note that it isn't a requirement that any given compiler must support the use of explicit national language characters in specifying names. If it does, they must be mapped into the UCS form before processing. A compiler that conforms to the standard must in any event support names in the basic character set plus the use of UCS characters in the somewhat unfriendly forms noted at the beginning of this section.

Namespaces

I'm sure that you noticed there was a line in the simple C++ program that I didn't explain in the preceding discussion. To understand it, you need to know what namespaces are, and for *those* to make any sense, I had to first to tell you about names. As a reminder, the line in question was

```
using namespace std;
```

Within the rules for identifiers that I discussed in the previous section, you can choose any names that you like for things in your programs. This obviously means that you might choose a name for something that's already used for some other purpose within the standard library. Equally, if two or more programmers are working concurrently on parts of a larger project, there is potential for name collisions. Clearly, using the same name for two or more different things is bound to cause confusion, and **namespaces** are there to alleviate this problem.

A namespace name is a bit like a family name or a surname. Each individual within a family has his or her own name, and within most families each family member has a unique name. In the Smith family, for instance, there may be Jack, Jill, Jean, and Jonah, and among family members they'll refer to each other using these names. However, members of other families may have the same names as members of the Smith family. Within the Jones family, for instance, there might be John, Jean, Jeremiah, and Jonah. When Jeremiah Jones refers to Jean, it's clear that he means Jean Jones. If he wants to refer to Jean in the Smith family, he'll use the fully qualified name: Jean Smith. If you're not a member of either family, you can only be sure that people know whom you're talking about if you use the full names of individuals, such as Jack Smith or Jonah Jones.

This is pretty much how namespaces work—a namespace name is analogous to a surname. Inside a namespace, you can use the individual names of things within the namespace. From outside the namespace, you can only refer to something within the namespace by a combination of the name of the particular entity and the namespace name. The purpose of a namespace is to provide a mechanism that minimizes the possibility of accidentally duplicating names in various parts of a large program and thereby creating confusion. In general, there may be several different namespaces within a program.

The entities in the C++ standard library are all defined within a namespace called std, so the names of all the entities within the standard libraries are qualified with std. The full name of cout, therefore, is actually std::cout. Those two colons together have a very fancy title: the **scope resolution operator**. I'll have more to say about it later on. In this example, it serves to separate the namespace name, std, from the name of the stream, cout.

The using directive at the beginning of the simple C++ program indicates that you want to refer to any of the things defined within the namespace called std without specifying the namespace name each time. Continuing this analogy, it makes your program file a sort of honorary member of the std family, so you can refer to everyone by his or her first name alone. One effect of this is to obviate the need to refer to cout as std::cout, making the program code little simpler. If you were to omit the using directive, you would have to write the output statement as

```
std::cout << "The best place to start is at the beginning";
```

Of course, although this does make the code look a little more complicated, it's really a much safer and therefore better way to write the code. The effect of the using directive is to allow you to refer *any* name in the namespace without qualifying it with the namespace name. This implies that you could do so accidentally. By explicitly qualifying cout with its namespace name, you avoid the need to make all the names in the namespace accessible in your program. This means that there's no possibility of clashes between names that you choose for things you might define in your program and names that are defined in the namespace.

The program code for this example is therefore somewhat better if you write it as follows:

```
// Program 1.1 A simple C++ program
#include <iostream>
int main() {
  std::cout << "The best place to start is at the beginning";
  return 0;
}
```

However, although this is much safer code, if you had a lot more references to std::cout in the code it might begin to look very cluttered. You also have the irritation of repeatedly typing std:: in many places throughout the program. In this case, you can use a form of the using directive that just introduces a single name from a namespace into your program source file. For instance, you can introduce the name cout from the std namespace into your program file with the following directive:

```
using std::cout;
```

With this directive, you can get the best of both worlds. You can use the name cout from the std namespace in its unqualified form, and you protect yourself from accidental conflicts in your code with other names in the std namespace because they're simply not accessible without using the std qualifier. The program now looks like this:

```
// Program 1.1A A simple C++ program
#include <iostream>
using std::cout;
int main() {
  cout << "The best place to start is at the beginning";
  return 0;
}
```

Of course, you can introduce just some names from the std namespace into your program file by means of a using directive for each name. You might do this for names that you refer to frequently in your code. You can then access other names from std that you refer to relatively rarely by their fully qualified names.

There's much more to namespaces and using directives than you've seen here. You'll explore them in depth in Chapter 10.

Keywords

There are reserved words in C++, called **keywords**, that have special significance within the language. The words return and namespace that you saw earlier are examples of keywords.

You'll see many more keywords as you progress through the book. You *must* ensure that the names that you choose for entities in your program aren't the same as any of the keywords in C++. You'll find a list of all the keywords that are used in C++ in Appendix B.

NOTE *Keywords are case sensitive, as are the identifiers that you choose in your program.*

C++ Statements and Statement Blocks

Statements are the basic units for specifying what your program is to do and the data elements it acts upon. Most C++ statements end with a semicolon (;). There are quite a few different sorts of statements, but perhaps the most fundamental is a statement that introduces a name into your program source file.

A statement that introduces a name into a source file is called a **declaration**. A declaration just introduces the name and specifies what kind of thing the name refers to, as opposed to a **definition**, which results in allocation of some memory to accommodate whatever the name refers to. As it happens, most declarations are also definitions.

A **variable** is a place in memory in which you can store an item of data. Here's an example of a statement that declares a name for a variable, and defines and initializes the variable itself:

```
double result = 0.0;
```

This statement declares the name `result` will be used to refer to a variable of type `double` (declaration), causes memory to be allocated to accommodate the variable (definition), and sets its initial value to 0.0 (initialization).

Here's an example of another kind of statement called a **selection statement**:

```
if (length > 25)
  boxLength = size + 2;
```

This statement tests the condition "Is the value of `length` greater than 25?" and then executes the statement on the second line if that condition is true. The statement on the second line adds 2 to the value stored in the variable `size` and stores the result in the variable `boxLength`. If the condition tested isn't true, then the second line won't be executed, and the program will continue on its merry way by executing whatever comes next in the program.

You can enclose several statements between a pair of curly braces, { }, in which case they're referred to as a **statement block**. The body of a function is an example of a block, as you saw in the first example program where the statements in the body of the `main()` function appear between curly braces. A statement block is also referred to as a **compound statement**, because in many circumstances it can be considered as a single statement, as you'll see when we look at C++'s decision-making capabilities in Chapter 4. In fact, wherever you can put a single statement in C++, you can equally well put a block of statements between braces. As a consequence, blocks can be placed inside other blocks—this concept is called **nesting**. In fact, blocks can be nested, one within another, to any depth you need.

A statement block also has important effects on the variables that you use to store data items, but I defer discussion of this until Chapter 3, where I cover **variable scope**.

Code Presentation Style

The way in which you arrange your code visually can have a significant effect on how easy it is to understand. There are two basic aspects to this. First, you can use tabs and/or spaces to indent program statements in a manner that provides visual cues to their logic, and you can arrange matching braces that define program blocks in a consistent way so that the relationships between the blocks are apparent. Second, you can spread a single statement over two or more lines when that will improve the readability of your program. A particular convention for arranging matching braces and indenting statements is a **presentation style**.

There are a number of different presentation styles in use. The following code shows three examples of how the same code might look in three commonly used styles:

```
namespace mine {        namespace mine          namespace mine {
int test()              {                         int test()
{                       int test()                {
  if(isGood) {          {                           if(isGood) {
    good();               if(isGood)                  good();
    return 0;              good();                    return 0;
  } else                  return 0;                 } else
    return 1;           } else                       return 1;
}                         return 1;               }
}                       }                         }
--                      }                         --
                        }
```

In this book I have used the style shown on the right for all the examples. I chose this because I think it is clear without being too extravagant on space. It doesn't matter much which style you use as long as you are consistent.

Program Structure

Each of your C++ programs will consist of one or more files. By convention, there are two kinds of file that you can use to hold your source code: **header files** and **source files**. You use header files to contain code that *describes* the data types that your program needs, as well as some other sorts of declarations. These files are referred to as **header files** because you usually include them at the beginning (the "head") of your other source files. Your header files are usually distinguished by having the filename extension .h, although this is not mandatory, and other extensions, such as .hxx, are used to identify header files in some systems.

Your source files, which have the filename extension .cpp, contain function definitions—the executable code for your program. These will usually refer to declarations or definitions for data types that you have defined in your own header files. The compiler will need to know about these when it compiles your code so you specify the .h files that are needed in a .cpp file by means of #include directives at the beginning of the file. An #include directive is an instruction to the compiler to insert the contents of a particular header file into your code. You'll also need to add #include directives for any standard library header files that your code requires.

Figure 1-3 shows a program in which the source code is contained in two .cpp files and three header files. The first .cpp file uses the information from the first two header files, and the second .cpp file requires the contents of the last two header files. You'll learn more about the #include directives that do this in Chapter 10.

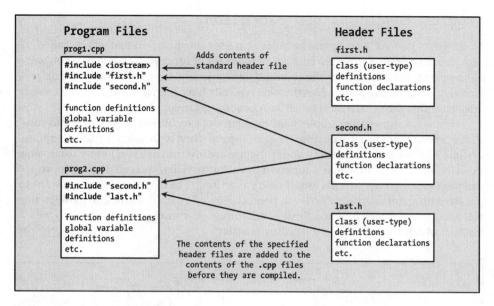

Figure 1-3. Source files in a C++ program

A number of **standard headers** are supplied with your compiler and contain declarations that you need in order to use the standard library facilities. They include, for example, declarations for the available standard library functions. The first .cpp file in Figure 1-3 includes the <iostream> header, which you met in the example C++ program. As you may have noticed, in this instance the name for the header has no extension. In fact, to distinguish them from other header files that you may use, the standard header names for C++ have no extension. The standard headers are often referred to as standard header *files* because that's how they're usually implemented. However, the C++ standard doesn't require that the headers be files, so they may not be in some implementations.

NOTE *Appendix C provides details on the ANSI/ISO standard library headers.*

Your compiler system may have a whole range of other header files, providing the definitions necessary to use operating system functions, or other goodies to save you programming effort. This example shows just a few header files in use, but in most serious C++ applications many more will be involved.

Program Functions and Execution

As already noted, a C++ program consists of at least one function that will be called main(), but typically a program consists of many other functions—some that you will have written and others from the standard library. Your program functions will be stored in a number of source files that will typically have filenames with the extension .cpp, although other extensions such as .cxx and .cc are common.

Figure 1-4 shows an example of the sequence of execution in a program that consists of several functions. Execution of main() starts when it's invoked by the operating system. All the other functions in your program are invoked by main() or by some other function in the set. You invoke a function by *calling* it. When you call a function, you can pass items of data to it for use while it's executing. The data items that you want to pass to a function are placed between parentheses following the function name in the call operation. When a function finishes executing, execution control returns to the point at which it was called in the calling function.

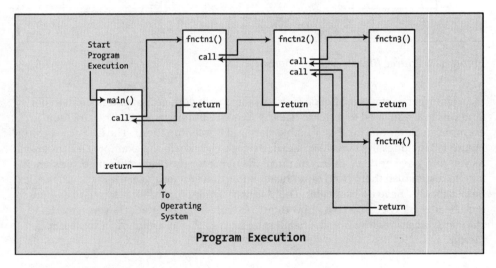

Figure 1-4. How program functions execute

A function can also return a value to the calling point when it finishes executing. The value returned can be stored for use later or it can participate in a calculation of some kind—in an arithmetic expression, for example. You'll have to wait until Chapter 8 to learn how you can create your own functions, but you'll use functions from the standard library early in the next chapter.

Creating an Executable from Your Source Files

Creating a program module that you can execute from your C++ source code is essentially a two-step process. In the first step, your **compiler** converts each .cpp file to an **object file** that contains the machine code equivalent of the source file contents. In the second step, the **linker** combines the object files produced by the compiler into a file containing the complete executable program.

Figure 1-5 shows three source files being compiled to produce three corresponding object files. The filename extension that's used to identify object files varies between different machine environments, so it isn't shown here. The source files that make up your program may be compiled independently in separate compiler runs, or most compilers will allow you to compile them in a single run. Either way, the compiler treats each source file as a separate entity and produces one object file for each .cpp file. The link step then combines the object files for a program, along with any library functions that are necessary, into a single executable file.

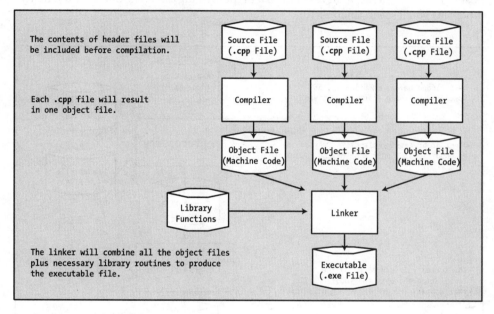

Figure 1-5. The compile and link process

In practice, compilation is an iterative process, as you're almost certain to have made typographical and other errors in the source code. Once you've eliminated these from each source file, you can progress to the link step, where you may find that yet more errors surface! Even when the link step produces an executable module, your program may still contain logical errors; that is, it doesn't produce the results you expect. To fix these, you must go back and modify the source code and start trying to get it to compile once more. You continue this process until your program works as you think it should. As soon as you declare to the world at large than your program works, someone will discover a number of obvious errors that you should have found. It hasn't been proven beyond doubt so far as I know, but it's widely believed that if a program is sufficiently large, it will always contain errors. It's best not to dwell on this thought when flying.

Let's take a closer look at what happens during the two basic steps, compiling and linking, because there are some interesting things going on under the covers.

Compiling

The compilation process for a source file has two main stages, as illustrated in Figure 1-6, but the transition between them is automatic. The first stage is the **preprocessing phase**, which is carried out before the compilation phase proper. The preprocessing phase modifies the contents of the source file according to the preprocessing directives that you have placed in the file. The #include directive, which adds the contents of a header file to a .cpp file, is an example of a preprocessing directive, but there are many others (as you'll see in Chapter 10).

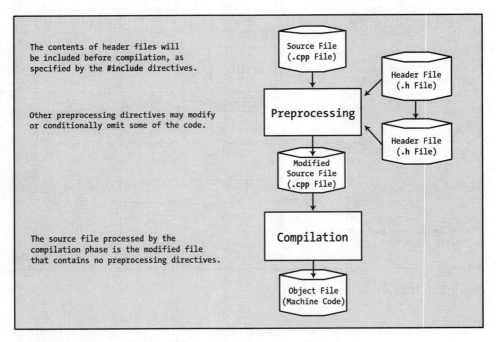

Figure 1-6. Details of the compilation process

This facility for modifying the source file before it is compiled provides you with a lot of flexibility in accommodating the constraints of different computers and operating system environments. The code you need in one environment may be different from that required for another because of variations in the available hardware or the operating system. In many situations, you can put the code for several environments in the same file and arrange for the code to be tailored to the current environment during the preprocessor phase.

Although preprocessing is shown in Figure 1-6 as a distinct operation, you don't execute it independent of the compiler. Invoking the compiler will perform preprocessing automatically, before compiling your code.

Linking

Although the output from the compiler for a given source file is machine code, it's quite a long way from being executable. For one thing, there will be no connection established between one object file and another. The object file corresponding to a particular source file will contain references to functions or other named items that are defined in other source files, and these will still be unresolved. Similarly, links to library functions will not yet be established; indeed, the code for these functions will not yet be part of the file. Dealing with all these things is the job of the **linker** (sometimes called the **linkage editor**).

As Figure 1-7 illustrates, the linker combines the machine code from all of the object files and resolves any cross-references between them. It also integrates the code for any library functions that the object modules use. This is actually a simplified representation of what the linker does, as we're assuming that all the links between modules are established *statically* within the executable module. It's also possible for some links to be *dynamic;* that is, they're established only when the program executes.

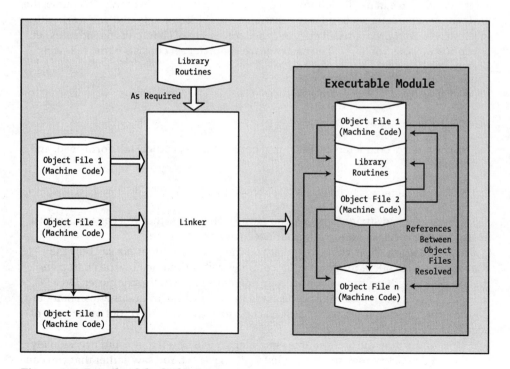

Figure 1-7. Details of the linking process

As I said, the linker establishes links to functions statically—that is, before the program executes. This is done for all the functions contained in the source files that make up the program. Functions linked to dynamically—that is, during program execution—are compiled and linked separately to create a different kind of executable module called a **dynamic link library (DLL)**. A link to a function in a DLL is established when the executable module for your program calls the function, and not before.

DLLs present several important advantages. A primary one is that the functions in the DLL can be shared between several programs that are executing concurrently. This saves using up memory with duplicates of the same function when more than one program is executing that requires the services provided by the functions in the DLL. Another advantage is that the DLL won't be loaded into memory *until* one of the functions it contains is called. This implies that if you don't use a function from a given DLL, it won't occupy space in memory. DLLs are a system capability that ties in closely with your operating system, so I don't discuss them further in this book.

C++ Source Characters

You write C++ statements using a **basic source character set**. This is simply the set of characters that you're allowed to use explicitly in a C++ source file. Obviously, the character set that you can use to define a name is going to be a subset of this. Of course, the basic source character set in no way constrains the character data that you work with in your code. Your program can create strings consisting of characters outside this set in various ways, as you'll see. The basic source character set consists of the following characters:

- The letters *a* to *z* and *A* to *Z*

- The digits 0 to 9

- The control characters representing horizontal tab, vertical tab, form-feed, and newline

- The characters _ { } [ ] # ( ) < > % : ; . ? * + - / ^ & | ~ ! = , \ " '

This is easy and straightforward. You have 96 characters that you can use, and it's likely that these will accommodate your needs most of the time.

This definition of the characters that you can use in C++ does *not* say how the characters are encoded. Your particular compiler will determine how the characters that you use to write your C++ source code are represented in the computer. On a PC, these characters will typically be represented in the machine by an American Standard Code for Information Interchange (ASCII) code such as ISO Latin-1, but other ways of encoding characters may be used.

Most of the time the basic source character set will be adequate, but occasionally you'll need characters that aren't included in the basic set. You saw earlier that you can include UCS characters in a name. You can also include UCS characters in other parts of your program, such as when you specify character data. In the next section I elaborate a little on what UCS is all about.

The Universal Character Set

UCS is specified by the standard ISO/IEC 10646, and it defines codes for characters used in all the national languages that are current and many more besides. The ISO/IEC 10646 standard defines several character-encoding forms. The simplest is UCS-2, which represents characters as 16-bit codes, so it can accommodate 65,536 different character codes that can be written as four hexadecimal digits, dddd. This encoding is described as the **basic multilingual plane** because it accommodates all of the languages in current use, and the likelihood of you ever wanting more than this is remote. UCS-4 is another encoding within the ISO/IEC 10646 standard that represents characters as 32-bit codes that you can express as eight hexadecimal digits, dddddddd. With more than 4 billion different codes, UCS-4 provides the capacity for accommodating all the character sets that you might ever need.

This isn't all there is to UCS, though. For example, there's another 16-bit encoding called UTF-16 (UTF stands for Unicode Transformation Format) that is different from UCS-2 in that it accommodates more than 65,535 characters by encoding characters outside of the first 65,536 by what are referred to as **surrogate pairs** of 16-bit code values. There are other character encodings with UCS too. Generally, a given character will have a code with the same value in any UCS encoding that you choose. The values of codes in US_ASCII are the same as those in UCS character encodings.

Regardless of whether a compiler supports an extended character set for writing source statements, you can include characters from the UCS in your source code by specifying them in the form of a hexadecimal representation of their codes, either as \udddd or \Udddddddd, where d is a hexadecimal digit. Note the lowercase *u* in the first case and the uppercase *U* in the second. However, you must not specify any of the characters in the basic source character set in this way. This is because the codes for these characters will be determined by the compiler, and they may not be consistent with the UCS codes.

If your compiler supports an extended character set with characters outside the base source character set, you'll be able to use these characters in your source code and the compiler will translate the characters to the internal representation before compilation begins.

 NOTE *The character codes defined by the UCS standard are identical to codes defined by Unicode, so Unicode is essentially UCS by another name. If you are keen to explore the delights of UCS and Unicode in detail,* http://www.unicode.org *is a good place to start.*

Trigraph Sequences

You're unlikely to see this in use very often—if ever—but the C++ standard allows you to specify certain characters as **trigraph sequences**. A trigraph sequence is a sequence of three characters that's used to identify another character. This was necessary way back in the dark ages of computing to accommodate characters that were missing from some keyboards. Table 1-1 shows the characters that may be specified in this way in C++.

Table 1-1. Trigraph Sequence Characters

Character	Trigraph Sequence
#	??=
[	??(
]	??)
\	??/
{	??<
}	??>
^	??'
|	??!
~	??-

The compiler will replace all trigraph sequences with their equivalent characters before any other processing of the source code.

Escape Sequences

When you want to use character constants in a program, certain characters can be problematic. A **character constant** is a data item that your program will use in some way, and it can be either a single character or a character string such as the one in the earlier simple example. Obviously, you can't enter characters such as newline or tab directly as character constants, as they'll just do what they're supposed to do: go to a new line or tab to the next tab position in your source code file. What you want in a character constant is the appropriate code for the character.

You can enter control characters as constants by means of an **escape sequence**. An escape sequence is an indirect way of specifying a character, and it always begins with a backslash (\). Table 1-2 shows the escape sequences that represent control characters.

Table 1-2. Escape Sequences That Represent Control Characters

Escape Sequence	Control Character
\n	Newline
\t	Horizontal tab
\v	Vertical tab
\b	Backspace
\r	Carriage return
\f	Form feed
\a	Alert/bell

There are some other characters that are a problem to represent directly. Clearly, the backslash character itself is difficult, because it signals the start of an escape sequence, and there are others with special significance too. Table 1-3 shows the "problem" characters you can specify with an escape sequence.

Table 1-3. Escape Sequences That Represent "Problem" Characters

Escape Sequence	"Problem" Character
\\	Backslash
\'	Single quote
\"	Double quote
\?	Question mark

Because the backslash signals the start of an escape sequence, the only way to enter a backslash as a character constant is by using two successive backslashes (\\).

Escape sequences also provide a general way of representing characters such as those in languages other than the one your keyboard supports, because you can use a hexadecimal (base 16) or octal (base 8) number after the backslash to specify the code for a character. Because you're using a numeric code, you can specify any character in this way. In C++, hexadecimal numbers start with x or X, so \x99A and \XE3 are examples of escape sequences in this format.

You can also specify a character by using up to three octal digits after the backslash—\165, for example. The absence of x or X determines that the code will be interpreted as an octal number.

··

Try It Out: Using Escape Sequences

You can produce an example of a program that uses escape sequences to specify a message to be displayed on the screen. To see the results, you'll need to enter, compile, link, and execute the following program.

As I explained in the Introduction, exactly how you perform these steps will depend on your compiler, and you'll need to consult your compiler's documentation for more information. If you look up "edit", "compile", and "link" (and, with some compilers, "build"), you should be able to find out what you need to do.

```
// Program 1.2 Using escape sequences
#include <iostream>
using std::cout;

int main() {
  cout << "\n\"Least said\n\t\tsoonest mended.\"\n\a";
  return 0;
}
```

(Continued)

When you do manage to compile, link, and run this program, you should see the following output displayed:

```
"Least said
                soonest mended."
```

You should also hear a beep or some equivalent noise from whatever sound output facility your computer has.

HOW IT WORKS

The output you get is determined by what's between the outermost double quotes in the statement

```
cout << "\n\"Least said\n\t\tsoonest mended.\"\n\a";
```

In principle, *everything* between the outer double quotes in the preceding statement gets sent to cout. A string of characters between a pair of double quotes is called a **string literal**. The double quote characters just identify the beginning and end of the string literal; they aren't part of the string. I said "in principle" because any escape sequence in the string literal would have been converted by the compiler to the character it represents, so the character will be sent to cout, not the escape sequence itself. A backslash in a string literal *always* indicates the start of an escape sequence, so the first character that's sent to cout is a newline character. This positions the screen cursor at the beginning of the next line.

The next character in the string is specified by another escape sequence, \", so a double quote will be sent to cout and displayed on the screen, followed by the characters Least said. Next is another newline character corresponding to \n, so the cursor will move to the beginning of the next line. You then send two tab characters to cout with \t\t, so the cursor will be moved two tab positions to the right. The characters soonest mended. will then be displayed from that point on, followed by another double quote from the escape sequence \". Lastly, you have another newline character, which will move the cursor to the start of the next line, followed by the character equivalent of the \a escape sequence that will cause the beep to sound.

The double quote characters that are interior to the string aren't interpreted as marking the end of the string literal because each of them is preceded by a backslash and is therefore recognized as an escape sequence. If you didn't have the escape sequence, \", available, you would have no way of outputting a double quote because it would otherwise be interpreted as indicating the end of the string.

(Continued)

The name `endl` is defined in the `<iostream>` header, and its effect when you use it in an output statement is to write a single newline character so you can use `endl` instead of \n. \n and `endl` aren't exactly equivalent, though, because using `endl` will result in the output buffer being flushed so any characters still in memory will be written to the output device. This won't be the case with \n. Obviously, you can't include `endl` in a string literal because it would be interpreted as simply four letters, e, n, d, and l.

 CAUTION *Be aware that the final character of* `endl` *is the* letter l, *not the* number 1. *It can sometimes be difficult to tell the two apart.*

Using `endl`, the statement in the preceding code to output the string could be written as follows:

```
cout << endl
     << "\"Least said"
     << endl
     << "\t\tsoonest mended.\"\a"
     << endl;
```

This statement sends five separate things in sequence to `cout`: `endl`, `"\"Least said"`, `endl`, `"\t\tsoonest mended.\"\a"`, and `endl`. This will produce exactly the same output as the original statement. Of course, for this statement to compile as written, you would need to add another `using` directive at the beginning of the program:

```
using std::endl;
```

You don't have to choose between using either `endl` or the escape sequence for newline. They aren't mutually exclusive, so you can mix them to suit yourself. For example, you could produce the same result as the original again with this statement:

```
cout << endl
     << "\"Least said\n\t\tsoonest mended.\"\a"
     << endl;
```

Here you've just used `endl` for the first and last newline characters. The one in the middle is still produced by an escape sequence. Of course, each instance of `endl` in the output will result in the output buffer being flushed after writing a newline character to the stream.

Whitespace in Statements

As you learned earlier, **whitespace** is the term used in C++ to describe spaces, horizontal and vertical tabs, newline, and form-feed characters. In many instances, whitespace separates one part of a statement from another and enables the compiler to identify where one element in a statement ends and the next element begins. For example, look at the following line of code:

```
int fruit;
```

This statement involves `int`, which is a type name, and `fruit`, which is the name of a variable. There must be at least one whitespace character (usually a space) between `int` and `fruit` for the compiler to be able to distinguish them. This is because `intfruit` would be a perfectly acceptable name for a variable or indeed anything else, and the compiler would interpret it as such.

On the other hand, consider this statement:

```
fruit = apples + oranges;
```

No whitespace characters are necessary between `fruit` and `=`, or between `=` and `apples`, although you're free to include some if you wish. This is because the equals sign (=) isn't alphabetic or numeric, so the compiler can separate it from its surroundings. Similarly, no whitespace characters are necessary on either side of the plus sign (+). In fact, you're free to include as little or as much whitespace as you like, so you could write the previous statement as follows:

```
fruit
 =
apples
 +
oranges;
```

If you do this, it's unlikely you'll be congratulated for good programming style, but the compiler won't mind.

Apart from its use as a separator between elements in a statement, or when it appears in a string between quotes, the compiler ignores whitespace. You can, therefore, include as much whitespace as you like to make your program more readable. In some programming languages, the end of a statement is at the end of the line, but in C++ the end of a statement is wherever the semicolon occurs. This enables you to spread a statement over several lines if you wish, so you can write a statement like this:

```
std::cout << std::endl << "\"Least said" << std::endl
                << "\t\tsoonest mended.\"\a" << std::endl;
```

or like this:

```
std::cout << std::endl
          << "\"Least said"
          << std::endl
          << "\t\tsoonest mended.\"\a"
          << std::endl;
```

Documenting Your Programs

Documenting your program code is extremely important. Code that seems crystal clear when you write it can look extraordinarily obscure when you've been away from it for a month. You can document your code using **comments**, of which there are two sorts in C++: single-line comments and multiline comments (that is, comments that can span several lines).

You begin a single-line comment with a double slash (//), for example

```
// Program to forecast stock market prices
```

The compiler will ignore everything on the line following the double slash, but that doesn't mean the comment has to fill the whole line. You can use this style of comment to explain a statement:

```
length = shrink(length, temperature);        // Compensate for wash shrinkage
```

You can also temporarily remove a line of code from your program just by adding a double slash to the beginning of the line:

```
// length = shrink(length, temperature);        // Compensate for wash shrinkage
```

This converts the statement to a comment, which is something you might want to do during the testing of a program, for example. Everything from the first // in a line to the end of the line is ignored, including any further occurrences of //.

The multiline comment is sometimes used for writing more verbose, general descriptive material—explaining the algorithm used within a function, for example. Such a comment begins with /*, ends with */, and everything between these two is ignored. This enables you to embellish multiline comments to highlight them, for example

```
/************************************************
 * This function predicts future stock prices     *
 * using advanced tea leaf simulation techniques. *
 ************************************************/
```

You can also use this comment style for temporarily disabling a *block* of code. Just put /* at the beginning of the block and */ at the end. However, you must take particular care not to nest /* ... */ comments; you'll cause error messages from your compiler if you do. This is because the closing */ of the *inner* nested comment will match the opening /* of the *outer* comment:

```
// You must not nest multiline comments
/* This starts an outer comment
/* This is an inner comment, but the start will not be recognized
   because of the outer comment.
   Instead, the end of the inner comment will be interpreted as the end
   of the outer comment. */
   This will cause the compiler to try to compile this part of the
   outer comment as C++ code. */
```

The last part of the outer comment is left "dangling," and the compiler will try to compile it, which will inevitably result in failure. For this reason, the // form of comment is the most widely used in C++ programs.

NOTE *You may also hear multiline comments being described as "C-style" comments. This is because the /* ... */ syntax is the only one available for creating comments in the C language.*

The Standard Library

The standard library contains a substantial number of functions and other things that support, augment, and extend the basic language capabilities of C++. The contents of the standard library are just as much a part of C++ as the syntax and semantics of the language itself. The standard for C++ defines both, and so *every* compiler that conforms to the standard will supply the complete standard library.

Bearing this in mind, the scope of the standard library is extraordinary. You get a vast range of capability, from essential elements such as basic language support, input and output functions, and exception handling (an exception is an unusual occurrence during program execution—often an error of some kind) to utility functions, mathematical routines, and a wide range of prewritten and tested facilities that you can use to store and manage data during execution of your program.

To use C++ most effectively, you should make sure that you have a good familiarity with the contents of the standard library. You'll be introduced to many of the capabilities of the standard library as you learn the C++ language in this book, but the degree of coverage within the book will inevitably be incomplete. It would take another book comparable with the size of this one to cover the capability and use of the standard library comprehensively.

The definitions and declarations necessary to use standard library facilities appear in the standard headers touched upon earlier. There are a few cases in which the standard headers will be included in your program files by default, but in most instances you must add an #include directive for the appropriate header for the library facilities that you want to use. You'll find a comprehensive list of the standard headers in Appendix C, with a brief description of what sort of functionality each one supports.

Almost everything in the C++ standard library is defined within the namespace std. This means that all the names that you'll use from the library are prefixed with std. As you saw at the beginning of the chapter, when you reference something from the standard library, you can prefix the name with std, as in the following statement:

```
std::cout << "The best place to start is at the beginning";
```

Alternatively, you can put a using directive at the beginning of your source file:

```
using std::cout;
```

This allows you to use the name cout without its std prefix so you can write that statement as follows:

```
cout << "The best place to start is at the beginning";
```

You also saw earlier that you have a blanket capability for introducing names from the std namespace into a program file:

```
using namespace std;
```

This allows you to omit the std prefix for any standard library names that are defined in the headers you've included in your program. However, it has the serious disadvantage that it allows potential clashes between names you've defined and identical names in the standard library headers that you've included.

In this book I always include the std namespace prefix where necessary in code fragments. In complete working programs, you'll generally add using statements for standard library names that you use repeatedly in code. Names that you use once or twice you'll just qualify with the namespace name.

Programming in C++

Because C++ inherits and enhances the power and flexibility of the original C language, you have a comprehensive capability for handling time-critical, low-level programming tasks and for dealing with problems for which a traditional procedural approach may be preferable. The major strengths of C++, though, are its powerful and extensive object-oriented features. These provide the potential for writing programs that are less error-prone, less time-consuming to maintain, simpler to extend, and easier to understand than their equivalent procedural solutions.

There are fundamental differences between these two programming methodologies, so let's contrast them to highlight just *how* they're different and see some of the reasons why an object-oriented approach can be so attractive.

Procedural and Object-Oriented Programming

Historically, procedural programming is the way almost all programs have been written. To create a procedural programming solution to a problem, you focus on the process that your program must implement to solve the problem. A rough outline of what you do, once the requirements have been defined precisely, is as follows:

- You create a clear, high-level definition of the overall process that your program will implement.

- You segment the overall process into workable units of computation that are, as much as possible, self-contained. These will usually correspond to functions.

- You break down the logic and the work that each unit of computation is to do into a detailed sequence of actions. This is likely to be down to a level corresponding to programming language statements.

- You code the functions in terms of processing basic types of data: numerical data, single characters, and character strings.

Apart from the common requirement of starting out with a clear specification of what the problem is, the object-oriented approach to solving the same problem is quite different:

- From the problem specification, you determine what types of **objects** the problem is concerned with. For example, if your program deals with baseball players, you're likely to identify BaseballPlayer as one of the types of data your program will work with. If your program is an accounting package, you may well want to define objects of type Account and type Transaction. You also identify the set of **operations** that the program will need to carry out on each type of object. This will result in a set of application-specific data types that you will use in writing your program.

- You produce a detailed design for each of the new data types that your problem requires, including the operations that can be carried out with each object type.

- You express the logic of the program in terms of the new data types you've defined and the kinds of operations they allow.

The program code for an object-oriented solution to a problem will be completely unlike that for a procedural solution and almost certainly easier to understand. It will certainly be a lot easier to maintain. The amount of design time required for an object-oriented solution tends to be greater than for a procedural solution. However, the coding and testing phase of an object-oriented program tends to be shorter and less troublesome, so the overall development time is likely to be roughly the same in either case.

Let's try to get an inkling of what an objected-oriented approach implies. Suppose that you're implementing a program that deals with boxes of various kinds. A feasible requirement of such a program would be to package several smaller boxes inside another, larger box. In a procedural program, you would need to store the length, width, and height of each box in a separate group of variables. The dimensions of a new box that could contain several other boxes would need to be calculated explicitly in terms of the dimensions of each of the contained boxes, according to whatever rules you had defined for packaging a set of boxes.

An object-oriented solution might involve first defining a Box data type. This would enable you to create variables that can reference objects of type Box and, of course, create Box objects. You could then define an operation that would add two Box objects together and produce a new Box object that could contain the first two. Using this operation, you could write statements like this:

```
bigBox = box1 + box2 + box3;
```

In this context the + operation means much more than simple addition. The + operator applied to numerical values will work exactly as before, but for Box objects it has a special meaning. Each of the variables in this statement is of type Box. The preceding statement would create a new Box object big enough to contain box1, as well as box2 and box3.

Being able to write statements like this is clearly much easier than having to deal with all the box dimensions separately, and the more complex the operations on boxes you take on, the greater the advantage is going to be. This is a trivial illustration, though, and there's a great deal more to the power of objects than that you can see here. The purpose of this discussion is just to give you an idea of how readily problems solved using an object-oriented approach can be understood. Object-oriented programming is essentially about solving problems in terms of the entities to which the problems relates rather than in terms of the entities that computers are happy with—numbers and characters. You'll explore object-oriented programming in C++ fully starting in Chapter 11.

Summary

This chapter's content has been broad-brush to give you a feel for some of the general concepts of C++. You'll encounter everything discussed in this chapter again, and in much more detail, in subsequent chapters. However, some of the basics that this chapter covered are as follows:

- A program in C++ consists of at least one function, which is called main().

- The executable part of a function is made up of statements contained between a pair of braces.

- A pair of curly braces is used to enclose a statement block.

- In C++, a statement is terminated by a semicolon.

- Keywords are a set of reserved words that have specific meanings in C++. No entity in your program can have a name that coincides with any of the keywords in the language.

- A C++ program will be contained in one or more files.

- The code defining functions is usually stored in files with the extension .cpp.

- The code that defines your own data types is usually kept in header files with the extension .h.

- The C++ standard library provides an extensive range of capabilities that supports and extends the C++ language.

- Input and output in C++ are performed using streams and involve the use of the insertion and extraction operators, << and >>.

- Object-oriented programming involves defining new data types specific to your problem. Once you've defined the data types that you need, a program can be written in terms of the new data types.

Exercises

The following exercises enable you to try out what you've learned in this chapter. If you get stuck, look back over the chapter for help. If you're still stuck after that, you can download the solutions from the Apress website (http://www.apress.com/book/download.html), but that really should be a last resort.

Exercise 1-1. Create a program that will display the text "Hello World" on your screen.

Exercise 1-2. Change your program so that it uses the hexadecimal values of the characters to spell out the phrase. If you're working on a computer that uses ASCII to encode its characters, you'll find a table of the values you need in Appendix A. (Hint: When you're using hexadecimal ASCII values, "He" can be displayed by the statement std::cout << "\x48\x65";.)

Exercise 1-3. The following program produces several compiler errors. Find these errors and correct them so the program can compile cleanly and run.

```
#include <iostream>
using namespace std;
int main() {
  cout << endl
       << "Hello World"
       << endl

  return0;
)
```

Exercise 1-4. What will happen if you remove the using directive from the program in Exercise 1-3? Apart from restoring the using directive, how else could you fix the problem that occurs? Why is your solution better that restoring the original using directive?

NOTE *You'll find model answers to all exercises in this book in the Downloads section of the Apress website at* http://www.apress.com/book/download.html.

Basic Data Types and Calculations

IN THIS CHAPTER, you'll look at some of the basic data types that are built into C++ and that you're likely to use in all your programs. You'll also investigate how to carry out simple numerical computations. All of C++'s object-oriented capability is founded on the basic data types built into the language, because all the data types that you'll create are ultimately defined in terms of the basic types. It's therefore important to get a good grasp of using them. By the end of the chapter, you'll be able to write a simple C++ program of the traditional form: input – process – output.

In this chapter, you'll learn about

- Data types in C++

- What literals are and how you define them in a program

- Binary and hexadecimal representation for integers

- How you declare and initialize variables in your program

- How calculations using integers work

- Programming with values that aren't integers—that is, floating-point calculations

- How you can prevent the value stored in a variable from being modified

- How to create variables that can store characters

Data and Data Types

C++ is a **strongly typed language**. In other words, every data item in your program has a **type** associated with it that defines what it is and your C++ compiler will make extensive checks to ensure that, as far as possible, you use the right data type in any given context and that when you combine different types, they're made to be compatible. Because of this type checking, the compiler is able to detect and report most errors that would arise from the accidental interpretation of one type of data as another or from attempts to combine data items of types that are mutually incompatible.

The numerical values that you can work with in C++ fall into two broad categories: integers (in other words, whole numbers) and floating-point values, which can be fractional. You can't conclude from this that there are just two numerical data types, however. There are actually several data types in each of these categories, and each type has its own permitted range of values that it can store. Before I get into numerical types in detail, let's look at how you carry out arithmetic calculations in C++, starting with how you can calculate using integers.

Performing Simple Calculations

To begin with, let's get some bits of terminology out of the way. An operation (such as a mathematical calculation) is defined by an **operator**— + for addition, for example, or * for multiplication. The values that an operator acts upon are called **operands**, so in an expression such as 2*3, the operands are 2 and 3.

Because the multiplication operator requires *two* operands, it is called a **binary operator**. Some other operators only require *one* operand, and these are called **unary operators**. An example of a unary operator is the minus sign in -2. The minus sign acts on one operand—the value 2—and changes its sign. This contrasts with the binary subtraction operator in expressions such as 4 - 2, which acts on two operands, the 4 and the 2.

Introducing Literals

In C++, fixed values of any kind, such as 42, or 2.71828, or "Mark Twain", are referred to as **literals**. In Chapter 1, when you were outputting text strings to the screen, you used a **string literal**—a constant defined by a series of characters between a pair of double quotes, of which "Mark Twain" is an example. Now you'll investigate the types of literals that are numeric constants. These are the ordinary numbers you meet every day: your shoe size, the boiling point of lead, the number of angels that can sit on a pin—in fact, any defined number.

There are two broad classifications of numeric constants that you can use in C++:

- **Integer literals** are whole numbers and are written without a decimal point.

- **Floating-point literals** (commonly referred to as **floating-point numbers**) are numbers that can be nonintegral values and are always written with a decimal point, or an exponent, or both. (You'll look into exponents a little later on.)

You use an integer when you're dealing with what is evidently a whole number: the number of players on a team, for example, or the number of pages in a book. You use a floating-point value when the values aren't integral: the circumference of a circle divided by its diameter, for example, or the exchange rate of the UK£ against the US$.

Floating-point numbers are particularly helpful when you're dealing with very small or very large quantities: the weight of an electron, the diameter of the galaxy, or the velocity of a bat out of hell, perhaps. The term "floating-point number" is used because while these values are represented by a fixed number of digits, called the **precision**, the decimal point "floats" and can be moved in either direction in relation to the fixed set of digits.

Letting the Point Float

Look at these two numbers:

0.000000000000000000001234567	1.234567×10^{-21}
123456700000000000000000000.0	$1.234567 \times 10^{+26}$

Both numbers have seven digits of precision, but they're very different numbers, the first being an extremely small number and the second being very large. A floating-point representation of each number on the left is shown to its right. Multiplying the number by a power of 10 shifts the decimal point in the base number, 1.234567. This flexibility in positioning the decimal point allows a huge range of numbers to be represented and stored, from the very small to the very large, in a modest amount of memory.

You'll look at how to use integers first, as they're the simpler of the two. You'll come back to working with floating-point values as soon as you're done with integers.

Integer Literals

You can write integer literals in a very straightforward way. Here are some examples:

```
-123    +123    123    22333
```

Here, the + and - signs in the first two examples are examples of the unary operators I mentioned earlier. You could omit the + in the second example, as it's implied by default, but if you think putting it in makes things clearer, that's not a problem. The literal +123 is the same as 123. The fourth example is the number that you would normally write as 22,333, but you must not use commas within an integer literal. If you include a comma, the compiler is likely to treat your number as two numbers separated by the comma.

You can't write just any old integer value that you want, either. To take an extreme example, an integer with 100 digits won't be accepted. There are upper and lower limits on integer literals, and these are determined by the amount of memory that's devoted to storing each type of integer value on the computer that you're using. I come back to this point a little later in the chapter when I discuss integer variables, and I also cover some further options for specifying integer literals.

Of course, although I've written the examples of integer literals as decimal values, inside your computer they're stored as binary numbers. Understanding binary arithmetic is quite important in programming, so in case you're a little rusty on how binary numbers work, I've included a brief overview in Appendix E. If you don't feel comfortable with binary and hexadecimal numbers, I suggest you take a look at the overview in Appendix E before continuing with the next section.

Hexadecimal Integer Literals

The previous examples of integer literals were decimal integers, but you can also write integers as hexadecimal values. To indicate that you're writing a hexadecimal value, you prefix the number with 0x or 0X, so if you write 0x999, you're writing a hexadecimal number with three hexadecimal digits. Plain old 999, on the other hand, is a decimal value with decimal digits, so the value will be completely different. Here are some more examples of integer literals written as hexadecimal values:

Hexadecimal values	0x1AF	0x123	0xA	0xCAD	0xFF
Corresponding decimal expression	$1*16^2$	$1*16^2$	$10*16^0$	$12*16^2$	$15*16^1$
	$+10*16^1$	$+2*16^1$		$+10*16^1$	$+15*16^0$
	$+15*16^0$	$+3*16^0$		$+13*16^0$	
Decimal value	431	291	10	3245	255

You'll remember that in Chapter 1 you saw hexadecimal notation being used in escape sequences that defined characters. What you're looking at here is different—you're defining integers. You'll come back to defining character literals later in this chapter.

The major use for hexadecimal literals is when you want to define a particular pattern of bits. Because each hexadecimal digit corresponds to 4 bits in the binary value, it's easy to express a particular pattern of bits as a hexadecimal literal. You'll explore this further in the next chapter.

Octal Integer Literals

You can also write integers as **octal** values—that is, using base 8. You identify a number as octal by writing it with a leading zero. Here are some examples of octal values:

Octal values	0123	077	010101
Corresponding decimal integers	83	63	4161

Of course, octal numbers can only have digit values from 0 to 7. Octal is used very infrequently these days, and it survives in C++ largely for historical reasons from the time when there were computers around with a word length that was a multiple of 3 bits. However, it's important to be aware of the existence of octal numbers, because if you accidentally write a decimal number with a leading zero, the compiler will try to interpret it as octal.

 CAUTION *Don't write decimal integer values with a leading zero. The compiler will interpret such values as octal (base 8), so a value written as 065 will be equivalent to 53 in decimal notation.*

As far as your compiler is concerned, it doesn't matter which number base you choose when you write an integer value—ultimately, it will be stored in your computer as a binary number. The different ways available to you for writing an integer are there just for your convenience. You could write the integer value fifteen as 15, as 0xF, or as 017. These will all result in the same internal binary representation of the value, so you will choose one or other of the possible representations to suit the context in which you are using it.

Integer Arithmetic

The basic arithmetic operations that you can carry out on integers are shown in Table 2-1.

Table 2-1. Basic Arithmetic Operations

Operator	Operation
+	Addition
–	Subtraction
*	Multiplication
/	Division
%	Modulus (the remainder after division)

The operators in Table 2-1 work largely in the way you would expect, and notice that they are all *binary* operators. However, the division operation is slightly idiosyncratic, so let's examine that in a little more detail. Because integer operations always produce an integer result, an expression such as 11/4 doesn't result in a value of 2.75. Instead, it produces 2. **Integer division** returns the number of times that the denominator divides into the numerator. Any remainder is simply discarded. So far as the C++ standard is concerned, the result of division by zero is undefined, but specific implementations will usually have the behavior defined and, in some cases, will provide a programmatic means of responding to the situation, so check your product documentation.

Figure 2-1 illustrates the different effects of the division and modulus operators.

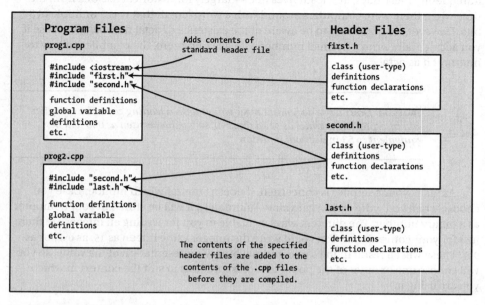

Program Files

prog1.cpp

```
#include <iostream>
#include "first.h"
#include "second.h"

function definitions
global variable
definitions
etc.
```

prog2.cpp

```
#include "second.h"
#include "last.h"

function definitions
global variable
definitions
etc.
```

Adds contents of
standard header file

The contents of the specified
header files are added to the
contents of the .cpp files
before they are compiled.

Header Files

first.h

```
class (user-type)
definitions
function declarations
etc.
```

second.h

```
class (user-type)
definitions
function declarations
etc.
```

last.h

```
class (user-type)
definitions
function declarations
etc.
```

Figure 2-1. Contrasting the division and modulus operators

The modulus operator, %, which is sometimes referred to as the **remainder operator**, complements the division operator in that it provides a means for you to obtain the remainder after integer division if you need it. The expression 11%4 results in the value 3, which is the remainder after dividing 11 by 4. When either or both operands of the modulus operator are negative, the sign of the remainder is up to the particular C++ implementation you're using, so beware of variations between different systems. Because applying the modulus operator inevitably involves a division, the result is undefined when the right operand is zero.

Let's see the arithmetic operators in action in an example.

Try It Out: Integer Arithmetic in Action

The following is a program to output the results of a miscellaneous collection of expressions involving integers to illustrate how the arithmetic operators work:

```
// Program 2.1 - Calculating with integer constants
#include <iostream>                      // For output to the screen
using std::cout;
using std::endl;


int main() {
   cout << 10 + 20          << endl; // Output is  30
   cout << 10 - 5           << endl; // Output is   5
   cout << 10 - 20          << endl; // Output is -10

   cout << 10 * 20          << endl; // Output is 200
   cout << 10/3             << endl; // Output is   3
   cout << 10 % 3           << endl; // Output is   1
   cout << 10 % -3          << endl; // Output is   1
   cout << -10 % 3          << endl; // Output is  -1
   cout << -10 % -3         << endl; // Output is  -1

   cout << 10 + 20/10 - 5   << endl; // Output is   7
   cout << (10 + 20)/(10 - 5) << endl; // Output is   6
   cout << 10 + 20/(10 - 5) << endl; // Output is 14
   cout << (10 + 20)/10 - 5 << endl; // Output is  -2

   cout << 4*5/3%4 + 7/3    << endl; // Output is   4
   return 0;                         // End the program
}
```

The output from this example on my system is as follows:

```
30
5
-10
200
3
1
1
-1
-1
7
6
14
-2
4
```

(Continued)

It doesn't look particularly elegant with that "ragged right" arrangement, does it? This is a consequence of the way that integers are output by default. Very shortly, you'll come back to find out how you can make it look prettier. First, though, let's look at the interesting parts of this example.

HOW IT WORKS

Each statement evaluates an arithmetic expression and outputs the result to the screen, followed by a newline character that moves the cursor to the beginning of the next line. All the arithmetic expressions here are **constant expressions**, because their values can be completely determined by the compiler before the program executes.

The first five statements are straightforward, and the reasons why they produce the results they do should be obvious to you:

```
cout << 10 + 20          << endl;  // Output is  30
cout << 10 - 5           << endl;  // Output is   5
cout << 10 - 20          << endl;  // Output is -10

cout << 10 * 20          << endl;  // Output is 200
cout << 10/3             << endl;  // Output is   3
```

Because integer operations always produce integer results, the expression 10/3 in the last line results in 3, as 3 divides into 10 a maximum of three times. The remainder, 1, that is left after dividing by 3 is discarded.

The next four lines show the modulus operator in action:

```
cout << 10 % 3           << endl;  // Output is   1
cout << 10 % -3          << endl;  // Output is   1
cout << -10 % 3          << endl;  // Output is  -1
cout << -10 % -3         << endl;  // Output is  -1
```

Here you're producing the remainder after division for all possible combinations for the signs of the operands. The output corresponding to the first line where both operands are positive is the only one guaranteed to be the same when you run it on your system. The results of the other three lines may have a different sign.

The next four statements show the effects of using parentheses:

```
cout << 10 + 20/10 - 5     << endl; // Output is   7
cout << (10 + 20)/(10 - 5) << endl; // Output is   6
cout << 10 + 20 /(10 - 5)  << endl; // Output is  14
cout << (10 + 20)/10 - 5   << endl; // Output is  -2
```

The parentheses override the "natural order" of execution of the operators in the expressions. The expressions within parentheses are always evaluated first, starting with the innermost pair if they're nested and working through to the outermost.

In an expression involving several different operators, the order in which the operators are executed is determined by giving some operators priority over others. The priority assigned to an operator is called its **precedence**. With the operators for integer arithmetic that you've seen, the operators *, /, and % form a group that takes priority over the operators + and -, which form another group. You would say that each of the operators *, /, and % has a **higher precedence** than + and -. Operators within a given group—+ and -, for example—have equal precedence. The last output statement in the example illustrates how precedence determines the order in which the operators are executed:

```
cout << 4*5/3%4 + 7/3 << endl;          // Output is    4
```

The + operator is of lower precedence than any of the others, so the addition will be performed last. This means that values for the two subexpressions, 4*5/3%4 and 7/3, will be calculated first. The operators in the subexpression 4*5/3%4 are all of equal precedence, so the sequence in which these will be executed is determined by their **associativity**. The associativity of a group of operators can be either **left** or **right**. An operator that is left associative binds first to the operand on the left of the operator, so a sequence of such operators in an expression will be executed from left to right. Let's illustrate this using the example.

In the expression 4*5/3%4, each of the operators is left associative, which means that the left operand of each operator is whatever is to its left. Thus, the left operand for the multiplication operation is 4, the left operand for the division operation is 4*5, and the left operand for the modulus operation is 4*5/3. The expression is therefore evaluated as ((4*5)/3)%4, which, as I said, is left to right.

Although the associativity of the operators in an expression is involved in determining the sequence of execution of operators from the same group, it doesn't say anything about the operands. For example, in the expression 4*5/3%4+7/3, it isn't defined whether the subexpression 4*5/3%4 is evaluated before 7/3 or vice versa. It could be either, depending on what your compiler decides. Your reaction to this might be "Who cares?" because it makes no difference to the result. Here, that's true, but there are circumstances in which it *can* make a difference, and you'll see some of them as you progress through this chapter.

Operator Precedence and Associativity

Nearly all operator groups are left associative in C++, so most expressions involving operators of equal precedence are evaluated from left to right. The only right associative operators are the unary operators, which I've already touched upon, and assignment operators, which you'll meet later on.

You can put the precedence and associativity of the integer arithmetic operators into a little table that indicates the order of execution in an arithmetic expression, as shown in Table 2-2.

Table 2-2. The Precedence and Associativity of the Arithmetic Operators

Operators	Associativity
unary + -	Right
* / %	Left
+ -	Left

Each line in Table 2-2 is a group of operators of equal precedence. The groups are in sequence, with the highest precedence operators in the top line and the lowest precedence at the bottom. As it only contains three lines, this table is rather simplistic, but you'll accumulate many more operators and add further lines to this table as you learn more about C++.

NOTE *The C++ standard doesn't define the precedence of the operators directly, but it can be determined from the syntax rules that are defined within the standard. In most instances it's easier to work out how a given expression will execute from the operator precedence than from the syntax rules, so I'll consider the precedence of each operator as I introduce it.*

If you want to see the precedence table for all the operators in C++, you can find it in Appendix D.

Try It Out: Fixing the Appearance of the Output

Although it may not appear so, the output from the previous example is right justified. The "ragged right" appearance is due to the fact that the output for each integer is in a **field width** that's exactly the correct number of characters to accommodate the value. You can make the output look tidier by setting the field width for each data item to a value of your choice, as follows:

```cpp
// Program 2.1A - Producing neat output
#include <iostream>          // For output to the screen
#include <iomanip>           // For manipulators
using std::cout;
using std::endl;
using std::setw;

int main() {
  cout << setw(10) << 10 + 20          << endl; // Output is  30
  cout << setw(10) << 10 - 5           << endl; // Output is   5
  cout << setw(10) << 10 - 20          << endl; // Output is -10

  cout << setw(10) << 10 * 20          << endl; // Output is 200
  cout << setw(10) << 10/3             << endl; // Output is   3
  cout << setw(10) << 10 % 3           << endl; // Output is   1
  cout << setw(10) << 10 % -3          << endl; // Output is   1
  cout << setw(10) << -10 % 3          << endl; // Output is  -1
  cout << setw(10) << -10 % -3         << endl; // Output is  -1
  cout << setw(10) << 10 + 20/10 - 5   << endl; // Output is   7
  cout << setw(10) << (10 + 20)/(10 - 5) << endl; // Output is   6

  cout << setw(10) << 10 + 20/(10 - 5) << endl; // Output is  14
  cout << setw(10) << (10 + 20)/10 - 5 << endl; // Output is - 2
  cout << setw(10) << 4*5/3%4 + 7/3    << endl; // Output is   4
  return 0;                                     // End the program
}
```

Now the output looks like this:

```
        30
         5
       -10
       200
         3
         1
         1
        -1
        -1
         7
         6
        14
        -2
         4
```

(Continued)

```
                        HOW IT WORKS
```

That's much nicer, isn't it? The tidy formatting is accomplished by the changes to the output statements. Each value to be displayed is preceded in the output by setw(10), as in the first statement:

```
    cout << setw(10) << 10 + 20                      << endl;  // Output is  30
```

setw() is called a **manipulator** because it enables you to manipulate, or control, the appearance of the output. A manipulator doesn't output anything; it just modifies the output process. Its effect is to **set** the field **w**idth for the next value to be output to the number of characters that you specify between the parentheses, which is 10 in this case. The field width that you set by using setw() only applies to the next value that is written to cout. Subsequent values will be presented in the default manner.

The additional #include statement for the standard header <iomanip> is necessary to make the setw() manipulator available in your program. I've also added a using declaration so you can use the setw name unqualified. There are other manipulators that you'll try out in other examples as you go along. Meanwhile, you can try out this example with different field widths to see their effect.

Using Variables

Calculating with integer constants is all very well, but you were undoubtedly expecting a bit more sophistication in your C++ programs than that. To do more, you need to be able to store data items in a program, and this facility is provided by variables. A **variable** is an area in memory that's identified by a name that you supply and that you can use to store an item of data of a particular type. Specifying a variable therefore requires two things: you must give it a name, and you must identify what kind of data you propose to store in it. First of all, let's consider what options you have for defining variable names.

Variable Names

As you saw in Chapter 1, the name that you give to a variable can consist of any combination of upper- or lowercase letters, underscores, and the digits 0 to 9, but it must *begin* with a letter or an underscore. As I said in Chapter 1, the ANSI standard says that a variable name can also include UCS characters, and although you could use this in defining your variable names, it's there to allow compilers to accommodate the use of national language characters that aren't in the basic set of upper- and lowercase letters (*A* to *Z*).

Don't forget, you must not express any character from the basic source character set as a UCS character. All characters from the basic source character set must appear as their explicit character representation.

You saw some examples of valid variable names in Chapter 1, but here are a few more:

```
value    monthlySalary    eight_ball    FIXED_VALUE    JimBob
```

Just to remind you of what I said in Chapter 1, a variable name can't begin with a digit, so names such as 8ball and 7Up aren't valid. Also, because C++ is a **case-sensitive** language, republican and Republican are different names. You shouldn't use variable names that begin with an underscore followed by a capital letter or that contain two successive underscores, as names of these forms are reserved for use within the standard libraries.

Generally, the names that you invent for your variables should be indicative of the kind of data that they hold. For instance, a name such as shoe_size is going to mean a whole lot more than ss—always assuming you're dealing with shoe sizes, of course. You'll find that you often want to use names that combine two or more words to make your program more understandable. One common approach for doing this uses the underscore character to link words in a single, for example:

```
line_count    pay_rise    current_debt
```

A convention that's frequently adopted in C++ is to reserve names that begin with a capital letter for naming **classes**, which are user-defined types. You'll learn how to define your own data types in Chapter 11. With this approach to names, Point, Person, and Program are all immediately recognizable as user-defined types and not variables. Of course, you're free to assign any names that you want (as long as they aren't keywords), but if you choose names that are meaningful and name your variables in a consistent manner, it will make your programs more readable and less error-prone. Appendix B contains a list of all the C++ keywords.

Integer Variables

Suppose you want to use a variable to record how many apples you have. You can create a variable with the name apples by means of a **declaration statement** for the variable, as shown in Figure 2-2.

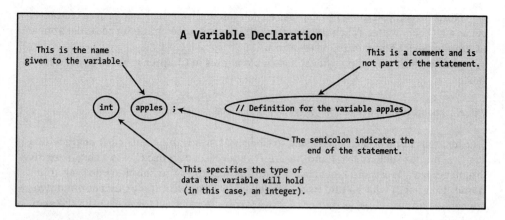

Figure 2-2. A variable declaration

The statement in Figure 2-2 is described as a **declaration** because it declares the name apples. *Any* statement that introduces a name into your program is a declaration for that name. The statement in the illustration is also called a **definition**, because it causes memory to be allocated for the variable apples. Later, you'll meet statements that *are* declarations but are *not* definitions. A variable is created by its definition, so you can only refer to it after the definition statement. If you attempt to refer to a variable prior to its definition, you'll get an error message from the compiler.

When you define a variable, you can also specify an initial value. For example,

```
int apples = 10;               // Definition for the variable apples
```

defines the variable called apples and sets its initial value as 10. The definition in the diagram had no initial value specified, so the memory assigned to the variable would contain whatever junk value was left over from previous use of the memory. Having junk values floating around in your program is a bad idea, and this leads to our first golden rule.

 GOLDEN RULE *Always initialize your variables when you define them. If you don't know what value a variable should have when you define it, initialize it to zero.*

You can use variables as operands of the arithmetic operators you've seen in exactly the same way as you've used literals. The value of the variable will be the operand value. If you apply the unary minus operator to a variable, the result is a value that has the opposite sign of the value of the variable, but the same magnitude. This doesn't change the value stored in the variable, though. You'll see how to do that very soon.

Let's try out some integer variables in a little program.

Try It Out: Using Integer Variables

Here's a program that figures out how your apples can be divided equally among a group of children:

```cpp
// Program 2.2 - Working with integer variables
   #include <iostream>            // For output to the screen
   using std::cout;
   using std::endl;

   int main() {
      int apples = 10;            // Definition for the variable apples
      int children = 3;           // Definition for the variable children

      // Calculate fruit per child
      cout << endl                // Start on a new line
          << "Each child gets "   // Output some text
          << apples/children      // Output number of apples per child
          << " fruit.";           // Output some more text

      // Calculate number left over
      cout << endl                // Start on a new line
          << "We have "           // Output some text
          << apples % children    // Output apples left over
          << " left over.";       // Output some more text

      cout << endl;
      return 0;                   // End the program
   }
```

I've been very liberal with the comments here, just to make it clear what's going on in each statement. You wouldn't normally put such self-evident information in the comments. This program produces the following output:

```
Each child gets 3 fruit.
We have 1 left over.
```

(Continued)

HOW IT WORKS

This example is unlikely to overtax your brain cells. The first two statements in main() define the variables apples and children:

```
int apples = 10;          // Definition for the variable apples
int children = 3;         // Definition for the variable children
```

The variable apples is initialized to 10, and children is initialized to 3. Had you wanted, you could have defined both variables in a single statement, for example:

```
int apples = 10, children = 3;
```

This statement declares both apples and children to be of type int and initializes them as before. A comma is used to separate the variables that you're declaring, and the whole thing ends with a semicolon. Of course, it isn't so easy to add explanatory comments here as there's less space, but you could split the statement over two lines:

```
int apples = 10,          // Definition for the variable apples
    children = 3;         // Definition for the variable children
```

A comma still separates the two variables, and now you have space for the comments at the end of each line. You can declare as many variables as you want in a single statement, and you can spread the statement over as many lines as you see fit. However, it's considered good style to stick to one declaration per statement.

The next statement calculates how many apples each child gets when the apples are divided up and outputs the result:

```
cout << endl              // Start on a new line
    << "Each child gets " // Output some text
    << apples/children    // Output number of apples per child
    << " fruit.";         // Output some more text
```

Notice that the four lines here make up a single statement, and that you put comments on each line that are therefore effectively in the middle of the statement. The arithmetic expression uses the division operator to obtain the number of apples that each child gets. This expression just involves the two variables that you've defined, but in general you can mix variables and literals in an expression in any way that you want.

The next statement calculates and outputs the number of apples that are left over:

```
cout << endl           // Start on a new line
     << "We have "     // Output some text
     << apples % children  // Output apples left over
     << " left over.";  // Output some more text
```

Here, you use the modulus operator to calculate the remainder, and the result is output between the text strings in a single output statement. If you wanted, you could have generated all of the output with a single statement. Alternatively, you could equally well have output each string and data value in a separate statement.

In this example, you used the int type for your variables, but there are other kinds of integer variables.

Integer Variable Types

The type of an integer variable will determine how much memory is allocated for it and, consequently, the range of values that you can store in it. Table 2-3 describes the four basic types of integer variables.

Table 2-3. Basic Integer Variable Types

Type Name	Typical Memory per Variable
char	1 byte
short int	2 bytes
int	4 bytes
long int	8 bytes

Apart from type char, which is always 1 byte, there are no standard amounts of memory for storing integer variables of the other three types in Table 2-3. The only thing required by the C++ standard is that each type in the sequence must occupy at least as much memory as its predecessor. I've shown the memory for the types on my system, and this is a common arrangement. The type short int is usually written in its abbreviated form, short, and the type long int is usually written simply as long. These abbreviations correspond to the original C type names, so they're universally accepted by C++ compilers. At first sight, char might seem an odd name for an integer type, but because its primary use is to store an integer code that represents a character, it does make sense.

You've already seen how to declare a variable of type int, and you declare variables of type short int and type long int in exactly the same way. For example, you could define and initialize a variable called bean_count, of type short int, with the following statement:

```
short int bean_count = 5;
```

As I said, you could also write this as follows:

```
int bean_count = 5;
```

Similarly, you can declare a variable of type long int with this statement:

```
long int earth_diameter = 12756000L; // Diameter in meters
```

Notice that I appended an L to the initializing value, which indicates that it's an integer literal of type long int. If you don't put the L here, it won't cause a problem. The compiler will automatically arrange for the value to be converted from type int to type long int. However, it's good programming practice to make the types of your initializing values consistent with the types of your variables.

Signed and Unsigned Integer Types

Variables of type short int, type int, and type long int can store negative and positive values, so they're implicitly **signed integer types**. If you want to be explicit about it, you can also write these types as signed short int, signed int, and signed long int, respectively. However, they're most commonly written without using the signed keyword.

You may see just the keyword signed written by itself as a type, which means signed int. However, you don't see this very often probably because int is fewer characters to type! Occasionally you'll see the type unsigned int written simply as unsigned. Both of these abbreviations originate in C. My personal preference is to always specify the underlying type when using the keywords signed or unsigned, as then there's no question about what is meant.

An unsigned integer variable can only store positive values, and you won't be surprised to learn that the type names for three such types are unsigned short int, unsigned int, and unsigned long int. These types are useful when you know you're only going to be dealing with positive values, but they're more frequently used to store values that are viewed as bit patterns rather than numbers. You'll see more about this in Chapter 3, when you look at the bitwise operators that you use to manipulate individual bits in a variable.

You need a way of differentiating unsigned integer literals from signed integer literals, if only because 65535 can be stored in 16 bits as an unsigned value, but as a signed value you have to go to 32 bits. Unsigned integer literals are identified by the letter U or u following the digits of the value. This applies to decimal, hexadecimal, and octal integer literals. If you want to specify a literal to be type unsigned long int, you use both the U or u and the L.

Figure 2-3 illustrates the difference between 16-bit signed and unsigned integers. As you've seen, with signed integers, the leftmost bit indicates the sign of the number. It will be 0 for a positive value and 1 for a negative value. For unsigned integers, *all* the bits can be treated as data bits. Because an unsigned number is always regarded as positive, there is no sign bit—the leftmost bit is just part of the number.

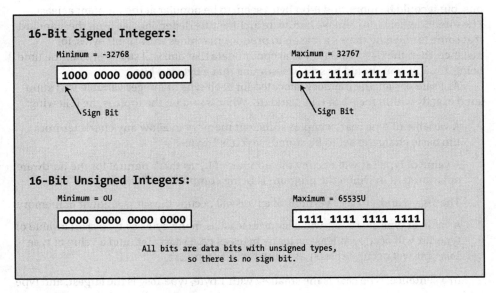

Figure 2-3. Signed and unsigned integers

If you think that the binary value for −32768 looks strange, remember that negative values are normally represented in 2's complement form. As you'll see if you look in Appendix E, to convert a positive binary value to a negative binary value (or vice versa) in 2's complement form, you just flip all the bits and then add 1. Of course, you can't represent +32768 as a 16-bit signed integer, as the available range only runs from −32768 to +32767.

Signed and Unsigned Char Types

Values stored as type char may actually be signed or unsigned, depending on how your compiler chooses to implement the type, so it may be vary between different computers or even between different compilers on the same computer. If you want a single byte to store integer values rather than character codes, you should explicitly declare the variable as either type signed char or type unsigned char.

Note that although type char will be equivalent to either signed char or unsigned char in any given compiler context, all three are considered to be different types. Of course, the words char, short, int, long, signed, and unsigned are all keywords.

Integer Ranges

The basic unit of memory in C++ is a byte. As far as C++ is concerned, a byte has suffi-cient bits to contain any character in the basic character set used by your C++ compiler, but it is otherwise undefined. As long as a byte can accommodate at least 96 characters, then it's fine according to the C++ standard. This implies that a byte in C++ is at least 7 bits, but it could be more, and 8-bit bytes seem to be popular at the moment at least. The intention here is to remove hardware architecture dependencies from the standard. If at some future date there's a reason to produce machines with 16-bit bytes, for instance, then the C++ standard will accommodate that and will still apply. For the time being, though, you should be safe in assuming that a byte is 8 bits.

As I said earlier, the memory allocated for each type of integer variable isn't stipu-lated exactly within the ANSI C++ standard. What *is* said on the topic is the following:

A variable of type char occupies sufficient memory to allow any character from the basic character set to be stored, which is 1 byte.

A value of type int will occupy the number of bytes that's natural for the hardware environment in which the program is being compiled.

The signed and unsigned versions of a type will occupy the same amount of memory.

A value of type short int will occupy at least as many bytes as type char; a value of type int will occupy at least as many bytes as type short int; and a value of type long int will occupy at least as many bytes as type int.

In a sentence, type char is the smallest with 1 byte, type long is the largest, and type int is somewhere between the two but occupies the number of bytes best suited to your computer's integer arithmetic capability. The reason for this vagueness is that the number of bytes used for type int on any given computer should correspond to that which results in the most efficient integer arithmetic. This will depend on the architec-ture of the machine. In most machines, it's 4 bytes, but as the performance and archi-tecture of computer hardware advances, there's increasing potential for it to be 8 bytes.

The actual number of bytes allocated to each integer type by your compiler will determine the range of values that can be stored. Table 2-4 shows the ranges for some typical sizes of integer variables.

Table 2-4. Ranges of Values for Integer Variables

Type	Size (Bytes)	Range of Values
char	1	−128 to 127
unsigned char	1	0U to 255U
short	2	−32768 to 32767
unsigned short	2	0U to 65535U
int	4	−2147483648 to 2147483647
unsigned int	4	0U to 4294967295U
long	8	−9223372036854775808L to 9223372036854775807L
unsigned long	8	0 to 18446744073709551615UL

The Type of an Integer Literal

I've introduced the idea of prefixes being applied to an integer value to affect the number base for the value. I've also informally introduced the notion of the suffixes U and L being used to identify integers as being of an unsigned type or of type long. Let's now pin these options down more precisely and understand how the compiler will determine the type of a given integer literal.

First, Table 2-5 presents a summary of the options you have for the prefix and suffix to an integer value.

Table 2-5. Suffixes and Prefixes for Integer Values

Suffix/Prefix	Description
No prefix	The value is a decimal number.
Prefix of 0x or 0X	The value is a hexadecimal number.
Prefix of 0 (a zero)	The value is an octal number.
Suffix of u or U	The value is of an unsigned type.
Suffix of L or l (lowercase *L*)	The value is of type long.

The last two items in the table can be combined in any sequence or combination of upper- and lowercase U and L, so UL, LU, uL, Lu, and so on are all acceptable. Although you can use the suffix l, which is a lowercase *L*, you should avoid doing so because of the obvious potential for confusion with the digit 1.

Now let's look at how the various combinations of prefixes and suffixes that you can use with integer literals will be interpreted by the compiler:

- A decimal integer literal with no suffix will be interpreted as being of type int if it can be accommodated within the range of values provided by that type. Otherwise, it will be interpreted as being of type long.

- An octal or hexadecimal literal with no suffix will be interpreted as the first of the types int, unsigned int, long, and unsigned long in which the value can be accommodated.

- A literal with a suffix of u or U will be interpreted as being of type unsigned int if the value can be accommodated within that type. Otherwise, it will be interpreted as type unsigned long.

- A literal with a suffix of l or L will be interpreted as being of type long if the value can be accommodated within that type. Otherwise, it will be interpreted as type unsigned long.

- A literal with a suffix combining both U and L in upper- or lowercase will be interpreted as being of type unsigned long.

If the value for a literal is outside the range of the possible types, then the behavior is undefined but will usually result in an error message from the compiler.

You'll undoubtedly have noticed that you have no way of specifying an integer literal to be of type short int or unsigned short int. When you supply an initial value in a declaration for a variable of either of these types, the compiler will automatically convert the value of the literal to the required type, for example:

```
unsigned short n = 1000;
```

Here, according to the preceding rules, the literal will be interpreted as being of type int. The compiler will convert the value to type unsigned short and use that as the initial value for the variable. If you used -1000 as the initial value, this couldn't be converted to type unsigned short because negative numbers are by definition outside the range of this type. This would undoubtedly result in an error message from the compiler.

Remember that the range of values that can be stored for each integer type is dependent on your compiler. Table 2-4 shows "typical" values, but your compiler may well allocate different amounts of memory for particular types, thus providing for different ranges of values. You also need to be conscious of the possible variations in types when porting an application from one system to another.

So far, I've largely ignored character literals and variables of type char. Because these have some unique characteristics, you'll deal with character literals and variables that store character codes later in this chapter and press on with integer calculations first. In particular, you need to know how to store a result.

The Assignment Operator

You can store the result of a calculation in a variable using the **assignment operator**, =. Let's look at an example. Suppose you declare three variables with the statements

```
int total_fruit = 0;
int apples = 10;
int oranges = 6;
```

You can calculate the total number of fruit with the statement

```
total_fruit = apples + oranges;
```

This statement will first calculate the value on the right side of the =, the sum of apples and oranges, and then store the result in the total_fruit variable that appears on the left side of the =.

It goes almost without saying that the expression on the right side of an assignment can be as complicated as you need. If you've defined variables called boys and girls that will contain the number of boys and the number of girls who are to share the fruit, you can calculate how many pieces of fruit each child will receive if you divide the total equally between them with the statement

```
int fruit_per_child = 0;
fruit_per_child = (apples + oranges) / (boys + girls);
```

Note that you could equally well have declared the variable `fruit_per_child` and initialized it with the result of the expression directly:

```
int fruit_per_child = (apples + oranges) / (boys + girls);
```

You can initialize a variable with *any* expression, as long as all the variables involved have already been defined in preceding statements.

Try It Out: Using the Assignment Operator

You can package some of the code fragments from the previous section into an executable program, just to see them in action:

```
// Program 2.3 - Using the assignment operator
#include <iostream>
using std::cout;
using std::endl;

int main() {
  int apples = 10;
  int oranges = 6;
  int boys = 3;
  int girls = 4;

  int fruit_per_child = (apples + oranges)/(boys + girls);

  scout << endl
      << "Each child gets "
      << fruit_per_child << " fruit.";

  cout << endl;
  return 0;
}
```

This produces the following output:

```
Each child gets 2 fruit.
```

This is exactly what you would expect from the preceding discussion.

Multiple Assignments

You can assign values to several variables in a single statement. For example, the following code sets the contents of apples and oranges to the same value:

```
apples = oranges = 10;
```

The assignment operator is right associative, so this statement executes by first storing the value 10 in oranges and then storing the value in oranges in apples, so it is effectively

```
apples = (oranges = 10);
```

This implies that the expression (oranges = 10) has a value—namely, the value stored in oranges, which is 10. This isn't merely a curiosity. Occasions will arise in which it's convenient to assign a value to a variable within an expression and then to use that value for some other purpose. You can write statements such as this:

```
fruit = (oranges = 10) + (apples = 11);
```

which will store 10 in oranges, 11 in apples, then add the two together and store the result in fruit. It illustrates that an assignment expression has a value. However, although you *can* write statements like this, I don't recommend it. As a rule, you should limit the number of operations per statement. Always assume that one day another programmer will want to understand and modify your code. As such, it's your job to promote clarity and avoid ambiguity.

Modifying the Value of a Variable

Because the assignment operation first evaluates the right side and then stores the result in the variable on the left, you can write statements like this:

```
apples = apples * 2;
```

This statement calculates the value of the right side, apples * 2, using the current value of apples, and then stores the result back in the apples variable. The effect of the statement is therefore to double the value contained in apples.

The need to operate on the existing value of a variable comes up frequently—so much so, in fact, that C++ has a special form of the assignment operator to provide a shorthand way of expressing this.

The op= Assignment Operators

The op= assignment operators are so called because they're composed of an operator and an equals sign (=). Using one such operator, the previous statement for doubling the value of apples could be written as follows:

```
apples *= 2;
```

This is exactly the same operation as the statement in the last section. The `apples` variable is multiplied by the value of the expression on the right side, and the result is stored back in `apples`. The right side can be any expression you like. For instance, you could write

```
apples *= oranges + 2;
```

This is equivalent to

```
apples = apples * (oranges + 2);
```

Here, the value stored in `apples` is multiplied by the number of `oranges` plus 2, and the result is stored back in `apples`. (Though why you would want to multiply apples and oranges together is beyond me!)

The `op=` form of assignment also works with the addition operator, so to increase the number of `oranges` by 2, you could write

```
oranges += 2;
```

This has the same effect as the same as the statement

```
oranges = oranges + 2;
```

You should be able to see a pattern emerging by now. You could write the general form of an assignment statement using the `op=` operator as

```
lhs op= rhs;
```

Here, `lhs` is a variable and `rhs` is an expression. This is equivalent to the statement

```
lhs = lhs op (rhs);
```

The parentheses around `rhs` mean that the expression `rhs` is evaluated first and the result becomes the right operand for the operation `op`.

NOTE `lhs` *is an **lvalue**, which is an entity to which you can assign a value. Lvalues are so called because they can appear on the left side of an assignment. The result of every expression in C++ will be either an lvalue or an **rvalue**. An rvalue is a result that isn't an lvalue—that is, it can't appear on the left of an assignment operation.*

You can use a whole range of operators in the `op=` form of assignment. Table 2-6 shows the complete set, including some operators you'll meet in the next chapter.

Table 2-6. op= Assignment Operators

Operation	Operator	Operation	Operator
Addition	+	Bitwise AND	&
Subtraction	-	Bitwise OR		
Multiplication	•	Bitwise exclusive OR	^
Division	/	Shift left	<<
Modulus	%	Shift right	>>

Note that there can be no spaces between the operator and the =. If you include a space, it will be flagged as an error.

Incrementing and Decrementing Integers

You've seen how you can modify a variable using the assignment operator and how you can increment one with the += operator. I'm sure you've also deduced that you can decrement a variable with -=. However, there are two other rather unusual arithmetic operators that can perform the same tasks. They're called the **increment** and **decrement operators,** ++ and -- respectively.

These operators are more than just other options, and you'll find them to be quite an asset once you get further into applying C++ in earnest. The increment and decrement operators are unary operators that can be applied to an integer variable. For example, assuming the variables are of type int, the following three statements all have exactly the same effect:

```
count = count + 1;
count += 1;
++count;
```

The preceding statements each increment the variable count by 1. The last form, using the increment operator, is clearly the most concise. The action of this operator is different from the other operators that you've seen, in that it *directly* modifies the value of its operand. The effect in an expression is to increment the value of the variable and then to use that incremented value in the expression. For example, suppose count has the value 5, and you execute this statement:

```
total = ++count + 6;
```

The increment and decrement operators are of higher precedence than all the binary arithmetic operators. Thus, count will be first incremented to the value 6, and then this value will be used in the evaluation of the expression on the right side of the assignment operation. The variable total will therefore be assigned the value 12.

You use the decrement operator in the same way as the increment operator:

```
total = --count + 6;
```

Assuming count is 6 before executing this statement, the decrement operator will reduce it to 5, and this value will be used to calculate the value to be stored in total, which will be 11.

Postfix Increment and Decrement Operations

So far, you've written the operators in front of the variables to which they apply. This is called the **prefix** form. The operators can also be written *after* the variables to which they apply; this is the **postfix** form, and the effect is slightly different. When you use the postfix form of ++, the variable to which it applies is incremented *after* its value is used in context. For example, you can rewrite the earlier example as follows:

```
total = count++ + 6;
```

With the same initial value of 5 for count, total is assigned the value 11, because the *initial* value of count is used to evaluate the expression before the increment by 1 is applied. The variable count will then be incremented to 6. The preceding statement is equivalent to the following two statements:

```
total = count + 6;
++count;
```

In an expression such as a++ + b, or even a+++b, it's less than obvious what is meant, or indeed what the compiler will do. These two expressions are actually the same, but in the second case you might really have meant a + ++b, which has a different meaning—it evaluates to one more than the other two expressions. It would be clearer to write the preceding statement as follows:

```
total = 6 + count++;
```

Alternatively, you can use parentheses:

```
total = (count++) + 6;
```

The rules that I've discussed in relation to the increment operator also apply to the decrement operator. For example, suppose count has the initial value 5, and you write the statement

```
total = --count + 6;
```

This results in total having the value 10 assigned, whereas if you write the statement

```
total = 6 + count-- ;
```

the value of total is set to 11.

You should avoid using the prefix form of these operators to operate on a variable more than once in an expression. Suppose the variable count has the value 5, and you write

```
total = ++count * 3 + ++count * 5;
```

First, it looks rather untidy, but that's the least of the problems with this. Second, and crucially, the statement modifies the value of a variable more than once and the result is *undefined* in C++. You could and should get an error message from the compiler with this statement, but in some instances you won't. This isn't a desirable feature in a program to say the least, so don't modify a variable more than once in a statement.

Note also that the effects of statements such as the following are undefined:

```
k = ++k + 1;
```

Here you're incrementing the value of the variable that appears on the right of the assignment operator, so you're attempting to modify the value of the variable k twice within one expression. Each variable can be modified only once as a result of evaluating a single expression, and the prior value of the variable may only be accessed to determine the value to be stored. Although such expressions are undefined according to the C++ standard, this doesn't mean that your compiler won't compile them. It just means that there is no guarantee of consistency in the results.

The increment and decrement operators are usually applied to integers, particularly in the context of **loops**, as you'll see in Chapter 5, and you'll see later in this chapter that they can be applied to floating-point values too. In later chapters, you'll explore how they can also be applied to certain other data types in C++, in some cases with rather specialized (but very useful) effects.

The const Keyword

You'll often feel the need to use constants of one kind or another in your programs: the number of days in January, perhaps, or π, the ratio of the circumference of a circle to its diameter, or even the number of buns in a baker's dozen. However, you should avoid using numeric literals explicitly within calculations; it's much better to use a variable that you've initialized to the appropriate value instead. For example, multiplying a value by 3 doesn't necessarily communicate that you're converting from yards to feet, but multiplying by a variable with the name feet_per_yard that you've initialized to the value 3 makes it absolutely clear what you're doing. Explicit numeric literals in a program are sometimes referred to as **magic numbers**, particularly when their purpose and origin is less than obvious.

Another good reason for using a variable instead of a magic number is that you reduce the number of maintenance points in your code. Imagine that your magic number represents something that changes from time to time—an interest rate, for instance—and that it crops up on several occasions in your code. When the rate changes, you could be faced with a sizable task to correct your program. If you've defined a variable for the purpose, you only need to change the value once, at the point of initialization.

Of course, if you use a variable to hold a constant of this kind, you really want to nail the value down and protect it from accidental modifications. You can use the keyword const to do this, for example:

```
const int feet_per_yard = 3;        // Conversion factor yards to feet
```

You can declare any kind of "variable" as const. The compiler will check that you don't attempt to alter the value of such a variable. For example, if you put something const on the left of an assignment operator, it will be flagged as an error. The obvious consequence of this is that you must always supply an initial value for a variable that you declare as const.

Be aware that declaring a variable as const alters its type. A variable of type const int is quite different from a variable of type int.

Try It Out: Using const

You could implement a little program to convert a length entered as yards, feet, and inches into inches:

```
// Program 2.4 - Using const
#include <iostream>
using std::cin;
using std::cout;
using std::endl;

int main() {
  const int inches_per_foot = 12;
  const int feet_per_yard = 3;
  int yards = 0;
  int feet = 0;
  int inches = 0;

  // Read the length from the keyboard
  cout << "Enter a length as yards, feet, and inches: ";
  cin >> yards >> feet >> inches;

  // Output the length in inches
  cout << endl
       << "Length in inches is "
       << inches + inches_per_foot * (feet + feet_per_yard * yards)
       << endl;
  return 0;
}
```

(Continued)

A typical result from this program is the following:

```
Enter a length as yards, feet, and inches: 2 2 11

Length in inches is 107
```

There's an extra using statement compared to previous examples:

```
using std::cin;
```

This introduces the name cin from the std namespace into the program file that refers to the standard input stream—the keyboard.

You have two conversion constants defined by the statements

```
const int inches_per_foot = 12;
const int feet_per_yard = 3;
```

Declaring them with the keyword const will prevent direct modification of these variables. You could test this by adding a statement such as

```
inches_per_foot = 15;
```

With a statement like this after the declaration of the constant, the program would no longer compile.

You prompt for input and read the values for yards, feet, and inches with these statements:

```
cout << "Enter a length as yards, feet, and inches: ";
cin >> yards >> feet >> inches;
```

Notice how the second line specifies several successive input operations from the stream, cin. You do this by using the extraction operator, >>, that I mentioned briefly in the last chapter. It's analogous to using cout, the stream output operation, for multiple values. The appearance of the insertion and extraction operators provides you with a visual cue as to the direction in which data flows.

The first value read from the keyboard will be stored in yards, the second in feet, and the third in inches. The input handling here is very flexible: you can enter all three values on one line, separated by spaces (in fact, by any whitespace characters), or you can enter them on several lines.

You perform the conversion to inches within the output statement itself:

```
cout << endl
     << "Length in inches is "
     << inches + inches_per_foot * (feet + feet_per_yard * yards)
     << endl;
```

As you can see, the fact that your conversion factors were declared as const in no way affects their use in expressions, just as long as you don't try to modify them.

Numerical Functions for Integers

I explain functions in detail in Chapter 8, but that won't stop us from making use of a few from the standard library before that. Let's do a quick reprise of what's going on when you use functions and cover some of the terminology they introduce.

A **function** is a named, self-contained block of code that carries out a specific task. Often, this will involve it performing some operation on data that you supply and then returning the result of that operation to your program. In those circumstances in which a function returns a value that is numeric, the function can participate in an arithmetic expression just like an ordinary variable. In general, a call to a function looks like this:

```
FunctionName(argument1, argument2, ... )
```

Depending on the function in question, you can supply zero, one, or more values for it to work with by placing them in parentheses after its name when you **call** it from your program. The values you pass to the function in this way are called **arguments**. Like all values in C++, the arguments you pass to a function, and the value it returns to your program, have types that you must take care to conform with in order to use the function.

You can access some numerical functions that you can apply to integers by adding an #include directive for the <cstdlib> header at the beginning of your source file. This header has the same contents as the original C library header, stdlib.h. You'll learn how each of these functions works by considering a few sample statements.

The abs() function returns the absolute value of the argument, which can be of type int or type long. The absolute value of a number is just its magnitude, so taking the absolute value of a negative number returns the number with a positive sign, whereas a positive number will be returned unchanged. The value returned by the abs() function will be of the same type as the argument, for example:

```
int value = -20;
int result = std::abs(value);  // Result is 20
```

The `<cstdlib>` header also defines the `labs()` function that will also produce the absolute value of an argument of type `long`. This function is there because older C programs may use it, but I suggest you just use the `abs()` function.

The `div()` function takes two arguments, both of type `int`. It returns the result of dividing the first argument by the second as well as the remainder from the operation in the form of a **structure** of type `div_t`. I go into structures in detail later on, so for the moment you'll just see how to access the quotient and the remainder from what is returned by the `div()` function through an example:

```
int value = 93;
int divisor = 17;
div_t results = std::div(value, divisor);       // Call the function
std::cout << "\nQuotient is " << results.quot;   // Quotient is 5
std::cout << "\n Remainder is " << results.rem;  // Remainder is 8
```

The first two statements define the variables `value` and `divisor` and give them the initial values 93 and 17, respectively. The next statement calls the `div()` function to divide `value` by `divisor`. You store the resulting structure of type `div_t` that is returned by the function in the variable `results`, which is also of type `div_t`. In the first output statement, you access the quotient from `results` by appending the name `quot` to `results`, separated by a period. The period is called the **member access operator**, and here you're using it to access the `quot` member of the `results` structure. Similarly, in the last statement you use the member access operator to output the value of the remainder, which is available from the `rem` member of the `results` structure. Any structure of type `div_t` will have members with the names `quot` and `rem`, and you always access them by using the member access operator.

Note that you could have used literals directly as arguments to the `div()` function. In this case, the statement calling the function would be

```
div_t results = std::div(93, 17);
```

The `ldiv()` function performs the same operation as the `div()` function, but on arguments of type `long`. The result is returned as a structure of type `ldiv_t`, which has members `quot` and `rem` that are of type `long`.

 CAUTION *The* `<cstdlib>` *header is inherited from C, so many implementations will have definitions of the original C functions defined outside of the* `std` *namespace so the function names can be used without the* `std` *qualifier. This is to allow C programs to be compiled and executed in the same environment, but you should use the functions with the* `std` *qualifier because your code is C++.*

Generating Random Numbers

Being able to generate random numbers in a program is very useful. You need to be able to build randomness into game programs, for instance; otherwise, they become very boring very quickly. The <cstdlib> header defines a function rand() that will generate random integers. To be more precise, it generates **pseudo-random** integers. Random numbers by definition aren't predictable, so any sequence of numbers produced by a numerical algorithm can't be truly random. It just has the appearance of being so. However, now that you understand that, you'll just refer to the numbers produced by the rand() function as random numbers. Note that rand() isn't an outstanding random number generator. For many applications, you'll probably want to use something that's rather more sophisticated.

The rand() function return a random integer as type int. The function doesn't require any arguments, so you can just use it like this:

```
int random_value = std::rand();  // A random integer
```

You store the integer that's returned by the rand() function here in the variable random_value, but you could equally well use it in an arithmetic expression, for example:

```
int even = 2*std::rand();
```

The value returned by the rand() function will be a value that is from 0 to RAND_MAX. RAND_MAX is a symbol that is defined in <cstdlib>. When you use RAND_MAX in your code, the compiler will replace it with an integer value. On my system it represents the value 0x7fff, but on other systems it may have a different value. It can be up to 0x3fffffff, which is the maximum integer you can store as type int. If this was the case, then you couldn't multiply the value produced by rand() by 2, as you did previously, without running the risk of getting an incorrect result. You'll see how you can get around this in the next chapter.

Because RAND_MAX is defined by a preprocessing macro (you'll learn what a preprocessing macro is in Chapter 10), it isn't within the std namespace, so you don't need to qualify the name when you use it. Any symbol that's defined by a macro won't be in the std namespace because it isn't a name that refers to something. By the time the compiler gets to compile the code, such a symbol will no longer be present because it will have already been replaced by something else during the preprocessing phase.

Making the Sequence Start at Random

Using rand() as you have so far, the sequence of numbers will always be the same. This is because the function uses a default seed value in the algorithm that generates the random numbers. This is fine for testing, but once you have a working game program, you'll really want different sequences each time the program runs. You can change the seed value that will be used to generate the numbers by passing a new seed value as an integer argument to the srand() function that is defined in <cstdlib>, for example:

```
std::srand(13); // Set seed for rand to 13
```

The argument to the srand() function must be a value of type unsigned int. Although the preceding statement will result in rand() generating a different sequence from the default, you really need a random seed to get a different sequence from rand() each time you execute a program. Fortunately, the clock on your computer provides a ready-made source of random seed values.

The <ctime> standard library header defines several functions relating to the data and the time. You'll just look at the time() function here because that's precisely what you need to obtain a more or less random seed value. The time() function returns a value that's the number of seconds that have elapsed since midnight on January 1, 1970, so if you use that as a seed, you can be certain that a program will use a different seed value each time it executes. The value is returned as type time_t, which is a type defined in the standard library to be equivalent to an integer type, usually type long. The return type is specified as type time_t to allow flexibility in the type of the return value in different C++ implementations. You can use the time() function to create the seed for a random number sequence like this:

```
std::srand((unsigned int)std::time(0));
```

There are a few things that you'll have to take on trust for the moment. The argument to the time() function here is 0. There's another possibility for the argument, but you don't need it here so you'll ignore it. The subexpression (unsigned int) serves to convert the value returned by the time() function to type unsigned int, which is the type required for the argument to the srand() method. Without this, the statement wouldn't compile. Type conversion is something else that you'll look into later.

Let's put a working example together that makes use of random number generation.

....

Try It Out: Generating Random Integers

Here's the code:

```
// Program 2.5 Using Random Integers
#include <iostream>
#include <cstdlib>
#include <ctime>
using std::cout;
using std::endl;
using std::rand;
using std::srand;
using std::time;

int main() {
  const int limit1 = 500;   // Upper limit for on set of random values
  const int limit2 = 31;    // Upper limit for another set of values
```

```
   cout << "First we will use the default sequence from rand().\n";
   cout << "Three random integer from 0 to " << RAND_MAX << ": "
        << rand() << " " << rand() << " " << rand()<< endl;

   cout << endl << "Now we will use a new seed for rand().\n";
   srand((unsigned int)time(0));                // Set a new seed

   cout << "Three random integer from 0 to " << RAND_MAX << ": "
        << rand() << " " << rand() << " " << rand()<< endl;
   return 0;
}
```

On my system I get the following output:

```
First we will use the default sequence from rand().
Three random integer from 0 to 32767: 6334 18467 41

Now we will use a new seed for rand().
Three random integer from 0 to 32767: 4610 32532 28452
```

HOW IT WORKS

This is a straightforward use of the rand() function, first with the default seed to start the sequence:

```
   cout << "A random integer from 0 to " << RAND_MAX << ": "
        << rand() << endl;
```

Each call to rand() returns a value that will be from 0 to RAND_MAX, and you call the function three times to get a sequence of three random integers.

Next, you set the seed value as the current value of the system clock with this statement:

```
   srand((unsigned int)time(0));                // Set a new seed
```

This statement will generally result in a different seed being set each time you execute the program. You then repeat the statement that you executed previously with the default seed set. Thus, each time you run this program, the first set will always produce the same output, whereas with the second set, the output should be different.

Floating-Point Operations

Numerical values that aren't integers are stored as **floating-point** numbers. Internally, floating-point numbers have three parts: a sign (positive or negative), a mantissa (which is a value greater than or equal to 1 and less than 2 that has a fixed number of digits), and an exponent. Inside your computer, of course, both the mantissa and the exponent are binary values, but for the purposes of explaining how floating-point numbers work, I'll talk about them as decimal values.

The value of a floating-point number is the signed value of the mantissa, multiplied by 10 to the power of the exponent, as shown in Table 2-7.

Table 2-7. Floating-Point Number Value

Sign(+/-)	Mantissa	Exponent	Value
-	1.2345	3	-1.2345×10^3 (which is -1234.5)

You can write a floating point literal in three basic forms:

- As a decimal value including a decimal point (for example, 110.0).

- With an exponent (for example, 11E1) in which the decimal part is multiplied by the power of 10 specified after the *E* (for exponent). You have the option of using either an upper- or a lowercase letter *E* to precede the exponent.

- Using both a decimal point and an exponent (for example, 1.1E2).

All three examples correspond to the same value, 110.0. Note that spaces aren't allowed within floating-point literals, so you must not write 1.1 E2, for example. The latter would be interpreted by the compiler as two separate things: the floating-point literal 1.1 and the name E2.

 NOTE *A floating-point literal must contain a decimal point, or an exponent, or both. If you write a numeric literal with neither, then you have an integer.*

Floating-Point Data Types

There are three floating-point data types that you can use, as described in Table 2-8.

Table 2-8. Floating-Point Data Types

Data Type	Description
float	Single precision floating-point values
double	Double precision floating-point values
long double	Double-extended precision floating-point values

The term "precision" here refers to the number of significant digits in the mantissa. The data types are in order of increasing precision, with float providing the lowest number of digits in the mantissa and long double the highest. Note that the precision only determines the number of digits in the *mantissa*. The range of numbers that can be represented by a particular type is determined by the range of possible exponents.

The precision and range of values aren't prescribed by the ANSI standard for C++, so what you get with each of these types depends on your compiler. This will usually make the best of the floating-point hardware facilities provided by your computer. Generally, type long double will provide a precision that's greater than or equal to that of type double, which in turn will provide a precision that is greater than or equal to that of type float.

Typically, you'll find that type float will provide 7 digits precision, type double will provide 15 digits precision, and type long double will provide 19 digits precision, although double and long double turn out to be the same with some compilers. As well as increased precision, you'll usually get an increased range of values with types double and long double.

Typical ranges of values that you can represent with the floating-point types on an Intel processor are shown in Table 2-9.

Table 2-9. Floating-Point Type Ranges

Type	Precision (Decimal Digits)	Range (+ or -)
float	7	1.2×10^{-38} to 3.4×10^{38}
double	15	2.2×10^{-308} to 1.8×10^{308}
long double	19	3.3×10^{-4932} to 1.2×10^{4932}

The numbers of decimal digits of precision in Table 2-9 are approximate. Zero can be represented exactly for each of these types, but values between zero and the lower limit in the positive or negative range can't be represented, so these lower limits for the ranges are the smallest *nonzero* values that you can have.

Simple floating-point literals with just a decimal point are of type double, so let's look at how to define variables of that type first. You can specify a floating-point variable using the keyword double, as in this statement:

```
double inches_to_mm = 25.4;
```

This declares the variable inches_to_mm to be of type double and initializes it with the value 25.4. You can also use const when declaring floating-point variables, and this is a case in which you could sensibly do so. If you want to fix the value of the variable, the declaration statement might be

```
const double inches_to_mm = 25.4;   // A constant conversion factor
```

If you don't need the precision and range of values that variables of type double provide you can opt to use the keyword float to declare your floating-point variable, for example:

```
float pi = 3.14159f;
```

This statement defines a variable pi with the initial value 3.14159. The f at the end of the literal specifies it to be a float type. Without the f, the literal would have been of type double, which wouldn't cause a problem in this case, although you may get a warning message from your compiler. You can also use an uppercase letter *F* to indicate that a floating-point literal is of type float.

To specify a literal of type long double, you append an upper- or lowercase *L* to the number. You could therefore declare and initialize a variable of this type with the statement

```
long double root2 = 1.4142135623730950488L;      // Square root of 2
```

Floating-Point Operations

The modulus operator, %, can't be used with floating-point operands, but all the other binary arithmetic operators that you have seen, +, -, *, and /, can be. You can also apply the prefix and postfix increment and decrement operators, ++ and --, to a floating-point variable with the same effect as for an integer—the variable will be incremented or decremented by 1.

As with integer operands, the result of division by zero is undefined so far as the standard is concerned, but specific C++ implementations generally have their own way of dealing with this, so consult your product documentation.

With most computers today, the hardware floating-point operations are implemented according to the IEEE 754 standard (also known as IEC 559). Although IEEE 754 isn't required by the C++ standard, it does provide for identification of some aspects of floating-point operations on machines on which IEEE 754 applies. The floating-point standard defines special values having a binary mantissa of all zeros and an exponent of all ones to represent +infinity or -infinity, depending on the sign. When you divide a positive nonzero value by zero, the result will be +infinity, and dividing a negative value by zero will result in -infinity. Another special floating-point value defined by IEEE 754 is called Not a Number, usually abbreviated to NaN. This is used to represent a result that isn't mathematically defined, such as arises when you divide zero by zero or you divide infinity by infinity.

Any subsequent operation in which either or both operands are a value of NaN results in NaN. Once an operation in your program results in a value of ±infinity, this will pollute all subsequent operations in which it participates. Combining a normal value with ±infinity results in ±infinity. Dividing ±infinity by ±infinity or multiplying ±infinity by zero results in NaN. Table 2-10 summarizes all these possibilities.

Table 2-10. Floating-Point Operations with NaN Operands

Operation	Result	Operation	Result
±N/0	±Infinity	0/0	NaN
±Infinity±N	±Infinity	±Infinity/±Infinity	NaN
±Infinity*N	±Infinity	Infinity-Infinity	NaN
±Infinity/N	±Infinity	Infinity*0	NaN

Using floating-point variables is really quite straightforward, but there's no substitute for experience, so let's try an example.

Try It Out: Floating-Point Arithmetic

Suppose that you want to construct a circular pond in which you want to keep a number of fish. Having looked into the matter, you know that you must allow 2 square feet of surface area on the pond for every 6 inches of fish length. You need to figure out the diameter of the pond that will keep the fish happy. Here's how you can do it:

```
// Program 2.6 Sizing a pond for happy fish
#include <iostream>
#include <cmath>                        // For square root calculation
using std::cout;
using std::cin;
using std::sqrt;

int main() {
  const double fish_factor = 2.0/0.5; // Area per unit length of fish
  const double inches_per_foot = 12.0;
  const double pi = 3.14159265;

  double fish_count = 0.0;           // Number of fish
  double fish_length = 0.0;          // Average length of fish

  cout << "Enter the number of fish you want to keep: ";
  cin >> fish_count;
  cout << "Enter the average fish length in inches: ";
  cin >> fish_length;
  fish_length = fish_length/inches_per_foot; // Convert to feet

  // Calculate the required surface area
  double pond_area = fish_count * fish_length * fish_factor;

  // Calculate the pond diameter from the area
  double pond_diameter = 2.0 * sqrt(pond_area/pi);

  cout << "\nPond diameter required for " << fish_count << " fish is "
       << pond_diameter << " feet.\n";
  return 0;
}
```

(Continued)

With input values of 20 fish with an average length of 9 inches, this example produces the following output:

```
Enter the number of fish you want to keep: 20
Enter the average fish length in inches: 9
Pond diameter required for 20 fish is 8.74039 feet.
```

HOW IT WORKS

You first declare three const variables that you'll use in the calculation:

```
const double fish_factor = 2.0/0.5; // Area per unit length of fish
const double inches_per_foot = 12.0;
const double pi = 3.14159265;
```

Notice the use of a constant expression to specify the value for fish_factor. You can use any expression that produces a result of the appropriate type to define an initializing value for a variable. You have declared fish_factor, inches_per_foot, and pi as const because you don't want to allow them to be altered.

Next, you declare variables in which you'll store the user input:

```
double fish_count = 0.0;           // Number of fish
double fish_length = 0.0;          // Average length of fish
```

You don't have to initialize these, but it's good practice to do so.

Because the input for the fish length is in inches, you need to convert it to feet before you use it in the calculation for the pond:

```
fish_length = fish_length/inches_per_foot; // Convert to feet
```

This stores the converted value back in the original variable.

You get the required area for the pond with the following statement:

```
double pond_area = fish_count * fish_length * fish_factor;
```

The product of fish_count and fish_length gives the total length of all the fish, and multiplying this by fish_factor gives the required area.

The area of any circle is given by the formula πr^2, where r is the radius. You can therefore calculate the radius of the pond as the square root of the area divided by π. The diameter is then twice the radius, and the whole calculation is carried out by this statement:

```
pond_diameter = 2.0 * sqrt(pond_area / pi);
```

You obtain the square root using a function that's declared in the standard header <cmath>. The sqrt() function returns the square root of the value of the expression placed between the parentheses after the function name. In this case, the value returned is of type double because the value of the expression is of type double, but there's also a version that returns the square root of a float value as type float. The <cmath> header contains declarations for many other standard library numerical functions, as you'll see a little later in this chapter. You'll look into functions in detail, including how you can define your own functions, in Chapter 8. Of course, like almost all the other names in the standard library, sqrt is defined within the std namespace, so you have a using declaration for the name at the beginning of your program file.

The last step before exiting main() is to output the result:

```
cout << "\nPond diameter required for " << fish_count << " fish is "
    << pond_diameter << " feet.\n";
```

This outputs the pond diameter required for the number of fish specified.

Working with Floating-Point Values

For most computations using floating-point values, you'll find that type double is more than adequate. However, you need to be aware of the limitations and pitfalls of working with floating-point variables. If you're not careful, your results may be inaccurate, or even incorrect. The following are common sources of errors when using floating-point values:

- Many decimal values don't convert exactly to binary floating-point values. The small errors that occur can easily be amplified in your calculations to produce large errors.

- Taking the difference between two nearly identical values can lose precision. If you take the difference between two values of type float that differ in the sixth significant digit, you'll produce a result that may have only one or two digits of accuracy. The other significant digits that are stored may represent errors.

- Dealing with a wide range of possible values can lead to errors. You can create an elementary illustration of this by adding two values stored as type float with 7 digits of precision but in which one value is 10^8 times larger that the other. You can add the smaller value to the larger as many times as you like, and the larger value will be unchanged. The <cfloat> header defines constants for the floating-point types that are the smallest values that you can add to 1.0 and get a different result. The constants are FLT_EPSILON, DBL_EPSILON, and LDBL_EPSILON.

Let's see how these errors can manifest themselves in practice, albeit in a somewhat artificial situation.

....

Try It Out: Errors in Floating-Point Calculations

Here's an example contrived to illustrate how the first two points can combine to produce errors:

```
// Program 2.7 Floating point errors
#include <iostream>
using std::cout;
using std::endl;

int main() {
  float value1 = 0.1f;
  float value2 = 2.1f;
  value1 -= 0.09f;                    // Should be 0.01
  value2 -= 2.09f;                    // Should be 0.01
  cout << value1 - value2 << endl;    // Should output zero
  return 0;
}
```

The value displayed should be zero, but on my computer this program produces the following:

7.45058e-009

HOW IT WORKS

The reason for the error is that none of the numerical values is stored exactly. If you add code to output the values of value1 and value2 after they've been modified, you should see a discrepancy between them.

Of course, the final difference between the values of value1 and value2 is a very small number, but you could be using this totally spurious value in other calculations in which the error could be amplified. If you multiply this result by 10^{10}, say, you'll get an answer around 7.45, when the result should really be zero. Similarly, if you compare these two values, expecting them to be equal, you don't get the result you expect.

 CAUTION *Never rely on an exact floating-point representation of a decimal value in your program code.*

....

Tweaking the Output

The previous program outputs the floating-point value in a very sensible fashion. It gave you 5 decimal places, and it used scientific notation (that is, a mantissa and an exponent). However, you could have chosen to have the output displayed using "normal" decimal notation by employing some more output manipulators.

Try It Out: Yet More Output Manipulators

Here's the same code as in the previous "Try It Out" exercise, except that it uses additional manipulators to improve the appearance of the output:

```
// Program 2.8 Experimenting with floating point output
#include <iostream>
#include <iomanip>
using std::setprecision;
using std::fixed;
using std::scientific;
using std::cout;
using std::endl;

int main() {
  float value1 = 0.1f;
  float value2 = 2.1f;
  value1 -= 0.09f;                          // Should be 0.01
  value2 -= 2.09f;                          // Should be 0.01

  cout << setprecision(14) << fixed;        // Change to fixed notation
  cout << value1 - value2 << endl;          // Should output zero

  cout << setprecision(5) << scientific;    // Set scientific notation
  cout << value1 - value2 << endl;          // Should output zero

  return 0;
}
```

When I run the modified program, this is the output I get:

```
0.00000000745058
7.45058e-009
```

(Continued)

This code uses three new manipulators. The setprecision() manipulator specifies how many decimal places should appear after the decimal point when you're outputting a floating-point number. The fixed and scientific manipulators complement one another and choose the format in which a floating-point number should be displayed when they're written to the stream.

By default, your C++ compiler will select either scientific or fixed, depending on the particular value you're outputting, and you saw in the first version of this program that it performed that task admirably. The default number of decimal places isn't defined in the standard, but five is common.

Let's look at the changes made. Apart from the #include for <iomanip>, just as you needed when you were using setw() earlier in the chapter and the additional using declarations, the interest is in these four lines of code:

```
cout << setprecision(14) << fixed;       // Change to fixed notation
cout << value1 - value2 << endl;         // Should output zero

cout << setprecision(5) << scientific;   // Set scientific notation
cout << value1 - value2 << endl;         // Should output zero
```

The first line is easy: you use the manipulators like you used setw(), by sending them to the output stream with the insertion operator. Their effects can then clearly be seen in the first line of output: you get a floating-point value with 14 decimal places and no exponent.

Note that these manipulators differ from setw() in that they're **modal**. In other words, they remain in effect for the stream until the end of the program, unless you set a different option. That's the reason for the third line in the preceding code—you have to set scientific mode and a precision of 5 *explicitly* in order to return to "default" behavior. You can see that you've succeeded, though, because the second line of output is the same as the one produced by the original program.

 NOTE *Actually, the* <iomanip> *header is only required here for the* setprecision() *manipulator. Both* fixed *and* scientific *are defined in* <iostream>. *There are more manipulators to discuss, but the rule is that the ones requiring values (such as* setw() *and* setprecision()) *are defined in* <iomanip>, *whereas the others are defined in* <iostream>.

Mathematical Functions

The <cmath> standard library header defines a range of trigonometric and numerical functions that you can use in your programs. You've already seen the sqrt() function. Table 2-11 presents some other numerical functions from this header that you may find useful.

Table 2-11. <cmath> Numerical Functions

Function	Description
abs(arg)	Returns the absolute value of arg as the same type as arg, where arg can be of any floating-point type. There are versions of the abs() function declared in the <cstdlib> header file for arguments of type int and type long.
fabs(arg)	Returns the absolute value of arg as the same type as the argument. The argument can be int, long, float, double, or long double.
ceil(arg)	Returns a floating-point value of the same type as arg that is the smallest integer greater than or equal to arg, so ceil(2.5) produces the value 3.0. arg can be of any floating-point type.
floor(arg)	Returns a floating-point value of the same type as arg that is the largest integer less than or equal to arg so the value returned by floor(2.5) will be 2.0. arg can be of any floating-point type.
exp(arg)	Returns the value of e^{arg} as the same type as arg. arg can be of any floating-point type.
log(arg)	The log function returns the natural logarithm (to base e) of arg as the same type as arg. arg can be any floating-point type.
log10(arg)	The log10 function returns the logarithm to base 10 of arg as the same type as arg. arg can be any floating-point type.
pow(arg1, arg2)	The pow function returns the value of arg1 raised to the power arg1, which is $arg1^{arg2}$. Thus the result of pow(2, 3) will be 8, and the result of pow(1.5, 3) will be 3.375. The arguments can be both of type int or any floating-point type. The second argument, arg2, may also be of type int with arg1 of type int, or long, or any floating-point type. The value returned will be of the same type as arg1.

Table 2-12 shows the trigonometric functions that you have available in the <cmath> header.

Table 2-12. <cmath> Trigonometric Functions

Function	Description
cos(angle)	Returns the cosine of the angle expressed in radians that is passed as the argument.
sin(angle)	Returns the sine of the angle expressed in radians that is passed as the argument.
tan(angle)	Returns the tangent of the angle expressed in radians that is passed as the argument.
cosh(angle)	Returns the hyperbolic cosine of the angle expressed in radians that is passed as the argument. The hyperbolic cosine of a variable x is given by formula $(e^x-e^{-x})/2$.
sinh(angle)	Returns the hyperbolic sine of the angle expressed in radians that is passed as the argument. The hyperbolic sine of a variable x is given by the formula $(e^x+e^{-x})/2$.
tanh(angle)	Returns the hyperbolic tangent of the angle expressed in radians that is passed as the argument. The hyberbolic tangent of a variable x is given by the hyperbolic sine of x divided by the hyperbolic cosine of x.
acos(arg)	Returns the inverse cosine (arccosine) of arg. The argument must be between -1 and $+1$. The result is in radians and will be from 0 to π.
asin(arg)	Returns the inverse sine (arcsine) of the argument. The argument must be between -1 and $+1$. The result is in radians and will be from $-\pi/2$ to $+\pi/2$.
atan(arg)	Returns the inverse tangent (arctangent) of the argument. The result is in radians and will be from $-\pi/2$ to $+\pi/2$.
atan2(arg1, arg2)	This function requires two arguments of the same floating-point type. The function returns the inverse tangent of arg1/arg2. The result will be in the range from $-\pi$ to $+\pi$ radians and of the same type as the arguments.

The arguments to these functions can be of any floating-point type and the result will be returned as the same type as the argument(s).

Let's look at some examples of how these are used. Here's how you can calculate the sine of an angle in radians:

```
double angle = 1.5;                // In radians
double sine_value = std::sin(angle);
```

If the angle is in degrees, you can calculate the tangent by using a value for π to convert to radians:

```
float angle_deg = 60.0f;    // Angle in degrees
const float pi = 1.14159f;
const float pi_degrees = 180.0f;
float tangent = std::tan(pi*angle_deg/pi_degrees);
```

If you know the height of the church steeple is 100 feet and you're standing 50 feet from the base of the steeple, you can calculate the angle in radians of the top of the steeple like this:

```
double height = 100.0;              // Steeple height- feet
double distance = 50.0;             // Distance from base
angle = std::atan2(height, distance);  // Result in radians
```

You can use this value in `angle` and the value of `distance` to calculate the distance from your toe to the top of the steeple:

```
double toe_to_tip = distance*std::cos(angle);
```

Of course, fans of Pythagoras of Samos could obtain the result much more easily, like this:

```
double toe_to_tip = std::sqrt(std::pow(distance,2) +
                                       std::pow(height, 2);
```

Working with Characters

Variables of type `char` are primarily used to store a code for a single character and occupy 1 byte in memory. The C++ standard doesn't specify the character encoding to be used for representing the basic character set, so this is determined by a particular compiler. It's typically, but not exclusively, ASCII.

You declare variables of type `char` in the same way as variables of the other types that you've seen, for example:

```
char letter;
char yes, no;
```

The first statement declares a single variable of type `char` with the name `letter`. The second variable declares two variables of type `char` having the names `yes` and `no`. Each of these variables can store the code for a single character. Because you haven't provided initial values for these variables, they'll contain junk values.

Character Literals

When you declare a variable of type `char`, you can initialize it with a character literal. You write a character literal as the character that you require between single quotes. For example, `'z'`, `'3'`, and `'?'` are all character literals.

Some characters are problematical to enter as literals. Obviously, a single quote presents a bit of a difficulty because it's a delimiter for a character literal. In fact, it isn't legal in C++ to put either a single quote or a backslash character between single quotes. Control characters such as newline and tab are also a problem because they result in an effect when you press the key for the appropriate character rather than entering the character as data. You can specify all of these problem characters by using escape sequences that begin with a backslash, as shown in Table 2-13.

Table 2-13. Escape Sequences for Problem Characters

Character		Escape Sequence
Newline	NL(LF)	\n
Horizontal tab	HT	\t
Vertical tab	VT	\v
Backspace	BS	\b
Carriage return	CR	\r
Form feed	FF	\f
Alert	BEL	\a
Backslash	\	\\
Single quote	'	\'
Double quote	"	\"
Question mark	?	\?

To specify a character literal corresponding to any of these characters, you just type in the corresponding escape sequence between single quotes. For instance, new-line is '\n' and backslash is '\\'.

There are also escape sequences that you can use to specify a character by its code expressed as either an octal or a hexadecimal value. The escape sequence for an octal character code is one to three octal digits preceded by a backslash. The escape sequence for a hexadecimal character code is one or more hexadecimal digits preceded by \x. You write both forms between single quotes when you want to define a character literal. For example, the letter 'A' could be written as hexadecimal '\x41' or octal '\81' in US-ASCII code. Obviously, you could write codes that won't fit within a single byte, in which case the result is implementation defined.

If you write a character literal with more than one character between the single quotes and the characters don't represent an escape sequence—'abc' is an example— then the literal is described as a **multicharacter literal** and will be of type int. The numerical value of such a literal is implementation defined but will usually be the result of placing the 1-byte codes for the characters in successive bytes of the int value. If you specify a multicharacter literal with more than four characters, this will usually result in an error message from the compiler.

You now know enough about character literals to initialize your variables of type char properly.

Initializing char Variables

You can define and initialize a variable of type char with the statement

```
char letter = 'A';        // Stores a single letter 'A'
```

This statement defines the variable with the name letter to be of type char with an initial value 'A'. If your compiler represents characters using US-ASCII codes, this will have the decimal value 65.

You can declare and initialize multiple variables in a single statement:

```
char yes = 'y', no = 'n', tab = '\t';
```

Because you can treat variables of type char as integers, you could equally well declare and initialize the variable letter with this statement:

```
char letter = 65;          // Stores the ASCII code for 'A'
```

Remember that type char may be signed or unsigned by default, depending on the compiler, so this will affect what numerical values can be accommodated. If char is unsigned, values can be from 0 to 255. If it's signed, values can be from –128 to +127. Of course, the range of bit patterns that can be stored is the same in both cases. They're just interpreted differently.

Of course, you can use the variable letter as an operand in integer operations, so you can write

```
letter += 2;
```

This will result in the value stored in letter being incremented to 67, which is 'C' in US-ASCII. You can find all the US-ASCII codes in Appendix A of this book.

 CAUTION *Although I've assumed US-ASCII coding in the examples, as I noted earlier although this is usually the case this doesn't have to be so. On older mainframe computers, for instance, characters may be represented using Extended Binary Coded Decimal Interchange Code (EBCDIC), in which the codes for some characters are different from US-ASCII.*

You can explicitly declare a variable as type signed char or unsigned char, which will affect the range of integers that can be represented. For example, you can declare a variable as follows:

```
unsigned char ch = 0U;
```

In this case, the numerical values can range from 0 to 255.

When you read from a stream into a variable of type char, the first nonwhitespace character will be stored. This means that you can't read whitespace characters in this way—they're simply ignored. Further, you can't read a numerical value into a variable of type char—if you try, you'll find that the character code for the first digit will be stored. When you output a variable of type char to the screen, it will be as a character, not a numerical value. You can see this demonstrated in the next example.

Try It Out: Handling Character Values

This example reads a character from the keyboard, outputs the character and its numerical code, increments the value of the character, and outputs the result as a character and as an integer:

```
// Program 2.9 - Handling character values
#include <iostream>
using std::cin;
using std::cout;
using std::endl;

int main() {
  char ch = 0;
  int ch_value = 0;

  // Read a character from the keyboard
  cout << "Enter a character: ";
  cin >> ch;
  ch_value = ch;                     // Get integer value of character

  cout << endl
       << ch << " is " << ch_value;

  ch_value = ++ch;                   // Increment ch and store as integer
  cout << endl
       << ch << " is " << ch_value
       << endl;

  return 0;
}
```

Typical output from this example is as follows:

```
Enter a character: w

w is 119
x is 120
```

HOW IT WORKS

After prompting for input, the program reads a character from the keyboard with the statement

```
cin >> ch;
```

Only nonwhitespace characters are accepted, so you can press Enter or enter spaces and tabs and they'll all be ignored.

Stream output will always output the variable ch as a character. To get the numerical code, you need a way to convert it to an integer type. The next statement does this:

```
ch_value = ch;                // Get integer value of character
```

The compiler will arrange to convert the value stored in ch from type char to type int so that it can be stored in the variable ch_value. You'll see more about automatic conversions in the next chapter, when I discuss expressions involving values of different types.

Now you can output the character as well as its integer code with the following statement:

```
cout << endl
     << ch << " is " << ch_value;
```

The next statement demonstrates that you can operate with variables of type char as integers:

```
ch_value = ++ch;              // Increment ch and store as integer
```

This statement increments the contents of ch and stores the result in the variable ch_value, so you have both the next character and its numerical representation. This is output to the display with exactly the same statement as was used previously. Although you just incremented ch here, variables of type char can be used with all of the arithmetic operators, just like any of the integer types.

Working with Extended Character Sets

Single-byte character codes such as ASCII or EBCDIC are generally adequate for national language character sets that use Latin characters. There are also 8-bit character encodings that will accommodate other languages such as Greek or Russian. However, if you want to work with these and Latin characters simultaneously, or if you want to handle character sets for Asian languages that require much larger numbers of character codes than the ASCII set, 256 character codes doesn't go far enough.

The type wchar_t is a character type that can store all members of the largest extended character set that's support by an implementation. The type name derives from **wide char**acters, because the character is "wider" than the usual single-byte character. By contrast, type char is referred to as "narrow" because of the limited range of character codes that are available. The size of variables of type wchar_t isn't stipulated by the C++ standard, except that it will have the same characteristics as one of the other integer types. It is often 2 bytes on PCs, and typically the underlying type is unsigned short, but it can also be 4 bytes with some compilers, especially those implemented on Unix workstations.

Wide-Character Literals

You define wide-character literals in the same way as narrow character literals that you use with type char, but you prefix them with the letter *L*. For example,

```
wchar_t wide_letter = L'Z';
```

defines the variable wide_letter to be of type wchar_t and initializes it to the wide-character representation for *Z*.

Your keyboard may not have keys for representing other national language characters, but you can still create them using hexadecimal notation, for example:

```
wchar_t wide_letter = L'\x0438';  // Cyrillic и
```

The value between the single quotes is an **escape sequence** that allows you to specify a character by a hexadecimal representation of the character code. The backslash indicates the start of the escape sequence, and the x after the backslash signifies that the code is hexadecimal. The absence of x or X would indicate that the characters that follow are to be interpreted as octal digits.

Of course, you could also use the notation for UCS character literals:

```
wchar_t wide_letter = L'\u0438';  // Cyrillic и
```

If your compiler supports 4-byte UCS characters, you could also initialize a variable of type wchar_t with a UCS character specified as \Udddddddd, where d is a hexadecimal digit.

Wide-Character Streams

The streams cin and cout that you've been using are narrow-character streams. They only handle characters that consist of a single byte, so you can't extract from cin into a variable of type wchar_t. The <iostream> header defines special wide-character streams, wcin and wcout for input and output of wide characters. You use the wide streams in the same way as the narrow streams. For instance, you can read a wide character from wcin like this:

```
wchat_t wide_letter = 0;
std::wcin >> wide_letter; // Read a wide character
```

Although you'll always be able to write wide characters to wcout, this doesn't mean that such characters will display correctly or at all. It depends on if your operating system recognizes the character codes.

Functional Notation for Initial Values

An alternative notation for specifying the initial value for a variable when you declare it is called **functional notation**. The term stems from the fact that you put the initial value between parentheses after the variable name, so it looks like a function call, as you'll discover later on.

Let's look at an example. Instead of writing a declaration as

```
int unlucky = 13;
```

you have the option to write the statement as

```
int unlucky(13);
```

Both statements achieve exactly the same result: they declare the variable unlucky as type int and give it an initial value of 13.

You can initialize other types of variables using functional notation. For instance, you could declare and initialize a variable to store a character with this statement:

```
char letter('A');
```

However, functional notation for initializing variables is primarily used for the initialization of variables of a data type that you've defined. In this case, it really does involve calling a function. The initialization of variables of the fundamental types in C++ normally uses the approach you have taken up to now. You'll have to wait until Chapter 11 to find out about creating your own types and how those kinds of variables get initialized!

Summary

In this chapter, I covered the basics of computation in C++. You learned about most of the fundamental types of data that are provided for in the language. The essentials of what I've discussed up to now are as follows:

- Numeric and character constants are called literals.

- You can define integer literals as decimal, hexadecimal, or octal values.

- A floating-point literal must contain a decimal point, or an exponent, or both.

- Named objects in C++, such as variables, can have names that consist of a sequence of letters and digits, the first of which is a letter, and where an underscore is considered to be a letter. Upper- and lowercase letters are distinguished.

- Names that begin with an underscore followed by a capital letter, and names that contain two successive underscores, are reserved for use within the standard library, so you shouldn't use them for names of your own variables.

- All literals and variables in C++ are of a given type.

- The basic types that can store integers are short, int, and long. These store signed integers by default, but you can also use the type modifier unsigned preceding any of these type names to produce a type that occupies the same number of bytes but only stores unsigned integers.

- A variable of type char can store a single character and occupies 1 byte. The type char may be signed or unsigned by default, depending on your compiler. You can also use variables of the types signed char and unsigned char to store integers.

- The type wchar_t can store a wide character and occupies either 2 or 4 bytes, depending on your compiler.

- The floating-point data types are float, double, and long double.

- The name and type of a variable appear in a declaration statement ending with a semicolon. A declaration for a variable that results in memory being allocated is also a definition of the variable.

- Variables may be given initial values when they're declared, and it's good programming practice to do so.

- You can protect the value of a "variable" of a basic type by using the modifier const. The compiler will check for any attempts within the program source file to modify a variable declared as const.

- An lvalue is an object or expression that can appear on the left side of an assignment. Non-const variables are examples of lvalues.

Although I discussed quite a few basic types in this chapter, don't be misled into thinking that's all there are. There are some other basic types, as well as more complex types based on the basic set, as you'll see, and eventually you'll be creating original types of your own.

Exercises

The following exercises enable you to try out what you've learned in this chapter. If you get stuck, look back over the chapter for help. If you're still stuck, you can download the solutions from the Downloads area of the Apress website (http://www.apress.com), but that really should be a last resort.

Exercise 2-1. Write a program that will compute the area of a circle. The program should prompt for the radius of the circle to be entered from the keyboard, calculate the area using the formula area = pi * radius * radius, and then display the result.

Exercise 2-2. Using your solution for Exercise 2-1, improve the code so that the user can control the precision of the output by entering the number of digits required. (Hint: Use the setprecision() manipulator.)

Exercise 2-3. Create a program that converts inches to feet-and-inches— for example, an input of 77 inches should produce an output of 6 feet and 5 inches. Prompt the user to enter an integer value corresponding to the number of inches, and then make the conversion and output the result. (Hint: Use a const to store the inches-to-feet conversion rate; the modulus operator will be very helpful.)

Exercise 2-4. For your birthday you've been given a long tape measure and an instrument that allows you to determine angles—the angle between the horizontal and a line to the top of a tree, for instance. If you know the distance, d, you are from a tree, and the height, h, of your eye when peering into your angle-measuring device, you can calculate the height of the tree with this formula:

h+d*tan(angle)

Create a program to read h in inches, d in feet and inches, and angle in degrees from the keyboard, and output the height of the tree in feet.

NOTE *There is no need to chop down any trees to verify the accuracy of your program. Just check the solutions on the Apress website* (http://www.apress.com/book/download.html).

Exercise 2-5. Here's an exercise for puzzle fans. Write a program that will prompt the user to enter two different positive integers. Identify in the output the value of the larger integer and the value of the smaller integer. (This *can* be done with what you've learned in this chapter!)

More on Handling Basic Data Types

IN THIS CHAPTER, I expand on the types that I discussed in the previous chapter and explain how variables of the basic types interact in more complicated situations. I also introduce some new features of C++ and discuss some of the ways that these are used.

In this chapter you'll learn

- How expressions involving mixed types of data are evaluated

- How you can convert a value from one basic type to another

- What the bitwise operators are and how you can use them

- How you can define a new type that limits variables to a fixed range of possible values

- How you can define alternative names for existing data types

- What the storage duration of a variable is and what determines it

- What variable scope is and what its effects are

Mixed Expressions

You're probably aware that your computer can only perform arithmetic operations on pairs of values of the same type. It can add two integers, and it can add two floating-point values, but it can't directly add an integer to a floating-point value. The expression 2 + 7.5, for example, can't be evaluated as it stands because 2 is an integer and 7.5 is a floating-point number.

The only way you can do this calculation is to convert one of the values into the same type as the other—typically, the integer value will be converted to its floating-point equivalent, so the expression will be calculated as 2.0 + 7.5. The same applies to mixed expressions in C++. Each binary arithmetic operation requires both operands to be of the same type; if they're different, one of them must be converted to the type of the other. Consider the following sequence of statements:

```
int value1 = 10;
long value2 = 25L;
float value3 = 30.0f;
double result = value1 + value2 + value3;     // Mixed calculation
```

The value of `result` is calculated as the sum of three different types of variables. For each add operation, one of the operands will be converted to the type of the other before the addition can be carried out. The conversion to be applied, and which operand it applies to, is determined by a set of rules that are checked in sequence until one is found that applies to the operation to be carried out. The preceding statement is actually executed with the following steps:

1. `value1 + value2` is calculated by converting `value1` to type `long` before the addition. The result is also of type `long`, so the calculation is `10L + 25L = 35L`.

2. The next operation is `35L + value3`. The previous result, `35L`, is converted to type `float` before it's added to `value3`. The result is of type `float`, so the operation will be `35.0f + 30.0f = 65.0f`.

3. Finally, the previous result is converted to type `double` and stored in `result`.

The rules for dealing with mixed expressions only come into play when the types of the operands for a binary operator are different. These rules, in the sequence in which they're applied, are as follows:

1. If either operand is of type `long double`, the other is converted to `long double`.

2. If either operand is of type `double`, the other is converted to `double`.

3. If either operand is of type `float`, the other is converted to `float`.

4. Any operand of type `char`, `signed char`, `unsigned char`, `short`, or `unsigned short` is converted to type `int`, as long as type `int` can represent all the values of the original operand type. Otherwise, the operand is converted to type `unsigned int`.

5. An enumeration type is converted to the first of `int`, `unsigned int`, `long`, or `unsigned long` that accommodates the range of the enumerators.

6. If either operand is of type `unsigned long`, the other is converted to `unsigned long`.

7. If one operand is of type `long` and the other is of type `unsigned int`, then provided type `long` can represent all the values of an `unsigned int`, the `unsigned int` is converted to type `long`. Otherwise, both operands are converted to type `unsigned long`.

8. If either operand is of type `long`, the other is converted to type `long`.

You haven't seen enumeration types yet, but you'll look at them little later in this chapter. They appear here so you have the complete set of rules. This all looks rather complicated, but it really isn't. Some of the apparent complexity arises because the range of values for integer types can be implementation dependent, so the rules need to accommodate that. The compiler checks the rules in sequence until it finds one that applies. If the operands are the same type after applying that rule, then the operation is carried out. If not, another rule is sought.

The basic idea is very simple. With two operands of different types, the type with the lesser range of values is converted to the other. The formal rules roughly boil down to the following:

1. If the operation involves two different floating-point types, the one with the lesser precision will be promoted to the other.

2. If the operation involves an integer and a floating-point value, the integer will be promoted to the floating-point type.

3. If the operation involves mixed integer types, the type with the more limited range will be promoted to the other.

4. If the operation involves enumeration types, they'll be converted to a suitable integer type.

The term **conversion** means an automatic conversion of one type to another. The term **promotion** generally means a conversion of a data value from a type with a lesser range to a type with a greater range. You'll see shortly that you can convert explicitly from one data type to another. Such a conversion is referred to as a **cast**, and the action of explicitly converting a value to a different type is called **casting**.

Just because C++ supports expressions involving mixed types doesn't mean it's a good idea in general. The results are often not what you expect, especially if you mix signed and unsigned types, so you should avoid writing mixed expressions as far as possible.

Assignments and Different Types

If the type of an expression on the right of an assignment operator is different from that of the variable on the left, the result of evaluating the expression on the right side will automatically be converted to the type of the variable on the left before it's stored. In many cases, you can lose information in this way. For example, suppose you have a floating-point value defined as

```
double root = 1.732;
```

If you now write the statement

```
int value = root;
```

the conversion of the value of root to int will result in 1 being stored in value. A variable of type int can only store a whole number, so the fractional part of the value stored in root is discarded in the conversion to type int. You can even lose information with an assignment between different types of integers:

```
long count = 60000;
short value = count;
```

If short is 2 bytes and long is 4 bytes, the former doesn't have the range to store the value of count, and an incorrect value will result.

Many compilers will detect these kinds of conversions and provide you with a warning message when they occur, but don't rely on this. To prevent these kinds of problems, you should, as far as possible, avoid assigning a value of one type to a variable of a type with a lesser range of values. Where such an assignment is unavoidable, you can specify the conversion explicitly to demonstrate that it's no accident and that you really meant to do it. Let's see how that works.

Explicit Casts

With mixed arithmetic expressions involving the basic types, your compiler automatically arranges conversions of operands where necessary, but you can also force a conversion from one type to another by using an **explicit cast**. To cast the value of an expression to a given type, you write the cast in the following form:

```
static_cast<the type to convert to>(expression)
```

The keyword `static_cast` reflects the fact that the cast is checked statically—that is, when your program is compiled. Later, when you get to deal with classes, you'll meet *dynamic* casts, where the conversion is checked dynamically—that is, when the program is executing. The effect of the cast is to convert the value that results from evaluating `expression` to the type that you specify between the angled brackets. The `expression` can be anything from a single variable to a complex expression involving lots of nested parentheses.

Here's a specific example of the use of `static_cast<>()`:

```
double value1 = 10.5;
double value2 = 15.5;
int whole_number = static_cast<int>(value1) + static_cast<int>(value2);
```

The initializing value for the variable `whole_number` is the sum of the integral parts of `value1` and `value2`, so they're each explicitly cast to type int. The variable `whole_number` will therefore have the initial value 25. The casts do *not* affect the values stored in `value1` and `value2`, which will remain as 10.5 and 15.5, respectively. The values 10 and 15 produced by the casts are just stored temporarily for use in the calculation and then discarded. Although both casts cause a loss of information in the calculation, the compiler will always assume that you know what you're doing when you explicitly specify a cast.

In the situation that I referred to earlier relating to assignments with different types, you can always make it clear that you know the cast is necessary by making it explicit:

```
int value = static_cast<int>(root);
```

Generally, the need for explicit casts should be rare, particularly with basic types of data. If you have to include a lot of explicit casts in your code, it's often a sign that you could choose more suitable types for your variables. Still, there are circumstances when casting is necessary, so let's look at a simple example of this situation.

Try It Out: Explicit Casting

Suppose you need to be able to convert a length in yards (as a decimal value) to yards, feet, and inches (as integer values). You can put together a program to do this:

```
// Program 3.1 Using Explicit Casts
#include <iostream>
using std::cin;
using std::cout;
using std::endl;

int main() {
  const long feet_per_yard = 3;
  const long inches_per_foot = 12;

  double yards = 0.0;              // Length as decimal yards
  long yds = 0;                    // Whole yards
  long ft = 0;                     // Whole feet
  long ins = 0;                    // Whole inches

  cout << "Enter a length in yards as a decimal: ";
  cin >> yards;

  // Get the length as yards, feet, and inches
  yds = static_cast<long>(yards);
  ft = static_cast<long>((yards - yds) * feet_per_yard);
  ins = static_cast<long>
                    (yards * feet_per_yard * inches_per_foot) % inches_per_foot;

  cout << endl
       << yards << " yards converts to "
       << yds   << " yards "
       << ft    << " feet "
       << ins   << " inches.";

  cout << endl;
  return 0;
}
```

Typical output from this program will be:

Enter a length in yards as a decimal: 2.75

2.75 yards converts to 2 yards 2 feet 3 inches.

(Continued)

HOW IT WORKS

The first two statements in main() declare a couple of conversion constants that you'll use:

```
const long feet_per_yard = 3;
const long inches_per_foot = 12;
```

You declare these variables as const to prevent them from being modified accidentally in the program, and you use the type long to be consistent with the other values. Although the type short would have been adequate to store these values, using it may actually increase (rather than decrease) the size of your program in the long run. This is because of additional, implicit conversions that may be necessary when using them in expressions with other integer types.

The next four declarations define the variables you'll use in the calculation:

```
double yards = 0.0;             // Length as decimal yards
long yds = 0;                   // Whole yards
long ft = 0;                    // Whole feet
long ins = 0;                   // Whole inches
```

You prompt for the required input and then read a value from the keyboard with these statements:

```
cout << "Enter a length in yards as a decimal: ";
cin >> yards;
```

The next statement computes the whole number of yards from the input value with an explicit cast:

```
yds = static_cast<long>(yards);
```

The cast to type long discards the fractional part of the value in yards and stores the integral result in yds. If you omit the explicit cast here, some compilers will compile the program without warning you that they've inserted the required conversion, even though there's clearly a potential loss of data in this conversion operation. You should always write an explicit cast in such cases to indicate that you intend this to happen. If you leave it out, it's not clear that you realized the need for the conversion and the potential loss of data.

You obtain the number of whole feet in the length with the following statement:

```
ft = static_cast<long>((yards - yds) * feet_per_yard);
```

You want the number of whole feet that aren't contained in the whole yards, so you subtract the value in yds from yards. The compiler will arrange for the value in yds to be converted automatically to type double for the subtraction, and the result will be of type double as well. The value of feet_per_yard will then be converted automatically to double to allow the multiplication to take place, and finally your explicit cast will be applied to the result to convert it from type `double` to type `long`.

The final part of the calculation is to obtain the residual number of whole inches:

```
ins = static_cast<long>
                    (yards * feet_per_yard * inches_per_foot) % inches_per_foot;
```

This is done by calculating the total number of inches in the original length, converting this to type `long` with an explicit cast, and then getting the remainder after dividing by the number of inches in a foot.

Lastly, you output the results with the following statement:

```
cout << std::endl
     << yards << " yards converts to "
     << yds   << " yards "
     << ft    << " feet "
     << ins   << " inches.";
```

Old-Style Casts

Prior to the introduction of `static_cast<>()` (and the other casts, `const_cast<>()`, `dynamic_cast<>()`, and `reinterpret_cast<>()`, which I discuss later in the book) into C++, an explicit cast of the result of an expression to another type was written like this:

```
(the_type_to_convert_to)expression
```

The result of `expression` is cast to the type between the parentheses. For example, the statement to calculate `ins` in the previous example could be written like this:

```
ins = (long)(yards * feet_per_yard * inches_per_foot) % inches_per_foot;
```

Essentially, there are four different kinds of casts, and the old-style casting syntax covers them all. Because of this, code using the old-style casts is more prone to error—it isn't always clear what you intended, and you may not get the result you expected. Although you'll still see old-style casting used extensively (it's still part of the language), I strongly recommend that you stick to using only the new casts in your code.

More on Pseudo-Random Number Generation

Now that you know about casting, you can make sure that you don't run into difficulties with using a value returned by the `rand()` in an arithmetic expression. I noted in the last chapter that `rand()` returns values from 0 to `RAND_MAX`, and `RAND_MAX` could be defined as any positive `int` value up to the maximum in the range. Assuming type `long` has a greater range than type int, you can avoid any possible problems when you want to perform arithmetic with a random integer by casting the value that is returned by the function to type long, for example:

```
long even = 2*static_cast<long>(std::rand());
```

With the value from rand() as type long, the multiply operation will be carried out after converting the value 2 to the same type. Thus the result of the multiplication will always be within range. You can produce the same effect by defining the literal as type long:

```
long even = 2L* std::rand();
```

Because 2L is of type long, the compiler will arrange to cast the value that is returned by rand() to type long before executing the multiply operation.

You could use rand() to obtain random integers in a more limited range than 0 to RAND_MAX. For instance, suppose you wanted random integers from to 0 to 10 inclusive. You could generate that from the value returned by the rand() function:

```
const int limit = 11;
int random_value = static_cast<int>(
                        (limit*static_cast<long>(std::rand()))/(RAND_MAX+1L));
```

What you're effectively doing here is dividing the range 0 to RAND_MAX into limit segments, in which all the values returned by rand() within a given segment will result in one of the values in the range 0 to limit-1 inclusive. You do this by multiplying limit by the ratio rand()/(RAND_MAX+1L). You divide by RAND_MAX+1L rather than RAND_MAX to deal with the case in which rand() returns a value that is exactly RAND_MAX. If you were to divide by RAND_MAX, the result would be limit in this singular case, instead of limit-1. The constant 1L that you add to RAND_MAX is of type long, so RAND_MAX will be converted to type long too before the addition is carried out. As I've already said, RAND_MAX is defined to be the largest possible integer of type int with some implementations of rand(). In this case, you can't add 1 and get a correct result without converting to type long first.

If you want your random values to be between 1 and some upper limit, rather than having a lower limit of 0, this is also very easy to arrange:

```
const int limit = 100;
int random_value = static_cast<int>(
                        1L+(limit*static_cast<long>(std::rand()))/(RAND_MAX+1L));
```

Here you use the same expression as you did previously to produce values from 0 to limit-1 inclusive, and you add 1 to produce values from 1 to limit.

As I said at the beginning, all this assumes that type `long` has a greater range than type `int`. If this isn't the case and you need to generate random values outside the range of type `int`, your only recourse is to cast the value returned by `rand()` to a floating-point type and store the result of your calculations as floating-point. For example, to produce values in a range from 0 to limit, you could use the following statements:

```
const double limit = 11.0;
double random_value = limit*std::rand()/(RAND_MAX+1.0);
```

Because you've declared `limit` to be of type `double`, the compiler will promote the integer that's returned by `rand()` to that type so you don't need to insert an explicit cast.

Finding Out About Types

I've mentioned several times that the number of bytes used for some types isn't specified in the C++ standard and that this is therefore set by your compiler. It's quite possible that you would want to know how many bytes particular types of variables will occupy in your compiler. You could hunt for this information in your compiler's documentation, but you can also get the information programmatically by using the `sizeof` operator.

`sizeof` is a unary operator, so it takes a single operand. It will return an integer value that is a measure of the amount of memory occupied by a particular variable, or by a type. The value returned by `sizeof` is actually defined as a multiple of the size of type `char`, but because variables of type `char` occupy 1 byte, the value returned will be a measure of the number of bytes that the operand occupies.

To obtain the number of bytes occupied by variables of type `type`, you use the expression `sizeof(type)`. You could therefore output the size of variables of type `int` with this statement:

```
std::cout << std::endl
          << "Size of type int is "
          << sizeof(int);          // Output the size of type int
```

The expression `sizeof(int)` returns the size of anything declared as type `int`, and you can find out the size of any data type in this way. To get the size of `long double` values, you could write this:

```
std::cout << std::endl
          << "Size of type long double is "
          << sizeof(long double);    // Output the size of type long double
```

You can also apply the sizeof operator to a particular variable, or even to an expression. In this case, the expression doesn't have to be between parentheses, although you can include them if you wish. Here's an example that will output the number of bytes occupied by the variable number:

```
long number = 999999999;
std::cout << std::endl
          << "Size of the variable number is "
          << sizeof number;          // Output the size of a variable
```

You can treat the value returned by the sizeof operator as an integer, but in fact it's of type size_t. This isn't really a new type, though. The word size_t is defined in the standard header as a synonym for one of the fundamental integer types, usually as unsigned int. Because it's a synonym and not a name for an entity in the standard library, the name is not within the std namespace, so you can use it as is. I can hear your next question already: "What's the point of having a different type name here? Why not just make it unsigned int?"

The reason for specifying the type returned by the sizeof operator is that it builds in flexibility. The sizeof operator always returns a value of type size_t, which your compiler may well define to be unsigned int, but it doesn't have to be so. It might be convenient for the developers of a C++ compiler for a particular hardware platform to define size_t to be equivalent to some other integral type, and they're free to do so. It won't affect your code, because your assumption is that its type is size_t. You'll see how to define a synonym for an existing type for yourself later in this chapter. Incidentally, the *t* in size_t stands for "type," so the name was chosen to indicate that it is a type for a size.

Try It Out: Finding the Sizes of Data Types

You can easily put together a program to list the sizes of all the data types you have seen:

```
// Program 3.2 Finding the sizes of data types
#include <iostream>
using std::cout;
using std::endl;

int main() {
  // Output the sizes for integer types
  cout << endl
       << "Size of type char is "
       << sizeof(char);
  cout << endl
       << "Size of type short is "
       << sizeof(short);
```

```
  cout << endl
       << "Size of type int is "
       << sizeof(int);
  cout << endl
       << "Size of type long is "
       << sizeof(long);

  // Output the sizes for floating-point types
  cout << endl
       << "Size of type float is "
       << sizeof(float);
  cout << endl
       << "Size of type double is "
       << sizeof(double);
  cout << endl
       << "Size of type long double is "
       << sizeof(long double);
  cout << endl;
  return 0;
}
```

On my computer, this program produces the following output:

```
Size of type char is 1
Size of type short is 2
Size of type int is 4
Size of type long is 4
Size of type float is 4
Size of type double is 8
Size of type long double is 8
```

You could modify this example to use the sizeof operator to obtain the sizes of sample variables and expressions, too.

Finding the Limits

There are occasions when you may want to know more about a particular type than just its size. You might want to know what the upper and lower limits on the values it can hold are, for instance. The standard header called <limits> makes this kind of information available for all the standard data types. The information is provided through a class for each type, and because I haven't discussed classes yet, the way this works won't be obvious to you at this point. However, you'll look at how you get the information using the facilities provided by the <limits> header, and I'll leave the detail explanations until I cover classes specifically in Chapter 13.

Let's look at an example. To display the maximum value you can store in a variable of type double, you could write this:

```
std::cout << std::endl
    << "Maximum value of type double is "
    << std::numeric_limits<double>::max();
```

The expression std::numeric_limits<double>::max() produces the value you want. By putting different type names between the angled brackets, you can obtain the maximum values for other data types. You can also replace max() with min() to get the minimum value that can be stored, but the meaning of minimum is different for integer and floating-point types. For an integer type, min() results in the true minimum, which will be a negative number for a signed integer type. For a floating-point type, min() returns the minimum positive value that can be stored.

You can retrieve many other items of information about various types. The number of binary digits, for example, is returned by this expression:

```
std::numeric_limits<type_name>::digits
```

You just insert the type_name in which you're interested between the angled brackets. For floating-point types, you'll get the number of binary digits in the mantissa. For signed integer types, you'll get the number of binary digits in the value—that is, *excluding* the sign bit.

To see this sort of thing in action, you can put together another little example to display the maximums and minimums for the numerical data types.

Try It Out: Finding Maximum and Minimum Values

Here's the program code:

```
// Program 3.3 Finding maximum and minimum values for data types
#include <limits>
#include <iostream>
using std::cout;
using std::endl;
using std::numeric_limits;

int main() {
  cout << endl
      << "The range for type short is from "
      << numeric_limits<short>::min()
      << " to "
      << numeric_limits<short>::max();
  cout << endl
      << "The range for type int is from "
      << numeric_limits<int>::min()
      << " to "
      << numeric_limits<int>::max();
```

```
        cout << endl
             << "The range for type long is from "
             << numeric_limits<long>::min()
             << " to "
             << numeric_limits<long>::max();
      cout << endl
             << "The range for type float is from "
             << numeric_limits<float>::min()
             << " to "
             << numeric_limits<float>::max();
      cout << endl
             << "The range for type double is from "
             << numeric_limits<double>::min()
             << " to "
             << numeric_limits<double>::max();
      cout << endl
             << "The range for type long double is from "
             << numeric_limits<long double>::min()
             << " to "
             << numeric_limits<long double>::max();
      cout << endl;
      return 0;
}
```

On my computer, this program produces the following output:

```
The range for type short is from -32768 to 32767
The range for type int is from -2147483648 to 2147483647
The range for type long is from -2147483648 to 2147483647
The range for type float is from 1.17549e-038 to 3.40282e+038
The range for type double is from 2.22507e-308 to 1.79769e+308
The range for type long double is from 2.22507e-308 to 1.79769e+308
```

HOW IT WORKS

This is a straightforward application of what you learned in the previous section. The values retrieved in the manner you've used in this example have a type and are therefore type-checked by the compiler when you use them.

Just so that you're aware of them, the range limits for numeric data types are also defined by macros in headers that are inherited from C. The <cfloat> header defines symbols for floating-point limits and the <climits> header defines symbols relating to limits for integer types. For example, in the <climits> header, the symbol INT_MAX represents the maximum value of a value of type int, and SCHAR_MIN represents the minimum value of a signed char. There are type_MAX and type_MIN symbols for the other types too. However, these are just symbols that the compiler will replace in your code by the equivalent number as a literal. For this reason, it's usually better to use the runtime_limits<> mechanism when you're accessing limits for types at runtime.

Bitwise Operators

As their name suggests, the **bitwise operators** enable you to operate on an integer variable at the bit level. You can apply the bitwise operators to any type of integer, both signed and unsigned, including the type char. However, they're usually applied to unsigned integer types.

A typical application for these operators is when you want to use individual bits in an integer variable to store information. An example of this would be **flags**, which is the term used to describe binary state indicators. You can use a single bit to store any value that has two states: on or off, male or female, true or false.

You can also use the bitwise operators to work with several items of information stored in a single variable. For instance, color values are often recorded as three 8-bit values for the intensities of the red, green, and blue components in the color. These are usually packed into 3 bytes of a 4-byte word. The fourth byte is not wasted either; it often contains a value that is a measure of the transparency of a color. Obviously, to work with individual color components, you need to be able to separate out the individual bytes from a word, and the bitwise operators are just the tool for this.

Let's consider another example. Suppose that you need to record information about fonts. You might want to store information about the style and the size of each font, plus whether it's bold or italic. You could pack all of this information into a 2-byte integer variable, as shown in Figure 3-1.

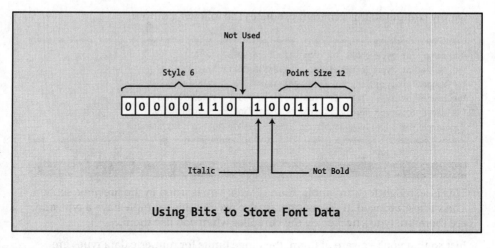

Figure 3-1. Packing font data into 2 bytes

You could use 1 bit to record whether the font is italic—a 1 value signifies italic and 0 signifies normal. In the same way, another bit could be used to specify whether the font is bold. You could use a byte to select one of up to 256 different styles. With another five bits, you could record the point size up to 32. Thus, in one 16-bit word you have four separate pieces of data recorded. The bitwise operators provide you with the means of accessing and modifying the individual bits and groups of bits from an integer very easily so they provide you with the means of assembling and disassembling the 16-bit word.

The Bitwise Shift Operators

The bitwise **shift operators** shift the contents of an integer variable by a specified number of bits to the left or right. These are used in combination with the other bitwise operators to achieve the kind of operations I described previously. The >> operator shifts bits to the right, and the << operator shifts bits to the left. Bits that fall off either end of the variable are lost.

All the bitwise operations work with integers of any type, but you'll use 16-bit words in this chapter's examples, which should keep the illustrative diagrams simple. You can declare and initialize a variable called number with the statement

```
unsigned short number = 16387U;
```

As you saw in the last chapter, you should write unsigned literals with a letter U or u appended to the number.

You can shift the contents of this variable and store the result with the statement

```
unsigned short result = number << 2;    // Shift left two bit positions
```

The left operand of the shift operator is the value to be shifted and the right operand specifies the number of bit positions that the value is to be shifted by. Figure 3-2 shows the effect of the operation.

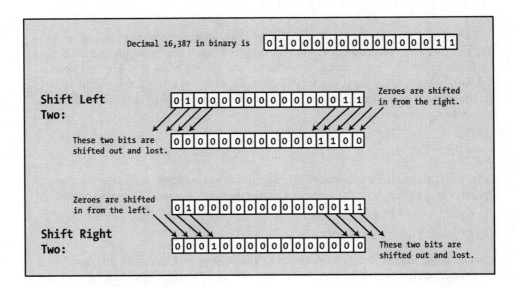

Figure 3-2. Shift operations

As you can see from Figure 3-2, shifting the value 16,387 two positions to the left produces the value 12. The rather drastic change in the value is the result of losing the high order bit.

To shift the value to the right, you can write

```
result = number >> 2;                 // Shift right two bit positions
```

This shifts the value 16,387 two positions to the right and produces the result 4,096. Shifting right two bits is effectively dividing the value by 4.

As long as bits aren't lost, shifting n bits to the left is equivalent to multiplying the value by 2, n times. In other words, it's equivalent to multiplying by 2^n. Similarly, shifting right n bits is equivalent to dividing by 2^n. But beware: As you saw with the left shift of the variable number, if significant bits are lost, the result is nothing like what you would expect. However, this is no different from the "real" multiply operation. If you multiplied the 2-byte number by 4 you would get the same result, so shifting left and multiplying are still equivalent. The incorrect answer arises because the value of the result of the multiplication is outside the range of a 2-byte integer.

When you want to modify the original value using a shift operation, you can do so by using an op= assignment operator. In this case, you would use the >>= or <<= operator, for example:

```
number >>= 2;          // Shift contents of number two positions to the right
```

This is equivalent to

```
number = number >> 2;  // Shift contents of number two positions to the right
```

You might imagine that confusion could arise between these shift operators and the insertion and extraction operators that you've been using for input and output. As far as the compiler is concerned, the meaning will generally be clear from the context. If it isn't, in most cases the compiler will generate a message, but you do need to be careful. For example, if you want to output the result of shifting a variable number left by two bits, you could write

```
cout << (number << 2);
```

Here, the parentheses are essential. Without them, the compiler will interpret the shift operator as a stream insertion operator so you won't get the result that you intended.

Shifting Signed Integers

You can apply the bitwise shift operators to both signed and unsigned integers. However, the effect of the right shift operator on signed integer types can vary between different systems, and it depends on your compiler's implementation. In some cases, the right shift will introduce "0" bits at the left to fill the vacated bit positions. In other cases, the sign bit is propagated to the right, so "1" bits fill the vacated bit positions to the left.

The reason for propagating the sign bit, where this occurs, is to maintain consistency between a right shift and a divide operation. You can illustrate this with a variable of type char, just to show how it works. Suppose you define value to be of type signed char with the value –104 in decimal:

```
signed char value = -104;
```

Its binary value is 10011000. You can shift it two bits to the right with this operation:

```
value >>= 2;        // Result 11100110
```

The binary result when the sign is propagated is shown in the comment. Two 0s are shifted out at the right end, and because the sign bit is 1, further 1s are inserted on the left. The decimal value of the result is –26, which is the same as if you had divided by 4, as you would expect. With operations on unsigned integer types, of course, the sign bit isn't propagated and 0s are inserted on the left.

As I said, what *actually* happens when you right-shift negative integers is implementation defined, so you must not rely on it working one way or the other. Because for the most part you'll be using these operators for operating at the bit level—where maintaining the integrity of the bit pattern is important—you should always use unsigned integers to ensure that you avoid the high-order bit being propagated.

Logical Operations on Bit Patterns

The four bitwise operators that you can use to modify bits in an integer value are shown in Table 3-1.

Table 3-1. Bitwise Operators

Operator	Description
~	This is the **bitwise complement operator**. This is a unary operator that will invert the bits in its operand, so 1 becomes 0 and 0 becomes 1.
&	This is the **bitwise AND operator**, which will AND the corresponding bits in its operands. If the corresponding bits are both 1, then the resulting bit is 1. Otherwise, it's 0.
^	This is the **bitwise exclusive OR operator**, which will exclusive-OR the corresponding bits in its operands. If the corresponding bits are different (that is, one is 1 and the other is 0), then the resulting bit is 1. If the corresponding bits are the same, the resulting bit is 0.
|	This is the **bitwise OR operator**, which will OR the corresponding bits in its operands. If either of the two corresponding bits is 1, then the result is 1. If both bits are 0, then the result is 0.

The operators appear here in order of precedence, so the bitwise complement operator has the highest precedence in this set, and the bitwise OR operator the lowest. As you can see in the complete operator precedence table in Appendix D, the shift operators << and >> are of equal precedence, and they're below the ~ operator but above the & operator.

If you haven't come across operators like these before, you're likely to be thinking, "Very interesting, but what are they *for*?" Let's put them into some kind of context.

Using the Bitwise AND

You'll typically use the bitwise AND operator to select particular bits or groups of bits in an integer value. To see what this means, you can reuse the example presented at the beginning of this section, which used a 16-bit integer to store the characteristics of a font.

Suppose you want to declare and initialize a variable to specify a 12-point, italic, style 6 font—in fact, the very same one illustrated in Figure 3-1. In binary, the style will be 00000110, the italic bit will be 1, the bold bit will be 0, and the size will be 01100. Remembering that there's an unused bit as well, you need to initialize the value of the font variable to the binary number 0000 0110 0100 1100.

Because groups of four bits correspond to a hexadecimal digit, the easiest way to do this is to specify the initial value in hexadecimal notation:

```
unsigned short font = 0x064C;            // Style 6, italic, 12 point
```

NOTE *When you set up bit patterns like this, hexadecimal notation is invariably more appropriate than using decimal values.*

To use the size, you need to be able to extract it from the font variable; the bitwise AND operator will enable you to do this. Because bitwise AND only produces 1 bit when both bits are 1, you can define a value that will "select" the bits defining the size when you AND it with font. All you need to do is define a value that contains 1s in the bit positions that you're interested in, and 0s in all the others. This kind of value is called a **mask**, and you can define such a mask with the statement

```
unsigned short size_mask = 0x1F;   // Mask is 0000 0000 0001 1111 to select size
```

The five low-order bits of font represent its size, so you set these bits to 1. The remaining bits are 0, so they will be discarded. (Binary 0000 0000 0001 1111 translates to hexadecimal 1F.)

You can now extract the point size from font with the statement

```
unsigned short size = font & size_mask;
```

Where both corresponding bits are 1 in an & operation, the resultant bit is 1. Any other combination of bits results in 0. The values therefore combine like this:

font	0000 0110 0100 1100
size_mask	0000 0000 0001 1111
font & size_mask	0000 0000 0000 1100

Showing the binary values in groups of four bits has no real significance other than making it easy to identify the hexadecimal equivalent; it also makes it easier to see how many bits there are in total. As you can see, the effect of the mask is to separate out the five rightmost bits, which represent the point size.

You could use the same mechanism to select out the style for the font, but you'll also need to use a shift operator to move the style value to the right. You can define a mask to select the left eight bits as follows:

```
unsigned short style_mask = 0XFF00;      // Mask is 1111 1111 0000 0000 for style
```

You can then obtain the style value with the statement

```
unsigned short style = (font & style_mask) >> 8;      // Extract the style
```

The effect of this statement is

font	0000 0110 0100 1100
style_mask	1111 1111 0000 0000
font & style_mask	0000 0110 0000 0000
(font & style_mask) >> 8	0000 0000 0000 0110

You should be able to see that you could just as easily isolate the bits indicating italic and bold by defining a mask for each, with the appropriate bit set to 1. Of course, you still need a way to test whether the resulting bit is 1 or 0, and you'll see how to do that in the next chapter.

Another use for the bitwise AND operator is to turn bits off. Part of the effect you saw previously is that any bit that is 0 in a mask will produce 0 in the result. To turn the italic bit off, for example, and leave the rest unchanged, you just bitwise-AND the font variable with a mask that has the italic bit as 0 and all the other bits as 1. You'll look at the code to do this in the context of the bitwise OR operator, for reasons that I'll explain next.

Using the Bitwise OR

You can use the bitwise OR operator for *setting* single or multiple bits. Continuing with your manipulations of the font variable, it's conceivable that you would want to set the italic and bold bits on demand. You can define masks to select these bits with the statements

```
unsigned short italic = 0X40U;          // Seventh bit from the right
unsigned short bold = 0X20U;            // Sixth bit from the right
```

Now you can set the bold bit with the statement

```
font |= bold;                           // Set bold
```

The bits combine here as follows:

font	0000 0110 0100 1100
bold	0000 0000 0010 0000
font | bold	0000 0110 0110 1100

Now, the font variable specifies that the font it represents is bold as well as italic. Note that this operation will result in the bit being set, regardless of its previous state. If it was on before, it remains on.

You can also set multiple bits by ORing the masks together, so the following statement will set both the bold and the italic bit:

```
font |= bold | italic;                  // Set bold and italic
```

It's easy to fall into the trap of allowing language to make you select the wrong operator. Because you say "Set italic *and* bold" there's a temptation to use the & operator, but this would be wrong. ANDing the two masks together would result in a value with all bits 0, so you wouldn't change anything.

As I said at the end of the last section, you can use the & operator to turn bits off—you just need a mask that contains a 0 at the position of the bit you want to turn off and 1 everywhere else. However, this raises the issue of *how* you specify such a mask. If you want to specify it explicitly, you'll need to know how many bytes there are in your variable—not exactly convenient if you want your program to be in any way portable. However, you can obtain the mask that you want by using the bitwise complement operator on the mask that you would normally use to turn the bit on. You can obtain the mask to turn bold off from the bold mask itself:

bold	0000 0000 0010 0000
~bold	1111 1111 1101 1111

The effect of the complement operator is that each bit in the original is flipped, 0 to 1 or 1 to 0. You should be able to see that this will produce the result you're looking for, regardless of whether the bold variable occupies 2, 4, or 8 bytes.

NOTE *The bitwise complement operator is sometimes called the NOT operator, because for every bit it operates on, what you get is* not *what you started with.*

Thus, all you need to do when you want to turn bold off is to bitwise-AND the complement of the mask, bold, with the variable, font. The following statement will do it:

```
font &= ~bold;                    // Turn bold off
```

You can also set multiple bits to 0 by combining several masks using the & operator, and then bitwise-ANDing the result with the variable you want to modify:

```
font &= ~bold & ~italic;          // Turn bold and italic off
```

This sets both the italic and bold bits to 0 in the font variable. Note that no parentheses are necessary here, because ~ has a higher precedence than &. However, if you're ever uncertain about operator precedence, put parentheses in to express what you want. It certainly does no harm, and it really does good when they're necessary.

Using the Bitwise Exclusive OR

The bitwise exclusive OR operator is used much less frequently than the & and | operators, and there are few common examples of its use. An important application, though, arises in the context of graphics programming. One way of creating the illusion of motion on the screen is to draw an object, erase it, and then redraw it in a new position. This process needs to be repeated very rapidly if you are to get smooth animation, and the erasing is a critical part of it. You don't want to erase and redraw the whole screen, as this is time consuming and the screen will flash. Ideally, you want to erase only the object or objects onscreen that you're moving. You can do this and get reasonably smooth animation by using what is called **exclusive OR mode**.

Exclusive OR mode is based on the idea that once you've drawn an object on the screen in a given color, it will then disappear if you redraw it in the background color. This is illustrated by the sequence in Figure 3-3.

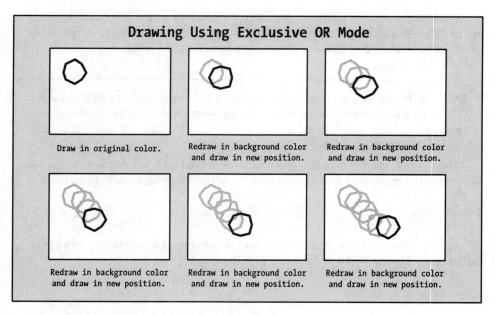

Figure 3-3. Drawing in exclusive OR mode

When you draw an object on the screen in exclusive OR mode, the color automatically alternates between the color you've selected for the object and the background color each time you draw the object. The key to achieving this is the use of the bitwise exclusive OR operator to alternate the colors rapidly and automatically. It uses a characteristic of the exclusive OR operation, which is that if you choose your values suitably, you can arrange to flip between two different values by repeated exclusive-OR operations. That sounds complicated, so let's see how it works by looking at a specific example.

Suppose you want to alternate between a foreground color (you'll use red), and a background color (white). As I noted earlier, color is often represented by three 8-bit values, corresponding to the intensities for each of red, blue, and green, and stored in a single 4-byte integer. By altering the proportions of red, blue, and green in a color, you can get around 16 million different colors in the range from white to black and everything in between. A bright red would be 0xFF0000, where the red component is set to its maximum and the intensities of the other two components for green and blue are zero. In the same scheme, green would be 0xFF00 and blue would be 0xFF. White has equal, maximum components of red, blue, and green, so it would be 0xFFFFFF.

You can therefore define variables representing red and white with the statements

```
unsigned long red = OXFF0000UL;        // Color red
unsigned long white = OXFFFFFFUL;      // Color white - RGB all maximum
```

Next, you'll create a mask that you can use to switch the color back and forth between red and white. You'll also initialize the variable containing the drawing color to red:

```
unsigned long mask = red ^ white;      // Mask for switching colors
unsigned long draw_color = red;        // Drawing color
```

The variable `mask` is initialized to the bitwise exclusive OR of the colors that you want to alternate, so it will be

red	1111 1111 0000 0000 0000 0000
white	1111 1111 1111 1111 1111 1111
mask (which is red ^ white)	0000 0000 1111 1111 1111 1111

If you exclusive-OR `mask` with `red` you'll get `white`, and if you exclusive-OR `mask` with `white` you'll get `red`. This is a very useful result. This means that having drawn an object using the color in `draw_color`, whichever it is, you can switch to the other color with the statement

```
draw_color ^= mask;                    // Switch the drawing color
```

The effect of this when `draw_color` contains `red` is as follows:

draw_color	1111 1111 0000 0000 0000 0000
mask	0000 0000 1111 1111 1111 1111
draw_color ^ mask	1111 1111 1111 1111 1111 1111

Clearly, you've changed the value of `draw_color` from red to white. Executing the same statement again will flip the color back to red:

```
draw_color ^= mask;                    // Switch the drawing color
```

This works as follows:

draw_color	1111 1111 1111 1111 1111 1111
mask	0000 0000 1111 1111 1111 1111
draw_color ^ mask	1111 1111 0000 0000 0000 0000

As you can see, `draw_color` is back to the value of red again. This technique will work with any two colors, although of course it has nothing to do with colors in particular at all—you can use it to alternate between any pair of integer values.

....

Try It Out: Using the Bitwise Operators

You can put together an example that exercises the bitwise operators, so that you can see them working together. You can also illustrate the use of the exclusive OR for switching between two values, and how you use masks to select and set individual bits. Here's the code:

```
// Program 3.4 Using the bitwise operators
#include <iostream>
#include <iomanip>
using std::cout;
using std::endl;
using std::setfill;
using std::setw;

int main() {
  unsigned long red = 0XFF0000UL;          // Color red
  unsigned long white = 0XFFFFFFUL;        // Color white - RGB all maximum

  cout << std::hex;                        // Set hexadecimal output format
  cout << setfill('0');                    // Set fill character for output

  cout << "\nTry out bitwise AND and OR operators.";
  cout << "\nInitial value   red       = " << setw(8) << red;
  cout << "\nComplement      ~red      = " << setw(8) << ~red;

  cout << "\nInitial value   white     = " << setw(8) << white;
  cout << "\nComplement      ~white    = " << setw(8) << ~white;

  cout << "\n Bitwise AND    red & white = " << setw(8) << (red & white);
  cout << "\n Bitwise OR     red | white = " << setw(8) << (red | white);

  cout << "\n\nNow we can try out successive exclusive OR operations.";

  unsigned long mask = red ^ white;

  cout << "\n          mask = red ^ white = " << setw(8) << mask;
  cout << "\n                  mask ^ red = " << setw(8) << (mask ^ red);
  cout << "\n                mask ^ white = " << setw(8) << (mask ^ white);

  unsigned long flags = 0xFF;              // Flags variable
  unsigned long bit1mask = 0x1;            // Selects bit 1
  unsigned long bit6mask = 0x20;           // Selects bit 6
  unsigned long bit20mask = 0x80000;       // Selects bit 20

  cout << "\n\nNow use masks to select or set a particular flag bit.";
  cout << "\nSelect bit 1 from flags    : " << setw(8) << (flags & bit1mask);
  cout << "\nSelect bit 6 from flags    : " << setw(8) << (flags & bit6mask);
  cout << "\nSwitch off bit 6 in flags  : " << setw(8) << (flags &= ~bit6mask);
  cout << "\nSwitch on bit 20 in flags  : " << setw(8) << (flags |= bit20mask);
  cout << endl;
  return 0;
}
```

This example produces the following output:

```
Try out bitwise AND and OR operators.
Initial value  red         = 00ff0000
Complement     ~red        = ff00ffff
Initial value  white       = 00ffffff
Complement     ~white      = ff000000
 Bitwise AND   red & white = 00ff0000
 Bitwise OR    red | white = 00ffffff

Now we can try out successive exclusive OR operations.
        mask = red ^ white = 0000ffff
              mask ^ red = 00ffffff
            mask ^ white = 00ff0000

Now use masks to select or set a particular flag bit.
Select bit 1 from flags   : 00000001
Select bit 6 from flags   : 00000020
Switch off bit 6 in flags : 000000df
Switch on bit 20 in flags : 000800df
```

HOW IT WORKS

There is an #include directive for the <iomanip> standard header, which you saw in the last chapter, because the code uses manipulators to control the formatting of the output. To start with, you define two integer variables containing values representing the colors that you'll use in subsequent bitwise operations:

```
unsigned long red = 0XFF0000UL;      // Color red
unsigned long white = 0XFFFFFFUL;    // Color white - RGB all maximum
```

You'll want to display your data as hexadecimal values, so you specify this with this statement:

```
cout << std::hex;               // Set hexadecimal output format
```

Here, hex is a manipulator that sets the output representation for integer values as hexadecimal. Note that this is modal—all subsequent integer output to the standard output stream in the program will now be in hexadecimal format. You don't need to keep sending hex to the output stream, cout. If necessary, you could change back to decimal output with this statement:

```
cout << std::dec;               // Set decimal output format
```

(Continued)

This uses the `dec` manipulator to reset integer output to the default decimal representation. Note that setting the output format to hexadecimal *only* affects integer values. Floating-point values will continue to be displayed in normal decimal form.

It would also make things clearer if you output your integers with leading zeros, and you set this mode with this statement:

```
cout << setfill('0');        // Set fill character for output
```

Here, `setfill()` is a manipulator that sets the fill character to whatever character you put between the parentheses. This is also modal, so any subsequent integer output will use this fill character when necessary. Both decimal and hexadecimal output is affected. If you wanted asterisks instead, you would use this:

```
cout << setfill('*');        // Set fill character for output
```

To set the fill character back to the default, you just use a space between the parentheses:

```
cout << setfill(' ');        // Set fill character for output
```

The value of red and its complement are displayed by these statements:

```
cout << "\nInitial value  red     = " << setw(8) << red;
cout << "\nComplement     ~red    = " << setw(8) << ~red;
```

You use the `setw()` manipulator that you saw in the last chapter to set the output field width to 8. If you make sure all your output values will be in a field of the same width, it will be easier to compare them. Setting the width is *not* modal; it only applies to the output from the next statement that comes after the point at which the width is set. From the output for red and white, you can see that the ~ operator is doing what you expect: flipping the bits of its operand.

You combine red and white using the bitwise AND and OR operators with these statements:

```
cout << "\n Bitwise AND  red & white = " << setw(8) << (red & white);
cout << "\n Bitwise OR   red | white = " << setw(8) << (red | white);
```

Notice the parentheses around the expressions in the output. These are necessary because the precedence of << is higher than & and |. Without the parentheses, the statements wouldn't compile. If you check the output, you'll see that it's precisely as discussed. The result of ANDing two bits is 1 if both bits are 1; otherwise the result is 0. When you bitwise-OR two bits, the result is 1 unless both bits are 0.

Next, you create a mask to use to flip between the values red and white by combining the two values with the exclusive OR operator:

```
unsigned long mask = red ^ white;
```

If you inspect the output for the value of mask, you'll see that the exclusive OR of two bits is 1 when the bits are different and 0 when they're the same. By combining mask with either of the two color values using exclusive OR, you can obtain the other, as demonstrated by these statements:

```
cout << "\n              mask ^ red = " << setw(8) << (mask ^ red);
cout << "\n            mask ^ white = " << setw(8) << (mask ^ white);
```

The last group of statements demonstrates how to use a mask to select a single bit from a group of flag bits. The mask to select a particular bit must have that bit as 1 and all other bits as 0. Thus, the masks to select bits 1, 6, and 20 from a 32-bit long variable are defined as follows:

```
unsigned long bit1mask = 0x1;            // Selects bit 1
unsigned long bit6mask = 0x20;           // Selects bit 6
unsigned long bit20mask = 0x80000;       // Selects bit 20
```

To select a bit from flags, you just need to bitwise-AND the appropriate mask with the value of flags, for example:

```
cout << "\nSelect bit 6 from flags    : " << setw(8) << (flags & bit6mask);
```

You can see from the output that the result of the expression (flags & bit6mask) is an integer with just bit 6 set. Of course, if bit 6 in flags was 0, the result of the expression would be 0.

To switch a bit off, you need to bitwise-AND the flags variable with a mask containing 0 for the bit you want to switch off and 1 everywhere else. You can easily produce this by applying the complement operator to a mask with the appropriate bit set, and bit6mask is just such a mask. The statement to switch off bit 6 in flags and display the result is as follows:

```
cout << "\nSwitch off bit 6 in flags  : " << setw(8) << (flags &= ~bit6mask);
```

Of course, if bit 6 were already 0, it would remain as such. To switch a bit on, you just OR flags with a mask having the bit you want to switch on as 1:

```
cout << "\nSwitch on bit 20 in flags  : " << setw(8) << (flags |= bit20mask);
```

This sets bit 20 of flags to 1 and displays the result. Again, if the bit were already 1, it would remain as 1.

More on Output Manipulators

Taking the last chapter into account, you've now seen five of the modal output manipulators that the `<iostream>` header defines: `scientific`, `fixed`, `dec`, `hex`, and `oct`. The time seems right, therefore, to list these and all the other similar manipulators in one place (see Table 3-2). Don't worry for now about the `bool` values mentioned in the last two entries—they're coming up in the next chapter.

Table 3-2. Output Manipulators

Manipulator	Action Performed
dec	Formats integer values as base 10 (decimal). This is the default representation.
hex	Formats integer values as base 16 (hexadecimal).
oct	Formats integer values as base 8 (octal).
left	Left-aligns values in the output field and pads them on the right with the fill character. The default fill character is a space, as you've seen.
right	Right-aligns values in the output field and pads them on the left with the fill character. This is the default alignment.
fixed	Outputs floating-point values in fixed-point notation—that is, without an exponent.
scientific	Outputs floating-point values in scientific notation—that is, as the mantissa plus an exponent. The default mode selects fixed or scientific notation, depending on the value to be displayed.
showpoint	Shows the decimal point and trailing zeros for floating-point values.
noshowpoint	The opposite of the `showpoint` manipulator. This is the default.
showbase	Prefixes octal output with 0 and hexadecimal output with 0x or 0X.
noshowbase	Shows octal and hexadecimal output without the prefix. This is the default.
showpos	Shows plus signs (+) for positive values.
noshowpos	Doesn't show plus signs for positive values. This is the default.
uppercase	Displays uppercase *A* through *F* for hexadecimal digits when outputting integers in hexadecimal format and 0X if `showbase` is set. Displays *E* for the exponent when outputting values in scientific notation, rather than using lowercase *e*.
nouppercase	Uses lowercase for the preceding items. This is the default.
boolalpha	Displays `bool` values as true and false.
noboolalpha	Displays `bool` values as 1 and 0.

You may want to set more than one of these modes at a time, and one way to do this is to insert multiple manipulators into the stream. For example, if you want to output your integer data as hexadecimal values that are left aligned in the output field, you could write

```
std::cout << std::hex << std::left << value;
```

which will output `value` (and all subsequent integers in the program, unless the settings are changed) as a left-justified hexadecimal number.

Table 3-3 shows the manipulators that expect you to supply an argument value.

Table 3-3. Output Manipulators That Require an Argument Value

Manipulator	Action Performed
setfill()	Sets the fill character as specified by the argument. The default fill character is a space.
setw()	Sets the field width as specified by the argument.
setprecision()	Sets the precision for floating-point values as specified by the argument. The precision is the number of decimal digits in the output.

Enumerated Data Types

You'll sometimes be faced with the need for variables that have a limited set of possible values that can be usefully referred to by name—the days of the week, for example, or the months of the year. There's a specific facility, called an **enumeration**, in C++ to handle this situation. When you define an enumeration, you're really creating a new type, so it's also referred to as an **enumerated data type**. Let's create an example using one of the ideas I just mentioned—a variable that can assume values corresponding to days of the week. You can define this as follows:

```
enum Weekday { Monday, Tuesday, Wednesday, Thursday, Friday, Saturday, Sunday };
```

This declares an enumerated data type called `Weekday`, and variables of this type can only have values from the set that appears between the braces, `Monday` through `Sunday`. If you try to set a variable of type `Weekday` to a value that isn't one of the values specified, it will cause an error. The symbolic names that are listed between the braces are called **enumerators**.

In fact, each of the names of the days will be automatically defined as representing a fixed integer value. The first name in the list, `Monday`, will have the value 0, `Tuesday` will be 1, and so on through to `Sunday` with the value 6. You can declare `today` as an instance of the enumeration type `Weekday` with the statement

```
Weekday today = Tuesday;
```

You use the Weekday type just like any of the basic types you've seen. This declaration for today also initializes the variable with the value Tuesday. If you output the value of today, the value 1 will be displayed.

By default, the value of each successive enumerator in the declaration of an enumeration is one larger than the value of the previous one, and the values begin at 0. If you would prefer the implicit numbering to start at a different value, a declaration like this one will make the enumerators equivalent to 1 through 7:

```
enum Weekday { Monday = 1, Tuesday, Wednesday, Thursday,
                                        Friday, Saturday, Sunday };
```

The enumerators don't need to have unique values. You could define Monday and Mon as both having the value 1, for example, with this statement:

```
enum Weekday { Monday = 1, Mon = 1, Tuesday, Wednesday,
                                 Thursday, Friday, Saturday, Sunday };
```

This allows the possibility of using either Mon or Monday as the value for the first day of the week. A variable, yesterday, that you've declared as type Weekday could then be set with this statement:

```
yesterday = Mon;
```

You can also define the value of an enumerator in terms of a previous enumerator in the list. Throwing everything you've seen so far into a single example, you could declare the type Weekday as follows:

```
enum Weekday { Monday,                Mon   = Monday,
               Tuesday   = Monday + 2,    Tues  = Tuesday,
               Wednesday = Tuesday + 2,   Wed   = Wednesday,
               Thursday  = Wednesday + 2, Thurs = Thursday,
               Friday    = Thursday + 2,  Fri   = Friday,
               Saturday  = Friday + 2,    Sat   = Saturday,
               Sunday    = Saturday + 2,  Sun   = Sunday
             };
```

Now, variables of type Weekday can have values from Monday to Sunday and from Mon to Sun, and the matching pairs of enumerators correspond to the integer values 0, 2, 4, 6, 8, 10, and 12.

If you'd like, you can assign explicit values to all the enumerators. For example, you could define this enumeration:

```
enum Punctuation { Comma = ',', Exclamation = '!', Question='?' };
```

Here, you've defined the possible values for variables of type Punctuation as the numerical equivalents of the appropriate symbols. If you look in the ASCII table in Appendix A, you'll see that the symbols are 44, 33, and 63, respectively, in decimal, which demonstrates that the values you assign don't have to be in ascending order. If you don't specify all of them explicitly, values will continue to be assigned by incrementing by 1 from the last specified value, as in the second Weekday example.

The values that you specify for enumerators must be **compile-time constants—** that is, constant expressions that the *compiler* can evaluate. Such expressions can only include literals, enumerators that have been defined previously, and variables that you've declared as const. You can't use non-const variables, even if you've initialized them.

Anonymous Enumerations

By declaring variables at the same time as you define the enumeration, you can omit the enumeration type, provided that you don't need to declare other variables of this type later on, for example:

```
enum { Monday, Tuesday, Wednesday, Thursday,
                      Friday, Saturday, Sunday } yesterday, today, tomorrow;
```

Here, you declare three variables that can assume values from Monday to Sunday. Because the enumeration type isn't specified, you can't refer to it. You can't declare other variables for this enumeration *at all*, because doing so would require you to name the enumeration type, which is simply not possible.

A common use of anonymous enumeration types is as an alternative way of defining integer constants, for example:

```
enum { feetPerYard = 3, inchesPerFoot = 12, yardsPerMile = 1760 };
```

This enumeration contains three enumerators with explicit values assigned. Although you've declared no variables of this enumerated data type, you can still use the enumerators in arithmetic expressions. You could write this statement:

```
std::cout << std::endl << "Feet in 5 miles = " << 5 * feetPerYard * yardsPerMile;
```

The enumerators are converted to type int automatically. It may look as if little (if anything) is to be gained by using an enumeration to define integer constants, but you'll see when you learn about classes that it provides a very useful way of including a constant within a class. For now, let's look a little more closely at the conversion of enumerated data types.

Casting Between Integer and Enumeration Types

In addition to the enumerators themselves, you can use a variable of an enumeration type in a mixed arithmetic expression. An enumerated data type will be cast automatically to the appropriate type, but the reverse isn't true; there's no automatic conversion from an integer type to an enumeration type. If you've declared the variable today to be of type Weekday that you defined previously, you can write

```
today = Tuesday;                    // Assign an enumerator value
int day_value = today + 1;          // Calculate with an enumerator type
```

The value of today is Tuesday, which corresponds to 1, so day_value will be set to 2. Although the enumerator Wednesday corresponds to the value 2, the following statement will *not* compile:

```
today = day_value;                  // Error - no conversion!
```

However, you can achieve the objective of this statement by putting in an explicit cast:

```
today = static_cast<Weekday>(day_value);   // OK
```

With an explicit cast, the integer value you're casting must be within the range of the enumerators, or the result is undefined. This doesn't mean that it must correspond to the value of an enumerator—just that it must be equal to or greater than the lowest enumerator, and less than or equal to the highest enumerator. For example, you could define an enumeration, Height, and declare a variable of that type with this statement:

```
enum Height { Bottom, Top = 20 } position;
```

The enumerator Bottom corresponds to the value 0, and Top corresponds to the value 20. The range is therefore from 0 to 20, so you could assign a value to the variable position with this statement:

```
position = static_cast<Height>(10);
```

The value assigned to position doesn't correspond to either of the enumerators, but it's nonetheless a legal value because it falls within the range of the minimum and maximum values of the enumerators. For a variable of the Punctuation type that you saw earlier, you could legally cast any integer from 33 to 63 to that type and store it, although in this instance it's difficult to see what purpose it would serve.

Try It Out: Enumerated Data Types

Enumerations become more obviously useful when you can make decisions by comparing the value of a variable of an enumerated data type against possible enumerators. You'll look at that in the next chapter, so here you can just work through a simple example to demonstrate some of the operations on enumerated data types you've seen so far:

```cpp
// Program 3.5 - Exercising an enumeration
#include <iostream>
using std::cout;

int main() {
  enum Language { English, French, German, Italian, Spanish };

  // Display range of enumerators
  cout << "\nPossible languages are:\n"
       << English << ". English\n"
       << French  << ". French\n"
       << German  << ". German\n"
       << Italian << ". Italian\n"
       << Spanish << ". Spanish\n";

  Language tongue = German;
  cout << "\n Current language is " << tongue;

  tongue = static_cast<Language>(tongue + 1);
  cout << "\n Current language is now " << tongue
       << std::endl;
  return 0;
}
```

This will display the following output:

```
Possible languages are:
0. English
1. French
2. German
3. Italian
4. Spanish

 Current language is 2
 Current language is now 3
```

(Continued)

You first define an enumeration, Language, with this statement:

```
enum Language { English, French, German, Italian, Spanish };
```

Variables of type Language can have any of the enumerators between the braces as a value. You list all the possible values with the next statement:

```
cout << "\nPossible languages are:\n"
     << English << ". English\n"
     << French  << ". French\n"
     << German  << ". German\n"
     << Italian << ". Italian\n"
     << Spanish << ". Spanish\n";
```

An enumerator is displayed as its numeric value, so you output a text string alongside each one to show what language it corresponds to.

You declare and initialize a variable of type Language with this statement:

```
Language tongue = German;
```

The value of this variable displays as 2, and then you give it a new value in the next statement:

```
tongue = static_cast<Language>(tongue + 1);
```

In the expression tongue + 1, the value of tongue is converted to type int, and then 1 is added to produce the value 3 as type int. This is then converted back to type Language by the explicit cast, before it gets stored back in tongue. Without the explicit cast, the statement wouldn't compile because there's no automatic conversion from an integer type to an enumeration type. Of course, the value of tongue then displays as 3.

Synonyms for Data Types

You've seen how enumerations provide a way to define your own data types. The typedef keyword enables you to specify your own data type *name* as an alternative to another type name. Using typedef, you can declare the type name BigOnes as being equivalent to the standard type long with the following declaration:

```
typedef long BigOnes;          // Defining BigOnes as a type name
```

Of course, this isn't defining a new type. This just defines BigOnes as an alternative type specifier for long, so you could declare a variable mynum as type long with this statement:

```
BigOnes mynum = 0;          // Declare & initialize a long int variable
```

There's no difference between this declaration and one using the standard built-in type name. You could equally well use this:

```
long int mynum = 0;         // Declare & initialize a long int variable
```

which has exactly the same result. In fact, if you declare your own type name (such as BigOnes), you can use both type specifiers within the same program to declare different variables that will end up having the same type. However, it's hard to come up with a justification for doing this.

Because typedef simply creates a synonym for a type that already exists, it may appear to be a bit superfluous. This isn't at all the case. One important use for typedef is to provide flexibility in the data types used by a program that may need to be run on a variety of computers. The standard library defines the type size_t that you saw earlier in this chapter by using typedef. Let's consider a particular instance in which you might want to use typedef.

Suppose you're writing a program that uses several variables to record values that count events of some kind—you could be recording the number of chocolate bars produced per hour on high-speed manufacturing machinery, for instance. You know that the typical values for these counts require 4-byte integers to be used.

On some computers, type int will be 2 bytes, which is insufficient for the range of integers in the program. On other computers, type int will be 4 bytes, which is just what you want. You could resolve this by using type long, which will generally be at least 4 bytes, but on some machines it may be 8 bytes, which is wasteful—particularly if your program stores a lot of integers. You can provide the flexibility to deal with this situation by declaring your own type for use throughout the program, for example:

```
typedef int Counter;       // Define the integer type for the program
```

Now you can write your program in terms of the type Counter, rather than the standard type, int. This gives you the advantage that should you want to compile your program on a machine on which the range for type int is insufficient, you can redefine Counter as

```
typedef long Counter;      // Define the integer type for the program
```

Now, all the integers that are declared as Counter within the program will be of type long.

You'll be able to do much better than this when you learn more about preprocessing directives. By using the information from the <climits> header, you can code a program so that it will automatically define your Counter type depending on the range of values available with each integer type.

You'll see later that typedef can also fulfill a very useful role in enabling you to simplify more complex type declarations than you've met so far. You'll also see later that classes provide you with a means of defining completely new data types, in which you have complete control over the properties and operations that apply to the new type.

The Lifetime of a Variable

All variables have a finite lifetime when your program executes. They come into existence from the point at which you declare them and then, at some point, they disappear—at the latest, when your program terminates. How long a particular variable lasts is determined by a property called its **storage duration**. A variable can have three different kinds of storage duration:

- Automatic storage duration

- Static storage duration

- Dynamic storage duration

The storage duration that a variable has depends on how you create the variable. I defer discussion of variables with dynamic storage duration until Chapter 7, but you'll look into the characteristics of the other two kinds of storage duration in this chapter.

Another property that variables have is **scope**. The scope of a variable is simply that part of your program in which the variable name is valid. Within a variable's scope, you can legally refer to it, set its value, or use it in an expression. Outside of the scope of a variable, you can't refer to its name—any attempt to do so will cause a compiler error. Note that a variable may still *exist* outside of its scope, even though you can't refer to it by name. You'll see examples of this situation a little later in this discussion.

All the variables that you've declared up to now have had automatic storage duration, and are therefore called **automatic variables**. Let's take a closer look at these first.

Automatic Variables

The variables that you've declared so far have been declared within a block—that is, between a pair of curly braces. These are called **automatic variables** and are said to have **local scope** or **block scope**. An automatic variable is "in scope" from the point at which it is declared until the end of the block containing its declaration.

An automatic variable is "born" when it's declared and automatically ceases to exist at the end of the block containing the declaration. This will be at the closing brace matching the first opening brace that precedes the declaration of the variable. Every time the block of statements containing a declaration for an automatic variable is executed, the variable is created anew, and if you specified an initial value for the automatic variable, it will be reinitialized each time it's created.

You can use the auto keyword to specify explicitly that a variable is automatic, but this keyword is rarely used because it's implied by default. Let's put together an example of what you've learned so far.

Try It Out: Automatic Variables

You can demonstrate the lifetime of automatic variables with the following example:

```cpp
// Program 3.6 Demonstrating variable scope
#include <iostream>
using std::cout;
using std::endl;

int main() {                             // Function scope starts here
  int count1 = 10;
  int count3 = 50;
  cout << endl << "Value of outer count1 = " << count1;

  {                             // New block scope starts here...
    int count1 = 20;            // This hides the outer count1
    int count2 = 30;
    cout << endl << "Value of inner count1 = " << count1;
    count1 += 3;               // This changes the inner count1
    count3 += count2;
  }                            // ...and ends here.

  cout << endl
       << "Value of outer count1 = " << count1
       << endl
       << "Value of outer count3 = " << count3;

  // cout << endl << count2;    // Uncomment to get an error
  cout << endl;
  return 0;
}                                        // Function scope ends here
```

The output from this example is as follows:

```
Value of outer count1 = 10
Value of inner count1 = 20
Value of outer count1 = 10
Value of outer count3 = 80
```

(Continued)

HOW IT WORKS

The first two statements declare and define two integer variables, count1 and count3, with initial values of 10 and 50, respectively:

```
int count1 = 10;
int count3 = 50;
```

Both of these variables exist from this point in the code to the closing brace at the end of the program. The scope of these variables also extends to the closing brace at the end of main().

NOTE *Remember that the lifetime and scope of a variable are two different things.* **Lifetime** *is the period of execution time over which a variable survives.* **Scope** *is the region of program code over which the variable name can be used. It's important not to get these two ideas confused.*

Following the variable definitions, the value of count1 is presented in the first line of output by this statement:

```
cout << endl << "Value of outer count1 = " << count1;
```

There's then a second opening brace that starts a new block. Two variables, count1 and count2, are defined within this block, with the values 20 and 30, respectively. The count1 variable declared here is *different* from the first count1. Although the first count1 still exists, its name is masked by the second count1. Any use of the name count1 following the declaration within the inner block refers to the count1 declared within that block.

I've duplicated names in this way only to illustrate what happens—it's not a good approach to programming in general. Doing this kind of thing in a real program would be confusing and unnecessary, and produce code that was extremely prone to error.

The output statement shows by the value in the second line that you're using the count1 in the inner scope—that is, inside the innermost braces:

```
{                                  // New block scope starts here...
    int count1 = 20;               // This hides the outer count1
    int count2 = 30;
    cout << endl << "Value of inner count1 = " << count1;
```

Had you still been using the outer count1, this statement would have output the value 10. The variable count1 is then incremented by this statement:

```
count1 += 3;                       // This changes the inner count1
```

The increment applies to the variable in the inner scope, because the outer one is still hidden. However, count3, which was defined in the outer scope, is incremented without any problem by the next statement:

```
count3 += count2;
```

This shows that the variables that were defined at the beginning of the outer scope are still accessible in the inner scope. They could have been defined *after* the second of the inner pair of braces and still be within the outer scope, but in that case they wouldn't exist at the point that you're using them.

After the brace ending the inner scope, count2 and the inner count1 cease to exist. Their lifetime has come to an end. The variables count1 and count3 are still there in the outer scope, and their values are displayed by this statement, demonstrating that count3 was indeed incremented in the inner scope:

```
cout << endl
     << "Value of outer count1 = " << count1
     << endl
     << "Value of outer count3 = " << count3;
```

If you uncomment the next line

```
// cout << endl << count2;    // uncomment to get an error
```

the program will no longer compile correctly, because it attempts to output a nonexistent variable.

Positioning Variable Declarations

You have great flexibility in where you place the declarations for your variables. The most important issue to consider is what scope the variables need to have. Beyond that, you should generally place a declaration close to where the variable is first to be used in a program. You should always write your programs with a view to making them as easy as possible for another programmer to understand, and declaring a variable close to its first point of use can be helpful in achieving that.

It's possible to place variable declarations outside all of the functions that make up a program. Let's look what effect that has on the variables concerned.

Global Variables

Variables declared outside of all blocks and classes are called **globals** and have **global scope** (which is also called **global namespace scope**). This means that they're accessible in all the functions in the source file, following the point at which they're declared. If you declare them at the very top, they'll be accessible from anywhere in the file.

Globals also have **static storage duration** by default. Global variables with static storage duration will exist from the start of execution of the program until execution of the program ends. If you don't specify an initial value for a global variable, it will be initialized with 0 by default. Initialization of global variables takes place before the execution of main() begins, so they're always ready to be used within any code that's within the variable's scope.

Figure 3-4 shows the contents of a source file, Example.cpp, and the arrows indicate the scope of each of the variables.

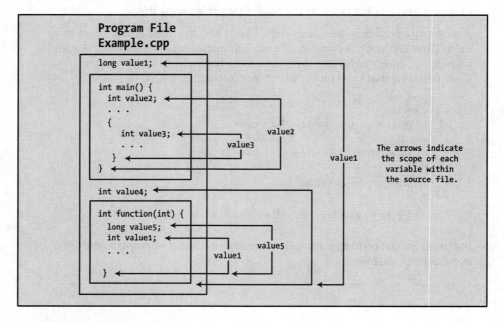

Figure 3-4. Variable scope

Figure 3-4 illustrates the extent of the scope of each variable in a file. The variable value1 that appears at the beginning of the file is declared at global scope, as is value4, which appears after the function main(). The global variables have a scope that extends from the point at which they're declared to the end of the file. Even though value4 exists when execution starts, it can't be referred to in main() because main() isn't within the variable's scope. For main() to use value4, you would need to move its declaration to the beginning of the file. Both value1 and value4 will be initialized with 0 by default, which isn't the case for the automatic variables. Remember that the local variable called value1 in function() will hide the global variable of the same name.

Because global variables continue to exist for as long as the program is running, this might raise the following question in your mind: "Why not make all variables global and avoid this messing about with local variables that disappear?" This sounds very attractive at first, but there are serious disadvantages that completely outweigh any advantages that you might gain.

Real programs are generally composed of a large number of statements, a significant number of functions, and a great many variables. Declaring all at the global scope greatly magnifies the possibility of accidental, erroneous modification of a variable, and it makes the job of naming them sensibly quite intractable. They'll also occupy memory for the duration of program execution. By keeping variables local to a function or a block, you can be sure they have almost complete protection from external effects. They'll only exist and occupy memory from the point at which they're defined to the end of the enclosing block, and the whole development process becomes much easier to manage.

Try It Out: The Scope Resolution Operator

As you've seen, a global variable can be hidden by a local variable with the same name. However, it's still possible to "get at" the global variable by using the **scope resolution operator** (::), which you saw in Chapter 1 when you learned about namespaces. Here's a demonstration of how this works with a revised version of the last example:

```
// Program 3.7 Using the scope resolution operator
#include <iostream>
using std::cout;
using std::endl;

int count1 = 100;               // Global version of count1

int main() {                          // Function scope starts here
  int count1 = 10;
  int count3 = 50;
  cout << endl << "Value of outer count1 = " << count1;
  cout << endl << "Value of global count1 = " << ::count1;

  {                               // New block scope starts here...
    int count1 = 20;              // This hides the outer count1
    int count2 = 30;
    cout << endl << "Value of inner count1 = " << count1;
    cout << endl << "Value of global count1 = " << ::count1;
    count1 += 3;                  // This changes the inner count1
    count3 += count2;
  }                               // ...and ends here.

  cout << endl
       << "Value of outer count1 = " << count1
       << endl
       << "Value of outer count3 = " << count3;

  // cout << endl << count2;      // Uncomment to get an error
  cout << endl;
  return 0;
}                                 // Function scope ends here
```

(Continued)

131

If you compile and run this example, you'll get the following output:

```
Value of outer count1 = 10
Value of global count1 = 100
Value of inner count1 = 20
Value of global count1 = 100
Value of outer count1 = 10
Value of outer count3 = 80
```

HOW IT WORKS

The lines in bold indicate the changes made to the previous example, and they're the only ones whose effects I need to discuss. The declaration of count1 prior to the definition of the function main() is global, so in principle it's available anywhere through the function main(). This global variable is initialized with the value of 100 in its declaration:

```
int count1 = 100;                   // Global version of count1
```

However, you have two other variables called count1 that are defined within main(), so the global count1 is hidden by the local count1 variables throughout the program. In fact, in the inner block it is hidden behind *two* variables called count1: the inner count1 and the outer count1.

The first new output statement is as follows:

```
int count1 = 10;
int count3 = 50;
cout << endl << "Value of outer count1 = " << count1;
cout << endl << "Value of global count1 = " << ::count1;
```

This uses the scope resolution operator, ::, to indicate to the compiler that you want to reference the global count1, *not* the local one. You can see that this works by the value displayed in the output. The global scope resolution operator also does its stuff within the inner block, as you can see from the output generated by this statement:

```
int count1 = 20;                    // This hides the outer count1
int count2 = 30;
cout << endl << "Value of inner count1 = " << count1;
cout << endl << "Value of global count1 = " << ::count1;
```

This outputs the value 100, as before—the long arm of the scope resolution operator used in this fashion always reaches a global variable.

You'll see a lot more of this operator when I cover object-oriented programming, where it's used extensively. I'll also talk further about namespaces, including how to create your own, in Chapter 10.

Static Variables

It's conceivable that you might want to have a variable that's defined and accessible locally within a block, but that also continues to exist after exiting the block in which it is declared. In other words, you need to declare a variable within a block scope, but give it static storage duration. The static keyword provides you with the means of doing just this, and the need for it will become more apparent when you begin to deal with functions in Chapter 8.

A variable that you declare as static will continue to exist for the life of a program, even though it's declared within a block and is only available from within that block (or its sub-blocks). It still has block scope, but it has static storage duration. To declare a static variable called count, you would write

```
static int count;
```

Variables with static storage duration are always initialized for you if you don't provide an initial value yourself. The variable count declared here will be initialized with 0. If you don't specify an initial value when you declare a static variable, it will always be initialized with 0 and converted to the type applicable to the variable. Remember that this is *not* the case with automatic variables. If you don't initialize your automatic variables, they'll contain junk values left over from the program that last used the memory they occupy.

The register Storage Class Specifier

The register specifier is used to indicate that a variable is critical to the speed of execution and should therefore be placed in a machine register. (A **register** is a special, high-speed storage facility located separately from main memory, usually on the processor chip.) Here's an example of how you use this modifier:

```
register int index = 0;
```

Here, you're requesting that the variable index use a register. The compiler is under no obligation to accede to this request, and in many compilers it won't result in a register being allocated for this purpose.

In general, you shouldn't use register unless you're absolutely sure of what you're doing. Most compilers will do a better job of deciding how registers should be used without any prompting.

The volatile Type Modifier

The volatile modifier is used to indicate that the value of a variable can be modified asynchronously by an external process, such as an interrupt routine:

```
volatile long data = 0L;   // Value may be changed by another process
```

The effect of using the volatile modifier is to inhibit the optimization that the compiler might otherwise carry out. For example, when a program references a non-volatile variable, the compiler might be able to reuse an existing value for that variable that was previously loaded into a register, to avoid the overhead of retrieving the same value from memory. If the variable was declared as volatile, its value will be retrieved every time it's used.

Declaring External Variables

You saw in Chapter 1 that programs can consist of several source files and most programs of any size will generally do so. If you have a program that consists of more than one source file, you may need to access a global variable from one source file that is declared in another. The extern keyword allows you to do this. Suppose you have one program file that contains the following:

```
// File1.cpp
int shared_value = 100;

// Other program code …
```

If you have code in another file that needs to access the shared_value variable, you can arrange for this as follows:

```
// File2.cpp
extern int shared_value;        // Declare variable to be external

int main() {
  int local_value = shared_value + 10;
..// Plus other code...
}
```

The first statement in File2.cpp declares shared_value to be external, so this is *only* a declaration, not a definition. The reference to shared_value in main() is then to the variable defined in the first file, File1.cpp.

You must not use an initializing value when declaring an external variable. If in the second file you wrote

```
extern int shared_value = 0;     // Wrong! Not an external declaration.
```

the variable would be defined locally, and the extern declaration would be ignored.

Precedence and Associativity

You have accumulated quite a number of new operators in this chapter. Table 3-4 summarizes the precedence and associativity of the operators you've seen so far.

Table 3-4. Operator Precedence and Associativity

Operator	Associativity
`static_cast<>()` Postfix ++ Postfix --	right
Unary + Unary - Prefix ++ Prefix -- ~	right
`*` `/` `%`	left
Binary + Binary -	left
`<<` `>>`	left
`&`	left
`^`	left
`|`	left
`=` `op=`	right

The operators in Table 3-4 appear in sequence from highest precedence to lowest, and each group in the table contains operators that have the same precedence. The sequence of execution of operators with the same precedence in an expression is determined from their associativity. As I mentioned previously, a table showing the precedence of all the C++ operators appears in Appendix D.

Summary

In this chapter, you learned some of the more complicated aspects of computation in C++. You also learned a little about how you can define data types of your own, although what you've seen here has nothing to do with the ability to define completely general types that I discuss in Chapter 11. The essentials of what you've learned in this chapter are as follows:

- You can mix different types of variables and constants in an expression. The compiler will arrange for variables to be automatically converted to an appropriate type where necessary.

- Automatic conversion of the type of the right side of an assignment to that of the left side will also be made where these are different. This can cause loss of information when the left-side type isn't able to contain the same information as the right-side type—double converted to int, for example, or long converted to short.

- You can explicitly convert a value of one basic type to another by using static_cast<>().

- By default, a variable declared within a block is automatic, which means that it only exists from the point at which it is declared to the end of the block in which its declaration appears, as indicated by the closing brace of the block that encloses its declaration.

- A variable may be declared as static, in which case it continues to exist for the life of the program. However, it can only be *accessed* within the scope in which it was defined. If you don't initialize a static variable explicitly, it will be initialized to 0 by default.

- Variables can be declared outside of all the blocks within a program, in which case they have global namespace scope and static storage duration by default. Variables with global scope are accessible from anywhere within the program file that contains them, following the point at which they're declared, except where a local variable exists with the same name as the global variable. Even then, they can still be reached by using the scope resolution operator (::).

- The keyword typedef allows you to define synonyms for other types.

- The extern keyword allows you to reference a global variable defined in another file.

Exercises

The following exercises enable you to try out what you've learned in this chapter. If you get stuck, look back over the chapter for help. If you're still stuck, you can download the solutions from the Downloads area of the Apress website (http://www.apress.com), but that really should be a last resort.

Exercise 3-1. Write a program that calculates the reciprocal of a nonzero integer entered by the user. (The reciprocal of an integer, n, is 1/n.) The program should store the result of the calculation in a variable of type double and then output it.

Exercise 3-2. Create a program that prompts the user to input an integer in decimal form. Then, invert the last bit of its binary representation. That is, if the last bit is 1, then change it to 0, and vice versa. The result should then be displayed as a decimal number. How does the adjustment affect the resulting integer value? (Hint: Use a bitwise operator.)

Exercise 3-3. Write a program to calculate how many square boxes can be contained in a single layer on a rectangular shelf, with no overhang. Use variables of type double for the length and depth of the shelf (in feet) and for the length of one side of a single box (in inches) and read values for these from the keyboard. You'll need to declare and initialize a constant to convert from feet to inches. Use a single statement to calculate the number of boxes that the shelf can hold in a single layer, assigning the answer to a variable of type long.

Exercise 3-4. Without running it, can you work out what the following code snippet will produce?

```
unsigned int k = 430U;
unsigned int j = (k >> 4) & ~(~0 << 3);
std::cout << j;
```

Exercise 3-5. Write a program to read four characters from the keyboard and pack them into a single 4-byte integer variable. Display the value of this variable as hexadecimal. Unpack the 4 bytes of the variable and output them in reverse order, with the low-order byte first.

Choices and Decisions in Your Programs

DECISION-MAKING IS FUNDAMENTAL to any kind of computer programming. If you didn't have the ability to alter the sequence of instructions in a program based on the result of comparing data values, you couldn't solve most problems with computer programs.

In this chapter, you'll explore how to make choices and decisions in your C++ programs. This'll enable you to check the validity of program input and write programs that can adapt their actions depending on the input data. Your programs will be able to handle problems where logic is fundamental to the solution. By the end of this chapter, you'll have learned the following:

- How to compare data values

- How to alter the sequence of program execution based on the result

- What logical operators and expressions are, and how you can apply them

- How to deal with multiple-choice situations

Comparing Data Values

To make decisions, you need a mechanism for comparing things, and you can make several kinds of comparisons. For instance, a decision such as, "If the traffic signal is red, stop the car," involves a comparison for equality. You compare the color of the signal with a reference color, red, and if they are equal, you stop the car. On the other hand, a decision like, "If the speed of the car exceeds the limit, slow down," involves a different relationship—here you check whether the speed of the car is greater than the current speed limit. Both of these comparisons are similar in that they result in one of two values: they are either **true** or **false**. This is precisely how comparisons work in C++.

You can compare data values using some new operators called relational **operators**. Table 4-1 lists the six fundamental operators for comparing two values.

Table 4-1. Relational Operators

Operator	Meaning
<	less than
<=	less than or equal to
>	greater than
>=	greater than or equal to
==	equal to
!=	not equal to

 CAUTION *Here, the equal to (==) comparison operator has two successive equal signs. This is not the same as the assignment operator (=), which consists of only a single equal sign. It's a very common mistake to use one equal sign instead of two when you intended to compare for equality. Unfortunately, this will not necessarily result in a warning message from the compiler because the expression may be perfectly valid but just not what you intended, so you need to take particular care to avoid this kind of error.*

Each of these binary operators compares two values and results in a `true` value if the comparison is true, or `false` if it is not. The values `true` and `false` are keywords in C++ and are also a new type of literal. They are called **Boolean literals** (after George Boole, the father of Boolean algebra), and they are of type `bool`.

If you cast the value `true` to an integer type, the result will be 1, and if you cast `false` to an integer, the result will be 0. You can also convert numerical values to type `bool` by using an explicit cast. Zero will convert to `false`, and any nonzero value will convert to `true`.

As with the other standard types, you can create a variable of type `bool` for the purpose of storing Boolean values. You declare these just like you would any other variable; here's an example:

```
bool decision = true;        // Declare, define, and initialize a logical variable
```

This declares and defines the variable `decision` as Boolean and assigns it an initial value of `true`.

Applying the Comparison Operators

You can see how comparisons work by looking at a few simple examples of applying the operators. Suppose you have two integer variables called i and j, with the values 10 and –5 respectively. You can use these in the following logical expressions:

```
i > j      i != j      j > -8      i <= j + 15
```

All of these expressions evaluate to true. Note that in the last expression, i <= j + 15, the addition operation j + 15 executes first because + has a higher precedence than <=.

You could store the result of any of these expressions in a variable of type bool. Here is an example:

```
decision = i > j;              // true if i is greater than j, false otherwise
```

If i is greater than j, the value true is stored in the bool variable decision, otherwise false is stored.

You can compare the values stored in variables of type char, too. First assume that you have the following variables defined:

```
char first = 'A';
char last = 'Z';
```

You can now write some examples of comparisons using these variables. Take a look at the following expressions:

```
first < last      'E' <= first      first != last
```

The first expression checks whether the value of first, which is 'A', is less than the value of last, which is 'Z'. This is always true. You can make sure this is the case for ASCII by looking at the codes for these characters in Appendix A—the uppercase letters are represented by an ascending sequence of numerical values from decimal 65 to 90, with 65 representing 'A' and 90 representing 'Z'. The result of the second expression is false, because 'E' is greater than the value of first. The last expression is true, because 'A' is definitely not equal to 'Z'.

You can output bool values just as easily as any other type of value—here's an example that shows how they look.

....

Try It Out: Comparing Data Values

This example reads two char values from the keyboard and outputs the result of their comparison:

```
// Program 4.1 Comparing data values
#include <iostream>
using std::cin;
using std::cout;
using std::endl;

int main() {
  char first = 0;                    // Stores the first character
  char second = 0;                   // Stores the second character
```
(Continued)

```
// Prompt for and read in the first character
cout << "Enter a character: ";
cin >> first;

// Prompt for and read in the second character
cout << "Enter a second character: ";
cin >> second;

cout << "The value of the expression first < second is: "
     << (first < second)
     << endl
     << "The value of the expression first == second is: "
     << (first == second)
     << endl;

return 0;
}
```

The following is an example of the output from this program:

```
Enter a character: p
Enter a second character: t
The value of the expression first < second is: 1
The value of the expression first == second is: 0
```

HOW IT WORKS

The prompting for input and reading of characters from the keyboard is standard stuff that you have seen before. You can output the results of applying the < and == operators in the following statement:

```
cout << "The value of the expression first < second is: "
     << (first < second)
     << endl
     << "The value of the expression first == second is: "
     << (first == second)
     << endl;
```

Note that the parentheses around the comparison expressions *are* necessary here; if they aren't there, the expressions don't mean what you think they mean and the compiler outputs an error message. The expressions compare the first and second characters that the user entered. From the preceding output you can see that the value true is displayed as 1, and the value false is displayed as 0.

The output values 1 and 0 for `true` and `false` are the default representations of these values. If you wanted the Boolean values actually to display as `true` and `false` on the screen, you could use the output manipulator `boolalpha` to do this. Just add this statement at the beginning of `main()`:

```
cout << std::boolalpha;
```

If you compile and run the example again, you get `bool` values displayed as `true` or `false`. To return output of Boolean values to the default setting within your program, use the `noboolalpha` manipulator.

Comparing Floating Point Values

Of course, you can also compare floating-point values. Let's consider some slightly more complicated numerical comparisons. First, define some variables with the following statements:

```
int i = -10;
int j = 20;
double x = 1.5;
double y = -0.25E-10;
```

Now take a look at the following logical expressions:

```
-1 < y      j < (10 - i)     2.0 * x >= (3 + y)
```

As you can see, you can use expressions that result in a numerical value as operands in comparisons. Because the comparison operators are all of lower precedence than the arithmetic operators (see Appendix D), none of the parentheses is strictly necessary, but they do help make the expressions clearer.

The first comparison produces the value `true`, because the variable y has a very small negative value (–0.000000000025), which is greater than –1. The second comparison results in the value `false`, because the expression 10 - i has the value 20, which is the same as j. The third expression is `true`, because 3 + y is slightly less than 3.

You can use relational operators to compare values of any of the basic types, so all you need now is a practical way of using the results of a comparison to modify the behavior of a program. Let's look into that immediately.

The if Statement

The basic if statement allows your program to execute a single statement, or a block of statements enclosed between braces if a given condition is true. This is illustrated in Figure 4-1:

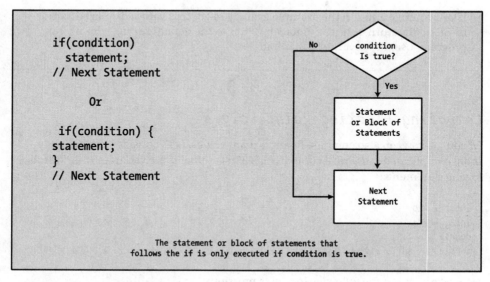

The statement or block of statements that
follows the if is only executed if condition is true.

Figure 4-1. Logic of the simple if statement

Here is a simple example of an if statement that tests the value of a variable called letter, of type char:

```
if(letter == 'A')
  std::cout << "The first capital, alphabetically speaking.\n";

  std::cout << "This statement always executes.\n";
```

If letter has the value 'A', the condition is true and these statements produce the following output:

```
The first capital, alphabetically speaking.
This statement always executes.
```

If the value of letter is not equal to 'A', only the second line appears in the output. You put the condition to be tested between parentheses immediately following the keyword, if. Notice the position of the semicolon (;) here. It goes after the statement following the if and the condition between the parentheses. A semicolon (;) must not appear after the condition in parentheses, because the if and the condition are bound with the statement or block that follows. They cannot exist by themselves.

You can also see how the statement following the if is indented to indicate that it only executes as a result of the condition being true. The indentation is not necessary for the program to compile, but it does help you recognize the relationship between the if condition and the statement that depends on it. Sometimes, you will see simple if statements like this one written on a single line:

```
if(letter == 'A') std::cout << "The first capital, alphabetically speaking\n.";
```

Generally, I prefer to write the statement (or block) bound to the if condition on a separate line; I think it is much clearer that way.

You could extend this example to change the value of letter if it contains the value 'A', as shown here:

```
if(letter == 'A') {
  std::cout << "The first capital, alphabetically speaking.\n";
  letter = 'a';
}

std::cout << "This statement always executes.\n";
```

Now all the statements in the block will be executed when the if condition is true. Without the braces, only the first statement would be the subject of the if, and the statement assigning the value 'a' to letter would always be executed. Note that there is a semicolon (;) after each of the statements in the block and not after the closing brace at the end of the block. You can have as many statements as you like within the block; you can even have nested blocks. Because letter has the value 'A', both statements within the block will be executed so its value will be changed to 'a' after the same message as before is displayed. Neither of these statements execute if the condition is false. Of course, the statement following the block always executes.

....

Try It Out: Making a Decision

Let's try out an if statement for real. You can create a program to range check the value of an integer entered from the keyboard:

```
// Program 4.2 Using an if statement
#include <iostream>
using std::cin;
using std::cout;
using std::endl;

int main() {
  cout << "Enter an integer between 50 and 100: ";

  int value = 0;
  cin >> value;
```

(Continued)

```
    if(value < 50)
      cout << "The value is invalid - it is less than 50." << endl;

    if(value > 100)
      cout << "The value is invalid - it is greater than 100." << endl;

    cout << "You entered " << value << endl;
    return 0;
}
```

The output depends on the value that you enter. For a value between 50 and 100, the output will be something like the following:

```
Enter an integer between 50 and 100: 77
You entered 77
```

Outside of the range 50 to 100, a message indicating that the value is invalid will precede the output showing the value entered. If it is below 50, the output will be

```
Enter an integer between 50 and 100: 27
The value is invalid - it is less than 50.
You entered 27
```

If the value is greater than 100, the output will be similar to this:

```
Enter an integer between 50 and 100: 270
The value is invalid - it is greater than 100.
You entered 270
```

HOW IT WORKS

After prompting for, and reading a value, the first if statement checks whether the value entered is below the lower limit of 50:

```
  if(value < 50)
    cout << "The value is invalid - it is less than 50." << endl;
```

The output statement is only executed if the if condition is true, which is when value is less than 50.

The next if statement checks the upper limit:

```
  if(value > 100)
    cout << "The value is invalid - it is greater than 100." << endl;
```

The output statement is executed if value is greater than 100.

The last output statement is

```
cout << "You entered " << value << endl;
```

This statement always executes.

Nested if Statements

The statement that executes when the condition in an if statement is true can itself be an if statement. This arrangement is called a **nested if**. The condition of the inner if is only tested if the condition for the outer if is true. An if that is nested inside another can *also* contain a nested if. Generally, you can continue nesting ifs like this, one inside the other, to whatever level you require.

Try It Out: Using Nested ifs

I can demonstrate the nested if with a working example that tests whether a character I enter is alphabetic. Although this example is a perfectly reasonable use of a nested if, it has some built-in assumptions that would be best avoided; see if you can spot the problem:

```
// Program 4.3 Using a nested if
#include <iostream>
using std::cin;
using std::cout;
using std::endl;

int main() {
  char letter = 0;                   // Store input in here

  cout << "Enter a letter: ";        // Prompt for the input
  cin >> letter;                     // then read a character

  if(letter >= 'A') {                // Test for 'A' or larger
    if(letter <= 'Z') {              // Test for 'Z' or smaller
      cout << "You entered an uppercase letter."
           << endl;
      return 0;
    }
  }
}
```

(Continued)

```
    if(letter >= 'a')                    // Test for 'a' or larger
      if(letter <= 'z') {                // Test for 'z' or smaller
        cout << "You entered a lowercase letter."
             << endl ;
        return 0;
      }
    cout << "You did not enter a letter." << endl;
    return 0;
}
```

Here is the typical output from this example:

```
Enter a letter: H
You entered an uppercase letter.
```

<h2>HOW IT WORKS</h2>

This program starts with the usual comment lines and the #include directive for the header supporting input/output, <iostream>, as well as the using declarations for the std names in your program. After allocating memory for the char variable letter and initializing it to zero, the function main() prompts you to enter a letter.

The if statement that follows the input checks whether the character entered is 'A' or larger:

```
  if(letter >= 'A') {                    // Test for 'A' or larger
    if(letter <= 'Z') {                  // Test for 'Z' or smaller
      cout << "You entered an uppercase letter."
           << endl;
      return 0;
    }
  }
```

If letter is greater than or equal to 'A', the nested if that checks for the input being 'Z' or less executes. If it *is* 'Z' or less, you can conclude that you have an uppercase letter, display a message, and you are done, so you execute a return statement to end the program. Both statements are enclosed between braces, so they both execute when the nested if condition is true.

This pair of nested ifs is built on two assumptions about the codes that are used to represent alphabetic characters. First, the letters A to Z are represented by a set of codes where the code for 'A' is the minimum and the code for 'Z' is the maximum. Second, the codes for the uppercase letters are contiguous, so no nonalphabetic characters lie between the codes for 'A' and 'Z'. It is not a good idea to build these kinds of assumptions into your code, because it limits the portability of your program. In EBCDIC coding (EBCDIC stands for Extended Binary Coded Decimal Interchange Code), for instance, the alphabetic character codes are not contiguous. You'll see how you can avoid this constraint in a moment.

The next if, using essentially the same mechanism as the first, checks whether the character entered is lowercase, displays a message, and returns, as shown here:

```
if(letter >= 'a')                    // Test for 'a' or larger
  if(letter <= 'z') {                // Test for 'z' or smaller
    cout << "You entered a lowercase letter."
         << endl ;
    return 0;
  }
```

If you were watching closely, you probably noticed that the test for a lowercase character contains only one pair of braces, whereas the uppercase test has two. The code block between the braces belongs to the inner if here. In fact, both sets of statements work as they should—remember that in C++, if(condition){...} is effectively a single statement and does not need to be enclosed within more braces. By the same token, if you feel the extra braces make the code clearer, by all means, use them. Finally, like the uppercase test, this code contains implicit assumptions about the order of codes for lowercase letters.

The output statement following the last if block only executes if the character entered was not a letter, and it displays a message to that effect. The return statement then executes. You can see that the relationship between the nested ifs and the output statement is much easier to follow because of the indentation applied to each. Indentation is generally used in C++ to provide visual cues to the logic of a program.

As I said at the start of this example, the program illustrates how a nested if works, but it is not a good way to test for characters. By using the standard library, you could write the program so that it would work independently of the character coding. Let's see how to do that.

Code-Neutral Character Handling

The standard library provides wide range of functions that you can use in your programs to perform a similarly wide range of tasks. These functions are listed in Table 4-2. By including the <cctype> header in your program, you can get access to an extremely useful set of functions for testing characters. In each case, you pass the function a variable or a literal of type int. If you pass a char type, it will automatically be converted to int.

Table 4-2. Functions for Testing Characters

Function	Action Carried Out
isupper()	Tests for an uppercase letter, by default 'A' to 'Z'.
islower()	Tests for a lowercase letter, by default 'a' to 'z'.
isalpha()	Tests for an upper- or lowercase letter.
isdigit()	Tests for a digit, 0 to 9.
isxdigit()	Tests for a hexadecimal digit, 0 to 9, 'a' to 'f', or 'A' to 'F'.
isalnum()	Tests for a letter or a digit (i.e., an alphanumeric character).
isspace()	Tests for whitespace, which can be a space, a newline, a carriage return, a form feed, or a horizontal or vertical tab.
iscntrl()	Tests for a control character.
isprint()	Tests for a printable character, which can be an upper- or lowercase letter, a digit, a punctuation character, or a space.
isgraph()	Tests for a graphic character, which is any printable character other than a space.
ispunct()	Tests for a punctuation character, which is any printable character that's not a letter or a digit. This will be either a space or one of the following: _ { } [ ] # ( ) < > % : ; . ? * + - / ^ & | ~ ! = , \ " '.

Each of these functions returns a value of type int. The value will be positive (true) if the character is of the type being tested for, and 0 (false) if it isn't. You may be wondering why these functions don't return a value of type bool, which would seem to make much more sense. The reason is that these functions were originally part of the C standard library and type bool was introduced later by C++.

The <cctype> header also provides two functions for converting between upper- and lowercase characters (see Table 4-3). You should pass the character to be converted to either function as type int. The result will be returned as type int.

Table 4-3. Functions for Converting Characters

tolower()	If you pass an uppercase letter, the lowercase equivalent is returned; otherwise the letter you pass returns unchanged.
toupper()	If you pass a lowercase letter, the uppercase equivalent is returned, otherwise the letter you pass returns unchanged.

You can use these functions to implement the previous example without any assumptions about the character coding. Different character codes in different environments are always taken care of by the standard library functions, so you don't need to worry about it. Using the standard library functions here also eliminates the need to use nested ifs, so the code will be simpler than before.

Note that all these character testing functions, except for isdigit() and isxdigit(), test the argument in the context of the current locale. A locale essentially determines how data that is locale dependent is handled. Different countries use different sets of characters for letters, so whether a particular character code is interpreted as a letter depends on the locale. Monetary units and the way decimal numbers are written also vary among locales. You can set the locale by calling the `setlocale()` function that is declared in the `<clocale>` header. This function accepts two arguments: the first specifies the category of function to which the locale is to apply, and the second specifies the locale. The value that you use for the first argument must be one of the values that are also declared in `<clocale>` for this purpose; see Table 4-4 for a list of these values.

Table 4-4. Values Defining Categories Affected by the Locale

Value	Description
LC_ALL	Specifies all categories.
LC_CTYPE	Specifies character handling.
LC_COLLATE	Specifies collating sequence in string comparisons.
LC_MONETARY	Specifies the formatting of monetary information.
LC_NUMERIC	Specifies the decimal point character.
LC_TIME	Specifies how time values are formatted.

The second argument to `setlocale()` is a string that specifies a particular locale. The string `"C"` is set as the default and corresponds to letters being the Latin `'A'` to `'Z'`. The set of strings that you can use to specify other locales are implementation defined but usually include quite straightforward country specifications such as "Germany."

The C++ header `<locale>` provides declarations for much more extensive capabilities for working with locale-dependent data, so you should explore this when you want to support multiple locales in a program.

....

Try It Out: Using Standard Library Character Conversions

When you modify the last example to use standard library functions, you might as well extend the capability of the program to try out the conversion functions as well:

```
// Program 4.4 Using standard library character testing and conversion
#include <iostream>
#include <cctype>                   // Character testing and conversion
using std::cin;
using std::cout;
using std::endl;

int main() {
  char letter = 0;                  // Store input in here

  cout << endl
       << "Enter a letter: ";       // Prompt for the input
  cin >> letter;                    // then read a character
  cout << endl;
```

(Continued)

```
    if(std::isupper(letter)) {                // Test for uppercase letter
        cout << "You entered a capital letter."
            << endl;
        cout << "Converting to lowercase we get "
            << static_cast<char>(std::tolower(letter)) << endl;
        return 0;
    }

    if(std::islower(letter)) {                // Test for lowercase letter
        cout << "You entered a small letter."
            << endl;
        cout << "Converting to uppercase we get "
            << static_cast<char>(std::toupper(letter)) << endl;
        return 0;
    }
    cout << "You did not enter a letter." << endl;
    return 0;
}
```

The typical output from this program is as follows:

```
Enter a letter: t

You entered a small letter.
Converting to uppercase we get T
```

HOW IT WORKS

The if expressions have been changed to use the standard library functions. You no longer need the nested ifs, because the two conditions you tested for earlier are now covered in one go by either the isupper() or the islower() function.

You really don't need to know how these functions work. In order to use them, you just need to know what they do, how many and what types of arguments to pass them, and what type of value they return. Armed with that information, you can use standard library functions to make your code much simpler and more generic. This version of the program works with whatever character coding is used for type char.

Notice how you can use the result returned from a conversion function directly in the output statements, as shown here:

```
    cout << "Converting to uppercase we get "
        << static_cast<char>(std::toupper(letter)) << endl;
```

The value returned by the toupper() function is of type int, so you cast it to type char and send it to the output stream, cout. If you want to store the returned character and remove the need for the explicit cast, you could save it back in the original variable, letter, with a statement such as the following:

```
letter = std::toupper(letter);
```

You could then output the converted character by using the variable letter in the output statement:

```
cout << "Converting to uppercase we get " << letter << endl;
```

If you need to use wide characters (of type wchar_t), you can include the <cwctype> header. This includes wide character equivalents of all the functions declared in <cctype>. Each of the testing function names has a 'w' after the 'is' in the function name, as demonstrated here:

iswupper()	iswdigit()	iswspace()	iswgraph()
iswlower()	iswxdigit()	iswcntrl()	iswpunct()
iswalpha()	iswalnum()	iswprint()	

character, and all return a value of type int.
conversion functions are called towlower()

....

he <cwtype> *headers in C++ are inherited from C.*
function is defined both inside and outside the std
rogram to be compiled and linked. In this case, using
without the std *qualifier will work, but because you*
ualify the names.

sing so far executes a statement *if* the condition
specified is true. Program execution then continues with the next statement in sequence. Of course, it might be that you want to execute a particular statement or block of statements only when the condition is false. To enable you to do this, you have an extension of the if that allows one course of action to be followed if the condition is true, and another to be executed if the condition is false. Execution then continues with the next statement in the sequence. This is described as an if-else statement.

The `if-else` combination provides a choice between two options. The general logic of the `if-else` is shown in Figure 4-2.

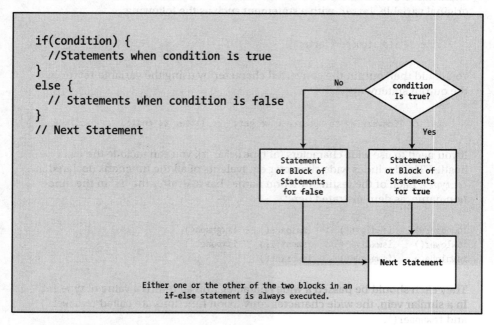

```
if(condition) {
  //Statements when condition is true
}
else {
  // Statements when condition is false
}
// Next Statement
```

Figure 4-2. The if-else statement logic

The flowchart in Figure 4-2 indicates the sequence in which statements are executed, depending on whether the `if` condition is `true` or `false`. As the illustration implies, and as you have seen before, you can always use a block wherever you can put a statement. This allows any number of statements to be executed for each option in an `if-else` statement.

Still using variables of type `char`, you could write an `if-else` statement that would report whether the character stored in the variable `letter` was alphanumeric:

```
if(std::isalnum(letter))
  std::cout << "It is a letter or a digit." << std::endl;
else
  std::cout << "It is neither a letter nor a digit." << std::endl;
```

This uses the function `isalnum()` from the header `<cctype>` that you saw earlier. If the variable `letter` contains a letter or a digit, the function `isalnum()` returns a positive integer. The `if` statement interprets this as `true`, so the first message is displayed. If `letter` contains something other than a letter or a digit, `isalnum()` returns 0. For the purposes of the `if`, this is automatically converted to `false`, and the output statement after `else` executes.

Try It Out: Extending the if

You can see the if-else statement in action in the following example. Let's try it with a numerical value this time:

```
// Program 4.5 Using the if-else
#include <iostream>
using std::cin;
using std::cout;
using std::endl;

int main() {
  long number = 0;                      // Store input here
  cout << "Enter an integer less than 2 billion: ";
  cin >> number;
  cout << endl;

  if(number % 2L == 0)                  // Test remainder after division by 2
    cout << "\nYour number is even."    // Here if remainder is 0
        << endl;
  else
    cout << "Your number is odd."       // Here if remainder is 1
        << endl;
  return 0;
}
```

Here is a typical example of output from this program:

```
Enter an integer less than 2 billion: 123456

Your number is even.
```

HOW IT WORKS

After reading the input value into number, the program tests the value in the if condition by taking the remainder that results from dividing by 2 (using the remainder operator, %, that we saw in Chapter 2) and checking to see whether it is 0. The remainder that results from dividing an integer by 2 can only be 1 or 0, and the code is commented to indicate this fact. If the remainder is equal to 0, then the if condition is true and the statement immediately following the if executes. If the remainder is 1, then the if condition is false, and the statement following the else keyword executes. After either outcome, the return statement executes to end the program.

(Continued)

NOTE *The* else *keyword is written without a semicolon (;), just like the* if *part of the statement. Again, you can use indentation as a visible indicator of the relationship between various statements. You can clearly see which statement is executed to produce a* true *result and which is executed for a* false *result. You should always indent the statements in your programs to show their logical structure.*

Here's an alternative way of coding the if condition in this example. Recall that any nonzero value produces true when converted to type bool, and a value of 0 converts to false. Therefore, you could use the result of the modulus operation as the condition and not bother with comparing it to 0. If you do that, the if-else statement could look like this:

```
if(number % 2L)                        // Test remainder after division by 2
   cout << "Your number is odd."    // Here if remainder is 1
         << endl;
else
   cout << "Your number is even."   // Here if remainder is 0
         << endl;
```

The if and the else clauses just need to be reversed; this is because if the value of number is even, then (number % 2L == 0) returns true, whereas (number % 2L) is converted to false. This may seem a little confusing at first, but remember that the first version of the condition was equivalent to

"Is it true that the remainder is 0?"

Whereas, if these are reversed, 1 will be converted to true, and the second version will be equivalent to

"Is the remainder 1?"

Nested if-else Statements

You have already seen that you can nest if statements within if statements. As you have no doubt anticipated, you can also nest if-else statements within ifs, ifs within if-else statements, and indeed if-else statements within other if-else statements. This provides you with plenty of versatility (and considerable room for confusion), so let's look at a few examples. Taking the first case first, an example of an if-else nested within an if might look like the following:

```
if(coffee == 'y')
   if(donuts == 'y')
      std::cout << "We have coffee and donuts."
              << std::endl;
```

```
    else
        std::cout << "We have coffee, but not donuts."
                    << std::endl;
```

Here, coffee and donuts are variables of type char that can have the value 'y' or 'n'. The test for donuts only executes if the result of the test for coffee is true, so the messages reflect the correct situation in each case. The else belongs to the if that tests for donuts. However, it is easy to get this confused.

If you write much the same thing, but with incorrect indentation, you can be trapped into the wrong conclusion about what happens here:

```
if(coffee == 'y')
    if(donuts == 'y')
        std::cout << std::endl
                    << "We have coffee and donuts.";
else                                        // This else is indented incorrectly.
    std::cout << "We have no coffee..."     // Wrong!
                << std::endl;
```

The indentation of the code now misleadingly suggests that you're looking at an if nested within an if-else, which is simply not the case. The first message is correct, but the output as a consequence of the else executing is quite wrong. This statement only executes if the test for coffee is true, because the else belongs to the test for donuts, not the test for coffee. This mistake is easy to see, but with larger and more complicated if structures, you need to keep in mind the following rule about which if owns which else.

> *An else always belongs to the nearest preceding if that's not already spoken for by another else. The potential for confusion here is known as the dangling else problem.*

Whenever a bunch of if-else statements looks a bit complicated in a program, you can apply this rule to sort things out. When you're writing your own programs, you can always use braces to make the situation clearer. It isn't really necessary in such a simple case, but you could write the preceding example as follows:

```
if(coffee == 'y') {
    if(donuts == 'y')
        std::cout << "We have coffee and donuts."
                    << std::endl;
    else
        std::cout << "We have coffee, but not donuts."
                    << std::endl;
}
```

Now it should be absolutely clear. The else definitely belongs to the if that is checking for donuts.

Understanding Nested ifs

Now that you know the rules, understanding the case of an if nested within an if-else should be easy:

```cpp
if(coffee == 'y') {
  if(donuts == 'y')
    std::cout << "We have coffee and donuts."
          << std::endl;
}
else if(tea == 'y')
  std::cout << "We have no coffee, but we have tea."
          << std::endl;
```

NOTE *Notice the formatting of the code here. When an* if *is nested beneath an* else, *writing* else if *on one line is the accepted convention, and I will be following it in this book.*

This time, the braces are essential. If you left them out, the else would belong to the if that's looking out for donuts. In this kind of situation, it is easy to forget to include the braces and thus create an error that may be hard to find. A program with this kind of error compiles without a problem, as the code is perfectly correct. It may even produce the right results some of the time, but it doesn't express what you intended.

If you removed the braces in this example, you'd get the right results only as long as coffee and donuts were both equal to 'y' so that the if(tea == 'y') check wouldn't execute.

Finally, you'll look at if-else statements nested in other if-else statements. This can get very messy, even with just one level of nesting. Let's beat the coffee and donuts analysis to death by using it again:

```cpp
if(coffee == 'y')
  if(donuts == 'y')
    std::cout << "We have coffee and donuts."
            << std::endl;
  else
    std::cout << "We have coffee, but not donuts."
            << std::endl;
else if(tea == 'y')
  std::cout << "We have no coffee, but we have tea, and maybe donuts..."
          << std::endl;
else
  std::cout << "No tea or coffee, but maybe donuts..."
          << std::endl;
```

The logic here doesn't look quite so obvious, even with the correct indentation. Braces aren't necessary, as the rule you saw earlier will verify, but it would look a bit clearer if you included them:

```
if(coffee == 'y') {
  if(donuts == 'y')
    std::cout << "We have coffee and donuts."
              << std::endl;
  else
    std::cout << "We have coffee, but not donuts."
              << std::endl;
}
else {
  if(tea == 'y')
    std::cout << " We have no coffee, but we have tea, and maybe donuts..."
              << std::endl;
  else
    std::cout << "No tea or coffee, but maybe donuts..."
              << std::endl;
}
```

You will find much better ways of dealing with this kind of logic in a program. Basically, if you put enough nested `if`s together, you can almost guarantee a mistake somewhere. The next section will help to simplify things.

Logical Operators

As you have just seen, using `if`s where you have two or more related conditions can be a bit cumbersome. You have tried your iffy talents on looking for coffee and donuts, but in practice, you may want to check much more complex conditions. For instance, you could be searching a personnel file for someone who is over 21, under 35, female, has a college degree, is unmarried, and who speaks Hindi or Urdu. Defining a test for this could involve the mother of all `if`s.

C++'s **logical operators** provide a neat and simple solution. Using logical operators, you can combine a series of comparisons into a single expression so that you end up needing just one `if`, almost regardless of the complexity of the set of conditions. What's more, you won't have trouble determining which one to use because there are just three of them (as shown in Table 4-5).

Table 4-5. Logical Operators

Operator	Functions As
&&	Logical AND
||	Logical OR
!	Logical negation (NOT)

The first two, `&&` and `||`, are binary operators that combine two operands of type `bool` and produce a result of type `bool`. The third operator, `!`, is unary, so it applies to a single operand of type `bool` and produces a `bool` result. In the following pages, first you'll learn what each of these is used for in general terms, then you'll look at an example. It's important that you separate in your mind the bitwise operators you saw earlier, which operate on the bits within integer operands, and these logical operators, which apply to operands of type `bool`.

Logical AND

You use the AND operator, &&, where you have two conditions that must both be `true` for a `true` result. For example, you want to be rich *and* healthy. When you were using a nested `if` earlier to determine whether a character was an uppercase letter, the value being tested had to be both greater than or equal to `'A'` *and* less than or equal to `'Z'`. Both conditions had to be `true` for the character to be an uppercase letter. The && operator *only* produces a `true` result if both operands are `true`. If either or both of the operands are `false`, then the result is `false`.

If you take the example of a value stored in a `char` variable called `letter`, you could replace the test using two `if`s with one that uses only a single `if` and the && operator:

```
if(letter >= 'A' && letter <= 'Z')
   std::cout << "This is an uppercase letter."
          << std::endl;
```

The output statement executes only if both of the conditions combined by the operator && are `true`. No parentheses are necessary in the expression because the precedence of each of the comparison operators is higher than that of &&. As usual, you're free to put parentheses in if you want. You could write the statement as follows:

```
if((letter >= 'A') && (letter <= 'Z'))
   std::cout << "This is an uppercase letter."
          << std::endl;
```

Now there can be no doubt that the comparisons between parentheses will execute first.

Logical OR

The OR operator, ||, applies when you have two conditions and you want a `true` result when either or both of them are `true`. The || operator only produces a `false` result when both of its operands are `false`. If either or both of the operands are `true`, then the result is `true`.

For example, you might be considered creditworthy enough for a loan from the bank if your income was at least $100,000 a year, or if you had $1,000,000 in cash. This could be tested using the following `if`:

```
if(income >= 100000.00 || capital >= 1000000.00)
   std::cout << "Of course, how much do you want to borrow?"
          << std::endl;
```

The response emerges when either or both of the conditions are `true`. (A better response might be, "*Why* do you want to borrow?" It's strange how banks will only lend you money when you don't need it.)

Logical Negation

The third logical operator, `!`, takes one operand with a logical value—`true` or `false`—and inverts its value. So, if the value of a Boolean variable, `test`, is `true`, then `!test` is `false`; if `test` is `false`, then `!test` results in the value `true`. For example, if x has the value 10, then this expression

```
!(x > 5)
```

is `false`, because x > 5 is `true`.

We could also apply the `!` operator to produce an expression that was a favorite of Charles Dickens:

```
!(income > expenditure)
```

If this expression is `true`, the result is misery—at least, as soon as the bank starts bouncing your checks.

You can apply all the logical operators to expressions that evaluate to `true` or `false`. Operands can be anything from a simple variable of type `bool` to a complex combination of comparisons and logical variables.

Try It Out: Combining Logical Operators

You can combine conditional expressions and logical operators to any degree to which you feel comfortable. For example, you can construct a questionnaire to decide whether a person is a good loan risk. Let's write this scenario as a working example:

```cpp
// Program 4.6 Combining logical operators
#include <iostream>
using std::cin;
using std::cout;
using std::endl;

int main() {
  int age = 0;                  // Age of the prospective borrower
  int income = 0;               // Income of the prospective borrower
  int balance = 0;              // Current bank balance
// Get the basic data
  cout << endl << "Please enter your age in years: ";
  cin >> age;
```

(Continued)

```
            cout << "Please enter your annual income in dollars: ";
            cin >> income;

            cout << "What is your current account balance in dollars: ";
            cin >> balance;
            cout << endl;

            // We only lend to people over 21, who make
            // over $25,000 per year, or have over
            // $100,000 in their account, or both.

            if(age >= 21 && (income > 25000 || balance > 100000)) {
              // OK, you are good for the loan - but how much?
              // This will be the lesser of twice income and half balance

              int loan = 0;                    // Stores maximum loan amount
              if(2 * income < balance / 2)
                loan = 2 * income;
              else
                loan = balance / 2;

              cout << "You can borrow up to $"
                   << loan
                   << endl;
            }
            else
              cout << "Sorry, we are out of cash today."
                   << endl;
            return 0;
          }
```

Here is an example of the output from this program:

```
Please enter your age in years: 25
Please enter your annual income in dollars: 28000
What is your current account balance in dollars: 185000

You can borrow up to $56000
```

HOW IT WORKS

First you declare three integer variables that you will use to store values entered via the keyboard:

```
int age = 0;                    // Age of the prospective borrower
int income = 0;                 // Income of the prospective borrower
int balance = 0;                // Current bank balance
```

Then you read in three values that determine the eligibility for a loan:

```
cout << endl << "Please enter your age in years: ";
cin >> age;

cout << "Please enter your annual income in dollars: ";
cin >> income;

cout << "What is your current account balance in dollars: ";
cin >> balance;
```

The if statement that follows determines whether or not a loan will be granted:

```
if(age >= 21 && (income > 25000 || balance > 100000))
```

The condition requires that the applicant's age be at least 21, and that either his or her income be greater than $25,000, or his or her balance be greater than $100,000. The parentheses around the expression

```
(income > 25000 || balance > 100000)
```

are necessary so that the result of ORing these income and balance conditions together is ANDed with the age test. Without the parentheses, the age test would be ANDed with the income test, and the result would be ORed with the balance test. This is because the && operator has a higher precedence than the || operator, as you can see from the table in Appendix D. Without the parentheses, the condition would have allowed anyone with a balance over $100,000 to get a loan, even if they were only 8 years old! That's not what was intended. Banks *never* lend to minors or mynahs.

If the if condition is true, the following block of statements executes:

```
// OK, you are good for the loan - but how much?
// This will be the lesser of twice income and half balance

int loan = 0;                    // Stores maximum loan amount
if(2 * income < balance / 2)
  loan = 2 * income;
else
  loan = balance / 2;

cout << "You can borrow up to $"
     << loan
     << endl;
```

In this block, you determine the maximum loan amount with another if statement. This determines that the maximum loan is the lesser of twice the salary and half the current bank balance.

(Continued)

Of course, if the first `if` condition is `false`, the `else` executes:

```
else
   cout << "Sorry, we are out of cash today."
        << endl;
```

As you can see, this outputs a message implying that the cash will not be forth-coming. It's obviously a lie, but at least they are letting you down lightly.

The Conditional Operator

The **conditional operator** is sometimes called the **ternary operator** because it involves three operands—the only operator to do so. It has similarities to the `if-else` statement, in that it selects one of two choices, depending on the value of a condition. However, whereas the `if-else` statement provides you with a way to select one of two statements to execute, the conditional operator lets you choose between two *values*. You can understand it best by looking at an example.

Suppose you have two variables, a and b, and you want to assign the value of the higher of the two to a third variable, c. You can do this with the following statement:

```
c = a > b ? a : b;          // Set c to the higher of a and b
```

The conditional operator has a logical expression as its first operand, in this case a > b. If this expression is `true`, the second operand—in this case a—is selected as the value resulting from the operation. If the first operand is `false`, the third operand—in this case b—is selected as the value. Thus, the result of the conditional expression is a if a is greater than b, and b otherwise. In the preceding statement, this value is stored in c. The assignment statement using the conditional operator is equivalent to the `if` statement:

```
if(a > b)
  c = a;
else
  c = b;
```

You can also use the conditional operator to select the lower of two values. In the previous program, you used an `if-else` to decide the value of the loan, but you can use this statement instead:

```
loan = 2*income < balance/2 ? 2*income : balance/2;
```

This produces exactly the same result, and you don't need parentheses because the precedence of the conditional operator is lower than that of the other operators in this statement. The condition is 2*income < balance/2. If this evaluates to `true`, then the expression 2*income evaluates and produces the result of the operation. If the condition is false, the expression balance/2 produces the result of the operation.

Of course, if you think parentheses would make things clearer, you can include them:

```
loan = (2*income < balance/2) ? (2*income) : (balance/2);
```

The conditional operator, which is often represented by ?:, can be written generally as follows:

```
condition ? expression1 : expression2
```

If condition evaluates as true, the result is the value of expression1; if it evaluates to false, the result is the value of expression2. If condition is an expression that evaluates to a numerical value, then it is automatically converted to type bool, with a nonzero value resulting in true and 0 resulting in false, as you've seen before.

Note that only one of expression1 or expression2 will be evaluated. This has significant implications for expressions such as the following:

```
a < b ? ++i+1 : i+1;
```

If a is less than b, i is incremented and the result of the conditional operation is the incremented value of i plus 1. The variable i is not incremented if a < b is false and, in this case, the result of the conditional operator is the current value of i plus 1.

....

Try It Out: Using the Conditional Operator with Output

You will find that you often use the conditional operator to control output, depending on the result of an expression or the value of a variable. You can vary a message by selecting one text string or another depending on the condition specified.

```
// Program 4.7 Using the conditional operator to select output.
#include <iostream>
using std::cin;
using std::cout;
using std::endl;

int main() {
  int mice = 0;            // Count of all mice
  int brown = 0;           // Count of brown mice
  int white = 0;           // Count of white mice

  cout << "How many brown mice do you have? ";
  cin >> brown;
```

(Continued)

```
    cout << "How many white mice do you have? ";
    cin >> white;

    mice = brown + white;

    cout << "You have "
         << mice
         << (mice == 1 ? " mouse " : " mice ")
         << "in total."
         << endl;
    return 0;
}
```

The output from this program might be as follows:

```
How many brown mice do you have? 2
How many white mice do you have? 3
You have 5 mice in total.
```

HOW IT WORKS

You've seen most of the operations in this program before. The only bit of interest is in the output statement that is executed after the numbers of mice have been entered:

```
    cout << "You have "
         << mice
         << (mice == 1 ? " mouse " : " mice ")
         << "in total."
         << endl;
```

The expression using the conditional operator evaluates to " mouse " if the value of the variable mice is 1, or " mice " otherwise. This allows you to use the same output statement for any number of mice and select singular or plural as appropriate.

You will encounter many other situations in which you can apply this sort of mechanism—for example, selecting between "is" and "are", or "he" and "she", or indeed any situation in which you have a binary choice. You can even combine two conditional operators to choose between three options on occasion. Here's an example:

```
    cout << (a < b ? "a is less than b." :
                     (a == b ? "a is equal to b." : "a is greater than b."));
```

This statement outputs one of three messages, depending on the relative values of the variables a and b. The second choice for the first conditional operator is the result of another conditional operator.

The switch Statement

Often, you're faced with a multiple-choice situation in which you need to execute a particular set of statements from a number of choices (that is, more than two), depending on the value of an integer variable or expression. An example of the sort of thing I'm talking about would be a lottery: you buy a numbered ticket, and if you're lucky, you win a prize. For instance, if your ticket number is 147, you've won first prize; if it's 387 you can claim second prize; ticket number 29 gets you third prize; any other ticket number wins nothing at all. The switch statement handles precisely this sort of situation.

The switch statement enables you to select from multiple choices based on a set of fixed values for a given expression. The choices are called **cases**. In the lottery example, you had four cases: one for each of the winning numbers, plus the "default" case for all losing numbers. Here's how you could write a switch statement to select a message for a given ticket number:

```
switch(ticket_number) {
  case 147:
    std::cout << "You win first prize!";
    break;
  case 387:
    std::cout << "You win second prize!";
    break;
  case 29:
    std::cout << "You win third prize!";
    break;
  default:
    std::cout << "Sorry, you lose.";
}
```

The switch statement is harder to describe than to use. The selection from a number of cases is determined by the value of an integer expression that you specify between parentheses following the keyword switch. The result of the selection expression can also be of an enumerated data type, because values of such types can be automatically converted to integers. In this example, it is simply the variable ticket_number, which must be an integer type—what else could it be?

You define the possible choices in a switch statement by using as many **case values** as you need. The case values appear in a **case label**, of the following form:

```
case case_value:
```

It's called a case *label* because it labels the statements it precedes. The statements following a particular case label execute if the value of the selection expression is the same as that of the case value. Each case value must be unique but doesn't need to be placed in any particular order, as you can see in the example.

The case value must be an **integer constant expression**, which is an expression that the *compiler* can evaluate, so that it can only involve literals, const variables, or enumerators. Furthermore, any literals that you do include must either be of an integer type or be cast to an integer type.

The default label in the example identifies the **default case**, which is a catchall; the statements that follow it are executed if the selection expression does not correspond to any of the case values. You don't have to specify a default case, though. If you don't and none of the case values is selected, the switch will do nothing.

The break statement that appears after each set of case statements is absolutely necessary for the logic here. It breaks out of the switch after the case statements execute, and causes execution to continue with the statement following the closing brace for the switch. If you omit the break statement for a case, the statements for all the following cases also execute. Notice that we *don't* need break after the final case (usually the default case) because execution leaves the switch at this point anyway, but it is considered good programming style to include it because it safeguards against accidentally falling through to another case that you might add to a switch later.

NOTE switch, case, default, *and* break *are all keywords.*

Try It Out: The switch Statement

You can examine how the switch statement works with the following example:

```
// Example 4.8 Using the switch statement
#include <iostream>
using std::cin;
using std::cout;
using std::endl;

int main() {
  int choice = 0;                              // Store selection value here

  cout << endl
       << "Your electronic recipe book is at your service." << endl
       << "You can choose from the following delicious dishes: "
       << endl
       << "1 Boiled eggs" << endl
       << "2 Fried eggs" << endl
       << "3 Scrambled eggs" << endl
       << "4 Coddled eggs" << endl
       << endl << "Enter your selection number: ";
  cin >> choice;
```

```
switch(choice) {
  case 1:
    cout << endl << "Boil some eggs." << endl;
    break;
  case 2:
    cout << endl << "Fry some eggs." << endl;
    break;
  case 3:
    cout << endl << "Scramble some eggs." << endl;
    break;
  case 4:
    cout << endl << "Coddle some eggs." << endl;
    break;
  default:
    cout << endl << "You entered a wrong number, try raw eggs." << endl;
  }
  return 0;
}
```

HOW IT WORKS

After defining your options in the output statement and reading a selection number into the variable choice, the switch statement executes with the selection expression specified simply as choice in parentheses, immediately following the keyword switch. The possible choices in the switch are enclosed between braces and are each identified by a case label. If the value of choice corresponds with any of the case values, then the statements following that case label execute. You only have one statement plus a break statement for each case in this example, but in general, you can have as many statements as you need following a case label, and you don't need to enclose them between braces.

The break statement at the end of each group of case statements transfers execution to the statement after the switch. The break isn't mandatory, but if you don't include it, all the statements for the cases following the one selected execute, which isn't usually what you want. You can demonstrate this for yourself by removing the break statements from the preceding example and seeing what happens.

If the value of choice doesn't correspond with any of the case values specified, the statements preceded by the default label execute. If you hadn't included a default case here and the value of choice was different from all of the case values, then the switch would have done nothing and the program would continue with the next statement after the switch—the return statement.

Try It Out: Sharing a Case

As I said earlier, each of the case values must be a compile-time constant and must be unique. The reason that no two case values can be the same is that if they are, the compiler has no way of knowing which statements should be executed if that particular value comes up. However, different case values don't need to have unique actions. Several case values can share the same action, as shown in the following example:

```cpp
// Example 4.9 Multiple case actions
#include <iostream>
#include <cctype>
using std::cin;
using std::cout;
using std::endl;

int main() {
  char letter = 0;
  cout << endl
       << "Enter a letter: ";
  cin >> letter;

  if(std::isalpha(letter))
    switch(std::tolower(letter)) {
      case 'a': case 'e': case 'i': case 'o': case 'u':
        cout << endl << "You entered a vowel." << endl;
        break;
      default:
        cout << endl << "You entered a consonant." << endl;
    }
  else
    cout << endl << "You did not enter a letter." << endl;

  return 0;
}
```

Here is an example of the output from this program:

```
Enter a letter: E

You entered a vowel.
```

HOW IT WORKS

In this example, you are using one of the standard library's character conversion routines in combination with a `switch` to determine whether a character entered is a vowel or a consonant. The `if` condition first checks that you really do have a letter and not some other character:

```
if(std::isalpha(letter))
```

If the value returned by `isalpha()` is nonzero, then the `switch` executes:

```
switch(tolower(letter)) {
    case 'a': case 'e': case 'i': case 'o': case 'u':
      cout << endl << "You entered a vowel." << endl;
      break;
    default:
      cout << endl << "You entered a consonant." << endl;
}
```

The `switch` is controlled by the value returned from the function `tolower()`. You can just use the variable `letter`, but then you need to specify all the uppercase vowels as case values, as well as the lowercase vowels. If `tolower()` returns a value that corresponds to a vowel, the message confirming that displays. Otherwise the `default` case executes, displaying the message that the character entered as a consonant.

If `isalpha()` returns 0, the switch doesn't execute, and the `else` executes to output the message that the character entered was not a letter.

It's possible to dispense with the `if` statement by combining the test for a letter with the conversion to lowercase, but it requires some trickery and does make the code more complicated. For example, you could write the `switch` as follows:

```
switch(std::tolower(letter) * (std::isalpha(letter) != 0)) {
  case 'a': case 'e': case 'i': case 'o': case 'u':
      cout << endl << "You entered a vowel." << endl;
      break;
  case 0:
      cout << endl << "You did not enter a letter." << endl;
      break;
  default:
      cout << endl << "You entered a consonant." << endl;
}
```

(Continued)

As you have seen, isalpha() returns an int that's zero if the argument is not a letter, and a positive integer *that is not necessarily 1* if the argument is a letter. The reason for the complicated selection expression in the switch is that the isalpha() function does not return a bool value. If the isalpha() function returned a bool value, you could simply use tolower(letter) * isalpha(letter), because this would evaluate to 0 when isalpha() returned false, and to the lowercase letter returned by tolower() otherwise, as true will convert to 1.

Another alternative would be to cast the value returned by isalpha() to type bool. Then, you could write the switch as follows:

```
switch(tolower(letter) * static_cast<bool>(isalpha(letter))) {
  case 'a': case 'e': case 'i': case 'o': case 'u':
    cout << endl << "You entered a vowel." << endl;
    break;
  case 0:
    cout << endl << "You did not enter a letter." << endl;
    break;
  default:
    cout << endl << "You entered a consonant." << endl;
}
```

This works because the integer returned by isalpha() is cast to bool, and the compiler arranges for this value to converted to int for the multiply operation, so it ends up as 0 or 1. However, these switch statements are beginning to get rather confusing. The original version using the if is certainly the clearest code, and is therefore preferable despite the clever logic of the other examples.

Unconditional Branching

The if statement provides you with the flexibility to choose to execute one set of statements or another, depending on a specified condition, so that the sequence of statement execution varies depending on the values of the data in the program. You have just seen that switch provides a way to choose from a fixed range of options depending on the value of an integer expression. The goto statement, in contrast, is a blunt instrument. It enables you to branch to a specified program statement unconditionally. The statement to be branched to must be identified by a **statement label**, which is an identifier defined according to the same rules as a variable name. This is followed by a colon and placed before the statement that you want to reference using the label. Here is an example of a labeled statement:

```
MyLabel: x = 1;
```

This statement has the label MyLabel, and an unconditional branch to this statement would be written as follows:

```
goto MyLabel;
```

Whenever possible, you should avoid using gotos in your program. They tend to encourage convoluted code that can be extremely difficult to follow. Note that a goto that branches into the scope of a variable but bypasses its declaration will cause an error message from the compiler.

NOTE *Because the* goto *statement is theoretically unnecessary—you always have an alternative to using* goto*—a significant cadre of programmers says that you should never use it. I don't subscribe to such an extreme view. It is a legal statement, after all, and you'll come across occasions when it can be convenient. However, I do recommend that you only use it where you can see an obvious advantage over the other options that are available.*

Decision Statement Blocks and Variable Scope

A switch statement generally has its own block between braces that encloses the case statements. An if statement also often has braces enclosing the statements to be executed if the condition is true, and the else part may have such braces too. You need to be conscious of the fact that these statement blocks are no different than any other blocks when it comes to defining variable scope. Any variable declared within a block ceases to exist at the end of the block, so you cannot reference it outside the block.

For example, consider the following rather arbitrary calculation:

```
if(value > 0) {
   int savit = value - 1;    // This only exists in this block
   value += 10;
}
else {
   int savit = value + 1;    // This only exists in this block
   value -= 10;
}
std::cout << savit;                  // This will not compile! savit does not exist
```

The output statement at the end causes an error message because the variable savit is undefined at this point. Any variable defined within a block can only be used within that block, so if you want to access data that originates inside a block from outside it, you must put the declaration for the variable storing that information in an outer block.

Note that declarations within a switch statement block must be reachable in the course of execution, and it must not be possible to bypass them, otherwise the code will not compile. The following code illustrates how illegal declarations can arise in a switch:

```
int test = 3;
switch(test) {
  int i = 1;                     // ILLEGAL - cannot be reached

  case 1:
  {
    int j = 2;                   // OK - can be reached and is not bypassed
    cout << endl << test + j;
    break;
  }

  int k = 3;                     // ILLEGAL - cannot be reached

  case 3:
    cout << endl << test;
    int m = 4;                   // ILLEGAL - can be reached but can be bypassed
    break;

  default:
    cout << endl << "Default reached.";
    break;

  int n = 5;                     // ILLEGAL - cannot be reached
}
```

In this switch statement, only one of the declarations—the one for j—is legal. For a declaration to be legal, it must first be possible for the declaration to be reached and thus executed in the normal course of execution of the program. This is not the case for variables i, k, and n. Secondly, it must not be possible during execution of the program to enter the scope of a variable while bypassing its declaration, which is the case for the variable m. Variable j, however, is only "in scope" from its declaration to the end of the enclosing block, so this declaration cannot be bypassed.

Summary

In this chapter, you have added the capability for decision-making to your programs. In fact, you now know how all the decision-making statements in C++ work. The essential elements of decision-making that you have learned about in this chapter are as follows:

- You can compare two values using one of the comparison operators. This will result in a value of type bool, which can be true or false.

- You can cast a bool value to an integer type—true will cast to 1 and false will cast to 0.

- Numerical values can be cast to type bool—a 0 value casts to false, and a nonzero value casts to true.

- The if statement can execute a statement or block of statements depending on the value of a condition expression. If the condition is true, or nonzero, the statement or statement block executes. If the condition is false or 0, it won't execute.

- The if-else statement provides an additional option over the simple if. The else statement is executed if the condition is false or 0.

- if and if-else statements can be nested.

- The switch statement provides a means of selecting between a fixed set of options, depending on the value of an integer expression.

- The conditional operator selects between two values depending on the value of an expression.

- You can branch unconditionally to a statement with a specified label by using a goto statement.

Exercises

The following exercises enable you to try out what you've learned in this chapter. If you get stuck, look back over the chapter for help. If you're still stuck after that, you can download the solutions from the Apress website (http://www.apress.com/book/download.html), but that really should be a last resort.

Exercise 4-1. Write a program that asks the user to input two integers and then uses an if-else statement to output a message that states whether or not the integers are the same.

Exercise 4-2. Create a program that asks the user to input an integer between 1 and 100. Use a nested if, first to check that the integer is within this range, and then, if it is, to determine whether or not the integer is greater than, less than, or equal to 50.

Exercise 4-3. Design a program that asks the user to input a letter. Use a library function to determine and output whether or not the letter is a vowel and whether it is lowercase or not. Finally, output the lowercase letter together with its character code as a binary value.

Exercise 4-4. Write a program that determines, using only the conditional operator, if an integer that is entered has a value that is 20 or less, is greater than 20 and not greater than 30, is greater than 30 but not exceeding 100, or is greater than 100.

Exercise 4-5. Create a program that prompts the user to enter an amount of money between $0 and $10 (decimal places allowed). Determine how many quarters (25c), dimes (10c), nickels (5c) and pennies (1c) are needed to make up that amount. Output this information to the screen and ensure that the output makes grammatical sense (for example, if you need only one dime then the output should be "1 dime" and not "1 dimes").

CHAPTER 5

Loops: Repeating One or More Statements

A LOOP IS another fundamental idea in programming. It provides you with a way to repeat one or more statements as many times as your application requires. You can employ a loop to handle any repetitive task, and for most programs of any consequence, loops are essential. Using a computer to calculate the company payroll, for example, would not be practicable without a loop.

C++ provides a number of ways to implement a loop, all of which have their own particular area of application. In this chapter, you'll begin by looking at the theory behind loops and then get down to their practical uses, including, of course, how to write them. Along the way, you will learn the following:

- The principles behind the different kinds of loop

- How the while loop works

- What the merits of the do-while loop are

- How to use a for loop

- What the break statement does in a loop

- What the continue statement is used for in a loop

- How to construct nested loops

Understanding Loops

A loop is a mechanism that enables you to execute the same statement or block of statements repeatedly until a particular condition is met. The statements inside a loop are sometimes called **iteration statements**. A single execution of the statement or statement block that is within the loop is described as an **iteration**.

Two essential elements make up a loop: the statement or block of statements that forms the body of the loop that is to be executed repeatedly, and a **loop condition** of some kind that determines when to stop repeating the loop.

A loop condition can take a number of different forms to provide different ways of controlling the loop. For example, you might want to

- Execute the loop a given number of times.

- Execute the loop until a given value exceeds another value.

- Execute the loop until a particular character is entered from the keyboard.

You can set the loop condition to suit the circumstances. In the final analysis, however, loops come in two basic flavors; these are illustrated in Figure 5-1.

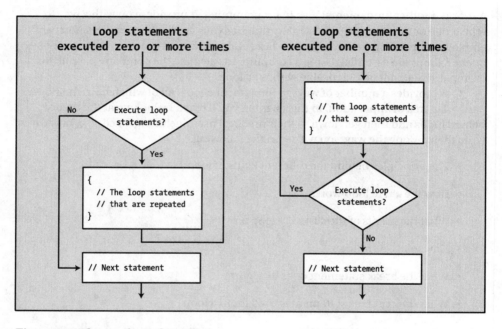

Figure 5-1. The two basic loop flavors

The difference between these two structures is evident at the point where you begin them. On the left, the loop condition is tested *before* the loop statements are executed; consequently, the loop statements are not executed if the test condition fails at the outset.

On the right, the test comes *after* the loop statements. The effect of this arrangement is that the loop statements are executed before the condition is tested for the first time, so this kind of loop always executes at least once.

The following are the three different kinds of loop in C++:

- The while loop

- The do-while loop

- The for loop

The while loop and the for loop have the same structure as the loop on the left side of Figure 5-1, so statements in the body of either of these loops may not execute at all. The do-while loop, on the other hand, has the structure shown on the right side of Figure 5-1, so the body of this type of loop is executed at least once. Let's start by looking at the detail of how the while loop works because it's the simplest of the three.

The while Loop

The while loop uses a logical expression to control execution of the loop body. The general form of the while loop is shown in Figure 5-2.

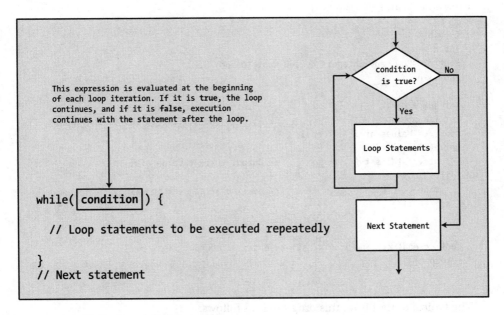

Figure 5-2. How the while loop executes

The flowchart in Figure 5-2 shows the logic of this loop. As long as the value of condition is true, the loop statement or block of loop statements is executed. When condition is false, execution continues with the statement following the loop. You can use any expression to control the loop, as long as it evaluates to a value of type bool, or to a value of an integer type.

 NOTE *If the condition expression controlling the loop results in an integer value, the loop continues as long as the value is nonzero. As you have seen, any nonzero integer is converted to type* bool *as* true, *and only 0 converts to* bool *as* false.

Of course, while is a keyword, so you can't use this word to name anything in your programs.

Try It Out: Using a while Loop

As a first example, you could use a while loop to calculate the sum of the integers from 1 to 10:

```
// Program 5.1 Using a while loop to sum integers
#include <iostream>
#include <iomanip>
using std::cin;
using std::cout;
using std::endl;

int main() {
  int n = 0;
  cout << "How many integers do you want to sum: ";
  cin >> n;

  int sum = 0;                        // Stores the sum of integers
  int i = 1;                          // Stores the integer to add to the total
  cout << "Values are: " << endl;
  while(i <= n) {
    cout << std::setw(5) << i;        // Output current value of i
    if(i%10 == 0)
      cout << endl;                   // Newline after ever 10 values
    sum += i++;
  }

  cout << endl << "Sum is " << sum << endl;  // Output final sum
  return 0;
}
```

The typical output from this program is as follows:

```
How many integers do you want to sum: 25
Values are:
    1    2    3    4    5    6    7    8    9   10
   11   12   13   14   15   16   17   18   19   20
   21   22   23   24   25
Sum is 325
```

HOW IT WORKS

The first two statements in `main()` deal with reading in the number of integers to be summed. The value of the variable n is used to determine when the `while` loop that does the summing ends.

Before you start the loop, you define and initialize a variable, i, that holds the current integer to be added to the total, and the variable, sum, which holds the sum.

```
int sum = 0;                    // Stores the sum of integers
int i = 1;                      // Stores the integer to add to the total
```

When the loop starts executing i will be 1 and sum will be 0.

The loop condition is the expression `i <= n`. This is true as long as i does not exceed n, and while this is the case, execution passes to the loop statements:

```
cout << std::setw(5) << i;      // Output current value of i
if(i%10 == 0)
  cout << endl;                 // Newline after ever 10 values
sum += i++;
```

First of all, you output the current value of i in a field width of 5 characters. In order to keep the output of values orderly, you output a newline character after every tenth output value. That way you should end up with ten to a line, and all nicely arranged in columns as long as the maximum has not got more than 5 decimal digits. The last statement here accumulates the total in sum. Because you're using the postfix form of the increment operator, the current value of i is added to sum, after which the value of i is incremented. This completes the loop block, so execution passes back to the beginning of the loop, and the condition is tested again with the new value of i.

I'm sure you can see that this pattern repeats with i having the values 1, 2, 3, 4, up to n. However, after the value n is added, i gets incremented to n+1, and the loop condition becomes `false`. When that happens, the loop ends and execution continues with the next statement after the loop, which outputs the sum:

```
cout << "Sum is " << sum << endl; // Output final sum
```

The net effect has been to repeat the loop n times, and thus to sum the integers from 1 to n.

 NOTE *Although this shows how a* `while` *loop works, if you happen to be of a mathematical bent, you'll know that you can calculate the sum of the integers from 1 to n with the formula* `n*(n+1)/2`, *so you don't really* need *a loop in this case!*

The do-while Loop

The do-while loop is similar to the while loop in that the loop continues for as long as the specified loop condition remains true. However, the difference is that the loop condition is checked at the *end* of the do-while loop, rather than at the beginning, so the loop statement is always executed at least once.

The logic and general form of the do-while loop are shown in Figure 5-3. Notice particularly the semicolon (;) that comes after the while statement, which is absolutely necessary. If you leave it out, the program won't compile.

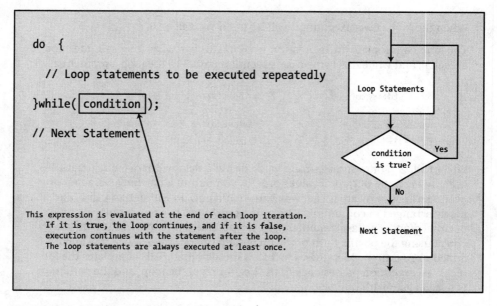

Figure 5-3. How a do-while loop executes

This kind of logic is ideal for situations where you have a block of code that you *always* want to execute once and may want to execute more than once. I can tell that you're not convinced that this is something that you'd ever need to do, so let's have another example.

Try It Out: Using a do-while Loop to Control Input

Suppose you want to calculate the average of an arbitrary number of input values—temperatures, for example, collected over a period of time. You have no way of knowing in advance how many values will be entered, but it's safe to assume that you'll always have at least one, because if you didn't, there'd be no point to running the program. That makes it an ideal candidate for a do-while loop. Here's the program:

```
// Program 5.2 Using a do-while loop to control input
#include <iostream>
using std::cin;
using std::cout;
using std::endl;

int main() {
  char ch = 0;              // Stores response to prompt for input
  int count = 0;            // Counts the number of input values
  double temperature = 0.0;   // Stores an input value
  double average = 0.0;       // Stores the total and average

  cout << endl;

  do {
    cout << "Enter a temperature reading: "; // Prompt for input
    cin >> temperature;                       // Read input value

    average += temperature;    // Accumulate total of values
    count++;                    // Increment value count

    cout << "Do you want to enter another? (y/n): ";
    cin >> ch;                             // Get response
    cout << endl;
  } while(ch == 'y');

  average /= count;          // Calculate the average
  cout << "The average temperature is " << average
       << endl;
  return 0;
}
```

A sample session with this program produces the following output:

```
Enter a temperature reading: 53
Do you want to enter another? (y/n): y

Enter a temperature reading: 65.5
Do you want to enter another? (y/n): y

Enter a temperature reading: 74
Do you want to enter another? (y/n): y

Enter a temperature reading: 69.5
Do you want to enter another? (y/n): n

Average temperature is 65.5
```

(Continued)

First, the program declares and initializes the variables required for the loop and the calculation:

```
char ch = 0;                // Stores response to prompt for input
int count = 0;              // Counts the number of input values
double temperature = 0.0;   // Stores an input value
double average = 0.0;       // Stores the total and average
```

The variable ch is used to store a response to a prompt for further input, which is tested at the end of the loop. As long as 'y' is entered, the program continues to read input values. (Ideally, the program would also accept 'Y'; you'll fix that shortly.) The purposes of the other three variables are clear from the comments.

Here is the loop that reads the input values:

```
do {
  cout << "Enter a temperature reading: "; // Prompt for input
  cin >> temperature;                       // Read input value

  average += temperature;    // Accumulate total of values
  count++;                   // Increment value count

  cout << "Do you want to enter another? (y/n): ";
  cin >> ch;                                 // Get response
  cout << endl;
} while(ch == 'y');
```

Because you're using a do-while loop, you'll always read at least one value. After prompting for input, the loop block reads a value from the keyboard and stores it in the temperature variable. This value is then added to average, so when the loop ends, average contains the sum of all the input values. You also increment count, because you'll need to know how many values there are in order to calculate the average. Finally in the loop, you prompt for a y or an n to be entered to indicate whether there are more values or not. When 'n' (in fact, any character other than 'y') is entered, the loop condition ch == 'y' will be false, and the loop will end. Execution then continues with the following statement:

```
average /= count;          // Calculate the average
```

This calculates the average by dividing the total that you accumulated in average by count, the number of values. The value stored in count will be automatically converted to double, the same type as average, before the division operation is carried out. Finally, you output the result and the program ends.

More Complex while Loop Conditions

Of course, you are not limited to a simple comparison for controlling a while (or a do-while) loop. *Any* expression that results in a true or false value can be used, or indeed any expression that yields an integer value. A problem with the previous example is that if you enter Y at the keyboard (instead of y), with the intention of entering another value, the program ends. This is not exactly foolproof programming. It would be better to allow input of either Y or y to continue the loop. You could do this quite easily by modifying the loop condition to

```
} while(ch == 'y' || ch == 'Y');
```

Now either an uppercase 'Y' or lowercase 'y' is acceptable as input to continue the loop.

Alternatively, you could use one of the standard library's character conversion functions, which I introduced in the last chapter. First, include the header at the top of your code:

```
// Program 5.2 Using a do-while loop to control input
#include <iostream>
#include <cctype>
```

Now you can substitute the following loop condition into the preceding program, which makes sure it's always the lowercase version of ch that gets compared with 'y':

```
} while(std::tolower(ch) == 'y');
```

As I explained earlier, you can also use an expression that evaluates to a numeric value as the loop condition. In this case, the compiler arranges that the result is converted to type bool. Remember that 0 converts to false, and *any* nonzero value, positive, or negative, converts to true. Thus, a while loop controlled by a numerical value only ends when the condition is 0.

The for Loop

You will primarily use the for loop to execute a statement or block of statements a predetermined number of times, but you can use it in other ways, as you shall see.

You control a for loop using three expressions separated by semicolons (;), which are placed between parentheses following the keyword for. These are shown in Figure 5-4.

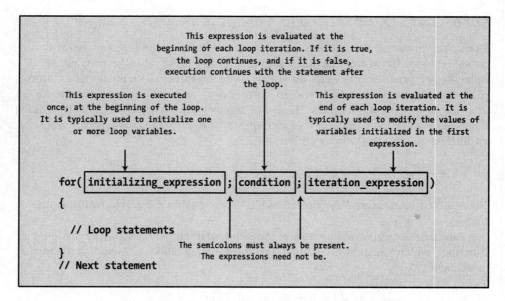

Figure 5-4. How a for loop is controlled

Any or all of the expressions controlling the for loop can be omitted, but you must always insert the semicolons. The reasons you might want to omit one or the other of the control expressions may not be immediately obvious, but leaving one or both of them out can be very useful; you'll explore some of the circumstances under which this is the case later in this chapter.

Figure 5-5 shows the logic of the for loop as a flowchart.

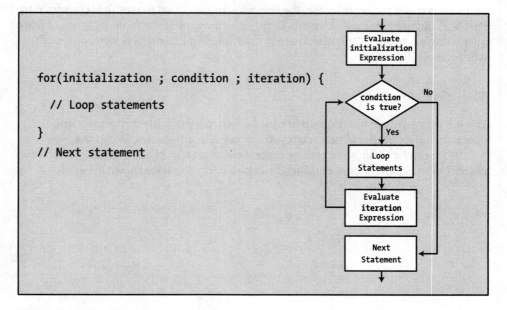

Figure 5-5. The logic of the for loop

The **initialization expression** is evaluated only once, at the beginning of the loop. The loop condition is checked next, and if it is true, the loop statement or statement block executes. On the other hand, if the condition is false, the loop statement is skipped and execution continues with the next statement after the loop. In this respect, the for loop is closer in operation to the while loop than to the do-while loop.

Presuming the condition is true and that the loop statement is therefore executed, the **iteration expression** is evaluated next; then the condition is checked once more to see if the loop should continue.

Try It Out: Using the for Loop

In the most typical use of the for loop, you use the first expression to initialize a counter, the second expression to check whether the counter has reached a given limit, and the third expression to increment the counter. You can demonstrate this in action by using a for loop to reimplement the program for summing integers.

```cpp
// Program 5.3 Using a for loop
#include <iostream>
using std::cin;
using std::cout;
using std::endl;

int main() {
  int sum = 0;                    // Accumulates the sum of integers
  int count = 0;                  // The number to sum

  cout << "How many integers do you want to sum? ";
  cin >> count;

  for(int i = 1 ; i <= count ; i++)
    sum += i;

  cout << endl
       << "The sum of the integers from 1 to " << count
       << " is " << sum << endl;

  return 0;
}
```

This program produces output something like this:

```
How many integers do you want to sum? 25

The sum of the integers from 1 to 25 is 325
```

(Continued)

HOW IT WORKS

You read the upper limit for the integers to be summed from the keyboard with these statements:

```
cout << "How many integers do you want to sum? ";
cin >> count;
```

The loop statement that accumulates the sum is indented, to show that it is part of the for loop:

```
for(int i = 1 ; i <= count ; i++)
   sum += i;
```

Because there's only one loop statement, you don't need any braces. The effect of this loop is to accumulate the sum of the integers from 1 to count in the variable, sum. The sequence of actions in the loop is as follows:

1. Execute the first expression. This declares the integer variable, i, and initializes it to 1.

2. Evaluate the second expression. This checks whether i is less than or equal to count. If i <= count evaluates to true, go to step 3. If it evaluates to false, go to step 6.

3. Execute the loop statement. This adds the current value of i to sum.

4. Execute the third expression. This increments the value of i.

5. Go back to step 2.

6. Leave the loop.

Thus, successive values of i are added to sum, starting with 1 and finishing with the value of count. Eventually, when i is incremented to count + 1, the for loop ends. Execution of the program then continues with the next statement after the loop, which outputs the total accumulated in sum.

Not only is it *legal* to declare variables within a for loop initialization expression, it is actually very common. This has some significant implications that you need to explore further.

Loops and Variable Scope

The for loop, like the while and do-while loops, defines a scope. The loop statement or block, as well as any expressions that control the loop, including all three expressions that you can use for control in the case of a for loop, *all* fall within the scope of a loop. In ANSI C++, any automatic variables declared within the scope of a loop do not exist outside the loop. Thus, the variable i that you declared in the loop initialization expression of the previous example is destroyed when the loop ends. If you try to reference the variable i after the loop, with a statement such as the following:

```
std::cout << std::endl
          << "The loop counter has the value " << i << std::endl;
```

the program no longer compiles, and you get an error message from an ANSI-compliant compiler to the effect that i does not exist.

But suppose that you really *need* the value of i after the loop. How can you get hold of it? You simply declare the variable i prior to the loop statement, as shown here:

```
int i = 1;                    // Declare & initialize loop counter
for( ; i <= count ; i++ ) // First expression is omitted
  sum += i;

std::cout << std::endl
          << "The sum of the integers from 1 to " << count
          << " is " << sum
          << std::endl;

std::cout << std::endl
          << "The loop counter has the value " << i << std::endl;
```

Now you can get at the value of i after the loop, because it's declared outside the loop's scope. Because i is also initialized prior to the execution of the loop, you don't need to include the loop initialization expression in this program. In general, however, it's a good idea to initialize the counter in the for statement—that way, you can always be confident of its value, no matter what changes you make to the rest of your program.

 CAUTION *Notice that despite the initialization expression being omitted, the semicolon (;) that separates the initialization expression from the loop condition must still be included.*

for Loops Before the ANSI Standard

Prior to the approval of the C++ standard, many C++ programs were written assuming the scope of a for loop variable extended beyond the end of the loop body. For this reason, many compilers that were otherwise ANSI compliant permitted a for loop variable to be referenced after the loop. I think most present-day ANSI-compliant compilers either do not support this old behavior, or support it through a compiler option that needs to be explicitly switched on. However, in case you run into a compiler of the old school let's take a quick look at the sorts of problems this can cause.

In ANSI C++, you can write the following code:

```
int count = 10;

// Calculate the sum of integers 1 to count
int count = 10;
long sum = 0;
for(int i = 1 ; i <= count ; i++)
    sum += i;

// Calculate the product of integers 1 to count
long product = 1;
for(int i = 2 ; i <= count ; i++)
    product *= i;
```

With a compiler that does not support ANSI standard behavior so far as loop variables are concerned, this will not compile. You'll get an error message to the effect that you are redeclaring the variable i. The reason for this is that the compiler is allowing the scope of i to extend beyond each loop in which it is declared to the end of the block that encloses the for loops (which of course is not shown in the preceding code). Thus, i declared within the first loop still exists when you attempt to declare the variable i in the second loop.

Controlling a for Loop with Floating-Point Values

The examples with the for loop so far have used an integer variable to control the loop, but in general, you can use anything you like. The following code fragment uses floating-point values to control a for loop:

```
const double pi = 3.14159265;
for(double radius = 2.5 ; radius <= 20.0 ; radius += 2.5)
  std:: cout << "radius = " << std::setw(12) << radius
             << "  area = " << std::setw(12)
             << pi * radius * radius << std::endl;
```

This loop is controlled by the radius variable, which is of type double. It has an initial value of 2.5 and is incremented on each loop iteration until it exceeds 20.0, whereupon the loop ends. The loop statement calculates the area of a circle for the current value of radius, using the standard formula πr^2, where r is the radius of the circle. You use the manipulator setw() in the loop statement to give each output value the same field width; this ensures that the output values line up nicely. Of course, to use the manipulators in a program, you need to include the header <iomanip>.

Be careful when you use floating-point variables to control for loops. As I explained in Chapter 2, fractional values may not be represented exactly as a binary floating-point number. This can lead to some unwanted side effects, as you shall see.

········

Try It Out: Using Floating-Point Variables for Loop Control

This program demonstrates the problem with floating-point values by using a slight variation of the previous loop:

```
// Program 5.4 Floating-point control in a for loop
#include <iostream>
#include <iomanip>
using std::cout;
using std::endl;

int main() {
  const double pi = 3.14159265;
  cout << endl;

  for(double radius = .2 ; radius <= 3.0 ; radius += .2)
    cout << "radius = " << std::setw(12) << radius
         << " area = " << std::setw(12) << pi * radius * radius
         << endl;
  return 0;
}
```

On my computer, this produces the following output:

```
radius =      0.2  area =      0.125664
radius =      0.4  area =      0.502655
radius =      0.6  area =       1.13097
radius =      0.8  area =       2.01062
radius =        1  area =       3.14159
radius =      1.2  area =       4.52389
radius =      1.4  area =       6.15752
radius =      1.6  area =       8.04248
radius =      1.8  area =       10.1788
radius =        2  area =       12.5664
radius =      2.2  area =       15.2053
radius =      2.4  area =       18.0956
radius =      2.6  area =       21.2372
radius =      2.8  area =       24.6301
```

(Continued)

HOW IT WORKS

On this occasion, it's more a case of why it doesn't! When you inspect the code, you might expect that you'd get the area of the circle with radius 3.0 at the end of this list. After all, the loop is specified to continue as long as radius is less than or equal to 3.0. But the last value displayed has the radius at 2.8; what's going wrong?

The loop ends earlier than you anticipate because when 0.2 is added to 2.8, the result is greater than 3.0. (This is an astounding piece of arithmetic at face value, but read on!) The reason for this is a very small error in the representation of 0.2 as a binary floating-point number; you cannot represent 0.2 exactly in binary floating point. The error is in the last digit of precision, so if your compiler supports 15-digit precision for type double, the error is of the order of 10^{-15}. Usually, this is of no consequence, but here you depend on adding 0.2 successively to get *exactly* 3.0—which doesn't happen.

You can see what the difference is by adding a statement in the loop to display the difference between 3.0 and the next value of radius:

```
for(double radius = .2 ; radius <= 3.0 ; radius += .2)
  cout << "radius = " << std::setw(6)  << radius
       << "  area = " << std::setw(12) << pi * radius * radius
       << "   delta to 3 = " << ((radius + .2) - 3.0)
       << endl;
```

On my machine, the last line of output is now this:

```
radius =    2.8  area =        24.6301  delta to 3 = 4.44089e-016
```

As you can see, radius + .2 is greater than 3.0 by around 4×10^{-16}, and so the loop terminates before the next iteration.

You might be wondering why the values of radius are output as nice, neat values in spite of the inaccuracy that we have just discussed. This is a result of the process that generates the displayed values. If you want a precise representation of the values of radius, you can output them in scientific notation—that is, in the form of the mantissa plus an exponent.

 NOTE *Any number that as a fraction has a denominator that is odd can't be represented exactly as a binary floating-point value.*

Try It Out: Displaying Numbers in Scientific Notation

To find out exactly what's going on in the loop, you can display the values in the previous example by modifying the program to use some of the floating-point output manipulators you saw in Chapter 2:

```cpp
// Program 5.5 Displaying numbers in scientific notation
#include <iostream>
#include <iomanip>
#include <limits>
using std::cout;
using std::endl;
using std::setprecision;
using std::numeric_limits;

int main() {
  const double pi = 3.14159265;
  cout << endl;

  for(double radius = .2 ; radius <= 3.0 ; radius += .2)
    cout << "radius = "
         << setprecision(numeric_limits<double>::digits10 + 1)
         << std::scientific << radius
         << "  area = "
         << std::setw(10) << setprecision(6)
         << std::fixed << pi * radius * radius
         << endl;
  return 0;
}
```

NOTE *By the way, don't puzzle over my choice of which* std *names I identify in* using *declarations and which I qualify explicitly. This is often determined by how I can best fit the code into the somewhat limited page width as much as anything else.*

With the revised version of the example, I get this output:

```
radius = 2.0000000000000001e-001  area =    0.125664
radius = 4.0000000000000002e-001  area =    0.502655
radius = 6.0000000000000009e-001  area =    1.130973
radius = 8.0000000000000004e-001  area =    2.010619
radius = 1.0000000000000000e+000  area =    3.141593
radius = 1.2000000000000000e+000  area =    4.523893
radius = 1.3999999999999999e+000  area =    6.157522
```

(Continued)

```
radius = 1.5999999999999999e+000    area =    8.042477
radius = 1.7999999999999998e+000    area =   10.178760
radius = 1.9999999999999998e+000    area =   12.566371
radius = 2.1999999999999997e+000    area =   15.205308
radius = 2.3999999999999999e+000    area =   18.095574
radius = 2.6000000000000001e+000    area =   21.237166
radius = 2.8000000000000003e+000    area =   24.630086
```

The number of digits displayed for the mantissa here is typical for an Intel PC; it could be different on other machines. As you can see, the radius values are not quite as exact as they appeared to be earlier.

HOW IT WORKS

You include the <limits> header because you need to access information about the number of (base 10) digits that a floating-point value of type double has in the mantissa. The output statement in the loop modifies the way in which the floating-point values are presented:

```
cout << "radius = "
     << setprecision(numeric_limits<double>::digits10 + 1)
     << std::scientific << radius
     << "  area = "
     << std::setw(10) << setprecision(6)
     << std::fixed << pi * radius * radius
     << endl;
```

By judicious use of the scientific and setprecision() manipulators, you can arrange to display the radius values in scientific notation. In order to guarantee that *all* the digits are shown, you have to use some of the information defined in the <limits> header, which you saw in Chapter 3. The integer value specified by numeric_limits<double>::digits10 is the number of decimal digits in the mantissa of a value of type double. This value typically reflects the number of *whole* decimal digits in the mantissa. Because the mantissa is really binary and does not necessarily correspond to a whole number of decimal digits, a couple of extra binary digits can still cause the output to be rounded. Therefore, you should add 1 to the number of digits to ensure that no rounding occurs.

Because you don't need the value for the area in scientific notation, you use the fixed manipulator to reset the output mode for floating-point values to present subsequent values without an exponent. You also set the field width for the area to 10 characters with the manipulator setw(10). Of course, the number of digits of precision is still going to be the maximum plus 1, and you don't need that either, so reset the number of digits to a more sensible value with the manipulator setprecision(6).

Using More Complex Loop Control Expressions

You're not limited to simple control expressions in the for loop. Let's look at a slightly more complex example. Return to the first code you saw in this chapter—it involved calculating the sum of the first ten integers—it is possible to perform the calculation in the for loop's iteration expression and dispense with the loop statement altogether, as shown here:

```
int count = 10;
int sum = 0;
for(int i = 1 ; i <= count ; sum += i++)
  ;
```

Notice the semicolon (;) on a line by itself after the loop control expressions. This is effectively an empty loop statement. The calculation is done in the iteration expression, sum += i++. This adds the current value of i to sum, and then the postfix increment operator adds 1 to i, ready for the next iteration. Using the third control expression in this way is quite convenient for simple loop operations, but you should not overuse this technique. The measure of when it is *in*appropriate is the degree to which it reduces the readability of your code.

You can also initialize multiple variables in the first for loop control expression. All you have to do is separate the initialization expressions with commas. Let's take a look at an example.

Try It Out: Initializing Multiple Loop Variables

In this program, three variables are initialized inside the loop control expression:

```
// Program 5.6 Multiple initializations in a loop expression
#include <iostream>
#include <iomanip>
using std::cout;
using std::cin;
using std::endl;
using std::setw;

int main() {
  int count = 0;
  cout << endl << "What upper limit would you like? ";
  cin >> count;

  cout << endl
       << "integer"                    // Output column headings
       << "      sum"
       << "        factorial"
       << endl;
```

(Continued)

```
for(long n = 1, sum = 0, factorial = 1 ; n <= count ; n++) {
  sum += n;                      // Accumulate sum to current n
  factorial *= n;                // Calculate n!
  cout << setw(4) << n   << "    "
       << setw(7) << sum << " "
       << setw(15) << factorial
       << endl;
}
return 0;
}
```

The program calculates the sum of the integers for each integer from 1 to count, where count is a value that you enter. It also calculates the factorial of each integer. (The factorial of an integer *n*, written *n*!, is simply the product of all the integers from 1 to *n*; for example, $5! = 1 \times 2 \times 3 \times 4 \times 5 = 120$.) Don't enter large values for count, as factorials grow very rapidly and easily exceed the capacity of even a long integer variable.

Typical output from this program is as follows:

```
What upper limit would you like? 10

integer    sum      factorial
   1        1           1
   2        3           2
   3        6           6
   4       10          24
   5       15         120
   6       21         720
   7       28        5040
   8       36       40320
   9       45      362880
  10       55     3628800
```

HOW IT WORKS

First, you read the value for count from the keyboard after displaying a prompt:

```
int count = 0;
cout << endl << "What upper limit would you like? ";
cin >> count;
```

For four-byte long values, anything over 13 produces a factorial outside the maximum value that you can store, so you'll get incorrect results.

The variables n, sum, and factorial are declared and initialized within the following loop expression:

```
for(long n = 1, sum = 0, factorial = 1 ; n <= 10 ; n++) {
```

Commas separate each variable from the next, just as in a declaration statement. In the loop itself, after the mathematical operations, different values are passed to the setw() manipulator for each variable to be output in the loop statement:

```
cout << setw(4) << n   << "    "
     << setw(7) << sum << " "
     << setw(15) << factorial
     << endl;
```

The field widths that are selected by the setw() manipulator have been chosen to align the values in columns under the headings that are displayed before the loop executes.

The Comma Operator

Although the comma looks as if it's just a humble separator, it is actually a binary operator. It combines two expressions into a single expression, where the value of the combined expression is the value that results when its right operand is evaluated. This means that anywhere you can put an expression, you can also put a series of expressions separated by commas. For example, consider the following statements:

```
int i = 1;
int value1 = 1;
int value2 = 1;
int value3 = 1;
value1 += ++i, value2 += ++i, value3 += ++i;
```

The first four statements initialize each of four variables to 1. The last statement consists of three assignment expressions, separated by the comma operator. Because the comma operator is left associative and has the lowest precedence of all the operators (see Appendix D), the statement will be executed as follows:

```
(((value1 += ++i), (value2 += ++i)), (value3 += ++i));
```

The effect of this statement will be that value1 will be set to 3, value2 will be set to 4, and value3 will be set to 5. The value of the composite expression is the value of the rightmost expression in the series, so the overall value (which is discarded here, because we don't assign it to anything) is 5. You can demonstrate the use of the comma operator by modifying the loop in the previous example to incorporate the calculations into the second loop control expression.

Try It Out: The Comma Operator

Here's the modified version of the last program:

```cpp
// Program 5.7 Demonstrating the comma operator
#include <iostream>
#include <iomanip>
using std::cout;
using std::cin;
using std::endl;
using std::setw;

int main() {
  int count = 0;
  cout << endl << "What upper limit would you like? ";
  cin >> count;

  cout << endl
       << "integer"                     // Output column headings
       << "     sum"
       << "        factorial"
       << endl;

  for(long n = 1, sum = 0, factorial = 1 ;
                   sum += n, factorial *= n, n <= count ; n++)
    cout << setw(4) << n    << "     "
         << setw(7) << sum << " "
         << setw(15) << factorial
         << endl;
  return 0;
}
```

For the same input, this program produces exactly the same output as the last example.

HOW IT WORKS

To illustrate the comma operator, I have put the calculations for the sum and factorial into the second loop expression:

```cpp
for(long n = 1, sum = 0, factorial = 1 ;
                 sum += n, factorial *= n, n <= count ; n++)
  cout << setw(4) << n    << "     "
       << setw(7) << sum << " "
       << setw(15) << factorial
       << endl;
```

Despite the identical output, the code and the computation that is carried out are different from the earlier example. The second loop control expression is evaluated at the *beginning* of each iteration, so sum is incremented and factorial is calculated each time. The value of the composite expression is the value of the expression n <= count, so this still determines when the loop ends. When this condition fails, you'll *already have calculated* sum and factorial with the current value of n, but these won't display because the loop statement won't be executed. In this case this isn't important—it's just a spurious calculation—but in many cases it could cause problems.

You could put the calculation in the third control expression, but this wouldn't produce the correct output. Because the loop statement executes before the iteration expression for the loop is evaluated, the values in sum and factorial won't correspond with the current value of n at the time of output.

You won't gain anything by coding this in this way here, and you should consider the example as a demonstration of syntax rather than good style. However, occasionally you'll come across situations in which the comma operator can be useful, for instance, when you need to evaluate several expressions in one.

Nested Loops

You can place a loop inside another loop. In fact, you can nest loops within loops to whatever depth you require to solve your problem. Furthermore, nested loops can be of any kind: you can nest a for loop inside a while loop inside a do-while loop, if you need to. They can be mixed in any way that you want.

The most common application of nested loops is in the context of arrays, which you'll meet in the next chapter, but they do have other uses. I'll illustrate how nesting works with an example that provides lots of opportunity for nesting loops.

Try It Out: Using a Nested Loop

Multiplication tables are the bane of many children's lives at school, but you can easily use a nested loop to generate one:

```
// Program 5.8 Generating multiplication tables
#include <iostream>
#include <iomanip>
#include <cctype>
using std::cout;
using std::cin;
using std::endl;
using std::setw;
```

(Continued)

```
int main() {
  int table = 0;                              // Table size
  const int table_min = 2;                    // Minimum table size
  const int table_max = 12;                   // Maximum table size
  char ch = 0;                                // Response to prompt

  do {
    cout << endl
         << "What size table would you like ("
         << table_min << " to " << table_max << ")? ";
    cin >> table;                             // Get the table size
    cout << endl;

    // Make sure table size is within the limits
    if(table < table_min || table > table_max) {
      cout << "Invalid table size entered. Program terminated."
           << endl;
      exit(1);
    }

    // Create the top line of the table
    cout << "     |";
    for(int i = 1 ; i <= table ; i++)
      cout << " " << setw(3) << i << " |";
    cout << endl;

    // Create the separator row
    for(int i = 0 ; i <= table ; i++)
      cout << "------";
    cout << endl;

    for(int i = 1 ; i <= table ; i++) {       // Iterate over rows
      cout << " " << setw(3) << i << " |";    // Start the row

      // Output the values in a row
      for(int j = 1 ; j <= table ; j++)
        cout << " " << setw(3) << i*j << " |"; // For each col.
      cout << endl;                            // End the row
    }

    // Check if another table is required
    cout << endl << "Do you want another table (y or n)? ";
    cin >> ch;
    cout << endl;
  } while(std::tolower(ch) == 'y');

  return 0;
}
```

Here is an example of the output produced by this program:

```
What size table would you like (2 to 12)? 10

      |  1 |  2 |  3 |  4 |  5 |  6 |  7 |  8 |  9 | 10 |
----------------------------------------------------------------
  1 |  1 |  2 |  3 |  4 |  5 |  6 |  7 |  8 |  9 | 10 |
  2 |  2 |  4 |  6 |  8 | 10 | 12 | 14 | 16 | 18 | 20 |
  3 |  3 |  6 |  9 | 12 | 15 | 18 | 21 | 24 | 27 | 30 |
  4 |  4 |  8 | 12 | 16 | 20 | 24 | 28 | 32 | 36 | 40 |
  5 |  5 | 10 | 15 | 20 | 25 | 30 | 35 | 40 | 45 | 50 |
  6 |  6 | 12 | 18 | 24 | 30 | 36 | 42 | 48 | 54 | 60 |
  7 |  7 | 14 | 21 | 28 | 35 | 42 | 49 | 56 | 63 | 70 |
  8 |  8 | 16 | 24 | 32 | 40 | 48 | 56 | 64 | 72 | 80 |
  9 |  9 | 18 | 27 | 36 | 45 | 54 | 63 | 72 | 81 | 90 |
 10 | 10 | 20 | 30 | 40 | 50 | 60 | 70 | 80 | 90 | 100 |

Do you want another table (y or n)? n
```

HOW IT WORKS

In this example, you have included three standard headers:

```
#include <iostream>
#include <iomanip>
#include <cctype>
```

Just as a refresher, the first is for stream input/output, the second is to get access to stream manipulators, and the third is because you'll be using the tolower() character conversion function.

You start the program proper by declaring some variables that you need:

```
int table = 0;               // Table size
const int table_min = 2;     // Minimum table size
const int table_max = 12;    // Maximum table size
char ch = 0;                 // Response to prompt
```

The second and third declarations define the limits on the size of the tables you want to support. These should not be altered anywhere, so you declare them as const to make sure. This also brings up the advantages I discussed in Chapter 2—removing magic numbers, and reducing maintenance points.

The program generates a table in the do-while loop, which allows additional tables to be generated if required. The loop performs four tasks, which are described by the comments here:

```
do {
    // Read the table size from the keyboard...
```

(Continued)

```
// Make sure the table size is within limits...

// Create and output the table...

// Get an indication whether another table is required...

} while(std::tolower(ch) == 'y');
```

Clearly, the variable ch stores the response entered when the prompt for another table displays. The code to read the table size is shown here:

```
cout << endl
     << "What size table would you like ("
     << table_min << " to " << table_max << ")? ";
cin >> table;                                    // Get the table size
cout << endl;
```

This uses the const values table_min and table_max to output the limits on the permitted size of tables. To deal with the situation of an invalid size for the table being entered, you just compare the value with the permitted limits:

```
if(table < table_min || table > table_max) {
  cout << "Invalid table size entered. Program terminated."
       << endl;
  exit(1);
}
```

If the value of table is less than the minimum or greater than the maximum allowed, you just display a message and end the program using the standard library exit() function. Later in the chapter, you'll see how you can handle this in a less brutal, more user-friendly fashion.

Next, the table is generated. The first for loop nested inside the do-while loop generates the top line of the table containing the multipliers:

```
cout << "    |";
for(int i = 1 ; i <= table ; i++)
  cout << " " << setw(3) << i << " |";
cout << endl;
```

The loop statement outputs multiplier values separated by spaces and vertical bars, from 1 to the size of the table. Each output column is six characters wide, so all the table entries need to be the same width to ensure everything lines up.

The next nested for loop generates a row of dashes to separate the top line from the rest of the table:

```
for(int i = 0 ; i <= table ; i++)
  cout << "------";
cout << endl;
```

Each iteration of this loop adds six dashes to the row. By starting the count at zero instead of one, you output a total of table + 1 sets in all: one for the left column of multipliers, and one for each of the columns of table entries.

The final loop, which itself contains a nested loop, outputs the left column of multipliers and the products that are the table entries:

```
for(int i = 1 ; i <= table ; i++) {      // Iterate over rows
  cout << " " << setw(3) << i << " |";    // Start the row

  // Output the values in a row
  for(int j = 1 ; j <= table ; j++)
    cout << " " << setw(3) << i*j << " |"; // For each col.
  cout << endl;                            // End the row
}
```

Including the outer do-while loop, you have three levels of nesting here. Each iteration of the middle for loop creates one row of the table. On each iteration, the output statement to start a new line and display the left multiplier executes. Then the inner loop executes, which generates the table entries for the current row. Each iteration of the inner for loop generates one entry, so the variable j is essentially a column number in the table. Because j varies from 1 to table, you'll have table entries in each row. The value to be displayed at each position is the product of the row number, i, and the column number, j.

When the complete table has been displayed, a prompt for whether another table is required appears:

```
cout << endl << "Do you want another table (y or n)? ";
cin >> ch;
cout << endl;
```

The character entered is stored in ch, and you use this in the do-while loop condition. If ch is 'y' or 'Y', another iteration of the do-while loop is executed to produce another table. Otherwise, the loop ends and so too does the program.

Skipping Loop Iterations

Sometimes, situations arise in which you want to skip one loop iteration and press on with the next one. The continue statement does this for you; you write it simply as follows:

```
continue;
```

When this statement executes within a loop, execution transfers immediately to the end of the current iteration, and as long as the loop control expression allows it, execution continues with the next iteration. This is best understood by using it in an example.

....

Try It Out: Using the continue Statement

Let's suppose you want to output a table of characters along with their corresponding character codes in hexadecimal and decimal format. Of course, you
don't want to output the characters that don't have a symbolic representation—
some of these, such as tabs and newline, mess up the output. So, you want a
program that outputs just the printable characters. Here's how you can do that:

```cpp
// Program 5.9 Using the continue statement
#include <iostream>
#include <iomanip>
#include <cctype>
#include <limits>
using std::cout;
using std::endl;
using std::setw;

int main() {
  // Output the column headings
  cout << endl
      << setw(13) << "Character   "
      << setw(13) << "Hexadecimal "
      << setw(13) << "Decimal    "
      << endl;

  cout << std::uppercase;                     // Uppercase hex digits

  unsigned char ch = 0;                       // Character code

  // Output characters and corresponding codes
  do {
    if(!std::isprint(ch))                     // If it does not print
      continue;                               // skip this iteration

    cout << setw(7)  << ch
        << std::hex                           // Hexadecimal mode
        << setw(13) << static_cast<int>(ch)
        << std::dec                           // Decimal mode
        << setw(13) << static_cast<int>(ch)
        << endl;
  } while(ch++ < std::numeric_limits<unsigned char>::max());
  return 0;
}
```

This outputs all the printable characters with code values from 0 to the maximum unsigned char value. On my computer, this displays the printable ASCII
characters.

You output headings for the columns of output with the statement:

```
cout << endl
    << setw(13) << "Character   "
    << setw(13) << "Hexadecimal "
    << setw(13) << "Decimal    "
    << endl;
```

Because you've used a field width of 13 for each heading, you'll need to take care to position the output values in the middle of each column.

To get the hexadecimal values displayed using uppercase digits, you use the following statement:

```
cout << std::uppercase;                    // Uppercase hex digits
```

This uses the uppercase output modifier to make all subsequent hexadecimal output use A to F rather than a to f.

Once you've set up a variable to hold the character codes, the really interesting bit is the do-while loop:

```
do {
  if(!std::isprint(ch))               // If it does not print
    continue;                         // skip this iteration

  cout << setw(7)  << ch
       << std::hex                    // Hexadecimal mode
       << setw(13) << static_cast<int>(ch)
       << std::dec                    // Decimal mode
       << setw(13) << static_cast<int>(ch)
       << endl;
} while(ch++ < std::numeric_limits<unsigned char>::max());
```

This iterates through character codes from 0 to the value produced by numeric_limits<unsigned char>::max(), which is the maximum value of type unsigned char.

Within the loop, first you check that the current value of ch represents a printable character using the function isprint(), which you saw in the last chapter. If isprint(ch) returns 0, the expression !isprint(ch) is true, and the continue statement executes. This skips the rest of the loop statements and goes straight to the next iteration. Thus, you only execute the output statement in the loop for printable characters.

In the output statements, you use the manipulators hex and dec to set the output mode for integers to what you require. In order to get the value of ch to display as a numeric value, you must cast it to int in the output statement. Left as it is, it always displays as a character.

(Continued)

Note that to keep the code simple, you have to use unsigned char rather than just char as the type for ch. Type char can be equivalent to (but not the same as) signed char or unsigned char, depending on the implementation, and you would need to program to allow for the possibility of type char turning out to be equivalent to signed char. One complication of signed values is that you cannot cover the whole range by counting up from 0, because adding 1 to the maximum value for signed char produces the minimum value, as Figure 5-6 shows.

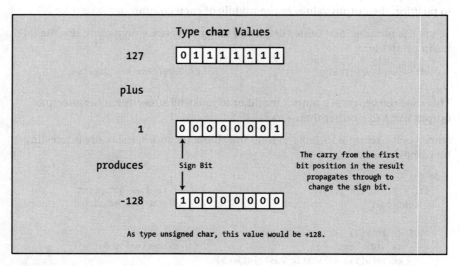

Figure 5-6. The effect of overflow with a signed variable

You could deal with this by setting the initial value of ch to the minimum for the type using numeric_limits<char>::min(), but when you cast the negative code values to int, of course you would get a negative result, so the hexadecimal codes would show the leading digits as F.

Note also that a for loop isn't suitable here. Because the condition is checked before the loop block executes, you might be tempted to write the loop as follows:

```
for(unsigned char ch = 0 ;
            ch <= std::numeric_limits<unsigned char>::max() ; ch++) {
  // Output character and code
}
```

This loop never ends, because after executing the loop block with ch at the maximum value, the next increment of ch gives it a value of 0, and the second loop control expression is never false.

Breaking Out of a Loop

Sometimes, you need to end a loop prematurely; something might arise within the loop statement that indicates there is no point in continuing. In this case, you can use the break statement. Its effect here is much the same as it was in the switch statement that you saw in the previous chapter: if you execute a break statement within a loop, the loop ends immediately and execution continues with the statement following the loop.

The break statement is used most frequently with an indefinite loop, so let's look next at what one of those looks like.

Indefinite Loops

An **indefinite loop** can potentially run forever. If you leave out the test condition in a for loop, for example, the loop is left with no way to stop itself. Unless there is some way to exit the loop from within the loop block itself, the loop runs indefinitely—that's how it gets its name.

Indefinite loops have several practical uses: for example, programs that monitor some kind of alarm indicator or that collect data from sensors in an industrial plant. You'll also find that an indefinite loop is useful when you don't know in advance how many loop iterations will be required, such as when you are reading a variable quantity of input data. In these circumstances, you arrange for the exit from the loop to be coded within the loop block, not within the loop control expression.

In the most common form of the indefinite for loop, all the control expressions are omitted, as shown here:

```
for( ; ; ) {
  // Statements that do something
  // There must be some way of ending the loop in here
}
```

Note that you still need the semicolons (;), even though no loop control expressions exist. The only way this loop can end is if some code within the loop terminates it.

You can have an indefinite while loop, too:

```
while(true) {
  // Statements that do something
  // There must be some way of ending the loop in here
}
```

Because the condition for continuing the loop is always true, you have an indefinite loop. Of course, you can also have a version of the do-while loop that is indefinite, but it has no advantages over the other two types of loop and is not normally used.

An obvious way to end an indefinite loop is to use the break statement, as I suggested at the start of this section. Executing break within a loop terminates the loop immediately, and execution continues with the statement following the loop. You'll often use this to handle invalid input and provide an opportunity for a correct value to be entered, or to repeat an operation such as playing a game until the user elects not to continue. Let me illustrate this with a new version of Program 5.8, which generated a multiplication table.

Try It Out: Using break

In Program 5.8, you terminated the program if an unacceptable table size was entered. You can now modify the program to allow the user three attempts to enter a correct value. Here's the new version of the program:

```cpp
// Program 5.10 Controlling input with an infinite loop
#include <iostream>
#include <iomanip>
#include <cctype>
using std::cout;
using std::cin;
using std::endl;
using std::setw;

int main() {
  int table = 0;                          // Table size
  const int table_min = 2;                // Minimum table size
  const int table_max = 12;               // Maximum table size
  const int input_tries = 3;
  char ch = 0;                            // Response to prompt

  do {
    for(int count = 1 ; ; count++) {      // Indefinite loop
      cout << endl
           << "What size table would you like ("
           << table_min << " to " << table_max << ")? ";
      cin >> table;                       // Get the table size
      cout << endl;

      // Make sure table size is within the limits
      if(table >= table_min && table <= table_max)
        break;                            // Exit the input loop
      else if(count < input_tries)
        cout << "Invalid input - Try again.";
      else {
        cout << "Invalid table size entered - for the third time."
             << "\nSorry, only three goes - program terminated."
             << endl;
        exit(1);
      }
    }
```

```
      // Create the top line of the table
   cout << "     |";
   for(int i = 1 ; i <= table ; i++)
     cout << " " << setw(3) << i << " |";
   cout << endl;

   // Create the separator row
   for(int i = 0 ; i <= table ; i++)
     cout << "------";
   cout << endl;

   for(int i = 1 ; i <= table ; i++) {       // Iterate over rows
     cout << " " << setw(3) << i << " |";    // Start the row

     // Output the values in a row
     for(int j = 1 ; j <= table ; j++)
       cout << " " << setw(3) << i*j << " |"; // For each col.
     cout << endl;                           // End the row
   }

   // Check if another table is required
   cout << endl << "Do you want another table (y or n)? ";
   cin >> ch;
   cout << endl;
 } while(std::tolower(ch) == 'y');

 return 0;
}
```

The normal output from this example is the same as the previous version of the program, but if you enter three successive invalid table sizes, you will get the following:

```
What size table would you like (2 to 12)? 1

Invalid input - Try again.
What size table would you like (2 to 12)? 14

Invalid input - Try again.
What size table would you like (2 to 12)? 46

Invalid table size entered - for the third time.
Sorry, only three goes - program terminated.
```

(Continued)

The maximum number of attempts at correct input is defined by the variable input_tries that you declare in this line:

```
const int input_tries = 3;
```

This is used in the only new feature in the program, which is the for loop that manages the input:

```
for(int count = 1 ; ; count++) {                // Indefinite loop
  cout << endl
       << "What size table would you like ("
       << table_min << " to " << table_max << ")? ";
  cin >> table;                                 // Get the table size
  cout << endl;

  // Make sure table size is within the limits
  if(table >= table_min && table <= table_max)
    break;                                      // Exit the input loop
  else if(count < input_tries)
    cout << "Invalid input - Try again.";
  else {
    cout << "Invalid table size entered - for the third time."
         << "\nSorry, only three goes - program terminated."
         << endl;
    exit(1);
  }
}
```

The for loop has no control expression to stop it, so it runs for an indefinite number of iterations until code in the loop body exits the loop. The variable count records the number of input attempts, so this determines when you give up on input. The first if statement within the loop causes break to execute if valid input is entered in response to the prompt. This ends the for loop and allows the rest of the program to execute.

If you enter invalid input, the second if, which checks the value of count, executes. As long as count is less than 3, a message displays and the loop goes to its next iteration to allow another try. Once three failed attempts have been made, the program terminates.

If you had declared and initialized count outside the input loop, you could have used an indefinite while loop:

```
int count = 1;
while(true) {
  // Read input as before...

  // Make sure table size is within the limits
  if(table >= table_min && table <= table_max)
    break;                                      // Exit the input loop
  else if(count++ < input_tries)
    cout << "Invalid input - Try again.";
```

```
    else {
       // Prompt and end the program as before...
    }
  }
```

Let's try another example that uses a for loop with no control expressions at all.

Try It Out: Using a for Loop with No Control Expressions

You can write another version of this program that calculates the average of several temperature samples. This time you'll use an indefinite for loop and a break statement to manage the input.

```cpp
// Program 5.11 Calculating an average in an indefinite loop
#include <iostream>
#include <cctype>
using std::cout;
using std::cin;
using std::endl;

int main() {
  char ch = 0;                      // Stores response to prompt for input
  int count = 0;                    // Counts the number of input values
  double temperature = 0.0;         // Stores an input value
  double average = 0.0;             // Stores the total and average

  for( ; ; ) {                      // Indefinite loop
    cout << "Enter a value: ";      // Prompt for input
    cin >> temperature;             // Read input value
    average += temperature;         // Accumulate total of values
    count++;                        // Increment value count

    cout << "Do you want to enter another? (y/n): ";
    cin >> ch;                      // Get response
    cout << endl;
    if(std::tolower(ch) == 'n')     // Check for no
      break;                        // if so end the loop
  }
  cout << endl
       << "The average temperature is " << average / count
       << endl;
  return 0;
}
```

Here's the typical output from this example:

```
Enter a value: 65.5
Do you want to enter another? (y/n): y

Enter a value: 67.9
Do you want to enter another? (y/n): y

Enter a value: 72.3
Do you want to enter another? (y/n): n

The average temperature is 68.5667
```

HOW IT WORKS

The only new aspect here is the means of exiting the loop:

```
for( ; ; ) {                          // Infinite loop
  cout << "Enter a value: ";          // Prompt for input
  cin >> temperature;                 // Read input value
  average += temperature;             // Accumulate total of values
  count++;                            // Increment value count

  cout << "Do you want to enter another? (y/n): ";
  cin >> ch;                          // Get response
  cout << endl
  if(std::tolower(ch) == 'n')         // Check for no
    break;                           // if so end the loop
}
```

This `for` loop has no control expressions, so it runs for an indefinite number of iterations. The `if` statement within the loop causes break to be executed when a user enters n or N in response to the prompt. This ends the loop and allows the average temperature to be calculated and displayed. Once again, you could just as easily use a `while` loop here:

```
while(true) {                         // Infinite loop
  cout << "Enter a value: ";          // Prompt for input
  cin >> temperature;                 // Read input value
  average += temperature;             // Accumulate total of values
  count++;                            // Increment value count

  cout << "Do you want to enter another? (y/n): ";
  cin >> ch;                          // Get response
  cout << endl;
  if(std::tolower(ch) == 'n')         // Check for no
    break;                           // if so end the loop
}
```

In this situation, you'll find no practical difference between the while loop and the for loop. Which you choose is just a question of which you prefer or find easier to read.

....

Summary

You will see further applications of loops in the next chapter, and almost any program of consequence involves a loop of some kind. Because they are so fundamental to programming, you need to be sure you have a good grasp of the ideas covered in this chapter. The essential points you have unearthed about loops are as follows:

- A loop is a mechanism for repeating a block of statements.

- There are three kinds of loop that you can use: the while loop, the do-while loop, and the for loop.

- The while loop repeats for as long as a specified condition is true.

- The do-while loop always performs at least one iteration, and continues for as long as a specified condition is true.

- The for loop is typically used to repeat a given number of times and has three control expressions. The first is an initialization expression, executed once at the beginning of the loop. The second is a loop condition, executed before each iteration, which must evaluate to true for the loop to continue. The third is executed at the end of each iteration and is usually used to increment a loop counter.

- Any kind of loop may be nested within any other kind of loop to any depth.

- Executing a continue statement within a loop skips the remainder of the current iteration and goes straight to the next iteration, as long as the loop control condition allows it.

- Executing a break statement within a loop causes an immediate exit from the loop.

- A loop defines a scope so that variables declared within a loop are not accessible outside the loop. In particular, variables declared in the initialization expression of a for loop are not accessible outside the loop.

Exercises

The following exercises enable you to try out what you've learned in this chapter. If you get stuck, look back over the chapter for help. If you're still stuck after that, you can download the solutions from the Apress website (http://www.apress.com/book/download.html), but that really should be a last resort.

Exercise 5-1. Write a program that outputs the squares of the odd integers from 1 up to a limit that is entered by the user.

Exercise 5-2. Write a program that uses a while loop to accumulate the sum of an arbitrary number of integers that are entered by the user. The program should output the total of all the values and the overall average as a floating-point value.

Exercise 5-3. Create a program that uses a do-while loop to count the number of non-whitespace characters entered on a line. The count will end when it first encounters the # character.

Exercise 5-4. Create a program that outputs a password consisting of sequence of eight random upper- or lowercase letters or digits. Duplicate characters are permitted.

Exercise 5-5. Create a program that loops 25 times and prints only the numbers 1 to 10, and 20 to 25.

Exercise 5-6. A lottery entry requires you to choose six different integers in the range 1 to 49 inclusive. Write a program that generates five lottery entries each time it runs.

CHAPTER 6

Arrays and Strings

SO FAR, I'VE COVERED all the fundamental data types and you've accumulated a basic knowledge of how to perform calculations and make decisions in a program. This chapter is about broadening the application of the basic programming techniques that you've learned so far, from using single data elements to working with whole collections of data items. You'll also look at string handling. In this chapter, you'll learn

- What an array is and how you can use it

- How to declare and initialize arrays of different types

- What a null-terminated string is

- How to use an array of type char to store a character string

- How to declare and use multidimensional arrays

- How to create and use arrays of type char as arrays of null-terminated strings

- How to create variables of type string

- What operations are available with objects of type string, and how you can use them

- How you can work with strings containing wide characters

Data Arrays

You already know how to declare and initialize variables of the basic types. Each variable can store only a *single* data item of the specified type—you can have a variable that stores an integer, or a variable that stores a character, and so on. An **array** can store *several* data items of the same type. You can have an array of integers or an array of characters—in fact, you can have an array of any type of data.

Here's an example of when you might need such a thing. Suppose you've already written a program to calculate an average temperature. But you also want to calculate how many samples are above the average and how many are below it. You'll need to retain the original sample data in order to do this, but storing each data item in a separate variable would be tortuous to code and utterly impractical for anything more than a very few items. An array provides you with the means of performing this task easily, and many other things besides.

Using an Array

An **array** is simply a number of memory locations, each of which can store an item of data of the same data type, and all of which are referenced through the same variable name. For example, you could store 366 temperature samples in an array declared as follows:

```
double temperatures[366];     // An array of temperatures
```

This declares an array of type double with the name temperatures, and with 366 **elements**. That means this array has 366 memory locations, each of which you can use to hold a value of type double. The number of elements specified between the brackets is called the **size** of the array.

You refer to the individual items in an array by using an integer that's usually referred to as an **index**. The index of a particular element is simply the offset from the first element in the array. The first element has an offset of 0 and therefore an index of 0, whereas an index value of 3 will refer to the fourth element of an array—three elements from the first. To reference an element, you put its index between square brackets after the array name, so to set the fourth element of the temperatures array to 99.0, you would write

```
temperatures[3] = 99.0;       // Set the fourth array element to 99
```

Let's look at another array. The basic structure of an array called height is illustrated in Figure 6-1.

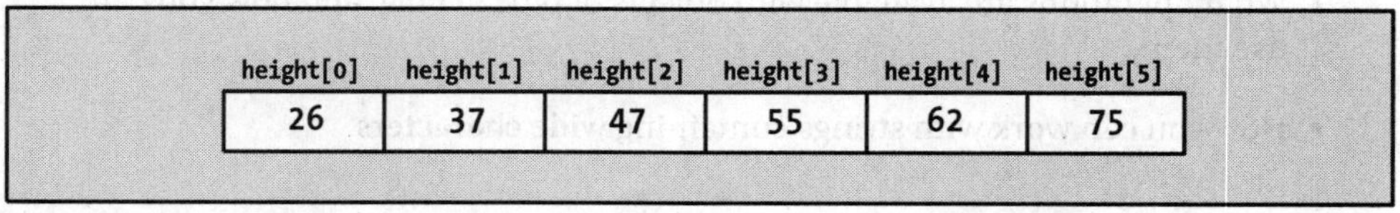

height[0]	height[1]	height[2]	height[3]	height[4]	height[5]
26	37	47	55	62	75

Figure 6-1. An array with six elements

The array in Figure 6-1 has six elements of type int. Each box represents a memory location holding the value of an array element. Each array element can be referenced using the expression above it. You can declare an array that has six elements of type int using this statement:

```
int height[6];                // Declare an array of six heights
```

The compiler will allocate six contiguous storage locations for storing values of type int as a result of this declaration (which is therefore also a definition). If a value of type int on your computer requires 4 bytes, then this array will occupy 24 bytes.

NOTE *The type of the array will determine the amount of memory required for storing each element. All the elements of an array are stored in one continuous block of memory.*

Of course, the declaration doesn't specify any initial values for the array, so they'll contain junk values.

In Figure 6-1, each element in the height array contains a different value. These might be the heights of the members of a family, for instance, recorded to the nearest inch. As there are six elements, the index values run from 0 through to 5. If you wanted to, you could sum the first three elements of height with the following statement:

```
int sum3 = height[0] + height[1] + height[2];    // The sum of three elements
```

Here, the individual elements of the array are behaving just like ordinary integer variables. However, you can't store the values stored in the elements of one array in the elements of another array in an assignment. You can only operate on the individual elements of an array. Thus, to copy the values of one array to another, you must copy the values one at a time. As you may have guessed, loops are very useful for working through all the elements in an array.

Try It Out: Using an Array

Let's jump straight in and see an array in action. You can use an integer array in a program to calculate the average height of a group of people and then work out how many are above average.

```
// Program 6.1 Using an array
#include <iostream>
#include <cctype>
using std::cout;
using std::cin;
using std::endl;

int main() {
  int height[10];                    // Array of heights
  int count = 0;                     // Number of heights
  char reply = 0;                    // Reply to prompt

  // Input loop for heights. Read heights till we are done, or the array is full
  do {
    cout << endl
        << "Enter a height as an integral number of inches: ";
    cin >> height[count++];
```

(Continued)

```
        // Check if another input is required
        cout << "Do you want to enter another (y or n)? ";
        cin >> reply;
    } while(count < 10 && std::tolower(reply) == 'y');

    // Indicate when array is full
    if(count == 10)
        cout << endl  << "Maximum number of heights reached." << endl;

    // Calculate the average and display it
    double average = 0.0;                       // Stores average height
    for(int i = 0; i < count ; i++)
        average += height[i];                   // Add a height
    average /= count;                           // Divide by the number of heights
    cout << endl
         << "Average height is " << average << " inches."
         << endl;

    // Calculate how many are above average height
    int above_average = 0;                      // Count of above average heights
    for(int i = 0 ; i < count ; i++)
        if(height[i] > average)                 // Greater than average?
            above_average++;                    // then increment the count

    cout << "There "
         << (above_average == 1 ? "is " : "are ")
         << above_average << " height"
         << (above_average == 1 ? " " : "s ")
         << "above average."
         << endl;
    return 0;
}
```

The typical output from this program is as follows:

```
Enter a height as an integral number of inches: 75
Do you want to enter another (y or n)? y

Enter a height as an integral number of inches: 56
Do you want to enter another (y or n)? y

Enter a height as an integral number of inches: 63
Do you want to enter another (y or n)? y

Enter a height as an integral number of inches: 42
Do you want to enter another (y or n)? y

Enter a height as an integral number of inches: 70
Do you want to enter another (y or n)? n

Average height is 61.2 inches.
There are 3 heights above average.
```

HOW IT WORKS

You start by declaring the array and two other variables that you'll need in the calculation:

```
int height[10];        // Array of heights
int count = 0;         // Number of heights
char reply = 0;        // Reply to prompt
```

The height array has a size of 10, so you can store a maximum of 10 integer values. You use the variable count to refer to the next free element in the array, and because the first array index is 0, this will also reflect the number of values stored in the array. Initially, the first element is free and there are no values stored, so count is 0.

You read the height values in a do-while loop:

```
do {
  cout << endl
       << "Enter a height as an integral number of inches: ";
  cin >> height[count++];

  // Check if another input is required
  cout << "Do you want to enter another (y or n)? ";
  cin >> reply;
} while(count < 10 && std::tolower(reply) == 'y');
```

After a prompt, you read a height value from the keyboard and store it in the element referenced by the current value of count. The variable count is then incremented to refer to the next free element. Next, you display a prompt to determine whether further heights are to be entered. The response is recorded in reply so that it can be tested in the loop condition. The do-while loop condition checks both the number of values stored against the size of the array and the reply to the prompt for more elements. If either the value of count has reached 10, which is the number of elements in the array, or the character in reply isn't 'y' or 'Y', the loop ends.

CAUTION *C++ doesn't check index values to ensure their validity. It's up to you to make sure that you don't reference elements outside the bounds of the array. If you store data using an index value that's outside the valid range for an array, you'll overwrite something in memory or cause a storage protection violation. Either way, your program will almost certainly come to a sticky end.*

(Continued)

After the loop ends, you check whether the value in count indicates that you filled the array; if so, you display a message. This will take care of the case in which someone attempts to enter more than the maximum number of values your program can accommodate. You then calculate the average height:

```
double average = 0.0;                    // Stores average height
for(int i = 0; i < count ; i++)
  average += height[i];                  // Add a height
average /= count;                        // Divide by the number of heights
cout << endl
     << "Average height is " << average << " inches."
     << endl;
```

You accumulate the sum of the heights in the variable average using a for loop. The loop will execute with values for i from 0 to count - 1, which is precisely the range of index values you need to access each of the elements in the array. When i is incremented to count, the loop ends. To calculate the average height, you simply divide the accumulated sum in average by the count of the number of heights (given by count).

The last calculation counts how many height values are above average:

```
int above_average = 0;                   // Count of above average heights
for(int i = 0 ; i < count ; i++)
  if(height[i] > average)                // Greater than average?
    above_average++;                     // then increment the count
```

This uses another for loop to compare each height with the value in average. If a value is greater than average, the count in above_average is incremented. Finally, you output the count of above-average heights with this statement:

```
cout << "There "
     << (above_average == 1 ? "is " : "are ")
     << above_average << " height"
     << (above_average == 1 ? " " : "s ")
     << "above average."
     << endl;
```

The conditional operators just adjust the output to deal with the difference between singular and plural heights. They choose between "is " and "are ", and whether "s " is appended to the word " height".

Avoiding Magic Numbers

I discussed the undesirability of magic numbers in your programs back in Chapter 2, but I let one slip through the net in the last example: the size of the height array. You could avoid this by declaring and initializing a constant with the array size that you want:

```
const int max_heights = 10;               // Array size
```

Now you can define the array with the size specified by max_heights:

```
int height[max_heights];                  // Array of heights
```

There are two other places in the code that you need to update to use this new constant: the loop condition of your do-while loop and the if statement loop that follows it:

```
do {
  cout << endl
       << "Enter a height as an integral number of inches: ";
  cin >> height[count++];

  // Check if another input is required
  cout << "Do you want to enter another (y or n)? ";
  cin >> reply;
} while(count < max_heights && std::tolower(reply) == 'y');

// Indicate when array is full
if(count == max_heights)
  cout << endl  << "Maximum height count reached." << endl;
```

Now the program has no magic numbers, and if you want to adjust the size of the array, you just need to modify the initial value of max_heights. Be aware that you *must* declare max_heights as const here. If you don't, the compiler won't accept it as a size for the array.

The size of an array can be any constant integral expression. The *compiler* must be able to evaluate the expression to produce an integer constant so that the appropriate amount of memory can be allocated. This implies that the expression can only contain literals, const variables, and enumerators.

Initializing Arrays

To initialize an array, you enclose the initializing values for the elements within braces and place them following an equal sign after the declaration of the array name. Here's an example of a declaration and initialization of an array:

```
int samples[5] = {2, 3, 5, 7, 11};
```

The values in the list correspond to successive index values of the array, so in this case samples[0] has the value 2, samples[1] has the value 3, samples[2] has the value 5, and so on. A list of initial values between braces is called an **aggregate initializer list**, or simply an **initializer list**. An array is one example of an **aggregate** in C++; there are others. You may see this bit of jargon used in error messages from your compiler.

   You must not specify more initializing values than there are elements in the array, but you *can* specify fewer. If there *are* fewer, the values are assigned to successive elements, starting with the first element, which has the index 0. The array elements for which you don't provide an initial value will be initialized with 0. This isn't the same as not supplying an initializer list. Without an initializer list, the array elements will contain junk values.

 NOTE *The syntax of C++ allows for an empty initializer list, in which case all elements will be initialized to zero. However, I recommend that you always put at least one initializing value in a list. Just a 0 will suffice to make it clear that all elements will be set to zero.*

Try It Out: Initializing an Array

The following, rather limited example illustrates the concepts in the preceding discussion. It outputs the values contained in two arrays:

```
// Program 6.2 Initializing an array
#include <iostream>
#include <iomanip>
using std::cout;
using std::endl;
using std::setw;

int main() {
  const int size = 5;
  int values[size] = {1, 2, 3};
  double junk[size];

  cout << endl;
```

```
  for(int i = 0 ; i < size ; i++)
    cout << " " << setw(12) << values[i];
  cout << endl;

  for(int i = 0 ; i < size ; i++)
    cout << " " << setw(12) << junk[i];
  cout << endl;

  return 0;
}
```

In this example you declare two arrays, the first of which, values, is initialized in part, and the second of which, junk, isn't initialized at all. The program generates two lines of output that look like this on my computer:

```
            1            2            3            0            0
4.24399e-314 2.2069e-312 1.11216e-306 1.81969e-307 1.99808e-307
```

The second line of output (corresponding to values of junk[0] to junk[4]) are likely to be different on your computer.

HOW IT WORKS

As you can see from the output, the first three elements of the values array contain the initializing values, and the last two elements have the default value of 0. In the case of the junk array, all the values are spurious because you didn't provide any initial values at all. The array elements will contain whatever values the program that last used these memory locations left there.

Setting Array Elements to Zero

Rather than having arrays sitting around containing junk values, it's easy to initialize a whole array to zero using a technique that I've already discussed. In the previous example, you could have arranged for all the elements of the junk array to be 0 with either this statement:

```
double junk[size] = {0};    // Initialize all elements to zero
```

or this one:

```
double junk[size] = {};    // Initialize all elements to zero
```

An initialization value of 0 will always be converted to the appropriate type for the array. The explicit value in the first of these statements is used to initialize the first element, and the remainder will be set to 0 too, as they have no initializing values. I prefer the first form because I think it makes your intention more obvious.

Defining the Array Size with the Initializer List

You can omit the size of the array in an array declaration when you supply initializing values. The number of elements in the array will then be the same as the number of initializing values. For example, consider the following array declaration:

```
int values[] = {2, 3, 4};
```

This defines an array with three elements of type int that will have the initial values 2, 3, and 4. It is equivalent to writing this:

```
int values[3] = {2, 3, 4};
```

The advantage of the first form here is that you can't get the array size wrong, because the compiler determines it for you. It's important to realize, though, that you can't have arrays without elements in C++, so the initializer list must always contain at least one initializing value if you omit the array size.

Determining the Size of an Array

You saw earlier how you could avoid magic numbers for the number of elements in an array by defining a constant initialized with the size of the array. Of course, you can't do that if you let the compiler decide the number of elements from the initializer list.

In Chapter 3, you saw that the sizeof operator can supply the number of bytes that a variable occupies. The sizeof operator can also help you figure out the number of elements in an array. Suppose you've declared an array as

```
int values[] = {2, 3, 5, 7, 11, 13, 17, 19};
```

The expression sizeof values will evaluate to the number of bytes occupied by the entire array. The expression sizeof values[0], on the other hand, will evaluate to the number of bytes occupied by a single element—the first element in this case, but any one would do because they're all the same. Thus, the expression sizeof values/sizeof values[0] will evaluate to the number of elements in the array. Let's try it out.

Try It Out: Getting the Number of Array Elements

Here's a very simple program that uses the technique described in this section:

```cpp
// Program 6.3 Obtaining the number of array elements
#include <iostream>
using std::cout;
using std::endl;

int main() {
  int values[] = {2, 3, 5, 7, 11, 13, 17, 19, 23, 29};

  cout << endl
       << "There are "
       << sizeof values/sizeof values[0]
       << " elements in the array."
       << endl;

  int sum = 0;
  for(int i = 0 ; i < sizeof values/sizeof values[0] ; sum += values[i++])
    ;

  cout << "The sum of the array elements is " << sum
       << endl;

  return 0;
}
```

This example produces the following output:

```
There are 10 elements in the array.
The sum of the array elements is 129
```

HOW IT WORKS

The number of array elements is determined by the compiler from the number of initializing values in the declaration:

```cpp
int values[] = {2, 3, 5, 7, 11, 13, 17, 19, 23, 29};
```

After the array declaration, you immediately output the number of elements with this statement:

```cpp
cout << endl
     << "There are "
     << sizeof values/sizeof values[0]
     << " elements in the array."
     << endl;
```

(Continued)

As discussed, you use the sizeof operator to calculate the number of elements. The array is type int here, so you could have used sizeof(int) in place of sizeof values[0], but the expression that you used is better because this expression will produce the correct number of elements regardless of the type of the array.

Just to prove that you can do it, you use the same expression again in the for loop condition:

```
int sum = 0;
for(int i = 0 ; i < sizeof values/sizeof values[0] ; sum += values[i++])
  ;
```

This loop sums the elements of the array in the third control expression, sum += values[i++]. This also increments the counter, i, after the current element has been added to sum. The loop statement itself is empty, a fact indicated by the semicolon that appears on its own on the next line.

Finally, you output the value of sum with this statement:

```
cout << "The sum of the array elements is " << sum
     << endl;
```

Arrays of Characters

An array of elements of type char can have a dual personality. It can simply be an array of characters, in which each element stores one character, *or* it can represent a string. In the latter case, each character in the string is stored in a separate array element, and the end of the string is indicated by a special string termination character, '\0', which is called the **null character**.

A character string that is terminated by '\0' is called a **C-style string**. This contrasts with the string type that is defined in the C++ standard library. Entities of type string don't need a string termination character and are much more flexible. For the moment, you'll just consider C-style strings in the context of arrays in general and come back to type string toward the end of this chapter. You'll find that using type string is much more powerful and convenient for string manipulation than using arrays of type char.

You can declare and initialize an array of characters with a statement like this:

```
char vowels[5] = {'a', 'e', 'i', 'o', 'u'};
```

This isn't a string—it's just an array of five characters. Each element of the array is initialized with the corresponding character from the initializer list. As with numeric arrays, if you provide fewer initializing values than there are array elements, the elements that don't have explicit initializing values will be initialized with zero—that is, the null character whose bits are all 0, not the zero character.

You could also leave it to the compiler to set the size of the array to the number of initializing values:

```
char vowels[] = {'a', 'e', 'i', 'o', 'u'};   // An array with five elements
```

This also defines an array of five characters initialized with the vowels in the initializer list.

You can also declare an array of type char and initialize it with a string literal, for example:

```
char name[10] = "Mae West";
```

Here you're creating a C-style string. Because you're initializing the array with a string literal, the null character will be appended to the characters in the string, so the contents of the array will be as shown in Figure 6-2.

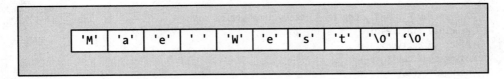

Figure 6-2. An initialized array of elements of type char

The last element will also be set to the null character, because there isn't an initializing value for it. Once again, you can leave the compiler to set the size of the array when you initialize it with a string:

```
char name[] = "Mae West";
```

This time, the array will have nine elements: eight elements to store the characters in the string, plus one extra element to store the string termination character. Of course, you could have used this approach when you declared the vowels array:

```
char vowels[] = "aeiou";                 // An array with six elements
```

There's a significant difference between this and the previous declaration for vowels. Here you're initializing the array with a string literal. This has '\0' appended to it to mark the end of the string, so the vowels array that is created will contain six elements. The array created as a result of the earlier declaration will only have five elements and can't be used as a string.

You can display a string that is stored in an array just by using the array name. The string in your name array, for example, could be displayed with this statement:

```
std::cout << name << std::endl;
```

This will display the entire string of characters, up to the '\0'. There *must* be a '\0' at the end. If there isn't, you'll continue to output characters from successive memory locations until a string termination character turns up or an illegal memory reference occurs.

 CAUTION *You can't output the contents of an array of a numeric type by just using the array name. This method only works for* char *arrays.*

Try It Out: Analyzing a String

Let's see how you could use an array of elements of type char in an example. This program reads a line of text and works out how many vowels and consonants are used in it:

```cpp
// Program 6.4 Analyzing the letters in a string
#include <iostream>
#include <cctype>
using std::cout;
using std::cin;
using std::endl;

int main() {
  const int maxlength = 100;                 // Array dimension
  char text[maxlength] = {0};                // Array to hold input string

  cout << endl << "Enter a line of text:" << endl;

  // Read a line of characters including spaces
  cin.getline(text, maxlength);

  cout << "You entered:" << endl << text << endl;

  int vowels = 0;                            // Count of vowels
  int consonants = 0;                        // Count of consonants
  for(int i = 0 ; text[i] != '\0' ; i++)
    if(std::isalpha(text[i]))                // If it is a letter
      switch(std::tolower(text[i])) {        // Test lowercase version
      case 'a': case 'e': case 'i':
      case 'o': case 'u':
        vowels++;                            // It is a vowel
        break;
      default:
        consonants++;                        // It is a consonant
      }
```

```
cout << "Your input contained "
     << vowels    << " vowels and "
     << consonants << " consonants."
     << endl;

  return 0;
}
```

Here's an example of the output from this program:

```
Enter a line of text:
A rich man is nothing but a poor man with money.
You entered:
A rich man is nothing but a poor man with money.
Your input contained 14 vowels and 23 consonants.
```

HOW IT WORKS

You declare an array of type char that has the number of elements defined by a const variable:

```
const int maxlength = 100;          // Array dimension
char text[maxlength] = {0};         // Array to hold input string
```

You'll store the input in the text array. However, you can't use your usual method for getting input, using the extraction operator (>>), because it won't do what you want in these circumstances. Consider this statement:

```
cin >> text;
```

This would certainly read characters into the text array, but only up to the first space. The extraction operator regards a space as a delimiter between input values, so it won't read an entire string containing spaces. You can't even use the extraction operator to read the input a character at a time, as *any* whitespace character, including '\n', is regarded as a delimiter. This means you can't store a newline character, and therefore you can't use it to indicate the end of the string. To read a whole line of text, including spaces, you need to use a different capability that is available with the standard input stream.

So, after prompting for input, you read from the standard input stream with this statement:

```
cin.getline(text, maxlength);
```

The getline() function for the cin stream reads in and stores a whole line of characters, including spaces. The input ends when a newline character, '\n', is read, which will be when you press the *Enter* key.

(Continued)

You can see that getline() is being passed *two* arguments. The input is stored in the location specified by the first of these; in this case, it's the text array. The second is the maximum number of characters that you want to store. This count includes the string termination character, '\0', which will be automatically appended to the end of the input string.

Although you haven't done so here, it's possible to pass a *third* argument to the getline() function. This enables you to specify an alternative character to '\n' to indicate the end of the input. For example, if you want to indicate the end of a string by entering an exclamation mark, you can use this statement:

```
cin.getline(text, maxlength, '!');
```

Why would you want to do this? One reason might be to allow multiple lines of text to be entered. With '!' indicating the end of the input instead of '\n', you can enter as many lines of text as you want, including '\n' characters. You just enter '!' when you're done. Of course, the total number of characters that you can enter in the read operation is still limited by maxlength.

Returning to the example, and simply to show that you can, you output the string that was entered using just the array name:

```
cout << "You entered:" << endl << text << endl;
```

Now that you've read and redisplayed the input line, you analyze the text string in quite a straightforward manner:

```
int vowels = 0;                          // Count of vowels
int consonants = 0;                      // Count of consonants
for(int i = 0 ; text[i] != '\0' ; i++)
  if(std::isalpha(text[i]))              // If it is a letter
    switch(std::tolower(text[i])) {      // Test lowercase version
      case 'a': case 'e': case 'i':
      case 'o': case 'u':
        vowels++;                        // It is a vowel
        break;
      default:
        consonants++;                    // It is a consonant
    }
```

You accumulate the counts of vowels and consonants in the two variables that you declare here. The for loop condition tests for finding the string termination character, rather than finding that a counter limit has been reached, which is the more typical test. Within the loop, you use the isalpha() library function to check for a letter. If you find one, you use the lowercase version of the letter as the selection expression in a switch statement. This avoids your having to write cases for uppercase as well as lowercase letters. Because you only get to the switch if text[i] is a letter, and because any letter that isn't a vowel must be a consonant, you can increment consonants as the default action.

Finally, you output the counts of vowels and consonants that you found in the text with this statement:

```
cout << "Your input contained "
     << vowels    << " vowels and "
     << consonants << " consonants."
     << endl;
```

Multidimensional Arrays

The arrays you've declared so far have required a single index value to select an element. Such an array is called a **one-dimensional array**, because varying one index can reference all the elements. However, you can also declare arrays that require two or more separate index values to access an element. These are referred to generically as **multidimensional arrays**. An array that requires two index values to reference an element is called a **two-dimensional array**. An array needing three index values is a **three-dimensional** array, and so on for as many dimensions as you think you can handle.

Suppose, as an avid gardener, that you want to record the individual weights of the carrots that you grow in your small vegetable garden. To store the weight of each of your carrots, which you planted in three rows of four, you could declare a two-dimensional array:

```
double carrots[3][4];
```

To reference a particular element of the carrots array, you need two index values. The first index value specifies the row, from 0 to 2, and the second index value specifies a particular carrot in that row, from 0 to 3. To store the weight of the third carrot in the second row, you could write

```
carrots[1][2] = 1.5;
```

Figure 6-3 shows the arrangement of this array in memory.

The rows are stored contiguously in memory. As you can see, the two-dimensional array is effectively a *one*-dimensional array of three elements, each of which is a one-dimensional array with four elements. You have an array of three arrays that each has four elements of type double.

As indicated in Figure 6-3, you can use the array name plus a *single* index value between square brackets to refer to an entire row in the array. You'll see this approach at its most useful when I discuss functions in Chapter 8.

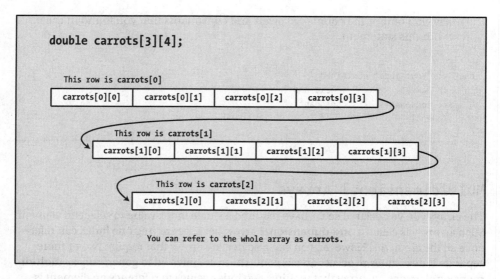

Figure 6-3. Elements in a two-dimensional array

When referring to an element, you use two index values. The right index value selects the element within a row and varies most rapidly. If you read the array from left to right, the right index corresponds to the column number. The left index selects the row, and therefore represents a row number. Figure 6-4 illustrates this concept. With arrays of more than two dimensions, the rightmost index value is always the one that varies most rapidly, and the leftmost index varies least rapidly.

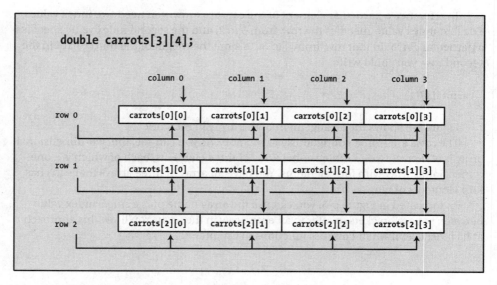

Figure 6-4. Rows and columns in a two-dimensional array

The array name by itself references the entire array. Note that with this array, you can't display the contents of either a row or the whole array using this notation. For example, the line

```
std::cout << carrots;                    // Not what you may expect!
```

will output a single hexadecimal value, which happens to be the address in memory of the first element of the array. You'll see why this is the case when I discuss pointers in the next chapter. Arrays of type char are a little different, as you saw earlier.

To display the entire array, one row to a line, you must write something like this:

```
for(int i = 0 ; i < 3 ; i++) {
  for(int j = 0 ; j < 4 ; j++)
    std::cout << std::setw(12) << carrots[i][j];
  std::cout << std::endl;
}
```

This uses magic numbers, 3 and 4, which you can avoid by using the sizeof operator:

```
for(int i = 0 ; i < sizeof carrots/sizeof carrots[0] ; i++) {
  for(int j = 0 ; j < sizeof carrots[0]/sizeof(double) ; j++)
    std::cout << std::setw(12) << carrots[i][j];
  std::cout << std::endl;
}
```

Of course, it would be better still not to use magic numbers for the array dimension sizes in the first place, so you *should* code this as the altogether tidier

```
const int nrows = 3;   // Number of rows in the array
const int ncols = 4;   // Number of columns which is number of elements per row
double carrots[nrows, ncols];
// Code to set values for the elements...

for(int i = 0 ; i < nrows ; i++) {
  for(int j = 0 ; j < ncols ; j++)
    std::cout << std::setw(12) << carrots[i][j];
  std::cout << std::endl;
}
```

Declaring an array of three dimensions just adds another set of square brackets. You might want to record three temperatures each day, seven days a week, for 52 weeks of the year. You could declare the following array to store such data as type long:

```
long temperatures[52][7][3];
```

The array stores three values in each row. There are seven such rows for a whole week's data and 52 sets of these for all the weeks in the year. This array will have a total of 1,092 elements of type long. To display the middle temperature for day 3 of week 26, you could write this:

```
std::cout << temperatures[25][2][1];
```

Remember that all the index values start at 0, so the weeks run from 0 to 51, the days run from 0 to 6, and the samples in a day run from 0 to 2.

Initializing Multidimensional Arrays

The way in which you specify initial values for a multidimensional array derives from the notion that a two-dimensional array is an array of one-dimensional arrays. The initializing values for a one-dimensional array are written between braces and separated by commas. Following on from that, you could declare and initialize your two-dimensional carrots array, for example, with this statement:

```
double carrots[3][4] = {
                        {2.5, 3.2, 3.7, 4.1},    // First row
                        {4.1, 3.9, 1.6, 3.5},    // Second row
                        {2.8, 2.3, 0.9, 1.1}     // Third row
                       };
```

I used explicit array dimensions to keep the code fragments short and simple here. Each row is a one-dimensional array, so the initializing values for each row are contained within their own set of braces. These three initializer lists are themselves contained within a set of braces, because the two-dimensional array is a one-dimensional array of one-dimensional arrays. You can extend this principle to any number of dimensions—each extra dimension requires another level of nested braces enclosing the initial values.

A question that may immediately spring to mind is, "What happens when you omit some of the initializing values?" The answer is more or less what you might have expected from past experience. Each of the innermost pairs of braces contains the values for the elements in the rows. The first list corresponds to carrots[0], the second to carrots[1], and the third to carrots[2]. The values between each pair of braces are assigned to the elements of the corresponding row. If there aren't enough to initialize all the elements in the row, then the elements without values will be initialized to 0. Let's look at an example:

```
double carrots[3][4] = {
                        {2.5, 3.2       },    // First row
                        {4.1            },    // Second row
                        {2.8, 2.3, 0.9  }     // Third row
                       };
```

The first two elements in the first row have values, whereas only one element in the second row has a value, and three elements in the third row have values. The elements will therefore be initialized as shown in Figure 6-5.

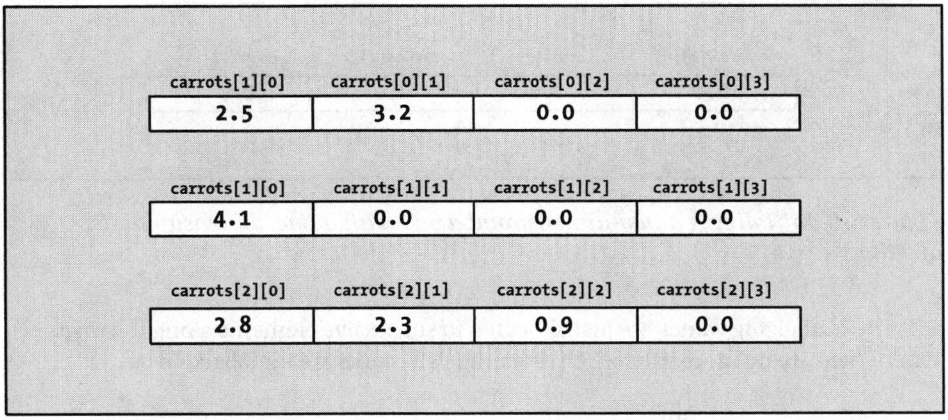

carrots[1][0]	carrots[0][1]	carrots[0][2]	carrots[0][3]
2.5	3.2	0.0	0.0

carrots[1][0]	carrots[1][1]	carrots[1][2]	carrots[1][3]
4.1	0.0	0.0	0.0

carrots[2][0]	carrots[2][1]	carrots[2][2]	carrots[2][3]
2.8	2.3	0.9	0.0

Figure 6-5. Omitting initial values for a two-dimensional array

As you can see, the elements without explicit initializing values in each row have all been set to 0. If you don't include sufficient sets of braces to initialize all of the rows in the array, the elements in the rows without initializing values will all be set to 0. You can deduce from this that you can zero *all* the elements in the array with the following statement:

```
double carrots[nrows][ncols] = {0};
```

If you include several initial values in the initializer list but omit the nested braces enclosing values for the rows, values are assigned sequentially to the elements, as they're stored in memory—with the rightmost index varying most rapidly. For example, suppose you declare the array like this:

```
double carrots[3][4] = {1.1, 1.2, 1.3, 1.4, 1.5, 1.6, 1.7};
```

The array will be set up with the values shown in Figure 6-6.

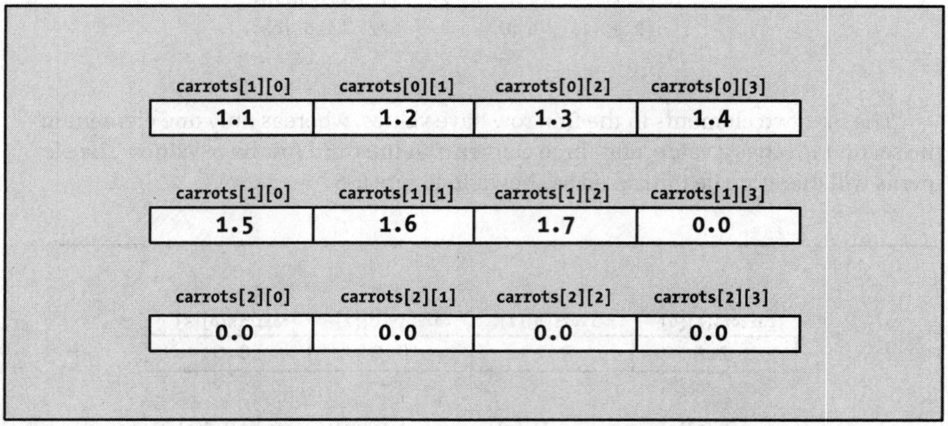

carrots[1][0]	carrots[0][1]	carrots[0][2]	carrots[0][3]
1.1	1.2	1.3	1.4

carrots[1][0]	carrots[1][1]	carrots[1][2]	carrots[1][3]
1.5	1.6	1.7	0.0

carrots[2][0]	carrots[2][1]	carrots[2][2]	carrots[2][3]
0.0	0.0	0.0	0.0

Figure 6-6. Initializing a two-dimensional array with a one-dimensional list of values

The initializing values are just allocated to successive elements along the rows. When there are no more values, the remaining elements are initialized to 0.

Setting Dimensions by Default

You can let the compiler determine the size of the first (leftmost) dimension of any array from the set of initializing values. Clearly, the compiler can only ever determine one of the dimensions in a multidimensional array, and it has to be the first. If you were to supply 12 initial values for a two-dimensional array, for instance, there's no way for the compiler to know whether the array should be three rows of four elements, six rows of two elements, or indeed any combination that amounts to twelve elements.

You could have declared your two-dimensional carrots array with this statement:

```
double carrots[][4] = {
                  {2.5, 3.2          },    // First row
                  {4.1               },    // Second row
                  {2.8, 2.3, 0.9     }     // Third row
              };
```

This will have three rows, as before, because there are three sets of braces within the outer pair. If there were only two sets, the array would have two rows, as in this statement:

```
double carrots[][4] = {
                    {2.5, 3.2          },     // First row
                    {4.1               }      // Second row
                };
```

This statement creates an array as though it was declared as follows:

```
double carrots[2][4] = {
                    {2.5, 3.2          },     // First row
                    {4.1               }      // Second row
                };
```

Arrays with more than two dimensions can also be declared such that the compiler sets the size of the first dimension from the set of initializing values. Here's an example of a three-dimensional array declaration:

```
int numbers[][3][4] = {
                    {
                        { 2,   4,   6,   8},
                        { 3,   5,   7,   9},
                        { 5,   8,  11,  14}
                    },
                    {
                        {12,  14,  16,  18},
                        {13,  15,  17,  19},
                        {15,  18,  21,  24}
                    }
                };
```

This array has three dimensions of sizes 2, 3, and 4. The outer braces enclose two further sets of braces, and each of these in turn contains three sets, each of which contains the four initial values for the corresponding row. As this simple example demonstrates, handling arrays of three dimensions or more gets increasingly complicated, and you need to take great care when placing the braces enclosing the initial values. The braces are nested to as many levels as there are dimensions in the array.

Multidimensional Character Arrays

You can declare arrays of two or more dimensions to hold any type of data. A two-dimensional array of type char is particularly interesting, because it can be an array of C-style strings. When you initialize a two-dimensional array of type char with character strings between double quotes, you don't need the braces around the string for a row—the double quotes do the job of the braces in this case, for example:

```
char stars[][80] = {
                    "Robert Redford",
                    "Hopalong Cassidy",
                    "Lassie",
                    "Slim Pickens",
                    "Boris Karloff",
                    "Oliver Hardy"
                 };
```

This array will have six rows because there are six string constants as initial values. Each row in the array stores a string containing the name of a movie star, and a terminating null character, '\0', will be appended to each string. Each row will actually accommodate up to 80 characters according to the row dimension you've specified.

....

Try It Out: Using a Two-Dimensional Character Array

You can demonstrate an array like this in an example. This program will select your lucky star, based on an integer that you enter:

```
// Program 6.5 Storing strings in an array
#include <iostream>
using std::cout;
using std::cin;
using std::endl;

int main() {
  char stars[][80] = {
                      "Robert Redford", "Hopalong Cassidy",
                      "Lassie",         "Slim Pickens",
                      "Boris Karloff",  "Mae West",
                      "Oliver Hardy",   "Sharon Stone"
                   };
  int choice = 0;

  cout << endl
       << "Pick a lucky star!"
       << " Enter a number between 1 and "
       << sizeof stars/sizeof stars[0] << ": ";
  cin >> choice;
```

```
if(choice >= 1 && choice <= sizeof stars/sizeof stars[0])
  cout << endl
      << "Your lucky star is " << stars[choice - 1];
else
  cout << endl                          // Invalid input
      << "Sorry, you haven't got a lucky star.";

cout << endl;
return 0;
}
```

A typical example of the output from this program is as follows:

```
Pick a lucky star! Enter a number between 1 and 8: 6

Your lucky star is Mae West
```

HOW IT WORKS

Apart from the example's incredible inherent entertainment value, the main point of interest is the declaration of the array stars. It's a two-dimensional char array, which can hold multiple strings, each of which can contain up to 80 characters, including the terminating null character that's automatically added by the compiler. The initializing strings for the array are enclosed between braces and separated by commas:

```
char stars[][80] = {
                "Robert Redford", "Hopalong Cassidy",
                "Lassie",         "Slim Pickens",
                "Boris Karloff",  "Mae West",
                "Oliver Hardy",   "Sharon Stone"
              };
```

Because you've omitted the size of the first array dimension, the compiler creates the array with the number of rows necessary to accommodate all the initializing strings. As you saw earlier, you can only omit the size of the first dimension; you must specify the sizes of any other dimensions that are required.

You prompt for an integer to be entered with this statement:

```
cout << endl
     << "Pick a lucky star!"
     << " Enter a number between 1 and "
     << sizeof stars/sizeof stars[0] << ": ";
```

(Continued)

The upper limit on the integer to be entered is given by the expression `sizeof stars/sizeof stars[0]`. This gives the number of rows in the array, so the statement automatically adapts to any changes you may make to the number of names in the list of initializing strings. You use the same technique in the `if` statement that arranges for the output to be displayed:

```
if(choice >= 1 && choice <= sizeof stars/sizeof stars[0])
   cout << endl
        << "Your lucky star is " << stars[choice - 1];
else
   cout << endl                          // Invalid input
        << "Sorry, you haven't got a lucky star.";
```

The `if` condition checks that the integer that was entered is within range before attempting to display a name. When you need to reference a string for output in the statement, you only need to specify the first index value. A single index value selects a particular 80-element subarray, and because this contains a string, the operation will output the contents of each element up to the terminating null character. The index is specified as `choice - 1` because the `choice` values start from 1, whereas the index values used to select a name from the array clearly need to start from 0. This is quite a common idiom when you're programming with arrays.

NOTE *One disadvantage of using arrays as you have in this example is the memory that is almost invariably left unused. All of your strings are less than 80 characters, and the surplus elements in each row of the array are wasted. You'll see a better way of dealing with situations like this in the next chapter.*

A Better Class of String

You've seen how you can use an array of type `char` to store a null-terminated (C-style) string, but there's a better alternative. The `<string>` header defines the `string` type, which has facilities that make it much easier to use than a null-terminated string. The `string` type is defined by a **class** (or to be more precise, a **class template**). The fact that I haven't yet discussed classes won't present any difficulty here because essentially a class simply introduces a new type into the language. In practice, using a class-defined type isn't profoundly different from using one of the basic data types that you're used to, so you'll just jump in and use them, and worry about the finer points of why they work the way they do later on.

An entity of a class type is usually referred to as an **object** (rather than a variable), so I'll use this terminology when I discuss the `string` type. There are one or two things in this section that you won't be able to explain fully yet, but the discussion *will* allow you to compare the string type with null-terminated strings and to see why it's generally better to use the string type.

The integer and floating-point types that you've seen (excluding enumerations) are described as **fundamental types**. The string type isn't one of the fundamental types. It's described as a **compound type**. A compound type is generally a type that's a composite of several data items that are ultimately defined in terms of fundamental types of data. A string object contains the characters that make up the string it represents, and it also contains other data, such as number of characters in the string. Enumerations and arrays are also examples of compound types.

As I said at the beginning of this section, the string type is defined in the <string> header, so you'll always need to include this header when you're using string objects. The string type name is also defined within the std namespace, so you need a using declaration to use the type name in its unqualified form. Because the string type is almost invariably used in its unqualified form, I'll assume a using declaration and write it as string rather than std::string in code fragments. Let's start by looking at how you create a string object.

Declaring string Objects

An object of type string contains a string of characters of type char, which can be an empty string if you choose. You can declare a variable of type string that refers to an empty string with the statement

```
string myString;  // An empty string
```

This statement declares a string object that you can refer to using the name myString. In this case, myString stores an *empty* string object—that is, it represents a string that contains no characters and has zero length.

You can declare and initialize a string object with a string literal:

```
string proverb = "Many a mickle makes a muckle.";
```

Here, proverb stores a string object that represents the string shown in the string literal. You could also use functional notation to initialize the object if you want, by writing the previous statement as follows:

```
string proverb("Many a mickle makes a muckle.");
```

The string that's stored doesn't need a string termination character. A string object keeps track of the length of the string that it represents, so no termination character is necessary. You can obtain the length of the string for a string object by using its length() function, which takes no arguments:

```
std::cout << proverb.length();
```

This statement calls the length() function for the proverb object and outputs the value returned using the insertion operator for the cout stream. This displays the length of the string stored in proverb, which in this case will be 29, the number of characters in the string.

The period in the expression proverb.length() is called the member **access operator**, or just the **dot operator**. It identifies the function length() as a **member** of the proverb object. You'll learn more about what this means when you investigate how to define your own data types in Chapter 11.

There are some other possibilities for initializing a string object. You can't initialize a string object with a single character between single quotes—a string constant must always appear between double quotes, even when it's just one character. However, you *can* initialize a string with a number of instances of the same character (including one instance!). You can declare and initialize a sleepy time string object with the statement

```
string sleeping(6, 'z');
```

The string object, sleeping, will contain the string "zzzzzz". If you want a string to suit a light sleeper with just one 'z', you could write this:

```
string light_sleep(1, 'z');
```

This will initialize light_sleep with the string literal "z". However, you *can't* write this:

```
string light_sleep = 'z';      // Wrong! Won't compile!
```

A further option for initializing a string object is to use an existing string object. Given you've declared proverb previously, you can write the following to declare another object:

```
string sentence = proverb;
```

The sentence object will be initialized with the same literal string as proverb, so it too will contain "Many a mickle makes a muckle." You could also use functional notation in this case if you want, so you could just as well have written the previous declaration as follows:

```
string sentence(proverb);
```

Characters within a string object are referenced using an index value starting from 0, just like an array. You can use this fact to select part of an existing string and use that to initialize a string object, for example:

```
string phrase(proverb, 0, 13);
```

This statement creates a new string object, phrase, and initializes it with part of the string that the proverb object contains, as shown in Figure 6-7.

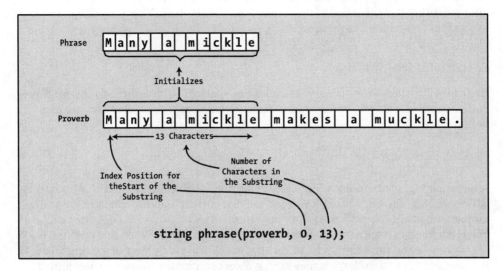

Figure 6-7. Creating a new string from part of an existing string

The first argument between the parentheses is the name of the string object you're using as the source of the initialization. The second argument is the starting index within that string object. The third argument is the number of characters to be selected as the initial value. So here you're selecting the first 13 characters of proverb, starting at the first character (with the index position 0), as the initial value for the phrase object. It will therefore contain "Many a mickle".

Operations with String Objects

Perhaps the simplest operation you can perform on a string object is assignment. You can assign the value of a string literal or another string object to a string object, for example:

```
string adjective = "hornswoggling";     // Declares a string
string word = "rubbish";                // Declares another string

word = adjective;                       // Modifies word
adjective = "twotiming";                // Modifies adjective
```

The third statement here assigns the value of adjective, which is "hornswoggling", to word, so "rubbish" is replaced. The last statement assigns the new string literal, "twotiming" to adjective, so the original value "hornswoggling" is replaced. Thus, after executing this sequence of statements, word will contain "hornswoggling" and adjective will contain "twotiming".

Concatenating Strings

You can join strings together using the addition operator—the technical term for this is **concatenation**. You can demonstrate concatenation using the objects that you just defined:

```
string description = adjective + " " + word + " whippersnapper";
```

After executing this statement, the description object will contain the string "twotiming hornswoggling whippersnapper". You can see that you can happily concatenate string literals with string objects using the + operator. This is because the + operator has been redefined to have a special meaning with string objects. When one operand is a string object and the other operand is either another string object or a string literal, the result of the + operation is a new string object containing the two strings joined into a single string.

Note that you *can't* concatenate two string literals by using the + operator. One of the operands must always be an object of type string. The following statement, for example, won't compile:

```
string description = " whippersnapper" + " " + word;  // Wrong!!
```

The problem here is that the compiler will try to evaluate the right side of the assignment as ((" whippersnapper" + " ") + word), and the + operator doesn't work with two string literals. However, judicious use of parentheses can make the statement legal:

```
string description = " whippersnapper" + (" " + word);
```

Here, the + operation between the parentheses *is* legal and produces a value of type string as a result, which can then be concatenated with the string literal " whippersnapper".

Try It Out: Concatenating Strings

That's quite enough theory for the moment—it's time for a bit of practice. This program reads your first and second name from the keyboard:

```cpp
// Program 6.6 Concatenating strings
#include <iostream>
#include <string>

using std::cout;
using std::cin;
using std::endl;
using std::string;

int main() {
  string first;                                 // Stores the first name
  string second;                                // Stores the second name

  cout << endl << "Enter your first name: ";
  cin >> first;                                 // Read first name

  cout << "Enter your second name: ";
  cin >> second;                                // Read second name

  string sentence = "Your full name is ";       // Create basic sentence
  sentence += first + " " + second + ".";       // Augment with names

  cout << endl
       << sentence                              // Output the sentence
       << endl;
  cout << "The string contains "                // Output its length
       << sentence.length()
       << " characters."
       << endl;

  return 0;
}
```

Here's some sample output from this program:

```
Enter your first name: Phil
Enter your second name: McCavity

Your full name is Phil McCavity.
The string contains 32 characters.
```

(Continued)

You first declare two `string` objects with these statements:

```
string first;                        // Stores the first name
string second;                       // Stores the second name
```

Because you haven't specified any initial values here, both of these will be initialized with empty strings. Next, you prompt for names to be entered, and you read the names from the keyboard:

```
cout << endl << "Enter your first name: ";
cin >> first;                        // Read first name

cout << "Enter your second name: ";
cin >> second;                       // Read second name
```

The stream extraction operator, >>, works with `string` objects in the same way that it does with arrays of type `char`. Characters are read until the first whitespace character is found, so you can't read a string containing spaces in this way. You'll see how you can overcome this limitation very soon.

After getting the names, you create another `string` object, but this time you initialize it explicitly with a string literal:

```
string sentence = "Your full name is ";      // Create basic sentence
```

The object `sentence` will be initialized with the string specified. You then use this object to assemble a string that contains a message you want to display:

```
sentence += first + " " + second + ".";      // Augment with names
```

The right side concatenates `first` with the literal `" "`, then `second` is appended to that, and finally the literal `"."` is appended to the result. With the sample input shown previously, the right side will evaluate to a `string` object containing `"Phil McCavity."`

As this statement demonstrates, the += operator also works with objects of type `string` in a similar way to what you've seen with the basic types. The statement is equivalent to this statement:

```
sentence = sentence + (first + " " + second + ".");       // Augment with names
```

Thus the effect of the += operator is to concatenate the `string` object resulting from the expression on the right side the `sentence` object on the left and then storing the final result back in `sentence`. Thus, after executing this statement, `sentence` will contain `"Your full name is Phil McCavity."`

When you use the += operator to append a value to a `string` object, the right side can be an expression resulting in a null-terminated string, or a single character of type `char`, or an expression that results in an object of type `string`.

Finally in the program, you use the stream insertion operator to output the contents of sentence and the length of the string:

```
cout << endl
     << sentence                     // Output the sentence
     << endl;
cout << "The string contains "       // Output its length
     << sentence.length()
     << " characters."
     << endl;
```

As this statement shows, you can output the value of a string object just like you can output the values of variables of any of the other types you've seen.

....

Accessing Characters in a String

You can refer to a particular character in a string by using an index value between square brackets, just as you do with an array. The first character in a string object has the index value 0. You could refer to the third character in sentence, for example, as sentence[2]. It's also possible to use such an expression on the left of the assignment operator, so you can *replace* individual characters as well as access them. The following statement changes all the characters in sentence to uppercase:

```
for(int i = 0 ; i < sentence.length() ; i++)
  sentence[i] = std::toupper(sentence[i]);
```

This applies the toupper() function to each character in the string in turn and stores the character that results from this back in the same position in the string. The index value for the first character is 0, and the index value for the last character is one less than the length of the string, so the loop continues as long as i<sentence.length() is true.

Note that you could get a warning message from your compiler as a result of the way the loop has been written. The loop variable, i, is of type int, whereas the integer returned by the length() function will be of type size_t. This implies that there could be a signed/unsigned mismatch in the comparison operation. This isn't going to cause any kind of problem here, but if you want to avoid getting the warning, you could write the loop as follows:

```
for(size_t i = 0 ; i < sentence.length() ; i++)
  sentence[i] = std::toupper(sentence[i]);
```

You can exercise this array-style access method in a version of the program you saw earlier that determined the number of vowels and consonants in a string. The new version will use a string object.

Try It Out: Accessing Characters

This program does essentially the same thing as Program 6.4, but it uses a string object rather than an array of type char:

```cpp
// Program 6.7 Accessing characters in a string
#include <iostream>
#include <string>
#include <cctype>
using std::cout;
using std::cin;
using std::endl;
using std::string;

int main() {
  string text;                              // Stores the input

  cout << endl << "Enter a line of text:" << endl;

  // Read a line of characters including spaces
  std::getline(cin, text);

  int vowels = 0;                           // Count of vowels
  int consonants = 0;                       // Count of consonants
  for(int i = 0 ; i<text.length() ; i++)
    if(std::isalpha(text[i]))               // Check for a letter
      switch(std::tolower(text[i])) {       // Test lowercase
        case 'a': case 'e': case 'i':
        case 'o': case 'u':
          vowels++;
          break;
        default:
          consonants++;
      }

  cout << "Your input contained "
       << vowels     << " vowels and "
       << consonants << " consonants."
       << endl;

  return 0;
}
```

Here's an example of the output from this program:

```
Enter a line of text:
A nod is as good as a wink to a blind horse.

Your input contained 14 vowels and 18 consonants.
```

HOW IT WORKS

When you compile this example, your compiler may issue a warning relating to this statement:

```
for(int i = 0 ; i<text.length() ; i++)
```

This warning arises because the integer returned by the length() function is size_t, which is defined to be unsigned integer type. If you want to eliminate the warning, you can declare the loop variable as type size_t:

```
for(size_t i = 0 ; itext.length() ; i++)
```

Although under normal circumstances you can ignore such messages, it's just as well to look at them—just in case. Similar warnings can also occur with the functions for string objects that return values that are positions in a string.

I confine the rest of this explanation to the new features introduced in the program. First, you declare your object of type string:

```
string text;                        // Stores the input
```

The text object, of type string, contains an empty string initially, but you'll read a line from the keyboard and store it here. After a prompt is displayed, the input is obtained using the getline() function:

```
getline(cin, text);
```

This version of getline() is declared in the <string> header. It reads characters from the stream specified by the first argument, cin in this case, until a newline character is read and the result is stored in the string object specified by the second argument, text in this case. Note that this time you don't need to worry about how many characters are in the input. The string object will automatically accommodate however many characters are entered.

You can change the delimiter that will signal the end of the input to a character other than '\n' by using a version of getline() with a third argument that specifies the delimiter for the end of the input:

```
getline(cin, text, '#');
```

This reads characters until '#' is found, indicating the end of the input. Because newline doesn't signal the end of input in this case, you can enter as many lines of input as you like, and they'll all be combined into a single string. The newline characters will still be present in the string, though.

Having read the text, you count the vowels and consonants in much the same way as you did in Program 6.4, with just a small change to the loop condition in the for loop:

```
for(int i = 0 ; i<text.length() ; i++)
```

(Continued)

You use the length() function of the text object to get the number of characters in the string, and this number controls the for loop. You can access each character by means of the index value, i, just as you could with your char array.

The major advantage of using a string object in this example is that you don't need to worry about the length of the string it contains.

Accessing Substrings

It's possible to extract a substring from a string object by using the substr() function. The function requires two arguments. You specify the index position where the substring starts as the first argument and the number of characters in the substring as the second argument. The function returns a string object containing the substring, for example:

```
string phrase = "The higher the fewer";
string word = phrase.substr(4, 6);
```

This extracts the six-character substring from phrase that starts at index position 4, so word will contain "higher" after the second statement executes.

If the length you specify overruns the end of the string object, then the substr() function just returns all the characters up to the end of the string. The following statement demonstrates this behavior:

```
string word = phrase.substr(4, 100);
```

Of course, there aren't 100 characters in the whole of phrase, let alone in a substring. In this case, the result will be that word will contain the substring from index position 4 to the end, which is "higher the fewer".

You could obtain the same result by omitting the length altogether and just supplying the first argument, where the substring starts:

```
string word = phrase.substr(4);
```

This also returns the substring from index position 4 to the end. If you omit both arguments to the substr() function, the whole of phrase will be selected as the substring.

If you specify a starting index position for the substring that falls outside the valid range for the string object you're dealing with, an **exception** will be thrown and your program will terminate abnormally—unless, that is, you've implemented some code to handle the exception. I discuss exceptions and how to handle them in Chapter 16.

Comparing Strings

You saw in the last example how you can use an index to access individual characters in a `string` object for comparison purposes. When you access an individual character using an index value, the result is of type `char`, so you can use the comparison operators to compare individual characters.

When you need to compare entire strings, you can *also* use any of the comparison operators, with `string` objects as operands. Just to remind you, the comparison operators I'm talking about here are as follows:

```
>      >=      <      <=      ==      !=
```

You can use these operators with strings in several ways. You can use them to compare two objects of type `string`, or to compare an object of type `string` with a string literal or a C-style string stored in an array of type `char`. The operands are compared character by character, until either the characters are different or the end of either or both operands is reached. When differing characters are found, numerical comparison of the character codes determines which of the strings has the lesser value. If no differing characters are found and the strings are of different lengths, then the shorter string is "less than" the longer string. Two strings are equal if they contain the same number of characters and all corresponding character codes are equal. Because you're comparing character codes, the comparisons are obviously going to be case sensitive.

You can compare two `string` objects using an `if` statement as follows:

```cpp
string word1 = "age";
string word2 = "beauty";
if(word1 < word2)
  std::cout << word1 << " comes before " << word2;
else
  std::cout << word2 << " comes before " << word1;
```

Executing these statements will result in the following output:

```
age comes before beauty
```

This shows that the old saying must be true.

The preceding code looks like a good candidate for using the conditional operator. You can produce the same result with the following statement:

```cpp
std::cout << word1
          << (word1 < word2 ? " comes " : " does not come ")
          << "before " << word2;
```

Let's do some practical string comparisons in a working example.

Try It Out: Comparing Strings

This program reads a number of names and finds the maximum and minimum of those entered:

```cpp
// Program 6.8 Comparing strings
#include <iostream>
#include <string>
#include <cctype>
using std::cout;
using std::cin;
using std::endl;
using std::string;

int main() {
  const int max_names = 6;                    // Maximum number of names
  string names[max_names];                    // Array of names
  int count = 0;                              // Number of names
  char answer = 0;                            // Response to a prompt

  do {
    cout << "Enter a name: ";
    cin >> names[count++];                    // Read a name

    cout << "Do you want to enter another name? (y/n): ";
    cin >> answer;                            // Read response
  } while(count < max_names && std::tolower(answer) == 'y');

  // Indicate when array is full
  if(count == max_names)
    cout << endl << "Maximum name count reached." << endl;

  // Find the minimum and maximum names
  int index_of_max = 0;
  int index_of_min = 0;

  for(int i = 1 ; i < count ; i++)
    if(names[i] > names[index_of_max])        // Current name greater?
      index_of_max = i ;                      // then it is new maximum
    else if(names[i] < names[index_of_min])   // Current name less?
      index_of_min = i;                       // then it is new minimum

  // Output the minimum and maximum names
  cout << endl
       << "The minimum name is " << names[index_of_min]
       << endl;
  cout << "the maximum name is " << names[index_of_max]
       << endl;
  return 0;
}
```

Here's some sample output from this example:

```
Enter a name: Meshak
Do you want to enter another name? (y/n): y
Enter a name: Eshak
Do you want to enter another name? (y/n): y
Enter a name: Abednego
Do you want to enter another name? (y/n): n


The minimum name is Abednego
The maximum name is Meshak
```

HOW IT WORKS

The names are stored in an array of type string that you declare using a constant to define the array size:

```
const int max_names = 6;                          // Maximum number of names
string names[max_names];                          // Array of names
```

Declaring an array of type string is the same as declaring any other kind of array. This declaration creates an array of max_names elements, in which each element is a string object containing an empty string.

You could initialize the array in the same way you did with two-dimensional arrays of type char, for example:

```
string names[max_names] = {"Zeus", "Venus"};      // Array of names
```

This statement initializes the first two elements of the names array with the string literals between the braces. The remaining elements are empty strings.

Because you expect at least one name to be entered, a do-while loop is a good choice for managing the input:

```
do {
  cout << "Enter a name: ";
  cin >> names[count++];                          // Read a name

  cout << "Do you want to enter another name? (y/n): ";
  cin >> answer;                                  // Read response
} while(count<max_names && std::tolower(answer) == 'y');
```

You've seen this sort of thing before—it's a straightforward mechanism for reading a number of data items. A name is read from the keyboard into the current element of the names array. The extraction operator reads characters up to the first whitespace character. The loop condition ends the loop if 'n' or 'N' is entered, or if the maximum capacity of the array of string objects is reached.

(Continued)

When you've read all the input—or as much as you have capacity for—you find the index values for the array elements that contain the maximum and minimum strings. You arbitrarily assume that the first string is both the minimum and maximum by setting the index values as 0. You then compare these to the other strings in the array. You do this in a for loop:

```
for(int i = 1 ; i < count ; i++)
  if(names[i] > names[index_of_max])          // Current name greater?
    index_of_max = i ;                          // then it is new maximum
  else if(names[i] < names[index_of_min])      // Current name less?
    index_of_min = i;                           // then it is new minimum
```

Within the loop, the nested if statement uses the > and < comparison operators for string objects to check whether the current array element is greater than the current maximum or less than the current minimum. If you find a new maximum, you avoid checking for a new minimum by placing the test for a new minimum in the else clause. Clearly, a new maximum can't also be a new minimum. Note that the loop counter starts at 1 because you assumed initially that the string at index position 0 is both the minimum and the maximum.

Finally, you output the maximum and minimum names that you've found with the following statements:

```
cout << endl
     << "The minimum name is " << names[index_of_min]
     << endl;
cout << "The maximum name is " << names[index_of_max]
     << endl;
```

The compare() Function

Given an object of type string, you can call the compare() function to compare the object with another object of type string, or a string literal, or a null-terminated string stored in an array of type char. To call the compare() function for a string object, object_name, you write

```
object_name.compare(other_object)
```

The period following the object name is the dot operator, which you met earlier in conjunction with the length() function. The object that your string is to be compared with, other_object, goes between the parentheses.

Here's an example of an expression that calls the compare() function for an object called word and compares it with a string literal:

```
word.compare("and")
```

Here, the function compares the contents of word with the string "and", and returns a value of type int. The function returns a positive integer if word is greater than "and"; zero if word is equal to "and"; and a negative integer if word is less than "and".

In the last example, you could have used the compare() function in place of the comparison operators, but the code would have been less clear. The for loop would be

```
for(int i = 1 ; i < count ; i++)
  if(names[i].compare(names[index_of_max]) > 0)     // Current name greater?
    index_of_max = i;                                // then it is new maximum
  else if(names[i].compare(names[index_of_min]) < 0) // Current name less?
    index_of_min = i;                                // then it is new minimum
```

Sometimes, as this example demonstrates, using the compare() function makes it more difficult to follow what's going on than when you use the comparison operators. However, there are situations in which the compare() function *does* have an advantage.

You can compare() a substring of the original string with the string specified by an argument by passing two extra arguments to the compare() function that define the start index of the substring and the number of characters in it. Consider the following statements:

```
string word1 = "A jackhammer";
string word2 = "jack";
if(word1.compare(2, 4, word2) == 0)
  std::cout << "Equal" << std::endl;
```

The if statement compares the four-character substring of word1 that starts at index position 2 with the whole of word2. This is illustrated in Figure 6-8.

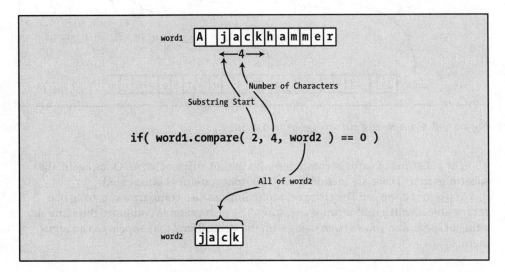

Figure 6-8. Using compare() *with a substring*

The first argument to compare() is the index position of the first character in the word1 substring that is to be compared with word2. The second argument is the number of characters in the substring. Because in this case word2 and the substring of word1 that you've specified are equal, the output statement is executed. Obviously, if word2 is a different length than the substring that you specify, they're unequal by definition.

You might want to compare a substring of one string with a substring of another using the compare() function, and there's a way to do that as well—it involves passing *five* arguments! For example:

```
string word1 = "A jackhammer";
string word2 = "It is a jack-in-the-box";
if(word1.compare(2, 4, word2, 8, 4) == 0)
    std::cout << "Equal" << std::endl;
```

The first three arguments to compare() are the same as before. The last two arguments are the index position of the substring in word2 and its length, as shown in Figure 6-9.

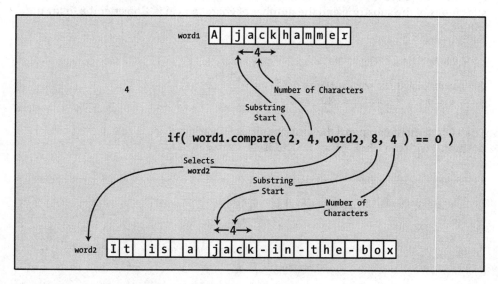

Figure 6-9. Comparing substrings of two strings

The substring of word1 is compared with the substring of word2. Once again, the substrings in this case are identical, so the output statement is executed.

You're not done yet! The compare() function can also compare a substring of a string object with a null-terminated string. The next example compares the same substring of word1 that you've been using with the string literal that appears as an argument:

```
if(word1.compare(2, 4, "jack") == 0)
    std::cout << "Equal" << std::endl;
```

Because the four-character substring of word1 that starts at index position 2 is again equal to "jack", the if expression is true and the output will occur.

Still another option is to select the first *n* characters from the null-terminated string by specifying the number of characters you want to use. This next statement compares the same substring from word1 with the first four characters from "jacket":

```
if(word1.compare(2, 4, "jacket", 4) == 0)
    std::cout << "Equal" << std::endl;
```

Naturally, in all of these examples, you can check the if statements for *in*equality by checking for the return value from compare() being nonzero. You could also test for word1 being less than the string specified by the argument(s) by looking for a result less than zero, or greater than the string specified by the argument(s) by looking for a result greater than zero.

Just to remind you how it works, if you declare word as

```
string word = "banana";
```

the expression word.compare("apple") returns a positive integer because "banana" is greater than "apple", and word.compare("orange") returns a negative integer because "banana" is less than "orange".

NOTE *In this section, you've seen the* compare() *function work quite happily with different numbers of arguments of various kinds. In fact, what you have here are lots of different functions with the same name. These are called* **overloaded functions**, *and you'll look at them further, and at how you can create your own, in Chapter 9.*

Comparisons Using substr()

Of course, if like me you have trouble remembering the sequence of arguments to the more complicated versions of the compare() function, you can just use the substr() function to extract the substrings you're interested in, and then use the comparison operators in many cases. For instance, to compare substrings in word1 and word2 as shown in Figure 6-9 in the previous section, you could write the test as follows:

```
if(word1.substr(2,4) == word2.substr(8,4))
    std::cout << "Equal" << std::endl;
```

This seems to me to be more readily understood than the equivalent operation using the compare() function.

Of course, by putting such comparisons in a loop and using the loop counter as the index for the start of a substring in the substr() function, you could search a string for an occurrence of a particular substring. I won't bother describing this in detail, though, as there are much easier ways of doing this.

Searching a String

You have many different methods available to you for searching a string object, and they all involve functions that return the index position of what you're looking for.

Let's start with the simplest sort of search. A string object has a function called find() that you can use to discover the index position of a substring within the string starts. You can also find the index position of a single character. The substring that you choose to search for can be another string object or a null-terminated string, for example:

```
string sentence = "Manners maketh man";
string word = "man";
std::cout << sentence.find(word) << std::endl;      // Outputs 15
std::cout << sentence.find("Man") << std::endl;      // Outputs 0
std::cout << sentence.find('k') << std::endl;        // Outputs 10
std::cout << sentence.find('x') << std::endl;        // Outputs string::npos
```

In each of the output statements, the sentence object is searched from the beginning using the find() function. The function returns the index position of the first character of the first occurrence of whatever is being sought.

In the last statement, 'x' doesn't occur in the string being searched, so the value string::npos is returned. This is a built-in constant that represents an illegal character position in a string and is used to signal a failure in a search operation. With my compiler, string::npos happens to have the value 4,294,967,295, but it may be different on your system.

Of course, you can use string::npos to check for a search failure with a statement such as this:

```
if(sentence.find('x') == string::npos)
    std::cout << "Character not found" << std::endl;
```

Another variation on the find() function allows you to search *part* of the string, starting from a specified position. For example, with sentence defined as before, you could write this:

```
std::cout << sentence.find("an", 1) << std::endl;      // Outputs 1
std::cout << sentence.find("an", 3) << std::endl;      // Outputs 16
```

Each of these statements searches sentence from the index position given by the second argument, to the end of the string. The first statement finds the first occurrence of "an" in the string, and the second statement finds the second occurrence because the search starts from index position 3 in sentence. You could use a string object as the first argument to specify the string you're searching for here, too. For example:

```
string sentence = "Manners maketh man";
string word = "an";
int count = 0;                              // Count of occurrences
size_t position = 0;                        // Stores a string index position
for(size_t i = 0 ; i<sentence.length()-word.length() ; ) {
  position = sentence.find(word, i);
  if(position == string::npos)
    break;
  count++;
  i = position+1;
}
std::cout << "\"" << word << "\" occurs in \"" << sentence
          << "\" " << count << " times.";
```

An index position in a string is of type `size_t`, so you declare the variable, `position`, that holds values returned by the `find()` function to be of that type. The loop index `i` is used to define the starting position for a `find()` operation so this is also of type `size_t`. Obviously, the last possible occurrence of `word` in `sentence` has to start `word.length()` positions back from the end of `sentence`, so you use that as the constraint on the maximum value of `i` in the loop. Note that there's no loop expression for incrementing the loop variable `i` because this is done in the loop body.

Within the loop, if `find()` returns `string::npos`, then `word` wasn't found, so you end the loop by executing the break statement. Otherwise, you increment the count and set `i` to one position beyond where `word` was found, ready for the next iteration. You might think you should set `i` to be `i+word.length`, but this wouldn't allow overlapping occurrences to be found such as if you were searching for `"anna"` in the string `"annannanna"`.

You can also search for a substring of a null-terminated, C-style string corresponding to a given number of characters in it. In this case, the first argument to `find()` is the null-terminated string, the second argument is the index position at which you want to start searching, and the third argument is the number of characters of the null-terminated string that you want to take as the string you're looking for, for example:

```
std::cout << sentence.find("akat", 1, 2) << std::endl;  // Outputs 9
```

This statement searches for the first two characters of `"akat"` (that is, `"ak"`) in `sentence`, starting from position 1. The following searches would both fail and return `string::npos`:

```
std::cout << sentence.find("akat", 1, 3) << std::endl;   // Outputs string::npos
std::cout << sentence.find("akat", 10, 2) << std::endl;  // Outputs string::npos
```

The first search fails because the string `"aka"` isn't in `sentence`. The second search is looking for `"ak"`, which *is* in `sentence`, but it fails because it doesn't occur after position 10 in `sentence`.

Try It Out: Searching a String

You can write a program that searches a `string` object for a given substring and works out how many times the substring occurs:

```cpp
// Program 6.9 Searching a string
#include <iostream>
#include <string>
using std::cout;
using std::endl;
using std::string;

int main() {
  // The string to be searched
  string text = "Smith, where Jones had had \"had had\", had had \"had\"."
                "\n \"Had had\" had had the examiners' approval.";

  string word = "had";                    // Substring to be found

  cout << endl  << "The string is: " << endl << text << endl;

  // Count the number of occurrences of word in text
  int count = 0;                          // Count of substring occurrences

  for( size_t index = 0 ;
       (index = text.find(word, index)) != string::npos ;
                       index += word.length(), count++)
     ;

  cout << "Your text contained "
       << count << " occurrences of \""
       << word  << "\"."
       << endl;

  return 0;
}
```

This program produces the following output:

```
The string is:
Smith, where Jones had had "had had", had had "had".
 "Had had" had had the examiners' approval.
Your input contained 10 occurrences of "had".
```

There are only 10 occurrences of "had". Of course, "Had" isn't found because it starts with an uppercase letter.

HOW IT WORKS

You declare the `string` object to be searched like this:

```
string text = "Smith, where Jones had had \"had had\", had had \"had\"."
               "\n \"Had had\" had had the examiners' approval.";
```

String literals are automatically concatenated in statements like this so you're able to spread the initializing string literal over two lines. Note that you have to use the escape sequence \" to put a double quote in the string, as a double quote by itself would be interpreted by the compiler as a delimiter.

You define the substring you're looking for as follows:

```
string word = "had";                    // Substring to be found
```

This declares another `string` object, word, which contains the character string "had". All the searching and counting is then done in the expressions controlling the for loop:

```
int count = 0;                           // Count of substring occurrences
for(size_t index = 0 ;
    (index = text.find(word, index)) != string::npos ;
                     index += word.length(), count++)
  ;
```

This is a slightly different approach to searching a string from the code fragment in the text. There is quite a lot happening in this loop, so to help you follow the action, the basic elements are shown in the diagram in Figure 6-10.

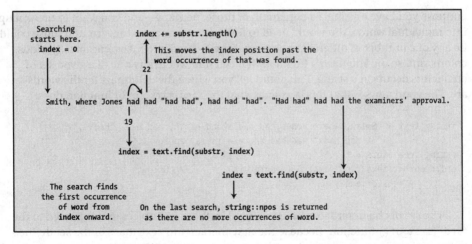

Figure 6-10. Searching a string

(Continued)

The first expression initializes the variable index, which is used to specify the position in text where each search operation is to begin. The expression that determines whether the loop continues or not is

```
(index = text.find(word, index)) != string::npos
```

This expression will search text, starting at position index, to find the first occurrence of word, and store the index position where word is found back into index. If the value stored in index is string::npos, then word wasn't found and the loop ends.

If word *was* found, the third for loop control expression is executed. This does two things: it increments the value in index with the expression index += word.length(), and because word was found, it increments the count of the number of occurrences of word by 1. The value word.length() is added to index to move the position in text past the copy of word that was just found, ready to start the next search. You increment in this way rather than by 1 because you're looking for whole words and want to exclude overlapping occurrences.

When the loop is done, you output the number of occurrences of word in text with this statement:

```
cout << "Your text contained "
     << count << " occurrences of \""
     << word  << "\"."
     << endl;
```

Searching a String for Characters from a Set

Suppose you have a string—a paragraph of prose, perhaps—and you want to break it up into individual words. You would need to find where the separators are, and those could be any of a number of different characters—there could be spaces, commas, periods, colons, and so on. You need a function that can find where any one of a given set of characters occurs in a string. This could tell you where the delimiters for the words are. The good news is that this is exactly what the find_first_of() function does:

```
string text = "Smith, where Jones had had \"had had\", had had \"had\"."
              " \"Had had\" had had the examiners' approval.";
string separators = " ,.\"";
std::cout << text.find_first_of(separators)        // Outputs 5
          << std::endl;
```

The set of characters sought are defined by the string object that is passed to the find_first_of() function. Because the first character in text that's in the set defined by separators is a comma, the last statement will output 5. You can define the argument here as a null-terminated string if you need to. If you want to find the first vowel in text, for example, you could write this:

```
std::cout << text.find_first_of("AaEeIiOoUu")      // Outputs 2
          << std::endl;
```

The given output results because the first vowel is 'i', at index position 2.

You can also search backward from the end of the string object to find the *last* occurrence of a character from a given set by using the find_last_of() function. For example, to find the last vowel in text, you could write this:

```
std::cout << text.find_last_of("AaEeIiOoUu")      // Outputs 92
          << std::endl;
```

The last vowel in text is the second 'a' in approval, at index position 92.

With the find_first_of() and find_last_of() functions, you can specify an extra argument that defines where the search process is to begin in the string being searched. If you use a null-terminated string as the first argument, you can also have a third argument specifying how many characters from the set are to be included.

A further option available to you is to find a character that's *not* in a given set. The find_first_not_of() and find_last_not_of() functions are your tools for this job. To find the position of the first character in text that isn't a vowel, you could write this:

```
std::cout << text.find_first_not_of("AaEeIiOoUu")  // Outputs 0
          << std::endl;
```

The first character that isn't a vowel is clearly the first, at index position 0. Let's try some of these functions in a working example.

Try It Out: Finding Characters from a Given Set

You'll write an example that will separate out all the words from a string containing prose. This involves combining the use of find_first_of() and find_first_not_of(). Here's the code:

```cpp
// Program 6.10 Searching a string for characters from a set
#include <iostream>
#include <string>
using std::cout;
using std::endl;
using std::string;

int main() {
  // The string to be searched
  string text = "Smith, where Jones had had \"had had\", had had \"had\"."
                " \"Had had\" had had the examiners' approval.";

  string separators = " ,.\"";                    // Word delimiters

  // Find the start of the first word
  size_t start = text.find_first_not_of(separators);
  size_t end = 0;                                 // Index for the end of a word
```

(Continued)

```
            // Now find and output the words
            int word_count = 0;                                  // Number of words
            while(start != string::npos) {
              end = text.find_first_of(separators, start + 1);   // Find end of word
              if(end == string::npos)                            // Found a separator?
                end = text.length();                             // No, so set to last + 1

              cout << text.substr(start, end - start)            // Output the word
                   << endl;
              word_count++;                                      // Increase the count

              // Find the first character of the next word
              start = text.find_first_not_of(separators, end + 1);
            }

            cout << "Your string contained "
                 << word_count << " words."
                 << endl;

            return 0;
          }
```

The output from this program is as follows:

```
Smith
where
Jones
had
had
had
had
had
had
had
Had
had
had
had
the
examiners'
approval
Your string contained 17 words.
```

HOW IT WORKS

You have seen the initial declarations of the string objects before, so the interesting part of this example is how the analysis of the string works. You need to find the first character of the first word, so you read past any separator characters at the beginning of text with this statement:

```
size_t start = text.find_first_not_of(separators);
```

As long as this returns a valid value—that is, a value other than string::npos—you know that start will contain the index position of the first character of the first word. In a moment, you'll find out where it ends.

You'll accumulate a count of the number of words in the variable word_count, which you declare as follows:

```
int word_count = 0;                          // Number of words
```

The while loop finds the end of the current word, displays it, and then finds the beginning of the next word:

```
while(start != string::npos) {
  end = text.find_first_of(separators, start + 1);
  if(end == string::npos)                    // Found a separator?
    end = text.length();                     // No, so set to last + 1

  cout << text.substr(start, end - start)    // Output the word
       << endl;
  word_count++;                              // Increase the count

  // Find the first character of the next word
  start = text.find_first_not_of(separators, end + 1);
}
```

The while condition will check the initial index position that is recorded in start. If text happens to be empty or contains only characters defined in separators, then the loop will end immediately. If not, then you have at least one word on your hands and the loop body is executed. You find the first position after start at which a character from the separators set occurs. This will be the position immediately following the end of the word. This is done with a search starting at position start + 1, using the find_first_of() function. The index position returned is stored in end. Figure 6-11 shows a diagram of the process.

(Continued)

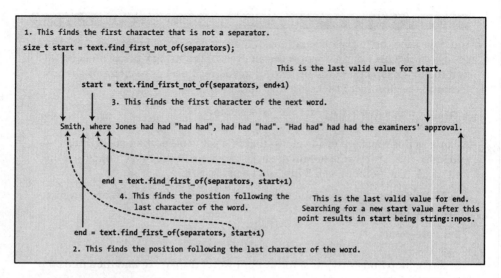

Figure 6-11. Finding all the words in a string

Of course, it's possible that this last search will fail, leaving end with the value string::npos. This can occur if the string text ends with a letter or indeed anything other than one of your specified separators. To deal with this, you check the value of end in the if statement, and if the search did fail, you set end to the length of text. This will be one character beyond the end of the string (because indexes start at 0, not 1), as you want end to correspond to the position *after* the last character in a word.

You then extract the word using the substr() function. The variable start contains the index position of the first letter in a word, and the expression end - start will be the number of characters in the word. When you've displayed the word, you increment word_count and look for the start of the next word with this statement:

```
start = text.find_first_not_of(separators, end + 1);
```

This statement searches again for the first character that isn't one of the separators, and the search starts one character *after* the character position recorded in end. If start contains a valid index, then there's another word and this will be displayed on the next iteration. If there are no more words, start will be set to string::npos and the loop will end.

Finally, you output the count of the number of words found with this statement:

```
cout << "Your string contained "
     << word_count << " words."
     << endl;
```

Searching a String Backward

The find() function searches forward through a string, either from the beginning or from a position that you specify. If you want to search backward, from the end of the string, you can use the rfind() function, perhaps named from **reverse find**.

The rfind() function comes in the same varieties as the find() function. You can search a whole string object for a substring defined as either another string object or a null-terminated string, or you can search for a character. For example:

```cpp
string sentence = "Manners maketh man";
string word = "an";
std::cout << sentence.rfind(word) << std::endl;    // Outputs 16
std::cout << sentence.rfind("man") << std::endl;   // Outputs 15
std::cout << sentence.rfind('e')   << std::endl;   // Outputs 11
```

Each of these searches finds the last incidence of the argument to the rfind() function and returns the position of the first character where it was found. Figure 6-12 illustrates the use of rfind().

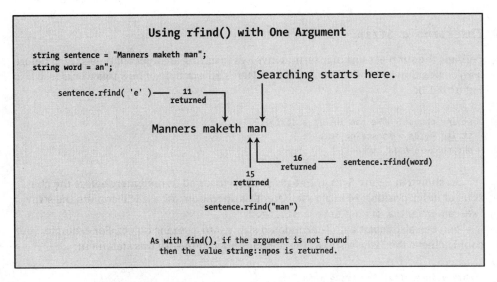

Figure 6-12. Searching backward through a string

Searching with word as the argument finds the last occurrence of "an" in the string. The rfind() function returns the index position of the first character in the substring sought.

If the substring isn't present, the value string::npos will be returned. For example, the following statement will result in this:

```cpp
std::cout << sentence.rfind("miners") << std::endl; // Outputs string::npos
```

Because sentence doesn't contain the substring miners, the value of string::npos will be returned and displayed by this statement. The other two searches illustrated in Figure 6-12 are similar to the first. They both search backward from the end of the string looking for the first occurrence of the argument.

Just as with the find() function, you can add an extra argument to rfind() to specify the starting position for the backward search, and you can add a third argument when the first argument is a C-style string. The third argument specifies the number of characters from the C-style string that are to be taken as the substring for which you're searching.

Modifying a String

Naturally, when you've searched a string and found what you're looking for, you may well want to change it in some way. You've already seen how you can use an index value within square brackets to modify a single character in a string object, but you can also insert a string into another string object or replace an existing substring. Unsurprisingly, you can insert a string by means of a function called insert(), and you can replace a substring in a string using a function called replace(). Let's look at inserting a string first.

Inserting a String

Perhaps the simplest sort of insertion involves inserting an object of type string before a given position in another string object. Here's an example of how this works (see also Figure 6-13):

```
string phrase = "We can insert a string.";
string words = "a string into ";
phrase.insert(14, words);
```

As shown in Figure 6-13, the words string is inserted immediately before the character at index position 14 in phrase. After this operation, phrase will contain the string "We can insert a string into a string."

You can also insert a null-terminated string into a string object. For example, you could achieve the same result as the previous operation with this statement:

```
phrase.insert(14, "a string into ");
```

Of course, the '\0' character is discarded from a null-terminated string before insertion, because it's a delimiter and not part of the string proper.

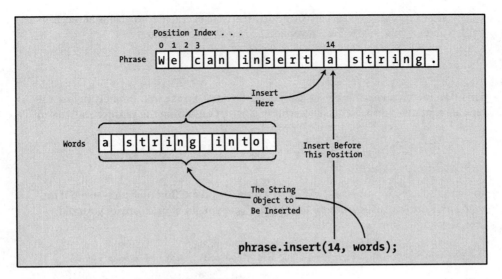

Figure 6-13. Inserting a string into another string

The next level of sophistication is the insertion of a substring of a `string` object into another object of type `string`. You just need to supply two extra arguments in the `insert()` function call: one specifies the index position of the first character in the substring, and the other specifies the number of characters in the substring. For example:

```
phrase.insert(13, words, 8, 5);
```

This inserts the five-character substring that starts at position 8 in words, into phrase. Given that they represent your original strings, this will insert " into" into "We can insert a string.", so that phrase becomes "We can insert into a string."

There is a similar facility for inserting a given number of characters from a null-terminated string into a `string` object. The following statement produces the same result as the last one:

```
phrase.insert(13, " into something", 5);
```

This statement inserts the substring consisting of first five characters of " into something" into phrase before the character at index position 13.

If you ever need to insert a string consisting of several identical characters into a string object, you have a special version of insert() to do that:

```
phrase.insert(16, 7, '*');
```

This statement causes five asterisks to be inserted in phrase immediately before the character at position 13. This will result in phrase containing the uninformative sentence "We can insert a *******string."

Replacing a Substring

You can replace any substring of a string object with a different string—even if the string and the substring have different lengths. If you go back to one of your old favorites and define text as follows:

```
string text = "Smith, where Jones had had \"had had\", had had \"had\".";
```

You can replace the name "Jones" with a less common name with this statement:

```
text.replace(13, 5, "Gruntfuttock");
```

This replaces five characters of text, starting from position 13, with the string "Gruntfuttock". If you now output text, it would display as follows:

```
Smith, where Gruntfuttock had had "had had" had had "had".
```

A more realistic application for this is to search for the substring to be replaced first, for example:

```
string separators = " ,.\"";                            // Word delimiters
size_t start = text.find("Jones");                      // Find the substring
size_t end = text.find_first_of(separators, start + 1); // Find the end
text.replace(start, end - start, "Gruntfuttock");
```

Here, you're finding the position of the first letter of "Jones" in text and storing the index value in start. You find the character following the last character of "Jones" by searching for one of the delimiters in separators with the find_first_of() function. You then use these index positions in the replace() operation.

The replacement string can be a string object or a null-terminated string. In the former case, you can specify a start index and a length to select a substring from the string object to use as the replacement string. For example, the previous replace operation could have been this:

```
string name = "Amos Gruntfuttock";
text.replace(start, end - start, name, 5, 12);
```

These two statements have the same effect as the previous use of replace(), because the replacement string starts at position 5 of name (which is the 'G') and contains 12 characters.

If the first argument is a null-terminated string, you can specify a number of characters to be selected from it to be the replacement string, for example:

```
text.replace(start, end - start, "Gruntfuttock, Amos", 12);
```

This time, the string to be substituted consists of the first 12 characters of "Gruntfuttock, Amos", so the effect is again exactly the same as the previous replace operation.

A further possibility, rather like the insert() function, is to specify the replacement string as consisting of a given character repeated a given number of times. For example, you could replace "Jones" by three asterisks with this statement:

```
text.replace(start, end - start, 3, '*');
```

This statement assumes that start and end are determined as before, and the result of it is that text will contain the following:

```
Smith, where *** had had "had had" had had "had".
```

Let's try the replace operation in an example.

··

Try It Out: Replacing Substrings

Here's a program that will replace a given word in a string with another word:

```cpp
// Program 6.11 Replacing words in a string
#include <iostream>
#include <string>
using std::cout;
using std::cin;
using std::endl;
using std::string;

int main() {
  // Read the string from the keyboard
  string text;
  cout << "Enter a string terminated by #:" << endl;
  std::getline(cin, text, '#');

  // Get the word to be replaced
  string word;
  cout << endl << "Enter the word to be replaced: ";
  cin >> word;
```

(Continued)

```
    // Get the replacement
    string replacement;
    cout << endl << "Enter the replacement word: ";
    cin >> replacement;

    if(word == replacement) {
      cout << endl
           << "The word and its replacement are the same." << endl
           << "Operation aborted." << cout;
      exit(1);
    }

    // Find the start of the first occurrence of word
    size_t start = text.find(word);

    // Now find and replace all occurrences of word
    while(start != string::npos) {
      text.replace(start, word.length(), replacement);          // Replace word
      start = text.find(word, start + replacement.length());
    }

    cout << endl
         << "Your string is now:" << endl
         << text << endl;

    return 0;
}
```

Here's a sample of output from this program:

```
Enter a string terminated by #:
A rose is a rose
is a rose.#

Enter the word to be replaced: rose

Enter the replacement word: dandelion

Your string is now:
A dandelion is a dandelion
is a dandelion.
```

HOW IT WORKS

You declare an object called text, of type string, that you'll use to hold a string in which you'll replace every instance of a given word. After prompting for the input, you read the string from the keyboard with this statement:

```
std::getline(cin, text, '#');
```

You've seen this function before. It reads from the stream specified by the first argument into the string object specified by the second argument. The third argument defines the character that signifies the end of the string. Specifying '#' as the string terminator allows multiple lines of text to be entered, so in this case all the newline characters that precede the terminating '#' will be stored in the string.

After prompting for the word to be replaced, you read it into the string object, word:

```
cin >> word;
```

This time, the first whitespace character will terminate the input, so you'll just store a single word. The word to be substituted is read into the replacement object in the same way.

The subsequent if statement just deals with the situation in which the word to be replaced and its replacement are the same:

```
if(word == replacement) {
  cout << endl
       << "The word and its replacement are the same." << endl
       << "Operation aborted." << cout;
  exit(1);
}
```

You could handle this in any way you wanted—you could even choose not to check, and just go through the motions of replacing identical words—but I chose to abort the program, just to remind the user who's in charge! It should also remind you that the comparison operators work with string objects.

Now you're ready to make the substitutions. First, you find the index position of the first occurrence of word with the following statement:

```
size_t start = text.find(word);
```

(Continued)

You declare start to be of type size_t because find() returns a value of that type. Just to remind you, this is a synonym for an integer type, usually unsigned int. If word doesn't happen to be in text, then start will contain the value string::npos. This will be dealt with in the while loop that does the replacing:

```
while(start != string::npos) {
    text.replace(start, word.length(), replacement);      // Replace word
    start = text.find(word, start + replacement.length());
}
```

If start contains string::npos at the outset, then the loop will terminate immediately. Assuming word *does* exist in text, the replace() function will be executed. Starting at the index position given by start, it replaces word.length() characters by the string replacement. Because replacement may well be a different length from word, you must take care in defining where to begin looking for the next occurrence of word. In the call to the find() function that does this, you specify the starting index position by adding the length of replacement to start. The loop will continue until word is no longer found in text.

Lastly, this statement displays the updated string:

```
cout << endl
     << "Your string is now:" << endl
     << text << endl;
```

Removing Characters from a String

You could remove a substring from a string object by using the replace() function. All you need to do is specify the replacement string as an empty string. However, there's also a specific function for this purpose: erase(). You can specify the substring to be erased by its starting index position and length. For example, to erase the first six characters from text, you could write this:

```
text.erase(0, 6);                        // Remove the first 6 characters
```

Again, you'll usually use this function to remove a specific substring that you had previously searched for. A more typical example of the usage of erase() might be as follows:

```
string word = "rose";
size_t index = text.find(word);
if(index != string::npos)
    text.erase(index, word.length());
```

Here, you attempt to find the position of word in text, and after confirming that it does indeed exist, you remove it using the erase() function. The number of characters in the substring to be removed is obtained by calling the length() function for word.

When you want to remove all the characters from a string, you can use the `clear()` function, for example:

```
text.clear();
```

This statement removes all the characters from the string, `text`, so it will then be an empty string.

Arrays of Type `string`

You used an array of `strings` in one of the earlier examples, but they bear a closer examination. You can have arrays of objects of type `string` in the same way that you can have arrays of any other type. For example, you can create an array of type `string` with this statement:

```
string words[] = {"this", "that", "the other"};
```

The array `words` will have three elements, as determined from the three initializing string literals that appear between the braces.

Of course, you could also have explicitly specified the array dimension, as in this statement:

```
string words[10] = {"this", "that", "the other"};
```

Now you have an array of ten elements of type `string`, where the first three are initialized with the string literals between the braces, and the remaining seven are empty strings.

There's no problem referencing individual characters in a `string` array element. In the `words` array, you can change the seventh character of the third element to `'t'` with this statement:

```
words[2][6] = 't';
```

You can now display this particular string with the following statement:

```
cout << words[2];
```

After the change, the string will display as follows:

```
the otter
```

Using an array of type `string` is very much like using any other kind of array. All the operations on a `string` array element are exactly the same as I've discussed for single `string` variables.

Wide-Character Strings

If you need your strings to contain characters of type wchar_t instead of characters of type char, you use the wstring type that is defined in the <string> header. You use objects of type wstring in essentially the same way as objects of type string. You could declare a wide string object with this statement:

```
wstring quote;
```

This assumes you have a using declaration for std::wstring in the file.

You write string literals that consist of characters of wchar_t between double quotes but with a prefix of L to distinguish them from string literals containing characters of type char. Thus you can declare and initialize a wstring variable like this:

```
wstring saying =
        L"The tigers of wrath are wiser than the horses of instruction.";
```

Note how you must use the L preceding the wide string literal consisting of characters of type wchar_t. Without it, you would have a char string literal and this statement wouldn't compile.

Of course, to output wide strings you must use the wcout stream, for example:

```
std::wcout << saying;
```

All the functions I've discussed in the context of string objects apply equally well for wstring objects, so I won't wade through them all again. You just must remember to use character variables of type wchar_t in operations with wstring objects and define the character and string literals that you need with the prefix L.

Summary

In this chapter, you saw how to create arrays of values, and you explored the special properties of arrays of type char, but you haven't finished with arrays yet. You'll see more on arrays, especially in the next chapter in which you'll explore the relationship between pointers and arrays.

In this chapter you also saw how you can use the string type that's defined in the standard library. In general, the string type is easier to use for string handling applications than arrays of type char, so it should be your first choice when you need to process character strings.

The important points this chapter discussed are as follows:

- An array is a named collection of values of the same type. It's stored contiguously in memory, whereas an individual value is accessed by means of one or more index values.

- A one-dimensional array requires one index value to reference its elements, a two-dimensional array requires two index values, and an *n*-dimensional array requires *n* index values.

- You can use elements of an array on the left of an assignment and in expressions in the same way that you can an ordinary variable of the same type.

- You can use a one-dimensional array of type char to store a null-terminated character string.

- You can allow the compiler to determine the size of the leftmost dimension of an array from the number of initializing values in the declaration statement.

- You can use a two-dimensional array of type char as a one-dimensional array of null-terminated character strings.

- The type string stores a character string without a termination character because a string object keeps track of the length of the string.

- Individual characters in a string object can be accessed and modified by using an index value between square brackets after the string variable name. Index values start at 0.

- You can concatenate a string object with a string literal, a character, or another string object using the + operator.

- Objects of type string have functions to search, modify, and extract substrings from them.

- Positions in a string are stored as integer values of type size_t.

- You can declare arrays of type string in the same way that you declare arrays of any other type.

- Objects of type wstring contain strings of characters of type wchar_t.

Exercises

The following exercises enable you to try out what you've learned in this chapter. If you get stuck, look back over the chapter for help. If you're still stuck after that, you can download the solutions from the Apress website (http://www.apress.com/book/download.html), but that really should be a last resort.

Exercise 6-1. Create an array to store the first names of up to 100 students. Create another array that stores the grade (0 to 100) of each student. Use a loop to prompt the user to enter names and grades into these arrays. Calculate the average grade, display it, and then display the names and grades of all the students in a table.

Exercise 6-2. A meteorologist friend of yours has to take three readings of air humidity per day (morning, midday, and evening), Monday to Friday. Write a program that allows the user to enter these readings, in chronological order, into a 5x3 array of values of type float. It should then calculate and output the average humidity for each day and the weekly average for each of the three times of day.

Exercise 6-3. Extend Program 6.9 so that the search for the substring "had" finds all instances of the word "had," regardless of case. (Hint: Make a copy of the original string.)

Exercise 6-4. Write a program that will read a text string of arbitrary length from the keyboard and then prompt for entry of a word that is to be found in the string. The program should find and replace all occurrences of this word that appear in the string, regardless of case, by as many asterisks as there are characters in the word. It should then output the new string. Note that only whole words are to be replaced. For example, if the user enters the string "Our house is at your disposal." and the word that is to be found is "our," then the resultant string should be: "*** house is at your disposal." and not "*** house is at y*** disposal."

Exercise 6-5. Write a program that prompts for input of two words and then tests them to determine whether one is an anagram of the other.

CHAPTER 7

Pointers

IT'S TIME FOR US to begin looking at **pointers**, which are a vital element of C++ programming. Pointers are important because they form the foundation that enables you to allocate and use memory *dynamically*. Pointers can also make your programs more effective and efficient in many other ways.

In this chapter you'll learn

- What a pointer is and how you declare one

- How to obtain the address of a variable

- How pointers relate to arrays

- How arithmetic with pointers works and what it's used for

- What standard library functions are available for processing null-terminated strings

- How to create memory for new variables while your program is executing

- How to release memory that you've allocated dynamically

- How you can convert from one type of pointer to another

What Is a Pointer?

Every variable and literal in your program has an **address** in memory—this is the location in the memory of your computer where the data is stored. Similarly, in order to execute, the functions your program uses must be located somewhere in memory; so a function has an address, too. These addresses will depend on where your program is loaded into memory when you run it, and they can therefore vary from one execution to the next.

A **pointer** is a variable that you can use to store a memory address. The address stored in a pointer usually corresponds to the position in memory where a variable is located, but it can also be the address of a function, as you'll see in the next chapter.

You can see from Figure 7-1 how a pointer gets its name: it "points to" the location in memory where something (a variable or a function) is stored. However, it's no use if your pointer just stores a memory address. In order to make use of whatever is stored at that particular address, you need to know exactly *what* it is, not just *where* it is. As you know, an integer has a very different representation from a floating-point value, and the number of bytes occupied by an item of data depends on what the data is. Thus, to use a data item stored at the address contained in a pointer, you also need to know the type of the data.

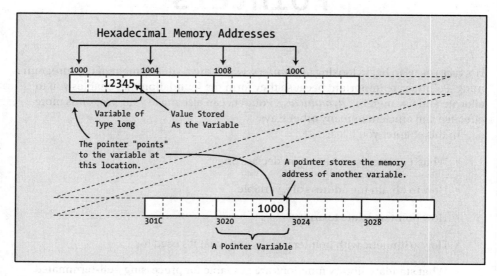

Figure 7-1. What a pointer is

As a consequence of this simple logic, a pointer isn't just "a pointer"; it's a pointer *to a particular type of data item*. This will become clearer when we get down to specifics, so let's look at how to declare a pointer.

Declaring a Pointer

The declaration of a pointer is similar to that of an ordinary variable, except that the type name has an asterisk following it to indicate that you're declaring a variable that's a pointer to that type. For example, to declare a pointer called pnumber that will "point to" values of type long, you could use the following statement:

```
long* pnumber;
```

This declares a pointer variable, pnumber, which can store the address of a variable of type long. The type of this variable is "pointer to long," and when the type is written alone (in a cast operation, for instance), it's usually written as long*.

The preceding declaration was written with the asterisk to the type name, but this isn't the only way of writing it. You can also write the declaration of a pointer with the asterisk adjacent to the variable name, as in this statement:

```
long *pnumber;
```

This declares precisely the same variable as before. The compiler will accept either notation, but the former is perhaps the more common, because it expresses the type, "pointer to long," more clearly. However, there's opportunity for confusion when you mix declarations of ordinary variables and pointers in the same statement. Try to guess what this statement does:

```
long* pnumber, number;
```

In fact, it declares a variable pnumber of type "pointer to long" and a variable number that's just of type long, although the notation that juxtaposes the asterisk and the type name makes this less than clear.

If you declared the same two variables in the alternative form:

```
long *pnumber, number;
```

this is rather less confusing, as the asterisk is now clearly associated with the variable pnumber.

However, the real solution to this difficulty is simply to avoid the problem in the first place. It's always better to declare all your variables on separate lines, as this will avoid any possibility of confusion:

```
long number;          // Declaration of long variable
long* pnumber;        // Declaration of variable of type 'pointer to long'
```

This has the added advantage that you can easily append comments to the declarations to explain their uses when necessary.

In this example, pnumber was the pointer variable name. It isn't obligatory, but it's a common convention in C++ to use variable names beginning with p to denote pointers. This makes it easier to see which variables in a program are pointers, which in turn can make your source code easier to follow.

Pointers to types other than long are declared in exactly the same way. To illustrate this, you can declare variables that are pointers to double and string with the following statements:

```
double* pvalue;       // Pointer to a double value
string* psentence;    // Pointer to a string value
```

Using Pointers

To use a pointer, you just need to store the address of another variable of the appropriate type in it, so let's see how you obtain the address of a variable in the first place.

The Address-Of Operator

The **address-of** operator, &, is a unary operator that obtains the address in memory where a variable is stored. You could declare a variable, number, and a pointer, pnumber, with these statements:

```
long number = 12345L;
long* pnumber;
```

Because the types of the variable number and the pointer pnumber are compatible, you can write the following assignment:

```
pnumber = &number;          // Store address of number in pnumber
```

The result of this statement is that pnumber now contains the address of number. The effect of this operation is illustrated in Figure 7-2.

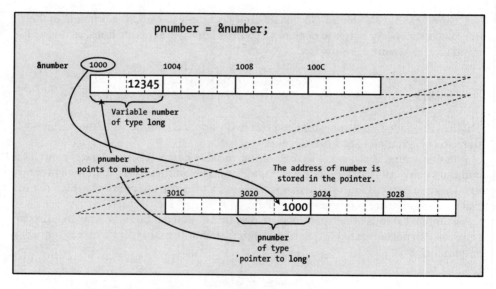

Figure 7-2. Storing an address in a pointer

You can use the & operator to obtain the address of any type of variable, but you have to store the address in a pointer of the appropriate type. If you want to store the address of a double variable, for example, the pointer must have been declared as type double*, which is "pointer to double." If you try to store an address in a pointer of the wrong type, then your program won't compile.

Taking the address of a variable and storing it in a pointer is all very well, but the really interesting aspect is how you can use it. Accessing the data in the memory location to which the pointer points is fundamental to using a pointer, and you do this using the indirection operator.

The Indirection Operator

The **indirection operator**, *, is used with a pointer variable to access the contents of the memory location pointed to. The name "indirection operator" stems from the fact that the data is accessed "indirectly." The same operator is sometimes also called the **dereference operator**, and the process of accessing the data in the memory location pointed to by a pointer is termed **dereferencing** the pointer.

To access the data at the address pointed to by the pointer, pnumber, you use the expression *pnumber. Let's see how this works in practice.

Try It Out: Using the Indirection Operator

This example demonstrates using the indirection operator, *, to display the value of the variable a pointer points to:

```
// Program 7.1 The indirection operator in action
#include <iostream>
using std::cout;
using std::endl;

int main() {
  long number = 50L;
  long* pnumber;                     // Pointer declaration
  pnumber = &number;                 // Store the address of number
  cout << endl
       << "The value stored in the variable number is "
       << *pnumber
       << endl;
  return 0;
}
```

When you compile and run the program, it will produce this output:

```
The value stored in the variable number is 50
```

HOW IT WORKS

You first declare a regular variable of type long, which is initialized to 50:

```
long number = 50L;
```

Next, you declare a pointer variable:

```
long* pnumber;                       // Pointer declaration
```

(Continued)

Because its type is long*, this variable can store addresses of variables of type long. You store the address of number in pnumber with the following statement:

```
pnumber = &number;                              // Store the address of number
```

The address-of operator, &, produces the memory address of number, and this is stored as the value of pnumber. You can now display the value stored in number by dereferencing pnumber:

```
cout << endl
    << "The value stored in the variable number is "
    << *pnumber
    << endl;
```

The indirection operator applied to a pointer refers to the contents of the address stored in the pointer. Because pnumber contains the address of number, *pnumber refers to the value of number.

....

An aspect of the indirection operator that can seem confusing is the fact that you now have several different uses for the same symbol, *. It's the multiplication operator and the indirection operator, and it's also used in the declaration of a pointer. Each time you use *, the compiler is able to distinguish its meaning by the context. When you multiply two variables—price * quantity, for instance—there's no meaningful interpretation of this expression for anything other than a multiplication operation. You'll see an example of this contextual interpretation of * in the next program in this chapter, Program 7.2.

Why Use Pointers?

A question that usually springs to mind at this point is "Why use pointers at all?" After all, taking the address of a variable you already know about and sticking it in a pointer so that you can come along and dereference it later on seems like an overhead you can do without. Don't be too hasty—there are several reasons why pointers are important.

First of all, as you'll see shortly, you can use pointer notation to operate on data stored in an array, which often executes faster than if you use array notation. Second, when you get to define your own functions later in the book, you'll see that pointers are used extensively for enabling access within a function to large blocks of data, such as arrays, that are defined outside the function.

Third, and most important, you'll also see later that you can allocate space for new variables dynamically—that is, during program execution. This sort of capability allows your program to adjust its use of memory depending on the input. You can create new variables while your program is executing, as and when you need them. Because you don't know in advance how many variables you're going to create dynamically, the only way you can do it is by using pointers, so make sure you get the hang of this chapter!

To get more of a feel for how pointers work, let's try another very simple example that just exercises the mechanics of using a pointer.

Try It Out: Using Pointers

You can try out the various aspects of pointer operation you've seen up to now with the following example:

```cpp
// Program 7.2 Exercising pointers
#include <iostream>
using std::cout;
using std::endl;

int main() {
  long* pnumber;                      // Pointer declaration
  long number1 = 55L;
  long number2 = 99L;                 // A couple of variables

  pnumber = &number1;                 // Store address in pointer
  *pnumber += 11;                     // Increment number1 by 11
  cout << endl
      << "number1 = "       << number1
      << "    &number1 = " << pnumber
      << endl;

  pnumber = &number2;                 // Change pointer to address of number2
  number1 = *pnumber * 10;            // 10 times number2

  cout << "number1 = "       << number1
      << "    pnumber = "   << pnumber
      << "    *pnumber = "  << *pnumber
      << endl;

  return 0;
}
```

On my computer, this program produces the following output:

```
number1 = 66     &number1 = 0012FEC8
number1 = 990    pnumber = 0012FEBC    *pnumber = 99
```

It's likely that the values for the addresses displayed will be different on your machine.

(Continued)

There's no input to this example; all operations are carried out with the values set in the program. After storing the address of number1 in the pointer pnumber, the value of number1 is incremented indirectly, through the pointer, in this statement:

```
*pnumber += 11;                          // Increment number1 by 11
```

The indirection operator determines that you're adding 11 to the contents of the variable pointed to, which is number1. This demonstrates that you can use a dereferenced pointer on the left of an assignment operation. If you forgot the *, the program would attempt to change the address stored in the pointer. (I discuss pointer arithmetic in detail a little later on.)

This statement displays the value of number1 and the address of number1 stored in pnumber:

```
cout << endl
     << "number1 = "     << number1
     << "   &number1 = " << pnumber
     << endl;
```

For a pointer to a numeric type, sending the pointer name by itself (in this case, pnumber) to the output stream produces the address value. Because it's a pointer type, the stored value is displayed as a hexadecimal value. Memory addresses are generally represented in hexadecimal notation—and that's not just in C++. Because number is an ordinary integer variable, its value is displayed in decimal.

After the first line of output, the contents of pnumber are set to the address of number2 with the following statement:

```
pnumber = &number2;                      // Change pointer to address of number2
```

Now pnumber points to the variable number2. The address of number1, which was previously contained in pnumber, has been overwritten. You can now change the variable number1 to the value of 10 times number2 through the pointer pnumber:

```
number1 = *pnumber * 10;                 // 10 times number2
```

The expression on the right of the assignment accesses the value of number2 indirectly through the pointer and multiplies it by 10. The compiler knows how to interpret the occurrences of * in this line, because it considers the context of each one.

The next output statement displays the results of these calculations:

```
cout << "number1 = "     << number1
     << "   pnumber = "  << pnumber
     << "   *pnumber = " << *pnumber
     << endl;
```

This displays the value of number1, the address stored in pnumber, and the value stored at the address contained in pnumber. Again, the value of pnumber displays as hexadecimal because it's an address. The expression *pnumber resolves to an ordinary integer value—the value stored in number2—so this displays as decimal.

Initializing Pointers

If anything, using pointers that aren't initialized is even more hazardous than using ordinary variables and arrays that aren't initialized. With a pointer variable containing a junk value, you can overwrite random areas of memory. The resulting damage just depends on how unlucky you are, so it's more than just a good idea always to initialize your pointers.

It's very easy to initialize a pointer to the address of a variable that has already been defined. You can initialize the pointer pnumber with the address of the variable number simply by using the address-of operator with the variable name as the initial value for the pointer:

```
int number = 0;          // Initialized integer variable
int* pnumber = &number;  // Initialized pointer
```

When you're initializing a pointer with another variable like this, remember that the variable must already have been declared prior to the pointer declaration. If this isn't so, your compiler will complain.

Of course, you may not want to initialize a pointer with the address of a specific variable when you declare it. In this case, you can initialize it with the pointer equivalent of zero:

```
int* pnumber = 0;        // Pointer not pointing to anything
```

This declaration ensures that pnumber doesn't point to anything. Consequently, if you try to dereference it before it has had a proper value assigned, your program will fail in a manner that clearly indicates that fact. A pointer initialized in this way is called a **null pointer**. However, you *can* test the pointer to see whether it's null before you try to dereference it:

```
if(pnumber == 0)
  std::cout << std::endl << "pnumber is null." << std::endl;
else
  std::cout << std::endl << "Value is " << *pnumber << std::endl;
```

Remember to use the double equal sign == in the comparison.
You could equally well use the following equivalent statement:

```
if(!pnumber)
  std::cout << std::endl << "pnumber is null." << std::endl;
else
  std::cout << std::endl << "Value is " << *pnumber << std::endl;
```

Of course, you can also use this form:

```
if(pnumber != 0)
  std::cout << std::endl << "Value is " << *pnumber << std::endl;
```

The symbol NULL is defined in the standard library as 0, and you'll often see this used to initialize null pointers. However, NULL is really there only for compatibility with C, and it's good practice in C++ to use 0, as I've done here.

Initializing Pointers to Type char

A variable of type "pointer to char" has the interesting property that it can be initialized with a string literal. For example, you can declare and initialize such a pointer with this statement:

```
char* pproverb = "A miss is as good as a mile.";   // Don't do this!
```

This looks very similar to initializing a char array with a string literal, and indeed it is. The statement creates a null-terminated string literal (actually, an array of type const char) from the character string appearing between the quotes, and it stores the address of the first character of the string literal in the pointer pproverb. This is shown in Figure 7-3.

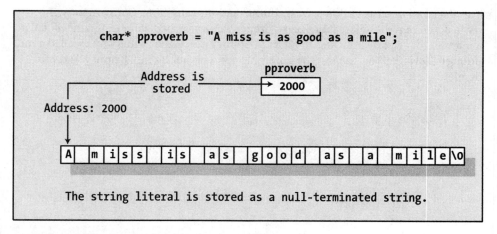

Figure 7-3. Initializing a pointer of type char*

Unfortunately, all is not quite as it seems. The type of the string literal is const, but the type of the pointer is not. The statement doesn't create a modifiable copy of the string literal; it merely stores the address of the first character. This means that if you write some code that attempts to modify the string, there will be trouble.

Look at this statement, which tries to change the first character of the string to 'X':

```
*pproverb = 'X';
```

The compiler won't complain, because it can see nothing wrong. The pointer, pproverb, wasn't declared as const, so the compiler is happy. However, when you try to *run* the program, you'll get an error, probably resulting in a program crash: the string literal in memory is still a constant, and you're not allowed to change it.

You might wonder, with good reason, why the compiler allowed you to assign a const value to a non-const type in the first place, when it causes these problems. The reason is that string literals only became constants with the release of the C++ standard, and there's a great deal of legacy code that relies on the "incorrect" assignment. Its use is deprecated, however, and the correct resolution of the problem is to declare the pointer like this:

```
const char* pproverb = "A miss is as good as a mile.";   ?? Do this instead!
```

This declares that pproverb points to variable that is const, in fact of type const char*, so the type is consistent with that of the string literal. There's plenty more to say about using const with pointers, so I'll come back to this subject later in this chapter. For now, let's see how using variables of type char* operates in another example.

....

Try It Out: Lucky Stars with Pointers

You could write a new version of our "lucky stars" example (Program 6.5) that uses pointers instead of an array, to see how that would work:

```
// Program 7.3 Initializing pointers with strings
#include <iostream>
using std::cout;
using std::cin;
using std::endl;

int main() {
  // The lucky stars referenced through pointers
  const char* pstar1 = "Mae West";
  const char* pstar2 = "Arnold Schwarzenegger";
  const char* pstar3 = "Lassie";
  const char* pstar4 = "Slim Pickens";
  const char* pstar5 = "Greta Garbo";
  const char* pstar6 = "Oliver Hardy";
  const char* pstr   = "Your lucky star is ";
```

(Continued)

```
    int choice = 0;                    // Star selector

cout << endl
    << "Pick a lucky star!"
    << " Enter a number between 1 and 6: ";
cin >> choice;

cout << endl;

switch(choice) {
  case 1:
    cout << pstr << pstar1;
    break;
  case 2:
    cout << pstr << pstar2;
    break;
  case 3:
    cout << pstr << pstar3;
    break;
  case 4:
    cout << pstr << pstar4;
    break;
  case 5:
    cout << pstr << pstar5;
    break;
  case 6:
    cout << pstr << pstar6;
    break;
  default:
    cout << "Sorry, you haven't got a lucky star.";
}
cout << endl;
return 0;
}
```

An example of output from this program is as follows:

```
Pick a lucky star! Enter a number between 1 and 6: 5

Your lucky star is Greta Garbo
```

HOW IT WORKS

The array of your original example has been replaced by six pointers, pstar1 to pstar6, each initialized with a name. You've also declared an additional pointer, pstr, initialized with the phrase that you want to use at the start of a normal output line. Because all these pointers are used to point to string literals, you've declared them as const.

Because you have discrete pointers, it's easier to use a switch statement to select the appropriate output message than the if statement that was employed in the original version. Any incorrect values that are entered are all taken care of by the default option of the switch.

Outputting the string pointed to by a pointer couldn't be easier. As you can see, you simply write the pointer name. Now, you may have noticed that the standard output stream cout treats pointer names differently, depending on what type the pointer points to. In Program 7.2, this code

```
cout << pnumber;
```

would have output the address contained in the pointer pnumber. In this example, on the other hand, the code

```
cout << pstar1;
```

outputs a string literal, not an address. The difference lies in the fact that pnumber is a pointer to a numeric type, whereas pstar1 is a "pointer to char." The output stream, cout, treats a variable that's a "pointer to char" as a null-terminated string and displays it as such.

Arrays of Pointers

So, what have you gained? Well, using pointers has eliminated the waste of memory that occurred with the array version of this program, because each string now occupies just the number of bytes necessary to accommodate it. However, the program does seem a little long-winded now. If you were thinking "There must be a better way," then you'd be right—you could use an array of pointers.

Try It Out: Using an Array of Pointers

With an array of pointers to type char, each element can point to an independent string, and the length of each of the strings can be different. You can declare an array of pointers in the same way that you declare any other array. Here's an alternative version of the previous example that uses a pointer array:

```cpp
// Program 7.4 Using an array of pointers to char
#include <iostream>
using std::cout;
using std::cin;
using std::endl;

int main() {
  const char* pstars[] = {                               // Initializing a pointer array
                     "Mae West", "Arnold Schwarzenegger", "Lassie",
                     "Slim Pickens", "Greta Garbo", "Oliver Hardy"
                  };
  const char* pstr = "Your lucky star is ";
  int choice = 0;

  const int starCount = sizeof pstars/sizeof pstars[0];   // Get array size

  cout << endl
       << "Pick a lucky star!"
       << " Enter a number between 1 and "
       << starCount
       << ": ";
  cin >> choice;

  cout << endl;
  if(choice >= 1 && choice <= starCount)                  // Check for valid input
    cout << pstr << pstars[choice - 1];                   // Output star name
  else
    cout << "Sorry, you haven't got a lucky star.";       // Invalid input

  cout << endl;
  return 0;
}
```

HOW IT WORKS

In this case, you're nearly getting the best of all possible worlds. You have a one-dimensional array of char pointers declared such that the compiler works out what the array size should be from the number of initializing strings:

```cpp
  const char* pstars[] = {                          // Initializing a pointer array
                     "Mae West", "Arnold Schwarzenegger", "Lassie",
                     "Slim Pickens", "Greta Garbo", "Oliver Hardy"
                  };
```

The memory usage that results from this statement is illustrated in Figure 7-4.

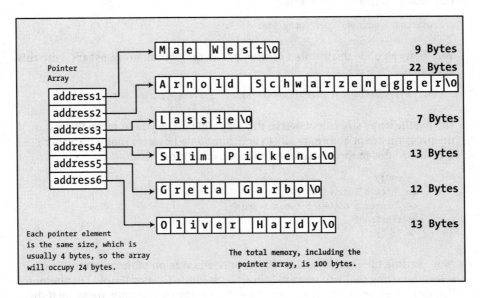

Figure 7-4. An array of pointers

As you can see, in addition to the memory required for each null-terminated string, memory is also occupied by the elements in the array, each of which is a pointer. That's a total of 100 bytes. Compared to using an array of type char, using the pointer array here requires less memory in total. With the old static array, each row must have at least the length of the longest string; six rows of 22 bytes each is 132 bytes, so by using a pointer array you've saved 32 bytes. Of course, the exact savings is dependent on how many strings you have and the diversity in their lengths. Sometimes there won't be any saving at all, but generally the pointer array is the more efficient choice.

Saving space isn't the only advantage that you get by using pointers. In many circumstances, you can save time too. For example, think of what happens if you want to swap "Greta Garbo" in fifth position with "Mae West" at the beginning. This is typical of the sort of operation you'd need to sort the strings into alphabetical order. With the previous pointer array, you just need to swap the pointers around—the strings themselves can stay right where they are.

If the strings were stored in an array of type char, then a great deal of copying would be necessary. You would need to copy the whole string "Greta Garbo" to a temporary location while you copied "Mae West" in its place, and then you would need to copy "Greta Garbo" to its new position, which would require significantly more time for the computer to execute. This logic applies equally to using objects of type string.

(Continued)

Getting back to the example, you store the address of the basic message for a star selection in another pointer:

```
const char* pstr = "Your lucky star is ";
```

You then calculate the number of elements in the pointer array, pstars, with this statement:

```
const int starCount = sizeof pstars/sizeof pstars[0];    // Get array size
```

Having the array size calculated in this way will enable you to make the rest of the program adapt automatically to accommodate however many stars there are. You do this in the prompt for the input value for choice:

```
cout << endl
     << "Pick a lucky star!"
     << " Enter a number between 1 and "
     << starCount
     << ": ";
```

After reading the choice value as in the previous version of the program, you select the string that you want to output by means of a very simple if statement. You display either a selection from the pstars array or a suitable message if the user enters an invalid value. The if condition uses the starCount variable as the upper limit for choice, so again, any number of star choices will be accommodated automatically. If you want more choices in the program, you can just add them to the list of initializing strings.

Sorting Strings Using Pointers

As I suggested in my discussion of the previous example, you can sort strings without having to move the strings around, if you use pointers to refer to them.

You could produce a new version of Program 6.10, in which you extract words from a text string. This will give you some useful experience in applying string objects and using arrays of pointers to string objects. At the same time, you'll get some practical experience of sorting using pointers.

Try It Out: Sorting Strings Using Pointers

You'll read a string of words from the keyboard and sort them into a well-defined order. Here's the code:

```
// Program 7.5 Sorting strings using pointers
#include <iostream>
#include <string>
using std::cout;
using std::cin;
```

```cpp
using std::endl;
using std::string;

int main() {
  string text;                                // The string to be sorted
  const string separators = " ,.\"\n";        // Word delimiters
  const int max_words = 1000;                 // Maximum number of words
  string words[max_words];                    // Array to store the words
  string* pwords[max_words];                  // Array of pointers to the words

  // Read the string to be searched from the keyboard
  cout << endl << "Enter a string terminated by #:" << endl;
  getline(cin, text, '#');

  // Extract all the words from the text
  int start = text.find_first_not_of(separators);  // Word start index
  int end = 0;                                      // End delimiter index
  int word_count = 0;                              // Count of words stored
  while(start != string::npos && word_count < max_words) {
    end = text.find_first_of(separators, start + 1);
    if(end == string::npos)                        // Found a separator?
      end = text.length();                         // No, so set to last + 1

    words[word_count] = text.substr(start, end - start); // Store the word
    pwords[word_count] = &words[word_count];       // Store the pointer
    word_count++;                                  // Increment count

    // Find the first character of the next word
    start = text.find_first_not_of(separators, end + 1);
  }

  // Sort the words in ascending sequence by direct insertion
  int lowest = 0;                                  // Index of lowest word
  for(int j = 0; j < word_count - 1; j++) {
    lowest = j;                                    // Set lowest

    // Check current against all the following words
    for(int i = j + 1 ; i < word_count ; i++)
      if(*pwords[i] < *pwords[lowest])             // Current is lower?
        lowest = i;

    if(lowest != j) {          // Then swap pointers...
      string* ptemp = pwords[j];                   // Save current
      pwords[j] = pwords[lowest];                  // Store lower in current
      pwords[lowest] = ptemp;                      // Restore current
    }
  }

  // Output the words in ascending sequence
  for(int i = 0 ; i < word_count ; i++)
    cout << endl << *pwords[i];

  cout << endl;
  return 0;
}
```

(Continued)

Here's an example of the output that this program can produce:

```
Enter a string terminated by #:
In this world nothing can be said to be certain, except death and taxes.#

In
and
be
be
can
certain
death
except
nothing
said
taxes
this
to
world
```

HOW IT WORKS

The text string containing the words to be sorted will be read into the variable declared as

```
string text;                                    // The string to be sorted
```

The constant separators contains all the characters that act as word delimiters; these are space, comma, period, double quote, and newline.

```
const string separators = " ,.\"\n";            // Word delimiters
```

You could add tab to this list if necessary. Alternatively, you could construct the string containing the separators by searching text for all the characters that are not letters, digits, or single quotes.

You'll store the words you extract from text in an array that will have a capacity for up to 1,000 words:

```
const int max_words = 1000;                     // Maximum number of words
string words[max_words];                        // Array to store the words
string* pwords[max_words];                      // Array of pointers to the words
```

The words array will store the words, whereas the array of pointers, pwords, will store the addresses of each of the elements in words. This is a little cumbersome, but you need the pointers if you want to avoid repeatedly copying the string objects when you're sorting them. You also have to allocate space for max_words string objects and pointers, even though you won't generally need them all. Later in this chapter you'll see a much better way to do this, using **dynamic memory allocation**.

You read multiple lines of text into text in the manner you've seen previously; input is terminated by entering #, so you can enter as many lines as you want:

```
cout << endl << "Enter a string terminated by #:" << endl;
getline(cin, text, '#');
```

Extracting individual words from text and storing them in the words array is done in the while loop:

```
// Extract all the words from the text
int start = text.find_first_not_of(separators);      // Word start index
int end = 0;                                          // End delimiter index
int word_count = 0;                                  // Count of words stored
while(start != string::npos && word_count < max_words) {
  end = text.find_first_of(separators, start + 1);
  if(end == string::npos)                            // Found a separator?
    end = text.length();                             // No, so set to last + 1

  words[word_count] = text.substr(start, end - start); // Store the word
  pwords[word_count] = &words[word_count];           // Store the pointer
  word_count++;                                       // Increment count

  // Find the first character of the next word
  start = text.find_first_not_of(separators, end + 1);
}
```

This also uses the approach you saw the last time that you did something of this kind. You find the index position of the first letter of a word and save it in start. You find the first separator following the word and store its index position in end. You then use the substr() function to extract the word as a string object, which you store in the next available element of the words array. You also store the *address* of that element of words in the corresponding element of the pwords array. The loop condition ensures that you stop searching for words if you reach the end of text or you fill the words array.

In preparation for the sort operation, you declare a variable called lowest to record the index position of the "lowest" word found during the sort:

```
int lowest = 0;                                       // Index of lowest word
```

The sorting of the words is done in the nested for loop:

```
for(int j = 0; j < word_count - 1; j++) {
  lowest = j;                                          // Set lowest

  // Check current against all the following words
  for(int i = j + 1 ; i < word_count ; i++)
    if(*pwords[i] < *pwords[lowest])                  // Current is lower?
      lowest = i;
```

(Continued)

```
   if(lowest != j) {            // Then swap pointers...
     string* ptemp = pwords[j];              // Save current
     pwords[j] = pwords[lowest];             // Store lower in current
     pwords[lowest] = ptemp;                 // Restore current
   }
 }
```

The operation rearranges the pointers in the pwords array so that they point to the words stored in the words array in ascending order. The process is very simple. The outer loop steps through the pwords array from the first element to the last. In the inner loop, you compare the word that each pointer points to with all the words pointed to by the following pointers to find the index position of the "lowest." If you find that the lowest pointer isn't the one you're considering, you swap the pointers, using ptemp as a temporary store. This process is repeated for each element in the pwords array.

By this method, the first element will contain the pointer to "lowest" word of all. The second element will point to the lowest bar the first, and so on for all the pointers that you've stored in the array. Note that in the output, "In" comes before "and" because my machine uses ASCII, in which the character code for 'I' is lower than that for 'a'.

Finally, you output the words in ascending order in the for loop:

```
for(int i = 0 ; i < word_count ; i++)
  cout << endl << *pwords[i];
```

The elements of the pwords array point to the words in ascending order. To output them in order, you just display the dereferenced pointers of the array.

TIDYING THE OUTPUT

Outputting one word to a line is fine for a short piece of text, but with a lot of text it's rather inconvenient. It would be nice to have all the words that begin with the same letter output as a group. If you're ready for a slightly more complicated output mechanism, you can replace the previous for loop with the following code:

```
// Output up to six words to a line in groups starting with the same letter
char ch = (*pwords[0])[0];               // First letter of first word
int words_in_line = 0;                   // Words in a line count
for(int i = 0; i < word_count ; i++) {
  if(ch != (*pwords[i])[0])              // New first letter?
  {
    cout << endl;                        // Start a new line
    ch = (*pwords[i])[0];                // Save the new first letter
    words_in_line = 0;                   // Reset words in line count
  }
  cout << *pwords[i] << "   ";
```

```
    if(++words_in_line == 6) {                  // Every sixth word
      cout << endl;                             // Start a new line
      words_in_line = 0;
    }
  }
}
```

This will again output all the words in ascending order, but this time words that begin with the same letter will be grouped together. Each group will start on a new line, with up to six words to a line.

The first letter for a group is stored in the variable ch. Notice how you refer to the first character of the first string object. The expression *pwords[0] dereferences the pointer in the first element of the pwords array to give the word that it points to. The expression (*pwords[0])[0] then gives the first letter of the word, because the additional set of square brackets outside the parentheses encloses the index of the letter in the word. The precedence of square brackets is higher than that of the indirection operator, *, so the parentheses are necessary here. The variable words_in_line keeps track of the number of words on the current line; when it reaches 6, you output a newline character. Of course, whenever the first letter of a word to be displayed is different from the character in ch, you're starting a new group, so you also output a newline in this instance as well as reset words_in_line to 0.

Constant Pointers and Pointers to Constants

When you were dealing with pointers to type char earlier in this chapter, you saw that using pointers to constants for handling string literals is the technique enforced by the C++ standard. In the "lucky stars" program, for example, you made sure that the compiler would pick up any attempts to modify the strings pointed to by elements of the pstars array by declaring the array using const:

```
const char* pstars[] = {
                        "Mae West", "Arnold Schwarzenegger", "Lassie",
                        "Slim Pickens", "Greta Garbo", "Oliver Hardy"
                       };
```

Here you're declaring the objects pointed to by elements of the pointer array as constant. The compiler inhibits any direct attempt to change these, so an assignment statement such as this one would be flagged as an error by the compiler, thus preventing a nasty problem at runtime:

```
*pstars[0] = 'X';
```

However, you could still legally write the next statement, which would copy the *address* stored in the element on the right of the assignment operator to the element on the left:

```
pstars[0] = pstars[5];
```

Now, those lucky individuals due to be awarded Ms. West would get Mr. Hardy instead, because both pointers now point to the same name. Note that this *hasn't* changed the values of the objects pointed to by the pointer array element—it has only changed the address stored in pstars[0], so your const specification hasn't been disobeyed.

You really ought to be able to inhibit this kind of change as well, because some people may reckon that good old Ollie may not have quite the same sex appeal as Mae West, and of course you can. Have a look at the following statement:

```
const char* const pstars[] = {
                      "Mae West", "Arnold Schwarzenegger", "Lassie",
                      "Slim Pickens", "Greta Garbo", "Oliver Hardy"
                   };
```

The extra const declares a **constant pointer**, and now the pointers *and* the strings they point to are being declared as constant. Nothing about this array can be changed.

To summarize, you can distinguish three situations arising from using const with pointers and the things to which they point:

- A **pointer to a constant.** Here, you can't modify what's pointed to, but you can set the pointer to point to something else:

  const char* pstring = "Some text that cannot be changed";

  Of course, this also applies to pointers to other types, for example:

  const int value = 20;
  const int* pvalue = &value;

  value is a constant and can't be changed. pvalue is a pointer to a constant, so you can use it to store the address of value. You couldn't store the address of value in a non-const pointer (because that would imply that you can modify a constant through a pointer), but you *could* assign the address of a non-const variable to pvalue. In the latter case, you would be making it illegal to modify the variable through the pointer.

  In general, it's always possible to strengthen const-ness in this fashion, but weakening it isn't permitted.

- **A constant pointer.** Here, the address stored in the pointer can't be changed, so a pointer like this can only ever point to the address it's initialized with. However, the *contents* of that address aren't constant and can be changed.

  You could take a numeric example to illustrate a constant pointer. Suppose you declare an integer variable value and a constant pointer pvalue as follows:

  ```
  int value = 20;
  int* const pvalue = &value;
  ```

  This declares that the pointer pvalue is const, so it can only ever point to value. Any attempt to make it point to another int variable will result in an error message from the compiler. The contents of value aren't const, though, and you can change them whenever you want. Again, if value was declared as const, you couldn't initialize pvalue with &value. The pointer pvalue can only point to a non-const variable of type int.

- **A constant pointer to a constant.** Here, both the address stored in the pointer and the thing pointed to have been declared as constant, so neither can be changed.

  Taking a numerical example, you can declare value as follows:

  ```
  const int value = 20;
  ```

  value is now a constant: you can't change it. You can still initialize a pointer with the address of value, though:

  ```
  const int* const pvalue = &value;
  ```

  pvalue is a constant pointer to a constant. You can't change what pvalue points to, and you can't change the value at the address it contains.

 NOTE *Naturally, this behavior isn't confined to the pointer to types* char *and* int *you've been dealing with so far. This discussion applies to pointers of any type.*

Pointers and Arrays

There is a close connection between pointers and array names. Indeed, there are many situations in which you can use an array name as though it were a pointer. Looking back at Chapter 6 and applying what you now know, you can see that an array name by itself can behave like a pointer when it's used in an output statement. If you try to output an array by just using its name (and as long as it isn't an array of type char), what you'll get is the hexadecimal address of the array in memory. Because an array name behaves like a pointer in this way, you can use one to initialize a pointer, for example:

```
double values[10];
double* pvalue = values;
```

This will store the address of the array values in the pointer pvalue so the array name actually stores an address.

Having noted the similarity between an array name and a pointer, I should emphasize that they're quite different entities, and you should remain conscious of this. The most significant difference between a pointer and an array name is that you can modify the address stored in a pointer, whereas the address that an array name refers to is fixed.

Pointer Arithmetic

You can perform operations on a pointer to alter the address it contains. In terms of arithmetic operators, you're limited to addition and subtraction, but you can also compare pointers to produce a logical result.

As far as addition goes, you can add an integer value (or an expression that evaluates to an integer) to a pointer. The result of the addition is an address. You can subtract an integer from a pointer, and that also results in an address. Finally, you can take the difference between two pointers, and in this case the result is an integer, not an address. No other arithmetic operations on pointers are legal.

Arithmetic with pointers works in a special way. Suppose you add 1 to a pointer with a statement such as this:

```
pvalue++;
```

This increments the pointer by 1. Exactly *how* you increment a pointer by 1 doesn't matter. You could use an assignment or the += operator if you wanted, so the effect would be just the same with this statement:

```
pvalue += 1;
```

The interesting point here is that the address stored in the pointer won't be incremented by 1 in the normal arithmetic sense. Pointer arithmetic implicitly assumes that the pointer points to an array and that the arithmetic operation is on the address contained in the pointer, which will correspond to one of the elements in the array.

Incrementing a pointer by 1 means incrementing it by one *element*. The compiler knows the number of bytes required to store one element of the array, and adding 1 to the pointer increments the address in the pointer by that number of bytes. In other words, adding 1 to the pointer increments the pointer so that it points to the next element in the array.

For example, if pvalue is "pointer to double," as in your previous declaration, and the compiler allocates 8 bytes for a variable of type double, then the address in pvalue will be incremented by 8. This is illustrated in the diagram shown in Figure 7-5.

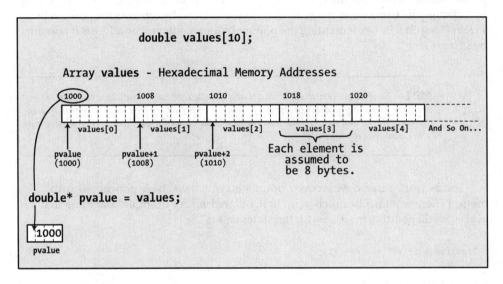

Figure 7-5. Incrementing a pointer

As Figure 7-5 shows, pvalue starts out with the address corresponding to the beginning of the array. Adding 1 to pvalue increments the address it contains by 8, so the result is the address of the next array element. It follows that incrementing the pointer by 2 moves the pointer two elements along. Of course, the pointer pvalue need not necessarily point to the beginning of the values array. You could assign the address of the third element of the array to the pointer with this statement:

```
pvalue = &values[2];
```

Following this, the expression pvalue + 1 would evaluate to the address of values[3], the fourth element of the values array, and you could make the pointer point to this element directly by writing this statement:

```
pvalue += 1;
```

This statement increments the address contained in pvalue by the number of bytes occupied by one element of the values array. In general, the expression pvalues + n, in which n can be any expression resulting in an integer, will produce a result by adding n * sizeof(double) to the address contained in the pointer pvalue, because pvalue was declared to be of type "pointer to double."

The same logic applies to subtracting an integer from a pointer. If pvalue contains the address of values[2], the expression pvalue - 2 evaluates to the address of the first element of the array, values[0]. In other words, incrementing or decrementing a pointer works in terms of the type of the object pointed to. Increasing a pointer to long by 1 changes its contents to the next long address, and so increments the address by sizeof(long) bytes. Decrementing the pointer by 1 decrements the address it contains by sizeof(long).

NOTE *The address resulting from an arithmetic operation on a pointer can be in a range from the address of the first element of the array to which it points to the address that's one beyond the last element. Outside of these limits, the behavior of the pointer is undefined.*

You can, of course, dereference a pointer on which you have performed arithmetic. (There wouldn't be much point to it, otherwise!) For example, assuming that pvalue is still pointing to values[2], the statement

```
*(pvalue + 1) = *(pvalue + 2);
```

is equivalent to this:

```
values[3] = values[4];
```

When you want to dereference a pointer after incrementing the address it contains, the parentheses are necessary because the precedence of the indirection operator is higher than that of the arithmetic operators, + and -. If you wrote the expression *pvalue + 1, instead of *(pvalue + 1), this would add 1 to the value stored at the address contained in pvalue, which is equivalent to executing values[2] + 1. Furthermore, because the result is a numerical value that's not an address (and therefore not an lvalue), its use in the previous assignment statement would cause the compiler to generate an error message.

Remember that an expression such as pvalue + 1 doesn't change the address in pvalue. It's simply an expression that evaluates to a result that is of the same type as pvalue. In this case, it's the address of the element following that pointed to by pvalue. Of course, if a pointer contains an invalid address (such an address is outside the limits of the array it relates to), and you store a value using the pointer, you'll attempt to overwrite the memory located at that address. This generally leads to disaster, with your program failing one way or another. It may not be obvious that the cause of the problem is the misuse of a pointer.

Taking the Difference Between Two Pointers

You can subtract one pointer from another, but this is only meaningful when they are of the same type and point to elements in the same array. Suppose you have a one-dimensional array, numbers, of type long declared as follows:

```
long numbers[] = {10L, 20, 30, 40, 50, 60, 70, 80};
```

You can declare and initialize two pointer variables:

```
long *pnum1 = &numbers[6];          // Points to seventh array element
long *pnum2 = &numbers[1];          // Points to second array element
```

Now you can calculate the difference between these two pointers as follows:

```
int difference = pnum1 - pnum2;           // Result is 5
```

The variable difference will be set to 5 because the calculation of the difference between the addresses is in terms of elements, not in terms of bytes.

Using Pointer Notation with an Array Name

You can use an array name as though it was a pointer for addressing the elements of an array. Suppose you have a one-dimensional array declared as follows:

```
long data[5];
```

Using pointer notation, you can refer to the element data[3], for example, as *(data + 3). This kind of notation can be applied generally, so that corresponding to the elements data[0], data[1], data[2], ..., you can write *data, *(data + 1), *(data + 2), and so on. The array name data by itself refers to the address of the beginning of the array, so an expression such as data + 2 produces the address of the element two elements along from the first.

You can use pointer notation with an array name in just the same way as you use the notation with an index value—in expressions or on the left of an assignment. You could set the values of the data array to even integers with this loop:

```
for(int i = 0 ; i < 5 ; i++)
  *(data + i) = 2 * (i + 1);
```

The expression *(data + i) refers to successive elements of the array: *(data + 0) corresponds to data[0], *(data + 1) refers to data[1], and so on. The loop will set the values of the array elements to 2, 4, 6, 8, and 10.

If you now want to sum the elements of the array, you could write this:

```
long sum = 0;
for(int i = 0 ; i < 5 ; i++)
  sum += *(data + i);
```

Let's try some of this in a practical context with a little more meat to it.

....

Try It Out: Array Names As Pointers

Because you've tried out pointers with strings, let's exercise this aspect of array addressing with a numerically oriented program that calculates prime numbers (a prime number is an integer that is divisible only by 1 and itself). Here's the program code:

```
// Program 7.6 Calculating primes
#include <iostream>
#include <iomanip>
using std::cout;
using std::endl;

int main() {
  const int max = 100;                   // Number of primes required
  long primes[max] = {2, 3, 5};          // First three primes defined
  int count = 3;                         // Count of primes found so far
  long trial = 5;                        // Candidate prime
  bool isprime = true;                   // Indicates when a prime is found

  do {
    trial += 2;                          // Next value for checking
    int i = 0;                           // Index to primes array

    // Try dividing the candidate by all the primes we have
    do {
      isprime = trial % *(primes + i) > 0;  // False for exact division
    } while(++i < count && isprime);

    if(isprime)                          // We got one...
      *(primes + count++) = trial;       // ...so save it in primes array
  } while(count < max);

  // Output primes 5 to a line
  for(int i = 0 ; i < max ; i++) {
    if(i % 5 == 0)                       // Newline on 1st line and after every 5th prime
      cout << endl;
    cout << std::setw(10) << *(primes + i);
  }
  cout << endl;
  return 0;
}
```

The output from this program is as follows:

2	3	5	7	11
13	17	19	23	29
31	37	41	43	47
53	59	61	67	71
73	79	83	89	97
101	103	107	109	113
127	131	137	139	149
151	157	163	167	173
179	181	191	193	197
199	211	223	227	229
233	239	241	251	257
263	269	271	277	281
283	293	307	311	313
317	331	337	347	349
353	359	367	373	379
383	389	397	401	409
419	421	431	433	439
443	449	457	461	463
467	479	487	491	499
503	509	521	523	541

HOW IT WORKS

You have the usual #include statements for <iostream> for input and output, and for <iomanip>, because you'll be using a stream manipulator to set the field width for output. You use the constant max to define the number of primes that you want the program to produce:

```
const int max = 100;        // Number of primes required
long primes[max] = {2, 3, 5};   // First three primes defined
int count = 3;              // Count of primes found
```

The primes array that stores the results has the first three primes already defined to start the process off. The variable count will record how many primes you have, so it's initialized to 3.

The test for primes uses the variables declared in the following statements:

```
long trial = 5;            // Candidate prime
bool isprime = true;        // Indicates when a prime is found
```

The variable trial will hold the next candidate to be tested, so you start it off at 5, as it will be incremented in the loop that follows. The Boolean variable isprime is a flag that you'll use to indicate when the value in trial is prime.

All the work is done in two loops: the outer do-while loop picks the next candidate to be checked and adds the candidate to the primes array if it's prime, and the inner loop actually checks the candidate to see whether or not it's prime. The outer loop will continue until you've filled the primes array.

(Continued)

Before the inner loop is executed, the trial variable is set to the next candidate to be tested with this statement:

```
trial += 2;                           // Next value for checking
```

The algorithm in the loop is very simple and is based on the fact that any number that isn't a prime must be divisible by a smaller number that *is* prime. You find the primes in ascending order, so at any point the primes array will contain all of the prime numbers lower than your current candidate. If none of the primes you have is a divisor of the candidate, then the candidate must be prime.

 NOTE *You only need to try dividing by primes that are less than or equal to the* square root *of the number in question, so this example isn't as efficient as it might be.*

Checking for whether the variable trial is prime is done in the inner loop:

```
do {
  isprime = trial % *(primes + i) > 0;  // False for exact division
} while(++i < count && isprime);
```

Within the loop, isprime is set to the value of the expression trial%*(primes + i)> 0. This finds the remainder after dividing trial by the prime number stored at the address primes + i. If the remainder is positive, it results in true.

The loop ends if i reaches count or whenever isprime is set to false. If any of the primes you have in the primes array divides into trial exactly, you know that trial isn't prime, so this will end the loop. If you try dividing all the primes into trial and none of them divides into it exactly, isprime will always be true and the loop will be ended by i reaching count.

After the inner loop ends, either because isprime was set to false or you exhausted the set of divisors in the primes array, you must decide whether or not the value in trial was prime. This is indicated by the value in isprime, which you test in the if statement:

```
if(isprime)                      // We got one...
  *(primes + count++) = trial;   // ...so save it in primes array
```

If isprime contains false, then one of the divisions was exact, so trial isn't prime. If isprime is true, the assignment statement stores the value from trial in primes[count] and then increments count with the postfix increment operator.

Once max primes have been found, you display them five to a line with a field width of ten characters as a result of these statements:

```
if(i % 5 == 0)              // Newline on 1st line and after every 5th prime
  cout << endl;
cout << std::setw(10) << *(primes + i);
```

This starts a new line when i has the values 0, 5, 10, and so on.

Using Pointers with Multidimensional Arrays

Using a pointer to store the address of a one-dimensional array is relatively straightforward, but with multidimensional arrays, things can get complicated. I should say that this subject is a little tricky, and you may want to skip over it on a first reading. However, if your previous experience is with C, this section is well worth a glance.

You can usually do everything you need to do with multidimensional arrays using array notation, and I recommend that you stick to it whenever you can. If you have to use a pointer with multidimensional arrays, you need to keep clear in your mind what is happening. By way of illustration, you can use an array called beans, declared as follows:

```
double beans[3][4];
```

You can declare and initialize the variable pbeans, of type "pointer to double," as follows:

```
double* pbeans = &beans[0][0];
```

Here, you're setting the pointer to the address of the first element of the array, which is of type double. You could also set the pointer to the address of the first *row* in the array with this statement:

```
double* pbeans = beans[0];
```

This is equivalent to using the name of a one-dimensional array, which is replaced by its address—you've seen this in an earlier discussion. However, because beans is a two-dimensional array, the following attempt to put an address in the pointer is illegal:

```
double* pbeans = beans;          // Will cause an error!!
```

The problem is one of type. The type of the pointer you have defined is double*, but the array is of type double[3][4]. A pointer to store the address of this array must be of type double*[4]. C++ associates the size of an array with its type, and the preceding statement is only legal if the pointer has been declared with the size required. This is done with a slightly more complicated notation than you've seen so far:

```
double (*pbeans)[4] = beans;
```

The parentheses here are essential; otherwise, you would be declaring an array of pointers. Now the initialization of the pointer to point to beans is legal, but note that this pointer can *only* be used to store addresses of an array with the dimensions shown.

Pointer Notation with Multidimensional Array Names

You can use pointer notation with an array name to reference elements of the array. You can reference each element of the array beans declared previously, which had three rows of four elements, in three ways:

- **Using the array name in the usual fashion, with two index values.** For example, beans[i][j]. This uses conventional array indexing to refer to the element with offset j in row i of the array.

- **Using the array name in pointer notation.** For example, *(*(beans + i) + j). You can determine the meaning of the expression by working from the inside outward. beans refers to the address of the first row of the array, so beans + i refers to row i of the array. The expression *(beans + i) is the address of the first element of row i, so *(beans+i) + j is the address of the element in row i with offset j. The whole expression *(*(beans+i) + j), therefore, refers to the value of that element. Unless you have a good reason for referencing the elements of an array in this way, it's best avoided. It isn't obvious what you mean, and your code will be that much harder to understand.

- **Using a mixture of pointer notation and an index value.** This is legal, but not recommended. The following are legal references to the same element of the array:

  *(beans[i] + j)
  (*(beans + i))[j]

  where you have mixed array and pointer notation.

....

Try It Out:
Using Pointer Notation with Multidimensional Arrays

Way back in Program 5.8, you generated a multiplication table. You can produce another version of this program that stores the table as an array. To avoid duplicating all the code that's no longer of interest, you'll simplify it to calculate a table of fixed size:

```
// Program 7.7 Using pointer notation with a multidimensional array
#include <iostream>
#include <iomanip>
#include <cctype>
using std::cout;
using std::endl;
using std::setw;

int main() {
  const int table = 12;                              // Table size
```

```
      long values[table][table] = {0};                    // Stores the table values

      // Calculate the table entries
      for(int i = 0; i < table ; i++)
        for(int j = 0; j < table ; j++)
          *(*(values + i) + j) = (i + 1) * (j + 1);        // Full use of pointer notation

      // Create the top line of the table
      cout << "     |";
      for(int i = 1 ; i <= table ; i++)
        cout << " " << setw(3) << i << " |";
      cout << endl;

      // Create the separator row
      for(int i = 0 ; i <= table ; i++)
        cout << "------";
      cout << endl;

      for(int i = 0 ; i < table ; i++) {                   // Iterate over the rows
        cout << " " << setw(3) << i + 1 << " |";           // Start the row

        // Output the values in a row
        for(int j = 0 ; j < table ; j++)
          cout << " " << setw(3) << values[i][j] << " |";  // Array notation
        cout << endl;                                      // End the row
      }

      return 0;
    }
```

This example produces the following output:

	1	2	3	4	5	6	7	8	9	10	11	12
1	1	2	3	4	5	6	7	8	9	10	11	12
2	2	4	6	8	10	12	14	16	18	20	22	24
3	3	6	9	12	15	18	21	24	27	30	33	36
4	4	8	12	16	20	24	28	32	36	40	44	48
5	5	10	15	20	25	30	35	40	45	50	55	60
6	6	12	18	24	30	36	42	48	54	60	66	72
7	7	14	21	28	35	42	49	56	63	70	77	84
8	8	16	24	32	40	48	56	64	72	80	88	96
9	9	18	27	36	45	54	63	72	81	90	99	108
10	10	20	30	40	50	60	70	80	90	100	110	120
11	11	22	33	44	55	66	77	88	99	110	121	132
12	12	24	36	48	60	72	84	96	108	120	132	144

(Continued)

You first declare the size of the array and the array itself:

```
const int table = 12;                            // Table size
long values[table][table] = {0};                 // Stores the table values
```

You must declare table as const because you use it to specify the size of table. An array size must be a constant expression, so non-const variables aren't allowed. The array will have 12 rows of 12 elements.

You use pointer notation to store the table entries in a nested for loop:

```
for(int i = 0; i < table ; i++)
  for(int j = 0; j < table ; j++)
    *(*(values + i) + j) = (i + 1) * (j + 1);    // Full use of pointer notation
```

The expression values + i refers to row i of the array, and *(values + i) refers to the address of the first element of row i. By adding j to that with the expression *(values + i) + j, you get the address of the jth element in row i. You dereference that with the expression *(*(values + i) + j) to refer to the *contents* of the jth element in row i of the array.

To output the entries in the table, you have another nested loop:

```
for(int i = 0 ; i < table ; i++) {               // Iterate over the rows
  cout << " " << setw(3) << i + 1 << " |";        // Start the row

  // Output the values in a row
  for(int j = 0 ; j < table ; j++)
    cout << " " << setw(3) << values[i][j] << " |"; // Array notation
  cout << endl;                                   // End the row
}
```

You use normal array notation to output the values stored in the array. The expression in pointer notation *(*(values + i) + j) is equivalent to values[i][j] in array notation. I'm sure you'll agree that array notation is a lot easier to understand in this situation!

Operations on C-Style Strings

In Chapter 4, you saw briefly the functions that are declared in the <cctype> header, which analyze and convert single characters. The standard library also contains some functions that you can use to analyze and transform null-terminated strings. The bulk of these are declared in the <cstring> header, which you must include in order to use them. Both the <cctype> and <cstring> header names begin with c, which indicates they are both libraries that are inherited from C.

CAUTION *Don't confuse the* <cstring> *header that you'll use here with the* <string> *header that you've already seen, which defines the* string *type.*

The functions in the <cstring> header make extensive use of pointers both as arguments and return values, and that's why I've deferred discussion of them to this point. They supply functionality for null-terminated strings similar to that you saw provided for string objects in the last chapter. In that sense, these functions are something of an anachronism, but they're still in the language, and you'll certainly see them used.

Operations on C-style strings are interesting here because they provide some exercise for pointer operations. There are a total of 22 functions in the <cstring> header, but you'll just take a look at the ones involved with concatenating null-terminated strings.

Concatenating Strings

In the last chapter, you saw that you could combine string objects simply by using the + operator. With null-terminated strings, it's not quite so easy. The <cstring> header declares two functions for concatenating null-terminated strings: strcat() and strncat().

The strcat() function takes two strings as arguments, of types char* and const char*, respectively, and appends the latter of these to the former, modifying the first argument in the process. It takes care of overwriting the '\0' at the end of the first string and adding '\0' to the end of the composite string, but you're responsible for making sure that the string pointed to by the first argument has enough space to hold the result. The first argument is also the return value of the function.

The strncat() function takes three arguments, the first two of which are the same as those for strcat(). The third argument is an integer that specifies how many characters from the second string should be added to the first; if you ask for more characters than are in the string, the whole string will be appended. Apart from that, the conditions of use and the return value are the same as for strcat().

These functions are quite easy to use. Suppose you declare two arrays of type char as follows:

```
char name[50] = "Bing";
char surname[] = "Crosby";
```

You could append a space to the string in name with this statement:

```
strcat(name, " ");
```

Then you could append the surname with this statement:

```
strcat(name, surname);
```

The result will be that name contains the string "Bing Crosby".

Because the functions always return the first argument, you could have done the whole thing in a single statement:

```
strcat(strcat(name, " "), surname);
```

This has the disadvantage that it's not as easy to figure out what's going on. In this statement, the first strcat() function call appends a space to name. The result of this is then used as the first argument to the outer strcat() function call, which appends the surname.

To help you verify that there is space in the first argument to hold the composite string, you can use the strlen() function, which returns the length of the string you pass as its only argument. You might use something like this:

```
if(sizeof name/sizeof name[0] > (strlen(name) + strlen(surname) + 1))
  std::cout << strcat(strcat(name, " "), surname);
```

The if condition works out how many characters name can hold and makes sure that this is greater than the length of the string you're going to construct (the extra + 1 in the if condition is for the space character).

The other functions defined in cstring perform operations such as copying (strcpy()), comparing (strcmp()) and searching (strchr()) null-terminated strings, and they're broadly similar in operation to the ones you've seen here. By taking pointers to char as arguments, the functions avoid the overhead of having to move and copy whole strings in memory; this is something you'll be seeing a lot more of in the next chapter and indeed in the rest of the book.

Remember that I've introduced these functions so that you'll recognize them if you see them, and because they're a small demonstration of how pointers can be useful. When you're writing your own code, I strongly recommend that you use string objects in preference to variables of type char* for your string-handling needs.

Dynamic Memory Allocation

All of the code you've written up to now allocates space for data at compile time. You specify the variables and the array sizes that you need in the source code, and that's what will be allocated when the program executes, whether you need it or not. Working with a fixed set of variables in a program can be very restrictive, and it's often wasteful.

When you were extracting words from a text string in Program 7.5, you allocated space for 1,000 words. A lot of the time you wouldn't need to store 1,000 words, and in those cases the excess space was allocated needlessly. It prevented some other program from using the space, even though it was completely unused by your program. On the other hand, if you tried to analyze a text string of 1,001 words, the program would be unable to handle it—even though, in all probability, there would be memory lying idle in the computer.

In another context, you might find that it would be appropriate to use a large integer array with one set of data, whereas a large floating-point array would be required for a different set of input data. If the arrays required were very large, you might not have enough memory in your machine to accommodate both at the same time. The solution to all these difficulties and disadvantages is to use **dynamic memory allocation**, which means that you allocate the memory you need to store the data you're working with when your program executes (runtime), rather than when you compile it (compile time). Figure 7-6 illustrates the difference between static and dynamic memory allocation.

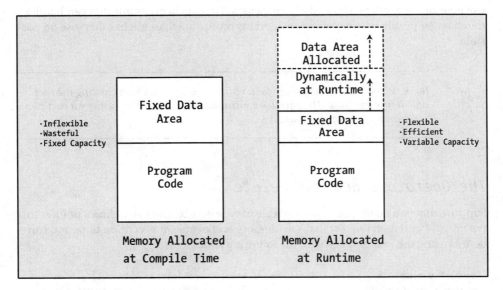

Figure 7-6. Static versus dynamic memory allocation

By definition, dynamically allocated variables can't be declared at compile time, and so they can't be named in your source program. When you allocate memory dynamically, the space that is made available by your request is identified by its address. The obvious (and only) place to store this address is in a pointer. With the power of pointers and the dynamic memory management tools in C++, writing this kind of flexibility into your programs is quick and easy.

Back in Chapter 3, I introduced the three kinds of storage duration that variables can have—automatic, static, and dynamic—and discussed how variables of the first two varieties are created. Variables allocated in the free store will always have *dynamic* storage duration.

The Free Store (aka the Heap)

In most instances, there is unused memory in your computer when your program is executed. In C++, this unused memory is called the **free store**, or sometimes the **heap**. You can allocate space within the free store for a new variable of a given type by using a special C++ operator that returns the address of the space allocated. This operator is new, and it's complemented by the operator delete, which deallocates memory that you've previously allocated with new.

You can allocate space in the free store for some variables in one part of a program, and then release the allocated space and return it to the free store once you've finished with the variables concerned. The memory then becomes available for reuse by other dynamically allocated variables later in the same program. This enables you to use memory very efficiently, and in many cases it results in programs that can handle much larger problems, involving considerably more data than might otherwise be possible.

 NOTE *When you allocate space for a variable using* new, *you're creating the variable in the free store. The variable continues to exist until the memory it occupies is released by the operator* delete.

The Operators new and delete

Suppose that you need space for a variable of type double. You can define a pointer to type double and then request that the memory is allocated at execution time. You can do this using the operator new with the following statements:

```
double* pvalue = 0;              // Pointer initialized with null
pvalue = new double;             // Request memory for a double variable
```

This is a good moment to recall that *all pointers should be initialized*. Using memory dynamically typically involves having a lot of pointers floating around, so it's particularly important that they not contain spurious values. You should always try to arrange that if a pointer doesn't contain a legal address, it should contain 0.

The new operator in the second line of the previous code returns the address of the memory in the free store allocated to a double variable, and this address is stored in the pointer pvalue. You can then use this pointer to reference the variable by using the indirection operator, as you've seen, for example:

```
*pvalue = 999.0;
```

Of course, under extreme circumstances the memory allocation may not be possible because the free store is all used up at the time of the allocation request. Alternatively, it could be that the free store is fragmented by previous usage, meaning that there's no area of the free store with a sufficient number of contiguous bytes to accommodate the variable for which you want to obtain space. This isn't likely with the space required to hold a double value, but it might just happen when you're dealing with entities that can be large, such as arrays or complicated class objects. This is clearly something that you need to consider, but just for the moment you'll assume that you always get the memory you request. I come back to this topic in Chapter 17, though, when I discuss **exceptions**.

You can initialize a variable that you create with new. Let's reconsider the previous example: the double variable allocated by new, with its address stored in pvalue. You could have initialized its value to 999.0 as it was created by using this statement:

```
pvalue = new double(999.0);          // Allocate a double and initialize it
```

When you no longer need a dynamically allocated variable, you can free up the memory that it occupied in the free store with the delete operator:

```
delete pvalue;                       // Release memory pointed to by pvalue
```

This ensures that the memory can be used subsequently by another variable. If you don't use delete, and you subsequently store a different address in the pointer pvalue, it will be impossible to free up the original memory location or to use the variable that it contains, because access to the address will have been lost.

It's important to realize that the delete operator frees the memory but does *not* change the pointer. After the previous statement has executed, pvalue still contains the address of the memory that was allocated, but the memory is now free and may immediately be allocated to something else—possibly by another program. To avoid the risk of attempting to use the pointer containing the now spurious address, and unless you're going to reassign it or it goes out of scope, you should always reset the pointer when you release the memory. To do this, you would write the following:

```
delete pvalue;                       // Release memory pointed to by pvalue
pvalue = 0;                          // Reset the pointer to 0
```

Dynamic Memory Allocation for Arrays

Allocating memory for an array dynamically is straightforward. Assuming that you've already declared pstring, of type "pointer to char," you could allocate an array of type char in the free store by writing the following:

```
pstring = new char[20];              // Allocate a string of twenty characters
```

This allocates space for a char array of 20 characters and stores its address in pstring.

To remove the array that you've just created in the free store, you must use the delete operator. The statement to do so looks like this:

```
delete [] pstring;                   // Delete array pointed to by pstring
```

CAUTION *The square brackets here are important: they indicate that what you're deleting is an array. When removing arrays from the free store, you should always include the square brackets, or the results will be unpredictable. Note also that you don't specify any dimensions here, simply* [ ].

Of course, you should also reset the pointer, now that it no longer points to memory that you own:

```
pstring = 0;                              // Reset the pointer
```

Let's see how dynamic memory allocation works, first with numeric data.

Try It Out: Using the Free Store

You can see how these operations work in practice by rewriting your earlier program that calculated 100 primes so that it will calculate an arbitrary number of primes. You'll use memory in the free store to store however many are required.

```
// Program 7.8 Calculating primes using dynamic memory allocation
#include <iostream>
#include <iomanip>
using std::cout;
using std::endl;
using std::cin;

int main() {
  int max = 0;                            // Number of primes required
  int count = 3;                          // Count of primes found
  long trial = 5;                         // Candidate prime
  bool isprime = true;                    // Indicates when a prime is found

  cout << endl
       << "Enter the number of primes you would like: ";
  cin >> max;                             // Number of primes required

  long* primes = new long[max];           // Allocate memory for them
  *primes = 2;                            // Insert three seed primes...
  *(primes + 1) = 3;
  *(primes + 2) = 5;

  do {
    trial += 2;                           // Next value for checking
    int i = 0;                            // Index to primes array
```

```
      // Try dividing the candidate by all the primes we have
      do {
        isprime = trial % *(primes + i) > 0;   // False for exact division
      } while(++i < count && isprime);

      if(isprime)                          // We got one...
        *(primes + count++) = trial;       // ...so save it in primes array
    } while(count < max);

    // Output primes 5 to a line
    for(int i = 0 ; i < max ; i++) {
      if(i % 5 == 0)           // Newline on 1st line and after every 5th prime
        cout << endl;
      cout << std::setw(10) << *(primes + i);
    }
    cout << endl;
    delete [] primes;                      // Free up memory
    return 0;
}
```

The output is essentially the same as the previous version of the program, except, of course, that you choose how many primes are calculated, so I won't reproduce it here.

HOW IT WORKS

Overall, the program is very similar to the previous version. After reading the number of primes required from the keyboard and storing it in the int variable, max, you allocate an array of that size in the free store using the operator new. You specify the size of the array required by putting the variable max between the square brackets following the array type specification:

```
long* primes = new long[max];            // Allocate memory for them
```

You store the address that's returned by new in the pointer, primes. This will be the address of the first element of an array of max elements of type long.

Next, you set the first three array elements to the values of the first three primes:

```
*primes = 2;                             // Insert three seed primes...
*(primes + 1) = 3;
*(primes + 2) = 5;
```

You have used pointer notation here, but you could equally well use array notation. If you prefer, you could write these statements as follows:

```
primes[0] = 2;                           // Insert three seed primes...
primes[1] = 3;
primes[2] = 5;
```

(Continued)

NOTE *You can't specify initial values for elements of an array that you've allocated dynamically. You have to use explicit assignment statements to set values for elements of such arrays.*

The calculation of the prime numbers is exactly as before. No changes are necessary, even though the memory that the primes will occupy has been allocated at runtime. Equally, the output process is the same. Acquiring space dynamically is really not a problem at all. Once the space has been allocated, it in no way affects how the computation is written.

Once you've finished with the array, you remove it from the free store using the delete operator, not forgetting to include the square brackets to indicate that it's an array you're deleting:

```
delete [] primes;                    // Free up memory
```

Because this is the end of the program, there's no possibility of misusing the pointer, so there's no need to reset it to 0. If the program continued, then naturally it would be a different matter.

Hazards of Dynamic Memory Allocation

There are two kinds of problems that can arise when you allocate memory dynamically. The first is called a **memory leak** and is caused by errors in your code. Unfortunately, memory leaks are quite common. The second is called **memory fragmentation** and is usually due to poor use of dynamic allocation. Memory fragmentation problems are relatively rare.

Memory Leaks

A memory leak occurs when you allocate memory using new and fail to release it when you're done with it. In this situation, it's common to lose the address of the memory block by overwriting the address in the pointer you were using to access it. This typically occurs in a loop, and it's easier to create this kind of problem than you might think. The effect is that your program gradually consumes more and more of the free store, with the program potentially failing at the point when all of the free store has been allocated and yet another request for memory is made. The effect of memory leaks is illustrated in Figure 7-7.

It's relatively easy to see where you've simply forgotten to use delete to free memory in a program as long as use of the memory ceases at a point in your code that's close to where you allocated it. It becomes more difficult to spot the omission in complex programs, in which memory may be allocated in one part of a program but should be released in a quite separate part. A good strategy for dealing with this is to add the `delete` operation at an appropriate place in your program immediately after you've used the `new` operator.

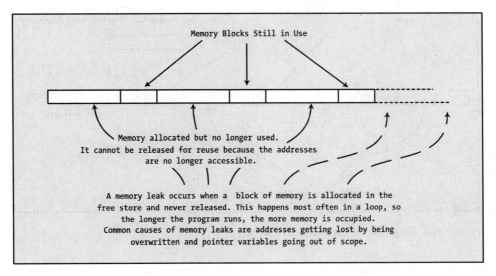

Figure 7-7. Memory leaks

Pointers and Variable Scope

When it comes to scope, pointers are just like any other variable. A pointer variable exists from the point at which you declare it in a block to the closing brace of the block. After that it no longer exists, and so the address it contained is no longer accessible.

This relates to the discussion of memory leaks. If a pointer contains the address of a block of memory in the free store, and the pointer goes out of scope, then it's no longer possible to `delete` the memory. It's most important to keep in mind the scope of your pointers, particularly when you're using dynamically allocated memory.

Fragmentation of the Free Store

Memory fragmentation can arise in programs that allocate and release memory blocks frequently. Each time the `new` operator is used, it allocates a contiguous block of bytes in the free store. If you create and destroy many variables of different sizes, it's possible to arrive at a situation in which the allocated memory that's still in use is interspersed with small blocks of free memory, none of which is large enough to accommodate a new dynamic variable that your program (or some other program that's executing concurrently) needs to allocate. The aggregate of the free memory can be quite large, but all the individual blocks may be quite small—too small for the current requirements. The effect of memory fragmentation is illustrated in Figure 7-8.

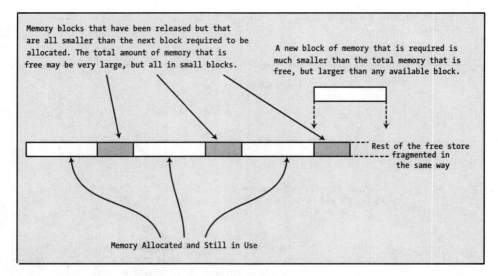

Figure 7-8. Fragmentation of the free store

This problem arises relatively infrequently these days, with virtual memory providing very large amounts of memory even on quite modest computers. When it does occur, the solution is to avoid allocating small blocks of memory. Instead, allocate larger blocks and manage the use of the memory yourself.

Try It Out: Sorting Strings Again

I began this discussion of dynamic memory allocation by criticizing the carefully crafted program for extracting and sorting words from a text string, and you're now in a position to be able to do something about it. The version that you'll construct here won't impose that arbitrary 1,000-word limit on your text and won't waste memory if you enter fewer than 1,000 words. To get an appreciation of the individual changes to the original code, you'll assemble the new version by modifying the old, step by step.

As you put this example together, you'll see once again that using dynamically allocated memory doesn't require many alterations to the mechanics of a program. I explain the changes from Program 7.5, which in large measure have to do with the *management* of dynamic memory, by breaking the code into sections and highlighting the new lines and amendments.

READING AND COUNTING THE WORDS IN A MULTILINE STRING

In fact, you can read the string from the keyboard in *exactly* the same way as in Program 7.5. The difference here is in when and how pointers are assigned to the words in the string. Last time, you created a fixed array of pointers before the string was entered, and you assigned the pointers to the words as you counted them. This time, you can defer creation of the pointers until after the text has been input, but in order to do that, you still need to find out how many words there are:

```cpp
// Program 7.9 Sorting strings using dynamic memory allocation
#include <iostream>
#include <string>
using std::cout;
using std::cin;
using std::endl;
using std::string;

int main() {
  string text;                                    // The string to be sorted
  const string separators = " ,.\"\n";            // Word delimiters

  // Three lines deleted that allocated the array

  // Read the string to be searched from the keyboard
  cout << endl << "Enter a string terminated by #:" << endl;
  std::getline(cin, text, '#');

  // Count the words in the text
  size_t start = text.find_first_not_of(separators);  // Word start index
  size_t end = 0;                                      // End delimiter index
  int word_count = 0;                                 // Count of words stored

  while(start != string::npos) {  // Deleted the check on the size of the array
    end = text.find_first_of(separators, start + 1);
    if(end == string::npos)                           // Found a separator?
      end = text.length();                            // No, so set to last + 1

    // Two lines deleted that stored each and its pointer

    word_count++;                                     // Increment count

    // Find the first character of the next word
    start = text.find_first_not_of(separators, end + 1);
  }
```

All the changes here are deletions. The five lines that you've removed had to do with the creation and assignment of fixed-size arrays of words and pointers to words, which you no longer require at this stage of the program. You've also been able to get rid of the condition on the while loop that restricted the number of words your program can handle. At the end of this code, you've got a string in text and a count of the number of words in it in word_count, so you know exactly how much memory you need to allocate.

(Continued)

CREATING THE ARRAY OF POINTERS TO THE WORDS

Now it's time to write some new code. You need an array of word_count pointers to refer to the words in text. There's only one line of code necessary to create this array:

```
// Allocate an array of pointers to strings in the free store
string** pwords = new string*[word_count];
```

The operator new creates an array of word_count elements of type string*, which is type "pointer to string." You need to store the address returned by new in pwords, so pwords must also be a pointer. Because what it points to is an array of elements of type string*, the type of pwords has to be string**, which is type "pointer to pointer to string."

CREATING OBJECTS FOR THE WORDS

With the array of pointers to the words available, you're ready to create the string objects that will represent the words. You'll create a string object for a word from the substring containing all the characters of a word, so you need to find the index position of the start of a word and the count of the number of characters in the word. In the interest of code reuse, you can perform this task with a loop that's almost identical to the one you used for counting the words in text in the first place:

```
// Create words in the free store and store the addresses in the array
start = text.find_first_not_of(separators);       // Start of first word
end = 0;                                           // Index for the end of a word
int index = 0;                                     // Pointer array index

while(start != string::npos) {
  end = text.find_first_of(separators, start + 1);
  if(end == string::npos)                          // Found a separator?
    end = text.length();                           // No, so set to last + 1
  pwords[index++] = new string(text.substr(start, end - start));
  start = text.find_first_not_of(separators, end+1); // Find start of next word
}
```

The variable start holds the index position of the first character of each word in turn, and end contains the position of the first separator after the word that begins at start. The length of the word is therefore given by the expression end - start, and you can use that fact to create the string object for a word in the free store, in the line that's the only one to change from your word-counting loop.

You initialize the string object with a word that you extract from text by using the substr() function. The operator new returns the address of the memory for the object, which you store in pwords[index]. You also increment index to the position of the next free array element, using the postfix increment operator.

SORTING AND OUTPUTTING THE WORDS

Apart from the fact that it was created dynamically, pwords is an array of pointers like any other. That means you can use exactly the same code for sorting and outputting the words that you did in Program 7.5. So that you've got it all in one place, here it is again:

```
// Sort the words in ascending sequence by direct insertion
int lowest = 0;                              // Index of lowest word
for(int j = 0 ; j < word_count - 1 ; j++) {
  lowest = j;                                // Set lowest

  // Check current against all the following words
  for(int i = j + 1 ; i < word_count ; i++)
    if(*pwords[i] < *pwords[lowest])         // Current is lower?
      lowest = i;

  if(lowest != j) {           // Then swap pointers...
    string* ptemp = pwords[j];               // Save current
    pwords[j] = pwords[lowest];              // Store lower in current
    pwords[lowest] = ptemp;                  // Restore current
  }
}

// Output up to six words to a line in groups starting with the same letter
char ch = (*pwords[0])[0];                   // First letter of first word
int words_in_line = 0;                       // Words in a line count
for(int i = 0 ; i < word_count ; i++) {
  if(ch != (*pwords[i])[0]) {                // New first letter?
    cout << endl;                            // Start a new line
    ch = (*pwords[i])[0];                    // Save the new first letter
    words_in_line = 0;                       // Reset words in line count
  }
  cout << *pwords[i] << "  ";
  if(++words_in_line == 6) {                 // Every sixth word
    cout << endl;                            // Start a new line
    words_in_line = 0;
  }
}
```

RELEASING FREE STORE MEMORY

This time around you aren't done when you've produced the output. You must use the delete operator to release the memory that you allocated for the words and for the pointer array:

```
// Delete words from free store
for(int i = 0 ; i < word_count ; i++)
  delete pwords[i];

// Now delete the array of pointers
delete[] pwords;

return 0;
}
```

(Continued)

You delete the string objects containing the words in the for loop. You then delete the pointer array, pwords. Note that because you're deleting an array here, you must put square brackets after the keyword delete.

If you piece together all the preceding sections of code, you should be able to get the resulting program to produce the following output:

```
Enter a string terminated by #:
Little Willie from his mirror
Licked the mercury right off,
Thinking, in his childish error
It would cure the whooping cough.
At the funeral Willie's mother
Brightly said to Mrs Brown,
"Twas a chilly day for Willie
When the mercury went down."#

At
Brightly   Brown
It
Licked   Little
Mrs
Thinking   Twas
When   Willie   Willie   Willie's
a
childish   chilly   cough   cure
day   down
error
for   from   funeral
his   his
in
mercury   mercury   mirror   mother
off
right
said
the   the   the   the   to
went   whooping   would
```

Isn't that nice?

Converting Pointers

The reinterpret_cast<>() operator allows you to cast between any pointer types, with the constraint that if the pointer type you're casting was declared as const, you can't cast it to a type that isn't const. You can also convert any integer numeric value to a pointer type, and vice versa. This doesn't change the values involved; it only changes the way the value is interpreted. Consequently, this is a very risky operator, so you should use it only when absolutely necessary.

The general form of the `reinterpret_cast<>()` operator is as follows:

```
reinterpret_cast<pointer_type>(expression)
```

The `expression` between the parentheses is interpreted as the `pointer_type` between the angled brackets. To illustrate the general conversion potential, you could suppose that, for some strange reason, you wanted to interpret a `float` value as a `long`. You could do this with the following statements:

```
float value = 2.5f;
float* pvalue = &value;
long* pnumber = reinterpret_cast<long*>(pvalue);
```

After these statements have been executed, the pointer pnumber points to the value in `value` (which is 2.5), but it will *interpret* it as type `long`. The value itself is unchanged—it has exactly the same bit pattern as before. You could output the value interpreted as type `long` with this statement:

```
std::cout << std::endl << *pnumber;
```

On my computer, this demonstrates that the floating-point value 2.5 looks like 1,075,838,976 as type `long`. The reverse process—storing a `long` value and then interpreting it as type `float`—will almost certainly produce a floating-point value that isn't properly formed.

At the risk of laboring the point, I want to repeat that the `reinterpet_cast<>()` operator is very hazardous, because it provides the means of arbitrarily interpreting a value of one type as another. You should avoid using this operator unless it's absolutely essential to the solution of your problem, and you know precisely what you're doing.

Summary

You've explored some very important concepts in this chapter. You'll make extensive use of pointers in your C++ programs, so make sure that you have a good grasp of them—you'll see a lot more of them throughout the rest of the book.

The vital points this chapter covered are as follows:

- A pointer is a variable that contains an address.

- You obtain the address of a variable using the address-of operator, &.

- To refer to the value pointed to by a pointer, you use the indirection operator, *. This is also called the dereference operator.

- You can add integer values to or subtract integer values from the address stored in a pointer. The effect is as though the pointer refers to an array, and the pointer is altered by the number of array elements specified by the integer value.

- The operator new allocates a block of memory in the free store and makes it available for use in your program by returning the address of the memory allocated.

- You use the operator delete to release a block of memory that you've allocated previously using the operator new.

- The reinterpret_cast<>() operator converts from one type of pointer to another.

Exercises

The following exercises enable you to try out what you've learned in this chapter. If you get stuck, look back over the chapter for help. If you're still stuck after that, you can download the solutions from the Apress website (http://www.apress.com/book/download.html), but that really should be a last resort.

Exercise 7-1. Write a program that declares and initializes an array with the first 50 even numbers. Output the numbers from the array ten to a line using pointer notation, and then output them in reverse order also using pointer notation.

Exercise 7-2. Write a program that reads an array size from the keyboard and dynamically allocates an array of that size to hold floating-point values. Using pointer notation, initialize all the elements of the array so that the value of the element at index position n is $1.0/(n+1)^2$. Calculate the sum of the elements using pointer notation, multiply the sum by 6, and output the square root of that result. Try the program for large array size—more than 100,000 elements, say. Do you notice anything interesting about the result?

Exercise 7-3. Amend your solution to Exercise 6-1 to allocate memory dynamically to store each student's details so that the program will deal with any number of students.

Exercise 7-4. You know that a two-dimensional array is an "array of arrays." You also know that you can create an array dynamically using a pointer. If the elements of the array that you create dynamically are also pointers, then each element in the array could store the address of an array. Using this concept, create an array of three pointers to arrays, in which each array can store six values of type int. Set the first array of integers to values 1 to 6, the next array to the squares (N×N) of the values stored first array, and the next the cubes (N×N×N) of the values stored in the first array of integers. Output the contents of the three arrays, and then delete the memory you've allocated.

CHAPTER 8

Programming with Functions

DIVIDING YOUR PROGRAM into manageable chunks of code is an idea that's fundamental to programming in every language. A **function** is a basic building block in all C++ programs. So far, you've made use of some of the functions from the standard library, but the only functions you've written yourself are the ones called main(). This chapter is all about defining your own functions with names that you choose.

In this chapter you will learn:

- What a function is, and why you should segment your programs into functions

- How to declare and define functions

- How arguments are passed to a function, and how a value is returned

- What pass-by-value means

- How specifying a parameter as a pointer affects the pass-by-value mechanism

- How using const as a qualifier for a parameter type affects the operation of a function

- What pass-by-reference means, and how you can declare a reference in your program

- How to return a value from a function

- What an inline function is

- The effect of declaring a variable as static within a function

Segmenting Your Programs

All the programs you have written so far have consisted of just one function, main(). As you know, all C++ programs must have a function called main()—it's where program execution starts. However, C++ allows you to include as many other functions in your programs as you need, and I've already used quite a few functions from the standard library in my examples. Defining and using your own functions is just as easy. An illustration of the overall structure of an arbitrary program that has been implemented as several functions is shown in Figure 8-1.

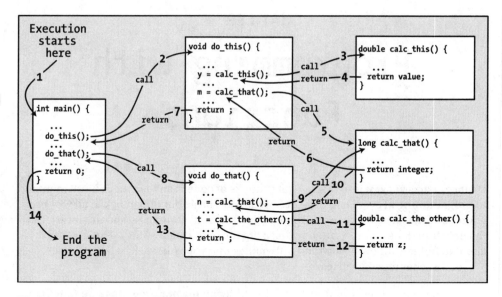

Figure 8-1. Functions calling functions

The sequence in which the functions shown in Figure 8-1 execute is indicated by the numbers on the arrows. Generally, when you call a function at a given point in your program, the code that the function contains executes; when it finishes, program execution continues immediately after the point where the function was called. Any function can call other functions—that's what main() does, after all—that may in turn call other functions, so a single function call could result in several functions being executed.

When one function calls another, which calls another, and so on, you have a situation where several functions are still in action, and each function is waiting for the function that it called to return. In Figure 8-1, main() calls do_that(), which calls calc_that(), so all three functions are in progress simultaneously. While the calc_that() function is executing, the do_that() function is waiting for it to return, and main() is waiting for do_that() to return.

For a function to execute, the code for it must reside somewhere in memory. Now, it's all very well saying that one function "waits for another to return," but in order for that to happen, something must keep track of from where in memory calls were made, and where functions must return. This information is all recorded and maintained automatically in the **call stack**. The call stack contains information on all the outstanding function calls at any given time, as well as details of the arguments passed to each function. The debugging facilities that come with most C++ development systems usually provide ways for you to view the call stack while your program executes.

Why You Should Segment Your Programs into Functions

You may have several reasons for segmenting your program into a number of functions.

First, it makes programs much easier to read and manage. It is easy to visualize how main() could become an unmanageable size by taking an extreme example. Many applications these days run to hundreds of thousands of lines of code, and some into millions of lines. Just imagine trying to deal with main() if it contained 100,000 lines of code! Grasping the logic of the program would be just about impossible, as would be tracking down anything but the simplest bug. It is absolutely essential that you divide up the code for a program of this size into a number—in this case a *large* number—of functions.

Second, you can reuse functions. For example, suppose that you wrote a function to sort strings in one particular program. Nothing prevents you from using that same function in another context. The standard library is a powerful example of the benefits of reusing functions. Thousands of hours of programming and testing effort have been invested into developing the standard library, but you have immediate access to the functionality that it provides and you can use it as often and in as many different programs as you like.

Third, breaking your program down into several functions can reduce the amount of memory you need to run it. Most applications involve some calculation that is used repeatedly. If the code for such a calculation is contained in a function that you call when you need it, then the code for that calculation appears just once. Without such a function, you would have to repeat the code each time you needed it, and so the compiled program would be larger.

Fourth, the process of deciding how you are going to implement a program to solve a given problem inevitably involves breaking down the problem into smaller units. Generally the design process for a program leads directly to code units that are relatively self-contained, and it invariably makes sense to program these as separate units that each involve one or more functions.

Understanding Functions

You have written quite a few main() functions by now, so you should have a pretty good idea of what a function looks like, but I'll go over the basic ideas just to be sure everything is clear. First let's look at the broad principles of how a function works.

A function is a self-contained block of code with a specific purpose. The immediate implication of this is that you need a reasonably clear idea of how the solution to your programming problem breaks down into functional units. With C++, there's actually more to it than that, but I'm going to defer detailed discussion until I begin to talk about how you define your own data types in Chapter 11. You'll find that this will have a profound effect on the approach that you take to designing a program.

For the time being, let's look at how to put a function together. During the discussion, it will help if you have the example illustrated in Figure 8-2 in mind.

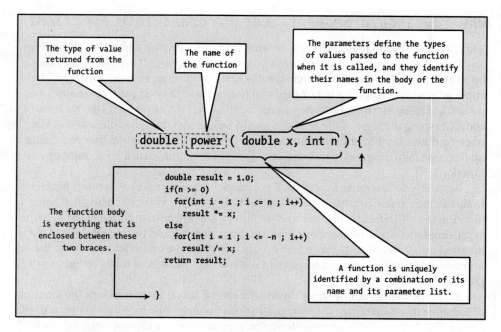

Figure 8-2. An example of a function definition

Defining a Function

You specify what a function does in a **function definition**; Figure 8-2 shows an example. A function definition has two parts: the **function header**, which is the first line of the definition, excluding the opening brace, and the **function body**, which lies between the braces. As you know from your experience with main(), the function body contains the code that executes when you call the function.

The Function Header

Let's first examine the function header of the example shown in Figure 8-2. This is the first line of the function:

```
double power(double x, int n)
```

It consists of three parts: the data type of the **return value** (which is double in this case); the name of the function, power; and the function's **parameter list**, enclosed between parentheses. The names of the parameters here are x and n, and these names will be used in the statements that specify what the function does. They correspond to the arguments passed when the function is called. The parameter x is of type double, and the parameter n is of type int, so when the function is called, values of these types should be passed to it.

NOTE *You must not place a semicolon at the end of the function header.*

The General Form of a Function Header

The general form of a function header can be written as follows:

```
return_type  function_name(parameter_list)
```

The function_name is the name that you use to call the function in a program. You usually give each of your functions a different name, but as you saw with some of the standard library functions in Chapter 2, several different functions can have the same name, as long as each has a different parameter list. Such functions normally all provide essentially the same operations, but with a different set of parameters.

Function names are governed by the same rules as variable names. Therefore, a function name is a sequence of letters and digits, the first of which is a letter, and where an underscore counts as a letter. The name of your function should generally reflect what it does, so you might call a function that counts beans count_beans(), whereas you'd name a function that calculates the result of raising a value to a given power power().

The **return_type** sets the data type of the value to be returned by the function, and it can be any legal data type—including any data types that you've created yourself. If the function does not return a value, the return type is specified by the keyword void.

The **parameter_list** identifies what the calling function can pass to your function and specifies the type and name of each parameter. You use a parameter name within the body of the function to access the item of data that is passed to it by the calling function when it executes. In some cases, a function may not have any parameters. You can indicate this with an empty parameter list, or by placing the keyword void between the parentheses. A function that has no parameters and does not return a value would therefore have the following header:

```
void my_function()
```

or alternatively:

```
void my_function(void)
```

Note that the type of a parameter cannot be void.

NOTE *Because a function with a return type specified as* void *doesn't return a value, it can't be used in an expression in the calling program. The function doesn't evaluate to anything, so trying to test its value or assign it to something wouldn't make sense. Attempting to use such a function in this way will cause the compiler to generate an error message.*

The Function Body

When you call a function, the statements in the function body execute. In the example in Figure 8-2, the first line of function body declares a double variable called result, which is initialized with the value 1.0. The variable, result, is an automatic variable: it's defined locally in the function, and it only exists within the body of the function. This means that the variable result ceases to exist after the function finishes executing.

The calculation is performed in one of the two for loops, depending on the value of the parameter, n. The value of n is the value of the second of the two arguments that are passed to the function when it is called. If n is greater than or equal to zero, the first for loop executes. If the value of n happens to *be* zero, the body of the loop doesn't execute at all because the loop condition immediately becomes false. In this event, result is left at 1.0. Otherwise, the loop control variable i assumes successive values from 1 to n, and the variable result is multiplied by x once for each loop iteration, which generates the required value. If n is negative, the second for loop executes, which divides result by x for each loop iteration.

Always remember that the variables you declare within the body of a function, and all the function parameters, are local to the function. You can use the names of the variables and parameters that you use in this function quite legally in other functions for quite different purposes if you so desire. The scope of variables that you declare within a function is determined in the way that you have already seen: a variable is created at the point at which it is defined, and it ceases to exist at the end of the block that contains it. The only exceptions to this rule are variables that you declare as static; I'll discuss these a little later in the chapter.

Before I discuss arguments, parameters, and return values in more depth, let's give the power() function a whirl in a complete program.

Try It Out: Using a Function

You can exercise the function power() with the following example:

```
// Program 8.1 Calculating powers
#include <iostream>
#include <iomanip>
using std::cout;
using std::endl;
```

```
// Function to calculate x to the power n
double power(double x, int n) {
  double result = 1.0;
  if(n >= 0)
    for(int i = 0 ; i < n ; i++)
      result *= x;
  else
    for(int i = 0 ; i < -n ; i++)
      result /= x;
  return result;
}

int main() {
  cout << endl;

  // Calculate powers of 8 from -3 to +3
  for(int i = -3 ; i <= 3 ; i++)
    cout << std::setw(10) << power(8.0, i);

  cout << endl;
  return 0;
}
```

This program produces the following output:

```
0.00195313  0.015625     0.125         1       8      64      512
```

<hr>

HOW IT WORKS

All the action occurs in the for loop in main():

```
  for(int i = -3 ; i <= 3 ; i++)
    cout << setw(10) << power(8.0, i);
```

The power() function is called seven times. The first argument is 8.0 on each occasion, but the second argument has successive values of i, from –3 to +3. Thus, seven values are output; these correspond to 8^{-3}, 8^{-2}, 8^{-1}, 8^0, 8^1, 8^2, and 8^3.

Parameters and Arguments

You pass information to a function by means of the **arguments** that you specify when you invoke it. The arguments are placed between parentheses following the function name in the call, as in this line from the Program 8.1:

```
    cout << std::setw(10) << power(8.0, i);
```

The values of the arguments that you specify when you call a function are assigned to the parameters that you used in its definition. The code in the function then executes as though it was written using your argument values to initialize the corresponding parameters. The relationship between the arguments in a call to a function and the parameters that appear in its definition is illustrated in Figure 8-3.

```
cout << power( 3.0 , 2 );    The arguments in a function call map
                             to the parameters in its definition.

                        double power( double x, int n) {

                          double result = 1.0;
The value 9.0 is returned to the    if(n >= 0)
 calling function when the            for(int i = 1 ; i <= n ; i++)
function completes execution.            result *= x;
This return value will then be     else
used within the expression in        for(int i = 1 ; i <= -n ; i++)
  which the function call              result /= x;
        appeared.                   return result;        When the code in the body
                                                          of the function executes,
                        }                                 the parameters will have
                                                          values corresponding to
                                                          the arguments that
                                                          appeared in the function
                                                          call statement.
```

Figure 8-3. Calling a function

NOTE *The difference between arguments and parameters is quite subtle. A parameter appears in a function definition and specifies the data type expected by the function. An argument is the actual value passed to the function when you call it.*

The sequence of the arguments in the function call must correspond to the sequence of the parameters in the parameter list in the function definition. You should also make sure that the data types of your arguments correspond to those demanded by the parameter list: the compiler doesn't necessarily warn you if it needs to make implicit type conversions, and so you run the risk of losing information.

C++ allows you to define several functions with the same name within a program. Functions that share a common name must have different parameter lists. The combination of the function's name and parameter list is called the **function signature**. When a program contains multiple functions with the same name, the compiler uses the function signature to establish which of the functions has been called in any particular instance. This is another good reason to ensure that your argument and parameter types correspond.

Return Values

In general, when a function with a return type other than void is called, it must return a
single value of the type specified in the function header. The return value is calculated
within the body of the function and is returned when execution of the function is
complete.

Thus, in any expression in which the function power() is called, power() acts as a
value of type double. However, you don't *have* to call a function that returns a value
from within an expression. You can just call the function by itself, with a statement
such as the following:

```
power(10.5, 2);
```

Here, the function executes and the value returned from it is discarded. Executing the
power() in this way is rather pointless, but this is not necessarily the case with all functions. For example, you might have a function that copies a file, and for which the
return value just provides additional information about the operation (success or failure, perhaps) that you may choose to discard occasionally. Of course, functions with a
return type of void are always called in a simple statement like this. Because they do
not return a value, they cannot be used in an expression.

The fact that a function can return only a single value might at first appear to be
a limitation, but this really isn't the case. The single value that is returned could be a
pointer to anything you like: an array of data, or even an array of pointers. A function
always returns a value of the type specified in the function header that is part of its
definition.

The return Statement

The return statement in Program 8.1 returns the value of result to the point where the
function was called. What might immediately strike you is that in the previous section I
said that result ceases to exist when the function finishes executing, so how is it returned?
The answer is that a *copy* of the value being returned is made automatically, and this copy
is made available to the calling point of the function.

The general form of the return statement is as follows:

```
return expression;
```

Here, expression must evaluate to a value of the type that is specified in the function
header for the return value. The expression can be anything you want, as long as you
end up with a value of the required type. It can include function calls and can even
include a call of the same function in which it appears, as you'll see in the next chapter.

If the return type is specified as void, no expression can appear in the return statement. It must be written simply as

```
return;
```

If the last statement in a function body executes so that the closing brace is reached, this is equivalent to executing a return statement with no expression. Of course, in a function with a return type other than void, this would be an error and the function would not compile.

Function Declarations

The previous example, Program 8.1, worked perfectly well, but let's try rearranging the code so that the function main() *precedes* the definition of the function power(). The code in the program file will look like this:

```
// Program 8.2 Calculating powers - rearranged
#include <iostream>
#include <iomanip>
using std::cout;
using std::endl;

int main() {
  cout << endl;

  // Calculate powers of 8 from -3 to +3
  for(int i = -3 ; i <= 3 ; i++)
    cout << setw(10) << power(8.0, i);

  cout << endl;
  return 0;
}

// Function to calculate x to the power n
double power(double x, int n) {
  double result = 1.0;
  if(n >= 0)
    for(int i = 0 ; i < n ; i++)
      result *= x;
  else
    for(int i = 0 ; i < -n ; i++)
      result /= x;
  return result;
}
```

If you attempt to compile this version of the program, you won't succeed. The compiler has a problem because the function power() is not defined when it is processing the function main(). Of course, you could simply abandon this version in favor of Program 8.1, but in other situations this won't solve the problem. You should understand two important issues here:

1. First, as you shall see later, a program can consist of several source files. In this situation, the definition of the function called may not precede the function doing the calling—for that matter, it may be contained in a completely separate file.

2. Second, suppose that you have a function A() that calls a function B(), which in turn calls the function A() again. Then, if you put the definition of A() first, it won't compile because it calls B(); the same problem arises if you define B() first because it calls A().

Naturally, a solution to these problems does exist. You can declare a function before you use or define it by means of a function prototype.

Function Prototypes

A **function prototype** is a statement that describes a function sufficiently for the compiler to be able to compile calls to it. It declares the name of the function, its return type, and the types of its parameters. A function prototype is often referred to as a **function declaration** and is similar to a variable declaration in that a function cannot be called within a program file unless the call is preceded in the file by a declaration. A definition of a function is also a declaration, which is why you didn't need a function prototype for power() in Program 8.1.

You could write the function prototype for your power() function as follows:

```
double power(double x, int n);
```

If you place the function prototype at the beginning of a program file that contains calls to the function, the compiler is able to compile the code regardless of where the definition of the function is. To get Program 8.2 to compile, you can just insert the prototype for the function power() before the definition of main():

```
// Program 8.2 Calculating powers - rearranged
#include <iostream>
#include <iomanip>
using std::cout;
using std::endl;

double power(double x, int n);          // Prototype for power function

int main() {
  // main() function as before
}

double power(double x, int n) {
  // power() function as before
}
```

The function prototype here is identical to the function header, with a semicolon appended. A function prototype is always terminated by a semicolon, but in general, it doesn't have to be *identical* to the function header. You can use different names for the parameters from those used in the definition (but not different types, of course). For instance:

```
double power(double value, int exponent);
```

This works just as well. The benefit of the names you have chosen here is marginal, but it does illustrate how it helps to use more explanatory names in the function prototype when such names are too cumbersome to use in the function definition.

Because the compiler only needs to know what *type* each parameter is, you can even omit the parameter names from the prototype, like this:

```
double power(double, int);
```

There is no particular merit in writing your function prototypes like this, and it is much less informative than the version with parameter names. If both function parameters were of the same type, then a prototype like this one would not give you any clue as to which parameter was which. Therefore, I recommend that you always include parameter names in your function prototypes.

Using Function Prototypes

You should get into the habit of writing a prototype for each function that you use in a program at the beginning of your program file—with the exception of main(), of course, which never requires a prototype. Doing this removes the possibility of compiler errors arising from the functions not being sequenced appropriately; also, it allows other programmers to get an overview of the functionality of your code.

I have been using library functions quite frequently, so where are the prototypes for these functions? In fact, they are in the standard headers that I have been including. One of the primary uses of headers is to collect together the function prototypes for a related group of functions. I will discuss this further in Chapter 10.

Passing Arguments to a Function

It is very important that you understand precisely *how* arguments are passed to a function because it affects how you write your functions and ultimately how they operate. You must also avoid a number of pitfalls, so you'll look at the mechanism for this quite closely.

As I have discussed, the arguments that you specify when you call a function correspond in type and sequence to the parameters appearing in the definition of the function. Although you have no latitude so far as the sequence is concerned, you do have some flexibility in the argument types. If you specify an argument in a function call with a type that doesn't correspond to the parameter type in the function definition, then the compiler converts the argument type to the parameter type (where possible). The rules for automatic conversions of this kind are the same as those that control automatic conversions in an assignment statement, as I discussed in Chapter 3. If an automatic conversion turns out not to be possible, you'll get an error message from the compiler.

Generally in C++ you have two mechanisms you can use to pass arguments to functions: the **pass-by-value** method, and the **pass-by-reference** method. I'll show you the pass-by-value mechanism first and then come back to the pass-by-reference method afterward.

The Pass-by-Value Mechanism

With the pass-by-value mechanism for transferring data to a function, the variables or constants that you specify as arguments are not actually passed to a function at all. Instead, just as with the return value, copies of the arguments are created, and these copies are used as the values to be transferred. This is illustrated in Figure 8-4, using the example of the power() function again.

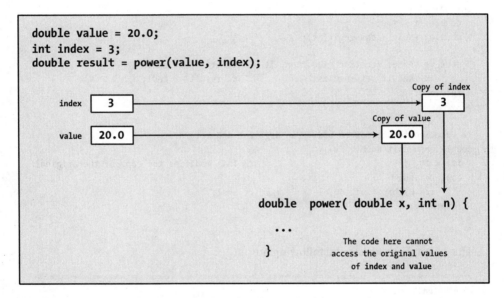

Figure 8-4. The pass-by-value mechanism for arguments to a function

Each time you call the power() function, the compiler arranges for copies of the arguments that you specify to be stored in a temporary location in memory, which is the call stack I mentioned earlier in this chapter. During execution, all references to the function parameters in the code making up the body of the function are mapped to these temporary copies of the arguments. Once the execution of the function is complete, the copies of the arguments are discarded.

I can demonstrate the effects of this with a simple example.

Try It Out: Passing Arguments to a Function

You can write a function that attempts to modify one of its arguments, and of course it fails miserably.

```cpp
// Program 8.3 Failing to modify the original value of a function argument
#include <iostream>
#include <iomanip>
using std::cout;
using std::endl;

double change_it(double it);              // Function prototype

int main() {
  double it = 5.0;
  double result = change_it(it);

  cout << "After function execution, it = " << it      << endl
       << "Result returned is "                  << result << endl;
  return 0;
}

// Function to attempt to modify an argument and return it
double change_it(double it) {
  it += 10.0;                                 // This modifies the copy of the original
  cout << endl
       << "Within function, it = " << it << endl;
  return it;
}
```

This example produces the following output:

```
Within function, it = 15
After function execution, it = 5
Result returned is 15
```

HOW IT WORKS

You can see from the output that adding 10 to the variable it in the function change_it() has no effect on the variable it in main(). The variable it in the function change_it() is local to the function, and it refers to a copy of whatever argument value was passed when the function was called. Figure 8-5 shows what is happening.

Of course, when the value of it that is local to change_it() is returned, a copy of *its* current value is made, and it's this copy that's returned to the calling program.

This pass-by-value mechanism is the default mechanism by which arguments are passed to a function. It provides quite a lot of security to the calling program by preventing the function from modifying variables owned by the calling program. However, suppose that you *do* want to modify values in the calling function. Can you find a way to do it when you need to? Sure you can—you can always use a pointer.

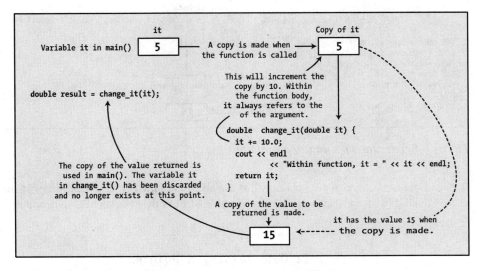

Figure 8-5. Modifying a pass-by-value parameter value

Passing a Pointer to a Function

When you use a pointer as an argument, the pass-by-value mechanism operates just as it did before. However, a pointer contains the address of another variable, and a copy of the pointer points to exactly the same place in memory as the original.

You could change the definition of your change_it() function to accept an argument of type double*. In main(), you can then pass the address of the variable it when you call the function. Of course, you must also change the code in the body of change_it() to dereference the pointer that is passed. The way this works is illustrated in Figure 8-6.

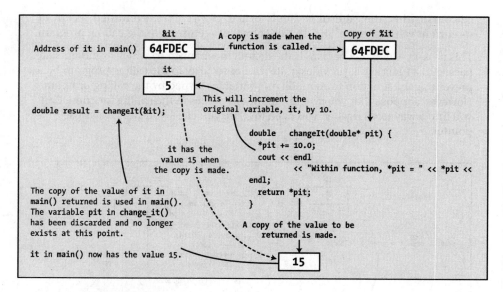

Figure 8-6. Passing a pointer to a function

Because the function change_it() now has the address of the original location of it in main() available in pit, it can modify the variable it directly. Let's see this in practice.

Try It Out: Passing a Pointer

Here, you change the last example to use a pointer to demonstrate the effect of passing an address instead of a value:

```cpp
// Program 8.4 Modifying the original value of a function argument
#include <iostream>
using std::cout;
using std::endl;

double change_it(double* pointer_to_it);  // Function prototype

int main() {
  double it = 5.0;
  double result = change_it(&it);          // Now we pass the address

  cout << "After function execution, it = " << it      << endl
       << "Result returned is "                  << result << endl;

  return 0;
}
```

```
// Function to modify an argument and return it
double change_it(double* pit) {
  *pit += 10.0;                            // This modifies the original it
  cout << endl
        << "Within function, *pit = " << *pit << endl;
  return *pit;
}
```

This version of the program produces the following output:

```
Within function, *pit = 15
After function execution, it = 15
Result returned is 15
```

HOW IT WORKS

Because the parameter type has been changed in the definition of change_it(), you have altered the function prototype:

```
double change_it(double* pointer_to_it);   // Function prototype
```

You have also used a different parameter name from the one used in the function definition, just to prove that you can.

In main(), after the variable it is declared and initialized, the address of the variable is passed to the change_it() function when it is called:

```
double result = change_it(&it);        // Now we pass the address
```

You don't need to create a pointer variable to hold the address of it. Because you only need the address to pass to the function, you can use the address-of operator in the function call.

The new version of the change_it() function uses the dereference operator to add 10 to the value stored in the it variable that was defined back in main():

```
*pit += 10.0;                          // This modifies the original it
```

The function also returns this modified value with the following statement:

```
return *pit;
```

A copy is still made of the value being returned; this always happens automatically for the value being returned from a function.

This version of change_it() serves only to illustrate how a pointer parameter can allow a variable in the calling function to be modified—it is not a model of how a function should be written. Because you are modifying the value of it directly, returning its value is somewhat superfluous here.

Passing Arrays to a Function

Because an array name is essentially an address, you can pass an array as an argument to a function, just by using its name. In this case, the address of the array is copied and passed to the function being called. This provides a number of advantages.

First, passing the address of an array is a very efficient way of passing an array to a function. If you were able to pass all the elements in an array by value, this could be very time consuming for large arrays because copies of every element would be made. In fact, you *can't* pass all the elements in an array by value as a single argument because each parameter represents a single item of data.

Second, and more importantly, because the function does not deal with the original array address, but with a copy of it, the function can treat a parameter representing an array as a pointer in the fullest sense—including modifying the address that it contains. This means that you can use the full power of pointer notation in the body of a function for parameters that are arrays. Before I get to that, let's try the most straightforward case first—handling an array parameter using array notation.

Try It Out: Passing an Array As a Function Argument

I can illustrate the use of an array parameter by writing a function to compute the average of a number of values that are passed to the function in an array when you call it.

```cpp
// Program 8.5 Passing an array
#include <iostream>
using std::cout;
using std::endl;

double average(double array[], int count);      // Function prototype

int main() {
  double values[] = {1.0, 2.0, 3.0, 4.0, 5.0, 6.0, 7.0, 8.0, 9.0, 10.0};

  cout << endl
       << "Average = "
       << average(values, (sizeof values)/(sizeof values[0]))
       << endl;
  return 0;
}

// Function to compute an average
double average(double array[], int count) {
  double sum = 0.0;                              // Accumulate total in here
  for(int i = 0 ; i < count ; i++)
    sum += array[i];                             // Sum array elements
  return sum/count;                              // Return average
}
```

This produces the following very brief output:

```
Average = 5.5
```

The function average() is designed to work with an array of any length. As you can see from the prototype, it accepts two arguments: the array, and a count of the number of elements in the array:

```
double average(double array[], int count);    // Function prototype
```

The type of the first parameter is specified as an array of values of type double. You can't specify the size of the array between the square brackets, nor would doing so have any effect even if you could. This is because the size of the first dimension of an array is not part of its type—you'll remember a similar issue arising when I discussed pointers to multidimensional arrays. In fact, you can pass *any* one-dimensional array of elements of type double as an argument to this function, which will rely on the correct value for the count parameter being supplied by the caller to indicate the number of elements in the array.

Within the body of the average() function, the computation is expressed in the way you would expect:

```
double average(double array[], int count) {
  double sum = 0.0;                      // Accumulate total in here
  for(int i = 0 ; i < count ; i++)
    sum += array[i];                     // Sum array elements

  return sum/count;                      // Return average
}
```

No significant difference exists between this and the way you would write the same computation if you implemented it directly in main(). The function has no way of checking that the array actually accommodates the number of elements indicated by count, and it will quite happily access memory locations outside the actual array if the value of count is greater than the length of the array. It is up to you to ensure that this doesn't happen.

The average() function is called in main() in the output statement:

```
cout << endl
     << "Average = "
     << average(values, (sizeof values)/(sizeof values[0]))
     << endl;
```

Here, the first argument to the average() function is the array name, values, and the second argument is an expression that evaluates to the number of elements in the array.

In this example, the elements of the array passed to average() were accessed in the body of the function using normal array notation. I've said that you can also treat an array passed to a function as a pointer and use pointer notation for the calculation. Let's try that out, too.

Try It Out: Using Pointer Notation When Passing Arrays

You can modify the function in Program 8.5 to work with pointer notation throughout, even though you are using an array. To do so, you'll change the function prototype and header to reflect the use of pointer notation—rather than array notation—for the first parameter, although this is not strictly necessary. You could use pointer notation in the body of the function with the type of the first argument still specified as an array. Here's the modified version of the program:

```cpp
// Program 8.6 Handling an array parameter as a pointer
#include <iostream>
using std::cout;
using std::endl;

double average(double* array, int count);      // Function prototype

int main() {
  double values[] = {1.0, 2.0, 3.0, 4.0, 5.0, 6.0, 7.0, 8.0, 9.0, 10.0};

  cout << endl
       << "Average = "
       << average(values, (sizeof values)/(sizeof values[0]))
       << endl;

  return 0;
}

// Function to compute an average
double average(double* array, int count) {
  double sum = 0.0;                             // Accumulate total in here
  for(int i = 0 ; i < count ; i++)
    sum += *array++;                            // Sum array elements
  return sum/count;                             // Return average
}
```

The output will be exactly the same as the previous version of the program.

HOW IT WORKS

As you can see, the program needed very few changes to make it work by using the array as a pointer. The prototype and the function header have been changed, although, in fact, neither change is absolutely necessary. (Try replacing the prototype and function header here with the corresponding lines from Program 8.5, but leaving the function body written in terms of a pointer. You'll find that it will work just as well.)

The most interesting aspect of this version of the program is the for loop statement:

```
sum += *array++;                        // Sum array elements
```

Here you appear to break a rule—that you can't modify an address specified as an array name—by incrementing the address stored in array. Of course, you are not really breaking the rule at all.

The pass-by-value mechanism makes a copy of the original array address, and passes that to the function. You are modifying the copy here, and the original array address will be quite unaffected. Generally, whenever you pass a one-dimensional array to a function, you are free to treat the value that is passed as a pointer in every sense and change the address in any way you wish.

---

const Pointer Parameters

You may wish to make sure that a function does not inadvertently modify elements of the array that is passed to it. All you need to do is use const in the specification of the parameter type. For instance, if you want to prevent the function average() from altering elements of its first parameter, you can write the function as follows:

```
double average(const double* array, int count) {
  double sum = 0.0;                     // Accumulate total in here
  for(int i = 0 ; i < count ; i++)
    sum += *array++;                    // Sum array elements
  return sum/count;                     // Return average
}
```

Now the compiler will verify that the elements of the array are not modified in the body of the function. Of course, you also need to modify the function prototype to reflect the new type for the first parameter; remember that const types are quite different from non-const types.

When you declare a pointer parameter as const, you are saying to the compiler, "When this function is called, whatever the pointer argument points to should be treated as a constant." This has two consequences: the compiler checks the code in the body of the function to make sure your claim is correct and that you don't try to change the value being pointed to; and it allows the function to be called with an argument that points to a constant.

NOTE *There is no purpose in declaring an ordinary parameter type, such as an* int, *as* const. *Because the pass-by-value mechanism makes a copy of the argument when the function is called, you can't modify the original value from within the body of the function.*

Passing Multidimensional Arrays to a Function

Given what you have already seen, passing a multidimensional array to a function is quite straightforward. For a two-dimensional array, declared as follows:

```
double beans[2][4];
```

You could write the prototype of a hypothetical function yield() like this:

```
double yield(double beans[2][4]);
```

You have explicitly specified the size of both dimensions here, but in fact, you have no way to check that the array's first dimension size is 2. With arrays, the size of the first dimension is not part of the type definition, so the type of the array beans is actually double[ ][4]. Any two-dimensional array with the second dimension size specified as 4 could be passed to this function.

How does the compiler know that the first parameter for the yield() function is an array and not a single array element? The answer is simple: you can't write a single array element as a parameter in a function definition or prototype, although of course you can pass one as an argument when you call a function. For a function accepting a single element of an array as an argument, the parameter itself would just have the type of that element. The array context doesn't apply.

When you're defining a multidimensional array as a parameter, you should omit the first dimension's size (unless you just want to indicate that your function is only intended to work with an array of a fixed size). Of course, the function then needs some way of knowing the size of the first dimension, and for this, you can employ the same method that you have been using for one-dimensional arrays in this chapter. You can add a second parameter to specify the size of the first dimension of the array:

```
double yield(double beans[][4], int size);
```

In case you're wondering, you can't circumvent the need for the extra parameter by using the sizeof operator within the function to determine the size of the array. Using sizeof on an array parameter name within the body of a function returns the size of the pointer to which the array name is equivalent.

Let's try passing a two-dimensional array to a function with a concrete example.

Try It Out: Passing Multidimensional Arrays

You can implement the yield() function to sum the elements of the array that is passed to it. Here's the code to do that and exercise the function:

```cpp
// Program 8.7 Passing a two-dimensional array to a function
#include <iostream>
using std::cout;
using std::endl;

double yield(double values[][4], int n);

int main() {
  double beans[3][4] = {
                        { 1.0,  2.0,  3.0,  4.0},
                        { 5.0,  6.0,  7.0,  8.0},
                        { 9.0, 10.0, 11.0, 12.0}
                       };

  cout << endl
       << "Yield = " << yield(beans, sizeof beans/sizeof beans[0])
       << endl;
  return 0;
}

// Function to compute total yield
double yield(double array[][4], int size) {
  double sum = 0.0;
  for(int i = 0 ; i < size ; i++)          // Loop through number of rows
    for(int j = 0 ; j < 4 ; j++)           // Loop through elements in a row
      sum += array[i][j];
  return sum;
}
```

This will produce the following output:

```
Yield = 78
```

HOW IT WORKS

The first parameter to the yield() function is defined as an array of an arbitrary number of rows, with each row having four elements. When you call the function, the first argument is the array beans, which has three rows. You specify the second argument as the total length of the array (in bytes) divided by the length of the first row. This will evaluate to the number of rows in the array.

(Continued)

The computation in the function is simply a nested for loop, with the inner loop summing elements of a single row, and the outer loop repeating this for each row.

In a function with a multidimensional array argument, pointer notation doesn't really apply particularly well. In the preceding example, when the array is passed, it passes an address that points to an array of four elements (a row). This doesn't lend itself to an easy pointer operation within the function. You'd need to modify the statement in the nested for loop to the following:

```
sum += *(*(array+i)+j);
```

I think you will agree that the computation is clearer in array notation!

The Pass-by-Reference Mechanism

A **reference** is simply an alias for another variable and a variable of a reference type stores a reference to some other variable. When you specify a function parameter as a reference type, your function uses the **pass-by-reference** mechanism to transfer the argument. When the function is called, the argument corresponding to a reference parameter is *not* copied, because the parameter name simply becomes an alias for the argument value in the calling program. Wherever the parameter name is used in the body of the function, it accesses the argument value in the calling function directly.

To specify a reference type, you just add & after the type name. To specify a type as "reference to int" for example, you write the type as int&. Figure 8-7 shows how calling a function with a reference parameter works:

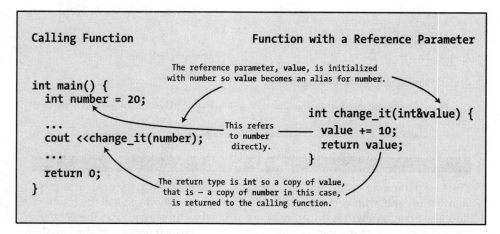

Figure 8-7. Using a reference parameter

Calling a function that has a reference parameter is no different from calling a function that has an ordinary parameter that is passed by value. Whenever the change_it() function is called, the reference parameter, value, is initialized with the specified argument, so while change-it() is executing, value becomes an alternative name for the variable, number, that was passed as the argument. If you call the function again later with a different argument, value then becomes an alias for that argument.

Specifying a function parameter as a reference has two major effects when the function is called. First, the argument is not copied, so the function accesses the argument in the calling function directly. Second, the absence of the copying process makes the function call faster, especially when the arguments are large complicated objects. This and other aspects will be of major importance when you consider passing class objects to a function. For now, let's look at using reference parameters a little more closely, and in particular, see how they compare with using pointers.

References Can Be Risky

In the rush to obtain the extra efficiency that you get by specifying reference parameters for your functions, it's easy to forget about the other aspect of their operation. Using a reference parameter enables the function to modify the original argument within the calling function, but the syntax of calling a function that has a reference argument makes doing so less obvious than when you use pointers for the same purpose. The potential for error by mistakenly assuming that an argument will be passed by value and is therefore protected against change is significant, and you do have safer options for changing original arguments within functions.

Figure 8-8 illustrates the differences between calling a function that uses a pointer parameter, and calling the same function when it has been implemented using a reference parameter.

Function with a Pointer Parameter

```
int change_it(int* value) {
  *value += 10;
  return *value;
}
```

When you call this function, the argument must be an address. In this case, it is obvious from the call that the following function might be able to alter the argument's value:

```
int number = 20;
cout << change_it(&number);
```

Function with a Reference Parameter

```
int change_it(int& value) {
  value += 10;
  return value;
}
```

Here the argument is passed in the form of a reference. The function call doesn't indicate that it is possible for the following function to alter the value of the argument:

```
int number = 20;
cout << change_it(number);
```

Figure 8-8. Pointer parameters versus reference parameters

With a function such as change_it() where the intention is to change the argument in the calling function, you have the option of declaring the parameter as a pointer or a reference. If you specify the parameter as a pointer, then the argument that is passed when the function is called must be an address, so it is obvious in the calling program that the argument may be changed. An argument corresponding to a reference parameter is just an ordinary variable name, so in this case, such a potential for change is not apparent.

How do you exploit the overhead-free nature of passing references to functions without compromising the security of your arguments? The answer is that you need to use const references, so let's investigate the effect of this in the next example.

Try It Out: Reference Parameters

Let's try a simple program that uses a function called larger(), which returns the larger of two values. You'll use this function in various forms to explore how reference parameters can affect the way a function operates. Here's the first version:

```
// Program 8.8 Using reference parameters
#include <iostream>
using std::cout;
using std::endl;

int larger(int& m, int& n);

int main() {
   int value1 = 10;
   int value2 = 20;
   cout << endl << larger(value1, value2) << endl;

   return 0;
}

// Function to the larger of two integers
int larger(int& m, int& n) {
   return m > n ? m : n;              // Return the larger value
}
```

The output of this program is simply the value 20, as you might expect.

HOW IT WORKS

Because the function larger() has reference parameters, it operates with the *original* values of the arguments value1 and value2 when it is called in main() with this statement:

```
   cout << endl << larger(value1, value2) << endl;
```

If you have any doubts about this, try adding a statement in the body of the larger() function to alter the second parameter value:

```
int larger(int& m, int& n) {
  n = 30;
  return m > n ? m : n;              // Return the larger value
}
```

If you then output the value of value2 after larger() has been called in main(), you'll see that its value has indeed been changed.

Suppose you wanted to compare value1 with some constant value—15, say—and return the larger of these values. You might try to add the following statement to main():

```
int main() {
  int value1 = 10;
  int value2 = 20;
  cout << endl << larger(value1, value2) << endl;
  cout << endl << larger(value1, 15) << endl;      // Won't compile!
  return 0;
}
```

With this statement in place, the program will no longer compile. The compiler won't allow a reference to be created to the constant 15, because it knows that the function has direct access to it and may modify it. You can draw the following significant conclusion from this:

You can't pass a constant as an argument to a function when the parameter has been specified as a non-const reference.

USING CONST REFERENCES

You can overcome this difficulty with larger() if you alter the function definition so that the parameters are const references. The prototype would then be as follows:

```
int larger(const int& m, const int& n);
```

Now the function will work with variables and constants. As long as you're not intending to modify the argument that is passed, you can always define the parameter as const. You've got direct access to the arguments that are passed from the calling function (avoiding copying), the compiler checks to make sure you have not included code to modify them, and the function works with variables and constant values. By using const reference parameters, you have been able to combine the greater performance and efficiency that reference parameters provide with the security of the pass-by-value method.

References versus Pointers

In most situations, using a reference parameter is preferable to using a pointer. You should declare reference parameters as const wherever possible, as this provides security for the caller arguments. Of course, if you *need* to modify a reference parameter within the body of a function, you can't declare it as const, but you should consider whether a pointer might be a better parameter type in this situation. The main reason for preferring a pointer is that it is always apparent to the caller that a pointer parameter can be modified.

An important difference between a pointer and a reference is that a pointer can be null, whereas a reference always refers to something—as long as it isn't an alias for a pointer that is null, of course. If you want to allow the possibility of a null argument, your only option is a pointer parameter. Of course, because a pointer parameter can be null, you must always test for null before dereferencing it. If you attempt to dereference a null pointer, your program will crash.

In Chapter 13, you'll begin to see that reference parameters provide some extraordinarily powerful facilities in the context of classes, and in some instances, they enable you to achieve results that would be impossible without them.

Declaring References

References don't only appear in the form of function parameters. A reference can exist in its own right, as an alias for another variable. Suppose that you have a variable declared as follows:

```
long number = 0;
```

You can declare a reference for the variable by using the following declaration statement:

```
long& rnumber = number;         // Declare a reference to variable number
```

The ampersand (&) following the type long indicates that a reference is being declared, and the initializing value following the equal sign is specified as the variable name number. Therefore, rnumber is of type "reference to long".

Just as when you're declaring pointers, you can also place the & adjacent to the variable name, so you could have written the previous statement as follows:

```
long &rnumber = number;         // Declare a reference to variable number
```

NOTE *The compiler doesn't mind which notation you use. In this book, I'll use the former, with & appended to the type name.*

The use of & in declaring a reference will seem a little confusing at first. Its use in the context of references looks similar to what you saw previously, when you were obtaining the address of a variable. However, with a little practice you'll soon appreciate the difference.

When you declare a reference, it must *always* be initialized with the name of the variable for which it is an alias. It is not possible to declare a reference without initializing it. A further constraint is that a reference is fixed—you can't change a reference once it has been declared; it will always be an alias for the same variable. The reason that a reference parameter in a function can appear to refer to different variables at different times is that it is an illusion. The reality is that the reference parameter is re-created and reinitialized each time the function is called, so for each function call, you have a completely new reference.

You can always use a reference in place of the original variable name. Here's an example:

```
rnumber += 10;
```

This statement has the effect of incrementing the variable number by 10, because rnumber is an alias for number.

To make sure that you have the difference clear in your mind, let's contrast the reference rnumber with the pointer, pnumber, declared in this statement:

```
long* pnumber = &number;        // Initialize a pointer with an address
```

This declares the pointer pnumber, and initializes it with the address of the variable number. You can then increment the variable with a statement such as the following:

```
*pnumber += 10;                 // Increment number through a pointer
```

I must point out a significant distinction here between using a pointer and using a reference: a pointer needs to be dereferenced to obtain or operate on the value of the variable to which it points. With a reference, you don't need to dereference it to access the value. In some ways, a reference is like a pointer that has already been dereferenced, although it can't be changed to refer to another variable. The reference is the complete equivalent of the variable for which it is a reference.

That's all I need to say about references for now, but it's far from the end of the matter. You'll be applying them extensively when you look at class operations in Chapter 13.

Arguments to main()

You can define the function main() to accept arguments that are entered on the command line when your program executes. The types of parameters that you can specify are standardized: you can either define main() with no parameters, as I have done in all the examples up to now, or you can define main() in the following form:

```
int main(int argc, char* argv[]) {
  // Code for main()
}
```

The first parameter, argc, is a count of the number of strings on the command line. The second parameter, argv, is an array that contains pointers to each of the strings that were entered on the command line, including the name of the program itself. The last element in the array argv (that is, argv[argc]) will always be 0, and the number of elements in argv will be argc + 1.

I'll give you a couple of examples to make this clear. Suppose that to run your program, you enter the following on the command line:

```
Myprog
```

In this case, argc will be 1 and argv[] will contain two elements. The first element will contain the address of the string "Myprog", and the second element will be 0.

Alternatively, suppose that you enter this:

```
Myprog 2 3.5 "Rip Van Winkle"
```

Now argc will be 4 and argv[] will have five elements. The first four elements will be pointers to the strings "Myprog.exe", "2", "3.5", and "Rip Van Winkle". The fifth element, argv[4], will be 0.

What you do with the command line arguments is entirely up to you. As an illustration of how to access the command line arguments, consider the following implementation of main():

```
// Program that lists its command line arguments
#include <iostream>
using std::cout;
using std::endl;

int main(int argc, char* argv[]) {
  for (int i = 0 ; i < argc ; i++)
    cout << endl << argv[i];

  cout << endl;
  return 0;
}
```

This just lists all the command line arguments, including the program name. Command line arguments can be anything at all—filenames to a file copy program, for example, or the name of a person to search for in a contact file—anything that is useful to have entered for your program when it executes.

Default Argument Values

You will find yourself in many situations in which it would be useful to assign default values to one or more of your function parameters. This means that you only need to specify a value for an argument in a function call when you want something different from the default.

A simple example might be a function that you use to output a standard error message. Most of the time, a default message will suffice, but occasionally you might want to specify an alternative. You can do this by specifying the default value for a parameter in the function prototype. You could write the definition for a function to output a message as follows:

```
// Output an error message to the command line
void show_error(const char* message) {
  cout << endl << message << endl;
}
```

To specify a default message, you'd write the string to be used as the default argument value in the *prototype* for this function, like so:

```
void show_error(const char* message = "Program Error");
```

If you want to use the function to output the default message, you call it without an argument value:

```
  show_error();            // Display default message
```

This displays the following output:

```
Program Error
```

When you want to provide a particular message, you can specify the argument to the following function:

```
  show_error("Nothing works!");
```

You could have defined the show_error() function using an argument of type string, instead of a C-style string. In this case, the prototype with a default value for the parameter would be written as follows:

```
void show_error(const string message = "Program Error");
```

Of course, in this case, you'd need to include the <string> header in the program to make the string type available.

Specifying a default parameter value in this way can make functions simpler to use, and you aren't limited to just one default parameter—you can have as many as you want. Let's explore that a little further.

Multiple Default Parameter Values

Any function parameters for which you specify default values must be placed at the *end* of the parameter list. The reason for this is simple. To use the default value of a parameter when calling the function, you omit the corresponding argument. Omitting arguments from the middle of the list would really confuse the compiler! The compiler assumes, therefore, that if any arguments are omitted in a function call, they correspond to the rightmost parameters.

Let's contrive an example of a function with several default parameter values. Suppose that you wrote a function to display one or more data values, several to a line, as follows:

```
void show_data(const int data[], int count, const string& title,
                                             int width, int perLine) {
  std::cout << std::endl << title;               // Display the title

  // Output the data values
  for(int i = 0 ; i < count ; i++) {
    if(i % perLine == 0)                          // Newline before the first
      std::cout << std::endl;                     // and after perLine
    std::cout << std::setw(width) << data[i];     // Display a data item
  }
  std::cout << std::endl;
}
```

The data parameter specifies the data values to be displayed, and count indicates how many there are. The third parameter is of type const string& and specifies a title that is to head the output. The fourth parameter determines the field width for each item, and the last parameter is the number of data items per line.

This long parameter list would be quite cumbersome in calls to the function—imagine having to specify all five parameters to output a single data item! You can use default values for some of the parameters to make it easier.

Try It Out: Using Multiple Default Parameter Values

Here's how you could use the function with defaults for all but the first parameter:

```cpp
// Program 8.9 Using multiple default parameter values
#include <iostream>
#include <iomanip>
#include <string>
using std::cout;
using std::endl;
using std::string;

// The function prototype including defaults for reference parameters
void show_data(const int data[], int count = 1,
            const string& title = "Data Values", int width = 10, int perLine = 5);

int main() {
  int samples[] = {1, 2, 3, 4, 5, 6, 7, 8, 9, 10, 11, 12};

  int dataItem = 99;
  show_data (&dataItem);

  dataItem = 13;
  show_data(&dataItem, 1, "Unlucky for some!");

  show_data(samples, sizeof samples/sizeof samples[0]);
  show_data(samples, sizeof samples/sizeof samples[0], "Samples");
  show_data(samples, sizeof samples/sizeof samples[0], "Samples", 14);
  show_data(samples, sizeof samples/sizeof samples[0], "Samples", 14, 4);

  return 0;
}

// Function to output one or more integer values
void show_data (const int data[], int count, const string& title,
                                            int width, int perLine) {
  cout << endl << title;                      // Display the title

  // Output the data values
  for(int i = 0 ; i < count ; i++) {
    if(i % perLine == 0)                       // Newline before the first
      cout << endl;                            // and after perLine

    cout << std::setw(width) << data[i];       // Display a data item
  }
  cout << endl;
}
```

(Continued)

This produces the following output:

```
Data Values
        99

Unlucky for some!
        13

Data Values
        1           2           3           4           5
        6           7           8           9          10
       11          12

Samples
        1           2           3           4           5
        6           7           8           9          10
       11          12

Samples
            1           2           3           4           5
            6           7           8           9          10
           11          12

Samples
            1           2           3           4
            5           6           7           8
            9          10          11          12
```

HOW IT WORKS

The prototype for the show_data() function specifies default values for all parameters except the first:

```
void show_data(const int data[], int count = 1,
          const string& title = "Data Values", int width = 10, int perLine = 5);
```

As you can see from the third parameter, you can supply default values for a reference parameter in the same way as you do for parameters of a non-reference type. Because the last four parameters all have default values, you have five ways to call the function: you can specify all five arguments, or omit the last one, or the last two, or the last three, or the last four. Remember that you can only omit arguments at the *end* of the list; you are not, for instance, allowed to omit the second and the fifth:

```
  show_data(samples, , "Samples", 15);        // Wrong!
```

In the function main(), you have an array of integers for sample output, defined as follows:

```
int samples[] = {1, 2, 3, 4, 5, 6, 7, 8, 9, 10, 11, 12};
```

You use this to exercise the show_data() function. The first application of the function outputs a single data value:

```
int dataItem = 99;
show_data(&dataItem);
```

Because the first parameter is an array of type int, you must pass the address of dataItem as the argument. The default value for count of 1 applies here, and the three other default parameter values also apply.

Next, you output a modified value for dataItem, along with a new title:

```
dataItem = 13;
show_data(&dataItem, 1, "Unlucky for some!");
```

You only want a different title, but if you specify a third argument, you must also specify the second. The value for count is the same as the default, because you are still outputting a single data item.

You then output the contents of the samples array four times in the next four statements:

```
show_data(samples, sizeof samples/sizeof samples[0]);
show_data(samples, sizeof samples/sizeof samples[0], "Samples");
show_data(samples, sizeof samples/sizeof samples[0], "Samples", 14);
show_data(samples, sizeof samples/ izeof samples[0], "Samples", 14, 4);
```

For an array, you need to specify the count argument; otherwise show-data() will output only the first element of the array. Each successive statement specifies an additional argument.

When you use several parameters with default values, you need to take care to sequence the parameters appropriately. The parameters should be ordered so that the one that is *least* likely to be specified comes last, with each preceding parameter being the next most likely to require an explicit value. Obviously, this will be a fine judgment in many instances.

Returning Values from a Function

As you already know, you can return a value of any type from a function. This is quite straightforward when you're returning a value of one of the basic types, but there are some pitfalls when you are returning a pointer.

Returning a Pointer

When you return a pointer from a function, you must make absolutely sure that the address it points to is either 0, or a location in memory that is still valid in the calling function. In other words, the variable pointed to must still be *in scope* after the return to the calling function. This implies the following golden rule.

 GOLDEN RULE *Never return the address of an automatic local variable from a function.*

Let's look at an illustration. Suppose you want to write a function that returns the address of the larger of two values. This function might be used on the left of an assignment, so that you could change the variable that contains the larger value, perhaps in a statement such as this:

```
*larger(value1, value2) = 100;      // Set the larger variable to 100
```

This sort of thing can easily lead you astray. Here's an implementation that doesn't work:

```
int* larger(int a, int b) {
  if(a > b)
    return &a;                  // Wrong!
  else
    return &b;                  // Wrong!
}
```

It's fairly easy to see what's wrong with this: a and b are local variables. Copies of the original integer argument values will be transferred to the local variables a and b, but when you return &a or &b, the variables at these addresses will be out of scope in the calling program. You should get a warning from your compiler if you try to compile this code.

What you can do is specify the parameters as pointers:

```
int* larger(int* a, int* b) {
  if(*a > *b)
    return a;                   // OK
  else
    return b;                   // OK
}
```

You could call this function with the statement:

```
*larger(&value1, &value2) = 100;    // Set the larger variable to 100
```

Writing a function to return the address of the larger of two values is unlikely to be particularly useful, but a function that returns the address of the largest element in an array might be of more interest.

··

Try It Out: Returning a Pointer

You could extend the idea slightly by writing two functions: one to return the address of the element in an array with the smallest value, and the other to return the element with the largest value. You can also use a version of your show_data() function. This program will modify an array of values of type double so that they fall within the interval 0 to 1. You might want to do this if you are only interested in the relative sizes of the values—scaling values to within a fixed range can make them easier to present graphically for example. Here is the code to scale a set of data values:

```cpp
// Program 8.10 Returning a pointer
#include <iostream>
#include <iomanip>
#include <string>
using std::cout;
using std::endl;
using std::string;

void show_data(const double data[], int count = 1,
          const string& title = "Data Values", int width = 10, int perLine = 5);
double* largest(double data[], int count);
double* smallest(double data[], int count);

int main() {
  double samples[] = {
                      11.0,   23.0,   13.0,   4.0,
                      57.0,   36.0,  317.0,  88.0,
                       9.0,  100.0,  121.0,  12.0
                     };

  const int count = sizeof samples/sizeof samples[0];

  show_data(samples, count, "Original Values");

  int min = *smallest(samples, count);

  // Shift range of values so smallest is zero
  for(int i = 0; i < count ; i++)
    samples[i] -= min;
```

(Continued)

```
    int max = *largest(samples, count);

    // Normalize range to 0 to 1.0
    for(int i = 0; i < count ; i++)
      samples[i] /= max;

    show_data(samples, count, "Normalized Values", 12);
    return 0;
}

// Function to find the largest of an array of double values
double* largest(double data[], int count) {
  int index_max = 0;
  for(int i = 1; i < count; i++)
    if(data[index_max] < data[i])
      index_max = i;
  return &data[index_max];
}

// Function to find the smallest of an array of double values
double* smallest(double data[], int count) {
  int index_min = 0;
  for(int i = 1; i < count; i++)
   if(data[index_min] > data[i])
     index_min = i;
  return &data[index_min];
}

// Function to display an array of double values
void show_data(const double data[], int count,
          const string& title, int width, int perLine) {
  cout << endl << title;
  for(int i = 0 ; i < count ; i++) {
    if(i % perLine == 0)
      cout << endl;
    cout << std::setw(width) << data[i];
  }
  cout << endl;
}
```

This program produces the following output:

```
Original Values
        11         23          13           4         57
        36        317          88           9        100
       121         12

Normalized Values
  0.0223642  0.0607029    0.028754           0    0.169329
   0.102236          1    0.268371   0.0159744    0.306709
   0.373802  0.0255591
```

This program uses two similar functions, largest() and smallest(), which return the addresses of the largest and smallest elements in a double array, respectively. The code for the function largest() is shown here:

```
double* largest(double data[], int count) {
  int index_max = 0;
  for(int i = 1; i < count; i++)
    if(data[index_max] < data[i])
      index_max = i;
  return &data[index_max];
}
```

This starts by assuming that the first element of the array is the largest, specified by setting the value of index_max to 0. The element at index position index_max is compared to each of the others in the for loop. If the index_max element is smaller than the current element within the loop, index_max is set to the current index value. The function returns the address of the largest element, given by the expression &data[index_max], which uses the address-of operator. The smallest() function differs only in the comparison operator used in the if condition.

In main(), you define an array called samples. Then, you assign the number of array elements to count. This means that you don't have to recalculate the value each time you need it:

```
const int count = sizeof sample /sizeof samples[0];
```

You display the original values for the elements with this statement:

```
show_data(samples, count, "Original Values");
```

Apart from the type of the first argument, the definition of the show_data() function is the same as you have seen previously. The prototype for the function defines default values for the last four parameters, and you use the defaults for the last two in this case.

You use the smallest() function to find the lowest value in the samples array with this statement:

```
int min = *smallest(samples, count);
```

To obtain the *value* of the lowest element, you apply the dereference operator, *, to the address that is returned by the function.

It's possible to shift the range of values so that the lowest value is zero by subtracting the current lowest value from each element in the array. Here you can see this done in the for loop:

```
for(int i = 0; i < count ; i++)
  samples[i] -= min;
```

(Continued)

Now that the range runs from zero to some highest value, you can modify the values so that they fall between 0 and 1 by dividing them by the current highest value, which is obtained using the `largest()` function:

```
int max = *largest(samples, count);
```

You then modify the values in another `for` loop, by dividing them by the current highest value:

```
for(int i = 0; i < count ; i++)
  samples[i] /= max;
```

Finally, you output the new values:

```
show_data(samples, count, "Normalized Values", 12);
```

This time, you override the default for the field width to accommodate the number of decimal places produced for each value.

As a final point in this section, it's worth noting that because the `largest()` and `smallest()` functions return an address, by applying the dereference operator you can convert the address that is returned to an *lvalue*, which you can then use on the left of an assignment operation, like this:

```
*largest(samples, count) *= 2.0;
```

This statement would double the value of the highest element in the `samples` array.

Returning a Reference

Returning a pointer from a function has certainly been useful, but it can be problematic, especially when you use the function on the left of an assignment operator in the way that I suggested at the end of the last section. Pointers can be null, and attempting to dereference a null pointer results in the failure of your program.

The solution, as you will surely have guessed from the title of this section, is to return a *reference* from a function. Because a reference is an alias for another variable, you can state a golden rule for references that's rather like the golden rule for pointers, and it applies for the same reasons of scope.

 GOLDEN RULE *Never return a reference to an automatic local variable from a function.*

Because a reference is an alias for another variable, it is by definition an lvalue. So by returning a reference from a function, you enable a call to the function to be used directly on the left of an assignment. In fact, returning a reference from a function is the *only* way you can enable a function to be used directly (without dereferencing) on the left of an assignment operation.

Suppose you define the larger() function as follows:

```
int& larger(int& m, int& n) {
  return m > n ? m : n;          // Return a reference to the larger value
}
```

Here, the return type is of type reference to int, and the parameters are non-const references. Because you want to return one or the other of the reference parameters, you must not declare the parameters as const.

You could now use the function to change the value of the larger of the two arguments with a statement like this:

```
  larger(value1, value2) = 50; // Change the value of the larger one to 50
```

With the function declared in this fashion, you can't use constants as arguments. Because your parameters are non-const references, the compiler simply won't allow it to happen. A reference parameter clearly permits the value to be changed, and changing a constant is not something the compiler will knowingly go along with.

You're not going to examine an extended example of using reference return types at this moment, but you can be sure that you'll meet them again before long. As you'll discover, reference return types become essential when you start creating your own data types using classes.

Returning a New Variable from a Function

You can create a new variable in the free store within a function and return it to the caller by means of a pointer return value. You just use the new operator to allocate the space, and return the address.

The hazard of using this technique is that you run the very real risk of creating a memory leak. Every time such a function is called, more memory is allocated in the free store, and it is left up to the *calling* function to take responsibility for releasing the memory by using the delete operator.

Inline Functions

With functions that are very short (the larger() function that I have been discussing with you is a good example), the overhead of the code the compiler generates to deal with passing arguments and returning a result is significant compared to the code involved in doing the actual calculation. The execution times of the two types of code may be similarly related.

In extreme cases, the code for calling the function may occupy *more* memory than the code in the body of the function. In such circumstances, you might want to suggest to the compiler that it replace a call to the function with the actual code from the body of the function, suitably adjusted to deal with local names. This could make the program shorter, or faster, or possibly both.

You can suggest that the compiler perform this task by using the `inline` keyword in the definition of the function, for example:

```
inline int larger(int m, int n) {
  return m > n ? m : n;
}
```

With this definition, you are suggesting that the compiler should replace calls with inline code. However, it is only a suggestion, and it depends on the compiler as to whether your suggestion is taken up. When you declare a function as `inline`, the definition must be available in every source file that calls the function. For this reason, the definition of an inline function usually appears in a header file rather than in a source file, and the header is included into each source file that uses the function.

Different compilers apply different rules to determine whether a function defined as `inline` has its calls replaced by inline code. A basic prerequisite is that such functions must be short and uncomplicated. Obviously, making a long function `inline` is likely to be counterproductive, especially if it's called many times in a program. Such folly could greatly increase the size of the program, with little or no improvement in execution time.

You may encounter a downside to declaring a function as `inline` if the compiler chooses not to make a function `inline` even though you have requested it to be so. In this situation, the function call compiles as a normal function call, but the compiler also typically treats the function as local to the source file, so each source file that uses it has its own compiled copy of the function. The result is that you have unnecessary duplication of the code for the function if it is used in several different source files.

Static Variables

In all the functions you have written so far, nothing is retained within the body of the function from one execution to the next. Suppose you want to count how many times a particular function has been called—how can you do that? One way is to define a variable at file scope and then increment it from within the function. A potential pitfall of this approach, however, is that *any* function can modify the variable within your program file, and you can't be sure that it's only being altered when it should be.

A better solution is to declare a variable within the function body as `static`, something I touched on briefly back in Chapter 3. A **static** variable is created on the first occasion that the statement that defines it is executed. Thereafter, it remains in existence until the program terminates. This means that you can carry over a value from one call of a function to the next.

To declare a variable as static, you just prefix the type name in the declaration of the variable with the keyword `static`. Here's an example:

```
static int count = 1;
```

When this statement executes, the static variable `count` is created and initialized to 1. Subsequent executions of the same statement have no further effect. The variable `count` continues to exist until the program terminates. If you omit the initializing value from the declaration, the static variable is initialized to 0.

Let's take a very simple example of a function that declares a static variable:

```
void nextInteger() {
  static int count = 1;
  cout << endl << count++;
}
```

This function increments the static variable `count` after displaying its current value. The first time the function is called, it displays the value 1. The second time, it displays the value 2. Each time the function is called, it displays an integer that is one larger than the previous value. The static variable `count` is created and initialized only once when the function is called for the first time. Subsequent calls of the function use whatever is the current value of `count`, which survives for as long as the program is executing.

You can declare any type of variable as `static`, and you can use a `static` variable for anything that you need to remember from one call of a function to the next. You might want to hold on to the number of the last file record that was read, for example, or the highest value of all the arguments that have been passed.

Here is an example that demonstrates a static variable in use.

....

Try It Out: Using a Static Variable in a Function

The Fibonacci sequence is a sequence of integers in which each number is the sum of the two preceding it. You'll write a function to return a number in the Fibonacci sequence by using static variables to recall the two previous numbers calculated by the function. Obviously, there are no "previous numbers" in the Fibonacci sequence before the program starts, so you'll initialize the two variables to 0 and 1. I wouldn't claim this method as a model of good programming style, but it does demonstrate the properties of static variables in a more complicated context.

```
// Program 8.11 Using a static variable
#include <iostream>
#include <iomanip>
using std::cout;
using std::endl;

long next_Fibonacci();
```

(Continued)

```
int main() {
  cout << endl << "The Fibonacci Series" << endl;
  for(int i = 0 ; i < 30 ; i++) {
    if(i % 5 == 0)                        // Every fifth number...
      cout << endl;                       // ...start a new line
    cout << std::setw(12) << next_Fibonacci ();
  }
  cout << endl;
  return 0;
}

// Function to generate the next number in the Fibonacci series
long next_Fibonacci () {
  static long last = 0;                   // Last number in sequence
  static long last_but_one = 1;           // Last but one number

  long next = last + last_but_one;        // Next is sum of the last two
  last_but_one = last;                    // Update last but one
  last = next;                            // Last is new one
  return last;                            // Return the new one
}
```

This produces the following output:

The Fibonacci Series

1	1	2	3	5
8	13	21	34	55
89	144	233	377	610
987	1597	2584	4181	6765
10946	17711	28657	46368	75025
121393	196418	317811	514229	832040

HOW IT WORKS

The function main() just calls the function nextFibonacci(), 30 times, in a loop:

```
for(int i = 0 ; i < 30 ; i++) {
  if(i % 5 == 0)                        // Every fifth number...
    cout << endl;                       // ...start a new line
  cout << std::setw(12) << nextFibonacci();
}
```

No arguments are passed, so the values returned are generated internally to the nextFibonacci() function. The two static variables declared in the function will hold the most recently generated number in the sequence, and the one before that:

```
static long last = 0;                   // Last number in sequence
static long last_but_one = 1;           // Last but one number
```

By judiciously initializing last to 0 and last_but_one to 1, you can kick the sequence off with two 1s. At each call of nextFibonacci(), the next number in the sequence is calculated by summing the previous two numbers in the sequence. The result is stored in the automatic variable next:

```
long next = last + last_but_one;        // Next is sum of last two
```

You can do this because last and last_but_one are static variables, which still carry the values assigned to them during the previous iteration of nextFibonacci().

Before returning the value next, you have to transfer the previous value in last to last_but_one, and the new value to last:

```
last_but_one = last;              // Update last but one
last = next;                      // Last is new one
```

Although static variables survive as long as the program does, they are only *accessible* within the block in which they are declared, so the variables last and last_but_one can only be accessed from within the body of the function nextFibonacci().

NOTE *The Fibonacci series may look like a bunch of rather dull numbers, but they crop up in all sorts of places. For example, plants grow successive leaves so that the angle between them is 2π times a ratio of alternate numbers in this sequence. So, plants grow their leaves at angles of 2π times 1/2 (the first and third numbers), 2π times 1/3 (the second and fourth numbers), 2π times 2/5 (the third and fifth numbers), and so on. Isn't that interesting?*

Summary

This chapter has introduced you to writing and using functions. However, you'll see more about functions in the next chapter, and more still in the context of user-defined types, which I will introduce starting in Chapter 11. The important bits that you should take away from this chapter are as follows:

- Functions are self-contained compact units of code with a well-defined purpose. A well-written program typically consists of a large number of small functions rather than a small number of large functions.

- A function definition consists of a function header defining the function name, the parameters, and the return type; and a function body containing the executable code for the function.

- A function prototype enables the compiler to process calls to a function even though the function definition has not been processed.

- The pass-by-value mechanism for passing arguments to a function passes copies of the original argument values, so the original argument values are not accessible from within the function.

- Passing a pointer to a function allows the function to change the value that is pointed to, even though the pointer itself is passed by value.

- Declaring a pointer parameter as const can prevent modification of the original value.

- You can pass the address of an array to a function as a pointer.

- Passing values to a function using a reference—the pass-by-reference mechanism—can avoid the copying that is implicit in the pass-by-value transfer of arguments. Any reference parameter that is not modified within a function should be specified as const.

- Specifying default values for function parameters allows arguments to be optionally omitted, whereupon the default value will be assumed.

- Returning a reference from a function allows the function to be used on the left of an assignment operator. Declaring the return type as a const reference prevents this.

Exercises

The following exercises enable you to try out what you've learned in this chapter. If you get stuck, look back over the chapter for help. If you're still stuck after that, you can download the solutions from the Apress website (http://www.apress.com/book/download.html), but that really should be a last resort.

Exercise 8-1. Write a function, valid_input(), that accepts two integer arguments and a string argument that identifies a value to be entered. The function should prompt for input of the value within the range specified by the arguments. The function should continue to prompt for input until the value entered by the user is valid.

Use the valid_input() function in a program to obtain the user's date of birth, and validate that the month, day, and year are all sensible. Finally, output the date to the screen in the form of this example:

```
November 21, 1977
```

The program should be implemented so that separate functions, month(), year(), and day() manage the input of the corresponding numerical values. Don't forget leap years!

Exercise 8-2. Write a function that accepts a string or array of characters as input and reverses it. What is the best sort of argument type to use? Provide a main() function to test your function by prompting the user for a string of characters, reversing them, and then outputting the reversed string.

Exercise 8-3. Write a program that accepts from two to four command line arguments. If it is called with less than two, or more than four arguments, output a message telling the user what they should do, and then exit. If the number of arguments is correct, write them to the command line, each on a separate line.

Exercise 8-4. Modify the program you wrote for Exercise 8-3 so that it will only accept two arguments and pass the second one to the string-reversing function that you wrote for Exercise 8-2. Output the reversed string.

Exercise 8-5. Write a function that returns a reference to the smaller of two integer variables of type long. Write another that returns a reference to the larger. Use these to generate as many numbers of the Fibonacci sequence as the user requests. You will recall from this chapter that the sequence is 1, 1, 2, 3, 5, 8, 13, ..., where each number is the sum of the two preceding it. (Hint: You need to store two numbers in the sequence n1 and n2, both of which start out as 1. If you store the sum of the two in the smaller of the two and then output the larger, you should get what you want. The hard bit may be figuring out why this works!)

CHAPTER 9

More on Functions

IN THIS CHAPTER, you'll explore some of the more subtle aspects of designing and using functions. You'll examine the way your choice of parameter types and the return type can affect how a function operates, and even where you can use it. You'll also investigate ways to create function definitions automatically.

In this chapter you will learn the following:

- How to implement several functions with the same name

- How you can use pointers and references as parameters

- The effect of declaring parameters with the const qualifier

- What function templates are, and how to use them

- How to define and use pointers to functions

- What recursive functions are and how they work

Function Overloading

Often, you'll find that you need two or more functions that do essentially the *same* thing, but with parameters of *different* data types. For example, you might need several versions of your function larger() to find the larger of two variables of any of the basic numeric data types. Ideally, of course, all of these functions would have the same name, larger(). The alternative would be to define a function larger_int() for variables of type int, and a function larger_float() for variables of type float, and so on; but this is clumsy and laborious. This is a case for **function overloading**.

With function overloading, you can have several functions in a program with the same name. For this to be legal, each function with a given name must have a different parameter list. By this I mean that the parameter *types* distinguish one parameter list from another; it is not sufficient simply to have different parameter names. Essentially, two functions with the same name are different if one of the following is true:

- The number of parameters for each function is different.

- The number of parameters is the same, but at least one pair of corresponding parameters has different types.

However, I need to drag some subtleties relating to this out in the open.

The Signature of a Function

The combination of the name of a function, together with its parameter types defines a unique characteristic called the **function signature**. The function signature serves to differentiate one function from another, so each function in your program must have a unique function signature. The function signature comes into play whenever you call a function in your program.

From the function prototypes or the function definitions, the compiler creates a function signature for each function in your program file. When you write a statement that includes a function call, the compiler uses the call to create a function signature and then compares it with the set of function signatures that are available from your function prototypes and/or definitions. If it finds a match, then it has established which function you called. If it doesn't find a match, then it checks to see whether any conversions on the arguments produce a match.

NOTE *The return type is* not *part of the function signature. In fact, this is logical. When you call a function, you are not obliged to store the value returned; therefore, the return type of the function is not necessarily determined by the calling statement.*

Try It Out: Overloading a Function

Let's try a very simple example that uses versions of the function `larger()` that you programmed in the previous chapter.

```
// Program 9.1 Overloading a function
#include <iostream>
using std::cout;
using std::endl;

// Prototypes for two different functions
double larger(double a, double b);
long larger(long a, long b);


int main() {
   double a_double = 1.5, b_double = 2.5;
   float a_float = 3.5f, b_float = 4.5f;
   long a_long = 15L, b_long = 25L;
   cout << endl;
   cout << "The larger of double values "
        << a_double << " and " << b_double <<" is "
        << larger(a_double, b_double) << endl;
   cout << "The larger of float values "
```

```
          << a_float << " and " << b_float <<" is "
          << larger(a_float, b_float) << endl;
  cout << "The larger of long values "
          << a_long << " and " << b_long <<" is "
          << larger(a_long, b_long) << endl;
return 0;
}

// Function to return the larger of two floating point values
double larger(double a, double b) {
  cout << "double larger() called" << endl;
  return a>b ? a : b;
}

// Function to return the larger of two integer values
long larger(long a, long b) {
  cout << "long larger() called" << endl;
  return a>b ? a : b;
}
```

This produces the following output:

```
double larger() called
The larger of double values 1.5 and 2.5 is 2.5
double larger() called
The larger of float values 3.5 and 4.5 is 4.5
long larger() called
The larger of long values 15 and 25 is 25
```

HOW IT WORKS

You have two overloaded versions of the function larger() and they both write a message to the command line when they are called. The first call in main() uses the version for arguments of type double:

```
  cout << "The larger of double values "
          << a_double << " and " << b_double <<" is "
          << larger(a_double, b_double) << endl;
```

An exact match for the function signature exists here, so the compiler has no problem selecting the correct function to use. The output shows that the function with parameters of type double was indeed chosen.

The next call is a little different, though:

```
  cout << "The larger of float values "
          << a_float << " and " << b_float <<" is "
          << larger(a_float, b_float) << endl;
```

(Continued)

This statement calls a function, `larger()`, with parameters of type `float`. You didn't define such a function. However, the compiler can convert from `float` to `double` with no data loss; this is an acceptable automatic conversion, so the compiler can use the version of `larger()` that accepts `double` arguments.

The next statement passes arguments of type `long` to the function `larger()`:

```
cout << "The larger of long values "
     << a_long << " and " << b_long <<" is "
     << larger(a_long, b_long) << endl;
```

Again, an exact match with the version accepts arguments of type `long`, and that is the version of `larger()` that is called.

Of course, type `int` converts to type `long` with no data loss, so you could use the version with `long` parameters in this case couldn't you? Well, give it a try by adding a few statements to `main()`:

```
int a_int = 15, b_int = 25;
cout << "The larger of int values "
     << a_int << " and " << b_int <<" is "
     << larger(a_int, b_int) << endl;
```

Didn't work, did it? The compiler just couldn't decide which version of `larger()` to use. Automatic casts from `int` to `long` or from `int` to `double` are both acceptable, so the compiler has no basis for a decision. In other words, your code is ambiguous. The compiler is not prepared to toss a coin here and expects you to decide. You can resolve this sort of problem by putting in explicit casts:

```
int a_int = 15, b_int = 25;
cout << "The larger of int values "
     << a_int << " and " << b_int <<" is "
     << larger(static_cast<long>(a_int), static_cast<long>(b_int))
     << endl;
```

Now this code shows an exact match with `long` arguments. It would have been sufficient to cast either of the arguments to `long`—the compiler would have been able to select the version with `long` parameters. However, by putting both casts in, your intentions are clear to anyone reading the code.

Overloading and Pointer Parameters

Obviously, pointers to different types are different, so the following prototypes declare two different overloaded functions:

```
int larger(int* pValue1, int* pValue2);
int larger(float* pValue1, float* pValue2);
```

You can use a parameter that is a pointer to a given type. Note that this is interpreted in the same way as an array of that type. Thus, for example, a parameter of type int* is treated in the same way as a parameter type of int[ ]. Hence, the following prototypes declare the same function, not two different functions:

```
int largest(int values[], int count);   // Identical signature to below
int largest(int* values, int count);    // Identical signature to above
```

With either parameter type, the argument that is passed is an address and you can implement the function using array notation or pointer notation.

Overloading and Reference Parameters

You need to be careful when you are overloading functions with reference parameters. For one thing, you can't overload a function with a parameter of a given type data_type, with a function that has a parameter of type *reference to data_type*. If you do this, the compiler won't be able to determine from a function call which function you want. To illustrate this, let's declare two function prototypes:

```
int do_it(int number);      // These are not
int& do_it(int& number);    // distinguishable
```

Now, assuming value is of type int, suppose you write a statement such as the following:

```
do_it(value);
```

This statement could call either function. You have no way to distinguish which function should be called, so you can't distinguish overloaded functions based on a parameter for one version being of a given type, and the other being a reference to that type.

You should also be wary when you have overloaded a function by declaring two versions, one with a parameter *reference to type1* and another with a parameter *reference to type2*. The function called depends on the sort of arguments you use, but you may get some surprising results.

....

Try It Out: Overloaded Functions with Reference Parameters

Let's explore the use of reference parameters a little with a modified version of the last example:

```
// Program 9.2 Overloading a function with reference parameters
#include <iostream>
using std::cout;
using std::endl;

double larger(double a, double b);
long& larger(long& a, long& b);

int main() {
  double a_double = 1.5, b_double = 2.5;
  cout << endl;
  cout << "The larger of double values "
       << a_double << " and " << b_double <<" is "
       << larger(a_double, b_double) << endl;

  int a_int = 15, b_int = 25;
  cout << "The larger of int values "
       << a_int << " and " << b_int <<" is "
       << larger(static_cast<long>(a_int), static_cast<long>(b_int))
       << endl;
  return 0;
}


// Function to return the larger of two floating point values
double larger(double a, double b) {
  cout << "double larger() called" << endl;
  return a>b ? a : b;
}


// Return the larger of two long references
long& larger(long& a, long& b) {
  cout << "long ref larger() called" << endl;
  return a>b ? a : b;
}
```

This version of the program produces the following output:

```
double larger() called
The larger of double values 1.5 and 2.5 is 2.5
double larger() called
The larger of int values 15 and 25 is 25
```

HOW IT WORKS

The second line of the resulting output may not have been what you were antici-
pating. You really want the second output statement to call the version of larger()
with long& parameters:

```
cout << "The larger of int values "
    << a_int << " and " << b_int <<" is "
    << larger(static_cast<long>(a_int), static_cast<long>(b_int))
    << endl;
```

Instead, this statement has called the version with double parameters—but why?
After all, you *did* cast both arguments to long.

In fact, that is exactly where the problem lies. The arguments are not a_int and
b_int, but the temporary locations that contain the same values, converted to
type long. Behind the scenes, the compiler is not prepared to use a temporary
address to initialize a reference—it's just too risky. The code in larger() has free
rein on what it does with the reference parameters, and the theory is that either
of the reference parameters can be modified and/or returned. Using a temporary location in this way is not sensible, so the compiler won't do it.

What can you do about this? You have a couple of choices. You could declare
a_int and b_int as type long; then the compiler happily calls the version of
larger() that uses parameters of type *reference to long*.

If circumstances don't allow this, then you can declare the reference parameters
as const, as shown here:

```
long larger(const long& a, const long& b);
```

Remember to make this change in both the function prototype *and* the function
definition. This informs the compiler that the function won't modify the arguments; then the compiler allows this version to be called, instead of the version
with double parameters.

Note that you simply return type long now. If you insist on returning a reference,
you must declare the return type as const because the compiler cannot convert
from a const reference to a non-const reference. A const reference is never an
lvalue, so you can't use it on the left of an assignment. Thus, you have nothing to
lose by returning a value of type long in this instance.

Overloading and const Parameters

Note that const is only sufficient for distinguishing parameters in order to define the signature of a function for references and pointers. For a fundamental type such as int, for example, const int is identical to int from the point of view of overloading. Hence, the following prototypes result in the same function signature and declare the same function:

```
long& larger(long a, long b);
long& larger(const long a, const long b);
```

The compiler ignores the const aspect of the parameters in the second declaration. This is because the arguments are passed *by value*, meaning that a *copy* of each argument is passed into the function, and thus the original is protected from modification by the function.

NOTE *For any fundamental type* T, *a function with parameter type* const T *is interpreted as the same as its overloaded cousin with parameter type* T—*the* const *will be ignored.*

Overloading with const Pointer Parameters

Two overloaded functions are *different* if one of them has a parameter of type *pointer to type* and the other has a parameter of *pointer to const type*. The corresponding parameters are pointers to different things—effectively, they are different types. For example, these prototypes have different function signatures:

```
long* larger(long* a, long* b);                  // Pointer parameters
const long* larger(const long* a, const long* b); // Pointer to const parameter
```

When the modifier const is applied to the value that is being pointed to, it prevents the value from being modified. Without the const modifier, the original value can be modified through the pointer, and the pass-by-value mechanism does not inhibit this in any way. In this example, the former function is called with these statements:

```
long num1 = 1;
long num2 = 2;
long num3 = *larger(num1, num2);
```

The latter version of larger() with const parameters is called by the following code:

```
const long num10 =1;
const long num20 = 2;
const long num30 = *larger(num10, num20);
```

The compiler won't pass a const value to a function in which the parameter is just a pointer. Allowing a const value to be passed through a pointer would violate the const declaration of the variable. Thus, the compiler must select the latter version of larger() for this case.

In contrast to the previous example, two overloaded functions are *the same* if one of them has a parameter of type *pointer to type* and the other has a parameter *const pointer to type*. For example, take a look at the following:

```
long* larger(long* a, long* b);                // These are
long* const larger(long* const a, long* const b);    // identical
```

These two functions are not differentiated and won't compile. The reason is clear when you consider that the first prototype has a parameter of type *pointer to long*, and the second has parameter of type *const pointer to long*. If you think of *pointer to long* as a type, T, then the parameter types are T and const T—which are not differentiated (you'll remember that I covered this case at the beginning of this section).

Overloading and const Reference Parameters

Reference parameters are more straightforward when is comes to const. A reference to a type T and a const reference to a type T are always differentiated, so for example, type const int& is always different from type int&. This means that you can overload functions in the manner indicated by the following prototypes:

```
long& larger(long& a, long& b);
long larger(const long& a, const long& b);
```

Here, each function has the same function body, which returns the larger of the two parameters, but the functions behave differently. The first prototype declares a function that doesn't accept constants as arguments, but you can use the function on the left of an assignment to modify one or the other of the reference parameters. The second prototype declares a function that accepts constants (and nonconstants, of course) as arguments, but because the return type is not an lvalue, you can't use the function on the left of an assignment. This echoes what I discussed in the context of Program 9.2—this context to declaring the return type as a const reference has little point. It still doesn't represent an lvalue.

NOTE *Remember that the return value has no effect on the overloading. It is not considered when the signature of a function is generated. However, as described earlier, it does have an effect on where the function can be used.*

Overloading and Default Argument Values

From Chapter 8, you'll recall that you can specify default parameter values for a function. However, if you do this for overloaded functions, it can sometimes affect the compiler's ability to distinguish one call from another and may create an ambiguous situation. For example, suppose you had two versions of the show_error() function, which you used in Chapter 8 to display an error message. Here's one that is defined with a C-style string argument:

```
void show_error(const char* message) {
  std::cout << std::endl << message << std::endl;
}
```

The other is defined with a string argument:

```
void show_error(const string& message) {
  std::cout << std::endl << message << std::endl;
}
```

You can't now define a default argument for both functions because doing so would create an ambiguity. The statement to output the default message in either case would be

```
  show_error();
```

With this function call, the compiler has no way of knowing which function is required. Of course, this is a silly example: you have no reason to specify defaults for both functions. A default for just one of these two functions does everything that you need. However, circumstances can arise where it is not so silly, and overall, you must ensure that all function calls uniquely identify the function that should be called.

A Sausage Machine for Functions

In some of the earlier situations, you were writing overloaded functions that contained exactly the same code. It seems an unnecessary overhead to have to write the same code over and over, and indeed it is. In such situations, you can write the code just once, as a function template.

A **function template** is a blueprint or a recipe for a function. The compiler uses it to generate a new member of a family of functions. The new function is created when it is first required. A function that is generated from a function template is described as an **instance** or an **instantiation** of the template. A more technical way of describing a function template is as a parametric function definition, where a particular function is selected by one or more parameters. The parameters are usually data types (but not always; for example, you might find it useful to supply sizes by passing integer values). I can cast a little light into the shadows of function templates with a specific example.

The larger() function that you have been playing with is a good candidate for a template. A definition of a template for this function is shown in Figure 9-1.

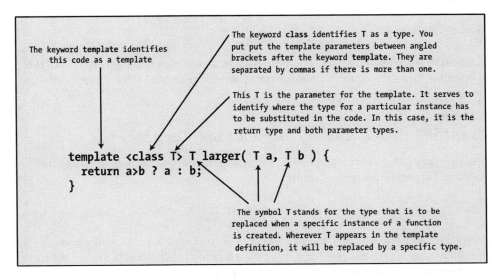

Figure 9-1. A simple function template

The function template starts with the keyword template to identify it as such. This is followed by a pair of angled brackets, which contains a list of parameters. In this case, you have just one, the parameter T. T is commonly used as a name for a parameter, probably because most parameters are types and because T is the first letter of the word type. In fact, you can use whatever name you like for the parameter: names such as replace_it or my_type are equally valid.

The word class is a keyword that identifies that T is a type. This doesn't imply that T has to be a class type. T can be any of the fundamental types such as int or long, or it could be a user-defined type (a class, in other words). You'll learn how to create your own types when I discuss classes.

NOTE *In the context of template definitions, you may come across the keyword* typename *between the angled brackets. This is a common alternative to the keyword* class, *and it has the same purpose in this context. In this book, I use the keyword* class *(in preference to* typename*) for this purpose.*

The rest of the definition is just like the definition of a normal function, except that you have the parameter, in this case T, sprinkled around. The compiler creates a new version of the function by replacing T throughout the template definition with the particular type that it must have to create a particular instance from the template.

You can place the template in your code in the same way you would a normal function definition; you can even have a template function prototype. In this case, it would be

```
template<class T> T larger(T a, T b);
```

You must ensure that either a declaration (that is, a prototype) or the definition of the template appears in the source file, before a function generated from a template is used.

Creating Instances of a Function Template

The compiler can create instances of the function from any statement that uses the function larger(). Here's an example:

```
cout << "Larger of 1.5 and 2.5 is " << larger(1.5, 2.5) << endl;
```

As you see, you can just use the function in the normal way. In particular, you don't specify a value for the template argument T—the compiler deduces the value of T from the arguments to the function call. Here, the arguments to larger() are literals of type double, so this call causes the compiler to search for an existing version of larger() with double parameters. If it doesn't find one, then the compiler creates this version of larger() from the template by substituting type double for T in the template definition.

The resulting template function accepts arguments of type double and returns a double value. With double plugged into the template in place of T, the template instance will effectively be as follows:

```
double larger(double a, double b) {
  return a>b ? a : b;
}
```

 NOTE *The compiler only generates this instantiation of the template once. If a subsequent function call requires the same instance, then it calls the instance already created. Your program only ever includes a single copy of the definition of each instance, even if the same instance is generated in different source files.*

You should keep a couple of things in mind throughout the detailed discussion on function templates that follows. First, a function template does not do anything by itself. It is a recipe or blueprint that the compiler uses to create a function definition from a function call. Second, this all happens during compilation and linkage. The compiler uses a template to generate source code for a function definition, which it then compiles. The role of the linker is to link only a *single* instance of a function into the executable module, even if several different source files call the same instance. When your program executes, the existence (or nonexistence) of a template in the original source code is neither apparent nor relevant.

Now that you are familiar with the concepts, let's road test a function template for real in a program.

Try It Out: Using a Function Template

Using this template is very straightforward. Here's the code to exercise it in various ways:

```cpp
// Program 9.3 Using a function template
#include <iostream>
using std::cout;
using std::endl;

template<class T> T larger(T a, T b);        // Function template prototype

int main() {
  cout << endl;
  cout << "Larger of 1.5 and 2.5 is " << larger(1.5, 2.5) << endl;
  cout << "Larger of 3.5 and 4.5 is " << larger(3.5, 4.5) << endl;

  int a_int = 35;
  int b_int = 45;
  cout << "Larger of " << a_int << " and " << b_int << " is "
       << larger(a_int, b_int)
       << endl;


  long a_long = 9;
  long b_long = 8;
  cout << "Larger of "   << a_long << " and " << b_long << " is "
       << larger(a_long, b_long)
       << endl;

  return 0;
}

// Template for functions to return the larger of two values
template <class T> T larger(T a, T b) {
  return a>b ? a : b;
}
```

(Continued)

This produces the following output:

```
Larger of 1.5 and 2.5 is 2.5
Larger of 3.5 and 4.5 is 4.5
Larger of 35 and 45 is 45
Larger of 9 and 8 is 9
```

HOW IT WORKS

As I have said before, the definition or prototype for the template must appear before you can call any instances of the function; this rule is much the same as for an ordinary function. Therefore, I have defined the template prototype as follows:

```
template<class T> T larger(T a, T b);     // Function template prototype
```

This is essentially the same as the first line of the template definition, but with a semicolon (;) at the end.

You call the function larger() in main() for the first time in this statement:

```
cout << "Larger of 1.5 and 2.5 is " << larger(1.5, 2.5) << endl;
```

The compiler automatically creates a version of larger() that accepts arguments of type double as a result of this statement; then that version is called here. The next statement also requires a version of larger() that accepts double arguments:

```
cout << "Larger of 3.5 and 4.5 is " << larger(3.5, 4.5) << endl;
```

Here, the compiler does the sensible thing and uses the version that it generated for the previous statement.

The next use of larger() is in this statement:

```
cout << "Larger of " << a_int << " and " << b_int << " is "
     << larger(a_int, b_int)
     << endl;
```

Here, you call the function with arguments of type int so that a new version of larger() is generated to accept int arguments.

The last call of the function larger() has two arguments of type long:

```
cout << "Larger of "   << a_long << " and " << b_long << " is "
     << larger(a_long, b_long)
     << endl;
```

This time you get a new version with two arguments of type long. You end up with a total of three different versions of larger() (in the form of three different bits of object code) from just a single piece of source code in this program.

Explicitly Specifying a Template Parameter

You can specify the parameter for the template explicitly when you call the function. This allows you to control which version of the function is used. The compiler no longer tries to deduce the type to replace T; it simply accepts what you specify. You will find a number of situations in which this can be useful:

- In situations where the function call is ambiguous, the compilation fails. You can use this technique to help the compiler resolve the ambiguity.

- In certain cases, the compiler is unable to deduce the template arguments and hence is unable to choose which version of the function to use. (You'll see an example of this when you consider templates with multiple parameters.) In such cases, you must specify the template parameter explicitly.

- To avoid having too many versions of the function (and hence avoid excessive occupation of memory), you can force function calls to take certain versions of your function.

Here's an example. In Program 9.3, the arguments of type int could be handled by the version of larger() that accepts arguments of type long (because you'll need that later anyway). You can force this by specifying the template parameter type to be used when you call the function:

```
cout << "Larger of " << a_int << " and " << b_int << " is "
     << larger<long>(a_int, b_int)
     << endl;
```

In the function call in this statement, you define the template parameter value, long, between angled brackets following the function name. Therefore, the function corresponding to type long is generated from the template if it does not already exist, and is then used here. The compiler supplies automatic casts for the arguments to the types required by the function parameter specifications.

Alternatively, you might decide that the version with parameters of type double is satisfactory. In this case, you just specify double between the angled brackets; the compiler supplies that version, generating it from the template if it does not already exist. You could even force the compiler to use a version that is likely to cause data loss— type short, for example. The compiler usually warns you against potential loss of data, but the compiler implements and uses the version that you specify.

Here's another situation in which an explicit template parameter would be suitable:

```
cout << "Larger of " << a_long << " and " << a_int << " is "
     << larger(a_long, a_int)
     << endl;
```

Here, the variables a_long and a_int are of type long and int respectively, just as in Program 9.3. The two arguments have different types—this arrangement doesn't match the function template, and so the compiler is unable to generate a suitable function. To overcome this, you can explicitly specify the template parameter:

```
cout << "Larger of " << a_long << " and " << a_int << " is "
    << larger<long>(a_long, a_int)
    << endl;
```

Now, the compiler can make the substitution of long for T to generate the function, and then it can supply a cast for a_int to make the call complete.

An alternative solution to this situation is to cast one of the arguments in the function call to the type of the other. Then, the compiler interprets this as having two arguments of the same type and calls the appropriate version of the function.

Specialization of Templates

Suppose that you extended Program 9.3 to call the function larger() with arguments that are addresses:

```
cout << "Larger of "   << a_long << " and " << b_long << " is "
    << *larger(&a_long,&b_long)
    << endl;
```

As a result of this statement, the compiler creates a version of the function with the template parameter as type long*. This version has the following prototype:

```
long* larger(long*, long*);
```

The return value is an address, and you have to dereference it in order to output the value. However, having done all that, *the result is only correct by accident.* This is because the comparison in the body of the function is not correct. The function that is generated will be

```
long* larger(long* a, long* b) {
  return a>b ? a : b;
}
```

This compares the addresses, not the values. This function returns the higher-valued address when you wanted the address containing the higher-valued long integer. From this you can see how easy it is to create hidden errors using templates. You need to be particularly careful when using pointer types as parameter values in a template.

What can you do about this? Well, you could define a **specialization** of your template to deal with this particular case. For a *specific* parameter value (or set of values, in the case of a template with multiple parameters), a specialization of a template defines a behavior that is different from the standard template. The definition for a template specialization must come after a declaration or definition of the original template. If you put a specialization first, then your program won't compile.

Defining a Template Specialization

The definition of a specialization starts with the keyword template, but in this case, the parameter is omitted, so the angled brackets that surround the template parameter in the original declaration are empty here. You still have to define the value of the parameter for the specialization and you must place this between angled brackets immediately following the template function name. The definition for a specialization of larger() for type long* will be as follows:

```
template <> long* larger<long*>(long* a, long* b) {
  return *a>*b ? a : b;
}
```

The only change to the body of the function is to dereference the arguments a and b so that you compare the values rather than the addresses. Let's see how it works in practice.

Try It Out: Using an Explicit Specialization

You can adapt Program 9.3 to use an explicit specialization. Add the problem statement mentioned earlier—the one that passes addresses to larger()—and an explicit specialization to deal with arguments of type long*, as shown here:

```
// Program 9.4 Using function template specialization
#include <iostream>
using std::cout;
using std::endl;

template<class T> T larger(T a, T b);                   // Function template prototype
template<> long* larger<long*>(long* a, long* b); // Specialization

int main() {
  cout << endl;
  cout << "Larger of 1.5 and 2.5 is " << larger(1.5, 2.5) << endl;
  cout << "Larger of 3.5 and 4.5 is " << larger(3.5, 4.5) << endl;

  int a_int = 35;
  int b_int = 45;
  cout << "Larger of " << a_int << " and " << b_int << " is "
       << larger(a_int, b_int)
       << endl;

  long a_long = 9;
```

(Continued)

```
    long b_long = 8;
    cout << "Larger of "    << a_long << " and " << b_long << " is "
        << larger(a_long, b_long)
        << endl;

    cout << "Larger of "    << a_long << " and " << b_long << " is "
        << *larger(&a_long,&b_long)
        << endl;

return 0;
}

// Template for functions to return the larger of two values
template <class T> T larger(T a, T b) {
  cout << "standard version " << endl;
  return a>b ? a : b;
}

// Template specialization definitions
template <> long* larger<long*>(long* a, long* b) {
  cout << "specialized version " << endl;
  return *a>*b ? a : b;
}
```

Both the template and the specialization have a statement that outputs a trace when they are called, so you know which is called in each case. This program produces the following output:

```
standard version
Larger of 1.5 and 2.5 is 2.5
standard version
Larger of 3.5 and 4.5 is 4.5
standard version
Larger of 35 and 45 is 45
standard version
Larger of 9 and 8 is 9
specialized version
Larger of 9 and 8 is 9
```

HOW IT WORKS

At the beginning of the program file, you have a declaration for the template specialization, in addition to the declaration of the template that you had earlier:

```
template<> long* larger<long*>(long* a, long* b); // Specialization
```

This is necessary because main(), where the specialization is used, comes before the definition. In the program, the definition of the specialization is the same as in the preceding discussion—you've just added an output statement so that you can trace when it is used.

It works just as you might have anticipated. All the calls of `larger()` from the previous version of the program are repeated here. The last call is from this statement:

```
cout << "Larger of "    << a_long << " and " << b_long << " is "
     << *larger(&a_long,&b_long)
     << endl;
```

This uses the specialization of the template, as the output indicates.

....

Function Templates and Overloading

You will come across different ways to overload a function produced from a function template. One way, as you've just seen, is to overload the function with another function generated from the template. Alternatively, you can overload the function by directly defining other functions with the same name. Using overloading, you can define "overrides" for specific cases, and these get used in preference to the template. In this case, as always, each overloaded function must have a unique signature.

Let's reconsider the previous situation in which you need to overload the `larger()` function to take pointer arguments. Instead of using a template specialization, you could explicitly declare an overloaded function. If you take this approach, then you'd replace the specialization prototype in Program 9.4 with the following overloaded function prototype:

```
long* larger(long* a, long* b);        // overloaded function
```

In place of the specialization definition in Program 9.4, you'd use the following function definition:

```
long* larger(long* a, long* b) {
  cout << "overloaded version for long* " << endl;
  return *a>*b ? a : b;
}
```

Try making these changes to Program 9.4 and then run it again. When the function `larger()` is called with `long*` arguments, the compiler determines that a suitable version of `larger()` exists, so the template is not used in this case. Effectively, this function definition has overridden the template.

It is also possible to overload an existing template with another template. For example, you could extend Program 9.4 by adding an **overloaded template** to find the largest value contained in an array. The definition of the template might be similar to this:

```
template <class T> T larger (const T array[], int count) {
  cout << "template overload version for arrays " << endl;
```

```
    T result = array[0];
    for(int i = 1 ; i < count ; i++)
      if(array[i] > result)
        result = array[i];
    return result;
}
```

This finds the largest element in an array of any suitable type. You could try this out in Program 9.4 by adding a couple of statements to main():

```
double x[] = { 10.5, 12.5, 2.5, 13.5, 5.5 };
cout << "Largest element has the value "
     << larger(x, sizeof x/sizeof x[0])
     << endl;
```

You'll need to add a prototype for the additional template, of course.

Templates with Multiple Parameters

You've been using function templates with a single parameter, but you can have several parameters in a template. A classic application for a second type argument is to provide a way of controlling the return type from a function template. You could define yet another template for the function larger(), which allows the return type to be specified independently of the function parameter type:

```
// Template for functions to return the larger of two values
template <class TReturn, class TArg> TReturn larger(TArg a, TArg b) {
  return a>b ? a : b;
}
```

Note that the compiler can't deduce the type, TReturn, for the return value, so you must always specify it. However, the compiler *can* deduce the type for the arguments, so you can get away with specifying just the return type. Here's an example:

```
cout << "Larger of 1.5 and 2.5 is "
     << larger<int>(1.5, 2.5)
     << endl;
```

The return type is specified (between the angled brackets) as int; and the argument type is deduced from the arguments as double. The result of the function call is 2.

You can specify both TReturn and TArg if you like:

```
cout << "Larger of 1.5 and 2.5 is "
     << larger<double, double>(1.5, 2.5)
     << endl;
```

Here, the compiler creates the function that accepts arguments of type double and returns a result of type double.

Clearly, the sequence of template parameters in the template definition is important here. If you had defined the template with the return type as the second parameter, you'd always have to specify *both* parameters in a function call: if you tried to specify only one parameter, it would be interpreted as the argument type, leaving the return type undefined.

Non-Type Template Parameters

So far, all the template parameters you have dealt with have been data types. Your templates can also have **non-type parameters**; in this case, the function call uses non-type arguments. Arguments corresponding to non-type parameters must be either integral and compile-time constant, or references/pointers to objects with external linkage.

When declaring the template, you include any non-type template parameters in the parameter list (along with any other type parameters). You'll see an example in a moment. The type of a non-type template parameter can be one of the following:

An integral type, such as int, long, and so on

An enumeration type

A pointer or reference to an object type

A pointer or a reference to a function

A pointer to a class member

You haven't met the last two before. I'll introduce pointers to functions later in this chapter, and I'll discuss references to functions and pointers to class members when I cover classes. The application of non-type template parameters to these types is beyond the scope of this book. You'll only consider an elementary example here, with parameters of type int, just to see how it works.

Suppose you needed a function to perform range checking on a value. You could define a template to handle a variety of types:

```
template <class T, int upper, int lower> bool is_in_range(T value) {
  return (value <= upper) && (value >= lower);
}
```

With this template, the compiler can't deduce all of the template parameters from the use of the function. The following function call won't compile:

```
double value = 100.0;
std::cout << is_in_range(value);    // Won't compile - incorrect usage
```

Compilation fails because the parameters upper and lower are unspecified. To use this template, you must specify the template parameter values. The correct way to use this is as follows:

```
cout << is_in_range<double,0,500>(value); // OK - check 0 to 500
```

It might well be better to use function parameters, rather than template parameters, for the limits in this case. After all, function parameters give you the flexibility of being able to pass values that are calculated during runtime, whereas here you must supply the limits at compile time.

Pointers to Functions

As you know, a pointer stores an address value. Up to now, you have used pointers to store the address of another variable with the same basic type as the pointer. This has given you considerable flexibility in allowing you to use different variables at different times through a single pointer.

A pointer can also point to the address of a function. Such a pointer can point to different functions at different times during execution of your program. At any time during your program's execution, you can use your pointer to call a function; the function that is called will be the function whose address was last assigned to the pointer.

Obviously, a pointer to a function must contain the memory address of the function that you want to call. To work properly, however, the pointer must also store other information—namely, the types of the parameters in the parameter list for any function that it points to, as well as the return type. Consequently, when you declare a pointer to a function, you have to specify the parameter types and the return type of the functions that it can point to, in addition to the name of the pointer.

Clearly, the information required in the declaration of a pointer to a function will restrict the variety of functions to which your pointer can point. This is analogous to a pointer that stores the address of a data item. For example, a pointer to type int can *only* point to a location that contains a value of type int—if you want to store the address of a value of type long, then you need a different kind of pointer.

In the same way, let's suppose that you have declared a pointer to a function for functions that accept one argument of type int and return a value of type double. This pointer can only be used to store the address of a function that has *exactly* this form. If you want to store the address of a function that accepts two arguments of type int and returns type char, then you must define another pointer that has these characteristics. Basically, the only variation you have with a particular function pointer is the function name. The number and types of the parameters and the return type must always be the same for a given function pointer.

NOTE *Function pointers are used less frequently in C++ than they were in C. This is because C++ offers other facilities such as classes, function overloading, and so on, which are able to perform similar tasks. However, pointers to functions still hold their place in the C++ language.*

Declaring Pointers to Functions

Let's declare a pointer pfun that you can use to point to functions that take two arguments, of type long* and int, and return a value of type long. Here's the declaration:

```
long (*pfun)(long*, int);    // Pointer to function declaration
```

This may look a little weird at first because of all the parentheses.

NOTE *The parentheses around the pointer name,* pfun, *and the asterisk, are essential here—without them, this statement would declare a function rather than a pointer because the * will bind to the* long *in preference to the* pfun.

You can write the general form of a declaration of a pointer to a function as follows:

```
return_type (*pointer_name)(list_of_parameter_types);
```

Remember that the parentheses around the pointer name are essential; if you don't use them you'll finish up with a function prototype! The pointer can only point to functions with the same return_type and list_of_parameter_types as those specified in the declaration.

You can break the declaration down into three components that appear in sequence:

The return_type of the functions that can be pointed to

The pointer_name, which is preceded by an asterisk to indicate that it's a *pointer* enclosed between the parentheses

A list_of_parameter_types, enclosed between parentheses, for the functions that can be pointed to

NOTE *If you attempt to assign a function to a pointer that does not conform to the types in the pointer declaration, you'll get an error message from the compiler.*

Of course, you should always initialize a pointer when you declare it. You can initialize a pointer to a function with the name of a function, within the declaration of the pointer. Suppose you have a function with the following prototype:

```
long max_element(const long* array, int count);    // Function prototype
```

Then you can declare and initialize a pointer to a function with this statement:

```
long (*pfun)(long*, int) = max_element;
```

The pointer has been initialized to point to the function max_element(). You can subsequently set the pointer to point to any function with the same parameter and return types.

Of course, you can also initialize a pointer to a function by using an assignment statement. Assuming the pointer pfun has been declared as it was earlier, you could set the value of the pointer to a different function with these statements:

```
long min_element(const long* array, int count);    // Function prototype
pfun = min_element;                 // Set pointer to function minElement()
```

As with pointers to variables, you must ensure that a pointer to a function is initialized before you use it to call a function. Without initialization, catastrophic failure of your program is guaranteed.

NOTE *You can, if you wish, initialize a pointer to function with the value 0. However, if the pointer is pointing to 0 when you use it to call a function, the behavior is undefined, and catastrophic behavior will again result.*

If you now want to call the function min_element() using the pointer pfun, you just use the pointer name as though it were a function name. For example, you might use the following statements:

```
long data[] = { 23, 34, 22, 56, 87, 12, 57, 76 };
std::cout << "value of minimum is "
          << pfun(data, sizeof data/sizeof data[0]);
```

This will output the minimum value of the elements in the array data.

NOTE *The ideas behind function templates and function pointers are connected in an odd sort of way. In a sense, a function pointer is actually the inverse of a function template. A particular function pointer can point to any one of a set of functions that have different names but have the same parameter and return types. Conversely, a function template defines a set of functions with the same name but where the parameter types and possibly the return types may vary.*

Try It Out: Pointers to Functions

To get a proper feel for these newfangled pointers to functions and how they perform in action, let's try one out in a program:

```cpp
// Program 9.5 Exercising pointers to functions
#include <iostream>
using std::cout;
using std::endl;

long sum(long a, long b);               // Function prototype
long product(long a, long b);           // Function prototype

int main() {
  long (*pDo_it)(long, long) = 0;       // Pointer to function declaration

  pDo_it = product;
  cout << endl
       << "3*5 = " << pDo_it(3, 5);     // Call product thru a pointer

  pDo_it = sum;                         // Reassign pointer to sum()
  cout << endl
       << "3 * (4+5) + 6 = "
       << pDo_it(product(3, pDo_it(4, 5)), 6);  // Call thru a pointer twice

  cout << endl;
  return 0;
}

// Function to multiply two values
long product(long a, long b) {
  return a*b;
}

// Function to add two values
long sum(long a, long b) {
  return a+b;
}
```

(Continued)

This example produces the following output:

```
3*5 = 15
3 * (4+5) + 6 = 33
```

HOW IT WORKS

This is hardly a useful program, but it does show, very simply, how a pointer to a function is declared, assigned a value, and subsequently used to call a function.

After the usual preamble, you declare and initialize pDo_it—it's a pointer to a function, which can point to either of the two functions that you have defined, sum() or product():

```
long (*pDo_it)(long, long) = 0;        // Pointer to function declaration
```

You have initialized pDo_it to 0, but the pointer can only call a function if it's pointing to the function. Therefore, you assign the address of the function product() to pDo_it:

```
  pDo_it = product;
```

When you are initializing a function pointer, you supply the name of the function to be pointed to just by itself—no parentheses or other adornments are required. The function name is automatically converted to an address, which is stored in the pointer.

The function product() is then called indirectly through the pointer pDo_it in the output statement.

```
  cout << endl
       << "3*5 = " << pDo_it(3, 5);      // Call product thru a pointer
```

The name of the pointer is used just as if it were a function name and is followed by the arguments, between parentheses, exactly as they would appear if the original function name were being used directly.

Just to show that you can, you change the pointer to point to the function sum(). You then use it again in a ludicrously convoluted expression to do some simple arithmetic. This shows that a pointer to a function can be used in exactly the same way as the function that it points to. The sequence of actions in the expression is shown in Figure 9-2.

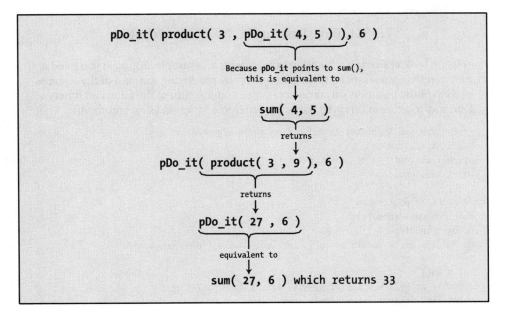

Figure 9-2. Execution of an expression using a function pointer

Passing a Function as an Argument

In fact, *pointer to function* is a perfectly reasonable type. Therefore, you could write a function which has a *pointer to function* as one of its parameters. Then, when the (outer) function uses its *pointer to function* parameter, it indirectly calls the function pointed to by the corresponding argument at the time the function is called.

Because you can make the pointer point to different functions in different circumstances, the calling program can determine the particular function that is to be called from inside the function that it calls.

When you call a function with a parameter of type *pointer to function*, the argument can be a pointer of the appropriate type containing the address of a function; alternatively you can pass a function explicitly by just using a function name as an argument. A function passed to another function as an argument is sometimes referred to as a **callback function**.

....

Try It Out: Passing a Function Pointer

You can look at passing a function pointer with an example. Suppose you need a
function that processes an array of numbers by producing the sum of the squares
of each of the numbers on some occasions, and the sum of the cubes on others.
One way to achieve this is by using a pointer to a function as an argument.

```cpp
// Program 9.6 A pointer to a function as an argument
#include <iostream>
using std::cout;
using std::endl;

// Function prototypes
double squared(double);
double cubed(double);
double sum_array(double array[], int len, double (*pfun)(double));

int main() {
  double array[] = { 1.5, 2.5, 3.5, 4.5, 5.5, 6.5, 7.5 };
  int len = sizeof array/sizeof array[0];

  cout << endl
       << "Sum of squares = "
       << sum_array(array, len, squared)
       << endl;

  cout << "Sum of cubes = "
       << sum_array(array, len, cubed)
       << endl;
  return 0;
}

// Function for a square of a value
double squared(double x) {
   return x*x;
}

// Function for a cube of a value
double cubed(double x) {
   return x*x*x;
}

// Function to sum functions of array elements
double sum_array(double array[], int len, double (*pfun)(double)) {
   double total = 0.0;      // Accumulate total in here

   for(int i = 0 ; i < len ; i++)
     total += pfun(array[i]);
   return total;
}
```

This example generates the following output:

```
Sum of squares = 169.75
Sum of cubes = 1015.88
```

HOW IT WORKS

The first statement of interest is the prototype for the function sum_array(). Its third parameter is a pointer to a function that has a parameter of type double, and returns a value of type double.

```
double sum_array(double array[], int len, double (*pfun)(double));
```

The sum_array() function processes each element of the array that is passed as its first argument, using whichever function is pointed to by its third argument. The function then returns the sum of the processed array elements.

The sum_array() function is called twice in main(). For the first call, the last argument is squared. For the second call, the last argument is cubed. In each case, it's the *address* corresponding to the function name that is used as the argument and is substituted for the function pointer in the body of the function sum_array(), so the appropriate function will be called within the for loop.

Obviously, you can find easier ways to achieve what this example does, but using a pointer to a function provides you with a lot of generality. You could pass any function to sum_array() that you care to define, so long as it takes one double argument and returns a value of type double.

Arrays of Pointers to Functions

You can declare an array of pointers to functions; it's similar to declaring an array of regular pointers. You can also initialize your array of function pointers, when you declare the array. Here is an example of declaring an array of pointers:

```
double sum(double, double);          // Function prototype
double product(double, double);      // Function prototype
double difference(double, double);   // Function prototype
double (*pfun[3])(double,double) =
          { sum, product, difference }; // Array of function pointers
```

Each of the elements in the array is initialized by the corresponding function address that appears in the initializing list between braces.

To call the function product() using the second element of the pointer array, you would write this:

```
pfun[1](2.5, 3.5);
```

The square brackets, which select the function pointer array element, appear immediately after the array name and before the arguments to the function being called. Of course, you can place a function call through an element of a function pointer array within any expression in which the original function might legitimately appear. The index value selecting the pointer can be any expression that produces a valid index value.

Recursion

Finally in this chapter, I'd like to delve into the world of **recursive functions**. You'll use recursive functions, at the end of this section, to reexamine the solution to the sorting problem that you saw in Chapter 7.

A function in C++ is permitted to call itself where appropriate. When a function contains a call to itself, it is referred to as a **recursive function**. A recursive function call can also be indirect—for example, where a function fun1() calls another function fun2(), which in turn calls the original function fun1().

Recursion may seem to be a recipe for a loop that executes indefinitely, and if you are not careful it certainly can be. A prerequisite for avoiding a loop of unlimited duration is that the function must contain some means of stopping the process.

What sort of things can recursion be used for? Unless you have come across the technique before, the answer may not be obvious. Data that is organized in a tree structure is one example. A tree structure is illustrated in Figure 9-3. This shows a tree that contains structures that can be regarded as subtrees. Data that describes a mechanical assembly such as a car is often organized as a tree. A car consists of subassemblies such as the body, the engine, the transmission, and the suspension. Each of these consists of further subassemblies and components until ultimately, the leaves of the tree are reached, which are all components with no further internal structure.

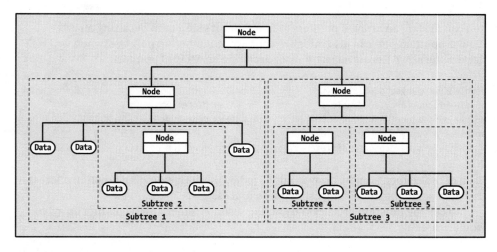

Figure 9-3. An example of a tree structure

When you need to process data that is organized as a tree, the tree can usually be traversed very effectively using recursion. Each branch of a tree can be regarded as a subtree, so a function for accessing each of the data items in a tree can simply call itself when a branch node is encountered. When a data item is encountered, the function does what is required with the data item and then returns to the calling point. Thus, when the function finds the leaf nodes of the tree—the data items—this provides the means by which the function stops the recursive calls of itself.

In physics and mathematics, you'll also find many things that you can think of as involving recursion. A simple example is the factorial of a positive integer. Factorials are really quite useful because the factorial of an integer n (written as $n!$) is the number of ways in which n things can be arranged. For a given positive integer, N, the factorial of N is the product $1 \times 2 \times 3 \times \ldots \times N$. To calculate this, you can define a recursive function like the following:

```
long factorial(long n) {
  if( n==1L)
    return 1L;
  return n*factorial(n-1);
}
```

If you visualize this function called with an argument value of 4, this executes the `else` clause that calls the function with a value of 3. If you use this process, ultimately the `factorial()` function will be called with an argument of 1, whereupon it will return and that value will be multiplied by 2, and so on, until the first call returns the value $4 \times 3 \times 2 \times 1$. This is very often the example given to show recursion in operation, but just to be different, I'll show you something even simpler in a working example.

Try It Out: A Recursive Function

At the start of the last chapter (see Program 8.1), you produced a function that would compute the integral power of a value—that is, it would compute x^n. For positive values of n, this is equivalent to 1 multiplied by x repeated n times; for negative values of n, it is 1 divided by x repeated n times. If n is 0 the result is 1. You can implement this as a recursive function as an elementary illustration of recursion in action.

```
// Program 9.7 recursive version of x to the power n
#include <iostream>
#include <iomanip>
using std::cout;
using std::endl;

double power(double x, int n);

int main() {
  cout << endl;
```

(Continued)

```
// Calculate powers of 8 from -3 to +3
for( int i = -3 ; i <= 3 ; i++)
  cout << std::setw(10) << power(8.0, i);

cout << endl;
return 0;
}


// Recursive function to calculate x to the power n
double power(double x, int n) {
  if(0 == n)
    return 1.0;
  if(0 < n)
    return x*power(x, n-1);

  return 1.0/power(x, -n);
}
```

The function main() is exactly the same as the Program 8.1, so if your function works, the output will also be the same:

```
0.00195313  0.015625     0.125          1         8        64       512
```

HOW IT WORKS

The first if statement returns the value 1.0 if *n* is 0. For positive *n*, the next if statement returns the result of the expression, $x*power(x, n-1)$. This causes a further call of the function power() with the index value reduced by 1. If, in this call, *n* is still positive, then power() is called again with *n* reduced by 1. Each call of the function is recorded in the call stack, along with the arguments for the call. This repeats until *n* is 0, whereupon 1 is returned and the successive outstanding calls unwind, multiplying by *x* in each case. In fact, for a given value of *n* greater than 0, the function calls itself *n* times. The mechanism is illustrated in Figure 9-4; here the value 3 is assumed for the index argument *n*.

As you see, you need a total of four calls of the power() function to generate x^3.

For negative powers of *n*, the reciprocal of x^n is calculated, so this uses the same process that I just described.

Incidentally, you could shorten the code for the power() function by using the conditional operator. In fact, the function body comes down to a single line:

```
double power(double x, int n) {
  return 0 == n ? 1.0 : (0 > n ? 1.0/power(x, -n) : x*power(x, n-1));
}
```

This doesn't improve the operation particularly, and perhaps it's not quite as clear what is happening. In fact, the recursive call process is very inefficient compared to a loop. Every function call involves a lot of housekeeping that includes obtaining and storing the return address, copying each of the arguments, and handing over the arguments to the function being called. If you implemented the function power() using a loop rather than recursive calls, it would execute a lot faster:

```
double power(double x, int n) {
  if(n == 0)
    return 1.0;
  if(n < 0) {
     x = 1.0/x;
     n = -n;
  }

  double result = x;
  for(int i = 1 ; i < n ; i++)
    result *= x;
  return result;
}
```

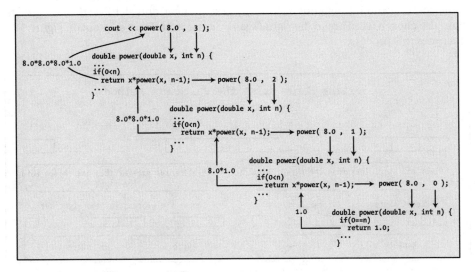

Figure 9-4. Recursive calls in executing the power() function

Using Recursion

Unless you have a problem that particularly lends itself to using recursive functions, or you have no obvious alternative, it is generally better to use a different approach, such as a loop. This is much more efficient than using recursive function calls for the reasons I explained in the context of the previous example. You also need to make sure that the depth of recursion necessary to solve your problem is not itself a problem. For instance, if a function calls itself a million times, the amount of memory you need to store copies of argument values and the return address will be considerable.

However, using recursion can often considerably simplify the coding; sometimes this gain in simplicity can be well worth the loss in efficiency that you get with recursion.

When you implement sorting and merging operations, you'll find that they provide you with a good example of when recursion is often favored. Often, sorting and merging sets of data is a recursive process in which you reapply the same algorithm to smaller and smaller subsets of the original data. Let's look at an example.

Implementing a Sort Recursively

In Program 7.9, you extracted words from some input text and sorted them in ascending sequence by initial letter, using an array of pointers. You could implement a recursive function to sort the words using a well-known sorting algorithm called **Quicksort**. Although this is an ancient method—it was invented more than 40 years ago—it is still the fastest general purpose sorting method around.

To apply the Quicksort algorithm to sorting the words, you first need to choose some arbitrary word from the set, such as the one in the middle. You can then arrange the remaining words so that all those that are "less than" the chosen word are to the left of the chosen word (though not necessarily in sequence), and all those that are "greater than" the chosen word are to the right (again, not necessarily in sequence). Figure 9-5 illustrates this process.

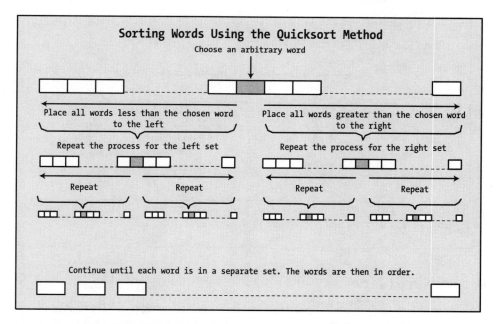

Figure 9-5. How the Quicksort algorithm works

After you have performed this process once, just repeat it for each of the two resulting sets to produce four sets. Repeat the process again, and continue until each word is in a separate set. Now the words are in ascending order. You reach the goal by repeatedly subdividing a set, always via the same process. This is a good indication that you should be able to implement the process using recursion.

Of course, you'll do this by rearranging addresses in an array, not by moving words around. Figure 9-6 shows a method for partitioning the addresses of the words into two sets, with the rearranged addresses in the original array.

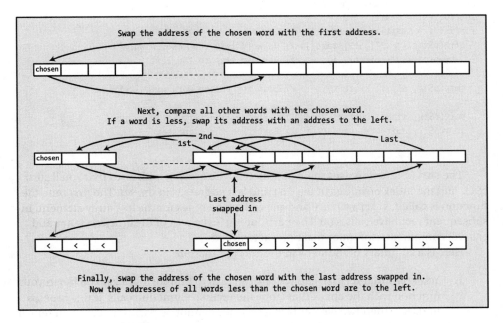

Figure 9-6 Swapping addresses in the Quicksort algorithm

You have to swap addresses in the array in several places, so it is a good idea to write a function to do this:

```
// Swap address at position first with address at position second
void swap(string* pStr[], int first, int second) {
  string* temp = pStr[first];
  pStr[first] = pStr[second];
  pStr[second] = temp;
}
```

You can use this to implement the Quicksort method by rearranging the elements in the address array in the manner illustrated in the diagram. The sorting algorithm itself should look something like this:

```
// Sort strings in ascending sequence
// Addresses of words to be sorted are from pStr[start] to pStr[end]
void sort(string* pStr[], int start, int end) {
```

```
// start index must be less than end index for 2 or more elements
if(!(start<end))
    return;                        // Less than 2 elements - nothing to do

// Choose middle address to partition set
swap(pStr, start, (start+end)/2); // Swap middle address with start

// Check words against chosen word
int current = start;
for(int i = start+1; i<=end ; i++)
    if(*(pStr[i]) < *(pStr[start])) // Is word less than chosen word?
        swap(pStr, ++current, i);   // Yes, so swap to the left

    swap(pStr, start, current);     // Swap the chosen word with last in

    sort(pStr, start, current-1);   // Partition the left set
    sort(pStr, current+1, end);     // Partition the right set
}
```

The sort() function uses three parameters: the array of addresses that you'll sort, pStr, and the index positions of the first and last addresses in the set. The *first* time the function is called, start will be 0 and end will be the index for the last array element. In subsequent recursive calls, you'll be partitioning just a part of the array, so start and end will contain interior index positions in many cases.

Here is a summary of the steps in the sort() function:

1. You know that recursive functions can lead to infinite loops, so you begin your function with the check that stops the recursive function calls. If this process finds less than two elements in a set, they cannot be partitioned, so you return from the function. With each recursion, you partition a set into two *smaller* sets—therefore, you must end up eventually with a set that has either one element or no elements.

2. Next, you swap the address in the middle of the set with the first address at index position start. The for loop compares the chosen word with words pointed to by the addresses following start. For any word that is *less than* the chosen word, its address is swapped into a position following start: the first goes into position start+1, the second to start+2, and so on. When the loop ends, current contains the index position of the address of the last of these swapped words. The address of the chosen word is still at position start, so you swap the address of the chosen word (at position start) with the address at current. As a result, the addresses of words less than the chosen word are to the left of current; and the addresses of words greater are to the right.

3. So far, you've partitioned a set of words; from here, sorting the whole set of words is easy. You simply have to sort the two subsets you have produced—to do this, just call the sort() function for each subset. The addresses of words less than the chosen word run from start to current-1, and the addresses of those greater run from current+1 to end.

When you use recursion, the code is relatively easy to follow, and it is much shorter and less convoluted than if you implemented the sort using loops. A loop is still faster, though.

··

Try It Out: Sorting Words Recursively

Let's produce another version of Program 7.9 that uses the sort() function that you just wrote. At the same time, you can make the program more manageable by breaking it up into functions. The original version of main() has three blocks of code that are candidates for separate functions: counting the words, creating string objects corresponding to the words, and displaying the words in sequence.

The first of these functions counts the words in the input text. This function needs access to the original text as well as the string object that contains the separator characters. It can return the word count as an int. Here is the prototype for this function:

```
int count_words(const string& text, const string& separators);
```

Both parameters should be const references, because the function doesn't need to modify them. You'll use the word count produced by this function to create an array of pointers of the appropriate size in the free store.

The next function extracts words from the input text. This function needs the array of addresses as a parameter, as well as the input text and the separators, so the prototype should look like this:

```
void extract_words(string** pStr, const string& text,
                                  const string& separators);
```

Obviously, the array parameter can't be declared as const here because the function stores the addresses obtained from new in the array. The function doesn't need to access the word count because the extracting process doesn't require it.

The last of these functions outputs the words. This function needs access to the pointer array and the word count as parameters, so its prototype should look like this:

```
void show_words(string** pStr, int count);
```

You can now use these functions, together with the sort() and swap() functions that you developed earlier, to define the function main():

```
// Program 9.8 Sorting strings recursively
#include <iostream>
#include <string>
using std::cout;
using std::cin;
using std::endl;
using std::string;
```

(Continued)

```
// Function prototypes
void swap(string* pStr[], int first, int second);
void sort(string* pStr[], int start, int end);
int count_words(const string& text, const string& separators);
void extract_words(string* pStr[], const string& text,
                                   const string& separators);
void show_words(string* pStr[], int count);

int main() {
  string text;                              // The string to be sorted
  const string separators = " ,.\"\n";      // Word delimiters

  // Read the string to be searched from the keyboard
  cout << endl << "Enter a string terminated by #:" << endl;
  getline(cin, text, '#');

  int word_count = count_words(text, separators); // Get count of words

  if(0 == word_count) {
    cout << endl << "No words in text." << endl;
    return 0;
  }

  string** pWords = new string*[word_count]; // Array of pntrs to words

  extract_words(pWords, text, separators);
  sort(pWords, 0, word_count-1);            // Sort the words
  show_words(pWords, word_count);           // Output the words

  // Delete words from free store
  for(int i = 0 ; i<word_count ; i++)
    delete pWords[i];

  // Now delete the array of pointers
  delete[] pWords;

  return 0;
}
```

To complete the program you just need the definitions for the three new functions in addition to sort() and swap(). Here's the code for the count_words() function:

```
// Function to count the words in the text
int count_words(const string& text, const string& separators) {
  size_t start = text.find_first_not_of(separators); // Word start index
  size_t end = 0;                                     // End delimiter index
  int word_count = 0;                                 // Count of words stored
  while(start != string::npos) {
    end = text.find_first_of(separators, start+1);
```

```
    if(end == string::npos)                    // Found one?
      end = text.length();                     // No, so set to last+1
    word_count++;                              // Increment count

    // Find the first character of the next word
    start = text.find_first_not_of(separators, end+1);
  }
  return word_count;
}
```

This is much the same as the original code, but you have packed it into a function. The same goes for the extract_words() function:

```
// Function to extract words from the text
void extract_words(string* pStr[], const string& text,
                                        const string& separators) {
  size_t start = text.find_first_not_of(separators); // Start 1st word
  size_t end = 0;                          // Index for the end of a word
  int index = 0;                           // Pointer array index

  while(start != string::npos) {
    end = text.find_first_of(separators, start+1); // Find end separator
    if(end == string::npos)                        // Found one?
      end = text.length();                         // No, so set to last+1
    pStr[index++] = new string(text.substr(start, end-start));
    start = text.find_first_not_of(separators, end+1); // Find next word
  }
}
```

To output the words in groups beginning with the same letter, with up to five words per line, you can implement show_words() as follows:

```
// Function to output the words
void show_words(string* pStr[], int count) {
  const int words_per_line = 5;            // Word_per_line
  cout << endl << "  " << *pStr[0];         // Output the first word
int words_in_line = 0;                      // Words in the current line
  for(int i = 1 ; i<count ; i++) {          // Output remaining words
    // Newline when initial letter changes or after 5 wrds per line
    if((*pStr[i])[0] != (*pStr[i-1])[0] ||
                        words_in_line++ == words_per_line) {
      words_in_line = 0;
      cout << endl;
    }
    cout << "  " << *pStr[i];                          // Output a word
  }
  cout << endl;
}
```

(Continued)

If you assemble all the functions to form a complete program, you'll have quite a good-sized example of a program split into several functions. If you run the program, it will work in the same way as the original version in Chapter 7, but the code will be much easier to understand with the structure that the functions provide. It would also be easier to modify the program if you needed to. Because you use an array here, the program must traverse the text looking for words twice, as you need to know how many elements are necessary in the pointer array. You can approach this in other ways that remove the need to know the number of words. One possibility involves storing the addresses in a linked list. Then you could use a single traversal of the text to create the word objects and add them to the list.

Summary

You should now have a reasonably comprehensive knowledge of how to write and use functions. However, you'll see more on functions in the context of user-defined types, which I'll introduce starting in Chapter 11.

Here are the important bits that you learned in this chapter:

- Overloaded functions are functions with the same name but with different parameter lists. Overloaded functions can't be differentiated by the return type alone.

- The signature of a function is defined by the function name together with the number and types of its parameters. When you call an overloaded function, the compiler determines the function signature of the call and compares it to the signatures of the available functions in order to select the appropriate function.

- A function template is a recipe for generating overloaded functions automatically.

- A function template has one or more parameters that are usually type variables but can also be non-type variables. An instance of the function template—that is, a function definition—is created by the compiler for each function call that corresponds to a unique set of template arguments.

- A function template can be overloaded with other functions or function templates.

- A pointer to a function stores the address of a function, plus information about the number and types of parameters and the return type for a function.

- You can use a pointer to a function to store the address of any function with the appropriate return type, and number and types of parameters.

- You can use a pointer to a function to call the function at the address it contains. You can also pass a pointer to a function as a function argument.

- A recursive function is a function that calls itself. Implementing an algorithm recursively can sometimes result in very elegant and concise code, but usually at the expense of execution time when compared to other methods of implementing the same algorithm.

Exercises

The following exercises enable you to try out what you've learned in this chapter. If you get stuck, look back over the chapter for help. If you're still stuck after that, you can download the solutions from the Apress website (http://www.apress.com/book/download.html), but that really should be a last resort.

Exercise 9-1. Create a function, plus(), that adds two values and returns their sum. Provide overloaded versions to work with int, double, and string types, and test that they work with the following calls:

```
int n = plus(3, 4);
double d = plus(3.2, 4.2);
string s = plus("he", "llo");
string s1 = "aaa"; string s2 = "bbb";
string s3 = plus(s1, s2);
```

What is the most efficient way to pass the arguments to the string version of the function? Can you explain why the following call doesn't work?

```
d = plus(3, 4.2);
```

Exercise 9-2. Turn the plus() function into a template, and test that it works for numeric types. Does your template work for the statement plus("he", "llo") in Exercise 9-1? Can you explain this behavior? Suggest a solution to the problem.

Exercise 9-3. The standard library provides trigonometry functions sin(), cos(), and tan(); each of them takes a double argument and returns a double value. To use them, you need to #include the standard library header <cmath>. Write a function calc() that takes two arguments—a double value and a pointer to a trig function—and returns the result of applying the function to the value as a double. Write a program to test your function; when this works, set up an array of function pointers to hold the three trig functions and test it using those.

Exercise 9-4. A recursive function called Ackerman's function is popular with lecturers of computer science and mathematics courses; it can be defined like this:

If m and n are integers, where $n >= 0$ and $m >= 0$,

then ack(m,n) = $n+1$, if $m == 0$;

ack(m,n) = ack($m-1$, 1), if $m > 0$;

and $n == 0$ack(m,n) = ack($m-1$, ack(m, $n-1$)), if $m>0$ and $n>0$.

Write a function to compute Ackerman's function recursively. Test your function for values of n between 0 and 5, and m between 0 and 3. One particular property of this function is that the depth of recursion increases dramatically for small increases in m and n. For instance, calculating Ackerman's function recursively for quite modest values such as $n > 8$ and $m > 3$ is extremely difficult if not impossible on most computers.

CHAPTER 10

Program Files and Preprocessing Directives

IN THIS CHAPTER, you'll look into subjects that relate to how multiple program files and header files interact, and to how you can manage and control the contents of your program files.

I have yet to discuss the major topic, classes. You'll begin to define your own data types in the next chapter, and this chapter will (in part) form a gentle introduction to classes. The material of this chapter has implications for how you define your data types; I'll discuss those implications as I come to them.

In this chapter you will learn the following:

- The details of how header files and program files interrelate

- What a translation unit is

- What linkage is and why it is important

- What namespaces are and how you create and use them

- What preprocessing is, and how to use the preprocessing directives that are available

- The basic ideas in debugging, and what debugging help you can get from preprocessing and the standard library

Working with Program Files

Way back in Chapter 1, I talked about how your C++ program will, in general, consist of multiple files. Let's recap a little. Two basic kinds of files are involved:

header files are commonly identified with the file name extension .h (note that some older systems use .hpp). These files contain type definitions and other code that is used in one or more source files in a program.

source files usually have the extension .cpp although .c, .cxx, and other extensions may also be used. These files contain the code that compiles to machine instructions—primarily function definitions. Any required header files are added to a source file by means of #include directives.

As you have seen, the *standard* headers for library functions in ANSI C++ (for example, <iostream>) have no extension, so it's always obvious whether or not an #include directive is for a standard header. You use a special notation in an #include directive where a standard library header name is enclosed between angled brackets:

```
#include <iostream>
```

NOTE *You also need to remember that you shouldn't add spaces between the angled brackets, otherwise the header name won't be recognized.*

Of course, you may come across other kinds of files that support the environment in which you are programming (defining resources of one kind or another, perhaps) but the .h and .cpp files are the ones that contain all your C++ code. This is illustrated in Figure 10-1.

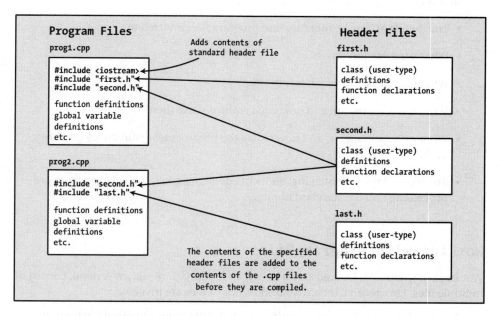

Figure 10-1. Your C++ program consists of .cpp *and* .h *files.*

The essential difference between a header file and a `.cpp` file is in how each is used. The rules governing what you put in header files and source files and how they are handled are the following:

- `.cpp` files primarily contain the code that determines what your program does, which consists of function definitions.

- `.h` files contain your function declarations (that is, the prototypes, but not the definitions), inline function definitions, enumerations, your own type definitions, and preprocessing directives. You should avoid putting function definitions in a `.h` file (`inline` functions are an exception to this rule), otherwise you may end up with duplicate definitions of such functions in your program, which will cause linkage errors.

- `.h` files can also contain definitions of constants that are to be shared between two or more `.cpp` files.

- Each `.cpp` must have an `#include` directive for each header file that it needs.

- When you compile your program, you compile just the `.cpp` files. The contents of the header files that your program uses are inserted into the `.cpp` files as determined by the `#include` directives.

- Each `.cpp` file that you compile produces an **object file**. The term object file has nothing to do with class objects. An object file is simply a file that contains the binary output from the compiler; it is often identified with the extension `.obj`. The object files are combined by the linker into a single executable module that usually has the extension `.exe`.

So far, you have only used headers that provide the declarations necessary for using the standard library. The program examples have been short and simple; consequently, they have not warranted the use of separate header files, which contain function declarations or constant definitions. In the next chapter, when you begin to define your own data types, the need for header files will become apparent. A typical practical C++ program involves a number of header files and `.cpp` files.

Each `.cpp` file in your program, along with the contents of all its header files included, is called a **translation unit.** The term translation unit is used because this does not need to be a file, although with the majority of C++ implementations it will be. The compiler processes each translation unit independently to generate an object file. These object files are then processed by the linker, which ties together any necessary connections between the object files to produce the executable program module.

The Scope of a Name

The **scope** of a name in your program is the range of statements over which the name is valid. You already know that a variable name or other name declared within a statement block (enclosed between braces) has **block scope**—this is also referred to as **local scope** because such a name is local to the block that contains the declaration and will not exist in any outer enclosing block. You can only use a name with block scope from the point at which it is declared up to the closing brace for the block. Here is an example:

```
int main() {
  const int limit = 10;
  for (int i = 1 ; i<= limit ; i++)
    std:: cout << std::endl <<  i << " squared is " << i*i;
}
```

Here the scope of the name limit is the entire body of the function main(). The scope of the loop variable, **i**, is just the extent of the for loop, which consists of the loop control expressions and the loop body.

Name Hiding

You are allowed to define a name in an outer scope that duplicates the name in the inner scope. In this case, the name that is defined in the inner scope hides the name that exists in the outer scope. Here is what this looks like:

```
int main() {
  const int limit = 10;                                 // Outer limit
  std::cout <<"Outer limit is " << limit << std::endl;   // Outer limit
  {
    const int limit = 5;                     // Hides limit with value 10
    std::cout <<"Inner limit is " << limit << std::endl; // Inner limit
    for (int i = 1 ; i<= limit ; i++)                    // Inner limit
      std:: cout << std::endl <<  i << " squared is " << i*i;
  }
}
```

In the inner block that contains the for loop, limit is the variable with the value 5. This hides the variable with the same name in the outer scope that has the value 10. Thus, the output statement in the inner loop produces 5 as the value of limit and the for loop executes five iterations.

Accessing Hidden Names

Suppose that in the previous code fragment you wanted the number of for loop iterations to be constrained by the value for the limit variable that is hidden. In this case, you can use the **scope resolution operator**, ::, to select the variable defined in the outer scope rather than the variable with the same name in the current scope. Here is an example:

```
int main() {
  const int limit = 10;                                 // Outer limit
  std::cout <<"Outer limit is " << limit << std::endl;   // Outer limit
```

```
  {
    const int limit = 5;                       // Hides limit with value 10
    std::cout <<"Inner limit is " << limit << std::endl; // Inner limit
    for (int i = 1 ; i<= ::limit ; i++)                   // Outer limit
      std::cout << std::endl <<  i << " squared is " << i*i;
  }
}
```

You are using the *unary* form of the scope resolution operator with the name, `limit`. You are also using the *binary* form of the operator to qualify the name `cout` for instance with its namespace name, `std`. The expression, `::limit`, in the `for` loop control expression specifies the `limit` variable that is in the outer scope, so the loop will execute ten iterations. The output statement immediately preceding the `for` loop refers to the inner variable, `limit`, so the value will be 5.

Global Scope

A name that is declared outside of all blocks and outside all named and unnamed namespaces (a function or a variable, for instance) is said to have **global namespace scope**, which is also referred to as **global scope**. The term **file scope** is also sometimes used for this because the name is valid from the point of its declaration until the end of the file (translation unit) that contains it, but global scope is preferable. Here's an example:

```
const int limit = 10;  // Global scope, also called file scope

int main() {
  for (int i = 1 ; i<= limit ; i++)
    std:: cout << std::endl <<  i << " squared is " << i*i;
}
```

In this example, the variable `limit` has global scope because its declaration is outside of any functions in the file. The scope of `limit` extends from its declaration to the end of the translation unit. You can access it from any function that is defined within the same translation unit. In this example, it is used within the `for` loop condition as the upper limit for the loop variable, `i`.

Of course, a name defined at global scope can be hidden by a local variable with the same name. You can see this happening in the following code:

```
const int limit = 10;  // Global scope, also called file scope
int main() {
  const in limit = 5;                       // Hides limit at global scope
  std::cout <<"Inner limit is " << limit << std::endl;   // Inner limit
  for (int i = 1 ; i<= limit ; i++)                      // Inner limit
    std:: cout << std::endl <<  i << " squared is " << i*i;
}
```

The limit variable defined in the body of main() hides the variable at global scope. If you want to access the global variable, limit, the scope resolution operator can help here too. Here's what this looks like:

```
const int limit = 10;  // Global scope, also called file scope

int main() {
  const int limit = 5;                    // Hides limit at global scope
  std::cout <<"Inner limit is " << limit << std::endl;   // Inner limit
  for (int i = 1 ; i<= ::limit ; i++)               // Outer limit
    std:: cout << std::endl <<  i << " squared is " << i*i;
}
```

Now the loop is controlled by the value of limit defined at global scope, whereas the statement preceding the loop outputs the value of the local limit variable. Here the loop executes ten iterations, whereas without the scope resolution applied to limit, it only executes five iterations.

Global variables are always initialized—by default, if necessary. If you don't supply an initial value for a global variable, it will be initialized with zero (0).

The "One Definition" Rule

Each variable, function, class type, enumeration type, or template in a translation unit (which is a .cpp file with the contents of all included header files added) that is not local to a block must only be *defined* once. You can have more than one *declaration* for a variable for instance, but you must always have a unique definition of what it represents.

Inline functions are an exception to this rule. A definition for an inline function must appear in every translation unit that calls the function, but all definitions of a given inline function in all translation units must be identical. For this reason, you should always define inline functions in a header file that you include in a source file when one is required.

Of course, your own data types will almost certainly be used in more that one translation unit, so you have some leeway here to allow different translation units to each include a definition for a given type, but only as long as these definitions are identical. In practice, you achieve this by placing the definition for a type in a single header file and then using an #include directive to add it to any source file that requires it. Of course, within a single translation unit, duplicate definitions for a given type are illegal. This means that you need to be careful how you define the contents of header files to avoid the possibility of duplicating definitions within a translation unit. You'll see how you do this later in this chapter.

Program Files and Linkage

Entities in one translation unit often need to be accessed from code in another translation unit. Functions are obvious examples of where this is the case, but you can have others—variables defined at global scope that are shared across several translation units, for instance. Because the compiler processes one translation unit at a time, such references can't be resolved by the compiler. Only the linker can do this when all the object files from the translation units in the program are available.

The way that names in a translation unit are handled in the compile/link process is determined by a property that a name can have called **linkage**. Linkage expresses where in the program code the entity that is represented by a name can be. Every name that you use in a program either has linkage, or doesn't. A name has linkage when you can use it to access something in your program that is *outside* the scope in which the name is declared. If this isn't the case, it has no linkage. If a name has linkage, then it can have **internal linkage** or **external linkage**. Therefore, every name in a translation unit has internal linkage, external linkage, or no linkage.

Determining Linkage for a Name

The linkage that applies to a name is not affected by whether its declaration appears in a header file or a source file. The linkage for each name in a translation unit is determined *after* the contents of any header files have been inserted into the .cpp file that is the basis for the translation unit. The three linkage possibilities for a name have the following meaning:

> **Internal linkage:** The entity that the name represents can be accessed from anywhere within the same translation unit. For example, the names of variables defined at global scope that have been declared as const have internal linkage by default.

> **External linkage:** With this type of linkage, a name can be accessed from another translation unit in addition to the one in which it is defined. In other words, the entity that the name represents can be shared and accessed throughout the entire program. All the functions that you have written so far, which have external linkage and non-const variables that are defined at global scope, also have external linkage.

> **No linkage:** When a name has no linkage, the entity that it refers to can only be accessed from within the scope that applies to the name. All names that are defined within a block—local names, in other words—have no linkage.

Now, the interesting question is this: From within a function, how do you access a variable that is defined in another translation unit? This comes down to how you declare a variable to be external.

External Names

In a program that is made up of several files, the linker establishes (or **resolves**) the connection between a function call in one source file and the function definition in another. Before the linker executes, the compiler has compiled a *call* to the function and to do this, it has to extract the information necessary to construct the call from the function prototype. The compiler doesn't really mind whether the function's *definition* occurs in the same file or in another .cpp file. This is because function names have external linkage by default. If a function is not defined within the translation unit in which it is called, the compiler flags the call as external and leaves it for the linker to take care of.

Variable names are different. The compiler needs some indication that the definition for a particular name is external to the current translation unit. If you want to use a name to access a variable that is defined *outside* the current translation unit, then you must declare the variable name using the extern keyword, as shown here:

```
extern double pi;
```

This statement declares that the name pi is a name that is defined outside of the current block. The type must correspond exactly to the type that appears in the definition. You can't have an initial value in an extern declaration.

Declaring a variable as extern implies that it is defined somewhere in another translation unit. This causes the compiler to mark the variable as having external linkage. It is the linker that actually makes the connection between the name and the variable to which it refers. Figure 10-2 illustrates the declaration of a variable name as extern.

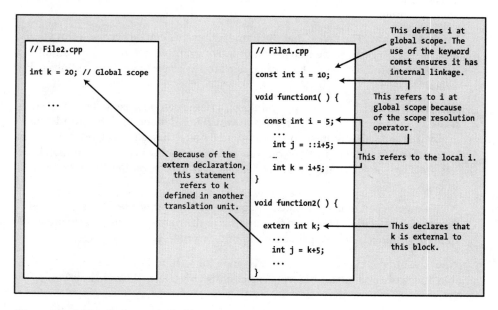

Figure 10-2. Declaring a variable as external

The extern declaration for the name k in function2() says that any subsequent use of k in that function refers to the k that is defined somewhere outside of the current block—the function block in this case. Note that the extern declaration does *not* define k, it merely indicates that it is defined somewhere else. Here, the name k has external linkage, because it refers to a variable in a separate translation unit. The compiler can't connect the name to the definition variable because the definition is in another translation unit. The compiler marks the variable as external so that the connection can be made by the linker when the object files are linked to create a single executable module.

Figure 10-2 also shows how you can access a global variable with internal linkage using the scope resolution operator, even when another variable with the same name has been defined at local scope. You can also access the local variable simply by using its name without the scope resolution operator.

Note that if you have an `extern` declaration for a name in a given block, you can't have a definition for that name in the same block. So, for instance, the following code doesn't compile:

```
int main() {
    int limit = 10;          // Illegal - redefinition!!
    std::cout <<"Local limit is " << limit << std::endl;
    extern int limit;        // External declaration of limit
        std::cout <<"External limit is " << limit << std::endl;
        for (int i = 1 ; i<= limit ; i++)
            std:: cout << std::endl <<  i << " squared is " << i*i;
    return 0;
}
```

Because the `extern` declaration and the definition for `limit` appear in the same block scope, the compiler flags this as an error. This is because you have two definitions for `limit`: the external definition and the local definition.

However, the following code does compile:

```
int main() {
    int limit = 10;      // OK - not in same block as external declaration.
    std::cout <<"Local limit is " << limit << std::endl;
    {
        extern int limit;        // External declaration of limit
            std::cout <<"External limit is " << limit << std::endl;
            for (int i = 1 ; i<= limit ; i++)
                std:: cout << std::endl <<  i << " squared is " << i*i;
    }
    return 0;
}
```

Suppose that `limit` is declared in another translation unit at global scope with this statement:

```
int limit = 15;  // External linkage
```

This causes the `for` loop body to execute 15 times.

Forcing const Variables to Have External Linkage

Let's take another example. Suppose you have variables defined as global in a file file1.cpp using these statements:

```
double pi = 3.14159265;
string days[] = {
                    "Sunday",    "Monday", "Tuesday", "Wednesday",
                    "Thursday", "Friday", "Saturday"
            };
```

These statements define the variable pi and the array days[], so duplicate definitions for the same variables can't exist elsewhere. However, you can access these variables from another function in a different source file (or, for that matter, in the same source file), by declaring the variables as external. For example, a function in the file file2.cpp could contain the following statements:

```
extern double pi;          // Variable is defined in another file
extern string days[];      // Array is defined in another file
```

These statements do not create the variables, they merely identify that they are defined elsewhere, so the compiler doesn't expect to find them within the present scope. The variables are used in file2.cpp, but their actual locations are determined by their definitions in file1.cpp. The linker establishes this connection when the object files are linked together.

 NOTE *Of course, if you declare a name as external, and its corresponding definition is not found, then you get an error message from the linker and no executable module is created.*

In this example, the names pi and days obviously represent constants, so you probably want to avoid the possibility of these variables being altered. Therefore, you might consider making each of them const when you define them in file1.cpp:

```
const double pi = 3.14159265;
const string days[] = {
                        "Sunday",    "Monday", "Tuesday", "Wednesday",
                        "Thursday", "Friday", "Saturday"
                };
```

However, declaring them as const has the effect of giving them internal linkage by default, and this makes them unavailable in other translation units. You can override this by using the extern keyword when you define them:

```
extern const double pi = 3.14159265;
  extern const string days[] = {
                            "Sunday",    "Monday", "Tuesday", "Wednesday",
                            "Thursday", "Friday", "Saturday"
                        };
```

These statements still define the const double variable and the const string array. The use of the keyword extern here tells the compiler that these variable names should have external linkage, even though they have been declared as const.

Now, when you want to access these in file2.cpp, you must declare them as const as well as external:

```
extern const double pi;        // Variable is defined in another file
extern const string days[];    // Array is defined in another file
```

Within the block in which these declarations appear, the use of the names pi and days refer to the constants defined in the other file. These declarations can appear in any translation unit that needs access to these names. They can appear either at global scope in a translation unit so that they are available throughout the code in the source file, or they can appear within a block in which case they are only available within that local scope.

Global variables can be useful for constant values that you want to share because they are accessible in any translation unit. By sharing constant values across all of the program files that need access to them, you can ensure that the same values are being used for the constants throughout your program. However, although up to now I have shown constants defined in source files, the best place for them is in a header file.

Let's see how some of what we have discussed works in practice.

....

Try It Out: Using External Variables

You can create a source file containing some data definitions:

```
// File data10_01.cpp
#include <string>
using std::string;

// The next two variables have external linkage
int count;                   // Will be initialized to 0 by default
float phi = 1.618f;          // The divine proportion or golden ratio

// Without the extern, the following would not be accessible
// from another file because they would have internal linkage
extern const double pi = 3.14159265;

extern const string days[] = {
                    "Sunday",    "Monday", "Tuesday", "Wednesday",
                    "Thursday", "Friday", "Saturday"
                        };
```

(Continued)

You can now access these from another source file:

```cpp
// Program 10.1 Accessing External Variables prog10_01.cpp
#include <iostream>
#include <string>
#include <iomanip>
using std::cout;
using std::endl;
using std::string;

// Declare external variables
extern float phi;
extern const double pi;
extern const string days[];
extern int count;

int main() {
  cout << std::setprecision(3) << std::fixed;
  cout << endl
       << "To 3 decimal places..." << endl;

  cout << "...a circle with a diameter of phi has an area of "
       << pi*phi*phi/4
       << endl;

  cout << "...phi squared is "        << phi*phi << endl;
  cout << "...in fact, phi+1 is also " << phi+1    << endl;

  cout << "Value of count is " << count << endl;

  count += 3;
  cout << "Today is " << days[count] << endl;
  return 0;
}
```

This example produces the following output:

```
To 3 decimal places...
...a circle with a diameter of phi has an area of 2.056
...phi squared is 2.618
...in fact, phi+1 is also 2.618
Value of count is 0
Today is Wednesday
```

HOW IT WORKS

Fortunately, it works exactly as we discussed. You can see that phi is demonstrably external because it is used in one file, in main(), but it is defined in another file. The constant pi and the constant array days also have external linkage because they are declared as extern. Try removing the extern keyword—you'll find out that the code won't compile.

You display the default value for count so that it has clearly been initialized to zero (0). Finally, you modify the value of count and use it to index the days array.

Note that the extern declarations in the prog10_01.cpp file make the names available to any function within that translation unit. If you wanted to limit access to these variables to a particular function, you could place the extern declarations in the body of that function.

Namespaces

With large programs, choosing unique names for all the entities that have external linkage can become difficult. This is particularly true when an application is being developed by several programmers working in parallel, or when a vendor wants to produce a library for sale to third parties. Without some kind of mechanism to prevent it, name clashes become highly likely. This is perhaps most likely in the context of user-defined types, or classes, which you will meet in the next few chapters. A **namespace** is designed to overcome this difficulty.

A namespace is a region within a program that attaches an extra name—a namespace name—to all the entity names within it. Two different namespaces can each contain entities with the same name, but the entities are differentiated because a different namespace name is attached to each of them. Figure 10-3 illustrates two namespaces defined within a single program, possibly within the same source file.

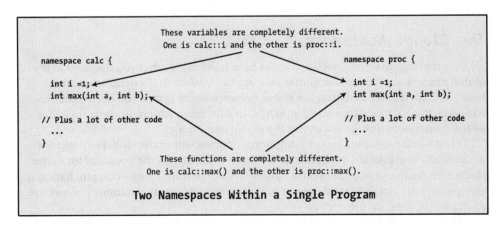

Figure 10-3. Using namespaces

In each namespace, a variable is defined with the name i, and a function is declared with the name max(). However, they each refer to *distinct* entities with no possibility of a clash between them because their names are qualified by the name of the namespace in which they are defined, which makes each name unique.

You'd typically use a separate namespace name within a single program for each collection of code that encompasses a common purpose. Each namespace would represent some logical grouping of functions, together with any related global variables and declarations. A namespace would also be used to completely contain a unit of release, such as a library.

You are already aware that the standard library is defined within the namespace std. This implies that every external name in the standard library is prefixed with std. For instance, the output stream name is std::cout, so to display the contents of a variable, value, you can write this:

```
std::cout << std::endl << value;
```

The operator :: here is the binary form of the **scope resolution operator**, that you saw earlier. The preceding statement **qualifies** the names cout and endl; it says to the compiler, "You'll find the definition of these names in the std namespace."

Of course, you have been doing this in the examples so far in this book for names in the std namespace, or else you've been adding a using declaration for the name like the one shown here:

```
using std::cout;
```

As I mentioned way back in Chapter 1, you can gain use of any name from a namespace by using a blanket using directive:

```
using namespace std;
```

However, this really defeats the purpose of using namespaces in the first place and increases the likelihood of errors due to the accidental use of a name in the std namespace. Therefore, it is much better to use qualified names or just add using declarations for those names in std that you are using.

The Global Namespace

All the programs that you've written so far have used names that you declared in the **global namespace**. The global namespace applies by default if a namespace hasn't been defined. All names within the global namespace are just as you declare them, without a namespace name being attached. In a program with multiple source files, all the names with linkage are within the global namespace.

With small programs, you can define your names within the global namespace without running into any problems. With larger applications, the potential for name clashes increases, so you should use namespaces to partition your code into logical groupings. That way, each code segment is self-contained from a naming perspective, and name clashes are prevented.

Of course, you need to know how to declare a namespace, so let's look at that next.

Defining a Namespace

You can define a namespace with these statements:

```
namespace myRegion {
  // Code you want to have in the namespace, including
  // function definitions and declarations, global variables,
  // templates, etc.
}
```

 NOTE *You do not need to place a semicolon after the closing brace at the end of the namespace definition.*

The namespace name that you have assigned here is myRegion. This uniquely identifies the namespace, and this name will be attached to all the entities declared within the namespace. The braces enclose the scope for the namespace myRegion, and every name within the namespace scope has the name myRegion attached to it.

 CAUTION *Of course, you wouldn't include the function* main() *within the namespace. The runtime environment expects* main() *to be defined in the global namespace, so you must always place the function* main() *outside of all your namespaces.*

You can extend a namespace scope by adding a second namespace definition in a file. For example, a program file might contain the following:

```
namespace calc {
  // This defines namespace calc
  // The initial code in the namespace goes here
}

namespace sort {
  // Code in a new namespace, sort
}

namespace calc {
  // This extends the namespace calc
  // Code in here can refer to names in the previous
  // calc namespace block without qualification
}
```

Here, you have two blocks defined as namespace calc, separated by a namespace sort. The second calc block is treated as a continuation of the first. Therefore, functions defined within each of the calc blocks all belong to the same namespace. The second block is referred to as an **extension namespace definition**, because it extends the original namespace definition. You could have further extension namespace definitions in the file, which would add more code within the same namespace.

Of course, you wouldn't usually organize a source file so that it contains multiple namespace blocks in this way. However, if you include several header files into your source file, and each header file contributes some code to the same namespace, then you may effectively end up with the sort of situation I just described. A common example of this is when you include a number of standard library headers (each of which contributes to the namespace std), interspersed with header files of your own (defined within a different namespace). Here's an example:

```
#include <iostream>      // In namespace std
#include "mystuff.h"     // In my namespace calc
#include <string>        // In namespace std - extension namespace
#include "morestuff.h"   // In my namespace calc - extension namespace
```

Finally, note that references to names within a namespace *from inside the same namespace* do not need to be qualified. For example, names that belong to the namespace calc can be referenced from within calc, without the need to qualify them with the namespace name.

Let's look at a simple example to illustrate the mechanics of declaring and using a namespace.

··

Try It Out: Using a Namespace

Here, you'll create a program that consists of two .cpp files. The first just contains definitions of some const variables that you defined earlier, but this time they are defined within a namespace:

```
// Program 10.2 Using a namespace    File: Data10_02.cpp
#include <string>
namespace data {
  extern const double pi = 3.14159265;
  extern const std::string days[] = {
                        "Sunday",   "Monday", "Tuesday", "Wednesday",
                        "Thursday", "Friday", "Saturday"
                                   };
}
```

Here you have defined pi and days[] within the namespace data. The array days[] is of type string, which is defined in the standard library, so you need to qualify the type name with the standard library namespace name, std.

To do this, you'll use these variables in another translation unit, which contains main():

```cpp
// Program 10.2 Using a namespace    File: Prog10_02.cpp
#include <iostream>
#include <string>

namespace data {
  extern const double pi;          // Variable is defined in another file
  extern const std::string days[]; // Array is defined in another file
}

int main() {
  std::cout << std::endl
            << "pi has the value "
            << data::pi << std::endl;

  std::cout << "The second day of the week is "
            << data::days[1] << std::endl;

  return 0;
}
```

If you compile and run this, it will produce the following output:

```
pi has the value 3.14159
The second day of the week is Monday
```

HOW IT WORKS

In the file containing main(), you must declare pi and days[] as external because they are defined in a separate translation unit. You do this with these statements:

```cpp
namespace data {
  extern const double pi;          // Variable is defined in another file
  extern const std::string days[]; // Array is defined in another file
}
```

You have placed the declarations for the external variables within the namespace data because the variables are defined within this namespace in the first .cpp file. This demonstrates the point that we discussed earlier—a namespace can be defined piecemeal. Even within a single file, you can have several namespace blocks that correspond to the same namespace name, and the contents of each will be in the same namespace. Because the type string is defined within the standard library namespace, you have to supply the qualified name std::string in the declaration.

(Continued)

This is not the best way to organize the code for this program. As a general rule, you should put the definitions for pi and days in a header file, data.h, for example. The contents of this header file would just be

```
// Declarations for globals in namespace data    File: data.h
#include <string>
namespace data {
  extern const double pi = 3.14159265;
  extern const std::string days[] = {
                        "Sunday",   "Monday", "Tuesday", "Wednesday",
                        "Thursday", "Friday", "Saturday"
                                  };
}
```

Then, to make the definitions available in the file containing main() (or any other file that needed access to these constants), you would simply add an #include directive at the beginning:

```
#include "data.h"
```

The name has the extension .h to identify that it is a header file. You'll see this in action in Program 10.3.

NOTE *The syntax for the* #include *is slightly different in this example. You should omit the* .h *extension* only *when you are including* standard library *headers. You'll see the significance of the double quotes rather than angled brackets when I discuss preprocessing later in this chapter. It's also important to ensure that the contents of a header file are not included more than once in a translation unit; you'll also see how this is done later on.*

Applying using Declarations

You are already aware of how a **using declaration** can declare a specific name from within a given namespace because I have been using this in all the examples. Just to formalize what you've been doing, a using declaration for a single name from a namespace is of the following form:

```
using namespace_name::identifier;
```

Here using is a keyword, namespace_name is the name of the namespace, and identifier is the name that you want to use unqualified. This declaration introduces a single name from the namespace, which might refer to several different things. For instance, a set of overloaded functions defined within a namespace can be introduced with a single using declaration.

Although I've placed the using declarations and directives at global scope in all the examples, you can also place them within a namespace, or within a function, or even within a statement block. In each case, the declaration or directive applies until the end of the block that contains it.

 NOTE *When you use an unqualified variable name, the compiler first tries to find the definition of the variable in the current scope, prior to the point at which it is used. If the compiler doesn't find the definition, then it looks in the immediately enclosing scope. This continues until the global scope is reached. If a definition for the variable is not found at global scope (which could be an* extern *declaration), the compiler concludes that the variable is not defined.*

Functions and Namespaces

For a function to exist within a namespace, it is sufficient for the function prototype to appear in a namespace. You can define the function elsewhere by simply using the qualified name for the function. In other words, the function definition doesn't have to be enclosed in a namespace block. Let's explore an example.

Suppose you want to write two functions, max() and min(), to return the maximum and minimum of an array of values. You can put the declarations for the functions in a namespace as follows:

```
// compare.h
namespace compare {
  double max(const double* data, int size);
  double min(const double* data, int size);
}
```

You could place this in a header file, compare.h, which would then be included by any source file that used the functions.

The definitions for the functions can now appear in a .cpp file. You can write the definitions without enclosing them in a namespace block, as long as the name of each function is qualified with the namespace name. The contents of the file would be

```
// compare.cpp
#include "compare.h"

// Function to find the maximum
double compare::max(const double* data, int size) {
  double result = data[0];
  for(int i = 1 ; i < size ; i++)
    if(result < data[i])
      result = data[i];
  return result;
}
```

```
// Function to find the minimum
double compare::min(const double* data, int size) {
  double result = data[0];
  for(int i = 1 ; i < size ; i++)
    if(result > data[i])
      result = data[i];
  return result;
}
```

You need the compare.h header file to be included so that the namespace is identified. This enables the compiler to deduce that the functions are within the namespace.

Of course you could place the code for the function definitions within the compare namespace directly. In this case, the contents of compare.cpp would be as follows:

```
// compare.cpp
namespace compare {
  // Function to find the maximum
  double max(const double* data, int size) {
    double result = data[0];
    for(int i = 1 ; i < size ; i++)
      if(result < data[i])
        result = data[i];
    return result;
  }

  // Function to find the minimum
  double min(const double* data, int size) {
    double result = data[0];
    for(int i = 1 ; i < size ; i++)
      if(result > data[i])
        result = data[i];
    return result;
  }
}
```

If you write the function definitions in this way, then you don't need to #include the file compare.h in this file. This is because the definitions are already within the namespace.

Using the functions is the same, however you have defined them. To confirm how easy it is, let's try it out with the functions that you've just defined.

Try It Out: The using Declaration

The function declarations go in the header file `compare.h` as we discussed earlier:

```
// compare.h
namespace compare {
  double max(const double* data, int size);
  double min(const double* data, int size);
}
```

You then put the definitions for the functions in a separate `.cpp` file that contains the following code:

```
// compare.cpp
#include "compare.h"

// Function to find the maximum
double compare::max(const double* data, int size) {
  double result = data[0];
  for(int i = 1 ; i < size ; i++)
    if(result < data[i])
      result = data[i];
  return result;
}

// Function to find the minimum
double compare::min(const double* data, int size) {
  double result = data[0];
  for(int i = 1 ; i < size ; i++)
    if(result > data[i])
      result = data[i];
  return result;
}
```

All you need now is a `.cpp` file containing the definition of `main()` to try the functions out:

```
// Program 10.3 Using functions in a namespace
#include <iostream>
#include "compare.h"

using compare::max;                     // Using declaration for max
using compare::min;                     // Using declaration for min
using std::cout;
using std::endl;

int main() {
  double data[] = {1.5, 4.6, 3.1, 1.1, 3.8, 2.1};
  const int dataSize = sizeof data/sizeof data[0];
```

(Continued)

```
    cout << endl;
    cout << "Minimum double is " << min(data, dataSize) << endl;
    cout << "Maximum double is " << max(data, dataSize) << endl;

    return 0;
}
```

If you compile the two .cpp files and link them, when you run the program, it produces the following output:

```
Minimum double is 1.1
Maximum double is 4.6
```

HOW IT WORKS

The declarations for the functions are introduced into the file containing main() with this directive:

```
#include "compare.h"
```

 CAUTION *If the file* compare.h *is in a different directory to the source files, then the* #include *directive must also contain the directory path from the source file to the header file. In this example, the header file* compare.h *is in the same directory as the source file.*

Then you have a using declaration for each function so that you can use the names without having to add the namespace name:

```
using compare::max;          // Using declaration for max
using compare::min;          // Using declaration for min
```

You could equally well have used a using directive for the compare namespace:

```
using namespace compare;
```

Because the namespace only contains the functions max() and min(), this would have been just as good, and one less line of code. However, in general, the effect of a using directive is quite different from the effect of a using declaration. The using directive allows any name from the namespace that is declared in the file to be used. The using declaration, on the other hand, only introduces one specific name.

Next you have the usual using declarations for cout and endl from the std namespace.

Within main(), you first define an array, data, that you'll pass as an argument to your two functions:

```
double data[] = {1.5, 4.6, 3.1, 1.1, 3.8, 2.1};
```

You need to pass the length of the data array to each function, so you compute this and store it in the constant dataSize:

```
const int dataSize = sizeof data/sizeof data[0];
```

Finally, you call the functions in the output statements that display the maximum and minimum values from the data array:

```
cout << "Minimum double is " << min(data, dataSize) << endl;
cout << "Maximum double is " << max(data, dataSize) << endl;
```

If you hadn't written the using declarations for the function names (or a using directive for the compare namespace), then you'd have had to qualify the functions as in these output statements:

```
cout << "Minimum double is " << compare::min(data, dataSize) << endl;
cout << "Maximum double is " << compare::max(data, dataSize) << endl;
```

Function Templates and Namespaces

You can define function templates in a namespace. The functions I just discussed are natural for generation from a template, so let's use those as an illustration. In this example, you'll put the template definitions in a namespace in a header file:

```
// tempcomp.h
namespace compare {
// Function template to find the maximum element in an array
template<class T> T max(const T* data, int size) {
    T result = data[0];
    for(int i = 1 ; i < size ; i++)
      if(result < data[i])
        result = data[i];
    return result;
  }

// Function template to find the minimum element in an array
template<class T> T min(const T* data, int size) {
    T result = data[0];
    for(int i = 1 ; i < size ; i++)
      if(result > data[i])
        result = data[i];
    return result;
  }
}
```

NOTE *If you wish, you can follow the recommended guidelines by placing the template definitions in a separate file,* tempcomp.cpp, *and writing only the template prototypes in the file* tempcomp.h. *Because you are using class templates, you'll need to prefix each of the template definitions with the keyword* export. *The code is then fully ANSI-compatible. However, some current compilers don't support usage of* export, *and you may find that the preceding code is more suitable to your C++ compiler.*

Of course, if you wanted to define special cases explicitly, for type char* for instance, you could put the prototype for the special case within the namespace just discussed, and put the definition in a .cpp file, either with a qualified function name, or within a namespace block.

Try It Out: Function Templates in a Namespace

You can exercise the template in the namespace compare with the following code:

```
// Program 10.4 Using function templates in a namespace
#include <iostream>
#include "tempcomp.h"

using compare::max;                    // Using declaration for max
using compare::min;                    // Using declaration for min
using std::cout;
using std::endl;

int main() {
  double data[] = {1.5, 4.6, 3.1, 1.1, 3.8, 2.1};
  int numbers[] = {23, 2, 14, 56, 42, 12, 1, 45};

  cout << endl;

  const int dataSize = sizeof data/sizeof data[0];
  cout << "Minimum double is " << min(data, dataSize) << endl;
  cout << "Maximum double is " << max(data, dataSize) << endl;

  const int numbersSize = sizeof numbers/sizeof numbers[0];
  cout << "Minimum integer is " << min(numbers, numbersSize) << endl;
  cout << "Maximum integer is " << max(numbers, numbersSize) << endl;

  return 0;
}
```

This program produces the following output:

```
Minimum double is 1.1
Maximum double is 4.6
Minimum integer is 1
Maximum integer is 56
```

HOW IT WORKS

This works in much the same way as the previous example, which defined each function explicitly. There is no .cpp file for the min() and max() function definitions because each required definition is generated by the compiler from the appropriate template. Because the template definitions appear within the compare namespace, the compiler generates the definition within that namespace.

You can use the function names without qualification in main() because you have using declarations for their names within the namespace compare. Without the using declarations, you'd need to qualify the function names in the output statements, as you did in the earlier example. For instance, the first two output statements would look like this:

```
cout << "Minimum double is " << compare::min(data, dataSize) << endl;
cout << "Maximum double is " << compare::max(data, dataSize) << endl;
```

The first argument in each function call is an array of type double, so the compiler generates definitions for versions of max() and min() that accept this argument type.

Extension Namespaces

Earlier we discussed how namespaces could be defined within several blocks. You could extend Program 10.4 to show an extension to an existing namespace in action.

Try It Out: Using an Extension Namespace

Here you'll add another header file containing a template for a function that normalizes an array of data—that is, the function adjusts the values so that they lie between 0 and 1. Here are the contents of the header file:

```
// normal.h
// Normalize an array of values to the range 0 to 1
#include "tempcomp.h"
```

(Continued)

```
namespace compare {
  template<class Toriginal, class Tnormalized>
      void normalize(Toriginal* data, Tnormalized* newData, int size) {
    Toriginal minValue = min(data, size);        // Get minimum element

      // Shift all elements so minimum is zero
      for(int i = 0 ; i < size ; i++)
        newData[i] = static_cast<Tnormalized>(data[i] - minValue);

      Tnormalized maxValue = max(newData, size);    // Get max of new set

      // Scale elements so maximum is 1
      for(int i = 0 ; i < size ; i++)
        newData[i] /= maxValue;
  }
}
```

To use this template, you can add a few statements at the end of the version of main() in the previous example:

```
// Program 10.5 Using a function template in a namespace extension
#include <iostream>
#include <iomanip>
#include "normal.h"

using compare::max;                    // Using declaration for max
using compare::min;                    // Using declaration for min
using std::cout;
using std::endl;

int main() {
  double data[] = {1.5, 4.6, 3.1, 1.1, 3.8, 2.1};
  int numbers[] = {23, 2, 14, 56, 42, 12, 1, 45};

  cout << endl;

  const int dataSize = sizeof data/sizeof data[0];
  cout << "Minimum double is " << min(data, dataSize) << endl;
  cout << "Maximum double is " << max(data, dataSize) << endl;

  const int numbersSize = sizeof numbers/sizeof numbers[0];
  cout << "Minimum integer is " << min(numbers, numbersSize) << endl;
  cout << "Maximum integer is " << max(numbers, numbersSize) << endl;

  double newData[numbersSize];                        // Array for result
  compare::normalize(numbers, newData, numbersSize);// Normalize

  // Output the normalized array values
  for(int i = 0 ; i < numbersSize ; i++) {
    if(i%5 == 0)
      cout << endl;
```

```
        cout << std::setw(12) << newData[i];
    }
    cout << endl;
    return 0;
}
```

This will produce the following output:

```
Minimum double is 1.1
Maximum double is 4.6
Minimum integer is 1
Maximum integer is 56


        0.4    0.0181818    0.236364            1    0.745455
        0.2            0         0.8
```

Let's examine the new header file first. You have an #include directive for the header file containing the templates for max() and min(), so after the contents have been included, your new header will contain the following:

```
namespace compare {
  // Templates for min() and max()
}
namespace compare {
  // Template for normalize()
}
```

The second namespace definition is an extension to the first.

Because the normalize() function is to store the results as an array with values between 0 and 1, the type Tnormalized must be able to accommodate a floating-point value, regardless of the type, Toriginal, of the original data values. The template header allows both the type of the original array, and the type of the result to be flexible:

```
template<class Toriginal, class Tnormalized>
    void normalize(Toriginal* data, Tnormalized* newData, int size)
```

The first parameter, data, is an array of elements of type Toriginal, and the second parameter, newData, is an array of the same size that stores values of type Tnormalized. Just to remind you, you could equally well use array notation for the parameters so that the header could be written:

```
template<class Toriginal, class Tnormalized>
    void normalize(Toriginal data[], Tnormalized newData[], int size)
```

(Continued)

The function templates for `normalize()`, `max()`, and `min()` are all in the same namespace; therefore the functions `max()` and `min()` can be used in `normalize()` without qualification. You can use the `min()` function template to get the value of the minimum element in the array passed as the first argument:

```
Toriginal minValue = min(data, size);        // Get minimum element
```

You can then declare `minValue` to be of type `Toriginal`, which is the same type as the array `data`. Next, subtract `minValue` from each of the elements in the `data` array. Store the results of this calculation in your new array `newData`, of type `Tnormalized`:

```
for(int i = 0 ; i < size ; i++)
    newData[i] = static_cast<Tnormalized>(data[i] - minValue);
```

Here, the result of subtracting `minValue` from an element of the `data` array is explicitly cast to type `Tnormalized`. After this operation, the minimum element in the new array will be zero and all the other elements will be positive.

Now you need the value of the maximum element in the new array:

```
Tnorm maxValue = max(newData, size);        // Get max of new set
```

This uses the `max()` function template to generate a function that accepts an array of type `Toriginal` as its first argument. In the next statement, I use a loop to divide each element of the new array by `maxValue`:

```
for(int i = 0 ; i < size ; i++)
    newData[i] /= maxValue;
```

After this operation, the minimum element is still zero and the maximum element is 1. All the other elements lie in between.

Now take a look at the main part of the program. The new statements in `main()` use a manipulator, so you have to add an #include directive for `<iomanip>`. I've replaced the #include directive for `tempcomp.h` by the following directive:

```
#include "normal.h"
```

Notice that I've *removed* the #include directive for `tempcomp.h` from the main source file. If you leave the directive in, then the definitions of `max()` and `min()` would be included twice: once directly, and once indirectly through the #include directive for `normal.h`. The multiple inclusion would cause a compilation error. Later in this chapter, you'll see how to prevent this from occurring, even when both directives are included.

You call the `normalize()` function to normalize the integer data values in the array `numbers`:

```
compare::normalize(numbers, newData, numbersSize);        // Normalize
```

The template for `normalize()` is within the namespace `compare`, and you have not added a `using` declaration or directive; therefore, the function name must be qualified here if the compiler is to recognize the name. The compiler will create a definition from the function template that accepts an array of type `int` as the first argument and an array of type `double` for the second argument.

Now that you have the array of normalized values, you can output them in the way that is familiar to you:

```
for(int i = 0 ; i < numbersSize ; i++) {
  if(i%5 == 0)
    cout << endl;
  cout << std::setw(12) << newData[i];
}
cout << endl;
```

Unnamed Namespaces

You don't have to assign a name to a namespace, but this doesn't mean it doesn't have a name. You can declare an unnamed namespace with the following code:

```
namespace {
  // Code in the namespace, functions, etc.
}
```

This creates a namespace that effectively has an internal name generated by the compiler. Only one "unnamed" namespace exists in a file, so any additional namespace declarations without a name will all be extensions of the first.

However, each unnamed namespace is unique *within a translation unit*. Unnamed namespaces within distinct translation units are distinct unnamed namespaces.

It is important to realize that an unnamed namespace is *not* within the global namespace. This fact, combined with the fact that an unnamed namespace is unique to a translation unit, has significant consequences. It means that functions, variables, and anything else declared within an unnamed namespace are local to the translation unit in which they are defined. They can't be accessed at all from any other translation unit.

Placement of function definitions within an unnamed namespace has the same effect as declaring the functions as `static` in the global namespace. Declaring functions and variables as `static` at global scope was a common way of ensuring they weren't accessible outside their translation unit. An unnamed namespace is a much better way of restricting accessibility where necessary, and using `static` in this way is now deprecated.

Namespace Aliases

In a large program with multiple development groups involved, you may well need to use long namespace names in order to ensure that you don't have any accidental name clashes. Left as they are, such long names may be unduly cumbersome to use. Having to attach names such as SystemGroup5_Process3_Subsection2 to every function call would be more than a nuisance.

To get over this, you can define an alias for a long namespace name on a local basis. The general form of the statement you'd use to define an alias for a namespace name is as follows:

```
namespace alias_name = original_namespace_name;
```

You can then use *alias_name* in place of *original_namespace_name* to access names within the namespace.

For example, to define an alias for the namespace name in the previous paragraph, you could write this:

```
namespace SG5P3S2 = SystemGroup5_Process3_Subsection2;
```

Now you can call a function within the original namespace with a statement such as the following:

```
 int maxValue = SG5P3S2::max(data, size);
```

Nested Namespaces

You can define one namespace inside another. The mechanics of handling this are easiest to understand if you take a specific context. For instance, suppose you have the following nested namespaces:

```
// outin.h
namespace outer {
  double max(double* data, const int& size) {
    // body code..
  }

  double min(double* data, const int& size) {
    // body code..
  }

  namespace inner {
    double* normalize(double* data, const int& size) {
      // ...
      double minValue = min(data, size);    // Calls max() in compare
      // ...
    }
  }
}
```

From within the namespace inner, the function normalize() can call the function min() (which is in the namespace outer) directly. This is because the declaration of normalize() contained within the inner namespace is in turn contained within the outer namespace—this means that the normalize() declaration is contained within the outer namespace.

To call min() from the global namespace, you qualify the function name in the usual way:

```
int result = outer::min(data, size);
```

Of course, you could also use a using declaration for the function name or specify a using directive for the namespace. In order to call normalize() from the global name-space, you need to qualify the function name with both namespace names:

```
double* newData = outer::inner::normalize(data, size);
```

The same applies if you include the function prototype within the namespace and supply the function definition separately. You could write just the prototype of normalize() within the namespace inner and place the definition of the function normalize() in the file outin.cpp:

```
// outin.cpp
#include "outin.h"
double* outer::inner::normalize(double* data, const int& size) {
  // ...
  double minValue = min(data, size);     // Calls max() in compare
  // ...
}
```

Of course, in order to compile this successfully, the compiler needs to know about the namespaces. Therefore, the header outin.h, which I #include here prior to the function definition, needs to contain the namespace declarations.

You have used a new form of the #include directive several times so far in this chapter. Now it's time you learned a bit more about how it works, along with the other preprocessing directives that are available.

Preprocessing Your Source Code

Preprocessing is usually an integral part of your compiler. It is a process executed by the compiler before your C++ program code is compiled into machine instructions. The job of preprocessing prepares your source code for the compile phase, according to instructions that you included in the source files; these instructions are called **pre-processing directives**. All preprocessing directives begin with the symbol #, so they are easy to distinguish from C++ language statements. Table 10-1 shows the complete set.

Table 10-1. Preprocessing Directives

Directive	Description
#include	Supports header file inclusion
#if	Enables conditional compilation
#else	else for #if
#elif	#else #if
#endif	Marks the end of an #if directive
#if defined (or #ifdef)	Does something if a symbol is defined
#if !defined (or #ifndef)	Does something if a symbol is not defined
#define	Defines a symbol
#undef	Deletes a symbol
#line	Redefines the current line number and/or filename
#error	Outputs a compile-time error message and stop the compilation
#pragma	Offers machine-specific features while retaining overall C++ compatibility

NOTE *Although all preprocessing directives begin with #, the converse is not true: for example,* #import *is not a preprocessing directive.*

The preprocessing phase analyzes, executes, and then removes all preprocessing directives from your source file (.cpp file). This generates the translation unit that consists purely of C++ statements. The compiler then begins the compile phase with the file that results, which (assuming that there are no errors) generates the object file that contains machine code. The linker must then process this object file, along with any other object files that are part of the program, to produce the finished executable module.

I have already used preprocessing directives in all the examples, so you should be very familiar with the #include directive by now. The other directives shown in Table 10-1 add considerable flexibility to the way in which you specify your programs. Keep in mind as you proceed that these are all preprocessing operations that occur before your program is compiled. They modify the set of statements that constitute your program and aren't involved in the execution of your program at all.

NOTE *The following discussion covers the basic syntax, examples of usage, and advice on how to use some of these preprocessing directives. You may wish to skip to the section entitled "Debugging Methods" later in this chapter and refer back to this section as necessary.*

Including Header Files in Your Programs

A header file is any external file, usually stored on disk, whose contents are included in your program when you use the #include preprocessing directive. You should be completely familiar with statements such as the following:

```
#include <iostream>
```

This fetches the contents of <iostream> (the standard library header that supports stream input/output operations) into your program. The contents of <iostream> replace the #include directive. This is a particular case of the general statement for including standard library header files into your program:

```
#include <standard_library_header_name>
```

Any standard library header name can appear between the angled brackets. If you include a header that you don't use, the primary effects are to take up more memory and extend the compilation time. It will also be slightly confusing for anyone else who reads the program.

You include your own header files into your program with a slightly different #include directive where you enclose the header file name between double quotes. A typical example might be

```
#include "myheader.h"
```

With this statement, the contents of the file named between double quotes are introduced into the program in place of the #include directive. The contents of any file can be included into your program this way. You simply specify the name of the file between quotes as I have shown in the example. With the majority of compilers, you can specify the file name using upper- and lowercase characters.

In theory, you can give whatever names you like to your own header files—you don't have to use the extension .h. However, it is a convention adhered to by most C++ programmers, and I'd recommend that you follow this convention.

The difference between specifying a file name between double quotes and enclosing it between angled brackets lies in the process that is used to find the file. The precise operation is compiler-dependent and is described in your compiler documentation. Usually, if you use *angled brackets*, the compiler only searches the default directories that contain the standard library headers. If the header name is between *double quotes*, then it searches the current directory (typically the directory containing the source file that is being compiled) followed by the directories containing the standard headers. If you put a header file in some other directory, then in order for it to be found, you must put the complete path for the header file between the double quotes. With some C++ implementations, you can specify the path relative to the directory containing the source file.

You can use the #include mechanism for dividing your program into several files, and of course for managing the declarations for any library functions of your own. It is common to use this facility to create a header file that contains all the function prototypes and global variables. These can then be managed as a separate unit and #included at the beginning of the program.

If you include more than one file in your program, then you need to avoid duplicating information. Duplicate code often causes compilation errors. Later in this chapter, you'll see how preprocessing provides some facilities for ensuring that any given block of code appears only once in your program, even if you inadvertently #include it several times.

NOTE *A file introduced into your source file by an* #include *statement may also contain other* #include *statements. If so, the additional* #include *statements are preprocessed in the same way as the first, and this continues until no more* #include *statements are in the code. You can see an example of this in Program 10.5.*

Substitutions in Your Program

Preprocessing directives allow you to use symbols in your source code that will be replaced in a predefined way during preprocessing. The process of symbol substitution can range from a simple one-to-one replacement of a symbol to complex macro expansions.

The simplest kind of symbol substitution you can define is to specify a sequence of characters that will replace a given symbol in a program file. You use the #define directive to do this. For example, you could arrange to replace the symbol PI by a sequence of characters that represents a numerical value, as follows:

```
#define PI 3.14159265
```

Here, although PI *looks* like a variable, this has nothing to do with variables, which is a serious disadvantage. Here PI is a symbol or **token**, which is exchanged for the specified sequence of characters before the program code is compiled. Note also that 3.14159265 is not a numerical value in the sense that no validation is taking place; it is merely a string of characters. During the preprocessing phase, the string PI will be replaced by its definition, the sequence of characters 3.14159265, wherever the preprocessing operation deems that the substitution makes sense.

NOTE *There is room for interpretation here. For example, the preprocessing operation deems that the substitution shouldn't be made wherever* PI *appears in a comment or as part of a character string (between double quotes). You'll look at this again a little later.*

In C, the #define directive is often used in this way to define symbolic constants; however, in C++, it is much better to define a suitable constant using const. Here's an example:

```
const long double pi = 3.14159265L;
```

Now pi is a constant value of a particular type. The compiler ensures that the value you have specified for pi is consistent with its type. You could place this definition in a header file for inclusion in any source file where the value is required.

Alternatively, you could define the constant with external linkage:

```
extern const long double pi = 3.14159265L;
```

Now you may access it from any translation unit just by adding an extern declaration for pi wherever it is required.

The general form of the #define preprocessing directive is as follows:

```
#define identifier sequence_of_characters
```

Here, identifier conforms to the usual definition of an identifier in C++—any sequence of letters and digits, the first of which is a letter, and where the underline character counts as a letter.

Note that sequence_of_characters can be any sequence of characters—not just digits. Let's look at one last example:

```
#define BLACK WHITE
```

As a result of this directive, any occurrence of the five-character sequence BLACK in your program will be replaced by the five-character sequence WHITE. No restriction exists on the sequence of characters that is used to replace the token identifier.

CAUTION *Using a* #define *directive has three major disadvantages:. it doesn't provide any type checking support, it doesn't respect scope, and the symbol name can't be bound within a namespace.*

Removing Tokens from a Program

In a #define directive, if you don't specify a substitution string for an identifier, then the identifier will be replaced with an empty token string—in other words, the identifier will be removed. For example, you could define an identifier with this directive:

```
#define VALUE
```

The effect of this is that all occurrences of the identifier VALUE that follow the directive will be removed from the statements in the program file.

Undefining a Macro Name

You may want to have the substitution resulting from a #define directive only apply to *part* of a program file. You can nullify the definition for an identifier by using the #undef directive. Suppose, having defined the identifier VALUE, you want to eliminate the effect at some point in the file. You can do this with this directive:

```
#undef VALUE
```

Subsequent to this directive, the identifier VALUE is undefined, so no substitutions for VALUE occur. The following code fragment is an example of this:

```
#define PI 3.142
// All occurrences of PI in code from this point will be replaced
// ...
#undef PI
// The identifier PI is no longer defined.
// Any references to PI will be left in the code from this point
```

Between the #define and #undef directives, preprocessing replaces appropriate occurrences of PI in the code with 3.142. Elsewhere, occurrences of PI are left as they are.

The combination of #define and #undef directives has another use, which you will explore when I deal with decision-making preprocessing directives later in this chapter.

Macro Substitutions

A **preprocessing macro** is based on the ideas implicit in the #define directive examples that you just saw, but it provides a greater range of possible results by allowing what we call multiple parameterized substitutions. This not only involves replacing a token identifier by a fixed sequence of characters, but it also allows parameters to be specified in the macro definition, which may themselves be replaced by argument values that you supply when you use the macro. Wherever a given parameter appears in the substitution sequence, it is replaced by the corresponding argument. Let's look at an example:

```
#define Print(var) cout << (var) << endl
```

This directive provides for two levels of substitution: the substitution for Print(var) by the string immediately following it in the #define statement, and the possible substitution of alternatives for var. For example, you could write the following in your source code:

```
Print(ival);
```

During preprocessing, this converts to

```
cout << (ival) << endl;
```

Here is the general form for the kind of substitution directive we just discussed:

```
#define identifier(list_of_identifiers) substitution_string
```

You can see from this that in the general case, any number of parameters is permitted, so you can define more complex substitutions.

 CAUTION *You must not leave a space between the first identifier and the left parenthesis; if you do, the parentheses will be interpreted as part of the substitution string.*

You could extend the previous macro directive to add a second parameter:

```
#define Print(var,digits) cout << setw(digits) << (var) << endl
```

This directive provides for the possible substitution of alternatives for myVar and for digits. For example, you could write

```
Print(ival,15);
```

which will be converted to

```
cout << setw(15) << (ival) << endl;
```

Of course, you would need the <iomanip> and <iostream> headers to be included, as well as some using declarations, for this statement to compile.

This sort of application of preprocessing macros used to be common, but in almost all cases, it is better to use an inline function or function template. This way you ensure appropriate type checking of the arguments and you reduce the possibility of errors. Instead of the previous macro, you could use a function template defined as follows:

```
template<class T> inline void Print(const T& var, const int& digits) {
  cout << setw(digits) << var << endl;
}
```

Now, if you write this statement:

```
Print(ival,15);
```

the compiler generates an inline function that accepts the appropriate type of argument from the template.

One common use for this kind of macro is to allow a very simple representation of a complicated function call in order to enhance the readability of a program.

 NOTE *Your C++ development system may provide further macro capabilities, such as the possibility of defining macros via the command line or within the compilation environment. These sorts of facilities are system specific and outside the scope of this book.*

Macros Can Cause Errors

To show the kind of errors inherent in using macros, I can define a macro for producing the maximum of two values with this directive:

```
#define max(x, y) x>y ? x : y
```

I can then generate a substitution by putting the following statement in my program:

```
result = max(myval, 99);
```

During preprocessing, this will be expanded to

```
result = myval>99 ? myval : 99;
```

This substitution works, and creates the illusion of a function. However, this is *not* a function, and it is important to be conscious of the substitution that is taking place. With a different statement, you can get some strange results—particularly if your substitution identifiers include explicit or implicit assignment. For example, the following modest extension of the last example can produce a result that you may not expect:

```
result = max(myval++, 99);
```

The substitution process generates this statement:

```
result = myval++>99 ? myval++ : 99;
```

Here, if the value of myval is larger than 99, myval will be incremented twice. Note that it does *not* help to use parentheses in this situation. Suppose that you write the statement as

```
result = max((myval++), 99);
```

This will be converted to

```
result = (myval++)>99 ? (myval++) : 99;
```

It is best to avoid writing macros that generate expressions of any kind. In general, you should use a template for an inline function rather than a macro. In this case, you can achieve the objective intended by this macro by using the standard library function max(), which returns the maximum of its two arguments. The max() function is defined as a template, so it works with arguments of various types.

In addition to the multiple substitution trap that you just saw, precedence rules can also catch you off guard when you are using macros. A simple example illustrates this. Suppose you write a macro for the product of two parameters:

```
#define product(m, n) m*n
```

And then try to use this macro with this statement:

```
result = product(x, y+1);
```

This compiles, but you don't get the result you want, because the macro expands to

```
result = x*y+1;
```

Of course, this evaluates to $(x*y)+1$, not $x*(y+1)$. Finding this bug could take a long time, because no external indication of what's going on ever appears. In the meantime, you are almost certain to have an erroneous value propagating through your program.

In this case, the solution is very simple. If you must use macros to generate expressions, then put parentheses around everything. The above example should be rewritten as follows:

```
#define product(m, n) ((m)*(n))
```

Now everything will work as it should. The inclusion of the outer parentheses may seem excessive, but because you don't know the context in which the macro expansion will be placed, it is better to include them. However, a far better solution would be to follow the next piece of advice:

> *To repeat what I have already said—unless you have a pressing reason for doing otherwise, always use inline functions rather than preprocessing macros.*

Preprocessing Directives on Multiple Lines

A preprocessing directive must be a single logical line, but this doesn't prevent you from spreading the directive over several physical lines. You just use the continuation character \, at the end of each line except the last. For instance, you could write this:

```
#define min(x, y) \
                ((x)<(y) ? (x) : (y))
```

Here, the directive definition continues on the second line, starting with the first non-whitespace character found, so you can position the text on the second line to make the most readable arrangement. Note that the \ must be the *final* character on the line, immediately before you press the Enter key.

Strings As Macro Arguments

String constants are a potential source of confusion when used with macros. The simplest string substitution is a single level definition such as this:

```
#define MYSTR "This string"
```

With this macro in place, the following statement

```
cout << MYSTR;
```

will be converted into this statement:

```
cout << "This string";
```

which is undoubtedly what you are expecting.

However, if you try to place the double quotes in the C++ statement (rather than in the #define directive), the substitution fails. Let me illustrate what I mean. If you write the directive as

```
#define MYSTR This string
```

and then write a statement such as this:

```
cout << "MYSTR";                    // Does not invoke the MYSTR macro
```

this time, no substitution occurs for MYSTR. Anything in quotes in your program is assumed to be a literal string, and so it will not be analyzed during preprocessing.

There is also a special way of specifying that the substitution for an argument to a preprocessing macro is to be implemented as a string. For example, you could specify a macro to display a string as follows:

```
#define PrintString(arg) cout << #arg
```

The character #, which precedes the appearance of the parameter arg in the macro expansion, indicates that the argument is to be surrounded by double quotes when the substitution is generated. Therefore, if you write this statement in your program

```
PrintString(Hello);
```

then preprocessing converts this to

```
cout << "Hello";
```

NOTE *This apparently quirky use of the # character was introduced into preprocessing because, without it, it's impossible to include a variable string in a macro definition. If you put the double quotes around the macro argument, then preprocessing doesn't interpret this as a variable but merely a string with quotes around it. On the other hand, if you put the quotes in the macro expansion, then the string between the quotes is not interpreted as a parameter variable identifier; it is just a string constant.*

One application of using the # character in this way is for converting a variable name to a string, such as in the following directive:

```
#define show(var) cout << #var << " = " (var) << endl
```

This macro creates a shorthand way of outputting the name of a variable and its value. If you now write

```
show(number);
```

this will generate the following statement:

```
cout << "number" << " = " (number) << endl;
```

You can also generate a substitution that allows you to display a string with double quotes included. Assuming you have defined the macro PrintString as shown earlier, you can write this statement:

```
PrintString("Output");
```

This will be preprocessed into this statement:

```
cout <<  "\"Output\"";
```

This is possible because preprocessing is clever enough to recognize the need to put \" at each end to get a string including double quotes to be displayed correctly.

Joining the Arguments in a Macro Expansion

You might wish to generate a macro that accepts two or more arguments and joins them together with no spaces between them. In this way, perhaps you could synthesize different variable names, depending on the arguments to the macro. Suppose you try to define a macro to do this:

```
#define join(a, b) ab
```

This can't work in the way you need it to. The definition of the expansion will be interpreted as the sequence of two characters, ab, not as the parameter a followed by the parameter b. If you separate them with a blank, then the result will also be separated with a blank, which isn't what you want either.

In fact, preprocessing provides you with another operator specifically designed to solve this problem. The solution is to specify this macro:

```
#define join(a, b) a##b
```

The presence of the operator comprising the two characters ## serves to separate the macro parameters and to indicate that the result of the two substitutions are to be joined without any spaces between them. For example, writing this statement:

```
strlen(join(var, 123));
```

will result in this statement:

```
strlen(var123);
```

This appears to be a rather limited capability at first sight, because you could always have written var123 rather than going to the trouble of using the macro. In fact, the capability to include decision-making in the instructions for preprocessing vastly increases the potential for this kind of directive.

Logical Preprocessing Directives

The ability to execute one block of directives rather than another raises the possibility of macro substitutions in which the arguments for one macro may be selected from substitutions defined in several others, depending on conditions that can be tested in the program file.

Preprocessing provides for this through directives that implement a logical #if capability. This works in essentially the same way as an if statement in C++ and vastly expands the scope of what you can do with preprocessing directives.

The Logical #if Directive

You have two ways in which you can use a logical #if directive. First, you can test whether or not a symbol has been previously defined by a #define directive. Second, you can test whether or not a constant expression is true. Let's look at testing for a symbol definition first, because this is the most commonly used tool.

To test whether an identifier exists (as a result of having been created in a previous #define directive), you use a directive of this form:

```
#if defined identifier
```

If the specified identifier has been defined, then the set of statements following the #if are included in the source file to be compiled. This set of statements is ended with the following directive:

```
#endif
```

If identifier has *not* been defined, then the statements between the #if and the #endif are skipped, and won't form part of the program. This is basically the same logical process that you use in C++ programming. Here you apply it to decide whether or not a block of statements is included as part of the program.

The block of statements between the #if and the #endif can include further preprocessing directives. These directives are executed if the identifier being tested by the #if is defined.

Let's put this into a concrete context. Suppose you put the following code in your program file:

```
// code that sets up the array data[]
  double average = 0.0;

#if defined CALCAVERAGE
int count = sizeof data/sizeof data[0];
for(int i = 0 ; i < count ; i++)
  average += data[i];
average /= count;
#endif

// rest of the program...
```

Here, the #if directive tests whether the symbol CALCAVERAGE has been defined by a previous preprocessing directive. If so, then the code between the #if and #endif directives is compiled as part of the program. If the symbol CALCAVERAGE has not been defined, then the code won't be included.

A shorthand form for testing whether an identifier has been defined does exist. Instead of writing the test as

```
#if defined CALCAVERAGE
```

you can write it as

```
#ifdef CALCAVERAGE
```

This is a little more concise and just as clear. A block of statements beginning with #ifdef should be terminated with #endif.

Preventing Code Duplication

You can also test for the absence of an identifier. The general form of this directive is

```
#if !defined identifier
```

Here, the statements following the #if down to the #endif are included in the source file to be compiled provided the identifier has not previously been defined. The shorthand version of this is

```
#ifndef identifier
```

NOTE *In fact,* #ifndef *tends to be used more frequently than* #ifdef *because it enables you to arrange that the contents of a header file (or any file) are not* #include*d more than once.*

As you've already seen, a header file that you include into a .cpp file using an #include directive can itself contain #include directives to incorporate other header files—this feature is used extensively in large programs. With a complex program involving many header files, there's a good chance that a header file may be #included more than once in your source files; indeed, in many situations, it becomes unavoidable. Of course, such code duplication can cause compiler errors, especially when the duplicated code contains definitions. Therefore, you must guard against the possibility.

So how do you use the #if directive to prevent duplication of code in your program? In fact, it's very simple: simply type the block of code that must not be duplicated, and start and end it as follows:

```
#if !defined MYHEADER_H
#define MYHEADER_H

// Block of code that must not be duplicated

#endif
```

The first time this code is met during preprocessing, the identifier MYHEADER_H will not have been previously defined and so the #if condition will be true. As a result, the block of code following the #if will be included in the program. This has two effects: first, MYHEADER_H will be defined through the #define directive; second, your block of code will be added to the code. Any subsequent occurrence of this same group of statements won't be included; this is because the identifier MYHEADER_H now exists, and the #if condition will be false. Therefore, your block of statements is included only once and is not duplicated.

Note that to define an identifier, the identifier only has to appear in a #define directive and doesn't need to have a value. It can be defined as empty as in this directive:

```
#define MYHEADER_H
```

The identifier MYHEADER_H is defined by this directive even though it doesn't have a value.

It is very much standard practice to put the #if/#endif combination (as shown earlier) around the entire contents of each header file. This ensures that the contents of each header file are never included in a source file more than once. It is usual to use the header file name as the identifier, because this ensures that the identifier is unique to each header file. For example, the header file compare.h (which you saw in the discussion of Program 10.3) would typically be

```
// compare.h
#ifndef COMPARE_H
#define COMPARE_H

namespace compare {
  double max(const double* data, int size);
  double min(const double* data, int size);
}
#endif
```

TIP *It's a good idea to get into the habit of protecting code in your own headers in this fashion as a matter of course. You'll be surprised how easy it is, once you have collected a few libraries of your own functions, to end up duplicating blocks of code accidentally.*

The #if directive is not limited to testing the existence of just one identifier. You can use logical operators to test whether multiple identifiers have been defined. For example, suppose you write this directive:

```
#if defined block1 && defined block2
```

This evaluates to true if both block1 and block2 have been defined previously; the code that follows such a directive won't be included unless this is the case. In a similar way, you can use the || operator, and even more complex expressions that combine several operators and use defined and !defined.

NOTE *The* #ifdef *and* #ifndef *are commonly used to include code specific to an operating system environment. For instance, you may run into a variety of Unix systems, each of which may have its own peculiarities that must be accommodated. By using the logical directives I've been discussing here, you can provide support for a variety of environments within a single set of source files. You just put the code specific to each environment in a separate block controlled by an* #ifdef *directive that tests for a unique symbol. You can then select a particular environment by defining the particular symbol that identifies it.*

Directives Testing for Specific Values

You can also use a form of the #if directive to test the value of a constant expression. If the value of the constant expression is true—or a non-zero value—then the following statements, down to the next #endif, are included. If the constant expression evaluates to false—or zero—then the statements down to the next #endif are skipped. You could write this form of the #if directive as shown here:

```
#if constant_expression
```

The constant_expression must be an integral constant expression that does not contain casts. It can contain preprocessing macros, but after all substitutions have been made, it must end up as an integer expression. All arithmetic operations are executed with the values treated as type long or unsigned long. If the value of constant_expression is non-zero, then statements following the #if directive, down to the #endif directive, will be included in the source code to be compiled.

This is frequently applied to test for a specific value being assigned to an identifier by a previous preprocessing directive. For example, you might have the following sequence of statements:

```
#if CPU == PENTIUM4
// Code taking advantage of Pentium 4 capability
#endif
```

The statements between the #if directive and #endif are only included in the program here if the identifier CPU has been defined as PENTIUM4 in a previous #define directive.

Multiple Choice Code Selection

To complement the #if directives, you have the #else directive. This works in exactly the same way as the C++ else statement, in that it identifies a group of directives to be executed, or statements to be included, if the #if directive condition fails. This provides you with a choice of two blocks of code, one of which will be incorporated into the final source. Here's an example:

```
#if CPU == PENTIUM4
cout << " PENTIUM4 code version." << endl;
// PENTIUM4 oriented code
#else
cout << "Older Pentium code version." << endl;
// code for older Pentium processors
#endif
```

In this case, one or other of the groups of statements will be included, depending on whether CPU has been defined as PENTIUM4 or not.

There is a special form of the #if for multiple choice selections, where you want to choose only one of several possible choices of statements for inclusion in your program or directives to be executed. This is the #elif directive, which has the following general form:

```
#elif constant_expression
```

Here is an example of how you would use this:

```
#if LANGUAGE == ENGLISH
#define Greeting "Good Morning."
#elif LANGUAGE == GERMAN
#define Greeting "Guten Tag."
#elif LANGUAGE == FRENCH
#define Greeting "Bonjour."
#else
#define Greeting "Hi."
#endif
std::cout << Greeting << std::endl;
```

With this sequence of directives, the output statement will display one of a number of different greetings, depending on the value assigned to the identifier LANGUAGE in a previous #define directive.

Another possible use for this is to include different code in a program depending on an identifier set to represent a version number:

```
#if VERSION == 3
// Code for version 3 here...
#elif VERSION == 2
// Code for version 2 here...
#else
// Code for original version 1 here...
#endif
```

This allows you to maintain a single source file that compiles to produce different versions of the program depending on how VERSION has been set in a #define directive.

Standard Preprocessing Macros

There are several standard predefined preprocessing macros that you can invoke when you wish. These are described in Table 10-2.

Table 10-2. Standard Predefined Preprocessing Macros

Macro	Description
__LINE__	The line number of the current source line as a decimal integer.
__FILE__	The name of the source file as a character string literal.
__DATE__	The date when the source file was processed as a character string literal in the form mmm dd yyyy. Here, mmm is the month in characters, (Jan, Feb, etc.); dd is the day in the form of a pair of digits 01 to 31, where single digit days are preceded by a blank; and yyyy is the year as four digits (such as 1994).
__TIME__	The time at which the source file was compiled, as a character string literal in the form hh:mm:ss, which is a string containing the pairs of digits for hours, minutes, and seconds separated by colons.
__STDC__	This is implementation dependent. It is usually defined if a compiler option has been set to compile standard C code; otherwise it is undefined.
__cplusplus	This will be defined to have at least the value 199711L when a C++ program is being compiled.

Note that each of the macro names start with two underscore (__) characters, and with the exception of the macro __cplusplus, they each end with two underscore characters.

The __LINE__ and __FILE__ macros enable you to display reference information relating to the source file. You can modify the line number using the #line directive. For example, if you wanted line numbering to start from 1000 at a particular point, you would add this directive:

```
#line 1000
```

You can use the #line directive to change the string returned by the __FILE__ macro. It usually produces the fully qualified file name, but you can change it to whatever you like. Here's an example:

```
#line 1000 "The program file"
```

This directive changes the line number of the next line to 1000, and alters the string returned by the __FILE__ macro to "The program file". This doesn't alter the actual file name—just the string returned by the macro. Of course, if you just wanted to alter the apparent file name and leave the line numbers unaltered, you could use the __LINE__ macro in the #line directive:

```
#line __LINE__ "The program file"
```

You could use the date and time macros to record when your program was last compiled with a statement such as this:

```
std::cout << std::endl
          << "Program last compiled at " << __TIME__
          << " on "                      << __DATE__
          << std::endl;
```

Once the program containing this statement has been compiled, the values displayed by the statement are fixed until you compile it again. On subsequent executions, the program outputs the time and date of the program's compilation.

The #error and #pragma Directives

The #error directive is intended to enable you to produce a diagnostic message when things go wrong during the preprocessing phase. For this reason, it is normally executed as a result of a directive that tests some condition, such as an #if directive. The effect of executing an #error is to display whatever you include on the directive line as a compiler error message, and to terminate the compilation immediately. For example, you could write this:

```
#ifndef __cplusplus
#error "Error - Should be C++"
#endif
```

You can, if you wish, include other preprocessing macros on the #error directive line. When you want to just include a string, as in the example, it is best to enclose it between double quotes. This prevents preprocessing from attempting to parse it as a macro. The precise form of the output is implementation defined.

The #pragma directive is specifically for implementation-defined options; it's effect is described in your compiler documentation. Any #pragma directive that is not recognized by the compiler is ignored.

Debugging Methods

Most of your programs will contain errors, or bugs, when you first complete them. You'll almost always find that debugging a program represents a substantial proportion of the total time required to write it.

The larger and more complex the program, the more bugs it's likely to contain, and the more time and effort you'll need to make it run properly. Very large programs—operating systems, for example, or complex applications such as word processing systems, or even the C++ program development system that you may be using at the moment—can be so complex that the system will never be completely bug free. You may already have some experience with this, with some of the systems on your own computer. Usually, residual bugs of this sort are relatively minor, and the system is programmed with ways to work around them.

Sometimes, the process of removing a bug can actually introduce new bugs into your program. Of course, this must not put you off—debugging is a crucial part of the programming process.

Your approach to writing a program can significantly affect how difficult it will be to test. A well-structured program that consists of compact functions, each with a well-defined purpose, is much easier to test than one without these attributes. Finding bugs will also be easier with a program that has well-chosen variable and function names, and extensive comments that document the operation and purpose of its component functions. Good use of indentation and statement layout can also make testing and fault finding simpler.

It is beyond the scope of this book to deal with debugging comprehensively, because we are concentrating on the C++ language. In any case, you'll probably be debugging your programs using tools that are specific to the C++ development system you have. Nevertheless, I'll introduce some basic ideas that are general and common to most debugging systems. You'll also take a look at the rather elementary debugging aids that come standard within the C++ library.

Integrated Debuggers

Most C++ compilers are supplied with extensive debugging tools built into the program development environment. These potentially powerful facilities can dramatically reduce the time you need to get a program working. They typically provide a varied range of aids to testing a program. Common facilities include the following:

Tracing Program Flow: This capability allows you to execute your program by tackling the source code one statement at a time. It operates by pausing execution after each statement has been executed; it continues with the next statement when you press a designated key. Other provisions of the debug environment usually allow you to display information at ease, pausing to show you what's happening to the data in your program. This is also known as **stepping through** your program.

Setting Breakpoints: If your program is large or complex, then stepping through it one statement at a time can be very tedious. It may even be impossible to step through your program in a reasonable period of time. If your program has a loop that executes 10,000 times, then stepping through it is an unrealistic proposition. Breakpoints provide an excellent alternative. You use breakpoints to define specific selected statements in your program; at each of these points, execution pauses and allows you to check what's happening. Execution continues to the next breakpoint when you press a specified key.

Setting Watches: This sort of facility allows you to specify variables—whose values you wish to track as execution progresses. The values of the selected variables are displayed at each pause point in your program. If you step through your program statement by statement, you can see the exact point at which values are changed, and sometimes when they unexpectedly don't change.

Inspecting Program Elements: You may be able to examine a wide variety of program components. For example: at breakpoints, inspection can show details of a function, such as its return type and its arguments. You can also see details of pointers, such as the pointer's address, the address stored by the pointer, and the data stored at that address. Access to the values of expressions and modifying variables may also be provided. Modifying variables can help you bypass problem areas, allowing you to execute subsequent areas with correct data.

Preprocessing Directives in Debugging

Although many C++ development systems provide powerful debug facilities, the addition of tracing code of your own can still be useful. By using conditional preprocessing directives, you can arrange for blocks of code to be included in your program to assist during testing. You can have complete control over the formatting of data that will be displayed for debugging purposes, and you can even arrange for the kind of output to vary according to conditions or relationships within the program.

Try It Out: Debugging with Preprocessing Directives

I'll illustrate how you can use preprocessing directive to help with debugging by using a somewhat contrived program that calls functions at random through an array of function pointers. This example also gives you a chance to review a few of the techniques that you should be familiar with by now. Just for this exercise you'll declare three functions that you'll use in the example within a namespace, fun. First, you'll put the namespace declaration in a header file:

```
// functions.h
#if !defined FUNCTIONS_H
#define FUNCTIONS_H
namespace fun {
  // Function prototypes
  int sum(int, int);        // Sum arguments
  int product(int, int);    // Product of arguments
```

(Continued)

```
    int difference(int, int);          // Difference between arguments
  }
  #endif
```

You'll need to enclose the contents of the file between an #if/#endif directive combination. This prevents the contents of this file from being #included into a translation unit more than once.

Now you can put the definitions for the functions in the file functions.cpp:

```
// functions.cpp

//#define TESTFUNCTION            // Uncomment to get trace output

#ifdef TESTFUNCTION
#include <iostream>              // Only required for trace output
#endif

#include "functions.h"

// Definition of the function sum
int fun::sum(int x, int y) {
  #ifdef TESTFUNCTION
  std::cout << "Function sum called." << std::endl;
  #endif

  return x+y;
}

// Definition of the function product
int fun::product(int x, int y) {
  #ifdef TESTFUNCTION
  std::cout << "Function product called." << std::endl;
  #endif

  return x*y;
}

// Definition of the function difference
int fun::difference(int x, int y) {
  #ifdef TESTFUNCTION
  std::cout << "Function difference called." << std::endl;
  #endif

  return x-y;
}
```

You need the standard header <iostream> here because you use stream output statements to provide trace information in each function.

The standard header <iostream> will only be included, and the output statements compiled, if the symbol TESTFUNCTION is defined in the file. Note that TESTFUNCTION isn't defined at present (the directive is commented out). You have explicit qualification of cout and endl, because you have no using declarations or directives in the file.

The code to call the functions goes in main(), which is in a separate .cpp file:

```cpp
// Program 10.6 Debugging using preprocessing directives
#include <iostream>
#include <cstdlib>              // For random number generator
#include <ctime>                // For time function

#include "functions.h"
using std::cout;
using std::endl;

#define TESTINDEX

// Function to generate a random integer 0 to count-1
int random(int count) {
return static_cast<int>(
           (count*static_cast<long>(std::rand()))/(RAND_MAX+1L));
}

int main() {
  int a = 10, b = 5;           // Starting values
  int result = 0;              // Storage for results

  // Declaration for an array of function pointers
  int (*pfun[])(int, int) = {fun::sum, fun::product, fun::difference};

  int fcount = sizeof pfun/sizeof pfun[0];
  int select = 0;                          // Index for function selection
  srand(static_cast<unsigned>(time(0))); // Seed random generator

  // Select function from the pointer array at random
  for(int i = 0 ; i < 10 ; i++)   {
    select = random(fcount);       // Generate random index 0 to fcount-1

    #ifdef TESTINDEX
    cout << "Random number = " << select << endl;
    if((select>=fcount) || (select<0)) {
      cout << "Invalid array index = " << select << endl;
      return 1;
    }
    #endif

    result = pfun[select](a, b);     // Call random function
```

(Continued)

```
        cout << "result = " << result << endl;
    }
    result = pfun[1](pfun[0](a, b), pfun[2](a, b));
    cout << endl
        <<"The product of the sum and the difference = " << result
        << endl;
    return 0;
}
```

This produces the following output:

```
Random number = 2
result = 5
Random number = 2
result = 5
Random number = 1
result = 50
Random number = 0
result = 15
Random number = 1
result = 50
Random number = 1
result = 50
Random number = 0
result = 15
Random number = 1
result = 50
Random number = 2
result = 5
Random number = 1
result = 50

The product of the sum and the difference = 75
```

In general, you should get something different. If you want to get the trace output for the functions in the namespace fun, you must uncomment the #define directive at the beginning of functions.cpp.

HOW IT WORKS

You have three #include directives for standard headers at the beginning of the file containing main():

```
#include <iostream>
#include <cstdlib>          // For random number generator
#include <ctime>            // For time function
```

The <cstdlib> header is necessary because you'll use the library function rand() to generate random numbers. The <ctime> header provides a declaration for the function `time()`, which you'll use to seed the random number generating process. You'll see how these work in a moment.

Next you have an `#include` directive for your header file:

```
#include "functions.h"
```

This adds the declarations for the functions `sum()`, `product()`, and `difference()`, which you'll call randomly in your source file. Remember that these are declared within the namespace `fun`. Your header file will be in the same directory as the source file, so you don't need to specify the path to the file.

The definition for the symbol `TESTINDEX` switches on diagnostic output in `main()`:

```
#define TESTINDEX
```

With this symbol defined, the code to output diagnostic information in `main()` will be included in the source that is compiled. If you remove this directive, then the trace code will not be included. Later on in the code, in the middle of the `for` loop, you'll find the code that is subject to this directive:

```
#ifdef TESTINDEX
  cout << "Random number = " << select << endl;
  if((select>=fcount) || (select<0)) {
    cout << "Invalid array index = " << select << endl;
    return 1;
  }
#endif
```

This checks to make sure you use a valid index for the array, `pfun`. Because you don't expect to generate invalid index values, you shouldn't get this output!

NOTE *It is easy to generate invalid index values and cause this diagnostic code to execute. To do this, simply persuade the* `random()` *function to generate a number other than 0, 1, or 2. Just add the* `++count;` *statement before the return statement in the definition of* `random()`. *Now you should get an erroneous index value produced roughly 25 percent of the time when the program runs.*

The *correct* definition of the function, `random()`, which generates random integers within a specific range, is as follows:

```
int random(int count) {
return static_cast<int>(
           (count*static_cast<long>(std::rand())))/(RAND_MAX+1L));
}
```

(Continued)

The standard library function rand() generates random numbers in the range 0 to RAND_MAX (where RAND_MAX is a symbol defined in <cstdlib>).

> **NOTE** *You might be tempted to use the modulus operator directly to produce the random values—for instance, by using the expression* rand()%count *to get a value between 0 and count. However, this effectively truncates the value returned from* rand() *to a few low order bits, and because of the way pseudo-random numbers are generated, these may not be random. By using the expression shown in the code, you can scale the range of values produced, so numbers in your range should be just as random as numbers in the original range.*

Just a reminder—you also can't rely on RAND_MAX being a value that you can increment. If you use an expression such as (count*rand())/(RAND_MAX+1) to scale the values returned by rand(), this will fail if RAND_MAX happens to be the maximum in the range for type int, as is the case with some implementations. If type long has the same range as type int, then the statement I have used won't work and you'll have to use floating-point arithmetic to scale the value produced by the rand() function. The following version of the random() function will always work:

```
int random(int count) {
return static_cast<int>(
          (count*static_cast<double>(std::rand()))/(RAND_MAX+1.0));
}
```

In main(), you declare and initialize an array of function pointers with this statement:

```
int (*pfun[])(int, int) = {fun::sum, fun::product, fun::difference};
```

The array is initialized with the names of the three functions declared in functions.h. Each function name in the initializing list is qualified with the namespace name, fun.

To get the size of the array, use this statement:

```
int fcount = sizeof pfun/sizeof pfun[0];
```

Getting the number of elements in an array of function pointers is no different from getting the number of elements in any other array. You'll have three pointers in the array, so fcount will be assigned the value 3.

After declaring and initializing the variable, select, that you'll use to index the array, pfun, call the srand() function to initialize the pseudo-random number generating process:

```
srand(static_cast<unsigned>(time(0)));   // Seed the random generator
```

The unsigned integer that is passed to srand() is used to start the process off. The standard library function, time(), returns the current time in seconds from the system clock, so this value will be different every time you run the program. In this way, you ensure that you start the pseudo-random number generation process off with a different seed each time. Commonly, the value returned is the number of seconds elapsed since midnight on January 1, 1970—although this is not specified by the C++ standard and is dependent on your library.

You call the functions from the namespace fun at random in the for loop in main():

```
for(int i = 0 ; i < 10 ; i++) {
  select = random(fcount);     // Generate random index 0 to fcount-1

  #ifdef TESTINDEX
  cout << "Random number = " << select << endl;
  if((select>=fcount) || (select<0)) {
    cout << "Invalid array index = " << select << endl;
    return 1;
  }
  #endif

  result = pfun[select](a, b);    // Call random function

  cout << "result = " << result << endl;
}
```

The function random() is used to generate a random index between 0 and fcount-1, which is stored in the variable, select. If TESTINDEX has been defined in a #define directive in this file, then the validation code will be executed. Within the validation code, you can conduct a test for an invalid index value; an invalid index will cause a message to be displayed before the program terminates in a controlled way by the return statement.

The program is completed with a potpourri of calls through function pointers and displays the following result:

```
result = pfun[1](pfun[0](a, b), pfun[2](a, b));
cout << endl
     <<"The product of the sum and the difference = " << result
     << endl;
```

If you define the symbol TESTFUNCTION in the file functions.cpp, you'll get trace output from each of the functions. This is a convenient way of controlling whether or not the trace statements are compiled into the program. You can see how this works by looking at one of the functions that may be called, product():

```
int fun::product(int x, int y) {
  #ifdef TESTFUNCTION
  std::cout << "Function product called." << std::endl;
  #endif

  return x*y;
}
```

(Continued)

The output statement simply displays a message, each time the function is called, but the output statement will *only* be compiled if TESTFUNCTION has been defined.

NOTE *The* #define *directive for a preprocessing symbol such as* TESTFUNCTION *is local to the file in which it appears, so each file that requires* TESTFUNCTION *needs to have its own* #define *directive. One potential inconvenience of this is the abundance of* #define *directives that you start to collect in all your program files. You can avoid this surplus by collecting all your symbol's controlling trace and other debug output into a separate header file, which you then include into all your* .cpp *files. In this way, you can alter the kind of debug output you get by making adjustments to this one header file.*

Of course, you can have as many different symbolic constants defined as you wish, as you have seen previously in this chapter. If you really need to, you can use more sophisticated control mechanisms to control which blocks of debug code are included, by combining them into logical expressions that you can test using the #ifdef or #ifndef conditional directives.

NOTE *All this diagnostic code is only included while you are testing the program. Once you think the program works, you quite sensibly leave it out. Therefore, you need to be clear that this sort of code is no substitute for error detection and recovery code that deals with unfortunate situations arising in your fully tested program (as they most certainly will).*

Using the assert() Macro

The assert() macro is another diagnostic aid that is provided in the standard library. It is declared in the library header <cassert>. This enables you to test logical expressions in your program;— assert(expression) causes the program to be terminated with a diagnostic message if the specified logical expression is false.

Try It Out: Demonstrating the assert() Macro

I can demonstrate how this works with a simple example:

```cpp
// Program 10.7 Demonstrating assertions
#include <iostream>
#include <cassert>
using std::cout;
using std::endl;
```

```
int main() {
  int x = 0;
  int y = 5;

  cout << endl;

  for(x = 0 ; x < 20 ; x++) {
    cout << "x = " << x << "   y = " << y << endl;
    assert(x<y);
  }
  return 0;
}
```

You should see an assertion message in the output when the value of *x* reaches 5.

HOW IT WORKS

Apart from the assert() statement, the program shouldn't need much explanation because it simply outputs the values of *x* and *y* in the for loop.

The program is terminated by the assert() macro, which calls abort() as soon as the condition *x<y* becomes false. The function abort() is from the standard library, and its effect is to terminate the program immediately. As you can see from the output, this happens when *x* reaches the value 5. The macro displays the output on the standard error stream, cerr, which is always the display screen. The message contains the condition that failed, and also the file name and line number in which the failure occurred. This is particularly useful with multifile programs, where the source of the error is pinpointed exactly.

Assertions are often used for critical conditions in a program where, if certain conditions are not met, disaster will surely ensue. You would want to be sure that the program wouldn't continue if such errors arise. You can use any logical expression as the argument to the assert() macro, so you have a lot of flexibility.

Program 10.6, which generates index values using a random number generator, contains exactly this kind of situation. With this sort of technique, you always have the possibility of a bug somewhere, resulting in an invalid index value, and if the index is outside the limits of the array pfun, then the result is pretty much guaranteed to be catastrophic.

In Program 10.6, you could use the assert() statement to verify the validity of the index value. Instead of the #ifdef block, you can simply write this statement:

```
assert((select>= 0) && (select < fcount));
```

Using assert() is very simple and effective, and when things go wrong, it provides sufficient information to pin down where the program has terminated.

Switching Off Assertions

You can also switch off the assertion mechanism when you recompile the program by defining the symbol NDEBUG at the beginning of the program file:

```
#define NDEBUG
```

This causes all assertions in the translation unit to be ignored. If you add this #define at the beginning of Program 10.7, you'll see that you get output for all the values of x from 0 to 19, and no diagnostic message. Note that this directive is only effective if it's placed *before* the #include statement for <cassert>.

 CAUTION *It is important to recognize that* assert() *is not an error-handling mechanism and that evaluation of the logical expression shouldn't cause side effects or be based on something beyond the programmer's control (e.g., the success, or lack there of, of opening a file). Your program should provide appropriate code to handle such conditions.*

Summary

This chapter has discussed capabilities that operate between, within, and across your program files. C++ programs typically consist of many files, and the larger the program, the more files you have to contend with. Therefore, it's vital that you really understanding namespaces and preprocessing if you are to develop real-world C++ programs.

The important points you have covered in this chapter include the following:

- Each entity in a program must have only one definition.

- A name can have internal linkage, meaning that the name is accessible throughout a translation unit; external linkage, meaning that the name is accessible from any translation unit; or it can have no linkage, meaning that the name is only accessible in the block in which it is defined.

- You use header files to contain definitions and declarations required by your source files. A header file can contain template and type definitions, enumerations, constants, function declarations, inline function definitions, and named namespaces. By convention, header files use file names with the extension .h.

- Your source files will contain function definitions and global variables. A C++ source file usually has the file name extension .cpp.

- You insert the contents of a header file into a .cpp files by using an #include directive.

- A .cpp file is the basis for a translation unit that is processed by the compiler to generate an object file.

- A namespace defines a scope; all names declared within this scope have the namespace name attached to them. All declarations of names that are not in an explicit namespace scope are in the global namespace.

- A single namespace can be made up of several separate namespace declarations with the same name.

- Identical names that are declared within different namespaces are distinct.

- To refer to an identifier that is declared within a namespace from *outside* the namespace, you need to specify the namespace name and the identifier, separated by the scope resolution operator, ::.

- Names declared within a namespace can be used without qualification from inside the namespace.

- The preprocessing phase executes directives to transform the source code in a translation unit prior to compilation of the code. When all directives have been processed, the translation unit will only contain C++ code, with no preprocessing directives remaining.

- You can use conditional preprocessing directives to ensure that the contents of a header file are never duplicated within a translation unit.

- You can use conditional preprocessing directives to control whether trace or other diagnostic debug code is included in your program.

- The assert() macro enables you to test logical conditions during execution and issue a message and abort the program if the logical condition is false.

Exercises

The following exercises enable you to try out what you've learned in this chapter. If you get stuck, look back over the chapter for help. If you're still stuck after that, you can download the solutions from the Apress website (http://www.apress.com/book/download.html), but that really should be a last resort.

Exercise 10-1. A program calls two functions, print-this(const string& s) and print_that(const string& s), each of which calls a third function, print(const string& s), to print the string that has been passed to it.

Implement each of the three functions and the main() function in separate source files, and provide three header files to contain the prototypes for print_this(), print_that(), and print(). Make sure that the header files are adequately guarded against being included more than once and that main.cpp contains the minimum number of #include statements.

Exercise 10-2. Modify the program so that the print() function uses a global integer variable to count the number of times it has been called. Output the value of this variable in main() after calls to print_this() and print_that().

Exercise 10-3. In the print.h header file, delete the existing prototype for print(), and instead create two namespaces, print1 and print2, each of which contains a function print(const string& s). The fact that these have identical function signatures means that the only way they can be told apart is by using their namespace names. Implement these two functions in the print.cpp file so that they print the namespace name and the string.

Now, make print_this() call the function declared in namespace print1, and print_that() call the version in namespace print2. Run the program, and verify that the right functions are being called.

Extra credit: You should be able to find three different ways (that is, three different forms of syntax) to call the print() functions from within print_this() and print_that().

Exercise 10-4. Modify the main() function so that print_this() is only called if a preprocessing symbol named DO_THIS is defined. If this is not the case, print_that() should be called.

Modify the code by defining a macro PRINT() so that PRINT(abc)—note the absence of quotes—calls print_this("abc") when DO_THIS is defined, and print_that("abc") when DO_THIS is not defined.

CHAPTER 11

Creating Your Own Data Types

THE GREAT STRENGTH OF C++ is its object-oriented nature. I'm implying a great deal by this statement, and I'll spend the next five chapters expanding on this topic. In this chapter and the next, I'll discuss the foundation of object-oriented programming—the ability to define your own data types—but there is much more to this than simply adding new types. Object-oriented programming provides you with a powerful approach to programming that is fundamentally different from what you have seen up to now. In Chapters 13, 14, and 15 you'll explore the detail of all the C++ techniques you might need to implement your own data types.

This chapter introduces some of the basic ideas behind objects and some of the simple ways in which you can use them. This information provides a knowledge base that will help you with the next chapter, in which you'll consider the principles of the object-oriented approach in more depth and learn to understand classes and how they are defined.

In this chapter you will learn the following:

- What an object is

- What a structure is and how structures are declared

- How the objects of a structure are defined and used

- How to handle the members of a structure object

- What a union is

Introducing Objects

A major part of the C++ language is about exploiting the advantages of object-oriented programming, and in this chapter you'll learn the basic concepts involved.

So what exactly is an object? In a sense, this is an easy question to answer because an object can be anything you like. It takes a little more time to elaborate on exactly how you define a particular type of object though.

When you write a program to solve a particular problem, the problem is usually described in terms of objects of various kinds. An invoicing program is probably concerned with customer objects, invoice objects, product objects, and account objects. A program to keep track of your CD collection is likely to involve CD objects and artist

481

objects. Each object of a particular type has a particular set of characteristics that identify it. A customer object might be defined by a name, an address, and a customer number, and each of these characteristics might also be an object. A CD object might be characterized by its title, its artist—which is another type of object—its recording date, and perhaps its classification (blues, rock, classical, or whatever). Object-oriented programming simply implements a program in terms of the problem-specific object types, rather than just the numbers and characters that your computer processes at the lowest level.

In C++ programming terms, an **object** is an instance of a data type. For example, suppose you define a variable as follows, as you have already done often:

```
string saying = "A good horse cannot be of a bad color.";
```

Here, you've defined a single instance of the type string and given a name to that instance by calling it saying. You can say that the variable saying is an object of type string.

The operations that you can perform on (and with) an object are precisely defined within the definition of the string type. For example, you can use your string object saying with the arithmetic operator +, comparison operators such as < and ==, and the subscript operator [ ].

You'll also come across some operations that you *can't* apply to a given object, simply because they aren't defined for that object type. For instance, subtraction doesn't work with string objects because the - operation has not been defined for them.

As you have seen, C++ gives you a number of fundamental data types for storing numerical data and characters, as well as a range of other types such as string type. You can also add new data types of your own and specify the operations that can be applied to them. The types that you define are usually referred to as **user-defined data types**, but this doesn't imply any particular limitations on them. Your data types can be as sophisticated and as complex as your application requires, and as you'll see, you can use them with the same operators that you apply to the fundamental data types.

A **class** is a definition of a user-defined data type, and for the most part, you define classes using the keyword class.

 CAUTION *Don't confuse what a class does with what the* typedef *statement or an enumeration does. A* typedef *statement does not create a new type; it simply defines an alias for an existing type. Each enumeration is a distinct type, but it is not a class. A class is an entirely new and original type that not only has a unique set of properties, but also has its own set of operations, which are applicable to objects of that class, that are defined entirely by you.*

While I am introducing you to classes, I'll show you two other ways of creating your own data types: by using **unions** and **structures**. You use the keywords union and struct respectively to create these. Technically, unions and structures are also classes;

however, I'll refer to a type that you define using the keyword `class` as a class, and the other two user-defined types as unions and structures respectively.

I'll discuss structures first and then taking a brief look at unions. A structure is very similar to a class, so understanding the basics of structures will help prepare you for classes, which I'll cover in depth over the next two chapters.

The Structure in C++

Historically, a **structure** was used in the C programming language, essentially as a named aggregate of data items of different data types. For instance, you might collect several variables—a variable `Name` of type `char*`, a variable `Age` of type `int`, and a variable `Gender` of type `char`—and store this cluster of data in a structure called `Person`.

In C++, you generally use a structure for the same purpose. However, a structure in C++ is capable of doing much more than a structure in C. Structures in C++ are blessed with the new facilities that were developed for classes. In fact, a class can functionally replace a C++ structure.

So why should you spend time and effort studying a capability such as a structure when it can be replaced by a class? Well, partly because a class and a structure are not identical, and because, like Everest to a mountaineer, it's there—part of the C++ language to be conquered. More importantly, it's still very pervasive in some environments. Further, your efforts to understand structures won't be wasted because structures' capabilities apply equally well to classes.

Understanding Structures

So far in this book, most of the variables and data types that you've seen have consisted of a single entity—a numerical value of some kind, or a character. Life, the universe, and everything are, however, more complicated than these fundamental data types allow by themselves—unless you're among those who believe the answer is 42, in which case all you'll ever need is an `int`!

In order to describe virtually anything in the real world, you need to define several values that are usually of a number of different types. From this idea comes the notion of a structure.

For instance, think about the information you need to describe something as simple as a book. You might consider the title, author, publisher, date of publication, number of pages, price, topic (or classification), and ISBN number, just for starters—you can probably come up with a few more properties, too. To identify a book in your program, you *could* specify separate variables, one to contain each of these characteristics. Ideally, though, you'd prefer to have a single data type—which we'll call `Book`—that embodies *all* of these properties.

This is exactly what a structure can do for you. A structure is a data type that defines a particular kind of object of your choosing.

Defining a Structure Type

Let's stick with the notion of a book. Suppose that you just want to include the title, author, publisher, and year of publication within your definition of a book. You could declare a structure type to accommodate this as follows:

```
struct Book {
    char title[80];
    char author[80];
    char publisher[80];
    int year;
};
```

 NOTE *This declaration does not define any variables; it specifies a new type called* Book. *The compiler uses this definition as a blueprint to create entities of type* Book.

The keyword struct declares that Book is a structure type. The elements that make up an object of type Book are those that you've declared between the curly braces. Note that the definition of each element in the struct is terminated by a semicolon and that a semicolon also appears after the closing brace—it's just like an ordinary declaration. The elements title, author, publisher, and year, which are enclosed between the braces in the definition, are referred to as **data members** (or, more generically, **members)** of the Book structure. Every object of type Book will contain the members title, author, publisher, and year. Figure 11.1 shows an example of a Book object.

```
            An Object of Type Book

  title        The Selfish Gene

  author       Richard Dawkins

  publisher    Oxford University Press

  year         1989
```

Figure 11-1. Example of a Book *object*

I have defined the string members of the *Book* structure as type char* so that they are C-style strings. In general it is always better to use type string, but I have chosen to use type char* here because it avoids a slight complication with type string that I want to defer discussing until a little later.

NOTE *The amount of memory that you need to store a structure object is the total memory you need to store each of the data members. For example, an object of type* Book *requires enough memory to contain three character arrays and an integer. You can use* sizeof *to measure the amount of memory occupied by a single object of a given data type. (In Chapter 12, I'll discuss a subtlety that can affect this, which involves something called boundary alignment.)*

The data members of a structure can be of any type, *except* the type of the structure being defined. Thus, for example, the structure definition for Book must not contain a data member of type Book. The reason for this is easy to see if you consider what would happen when you initialize a variable of type Book—you'd need to initialize the data member of type Book that it contained, which would also contain a data member of type Book that would need initializing, and so on. In fact, the size of your object would be infinite!

However, your declaration of the type Book could include a *pointer to Book*, which provides a very useful capability, as you'll see a little later on.

Declaring Variables of a Structure Type

Now that you have defined the structure Book, let's look at how to (and how not to) create variables of that type. You can create a variable of type Book in exactly the same way that you'd create variables of any other type:

```
Book paperback;          // Define variable paperback of type Book
```

This defines a variable paperback, which you can now use to store a Book object.

Optionally, you can use the keyword struct in the definition of a variable of a structure type. So you could have defined the variable paperback with this statement:

```
struct Book paperback;   // Define variable paperback of type Book
```

However, this is a hangover from C and is generally not practiced.

The next three statements define three variables:

```
Book novel;
Book* ptravel_guide;
Book language_guide[10];
```

The variable novel is of type Book, ptravel_guide is of type *pointer to Book*, and language_guide is an array with 10 elements of type Book. It's also possible (though not recommended) to define multiple variables of type Book in a single statement. For example, instead of the preceding statements, you would use the following:

```
Book novel, *ptravel_guide, language_guide[10];
```

Just as with variables of the basic types, this single statement is error prone and makes for unclear code. The set of three definition statements is entirely preferable.

Finally, you can define variables when you define the structure type:

```
struct Book {
    char title[80];
    char author[80];
    char publisher[80];
    int year;
} dictionary, thesaurus;
```

This statement defines the type, Book, and then defines two variables of that type: dictionary and thesaurus. However, even though this looks convenient, it's better programming practice to write a separate statement for the type definition and for each of the object declarations. Typically, you should put your type definitions in header files and include the appropriate header files into your .cpp files whenever you use any of your data types.

Creating Objects of a Structure Type

The first way you can create an object of type Book is to define the initial values for the data members in an initializer list. Suppose you want to initialize the variable novel with the data for a specific book. You could create an object to be stored in the variable novel and initialize its data members with the following statement:

```
Book novel =
{
    "Feet of Clay",                    // Initial value for title
    "Terry Pratchett",                 // Initial value for author
    "Victor Gollanz",                  // Initial value for publisher
    1996                               // Initial value for year
};
```

The initializing values appear between a set of braces, separated by commas, in much the same way that you defined initial values for members of an array. Obviously, the sequence of initial values needs to match the sequence of members in the structure definition. This statement initializes each member of the object novel with the corresponding value, as indicated in the comments. The name novel now refers to a particular object, namely a Book object with data members having the values you specified.

A type, such as Book, is called an **aggregate** when objects of that type can be initialized with a list of values between braces. Any entity initialized in this way is called an aggregate. Because arrays of elements of the fundamental types can be initialized by an initializer list they are also aggregates.

NOTE *You couldn't initialize a* Book *object in this way if the members of* Book *were of a class type such as* string. *The reason is that you can only create objects of a class type by calling a special function called a constructor, and this would imply that the structure is not an aggregate. You'll see more about constructors in the next chapter.*

If you supply fewer initial values in the declaration than there are data members of the structure variable, then the data members without initial values are initialized to 0.

You can also initialize an array of structure variables, in much the same way that you initialized multidimensional arrays. Just put the set of initial values for each array element between braces, and separate each set from the next with a comma. This statement declares and initializes an array:

```
Book novels[] = {
  { "Our Game" ,              "John Le Carre" , "Hodder & Stoughton", 1995 },
  { "Trying to Save Piggy Sneed" , "John Irving" ,   "Bloomsbury",        1993 },
  { "Illywhacker" ,           "Peter Carey" ,  "Faber & Faber ",    1985 }
            };
```

This declaration creates and initializes the array, novels, which is of type Book, and gives the novel array three elements.

Accessing the Members of a Structure Object

You use the **member access operator** (which is just a period so it is sometimes known as dot notation) to access individual data members of a structure object. To refer to a particular data member, write the structure variable name, follow it with a period, and follow the period with the name of the member that you want to access. For instance, you can assign the value 1994 to the member year of your structure novel like this:

```
novel.year = 1994;
```

You can use variable members of a structure in arithmetic expressions in exactly the same way as you'd use any other variable of the same type. For example, to increment the member year by two, write the following:

```
novel.year += 2;
```

Accessing members of a structure array element is also straightforward. For instance, you can calculate the time between the publication of the first and last books in the array novels with this statement:

```
int interval = novels[0].year - novels[2].year;
```

This calculates the difference between the year members of the first and last elements of the array.

Try It Out: Using Structures

Here, you'll take a very simple real-life item, which needs more than one value to represent it, and model it as a structure. Suppose you want to write a program that deals with boxes of various sizes. They could be candy boxes, shoe boxes, or any kind of box that is rectilinear in shape. In this example, you'll use three values to define a box: length, width, and height. The structure members reflect the representation of a box by its physical dimensions. You can declare a structure type to represent a box as shown in Figure 11-2.

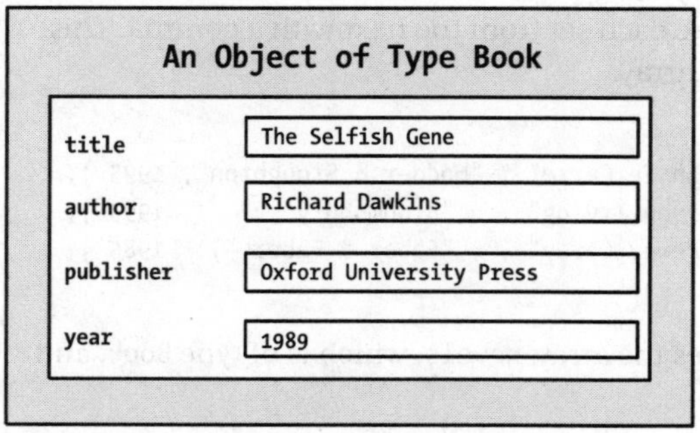

An Object of Type Book

title	The Selfish Gene
author	Richard Dawkins
publisher	Oxford University Press
year	1989

Figure 11-2. A structure to represent a box

Now you'll use your Box structure in a program that will create some boxes. You'll also define and use a global function to calculate volume of a box object.

```
// Program 11.1 Using a Box structure
#include <iostream>
using std::cout;
using std::endl;

// Structure to represent a box
struct Box {
  double length;
  double width;
  double height;
};

// Prototype of function to calculate the volume of a box
double volume(const Box& aBox);

int main() {
  Box firstBox = { 80.0, 50.0, 40.0 };
```

```
  // Calculate the volume of the box
  double firstBoxVolume = volume(firstBox);
  cout << endl;
  cout << "Size of first Box object is "
       << firstBox.length  << " by "
       << firstBox.width << " by "
       << firstBox.height
       << endl;
  cout << "Volume of first Box object is " << firstBoxVolume
       << endl;

  Box secondBox = firstBox;    // Create a second Box object the same as firstBox

  // Increase the dimensions of second Box object by 10%
  secondBox.length *= 1.1;
  secondBox.width *= 1.1;
  secondBox.height *= 1.1;

  cout << "Size of second Box object is "
       << secondBox.length << " by "
       << secondBox.width << " by "
       << secondBox.height
       << endl;
  cout << "Volume of second box object is " << volume(secondBox)
       << endl;

  cout << "Increasing the box dimensions by 10% has increased the volume by "
       << static_cast<long>
                    ((volume(secondBox)-firstBoxVolume)*100.0/firstBoxVolume)
       << "%"
       << endl;
  return 0;
}

// Function to calculate the volume of a box
double volume(const Box& aBox) {
  return aBox.length * aBox.width * aBox.height;
}
```

If you compile and run this program, you should get this output:

```
Size of first Box object is 80 by 50 by 40
Volume of first Box object is 160000
Size of second Box object is 88 by 55 by 44
Volume of second box object is 212960
Increasing the box dimensions by 10% has increased the volume by 33%
```

(Continued)

HOW IT WORKS

In this program, the structure definition appears at global scope. Generally, the structure definition is available within the scope in which it appears. If the structure definition for Box had appeared within the body of main(), then the function volume() (which is also defined at global scope) would be unable to recognize the parameter type Box&.

Putting the Box structure definition at global scope allows you to declare a variable of type Box anywhere in your .cpp file. In a program with several .cpp files, type definitions are normally stored in a header file and are then added into each .cpp file that uses the data types by means of an #include directive.

You declare the function, volume(), which you define later in the source file, with this prototype:

```
double volume(const Box& aBox);
```

The parameter is a const reference to a Box object. Because you define the parameter as a reference, the original Box object won't be copied when you call the function. This is important to remember with complex structure types (and also classes, which you'll see in the next chapter), because the time required to copy arguments that are complex objects can substantially reduce the efficiency of your program. In this case, you make the parameter type const because the function shouldn't modify the argument at all—it will just use the data members.

In main(), you declare and initialize a Box object with this statement:

```
Box firstBox = { 80.0, 50.0, 40.0 };
```

The values between the braces are used to initialize the corresponding members of the structure; so length will be 80, width will be 50, and height will be 40. Obviously it is important to get the initializing values in the correct order.

You calculate the volume of the box object firstBox with the following statement:

```
double firstBoxVolume = volume(firstBox);
```

You store the calculated volume in the variable firstBoxVolume because you'll need it again later in the program. I'll come back to how the function volume() works in a moment.

The next statement in main() displays the dimensions of firstBox:

```
cout << "Size of first Box object is "
     << firstBox.length  << " by "
     << firstBox.width << " by "
     << firstBox.height
     << endl;
```

Here, you access each member of firstBox simply by prefixing the member name with the object name and the member access operator, and you use this in the output statement in the normal way.

The next statement displays the volume of the box that you calculated earlier:

```
cout << "Volume of first Box object is " << firstBoxVolume
     << endl;
```

Next, you create a new Box object that will be the same as firstBox:

```
Box secondBox = firstBox;    // Create a second Box object the same as firstBox
```

This creates a new Box object, secondBox, and sets each member of secondBox to the same value as the corresponding member of firstBox.

You then change the values of each of the members of secondBox with these statements:

```
secondBox.length *= 1.1;
secondBox.width *= 1.1;
secondBox.height *= 1.1;
```

Here you use three separate statements to multiply the three data members by 1.1. This looks a little long-winded, doesn't it? Why can't you just write this?

```
secondBox *= 1.1;               // Wrong!!! Won't work!!!
```

In this case, the compiler would have a problem because secondBox is an object of type Box and the compiler does not know how a multiply operation is supposed to work with an object of type Box. On the other hand, the three separate statements you are using to compile because the data members are all of type double, and the compiler knows what you mean when you multiply a double by 1.1.

 NOTE *Generally, if you want to apply an operator to objects of a type that you have defined, you must define how the operator works. Only the assignment operator has a default definition, and that only applies when you assign one object of a user-defined type to another object of the same type. This operation is performed by assigning values member-by-member from the right operand to the left operand. You'll learn how to write operations for your own types in Chapter 14.*

(Continued)

With the members of secondBox incremented by 10 percent, you output the dimensions and the volume in the same way that you used for firstBox. Finally, you calculate the change in volume due to the increase in dimensions with this statement:

```
cout << "Increasing the box dimensions by 10% has increased the volume by "
    << static_cast<long>
                    ((volume(secondBox)-firstBoxVolume)*100.0/firstBoxVolume)
    << "%"
    << endl;
```

You cast the value of the percentage increase to type long so that the output is an integral percentage value.

Before moving on, look at how the function volume() works. Here is the definition of the function volume():

```
double volume(const Box& aBox) {
  return aBox.length * aBox.width * aBox.height;
}
```

A Box object is passed as a reference argument to the volume() function just like any other argument type. Within the function, the argument is represented by the parameter name aBox. To calculate the volume, multiply together the members of the Box object that is passed to the function. To access each member of aBox, use the member selection operator together with the member name. This combination identifies the member of the object that you pass to the function when you call it. The resulting product is returned from the function.

Member Functions of a Structure

In Program 11.1, you designed the structure Box simply as a compound data item containing three data members. This is a common way to use structures. Many programmers prefer to use structures simply as collections of data items, and use classes when they require more functionality. However, as I have already noted, a C++ structure *is* a class, and as such, it is also possible for a C++ structure object to support functionality.

In Program 11.1, you may have noticed that the volume() function only has relevance to Box objects. It has no purpose in any other context. For this reason, it would make sense if you include the function as an integral part of the Box type rather than allowing it to float around as an independent entity in the global namespace.

You can define the volume() function within the Box type definition. The function is then a member of the type Box and is an integral part of every Box object. Here's how the definition would look with volume() as a function member of the structure:

```
struct Box {
  double length;
  double width;
  double height;

  // Function to calculate the volume of a box
  double volume() {
    return length * width * height;
  }
};
```

The function is now an integral part of the type so you can only use this function with an object of type Box. You've made some significant changes to the function definition compared to the previous version. Now no parameter is specified for the function because no parameter is necessary. When you call the function, you call it as a member of a specific Box object and the operations carried out by the body of the function apply to that object. The body of the function has changed in that it now refers directly to the member names of the structure, and these represent the corresponding members of the object for which you call the function.

To call this function for an object, just use the member selection operator in the same way you did for data members. For example, with this definition for the type Box, declare an object firstBox of type Box, and then calculate its volume as follows:

```
Box firstBox = { 80.0, 50.0, 40.0 };
double firstBoxVolume = firstBox.volume();
```

This calls the function volume() for the object firstBox. The volume of firstBox is calculated, and the result is stored in firstBoxVolume. The length, width, and height data members used in the calculation are those of the object firstBox.

If you call the function for a different Box object, then clearly the data members of that object will be used. For example, to display the volume of a Box variable secondBox, you could write this:

```
cout << "Volume of second Box object is " << newBox.volume()
     << endl;
```

You can alter Program 11.1 so that it uses the volume() member function throughout, and if you do, the output from the program will be exactly the same.

Integrating the function with the type really changes the nature of the function. Every Box object now has the fundamental ability to calculate its own volume. Of course, the volume() function only applies to Box objects, and if you don't have a Box object, then you can't use the volume() function. (Of course, you could write another volume() function at global scope. You wouldn't be able to confuse them, because one can only be called when you are using a Box object, and the other can only be called if you are using the function name by itself.)

Placing the Member Function Definition

In the earlier example, the member function definition is contained within the structure definition. You can, instead, put a *declaration* for the member function within the structure definition and define the member function separately. In this case, the structure definition would be as follows:

```
struct Box {
  double length;
  double width;
  double height;

  double volume();            // Function to calculate the volume of a box
};
```

Now the function definition will be separate from the definition of the structure. In the function definition, you must tell the compiler that the function being defined is a member of the structure Box. For this, use the structure type name along with the scope resolution operator, ::, preceding the function name. The function definition would be

```
double Box::volume() {
  return length * width * height;
}
```

When you qualify the function name with the type name, Box, you identify that this function belongs to the Box structure. This is the same principle as qualifying a name that is defined within a namespace. You can still use the names of the members of the Box structure without qualification within the body of the function because the context of the entire function is defined by the Box qualifier that you've applied to the function name.

As I've said, every object of type Box will have its own volume() function. However, the code for this function will only appear once in memory, regardless of how many objects of type Box exist. They all share a single copy of the function, so no memory is wasted. This raises the question of how the data members of a particular object are associated with the data member names used within the body of the function when the function executes. I'll defer answering this question until the next chapter, when I get deeper into classes.

Of course, separating the definition of functions that are members of a structure from the definition of the structure itself is the preferred way of organizing the code. When you define a new type, you should place the type definition in a header file with just declarations for member functions within the type definition. Put the definitions for the member function in a separate source file. For your Box structure, for instance, put the type definition in a file with the name box.h and the member function definitions in a file with the name box.cpp. Always protect the contents of the header file from duplication in a source file by applying the technique using conditional preprocessing directives that I discussed in Chapter 10. You must also include the header file containing the type definition into any source file that contains definitions for the member functions of the type.

Using Pointers with a Structure

I have already mentioned that you can create a pointer to a variable of a structure type, or indeed to any user-defined type. For example, to define a pointer to a Box object, the declaration is what you might expect:

```
Box* pBox = 0;              // Define a null pointer to an object of type Box
```

This pointer can hold the address of an object of type Box; here you've initialized it with 0.

Assuming you have already defined a Box object called aBox, you can set your pointer to the address of this variable in the normal way, using the address-of operator:

```
pBox = &aBox;               // Set pointer to the address of aBox
```

The pointer pBox now contains the address of the object, aBox.

Creating Objects in the Free Store

You can also create objects of type Book in the free store by using the new operator. The process is essentially the same as what you've used to create string objects in the free store. Here's an example:

```
Book pDictionary = new Book;
```

This statement creates the pointer, pDictionary, that points to a Book object that has been created in the free store. Of course, when you're finished with this object, you must delete it from the free store in the usual way:

```
delete pDictionary;
```

The members of the object have not been initialized, so they'll contain junk values. To make the object useful, you need to set specific values for the members explicitly. To do that, you need to know how to access members of an object through a pointer.

Accessing Structure Members Through a Pointer

Suppose you define a Box object with this statement:

```
Box theBox = { 80.0, 50.0, 40.0 };
```

You can declare a pointer to a Box object and initialize it with the address of theBox in a single statement by writing the following:

```
Box* pBox = &theBox;
```

Using the pointer pBox to access the data members of the object to which it points is a two-step process. You must dereference the pointer to obtain the object and then use this with the member selection operator and the member name. For example, you could increment the height data member of theBox with this statement:

```
(*pBox).height += 10.0;              // Increment the height member by 10.0
```

After this statement executes, the height member will have the value 60.0, and the remaining members will be unchanged. Note that the parentheses in this statement are essential because the member selection operator takes precedence over the dereferencing operator. Without the parentheses, the compiler would interpret this statement as follows:

```
*(pBox.height) += 10.0;
```

This statement attempt to treat the pointer pBox as an object, access its height member, and dereference that. Since pBox is a pointer and not an object, this fails at the first step, so the statement won't compile.

The Pointer Member Access Operator

The two-step operation I've just described—dereferencing a *pointer to object* and accessing its members—crops up with great frequency in C++. However, the combination of the * and . operators looks clumsy; the operation requires judicious use of parentheses, and the expression that results doesn't immediately reflect what you're trying to do.

For all these reasons, the C++ language includes a special operator, called the **dereferencing operator**, ->, which enables you to express the same thing in a readable and intuitive form. The operator looks like an arrow and is formed from a minus sign (–) and a greater than (>) symbol. The dereferencing or arrow operator is used specifically for accessing members of an object of a user-defined type through a pointer.

Instead of this rather ugly statement

```
(*pBox).height += 10.0;              // Increment the height member by 10.0
```

you can use the dereferencing operator in a rather more elegant way:

```
pBox->height += 10.0;                // Increment the height member by 10.0
```

This is a much better expression of what is going on, isn't it? You can use this operator in the same way with objects of class types; you'll be seeing a lot more of this operator throughout the rest of the book.

Now if you return to your Book object in the free store referred to through the pointer pDictionary, you can now set values for the members like this:

```
pDictionary->title = "The Chambers Dictionary";
pDictionary->author = "various";
pDictionary->publisher = "Chambers Harrap";
pDictionary->year = 1994;
```

Having done that, you can use the object, but don't forget that you must delete it from the free store when you are done with it.

Of course, in addition to accessing data members, you can also use the dereferencing operator to call member functions of a structure through a pointer. Let's take pointers to objects for a test drive.

Try It Out: Using Pointers to Objects

This example involves three files: a header file containing the definition of the Box structure, a source file containing the definition for the function member of the Box structure, and finally the source file containing main(). Here's the code that goes in the header file:

```
// Program 11.2 Using pointers to Box objects,  File:  box.h
// Defines the Box structure type

#ifndef BOX_H
#define BOX_H
struct Box {
  double length;
  double width;
  double height;

  double volume();                    // Function to calculate the volume of a box
};
#endif
```

The conditional preprocessing directives here prevent accidental duplication of the contents of a header file in a source file.

Next you define box.cpp, which contains the definition of the function member of the Box structure:

```
// Program 11.2 Using pointers to Box objects.  File:  box.cpp
// Defines the Box member function
#include "box.h"

// Box function to calculate volume
double Box::volume() {
  return length * width * height;
}
```

(Continued)

Finally, you define the contents of ex11_2.cpp, which contains the function main(), to do some work with Box objects:

```cpp
// Program 11.2 Using pointers to Box objects File: ex11_2.cpp
#include <iostream>
#include "box.h"
using std::cout;
using std::endl;

int main() {
  Box aBox = { 10, 20, 30 };
  Box* pBox = &aBox;                         // Store address of aBox
  cout << endl
       << "Volume of aBox is " << pBox->volume() << endl;

  Box* pdynBox = new Box;                     // Create Box in the free store
  pdynBox->height = pBox->height+5.0;
  pdynBox->length = pBox->length-3.0;
  pdynBox->width = pBox->width-2.0;
  cout << "Volume of Box in the free store is " << pdynBox->volume() << endl;

  delete pdynBox;
  return 0;
}
```

This produces the following output:

```
Volume of aBox is 6000
Volume of Box in the free store is 4410
```

HOW IT WORKS

Before you look at how the pointers are working, notice that the Box structure definition in the header file, box.h, contains only a *declaration* of the volume() function. The *definition* of the function appears in box.cpp. The #include directive for box.h here ensures that the compiler makes the correct connection to your Box structure and the scope resolution operator (::) indicates that the function definition does indeed belong to the Box structure.

In the ex11_2.cpp file, you have #include directives for the standard library header iostream and your header that contains the definition of Box.

After creating and initializing the object aBox in main(), you store its address in the pointer pBox:

```cpp
  Box* pBox = &aBox;                         // Store address of aBox
```

You can now access the members of aBox indirectly, via the pointer pBox and the indirect member selection operator. In the following statement, you access the volume() function for aBox:

```
cout << endl
    << "Volume of aBox is " << pBox->volume() << endl;
```

Next, you create a Box object dynamically and store its address in another pointer:

```
Box* pdynBox = new Box;                  // Create Box in the free store
```

The address returned by new is stored in the pointer pdynBox. You have not yet initialized the data members of this new Box object, so they'll contain junk values. You assign values to the data members by using expressions that involve the values of the members of aBox:

```
pdynBox->height = pBox->height+5.0;
pdynBox->length = pBox->length-3.0;
pdynBox->width = pBox->width-2.0;
```

In these three statements, each member is referenced using the pointer, the dereferencing operator, and the member name. Now that you have some sensible values for the dimensions of the Box object, you can calculate its volume:

```
cout << "Volume of Box in the free store is " << pdynBox->volume() << endl;
```

Finally, delete the Box object from the free store:

```
delete pdynBox;
```

As you can see, using a pointer to an object with the dereferencing operator is quite intuitive, and the code is easy to read and understand.

Applications for Pointers to Objects

Pointers to objects of class types are very important, and in this section, I'll briefly mention three situations in which they are particularly useful.

The first is an application that you saw in action in Program 11.2. You must use a pointer when you create (or access) an object within the free store. More often than not, your programs need to accommodate a varying number of objects, and the best way to handle this is to create the objects dynamically.

The second application is a linked list. As I said earlier in the chapter, the data members of a structure *can't* include a member of the same structure type, so you can't define a Book structure that contains a Book data member. However, a structure *can* contain a *pointer to structure type*; and to take this a step further, the structure definition can include a *pointer to a structure of the* same *type*. Defining a member of a structure that is a pointer to a structure of the same type has several uses; one significant consequence is that it enables the creation of a powerful mechanism for storing a collection of objects called a **linked list**; and example of a linked list is shown in Figure 11-3.

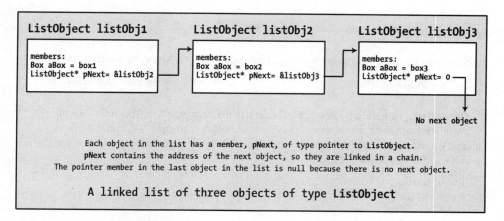

Figure 11-3. An example of a linked list

Figure 11-3 illustrates how a sequence of objects of a given type can be chained together: each object contains a pointer member that contains the address of the next. As long as you know the address of the first object in a chain, you can get to all the others by following the chain of pointer members from one object to the next. I'll show you this in more detail in the context of classes in Chapter 13.

The most important application of pointers to objects is the fundamental role that they play in making **polymorphism** possible. Polymorphism is an essential mechanism in object-oriented programming, which we shall discuss at length in Chapter 15.

Understanding Unions

A **union** is a data type that allows you to use the same block of memory to store values of different types at different times. The variables in a union are referred to as members of the union. You can use a union in one of three ways.

First, you can use a union to enable the same block of memory to store different variables (possibly of different types), at different points in a program. Originally, the idea behind this was simply to economize on the use of memory at a time when memory was limited in capacity and very expensive. However, this is happily no longer the case, and it's not worth the risk of error that is implicit in such an arrangement. Therefore, I don't recommend this application of a union, especially because you can achieve the same effect by allocating memory dynamically.

The second application, which concerns memory saving on a larger scale, involves arrays. Suppose that you have a situation in which a large array of data is required, but you don't know in advance of execution what the data type will be—it will be determined by the input data. A union allows you to have several arrays of different basic types as members, and each array occupies the same block of memory (rather than each having its own memory area). At compile time, you've covered all possibilities; and at execution time, the program will use whichever array is appropriate to the type of data entered. The unused arrays don't occupy any additional space. I recommend that you don't use unions in this manner either, because you can achieve the same result by using a couple of pointers of different types, and again, allocating the memory dynamically.

Third, you may want to use a union to interpret the same data in two or more different ways. For example, suppose you have a variable of type int, which you want to treat as four characters of type char. A color value is an example of where this might be applicable. A union provides a way to treat the int value representing a color as a 4-byte integer when you are copying it or otherwise treating it as a single unit, and as four separate bytes that you can access individually when you need to. Conversely, you can use a union to do the reverse—that is, treat a string of characters as a series of integers that you can use to produce a key of some kind. Unions make both cases very easy to deal with.

Don't be misled by this third application of unions. The fact that you can access the same data through variables of different types doesn't imply that any type conversion is occurring. In fact, the same bit pattern is simply being interpreted in different ways, with no checks on the validity of the data, and clearly, there are lots of situations in which this could prove disastrous.

In general, a member of a union can't be a class type unless it is an aggregate—that is, an object that can be initialized by an initialization list. In particular, a string object can't be a member of a union. For the most part, the data members of unions will be variables of fundamental types.

Let's look at how you declare a union.

Declaring Unions

As I said, you declare a union using the keyword union. Here's how it works:

```
union ShareLD {          // Sharing memory between long and double
  double dVal;
  long lVal;
};
```

This declares a data type, ShareLD, which allows the variables of type long and double to occupy the same memory. The union type name is sometimes referred to as a **tag name**. This statement is rather like a structure declaration, which is not surprising as a union is a struct in which all the members occupy the same space. You haven't actually defined a union instance yet, so you don't have any variables at this point. You're now in a position to declare an instance of the union ShareLD; call it myUnion:

```
ShareLD myUnion;
```

You could also have defined myUnion by including it in the union definition statement:

```
union ShareLD {          // Sharing memory between long and double
  double dVal;
  long lVal;
} myUnion;
```

When you want to refer to a member of the union, use the direct member selection operator (the period) with the union instance name, just as you did when you were accessing members of a class. So, with the following statement, you could set the long variable lVal to 100 in the union instance myUnion:

```
myUnion.lVal = 100;        // Using a member of a union
```

NOTE *When you use a union to store values of different types in the same memory, you encounter a basic problem. Because of the way a union works, you also need some way to determine which of the member values is current. This is usually achieved by maintaining another variable that acts as an indicator of the type of value stored.*

A union can contain more than two data members, if it needs to. You can define another union that shares a memory location between several variables. The union occupies the amount of memory required to store its largest member. For example, suppose I declare this union:

```
union ShareDLF {
    double dVal;
    long lVal;
    float fVal;
};
```

I can create an instance of this union with the following statement:

```
ShareDLF uinst = {1.5};
```

Note the way that I initialized the value of the union. When you initialize a union within the declaration statement, it is always the *first* data member that gets initialized. In this case, it is the data member dVal, which will contain the value 1.5. If you want to initialize the member fVal, then you must write separate statements for the declaration and assignment of the union:

```
ShareDLF uinst;
uinst.fVal = 1.5;
```

On my computer, uinst will occupy 8 bytes, as illustrated in Figure 11-4. Obviously a union is not going to be a particularly portable mechanism between different machines since the number of bytes occupied by the various numerical types is not fixed.

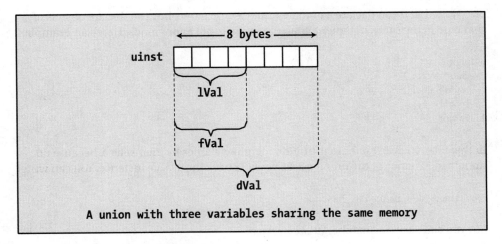

Figure 11-4. Sharing memory in a union

Anonymous Unions

You can declare a union without a union type name, in which case, an instance of the union is automatically defined. For example, you can define a union like this:

```
union {        // An anonymous union
   char* pVal;
   double dVal;
   long lVal;
};
```

This declares a union with no type name and also defines an instance of the union that has no name. Consequently, the members of the union may be referred to just by their member names as they appear in the union definition. You may find this more convenient than a union with a type name, but you need to be careful that you don't confuse the union members with ordinary variables. The members of this union still share the same memory.

Let's illustrate how this anonymous union works. In order to use the double member, you could write this statement:

```
dVal = 99.5;    // Using a member of an anonymous union
```

As you can see, nothing here indicates that the variable dVal is a union member. If you need to use anonymous unions, you could use a naming convention to make the members more obvious.

Note that if you declare a union without a type name, but you declare objects of that type in the same statement, then the union is not anonymous. Here's an example:

```
union {
    char* pVal;
    double dVal;
    long lVal;
} uvalue;
```

In this case, you can't refer to the union members names by themselves, because no unnamed instance of the union exists; you just have the uvalue instance. You can write

```
uvalue.dval = 10.0;
```

but you can't use the member name by itself:

```
dval = 10.0;      // Error!! Unnamed union instance does not exist!!
```

More Complex Structures

So far, the structures that you have considered have been very simple. In particular, you've used only basic data types for members of structures. In fact, the data members of a structure can be of other types, including unions and other structures. Let's look at an example—not a very practical example—but one that is sufficient to demonstrate the idea.

Suppose, having fallen on hard times, you are desperate to save memory and are forced to make your variables share memory wherever possible. You could define a union that provided for variables of several different types to occupy the same space in memory:

```
union Item {
    double dData;
    float fData;
    long lData;
    int iData;
};
```

You can use a variable of type Item to store a value of type double, float, long, or int, but only one at any given time.

Using this union is easy. Just write

```
Item value;             // Create Item instance
value.dData = 25.0;
```

This stores the floating-point value in dData. A little later you might write this:

```
value.lData = 5;
value.lData++;
```

This overwrites the floating-point value by storing the value 5 in lData. Using this technique is somewhat hair-raising. One tiny mistake—such as assuming a variable of type Item contains a long value when it actually stores a double value—and you have a recipe for disaster. If you really must get involved in this kind of thing, at least provide some way to check what the type is.

In order to identify the type of the value stored, you could use an enumeration like this one:

```
enum Type { Double, Float, Long, Int };
```

You could then declare a structure that has two members. The first member is a union that is capable of holding a variable of type double, float, long, or int. The second member is an enumeration variable of type Type. You can define the structure as follows:

```
struct SharedData {
    union {                        // An anonymous union
        double dData;
        float fData;
        long lData;
        int iData;
    };
    Type type;                     // Variable of the enumeration type Type
};
```

Note that the union member of SharedData is anonymous. This allows you to refer to the members of the union for an object of type SharedData without having to specify the union name. You can declare a variable of type SharedData as follows:

```
SharedData value = {25.0, Double}; // Initializes dData to 25.0 and type to Double
```

This initializes the value of dData to 25.0 because dData is the first member of the union. (Because you are initializing within the declaration statement, dData is the only union member that the compiler allows you to initialize.) The second value in the initializer list is the value for type. You can only specify one of the possibilities declared in the enumeration Type.

Note that you can omit the initial value for type and the result is still correct because the default value of zero correspond to Double, as shown here:

```
SharedData value = {25.0};         // Initializes dData to 25.0 and type to Double
```

This only works because Double appears first in the list of enumerators in the declaration of Type.

You can subsequently set value with these statements:

```
value.lData = 10;
value.type = Long;
```

Now as long as you remember to set the type every time you change the value, you can test the type of value that is stored to determine how to legally use it. Here's an example:

```
if(value.type == Long)
    value.lData++;
```

 NOTE *This example is designed to illustrate how pieces of related data can be bound together using a structure. Of course, in this hypothetical case, this whole process is rather counterproductive, because you are sharing the use of a trivially small memory area—typically 8 bytes for type* double. *You'd use more memory each time you test for the type than you'd save from sharing memory between different types!*

Structures with Structures As Members

So far, you've seen a union as a member of a structure. A structure can also be a data member of a structure type as long as the two structure types involved are not the same. Suppose you wanted a type to represent a person. You might want to record some of his or her personal details, such as name, address, phone number, date of birth—well, let's stop there. Think for a moment about how to store these data items.

The phone number could be stored as an integer, but it's more likely that you'll want the area code separate from the number. You might even want a country code if you want to record information on people living overseas. You can already see that storing the phone number is going to demand a structure itself. A cursory considera-tion of the other information you'll want to store within a Person object will show you that most of the members of a Person structure are going to be structures themselves. Let's look at what a cut down version of this might look like.

You could define a Person structure as follows:

```
struct Person {
  Name name;
  Date birthdate;
  Phone number;
};
```

As you can see here, just three data members define a Person type, but each of them is a structure in its own right.

The type to store a name might be defined as follows:

```
struct Name {
  char firstname[80];
  char surname[80];
};
```

> **NOTE** *Of course, it would be better to use* string *objects as members of the* Name *structure, but initializing a* Name *object would then need a capability called a constructor that you haven't learned about yet (I'll cover constructors in Chapter 12). Let's press on with clunky old null-terminated strings for now.*

For the Date structure, you can record a date as three integers that correspond to the day in the month, the month, and the year:

```
struct Date {
  int day;
  int month;
  int year;
};
```

For the Phone structure, you might well want to store the number as a character string, as this would be more convenient for dialing. For your purposes here, however, you can store just the area code and the number as integers:

```
struct Phone {
  int areacode;
  int number;
};
```

You declare a variable of type Person in much the same way as you've declared structure objects in this chapter:

```
Person him;
```

You can also initialize a variable of type Person when you declare it by using an initializer list:

```
Person her = {
            { "Letitia", "Gruntfuttock" },   // Initializes Name member
            {1, 4, 1965              },   // Initializes Date member
            {212, 5551234            }    // Initializes Phone member
          };
```

The list of initial values is arranged in a similar manner to that used for multidimensional arrays. The list corresponding to each member that is a structure is enclosed between braces, and each of these lists is separated from the next by commas. You are not obliged to include braces around the lists for each structure member, and if you leave them out, the values are just assigned in sequence. Of course, the potential for error is greater if you do it like this, and you can't omit a value for a member of an inner structure.

As it stands, you only have a limited range of things you can do with a variable of type Person. You could use an assignment to make the members of one Person object the same as another:

```
Person actress;
actress = her;                          // Copy members of her
```

In this case, the members of her (and their members) will be copied to the corresponding members of actress.

Of course, you can reference the value of a member using the member selection operator. For example, you could output the name of the person, her, with this statement:

```
std::cout << her.name.firstname << " " << her.name.surname << std::endl;
```

Displaying the name in this way is a little cumbersome, so you could include a member function for this sort of thing. Let's try this in a simple example.

Try It Out: Practicing with Persons

The structures that define the members of Person can contain functions as members. You could add a member to each of them to output their members. You can also add a function to the Person structure and put all four definitions together in a single header file, person.h:

```
// Person.h Definitions for Person and related structures
#ifndef PERSON_H
#define PERSON_H

// Structure representing a name
struct Name {
  char firstname[80];
  char surname[80];

  void show();        // Display the name
};

// Structure representing a date
struct Date {
  int day;
  int month;
  int year;

  void show();                // Display the date
};

// Structure representing a phone number
struct Phone {
```

```
  int areacode;
  int number;

  void show();            // Display a phone number
};

// Structure representing a person
struct Person {
  Name name;
  Date birthdate;
  Phone number;

  void show();            // Display a person
  int age(Date& date);    // Calculate the age up to a given date
};
#endif
```

In addition to the function show(), which outputs details of a Person object, you have also added a member function age() to calculate the age of the person up to the date passed as an argument.

Naturally, the definitions for each of the structures referred to in the definition of the Person structure must appear earlier in the file.

You can put the implementations of the function members of the structures in a source file, person.cpp:

```
// Program 11.5 Working with a person.     File: person.cpp
#include <iostream>
#include "person.h"
  // Display the name
  void Name::show() {
    std::cout << firstname << " " << surname << std::endl;
  }

  // Display the date
  void Date::show() {
    std::cout << month << "/" << day << "/" << year << std::endl;
  }

  // Display a phone number
  void Phone::show() {
    std::cout << areacode << " " << number << std::endl;
  }

  // Display a person
  void Person::show() {
    std::cout << std::endl;
    name.show();
    std::cout << "Born: ";
    birthdate.show();
```

(Continued)

```
      std::cout << "Telephone: ";
      number.show();
  }

  // Calculate the age up to a given date
  int Person::age(Date& date) {
    if(date.year <= birthdate.year)
      return 0;

    int years = date.year - birthdate.year;
    if((date.month>birthdate.month) ||
               (date.month == birthdate.month && date.day>= birthdate.day))
    return years;
      else
    return --years;
  }
```

You can now use this in a little program:

```
// Program 11.3 Working with a Person
#include <iostream>
#include "person.h"
using std::cout;
using std::endl;

int main() {
  Person her = {
                { "Letitia", "Gruntfuttock" },    // Initializes Name member
                {1, 4, 1965              },    // Initializes Date member
                {212, 5551234            }    // Initializes Phone member
              };

  Person actress;
  actress = her;                                  // Copy members of her
  her.show();
  Date today = { 15, 6, 2003 };

  cout << endl << "Today is ";
  today.show();
  cout <<  endl;

  cout << "Today " << actress.name.firstname << " is "
       << actress.age(today) << " years old."
       << endl;
  return 0;
}
```

This should produce the following output:

```
Letitia Gruntfuttock
Born: 4/1/1965
Telephone: 212 5551234

Today is 6/15/2003

Today Letitia is 38 years old.
```

You first create and initialize a Person object, her, using the statement you saw earlier, and then you copy the members of her to the Person object actress using an assignment. To output details of her, call the show() function for the her object:

```
her.show();
```

When the show() function executes, it accesses the name, birthdate, and number members of the her object. This function uses the show() functions for each of these objects in order to display the full details of the person, her.

You define a new Date object with this declaration:

```
Date today = { 15, 6, 2003 };
```

Then you output the date that this represents with these statements:

```
cout << endl << "Today is ";
today.show();
cout << endl;
```

Alternatively, you could have explicitly displayed each member of the today object with a statement such as this:

```
cout << endl << "Today is " << today.month << "/"
                            << today.day << "/"
                            << today.year << endl;
```

Finally, you output the age of the actress object with this statement:

```
cout << "Today " << actress.name.firstname << " is "
     << actress.age(today) << " years old."
     << endl;
```

(Continued)

This directly accesses a member of the name member of actress with the expression actress.name.firstname. It also uses the age() function for the actress object to calculate the age up to the date represented by today.

In this example, you've seen how to access a member of a structure that is itself a structure and how adding functions to a structure can make objects easier to work with. You may have noticed that you need a better way of creating an object and assigning initial values to its members than what you've seen so far. This discussion is leading you closer to the notion of a class object. Building functionality into a type is fundamental to object-oriented programming, and what you've looked at so far is merely a taste of the capability you'll learn about in the next two chapters.

Summary

In this chapter, you've used structures to introduce some of the practical aspects of programming with user defined data types and objects. In the next chapter, you'll use this foundation as we further explore object-oriented techniques and principles. The key points from this chapter include the following:

- A structure type is a new data type in your program.

- A structure object is an object with members that are publicly accessible by default. A structure can have both data members and function members.

- You can refer to a member of a structure object using the object name and the member name separated by a period—the period is called the **member selection operator**.

- A union is a data type whose objects allow you to use the same block of memory to store values for several different variables (possibly of different types) at different times.

- When you declare a union object, you can only supply an initial value of the type of the first member of the union.

- Data members of a structure can be of any type, including other structures, but a data member can't be of the same type as the containing structure.

- An aggregate is an entity that can be initialized when it is created by a list of values between braces.

- You can create objects dynamically in the free store, but you must store the address of such objects in a pointer.

- You can access members of an object by using the **dereference operator**, ->.

Exercises

The following exercises enable you to try out what you've learned in this chapter. If you get stuck, look back over the chapter for help. If you're still stuck after that, you can download the solutions from the Apress website (http://www.apress.com/book/download.html), but that really should be a last resort.

Exercise 11-1. Write a simple currency converter program using a structure object to represent a currency. For your purposes, a *currency object* needs to tie together two things: a currency type and a conversion factor that will convert the currency to dollars by multiplication. Design a structure that a user can use to represent currency objects, and write a program that allows the user to convert between any two supported currencies by choosing "from" and "to'" currency types from a list. The user should then be able to enter values (and get the converted value output) until he or she enters a negative value, at which point the program exits.

Exercise 11-2. (Harder) Provide a way for the user to add new currencies when running the program.

Exercise 11-3. Implement the SharedData structure described in the section of the chapter called "More Complex Structures." Extend the structure (and its associated enumerated type) so that it can store *pointers* to the four types as well. Make sure that you can store pointers to variables.

Exercise 11-4. Write a function that accepts any array of SharedData objects and print each element in the format [*array_element*] *type* = *value*. Here's an example:

```
[0]   double = 37.2
[1]   float* = 2.5
```

Test the function using a suitable version of main().

CHAPTER 12

Classes: Defining Your Own Data Types

IN THIS CHAPTER, I'll expand on the discussion of types defined as structures and look into one of the most fundamental tools in the C++ programmer's toolbox: **classes**. I'll also introduce some ideas that are implicit in object-oriented programming and start to show how these are applied in practice.

In this chapter you will learn the following:

- What the basic principles in objected-oriented programming are

- How you define a new data type as a class, and how you can use objects of a class

- What class constructors are, and how you write them

- What the default constructor is, and how you can supply your own

- What the default copy constructor is

- What a friend function is

- What privileges a friend class has

- What the pointer this is, and how and when you use it

Classes and Object-Oriented Programming

You define a new data type by a class, but before I get into the language, syntax, and programming techniques of classes, I'll start by considering how your existing knowledge relates to the concept of object-oriented programming.

The essence of **object-oriented programming** (commonly abbreviated to **OOP**) is that you write programs in terms of objects in the domain of the problem you are trying to solve, so part of the development process involves designing a set of types to suit the context. If you're writing a program to keep track of your bank account, you'll probably need to have data types such as Account and Transaction. For a program to analyze baseball scores, you may have types such as Player and Team. The variables of the basic types don't allow you to model real-world objects (or even imaginary objects) adequately. It's not possible to model a baseball player realistically in terms of just an int or a double, or any other basic data type. You'd need several values of a variety of types for any meaningful representation of a baseball player.

Structures provide a possible solution. You've seen how you can define a structure type that can be a composite of variables of several other types. A structure type can also have functions as an integral part of its definition. In the last chapter, you defined a structure called Box to represent a box, and with this new data type, you're able to define variables of type Box, just as you defined variables of the basic types. Then you're able to create and manipulate as many Box objects as you needed in your program. This goes quite a long way toward making programming in terms of real-world objects possible. Obviously, you can apply the idea of a structure to represent a baseball player, or a bank account, or anything else you require. By using structures, you can model whatever kinds of objects you want and write your programs around them. So, that's object-oriented programming all wrapped up then?

Well, not quite. A structure as I've defined it up to now is a big step forward, but there's more to it than that. As well as the notion of user-defined types, object-oriented programming implicitly incorporates a number of additional important ideas (famously *encapsulation* and *data hiding, inheritance,* and *polymorphism*). The struct doesn't quite fit the bill. Let's get a rough, intuitive idea of what these additional OOP concepts mean right now. This will provide a reference frame for the detailed C++ programming you'll be getting into in this and the next four chapters.

Encapsulation

In general, the definition of an object of a given type requires a combination of a specific number of different properties—the properties that make the object what it is. An object contains a specific set of data values that describe the object in sufficient detail for your needs. For a box, it could be just the three dimensions: length, width, and height. For an aircraft carrier, it is likely to be much more. An object also contains a set of functions that operate on it—functions that use or change the set of data values. They define the set of operations that can be applied to the object: what you can do with it, or to it. Every object of a given type incorporates the same combination of these things: the set of data values as data members, and the set of operations as member functions.

This packaging of data values and functions within an object is referred to as **encapsulation**. Figure 12-1 illustrates this with the example of an object that represents a loan account with a bank.

Every LoanAccount object has its properties defined by the same set of data members; in this case, one holds the outstanding balance and the other holds the interest rate. Each object also contains a set of member functions that define operations on the object; the one shown in Figure 12-1 calculates interest and adds it to the balance. The properties and operations are all encapsulated in every object of the type LoanAccount. Of course, this choice of what makes up a LoanAccount object is arbitrary. You might define it quite differently for your purposes, but however you define the LoanAccount type, all the properties and operations that you specify are encapsulated within every object of the type.

Note that I said earlier that the data values defining an object needed to be "sufficient for your needs," not "sufficient to define the object in general." A person could be defined very simply—perhaps just by the name, address, and phone number if you were writing an address-book application. A person as a company employee or as a medical patient is likely to be defined by many more properties and many more operations would be required. You just decide what you need in the contexts in which you intend to use the object.

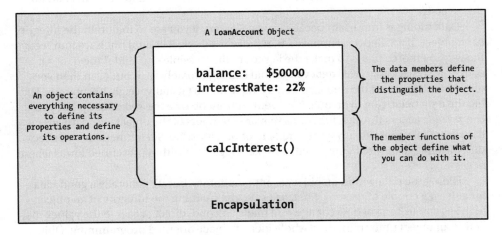

Figure 12-1. An example of encapsulation

Data Hiding

Of course, the bank wouldn't want the balance for a loan account (or the interest rate for that matter) changed arbitrarily from outside an object, as you were able to do with your structure objects in the Chapter 11. To permit this would be a recipe for chaos. Ideally, the data members of a LoanAccount object are protected from direct outside interference, and are only modifiable in a controlled way. The ability to make the data values for an object generally inaccessible is called **data hiding**. Figure 12-2 shows data hiding applied to a LoanAccount object.

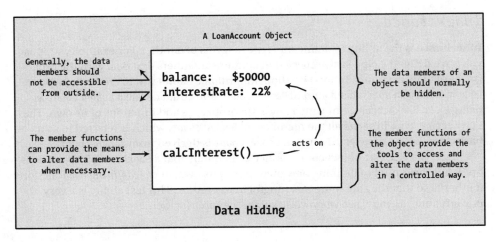

Figure 12-2. An example of data hiding

With a `LoanAccount` object, the member functions of the object can provide a mechanism that ensures any changes to the data members follow a particular policy, and that the values set are appropriate. Interest shouldn't be negative, for instance, and generally, the balance should reflect the fact that money is owed to the bank, and not the reverse.

Data hiding is important because it is necessary if you are to maintain the integrity of an object. If an object is supposed to represent a duck, it should not have four legs; the way to enforce this is to make the leg count inaccessible—to "hide" the data. Of course, an object may have data values that can legitimately vary, but even then you often want to control the range; after all, a duck doesn't usually weigh 300 pounds. Hiding the data belonging to an object prevents it from being accessed directly, but you can *provide* access through functions that are members of the object, either to alter a data value in a controlled way, or simply to obtain its value. Such functions can check that the change they're being asked to make is legal and within prescribed limits where necessary.

Hiding the data within an object is not mandatory, but it's generally a good idea for at least a couple of reasons. First, as I said, maintaining the integrity of an object requires you to control how changes are made. Second, direct access to the values that define an object undermines the whole idea of object-oriented programming. Object-oriented programming is supposed to be programming in terms of *objects*, not in terms of the bits that go to make up an object.

You can think of the data members as representing the **state** of the object, and the member functions that manipulate them as representing the object's **interface** to the outside world. Using the class then involves programming using the functions declared as the interface. A program using the class interface is only dependent on the function names, parameter types, and return types specified for the interface. The internal mechanics of these functions don't affect the program creating and using objects of the class. That means it's important to get the interface to a class right at the design stage, but you can subsequently change the implementation to your heart's content without necessitating any changes to programs that use the class.

Inheritance

Inheritance is the ability to define one type in terms of another. For example, suppose you have defined a type `BankAccount` that contains members that deal with the broad issues of bank accounts. In this situation, inheritance allows you to create the type `LoanAccount` as a specialized kind of `BankAccount`. You could define a `LoanAccount` as being like a `BankAccount`, but with a few extra properties and functions of its own. The `LoanAccount` type **inherits** all the members of `BankAccount`, which is referred to as its **base class**. In this case, you'd say that `LoanAccount` is **derived** from `BankAccount`.

Each `LoanAccount` object contains all the members that a `BankAccount` object does, but it has the option of defining new members of its own, or of *redefining* the functions it inherits so that they are more meaningful in its context. This last ability is a very powerful one, as you'll see when you explore the topic further.

Extending the current example, you might also want to create a new type called CheckingAccount by adding different characteristics to BankAccount. This whole situation is illustrated in Figure 12-3.

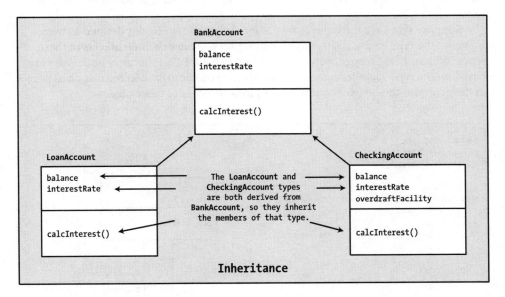

Figure 12-3. An example of inheritance

Both of the types LoanAccount and CheckingAccount are declared so that they are derived from the type BankAccount. They inherit the data members and member functions of BankAccount, but they are free to define new characteristics that are specific to their own type.

In this example, CheckingAccount has added a data member called overdraftFacility that is unique to itself, and both the derived classes have redefined the calcInterest() member function that they inherited from the base class. This is reasonable, because it's likely that calculating and dealing with the interest for a checking account involves something rather different than doing it for a loan account.

Polymorphism

The word **polymorphism** means the ability to assume different forms at different times. Polymorphism in C++ always involves calling a member function of an object, using either a pointer or a reference. Such a function call can have different effects at different times—a sort of Jekyll and Hyde function call. The mechanism only works for objects of types that are derived from a common type, such as your BankAccount type. Polymorphism means that objects belonging to a "family" of inheritance-related classes can be passed around and operated on using base class pointers and references.

In the earlier example, LoanAccount and CheckingAccount objects can both be passed around using a pointer or reference to BankAccount. The pointer or reference can then be used to call the inherited member functions of whatever object it refers to. The idea and implications of this will be easier to appreciate if you look at a specific case.

Suppose you have the types LoanAccount and CheckingAccount defined as before, based on the type BankAccount. Suppose also that you have defined objects of these types, debt and cash respectively, as illustrated in Figure 12-4. Because both types are based on the type BankAccount, a variable of type *pointer to BankAccount*, such as pAcc in the diagram, can be used to store the address of either of these objects.

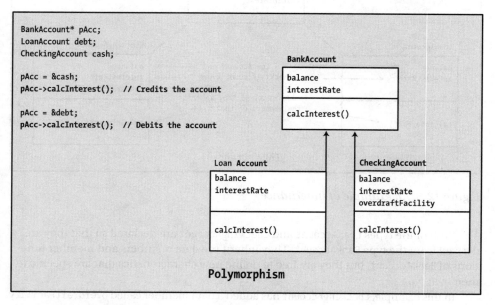

Figure 12-4. An example of polymorphism

 NOTE *The code in Figure 12-4 uses the notation you saw in the last chapter to call a function member of an object through a pointer.*

The beauty of polymorphism is that the function called by pAcc->calcInterest() varies depending on what pAcc points to. If it points to a LoanAccount object, then the calcInterest() function for that object is called and interest is debited from the account. If it points to a CheckingAccount object, the result is different because the calcInterest() function for that object is called and interest is credited to the account. The particular function called through the pointer is not decided when your program is compiled, but when it executes. Thus, the same function call can do different things depending on what kind of object the pointer points to. Figure 12-4 shows just two different types, but in general, you can get polymorphic behavior with as many different types as your application requires.

You need quite a bit of C++ language know-how to accomplish what I've described, and that's exactly what you'll be exploring in the rest of this chapter and throughout the next four chapters. You'll get hands-on experience using polymorphism in your programs in Chapter 16. The road starts here, though, with the more modest subject of using the keyword class to define a new type.

Terminology

Here's a summary of the terminology that I'll be using when I'm discussing classes in C++. It includes some terms that you've come across already:

- A **class** is a user-defined data type.

- The variables and functions declared within a class are called **members** of the class. The variables are called **data members** and the functions are called **member functions**. The member functions of a class are sometimes referred to as **methods**, but I'll not use this terminology in this book.

- Having defined a class, I can declare variables of the class type (also called **instances** of the class). Each instance is an **object** of the class.

- Defining an instance of a class is sometimes referred to as **instantiation**.

- **Object-oriented programming** is a programming style based on the idea of defining your own data types as classes. It involves the ideas of **encapsulation** of data, class **inheritance**, and **polymorphism**, which I've just discussed.

When you get into the detail of object-oriented programming, it may seem a little complicated in places. Getting back to the basics of what you are doing can often help make things clearer; so use this list to always keep in mind what objects are really about. Object-oriented programming is about writing programs in terms of the objects that are specific to the domain of your problem. All the facilities around classes in C++ are there to make this as comprehensive and flexible as possible. Let's get down to the business of understanding classes, starting with how you define a class.

Defining a Class

As I already said, a class, like a struct, is a user-defined type. The definition of a type using the class keyword is, in essence, the same as one using the struct keyword, but the effect is different. Let's look at how you can define a class to represent a box. You'll use this to investigate how the resulting class differs from the structure that you defined earlier. To create a class, just use the keyword class in place of the keyword struct:

```
class Box {
  double length;
  double width;
  double height;
```

```
    // Function to calculate the volume of a box
    double volume() {
      return length * width * height;
    }
};
```

Here, I've taken the definition of the Box structure from the previous chapter and replaced the keyword struct with the keyword class. In any program using objects of this type, a crucial difference between structures and classes immediately becomes apparent—you'd be unable to access any of the members of an object of this type. You'd also be unable to reference any of the data members or call the function volume() from outside the class. If you tried to, the code wouldn't compile.

When you create a class, all the members that you've defined are hidden by default so that they're not accessible outside the class. They're said to be **private** members of the class, and private members can *only* be accessed from within a member function of the same class.

For members of a class object to be accessible in a function that is *not* part of the class, you must declare them to be **public** members of the class by using the keyword public. In comparison, the members of a struct are public by default, so that's why they're always available.

 NOTE *The keywords* class *and* struct *are used to create data types that obey the principles of object-oriented programming. By default, the members of a* class *object are private, whereas the members of a* struct *object are public.*

Let's see how you can declare class members as public by modifying the definition of your Box class:

```
class Box {
  public:
    double length;
    double width;
    double height;

    // Function to calculate the volume of a box
    double volume() {
      return length * width * height;
    }
};
```

The keyword public is an **access specifier**. An access specifier determines whether class members are accessible in various parts of your program. Class members that are public can be accessed directly from outside the class, and therefore these members aren't hidden. To specify class members as public, you use the keyword public followed by a colon (:). All class members that follow this access specifier in the class definition are public, up to the point where another access specifier appears. Of course, objects of the class Box encapsulate the three data members and a function member. Every Box object contains all four, and because you've have declared them as public in the class, they'll all be directly accessible from outside.

There are two other keywords that are access specifiers: private and protected. Class members that are private or protected are hidden—that is, they're not directly accessible from outside the class. If you were to introduce the following line into the earlier class declaration:

```
private:
```

then all the members after the line would be private rather than public. I'll discuss the effects of the keyword private in more detail later in this chapter, and you'll see when to use the protected keyword in Chapter 15.

In general, you can repeat any of the access specifiers in a class definition as many times as you want. This allows you to place data members and member functions in separate groups within the class definition, each with their own access specifier. It can be easier to see the internal structure of a class definition if you arrange to group the data members and the member functions separately, according to their access specifiers.

You can see just how close a structure is to a class by revising the first example from the previous chapter to use the latter rather than the former. This won't produce a good design for a class by any means, but you can move toward that by progressively improving your class and seeing the positive effects of each new feature as you add it.

....

Try It Out: Using a Class

Here's a revised version of Program 11.1 from the previous chapter, using a class instead of a structure:

```cpp
// Program 12.1 Using a Box class     File: ex12_01.cpp
#include <iostream>
using std::cout;
using std::endl;

// Class to represent a box
class Box {
  public:
    double length;
    double width;
    double height;

    // Function to calculate the volume of a box
    double volume() {
      return length * width * height;
    }
};
```

(Continued)

```
int main() {
  Box firstBox = { 80.0, 50.0, 40.0 };

    // Calculate the volume of the box
    double firstBoxVolume = firstBox.volume();
    cout << endl;
    cout << "Size of first Box object is "
        << firstBox.length << " by "
        << firstBox.width << " by "
        << firstBox.height
        << endl;
    cout << "Volume of first Box object is " << firstBoxVolume
        << endl;

    Box secondBox = firstBox;   // Create 2nd Box object same as firstBox

    // Increase the dimensions of second Box object by 10%
    secondBox.length *= 1.1;
    secondBox.width *= 1.1;
    secondBox.height *= 1.1;

    cout << "Size of second Box object is "
        << secondBox.length << " by "
        << secondBox.width << " by "
        << secondBox.height
        << endl;
    cout << "Volume of second Box object is " << secondBox.volume()
        << endl;

    cout << "Increasing the box dimensions by 10% has increased the volume by "
        << static_cast<long>
            ((secondBox.volume()-firstBoxVolume)*100.0/firstBoxVolume)
        << "%"
        << endl;
    return 0;
}
```

This program produces exactly the same output as the previous version.

HOW IT WORKS

The code in main() is exactly the same as before. This is because, having
declared the class members as public, a class works in the same way as a structure. Everything we discussed previously in the context of structures applies
equally well to classes. You use the member access operator and the pointer
member access operator in exactly the same way with classes as you did with
structures.

However, one aspect of this code does not reflect the general usage of classes.
In the example, you've declared and initialized a class object with the following
initializer list:

```
Box firstBox = { 80.0, 50.0, 40.0 };
```

This statement is perfectly legal, at least in this particular case. However, the data members of class objects are typically *not* initialized in this way, because the data members are usually hidden. You can't initialize the hidden data members of a class using an initializer list. Instead, you create and initialize class objects through a special kind of member function, which *can* initialize hidden data members. This member is called a class constructor.

Constructors

A class **constructor** is a special kind of function in a class that differs in significant respects from an ordinary member function. A constructor is called when a new instance of the class is defined. It provides the opportunity to initialize the new object as it is created and to ensure that data members only contain valid values. Objects of classes in which the class definition contains a constructor can't be initialized with a set of data values between braces.

A class constructor always has the same name as the class in which it is defined. The function Box(), for example, is a constructor for your class Box. Also, a constructor does not return a value and therefore has no return type. It is wrong to specify a return type for a constructor; you must not even write it as void. The primary function of a class constructor is to assign and validate the initial values of all the data elements of the class object being created, and no return type is necessary or permitted.

Try It Out: Adding a Constructor to the Box Class

Let's extend the Box class from the previous example to incorporate a constructor and then check it out with a simpler version of main():

```
// Program 12.2 Using a class constructor      File: ex12_02.cpp
#include <iostream>
using std::cout;
using std::endl;

// Class to represent a box
class Box {
  public:
    double length;
    double width;
    double height;

    // Constructor
    Box(double lengthValue, double widthValue, double heightValue) {
      cout << "Box constructor called" << endl;
      length = lengthValue;
      width = widthValue;
      height = heightValue;
    }
```

(Continued)

```
      // Function to calculate the volume of a box
      double volume() {
         return length*width*height;
      }
};

int main() {
   Box firstBox(80.0, 50.0, 40.0);

   // Calculate the volume of the box
   double firstBoxVolume = firstBox.volume();
   cout << endl;
   cout << "Size of first Box object is "
        << firstBox.length  << " by "
        << firstBox.width << " by "
        << firstBox.height
        << endl;
   cout << "Volume of first Box object is " << firstBoxVolume
        << endl;

   return 0;
}
```

This example produces the following output:

```
Box constructor called
Size of first Box object is 80 by 50 by 40
Volume of first Box object is 160000
```

HOW IT WORKS

The constructor for the Box class has been defined with three parameters of type double, corresponding to the initial values for the length, width, and height members of an object:

```
Box(double lengthValue, double widthValue, double heightValue) {
   cout << "Box constructor called" << endl;
   length = lengthValue;
   width = widthValue;
   height = heightValue;
}
```

As you can see, no return type is specified and the name of the constructor is the same as the class name. The first statement in the constructor outputs a message so that you can tell when it's been called. You wouldn't do this in production programs but, because it's helpful in showing when a constructor is called, you'll often use the technique when you're testing a program. I'll use it regularly for illustration purposes, and to trace what is happening in the examples. The rest of the code in the body of the constructor is very simple. It just assigns the arguments passed to the corresponding data members. If necessary, you could also include checks that look for valid, nonnegative arguments that are supplied for the dimensions of a box. In the context of a real application, you'd probably want to do this, but here your primary interest is in seeing how a constructor works, so I'll keep it simple for now.

Within main(), declare the object firstBox with this statement:

```
Box firstBox(80.0, 50.0, 40.0);
```

The initial values for the data members length, width, and height appear between the parentheses following the object name and are passed as arguments to the constructor. When the constructor is called, it displays the message that appears as the first line of output, so you have evidence that the definition does indeed call the constructor that you have added to the class.

Because a constructor has now been declared in the class definition, you can no longer initialize the data members of an object using a list. The statement that you used to define a Box object in the previous example would now not compile:

```
Box firstBox = { 80.0, 50.0, 40.0 };  // Not legal! You must call a constructor.
```

CAUTION *You can't use an initializer list to create objects of classes that have one or more constructors defined. You must use a constructor to create objects of such classes.*

The next two statements in main() output the dimensions and volume of the box in the way you've seen previously, so you also have evidence that the data members have been set to the values specified as arguments to the constructor.

Placing Constructor Definitions Outside the Class

When you were playing with structures in the last chapter, you saw that the definition of a member function could be placed outside the class definition. This is also true for classes and for class constructors. You can define the class Box in a header file as follows:

```
// Box.h
#ifndef BOX_H
#define BOX_H

class Box {
  public:
    double length;
    double width;
    double height;
```

```
    // Constructor
    Box(double lengthValue, double widthValue, double heightValue);

    // Function to calculate the volume of a box
    double volume();
};

#endif
```

Now you can put the definitions of the member functions in a .cpp file. Each function name, including the names of any constructors, must be qualified with the class name Box, using the scope resolution operator:

```
// Box.cpp
#include <iostream>
#include "Box.h"

using std::cout;
using std::endl;

// Constructor definition
Box::Box(double lengthValue, double widthValue, double heightValue) {
  cout << "Box constructor called" << endl;
  length = lengthValue;
  width = widthValue;
  height = heightValue;
}

// Function to calculate the volume of a box
double Box::volume() {
  return length * width * height;
}
```

You have to include the header file containing the declaration of the Box class here, otherwise the compiler won't know that Box is a class. Separating the declarations of classes from the declarations of their member functions is consistent with the notion of what .h files and .cpp files are for, and it makes the code easier to manage. Any source file that needs to create objects of type Box just needs to include the header file Box.h.

A programmer using this class doesn't need access to the definitions of the member functions, only to the class definition in the header file. As long as the *class* definition remains fixed, you're free to change the implementations of the member functions without affecting the operation of programs that use the class.

Defining a member function outside the class definition is not exactly the same as placing the definition inside the class. Function definitions that appear *within* a class definition are implicitly declared as inline functions. (This does not necessarily mean that they'll turn out to be *implemented* as inline functions—the compiler still decides that, based on the characteristics of the function, as I discussed in Chapter 8.) Member functions with definitions *outside* the class can only be inline if you explicitly declare them as such.

The subsequent examples in this chapter assume that you now have the Box class split into .h and .cpp files, along with another file containing the main() function, that currently looks like this:

```
// Program 12.2a Using a class constructor    File: ex12_02a.cpp
#include <iostream>
#include "Box.h"

using std::cout;
using std::endl;

int main() {
  Box firstBox(80.0, 50.0, 40.0);

  // Calculate the volume of the box
  double firstBoxVolume = firstBox.volume();
  cout << endl;
  cout << "Size of first Box object is "
       << firstBox.length  << " by "
       << firstBox.width << " by "
       << firstBox.height
       << endl;
  cout << "Volume of first Box object is " << firstBoxVolume
       << endl;

  return 0;
}
```

This is exactly the same version of main() as in the previous example. The only difference in the code is the #include directive for the Box.h header file that contains the definition of the Box class.

The Default Constructor

The example and experimentation with a class constructor seems quite straightforward, but as ever, some subtleties lurk just beneath the surface. By defining a constructor for the class, you've modified the class in a way that is not immediately obvious. Let's look into that now.

Every class that you declare will have at least one constructor, because an object of a class is *always* created using a constructor. If you don't define a constructor for your class (as in Program 12.1), then the compiler supplies a **default constructor** that is used to create objects of your class.

The **default constructor** is a constructor that can be called without supplying any explicit arguments. When you declare a class, the compiler supplies a default constructor automatically, *but only as long as you do not define a constructor for the class yourself*. As soon as you add any constructor of your own, the compiler assumes that the default constructor is now your responsibility, and it doesn't supply one. The following example illustrates how the default constructor can affect your code.

Let's try defining a second Box object in your program but initializing it differently from firstBox. Change main() in Program 12.2 to the following:

```cpp
int main() {
  Box firstBox(80.0, 50.0, 40.0);

  // Calculate the volume of the box
  double firstBoxVolume = firstBox.volume();
  cout << endl;
  cout << "Size of first Box object is "
       << firstBox.length  << " by "
       << firstBox.width << " by "
       << firstBox.height
       << endl;
  cout << "Volume of first Box object is " << firstBoxVolume
       << endl;

  Box smallBox;       // Will not compile! Constructor already specified
  smallBox.length = 10.0;
  smallBox.width = 5.0;
  smallBox.height = 4.0;

  // Calculate the volume of the small box
  cout << "Size of small Box object is "
       << smallBox.length << " by "
       << smallBox.width << " by "
       << smallBox.height
       << endl;
  cout << "Volume of small Box object is " << smallBox.volume()
       << endl;

  return 0;
}
```

The new code attempts to create a new object, smallBox, with a declaration that doesn't supply initial values to the constructor. Instead, you set the data members explicitly with the three assignment statements. Unfortunately, this won't compile. The compiler's error message relates to the following line:

```cpp
  Box smallBox;       // Will not compile! Constructor already specified
```

Here, the compiler is looking for the default constructor—that is, the constructor that can be called with no explicit arguments. However, this program uses the class Box, which includes your user-defined constructor:

```
Box(double lengthValue, double widthValue, double heightValue) {
  cout << "Box constructor called" << endl;
  length = lengthValue;
  width = widthValue;
  height = heightValue;
}
```

Because you've declared a constructor for the class, the compiler won't generate a default constructor, and this is the cause of the error.

The default constructor that's generated by the compiler does relatively little—in particular, the default constructor does *not* initialize the data members of the object that's created that are not of a class type, and data members of a class type will only be initialized by calling their default constructors, assuming they exist. This is far from ideal: you must aim to have control over the values contained in your variables, so if you plan to use the default constructor to create objects, you'll want to supply your own anyway. To make the new version of main() work, you can add your own default constructor to the class definition.

....

Try It Out: Supplying a Default Constructor

Let's add your version of the default constructor to the last example. For now, just include code to register that the default constructor is called, and come back to initializing the data members later. Here is the next version of the class definition in Box.h:

```
class Box {
  public:
    double length;
    double width;
    double height;

    // Constructors
    Box();                                          // Default constructor
    Box(double lengthValue, double widthValue, double heightValue);

    // Function to calculate the volume of a box
    double volume();
};
```

You must also add the definition for the default constructor to Box.cpp.

```
// Default constructor definition
Box::Box() {
  cout << "Default constructor called" << endl;
  length = width = height = 1.0;        // Default dimensions
}
```

(Continued)

You can now use this with the following version of `main()`:

```cpp
// Program 12.3 Defining and using a default class constructor
//  File: ex12_03.cpp
#include <iostream>
#include "Box.h"

using std::cout;
using std::endl;

int main() {
Box firstBox(80.0, 50.0, 40.0);

  // Calculate the volume of the box
  double firstBoxVolume = firstBox.volume();
  cout << endl;
  cout << "Size of first Box object is "
       << firstBox.length  << " by "
       << firstBox.width << " by "
       << firstBox.height
       << endl;
  cout << "Volume of first Box object is " << firstBoxVolume
       << endl;

  Box smallBox;
  smallBox.length = 10.0;
  smallBox.width = 5.0;
  smallBox.height = 4.0;

  // Calculate the volume of the small box
  cout << "Size of small Box object is "
       << smallBox.length << " by "
       << smallBox.width << " by "
       << smallBox.height
       << endl;
  cout << "Volume of small Box object is " << smallBox.volume()
       << endl;

  return 0;
}
```

You'll now get this output:

```
Box constructor called
Size of first Box object is 80 by 50 by 40
Volume of first Box object is 160000
Default constructor called
Size of small Box object is 10 by 5 by 4
Volume of small Box object is 200
```

```
                              HOW IT WORKS
```

In this version of the program, you've supplied your own constructors, so the compiler doesn't supply a default constructor. Crucially, you have included your own version of the default constructor. No error messages from the compiler appear, and everything works. The program output indicates that the default constructor is being called for the declaration of smallBox.

You've designed your default constructor to initialize the data members of any new object that it creates:

```
length = width = height = 1.0;          // Default dimensions
```

You can now use the default constructor to define *and initialize* the Box object, smallBox:

```
Box smallBox;
```

A significant feature of a default constructor is that it can be called without specifying an argument list—it doesn't even need parentheses. The statement above just specifies the class type, Box, and the object name, smallBox, so this results in a call of the default constructor.

Defining a default constructor that sets values for the data members ensures that you don't have boxes floating around in which the data members contain junk values. Having safely defined and initialized smallBox, you can now adjust the dimensions as appropriate:

```
smallBox.length = 10.0;
smallBox.width = 5.0;
smallBox.height = 4.0;
```

An aspect of this example that you may have missed in all the excitement is that you have overloaded the constructor, just as you overloaded functions in Chapter 9. The Box class has two constructors that differ only in their parameter lists. One has three parameters of type double, and the other has no parameters at all.

Default Initialization Values

When I discussed "ordinary" functions in C++, you saw how to specify **default values** for the parameters in the function prototype. You can also do this for class member functions, including constructors. If you put the definition of the member function inside the class definition, then you can put the default values for the parameters in the function header. If you only include the declaration of a function in the class definition, then the default parameter values should go in the declaration, not in the function definition.

In your default constructor, you decided that the default size for a Box object was a unit box, with all sides of length 1. With this in mind, you could alter the class definition in the last example to the following:

```
class Box {
  public:
    double length;
    double width;
    double height;

    // Constructors
    Box();                                  // Default constructor
    Box(double lengthValue = 1.0, double widthValue = 1.0,
                                          double heightValue = 1.0);

    // Function to calculate the volume of a box
    double volume();
};
```

If you make this change to the last example, what happens? You get another error message from the compiler, of course! The compiler displays a message that basically says that you have multiple default constructors defined. The code in main() is likely to result in a message that says you have an ambiguous call to an overloaded function, caused by this line:

```
  Box smallBox;
```

The reason for the confusion is that this statement is a legal call to *either* constructor. A call made like this to the constructor with the default parameter values is indistinguishable from a call to the default constructor with no parameters. The failure to specify any parameters means that the compiler can't differentiate one from the other. In other words, the constructor with default parameter values *also serves as a default constructor*.

In this case, the obvious solution is to get rid of the constructor that accepts no parameters. If you do so, everything compiles and executes OK. However, don't assume that this is always the best way to implement the default constructor. You'll have many occasions when you won't want to assign default values in this way, in which case you *will* need to write a separate default constructor. You'll even have times when you don't want to have a default constructor at all, even though you've defined another constructor. This ensures that all objects of the class must have initializing values explicitly specified in their declarations.

Using an Initializer List in a Constructor

So far, you've initialized the members of an object in the body of a class constructor using explicit assignment. However, you can use a different technique that uses an **initializer list**. I can demonstrate this with an alternative version of the constructor for the class Box:

```
// Constructor definition using an initializer list
Box::Box(double lvalue, double wvalue, double hvalue) :
                          length(lvalue), width(wvalue), height(hvalue) {
  cout << "Box constructor called" << endl;
}
```

Now the values of the data members are not set in assignment statements in the body of the constructor. As in a declaration, they're specified as initializing values using functional notation and appear in the initializer list as part of the function header. The member length is initialized by the value of lvalue, for example. Note that the initializer list for the constructor is separated from the parameter list by a colon (:), and each initializer is separated from the next by a comma (,).

In fact, this is more than just a different notation. You'll find a fundamental difference in how the initialization is performed. When you initialize a data member using assignment statements in the body of the constructor, the data member is first created (using a constructor call if it is an instance of a class), and then the assignment is carried out as a separate operation. When you use an initializer list, on the other hand, the initial value is used to initialize the data member *as it is created*. This can be a much more efficient process than using assignments in the body of the constructor, particularly if the data member is a class instance. If you substitute this version of the constructor in the previous example, you'll see that it works just as well.

This technique for initializing parameters in a constructor is important for another reason. As you shall see, it is the *only* way of setting values for certain types of data members.

Use of the explicit Keyword

The hazard of class constructors that have a *single* parameter is that the compiler can use such a constructor as an implicit conversion from the type of the parameter to the class type. This can produce undesirable results in some circumstances. Let's consider a particular situation.

Suppose that you define a class that defines boxes that are cubes so that all the sides have the same length:

```
class Cube {
  public:
    double side;

    Cube(double side);                  // Constructor
    double volume();                    // Calculate volume of a cube
    bool compareVolume(Cube aCube);     // Compare volume of a cube with another
};
```

You can define the constructor as

```
Cube::Cube(double length) : side(length) {}
```

the function that calculates the volume of a cube as

```
double Cube::volume() {return side * side * side;}
```

and the compareVolume() member as

```
bool Cube::compareVolume(Cube aCube) {return volume() > aCube.volume();}
```

The constructor requires only one argument of type double. Clearly, the compiler could use the constructor to convert a double value to a Cube object, but under what circumstances is that likely to happen? Let's continue examining the Cube class.

The class also defines a volume() function and a function to compare the current object with another Cube passed as an argument, which returns true if the current object has the greater volume. You might use this in the following way:

```
Cube box1(5.0);
Cube box2(3.0);

if(box1.compareVolume(box2))
  std::cout << std::endl << "box1 is larger";
else
  std::cout << std::endl << "box1 is not larger";
```

This is all very straightforward, but look what happens if someone using this class writes

```
if(box1.compareVolume(50.0))
  std::cout << std::endl << "Volume of box1 is greater than 50";
else
  std::cout << std::endl << "Volume of box1 is not greater than 50";
```

The person writing this code has misunderstood the compareVolume() function and believes that it compares the volume of the current object with 50.0. The compiler knows that the argument to the compareVolume() function should be a Cube object, but it compiles this quite happily because a constructor is available that converts the argument 50.0 to a Cube object. The code the compiler produces is equivalent to

```
if(box1.compareVolume(Cube(50.0))
  std::cout << std::endl << "Volume of box1 is greater than 50";
else
  std::cout << std::endl << "Volume of box1 is not greater than 50";
```

The function is not comparing the volume of the box1 object with 50.0, but with 125000.0, the volume of Cube(50.0)! The result will be very different from what was expected.

Happily, you can prevent this nightmare from ever happening by declaring the constructor as explicit:

```
class Cube {
  public:
    double side;

    explicit Cube(double side);
    double volume();
    bool compareVolume(Cube aCube);
};
```

The compiler never uses a constructor declared as explicit for an implicit conversion. It can only be used explicitly in the program code to create an object. Because, by definition, an implicit conversion converts from one given type to another, you only need to use the explicit keyword with constructors that have a single parameter.

Private Members of a Class

One of the primary purposes of a constructor is to allow you to make sure that all the data members of an object are set to appropriate values. For example, you could ensure that all the dimensions for a Box object are positive values by adding a few checks to the constructor:

```
Box::Box(double lvalue, double wvalue, double hvalue) :
                        length(lvalue), width(wvalue), height(hvalue) {
  std::cout << "Box constructor called." << std::endl;

  // Ensure positive dimensions
  if(length <= 0.0)
    length = 1.0;
  if(width <= 0.0)
    width = 1.0;
  if(height <= 0.0)
    height = 1.0;
}
```

Now you are sure that whatever the argument values to the constructor, the Box object has legitimate dimensions. Of course, you might also want to output a message that explains that this kind of adjustment is being made.

Now that you have gone to such lengths to protect the integrity of the data members, you can't prevent them from being modified externally by statements such as the following:

```
Box theBox(10.0, 10.0, 5.0);
theBox.length = -20.0;                  // Set illegal box dimension
```

because the data members are declared using the keyword public. You can prevent this sort of thing by *hiding* the data members. All you need to do this is declare the data members of a class to be private. Class members that are private can, for the most part, only be accessed by member functions of a class. A normal function that is not a member of a given class has no direct way to access the private members of that class. This is illustrated in Figure 12-5.

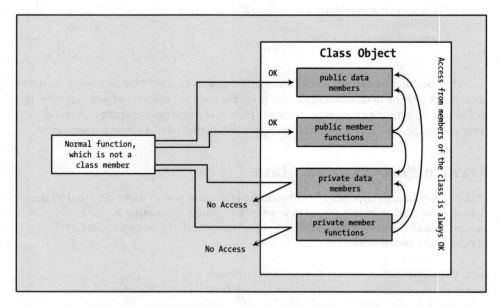

Figure 12-5. Hiding members of a class

In general, it is good object-oriented programming practice to keep the data members of a class private as much as you can. After all, the whole point of object-oriented programming is that you can write your solutions in terms of *objects*, and program using those objects, rather than messing around with their nuts and bolts.

The public members of a class, which typically are functions, are often referred to generically as the **class interface**. The class interface provides the means for manipulating and operating on objects of the class, so it determines what you can do with an object and what an object can do for you. By keeping the internals of a class private, you can later modify them in whatever way you want without necessitating modifications to code that uses the class through its public interface. Thus, the public interface is effectively separated from the implementation of the class.

Try It Out: Private Data Members

You can rewrite the Box class once again to make its data members private, and you can see how to use it in another example. Here are the changes to the header file, Box.h:

```cpp
// Box.h Definition of the Box class
#ifndef BOX_H
#define BOX_H

class Box {
  public:
    // Constructor
    Box(double lengthValue = 1.0, double widthValue = 1.0,
                                      double heightValue = 1.0);

    // Function to calculate the volume of a box
    double volume();

  private:
    double length;
    double width;
    double height;
};

#endif
```

You can also add your dimension-checking code to Box.cpp:

```cpp
// Box.cpp Box class member function definitions
#include <iostream>
#include "Box.h"

using std::cout;
using std::endl;

// Constructor
Box::Box(double lvalue, double wvalue, double hvalue) :
                       length(lvalue), width(wvalue), height(hvalue) {
  cout << "Box constructor called" << endl;

  // Ensure positive dimensions
  if(length <= 0.0)
    length = 1.0;
  if(width <= 0.0)
    width = 1.0;
  if(height <= 0.0)
    height = 1.0;
}

// Function to calculate the volume of a box
double Box::volume() {
  return length * width * height;
}
```

(Continued)

That the definitions of the member functions are outside the class doesn't affect the accessibility of the members of the class. All the members of a class can be accessed from the body of a function member of the class, regardless of where you place the definitions.

To try out the new version of the Box class, write a new main() function:

```cpp
// Program 12.4 Using a class with private data members
// File: ex12_04.cpp
#include <iostream>
#include "Box.h"

using std::cout;
using std::endl;

int main() {
  cout << endl;

  Box firstBox(2.2, 1.1, 0.5);
  Box secondBox;
  Box* pthirdBox = new Box(15.0, 20.0, 8.0);

  cout << "Volume of first box = "
       << firstBox.volume()
       << endl;

//   secondBox.length = 4.0;       // Uncomment this line to get an error

  cout << "Volume of second box = "
       << secondBox.volume()
       << endl;

  cout << "Volume of third box = "
       << pthirdBox->volume()
       << endl;

  delete pthirdBox;
  return 0;
}
```

Here is the output from this program:

```
Box constructor called
Box constructor called
Box constructor called
Volume of first box = 1.21
Volume of second box = 1
Volume of third box = 2400
```

HOW IT WORKS

Here, you use the keyword `public` to start a public section where you have the declarations for the member functions: a constructor and the function `volume()`. The placement of the declarations for the public members of the class before the private ones is quite deliberate—the public class members are usually of more interest to someone browsing the code, because they are accessible externally.

The definition of the class `Box` now declares the data members as private by using the `private` keyword followed by a colon (:). All member declarations after this point and until the next access specification will be private, and therefore inaccessible from outside the class. This is data hiding in action. If you uncomment this statement in `main()`:

```
// secondBox.length = 4.0;                // Uncomment this line to get an error
```

then the code won't compile because the attempt to use a private data member of a class from outside the class is not legal.

NOTE *The only way to get a value into a private data member of a* Box *object is to use a constructor or a member function. It's your responsibility to make sure that all the ways in which you might want to set or modify private data members of a class are provided through member functions.*

You can also put functions into a `private` section of a class, in which case they can only be called by other member functions. If you put the function `volume()` in the `private` section, then the statements that attempt to use it in the function `main()` result in error messages from the compiler. If you put the constructor in the `private` section, you won't be able to declare any objects of the class.

NOTE *Although there are no advantages to making any of the Box class functions private, you'll often find reasons why you want to make a class member function private in other situations. For instance, you might need a "helper" function that implements a capability that is used internally by several other member functions but is not relevant to the use of class objects.*

Now let's return to `main()`; first you declare two `Box` objects with the statements:

```
Box firstBox(2.2, 1.1, 0.5);
Box secondBox;
```

Both of these call the same constructor (well, actually, only one exists), but the declaration for `secondBox` use the default parameter values so that `secondBox` will be a cube of dimension 1.0.

(Continued)

The next statement declares a pointer to a Box object, pthirdBox, and creates a Box object in the free store using the operator new:

```
Box* pthirdBox = new Box(15.0, 20.0, 8.0);
```

The operator new calls the same Box constructor, as you can see from the output, and the address returned by new is stored in pthirdBox.

Now you output the volume of each Box object. For the object that you created dynamically, you use the pointer member access operator to call the function volume():

```
cout << "Volume of third box = "
    << pthirdBox->volume()
    << endl;
```

This demonstrates that the class is still working satisfactorily now that its data members are defined as having the access specifier private. The major difference is that they are now completely protected from unauthorized access and modification. Because all the data members are hidden, the only way to set or change the values is through a public member function of the class. In the case of your Box class, this boils down to just one: the constructor.

....

Accessing Private Class Members

On reflection, I've decided that declaring the data members of a class as private is rather extreme. It's all a good idea to protect them from unauthorized modification, but you've introduced a serious constraint: if you don't know what the dimensions of a particular Box object are, you have no way to find out. Surely it doesn't need to be that secret?

It doesn't, and you don't need to go back to exposing your data members with the public keyword. You can fix the problem by adding a member function to the class that returns the value of a data member. To provide access to the dimensions of a Box object, you just need to add three functions to the class definition:

```
class Box {
  public:
    // Constructor
    Box(double lengthValue = 1.0, double widthValue = 1.0,
                                        double heightValue = 1.0);

    // Function to calculate the volume of a box
    double volume();

    // Functions to provide the values of data members
    double getLength() {return length;}
    double getWidth() {return width;}
    double getHeight() {return height;}
```

```
  private:
    double length;
    double width;
    double height;
};
```

You've added functions to the class that return the values of data members. That means the values of the data members are fully accessible, but you can't change them, so the integrity of the class is preserved without the secrecy. Functions of this kind usually have their definitions within the class definition because they are short, and this makes them inline by default. Consequently, the overhead involved in getting hold of the value of a data member is minimal. Functions that retrieve the values of data members are often referred to as **accessor** member functions.

You could have you use these accessor functions in the previous example to output the dimensions of the Box object that you created dynamically:

```
cout << "Box size is "
     << pthirdBox->getLength() << " by "
     << pthirdBox->getWidth() << " by "
     << pthirdBox->getHeight()
     << endl;
```

You can use this approach for any class. All you need to do is write a function for each data member that you want to make available to the outside world, and then their values can be accessed without compromising the security of the class. Of course, if you put the definitions for these functions outside the class definition, you should declare them as inline. For instance, if you had simply declared getLength() in the class definition, you would've needed to define it in Box.cpp as follows:

```
inline double Box::getLength() {return length;}
```

You may find yourself in situations in which you *do* want to allow data members to be changed from outside the class. If you supply a member function to do this rather than exposing the data member directly, you have the opportunity to perform integrity checks on the value. For example, you could add a function to allow the height of a Box object to be changed:

```
class Box {
  public:
    // Constructor
    Box(double lengthValue = 1.0, double widthValue = 1.0,
                                    double heightValue = 1.0);

    // Function to calculate the volume of a box
    double volume();

    // Inline functions to provide the values of data members
    double getLength() {return length;}
```

```
       double getWidth() {return width;}
       double getHeight() {return height;}

       // Functions to set data member values
       void setHeight(double hvalue) {if(hvalue > 0) height = hvalue;}

    private:
       double length;
       double width;
       double height;
};
```

The `if` statement ensures that you only accept new values for `height` that are positive. If a new value is supplied for the `height` member that is zero or negative, it will be ignored. Member functions that allow data members to be modified are often referred to as **mutator** member functions.

The Default Copy Constructor

Suppose you declare and initialize a Box object `firstBox` with this statement:

```
Box firstBox(15.0, 20.0, 10.0);
```

Suppose further that you now want to create another Box object, identical to the first. Let me put it another way; you'd like to initialize the second Box object with `firstBox`. Let's see what happens when you use a Box object as a constructor argument.

....

Try It Out: Creating a Copy of an Object

You can use the definition of the Box class from the previous example just as it is for this experiment. Here's the code that you'd use to try to create a copy of a Box object:

```
// Program 12.5 Creating a copy of an object     File: ex12_05.cpp
#include <iostream>
#include "Box.h"

using std::cout;
using std::endl;

int main() {
  cout << endl;

  Box firstBox(2.2, 1.1, 0.5);
  Box secondBox(firstBox);

  cout << "Volume of first box = "
       << firstBox.volume()
```

```
        << endl;

  cout << "Volume of second box = "
       << secondBox.volume()
       << endl;

  return 0;
}
```

When you compile and run this, you should get this output:

```
Box constructor called
Volume of first box = 1.21
Volume of second box = 1.21
```

HOW IT WORKS

Clearly, the program is working as you hoped it would, with both boxes having the same volume. However, as you can see from the output, your constructor was called only once (for the creation of firstBox). Therefore, you are probably asking how the secondBox object was created.

The mechanism is similar to the situation when you had no constructor defined and the compiler supplies a default constructor that allows an object to be created. In this case, the compiler generates a default version of what is referred to as a **copy constructor**. A copy constructor does exactly what you are doing here—it creates an object of a class by initializing it with an existing object of the same class. The default version of the copy constructor creates the new object by copying the existing object, member by member. In fact, you can use the copy constructor in this way for any data type.

 NOTE *You don't have to create an object explicitly to cause a call to the copy constructor. Whenever you pass an object by value as an argument to a function, the compiler makes a copy of the object by calling the copy constructor.*

The default copy constructor is fine for simple classes, such as the Box class here, but for many classes—classes that have pointers as members, for example—it may produce undesirable effects. Indeed, with such classes, it can create serious errors in your program, and in these cases, you need to define your own copy constructor for the class.

A copy constructor is a constructor that creates a new object from an existing object of the same type; defining it requires a special approach that you will look into fully in the next chapter.

(Continued)

Friends

Under normal circumstances, you'll hide the data members of your classes by declaring them as private. You may well have private member functions of the class too. In spite of this, it is sometimes useful to treat certain, selected functions as "honorary members" of the class and allow them to access nonpublic members of a class object, just as though they were members of the class. Such functions are called **friends** of the class. A friend can access any of the members of a class object, regardless of their access specification.

You need to consider two situations that involve friends: an individual function can be specified as a friend of a class, or a whole class can be specified as a friend of another class. In the latter case, all the member functions of the friend class have the same access privileges as a normal member of the class. Let's first look at individual functions as friends.

The Friend Functions of a Class

A function that is not a member of a class but nonetheless can access all its members is called a **friend function** of that class. To make a function a friend function, you must declare it as such within the class definition, using the keyword friend.

 NOTE *A friend function of a class can be a global function or it can be a member of another class. However, a function can't be the friend of the class of which it is a member. Consequently, the access specifiers don't apply to the friends of a class.*

I should say right now that the need for friend functions in practice is limited. They are useful in situations in which a function needs access to the internals of two different kinds of objects, where making the function a friend of both classes makes that possible. I will use them here, however, in simpler contexts that don't necessarily reflect a situation where they are required, but that provide a convenient vehicle for demonstrating their operation.

Let's suppose that you want to implement a friend function in the Box class to compute the surface area of a Box object.

....

Try It Out: Using a Friend to Calculate the Surface Area

To make the function a friend, you must declare it as such within the class definition. You can adapt Program 12.4, first by changing the definition in Box.h to the following:

```
class Box {
  public:
    // Constructor
    Box(double lengthValue = 1.0, double widthValue = 1.0,
                                  double heightValue = 1.0);
```

```
   // Function to calculate the volume of a box
   double volume();

   // Friend function
   friend double boxSurface(const Box& theBox);

 private:
   double length;
   double width;
   double height;
};
```

This example also uses the file Box.cpp from Program 12.4 and the following main program code:

```
// Program 12.6 Using a friend function of a class   File: ex12_06.cpp
#include <iostream>
#include "Box.h"

using std::cout;
using std::endl;

int main() {
  cout << endl;

  Box firstBox(2.2, 1.1, 0.5);
  Box secondBox;
  Box* pthirdBox = new Box(15.0, 20.0, 8.0);

  cout << "Volume of first box = "
       << firstBox.volume()
       << endl;

  cout << "Surface area of first box = "
       << boxSurface(firstBox)
       << endl;

  cout << "Volume of second box = "
       << secondBox.volume()
       << endl;

  cout << "Surface area of second box = "
       << boxSurface(secondBox)
       << endl;

  cout << "Volume of third box = "
       << pthirdBox->volume()
       << endl;

  cout << "Surface area of third box = "
       << boxSurface(*pthirdBox)
       << endl;
```

(Continued)

```
    delete pthirdBox;
    return 0;
}

// friend function to calculate the surface area of a Box object
double boxSurface(const Box& theBox) {
    return 2.0 * (theBox.length * theBox.width +
                  theBox.length * theBox.height +
                  theBox.height * theBox.width);
}
```

Now you'll get this output:

```
Box constructor called
Box constructor called
Box constructor called
Volume of first box = 1.21
Surface area of first box = 8.14
Volume of second box = 1
Surface area of second box = 6
Volume of third box = 2400
Surface area of third box = 1160
```

HOW IT WORKS

You declare the function boxSurface() as a friend of the Box class by writing the function prototype using the keyword friend, within the class definition:

```
    friend double boxSurface(const Box& theBox);
```

You won't alter any aspect of the Box object passed as an argument to the function, so it is sensible to use a const reference parameter specification. It's also a good idea to be consistent when placing the friend declaration within the definition of the class. You can see that I've chosen to position this declaration at the end of all the public members of the class but before the private members. The rationale for this is that the function is part of the interface to the class because it has full access to members of the class. Remember, though, that a friend function is *not* a member of the class, so access specifiers do not apply to it.

The boxSurface() function itself is a global function, and its definition follows that of main(). You could put it in Box.cpp if you wanted because it is related to the Box class, but placing it in the main file helps indicate that it's a global function.

Notice that you have to specify access to the data members of the object within the definition of boxSurface() by using the Box object that is passed to the function as a parameter. Because a friend function is *not* a class member, the data members can't be referenced by their names alone. They each have to be qualified by the object name, in exactly the same way as they might in an ordinary function that accesses public members of a class. A friend function is the same as an ordinary function, except that it can access all the members of a class without restriction.

The main() function has been amended to call the friend function to output the surface area of each of the three objects you create. From the output you can see that it works as expected.

Although this example demonstrates how you write a friend function, it is not a very realistic use of one. You could have used accessor member functions to return the values of the data members; if you did this, then boxSurface() wouldn't have needed to be a friend function at all. In this case, perhaps the best option of all would have been to make boxSurface() a public member function of the class so that the capability for computing the surface area of a box becomes part of the class interface.

Friend functions are part of the interface to a class, but it is better programming practice to define the interface to a class entirely in terms of member functions if you can. As I explained at the beginning of this discussion, the only circumstances in which they are really necessary is when you need to access the non-public members of two different classes; even then, you may be able to do what you want without involving friend functions.

Friend Classes

You can also declare a whole class to be a friend of another class. All the member functions of the friend class will have unrestricted access to the members of the class of which it has been declared a friend.

For example, suppose you have defined a class, Carton, and want to allow the member functions of the Carton class to have access to the members of the Box class. To make this happen, you just need to include a statement within the Box class definition that declares Carton to be its friend:

```
class Box {
  // Public members of the class...

  friend class Carton;

  // Private members of the class...
};
```

Friendship is not a reciprocal arrangement. Whereas functions in the Carton class can now access all the members of the Box class, functions in the Box class have no access to the private members of the Carton class. Friendship amongst classes is not transitive either; just because class A is a friend of class B, and class B is a friend of class C, it doesn't follow that class A is a friend of class C.

A typical use for a friend class is where the functioning of one class is highly intertwined with that of another class. A linked list (like the one I discussed in the last chapter) basically involves two class types: a List class that maintains a list of objects (usually called nodes), and a Node class that defines what a node is. The List class needs to stitch the Node objects together by setting a pointer in each Node object so that it points to the next Node object. Making the List class a friend of the class that defines a node would enable members of the List class to access the members of the Node class directly.

The Pointer Named this

In your Box class, you wrote the function volume() in terms of the class member names in the definition of the class. When you think about it, though, *every* object of type Box that you create contains these members, so you must be able to find a way for the function to refer to the members of the particular object for which it has been called. In other words, when the code in the volume() function refers to the length member of the class, there has to be a way for length to refer to the member of the object for which the function is called, and not some other object.

When any class member function executes, it automatically contains a hidden pointer with the name this, which contains the address of the object for which the function was called. For example, suppose you write this statement:

```
cout << firstBox.volume();
```

The pointer this in the function volume() contains the address of firstBox. When you call the function for another Box object, this will be set to contain the address of that object.

This means that when the data member length is accessed in the function volume() during execution, it is actually referring to this->length, which is the fully specified reference to the object member that is being used. The compiler takes care of adding the necessary pointer name this to the member names in the function. In other words, the compiler implements the function as follows:

```
double Box::volume() {
  return this->length * this->width * this->height;
}
```

You could write the function explicitly using the pointer this if you wanted to, but it isn't necessary here. However, you will find yourself in situations where you *do* need to use it—for example, when a member function has multiple parameters of the same class type, or when you need to return the address of the current object. Let's see how the this pointer works in practice by using it explicitly in an example.

Try It Out: Explicit Use of this

Being able to compare the volumes of Box objects would be a very useful addition to your class, so let's add a public function to your class Box to do just that. The class definition in Box.h will be

```cpp
class Box {
  public:
    // Constructor
    Box(double lengthValue = 1.0, double widthValue = 1.0,
                                     double heightValue = 1.0);

    // Function to calculate the volume of a box
    double volume();

    // Function to compare two Box objects
    int compareVolume(Box& otherBox);

  private:
    double length;
    double width;
    double height;
};
```

You'll need to add the definition of compareVolume() to the Box.cpp file, alongside the other function definitions that you have there:

```cpp
// Function to compare two Box objects
// If the current Box is greater than the argument, 1 is returned
// If they are equal, 0 is returned
// If the current Box is less than the argument, -1 is returned
int Box::compareVolume(Box& otherBox) {
  double vol1 = this->volume();           // Get current Box volume
  double vol2 = otherBox.volume();        // Get argument volume
  return vol1 > vol2 ? 1 : (vol1 < vol2 ? -1 : 0);
}
```

You can now create a couple of Box objects and compare their volumes:

```cpp
// Program 12.7 Using the this pointer    File: ex12_07.cpp
#include <iostream>
#include "Box.h"

using std::cout;
using std::endl;

int main() {
  cout << endl;
```

(Continued)

```
    Box firstBox(17.0, 11.0, 5.0);
    Box secondBox(9.0, 18.0, 4.0);

    cout << "The first box is "
        << (firstBox.compareVolume(secondBox) >= 0 ? "" : "not ")
        << "greater than the second box."
        << endl;

    cout << "Volume of first box = "
        << firstBox.volume()
        << endl;

    cout << "Volume of second box = "
        << secondBox.volume()
        << endl;

    return 0;
}
```

From this program, you'll get this output:

```
Box constructor called
Box constructor called
The first box is greater than the second box.
Volume of first box = 935
Volume of second box = 648
```

HOW IT WORKS

The implementation of the member function compareVolume() involves working with two Box objects: the one for which the function is called, and the argument. To call the function volume() for the object for which the compareVolume() function was called, use the this pointer:

```
double vol1 = this->volume();       // Get current Box volume
```

 NOTE *Remember that you use the direct member access operator, . , when you're using an object to select a member; and you use the arrow operator, ->, when you're using a pointer to an object.* this *is a pointer, so it requires the arrow operator.*

I used the this pointer in this example simply to demonstrate its existence. It isn't actually necessary here, so it would have been just as acceptable to have written this:

```
double vol1 = volume();             // Get current Box volume
```

Within the body of compareVolume(), or indeed any member function, class member names that you use by themselves will automatically be accessed using the this pointer, so you'll always get the member belonging to the current object. You only need to use the this pointer explicitly in limited circumstances. One example where you might use this explicitly is to resolve ambiguity—if a function parameter had the same name as a data member, for example. You'd also use this if you wanted to return the address of the current object from a member function.

To get the volume of the object passed as an argument, just use the parameter name to call the function:

```
double vol2 = otherBox.volume();      // Get argument volume
```

The last statement in compareVolume() returns the appropriate integer value:

```
return vol1 > vol2 ? 1 : (vol1 < vol2 ? -1 : 0);
```

If vol1 is greater than vol2, then the conditional operator causes 1 to be returned. Otherwise, the conditional operation within parentheses is executed and returns −1 if vol1 is less than vol2, and 0 if it isn't.

You use the compareVolume() function in main() to check the relationship between the volumes of the objects firstBox and secondBox in this statement:

```
cout << "The first box is "
     << (firstBox.compareVolume(secondBox) >= 0 ? "" : "not ")
     << "greater than the second box."
     << endl;
```

The value returned by the compareVolume() function is used with a conditional operator to decide whether to include the string "not " in the output. The output then confirms that the firstBox object is larger than the secondBox object.

In fact, it is not essential to write the compareVolume() function as a class member. You could just as well have written it as an ordinary function, with the objects as arguments. Note that this is not true of the function volume(), because it needs to access the private data members of the class. Of course, if the function compareVolume() was implemented as an ordinary function, it wouldn't have the pointer this, but it would still be very simple:

```
// Comparing two Box objects - ordinary function version
int compareVolume(Box& box1, Box& box2) {
  double vol1 = box1.volume();                    // Get first Box volume
  double vol2 = box2.volume();                    // Get second Box volume
  return vol1 > vol2 ? 1 : (vol1 < vol2 ? -1 : 0);
}
```

(Conatinued)

Let's briefly compare this function to the class member version of `compareVolume()`. In this version, both objects are arguments, but the same values are returned. You'd use this version to perform the same operation as before with this statement:

```
cout << "The first box is "
    << (compareVolume(firstBox, secondBox) >= 0 ? "" : "not ")
    << "greater than the second box."
    << endl;
```

In this instance you can't conclude that one version of the `compareVolume()` function is significantly better than the other. However, there is a much better way to compare objects, as we will see later.

Returning this *from a Function*

If you specify the return type for a member function as a pointer to the class type, you can return this from the function. This gives you the very useful capability of calling a succession of member functions for an object one after another. Let's consider an example of where this would be useful.

Suppose you add mutator function to your Box class to set the length, width, and height of a box, and you make these functions return this:

```
class Box {
  public:
    // Constructor
    Box(double lengthValue = 1.0, double widthValue = 1.0,
                                        double heightValue = 1.0);

    // Function to calculate the volume of a box
    double volume();

    // Function to compare two Box objects
    int compareVolume(Box& otherBox);

    // Mutator functions
    Box* setLength(double lvalue);
    Box* setWidth(double wvalue);
    Box* setHeight(double hvalue);

  private:
    double length;
    double width;
    double height;
};
```

You can implement these in Box.cpp as follows:

```
// setXXX() functions
Box* Box::setLength(double lvalue) {
  if(lvalue > 0) length = lvalue;
     return this;
}

Box* Box::setWidth(double wvalue) {
  if(wvalue > 0) width = wvalue;
     return this;
}

Box* Box::setHeight(double hvalue) {
  if(hvalue > 0) height = hvalue;
     return this;
}
```

Now you can modify all the dimensions of a Box object in a single statement:

```
Box aBox(10,15,25);        // Create a box
Box* pBox = &aBox;         // and a pointer to aBox
pBox->setLength(20)->setWidth(40)->setHeight(10);  // Set all dimensions of aBox
```

Because your mutator functions return the this pointer, you can use the value returned by one function to call the next. Thus the pointer returned by setLength() is used to call setWidth(), which returns a pointer you can then use to call setHeight(). Isn't that nice?

Objects That Are const and const Member Functions

Before we leave the previous example, let's consider the compareVolume() member function once more. Because you don't modify the parameter, you really should have declared it as const in the class definition:

```
class Box {
  // Rest of the class as before...

  int compareVolume(const Box& otherBox);
};
```

Of course, you'll need to change the function definition in the same way. Try that out and run the example again. You should find that the compiler complains when it tries to link the parts of the program together. If your compiler complies with the C++ standard, you'll get an error message for this statement:

```
  double vol2 = otherBox.volume();     // Get argument volume
```

If you specify that an object is const, you are telling the compiler that you'll not modify it. Here, when you call the function volume() for the const object otherBox, the compiler has to pass the address of otherBox to the function via the this pointer, and it has no guarantee that the function will not modify the object. The error message is likely to be in terms of being unable to convert the this pointer, because the compiler can't cast away the const nature of the object by default.

For any object that you declare to be const, you can only call member functions that are also declared to be const. A const member function won't modify the object for which it is called. To declare a member function as const, you need to add the keyword const at the *end* of the function declaration in the class definition. For the compareVolume() function to work with a const parameter, you must declare the volume() function to be const. In this case, the class definition will be as follows:

```cpp
class Box {
  public:
    // Constructor
    Box(double lengthValue = 1.0, double widthValue = 1.0,
                                          double heightValue = 1.0);

    // Function to calculate the volume of a box
    double volume() const;

    // Function to compare two Box objects
    int compareVolume(const Box& otherBox);

  private:
    double length;
    double width;
    double height;
};
```

The keyword const must also appear in the function definition for volume() in Box.cpp:

```cpp
double Box::volume() const {
  return length * width * height;
}
```

The program will now compile and work as before. Declaring a member function as const essentially ensures that whatever the this pointer points to is a const—in other words, *this is const. You should always declare member functions that don't change the object for which they are called as const. This doesn't prevent them from being called for non-const objects, but it does allow you to use const objects more widely, which makes your code more efficient and less prone to error. In fact, based on this, you should declare the compareVolume() function in the Box class to be const too:

```cpp
class Box {
  public:
    // Constructor
```

```
    Box(double lengthValue = 1.0, double widthValue = 1.0,
                                  double heightValue = 1.0);


    // Function to calculate the volume of a box
    double volume() const;

    // Function to compare two Box objects
    int compareVolume(const Box& otherBox) const;

  private:
    double length;
    double width;
    double height;
};
```

Of course, it must also be const in the definition in Box.cpp:

```
int Box::compareVolume(const Box& otherBox) const {
  double vol1 = this->volume();         // Get current Box volume
  double vol2 = otherBox.volume();      // Get argument volume
  return vol1 > vol2 ? 1 : (vol1 < vol2 ? -1 : 0);
}
```

Other member functions that are prime candidates for being declared as const are the accessor functions. In fact, these should always be declared as const, because they just provide access to the value of a data member; they do not alter it.

Note that declaring a member function as const affects the function signature. This means that you can overload a function by adding a const version of the function. For example, suppose you had member functions with the following prototypes:

```
int Box::compareVolume(const Box& otherBox)
```

```
int Box::compareVolume(const Box& otherBox) const
```

These would be overloaded versions of the compareVolume() function. However, you should be careful about overloading a member function on the basis of const-ness, as it can be confusing to someone using a class.

Mutable Data Members of a Class

If you declare an object as const, then you can only call const member functions, as you have seen. You can't change the values of the data members of the object because they'll also be effectively const. However, you may find situations in which you need to allow certain, selected data members of a class to be altered, even if the object was declared as const.

For an example of such a circumstance, imagine an object that obtains data from a remote source—another computer, perhaps—and stores that data in a data member that provides an internal buffer. An object of the class may well need to be able to update its internal buffer, even if it has been declared to be const.

To accommodate these kinds of situations, you need two things: you need to be able to exempt a particular data member from the const-ness of an object, and you need to be able to alter the value of the exempt data member in a const member function and still have the const declaration of the member function unbroken. You can do both by declaring a data member as **mutable**.

To illustrate how this is applied, let's consider a simple context. Suppose that for security reasons, you want to record a timestamp in a data member of an object each time any member function is called. The object might represent controlled access to part of a building, for instance. You want to allow the object to be const, but you still want to timestamp the last use of the object.

The way to do this is to declare the data member storing the timestamp as mutable. This exempts the data member from the const-ness implied by a const declaration of an object of the class, and it also allows it to be altered by a const member function. To do this, just use the keyword mutable in the member declaration. Here's an example:

```
class SecureAccess {
  public:
    bool isLocked() const;
    // More of the class definition...

  private:
    mutable int time;
    // More of the class definition...
}
```

The member function isLocked() might be implemented something along the lines of this:

```
bool SecureAccess::isLocked() const {
  time = getCurrentTime();          // Store time of function call
  return lockStatus();              // Return the state of the door
}
```

Here, the lockStatus() function is assumed to return true if the door is locked and false otherwise. Because the data member, time, is declared as mutable, it can appear on the left of an assignment statement here. Only data members that have been declared as mutable can appear on the left of an assignment in a member function that is declared as const.

Now you can create an object of the class that you declare as const and call the isLocked() member for it:

```
const SecureAccess mainDoor;
bool doorState = mainDoor.isLocked();
```

Because the mainDoor object is const, you can only call its const member functions. Any const member function in the class SecureAccess can modify the value stored in the member time, regardless of whether an object is declared as const. If time is not declared as mutable, any const function member that tries to change it will cause a compilation error.

Casting Away const

Very rarely, circumstances can arise where a function is dealing with a const object, either passed as an argument or the object pointed to by this, and it is necessary to make it non-const. This could be because you want to pass it as an argument to another function, written by someone else, that has a non-const parameter. The const_cast<>() operator enables you to do this. The general form of using the const_cast<>() operator is

```
const_cast<Type>(expression)
```

Here, the type of expression must be either const Type or the same as Type. You *should not* use this operator to undermine the const-ness of an object. The only situations in which you should use it are those where you are sure the const nature of the object won't be violated as a result.

Arrays of Objects of a Class

As I indicated earlier, you can declare an array of objects of a class in exactly the same way that you declare an array of any other type. Each element of an array of class objects has to be created individually, and to do this, the compiler arranges for the default constructor to be called for each element. The compiler doesn't allow you to initialize your array within the definition statement. I can demonstrate that this is the case with an example.

....

Try It Out: Creating an Array of Box Objects

You can modify the previous definition of the Box class to include a specific default constructor. I'll illustrate the array declaration by declaring two constructors at the outset and tracking each constructor call via lines of output. The class definition will be

```
class Box {
  public:
    // Constructors
    Box();
    Box(double lengthValue, double widthValue, double heightValue);

    // Function to calculate the volume of a box
    double volume() const;

    // Function to compare two Box objects
    int compareVolume(const Box& otherBox) const;
```

(Continued)

```
      private:
        double length;
        double width;
        double height;
    };
```

Here you've removed the default parameter values from the original constructor so that you don't have a duplicate default constructor. The member function definitions in Box.cpp will be as they were at the end of the last section, although you'll need to restore the default constructor definition if you removed it when you stopped using it:

```
// Default constructor
Box::Box() {
  cout << "Default constructor called" << endl;
  length = width = height = 1.0;
}
```

The code to create and use a Box array is very simple:

```
// Program 12.8 Creating an array of Box objects   File: ex12_08.cpp
#include <iostream>
#include "Box.h"

using std::cout;
using std::endl;

int main() {
  cout << endl;

  Box firstBox(17.0, 11.0, 5.0);
  Box boxes[5];

  cout << "Volume of first box = "
       << firstBox.volume()
       << endl;

  const int count = sizeof boxes/sizeof boxes[0];

  cout << "The boxes array has " << count << " elements."
       << endl;

  cout << "Each element occupies " << sizeof boxes[0] << " bytes."
       << endl;

  for(int i = 0 ; i < count ; i++)
    cout << "Volume of boxes[" << i << "] = "
         << boxes[i].volume()
         << endl;

  return 0;
}
```

On my machine, this example generates the following output:

```
Box constructor called
Default constructor called
Default constructor called
Default constructor called
Default constructor called
Default constructor called
Volume of first box = 935
The boxes array has 5 elements.
Each element occupies 24 bytes.
Volume of boxes[0] = 1
Volume of boxes[1] = 1
Volume of boxes[2] = 1
Volume of boxes[3] = 1
Volume of boxes[4] = 1
```

HOW IT WORKS

The first line of output is produced by the constructor call in the declaration:

```
Box firstBox(17.0, 11.0, 5.0);
```

The next five lines of output originate from the declaration of the array:

```
Box boxes[5];
```

You can see from the output that the default constructor is called once for each array element. This statement defines five objects, each of type Box. Because you are defining an array, you can't supply arguments for a constructor. Because no arguments are supplied, the compiler uses the default constructor to create each of the five objects of the array.

After displaying the volume of firstBox, just to show there is nothing special about an array of Box objects, you can calculate the number of elements in the array using the sizeof operator:

```
const int count = sizeof boxes/sizeof boxes[0];
```

The value stored in count is displayed in the usual way by the next statement:

```
cout << "The boxes array has " << count << " elements."
     << endl;
```

The size of each element will be the size of a Box object, which is displayed by this statement:

```
cout << "Each element occupies " << sizeof boxes[0] << " bytes."
     << endl;
```

(Continued)

You can see from the output that the size of a Box object is 24 bytes, which corresponds to the memory required for storing three values of type double on my machine. The presence of member functions (or lack thereof) has no influence on the size of an object.

Finally in this example, the volume of each element of the Boxes array is displayed in a loop:

```
for(int i = 0 ; i < count ; i++)
  cout << "Volume of boxes[" << i << "] = "
       << boxes[i].volume()
       << endl;
```

It's clear from the output that the default constructor initialization is working satisfactorily, as the volume of each array element is 1.

The Size of a Class Object

As you saw in the last example, you can obtain the size of a class object by using the sizeof operator in exactly the way you have done previously with the basic data types. You can apply the operator either to a particular object, or to the class type. The size of a class object is generally the sum of the sizes of the data members of the class, although on some machines, it may turn out to be greater than this on occasion. This isn't something that should bother you, but it's nice to know why.

On some computers, for performance reasons, two-byte variables must be placed at an address that is a multiple of two, four byte variables must be placed on a boundary that is a multiple of four, and so on. A consequence of this is that sometimes, the compiler must leave gaps between the memory for one value and the next. If, on such a machine, you have three variables that occupy two bytes, followed by a variable that requires four bytes, a gap of two bytes may need to be left in order to place the fourth variable on the correct boundary. In this case, the total space required by all four is greater than the sum of the individual sizes. You can create an example that illustrates this on a PC and other systems that require **boundary alignment**.

Try It Out: Object Sizes Affected by Boundary Alignment

You can define a variation on the Box class called SizeBox, which is designed specifically to show the effect of boundary alignment on object sizes:

```
// SizeBox.h
#ifndef SIZEBOX_H
#define SIZEBOX_H

class SizeBox {
  public:
    SizeBox();
    int totalSize();                 // Sum of sizes of members
```

```
   private:
     char* pMaterial;
     double length;
     double width;
     double height;
};

#endif
```

Here are the definitions for the member functions:

```
// SizeBox.cpp
#include "SizeBox.h"

SizeBox::SizeBox() :
    length(1.0), width(1.0), height(1.0), pMaterial("Cardboard") {}

// Sum of sizes of members
int SizeBox::totalSize() {
  return sizeof(length)+sizeof(width)+sizeof(height)+sizeof(pMaterial);
}
```

You don't need the class to do very much other than be able to create instances of itself and supply the number of bytes occupied by its members, so the only member functions are the constructor and the function totalSize(). You have an extra data member that is a pointer to a null-terminated string that records the type of the material the box is made of. You can create objects and report the amount of memory they occupy with the following code:

```
// Program 12.9 Trying object sizes    File: ex12_09.cpp
#include <iostream>
#include "SizeBox.h"

using std::cout;
using std::endl;

int main() {
  SizeBox box;
  SizeBox boxes[10];
  cout << endl          << "The data members of a Box object occupy "
       << box.totalSize() << " bytes.";

  cout << endl          << "A single Box object occupies "
       << sizeof SizeBox << " bytes.";

  cout << endl          << "An array of 10 Box objects occupies "
       << sizeof(boxes)  << " bytes."
       << endl;
  return 0;
}
```

(Continued)

This will produce the following output:

```
The data members of a Box object occupy 28 bytes.
A single Box object occupies 32 bytes.
An array of 10 Box objects occupies 320 bytes.
```

HOW IT WORKS

The output demonstrates that things don't quite add up. The memory for a SizeBox object is made up of 24 bytes for the three double members, plus 4 bytes for the pointer member, pMaterial, which makes a total of 28 bytes, as reported in the first line of output. When you output the size of a SizeBox object, however, it turns out to be 32 bytes, and this is confirmed by the array of 10 objects.

The extra 4 bytes are due to boundary alignment. Figure 12-6 shows what is happening. As I described before, on many machines the compiler has to allocate addresses for 8-byte variables that are a multiple of 8, addresses for 4-byte variables that are a multiple of 4, and so on for performance reasons.

4 bytes	4 bytes	8 bytes	8 bytes	8 bytes
pMaterial	not used	length	width	height

Figure 12-6. Lost space due to boundary alignment

The SizeBox object consists of a pointer and three members of type double. The pointer pMaterial will be at an address that is a multiple of 4 because it occupies 4 bytes. The three 8-byte members must each occupy an address that is a multiple of 8. If the next available address is *not* a multiple of 8, then the compiler has to leave a gap—4 bytes in this case—to make the length member lie on an 8-byte boundary.

You might think that by rearranging the data members—by putting pMaterial last, for instance—you could make class objects occupy less space, but this is not usually the case. The compiler must take account of what happens in the case of an array of objects, and this requires that the object is on a boundary that is a multiple of 8 bytes.

Now that we've got that out of the way, let's get back to what we can do with a class!

Static Members of a Class

You can declare data members and member functions of a class as static. Static data members of a class are used to provide class-wide storage of data that is independent of any particular object of the class type, but is accessible by any of them. They record the properties of the class as a whole, rather than of individual objects. You can use static data members to store constants that are specific to a class, or you could store information about the objects of a class in general, such as how many there are in existence.

A static member function provides a computational ability that's independent of any individual class object, but can be invoked by any class object if necessary. It can also be invoked from outside the class if it is a public member. A common use of static member functions is to operate on static data members, regardless of whether any objects of the class have been declared.

Because the context is a class definition, there is a little more to this topic than the effect of the keyword static outside of a class, so you need to consider it in greater detail. Let's look into static data members first.

Static Data Members of a Class

Static data members of a class are associated with the class as a whole, not with any particular object of the class. When you declare a data member of a class as static, the effect is that the static data member is defined only once, and will exist *even if no objects of the class have been created*. Each static data member is accessible in any object of the class that has been created, and is shared among however many objects there are. An object gets its own independent copies of each of the ordinary data members of a class, but only one instance of each static data member ever exists, regardless of how many class objects have been defined.

You use static data members to record class-wide information. One use for a static data member is to count how many objects of a class actually exist. You could add a static data member to your Box class by adding the following statement to your class definition:

```
static int objectCount;          // Count of objects in existence
```

Figure 12-7 illustrates how the static member, objectCount, will be shared between all objects of the class.

Now you have a problem. How do you initialize the static data member? You can't put it in the class declaration—that's simply a blueprint for an object, and initializing values are not allowed. You don't want to initialize it in a constructor, because you want to increment it every time the constructor is called; and anyway, it exists even if no objects exist (and therefore no constructors have been called). Similarly, you can't initialize it in another member function, because a member function is associated with an object, and you want it initialized before any object is created.

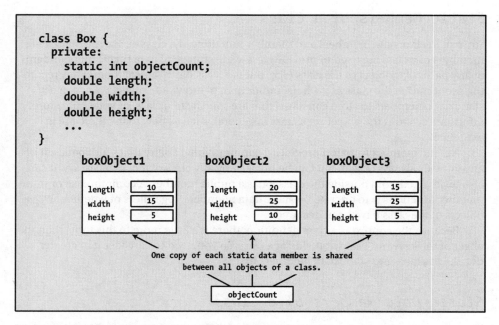

Figure 12-7. Static class members are shared between objects

The answer is to write the initialization outside of the class declaration with a statement like this:

```
int Box::objectCount = 0;              // Initialize static member of class Box
```

Even though the static data member is specified as private, you can still initialize it in this fashion. Indeed, this is the *only* way you can initialize it. Of course, because it's private, you can't then access objectCount directly from outside the class.

Because this statement defines and initializes the static member of the class, it must occur only once in your program. Therefore, the logical place to put it is the Box.cpp file.

NOTE *Notice that the keyword* static *is not included in the definition—indeed, you must not include it. However, you do need to qualify the member name by using the class name and the scope resolution operator so that the compiler understands that you are referring to a static member of the class. Otherwise, you'd simply create a global variable that has nothing to do with the class.*

Try It Out: Counting Instances

Let's add the static data member and the object counting capability to Program 12.8. You'll need just two extra statements in the class definition: one to declare the new static data member, and another to define a function that will retrieve its value:

```
class Box {
  public:
    // Constructors
    Box();
    Box(double lengthValue, double widthValue, double heightValue);

    // Function to calculate the volume of a box
    double volume() const;

    // Function to compare two Box objects
    int compareVolume(const Box& otherBox) const;

    int getObjectCount() const {return objectCount;}

  private:
    static int objectCount;            // Count of objects in existence
    double length;
    double width;
    double height;
};
```

The getObjectCount() function has been declared as const because it doesn't modify any of the data members of the class. You can add the statement to initialize the static member objectCount at the end of the Box.cpp file:

```
// Initialize static member of class Box
int Box::objectCount = 0;
```

You must also modify both constructors to update the count when an object is created:

```
// Default constructor
Box::Box() {
  cout << "Default constructor called" << endl;
  ++objectCount;
  length = width = height = 1.0;
}

// Constructor definition using an initializer list
Box::Box(double lvalue, double wvalue, double hvalue) :
                        length(lvalue), width(wvalue), height(hvalue) {
  cout << "Box constructor called" << endl;
  ++objectCount;
```

(Continued)

```
    // Ensure positive dimensions
    if(length <= 0)
      length = 1.0;
    if(width <= 0)
      width = 1.0;
    if(height <= 0)
      height = 1.0;
}
```

You can modify the version of main() from Program 12.8 to output the object count:

```
// Program 12.10 Counting Box objects        File: ex12_10.cpp
#include <iostream>
#include "Box.h"

using std::cout;
using std::endl;

int main() {
  cout << endl;

  Box firstBox(17.0, 11.0, 5.0);
  cout << "Object count is " << firstBox.getObjectCount() << endl;
  Box boxes[5];
  cout << "Object count is " << firstBox.getObjectCount() << endl;

  cout << "Volume of first box = "
       << firstBox.volume()
       << endl;

  const int count = sizeof boxes / sizeof boxes[0];

  cout <<"The boxes array has " << count << " elements."
       << endl;

  cout <<"Each element occupies " << sizeof boxes[0] << " bytes."
       << endl;

  for(int i = 0 ; i < count ; i++)
    cout << "Volume of boxes[" << i << "] = "
         << boxes[i].volume()
         << endl;

  return 0;
}
```

The program will now produce the following output:

```
Box constructor called
Object count is 1
Default constructor called
Default constructor called
Default constructor called
Default constructor called
Default constructor called
Object count is 6
Volume of first box = 935
The boxes array has 5 elements.
Each element occupies 24 bytes.
Volume of boxes[0] = 1
Volume of boxes[1] = 1
Volume of boxes[2] = 1
Volume of boxes[3] = 1
Volume of boxes[4] = 1
```

HOW IT WORKS

This code shows that, indeed, only one copy of the static member objectCount exists, and both of the constructors are updating it. You called the function getObjectCount() for the firstBox object on both occasions, but for the second call, you could have used any of the array elements and you would have gotten the same result.

Of course, you're only counting the number of objects that get created. You have no way to know when objects are destroyed, so the count won't necessarily reflect the number of objects that are around at any point. You'll find out in the next chapter how to account for objects that get destroyed.

Note that the size of a Box object is unchanged in the output compared to the previous example, even though you have added objectCount to the class definition. This is because static data members are not part of any object—they belong to the class. Because static data members are not part of a class object, member functions that you have declared as const can modify static data members of a class without violating their const-ness.

 CAUTION *You* must *define a static data member that appears within the definition of a class, or the compiler will complain. The declaration in the class definition doesn't define the static variable, so until you define it by initializing it outside the class, it doesn't exist.*

(Continued)

Accessing Static Data Members

Suppose that in a reckless moment, you declared the objectCount data member as public:

```
class Box {
  public:
    static int objectCount;              // Count of objects in existence

    // Constructors
    Box();
    Box(double lengthValue, double widthValue, double heightValue);

    // Function to calculate the volume of a box
    double volume() const;

    // Function to compare two Box objects
    int compareVolume(const Box& otherBox) const;

    int getObjectCount() const {return objectCount;}

  private:
    double length;
    double width;
    double height;
};
```

Now you don't need to use the getObjectCount() function. To output the number of objects in main(), just write this:

```
std::cout << "Object count is " << firstBox.objectCount << std::endl;
```

There's more: I claimed that a static variable exists even if no objects have been created. This means that you should be able to get the count *before* you create the first-Box object, but how do you refer to the data member? The answer is that you just use the class name, Box, as a qualifier with the scope resolution operator:

```
std::cout << "Object count is " << Box::objectCount << std::endl;
```

In fact, you can always use the class name to access a public static member of a class. It doesn't matter whether any objects exist or not. Try it out by modifying the last example; you'll see that it works as described.

A Static Data Member of the Same Type As the Class

A static data member is not part of each object of the class, so it can be of the same type as the class. The Box class can contain a static data member of type Box, for example. This might seem a little strange at first, but it can be useful. I can use the Box class to illustrate just how.

Suppose you want to have a standard "reference" box available for some purpose; you might want to relate Box objects in various ways to a standard box, for example. Of course, you could define a standard Box object outside the class, but if you are going to use it within member functions of the class, it creates an external dependency that it would be better to get rid of. The alternative solution is to make the standard Box a static member of the class:

```
class Box {
  public:
    // Constructors
    Box();
    Box(double lengthValue, double widthValue, double heightValue);

    // Function to calculate the volume of a box
    double volume() const;

    // Function to compare two Box objects
    int compareVolume(const Box& otherBox) const;

  private:
    const static Box refBox;          // Standard reference box
    double length;
    double width;
    double height;
};
```

Because refBox is a standard Box object that should not be changed, you also declare it as const. However, you must still initialize it outside the class for it to be defined. You could put a statement in Box.cpp to define refBox:

```
const Box Box::refBox(10.0, 10.0, 10.0);
```

This calls the constructor of the Box class to create refBox. Because the static data member of the class will be created before any objects are created in the program, at least one Box object will always exist.

Any of the member functions for objects of the class can access refBox, so it is available to all; however, it isn't accessible outside the class because you declared it to be a private member. A class constant is one situation where you might want to make the data member public if it has a useful role outside the class. As long as it is declared as const, it can't be modified.

Static Member Functions of a Class

By declaring a function member as static, you make it independent of any particular object of the class. Just like a static data member, a static function member of a class exists even if no class objects have been created. Declaring a static function in a class is easy: you simply use the keyword static, as you did with the data member objectCount. In fact, you could have declared the getObjectCount() function as static in the previous example:

```cpp
class Box {
  public:
    // Constructors
    Box();
    Box(double lengthValue, double widthValue, double heightValue);

    // Function to calculate the volume of a box
    double volume() const;

    // Function to compare two Box objects
    int compareVolume(const Box& otherBox) const;

    static int getObjectCount() {return objectCount;}

  private:
    static int objectCount;             // Count of objects in existence
    double length;
    double width;
    double height;
};
```

 CAUTION *Static member functions can't be declared as* const. *Because a static member function isn't associated with any object of a class, it has no* this *pointer, so the idea of* const *doesn't apply.*

Static member functions have the advantage that they exist and can be called even if no objects of the class exist. You can call a static member function using the class name as a qualifier. Here's an example:

```cpp
std::cout << "Object count is " << Box::getObjectCount() << std::endl;
```

Of course, if you have created objects of the class, you can call a static member function through an object of the class in the same way as you call any other member function. For instance:

```cpp
std::cout << "Object count is " << firstBox.getObjectCount() << std::endl;
```

The difference between this and an ordinary member function is that the static function has no access to the object for which it is called. In order for a static member function to access an object of the class, it would need to be passed as an argument to the function. Referencing members of a class object from within a static function must then be done using qualified names (as you would do with an ordinary global function accessing a public data member).

Of course, a static member function is a full member of the class in terms of access privileges. If an object of the same class is passed as an argument to a static member function, it can access `private` as well as `public` members of the object. It wouldn't make sense to do so, but just to illustrate the point, you could include a definition of a static function in the `Box` class as shown here:

```
static double sum(Box theBox) {
  return theBox.length + theBox.width + theBox.height;
}
```

Even though you are passing the `Box` object as an argument, the private data members can be accessed. Of course, it would make more sense to do this with a member function, rather than a static function.

Summary

In this and the previous chapter, I have covered the basic ideas behind classes in C++, and the ground rules for defining and using them. However, although I have covered a lot of ground, this is just the start. You have a great deal more to learn about implementing the operations applicable to objects of your classes, and about the subtleties of the internals of a class.

In subsequent chapters, you'll be building on what you have learned here, and you'll see more about how you can extend the capabilities of your classes. In addition, you'll explore more sophisticated ways to use classes in practice. The key points to keep in mind from this chapter are as follows:

- A **class** provides a way to define your own data types. Classes can reflect whatever types of **objects** your particular problem requires.

- A class can contain **data members** and **member functions**. The member functions of a class always have free access to the data members of the same class.

- Objects of a class are created and initialized using functions called **constructors**. A constructor is called automatically when an object declaration is encountered. Constructors may be overloaded to provide different ways of initializing an object.

- Members of a class can be specified as `public`, in which case they are freely accessible from any function in a program. Alternatively, they may be specified as `private`, in which case they may only be accessed by member functions or `friend` functions of the class.

- Data members of a class can be defined as static. Only one instance of each static data member of a class exists, no matter how many objects of the class are created.

- Although static data members of a class are accessible in a member function of a class object, they aren't part of the class object and don't contribute to its size.

- Static function members of a class exist and can be called, even if no objects of the class have been created.

- Every nonstatic function member of a class contains the pointer this, which points to the current object for which the function was called.

- A static function member of a class doesn't contain the pointer this.

- Member functions of a class declared as const can't modify data members of an object of the class unless the data members have been declared as mutable.

- Using references to class objects as arguments to function calls can avoid substantial overheads in passing complex objects to a function.

- A copy constructor is a constructor for an object that is initialized with an existing object of the same class. The compiler generates a default copy constructor for a class if you don't define one.

Exercises

The following exercises enable you to try out what you've learned in this chapter. If you get stuck, look back over the chapter for help. If you're still stuck after that, you can download the solutions from the Apress website (http://www.apress.com/book/download.html), but that really should be a last resort.

Exercise 12-1. Create a class called Integer that has an int as its single, private data member. Provide a constructor for the class, and use it to output messages that tell you when objects are created. Provide member functions of the class to get and set the data member, and to output its value. Write a test program to create and manipulate at least three Integer objects, and verify that you can't assign a value directly to the data member.

Exercise all the class functions in your test program by getting, setting, and outputting the value of the data member of each object.

Exercise 12-2. Modify the constructor for the Integer class in the previous example so that the data member is initialized to zero in the initialization list and implements a copy constructor for the class.

Now write a member function that compares the current object with an Integer object passed as an argument. The method should return –1 if the current object is less than the argument, 0 if they are equal, and +1 if the current object is greater than the argument. Try two versions of the function: first with the parameter passed to the function by value and then by reference. What do you see printed from the constructors when the function is called? Make sure that you understand why this is so.

You can't have both functions present in the class as overloaded functions. Why not?

Exercise 12-3. Implement member functions add(), subtract(), and multiply() for the Integer class that will add, subtract, and multiply the current object by the value of the argument of type Integer. Demonstrate the operation of these functions in your class with a version of main() that creates Integer objects encapsulating values 4, 5, 6, 7, and 8, and then uses these to calculate the value of $4 \times 5^3 + 6 \times 5^2 + 7 \times 5 + 8$. Implement the functions so that the calculation and the output of the result can be performed in a single statement.

Exercise 12-4. Change your solution for Exercise 12-2 so that it implements the compare() function as a friend of the Integer class.

CHAPTER 13

Class Operations

YOU'LL NEED TO UNDERSTAND the subtleties of creating and destroying class objects if operations on objects of your classes are to work safely and effectively. In this chapter, I'll cover the groundwork for creating and destroying class objects.

To demonstrate why some things need to be done in a particular way, I'll show you how to develop your classes incrementally over this chapter and the next. The intermediate stages we go through will sometimes have shortcomings that you'll need to overcome. Once you understand the shortcomings, you'll find that it's easier to see the reasons for particular approaches in some circumstances. I'll cover a lot in these chapters, but that's mainly because your classes have a lot of potential in terms of capability.

In this chapter you will learn the following:

- How to use pointers and references with class types

- What a class destructor is and when you should implement one

- How to deal with dynamic memory allocation within a class

- When you must implement a copy constructor and how you do it

- How to limit access to a class

- What a nested class is

Pointers and References to Class Objects

In the last chapter, you saw how to declare and use pointers and references to class objects in the same way that you use them for basic data types. Pointers and references to class objects are key features of object-oriented programming, and they each provide particular advantages.

You can use a pointer to a class object in three basic contexts:

1. As a means of invoking operations on an object—that is, calling functions using the dereference operator, ->

2. As an argument to a function

3. As a data member of a class

The first of these enables you to call a function polymorphically, where the function called depends on the type of the object that is being pointed to. I'll investigate this capability extensively in Chapter 16.

When you pass a pointer to an object as an argument to a function, you avoid the copying that is implicit in the pass-by-value mechanism. This can vastly improve the efficiency of your program—especially if large objects are involved—because copying large objects is time-consuming.

If a class contains a pointer to an object as one of its data members, it allows a series of objects to be linked together; it can even allow objects of different types to be linked. This is essential when you want to organize data into structures like graphs or trees, or into the linked lists that I referred to briefly in Chapter 11. I'll come back to linked lists in a moment.

References to objects have importance as parameter types for functions. In general, passing a large object by reference is much faster than passing it by value, because you avoid the copying that is inherent in the pass-by-value mechanism. References are also fundamental in the implementation of the copy constructor, as you'll see.

NOTE *Later in this chapter, you'll also see that returning a pointer from a function has its advantages.*

Pointers As Data Members

You'll find it simple to declare a pointer as a data member of a class. Let's look at an example that I introduced back in Chapter 11—a linked list of objects. You can use this idea to put together a working example that uses a pointer as a data member of a class and also to draw together some of the topics that I covered in Chapter 12. You'll also see how even a simple class can produce unexpected complications that you'll have to learn to recognize and deal with.

NOTE *I should say here and now that you don't need to create your own linked list classes; very flexible versions are already defined in the standard library, and you'll explore these eventually. However, you can learn a lot by trying to put your own classes together to do this, and you'll learn how linked lists work as well.*

I'll also show you how to define a class that represents a collection of an arbitrary number of Box objects (where Box is the class that was introduced in Chapter 12). In this case, a Box object represents a unit of a product to be delivered, and your collection of Box objects represents a truckload of boxes, so you'll call the class TruckLoad. The TruckLoad class will help you plan how the truck should be loaded so that the driver can unload his or her deliveries in the right order.

Ultimately, you might use this arrangement, for example, in a program that a distribution office uses. For instance, the office might take orders for a product and arrange for their dispatch. The method of dispatch is by truck. In this model, the order in which the truck is loaded at the depot is crucial because the truck driver must be able to unload the boxes in the correct order at the various destinations on route.

A linked list is appropriate for such an application. You could use an array, but a linked list has two significant advantages. First, an array must be fixed in size when you declare it, whereas a linked list can be as long or as short as you need it to be; this assures efficient memory management. Second, because the distribution office employees plan each consignment, they may need to add to the list at the beginning, or the end, or in the middle. You can implement this facility efficiently in a linked list but not in array.

You want to be able to create a new TruckLoad object from a single Box object or from an array of Box objects, be able to add Box objects to a TruckLoad object, and be able to retrieve all the Box objects in the TruckLoad. You'll build the class step by step.

First consider how you're going to collect Box objects together so that they represent a coherent whole—a truckload. You need a programming device that can tie an arbitrary number of Box objects together. A Box object has no built-in facility for linking it with another Box object, and to start altering the definition of the Box class to incorporate this capability would be inconsistent with the idea of a box—boxes aren't like that.

One way to collect Box objects into a group is to define another kind of object, which we'll call a Package. A Package object has two key facilities: it can "contain" a Box object (see Figure 13-1), and it can be linked to another Package object.

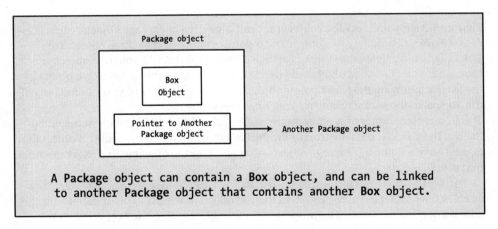

Figure 13-1. The contents of a Package object

Figure 13-1 shows how each Package object contains a Box object and also forms a link in a chain of Package objects, which are strung together using pointers. Hence, a Package object is simply an element that forms part of a list.

NOTE *The* Box/Package *relationship here illustrates how a* Package *acts as a container for a* Box *object and also provides a way to link to other* Package *objects. This concept is quite general and you could design container objects for objects of any kind in essentially the same way.*

In this case, a collection of Package objects, each containing a Box object, is created and managed by a TruckLoad object. The TruckLoad object represents an instance of a truckload of boxes. Any number of boxes may exist in the truckload and each box will be inside a package. The Package object provides the mechanism whereby the Truck-Load object can keep track of the Box objects it contains. The relationship between these objects is illustrated in Figure 13-2.

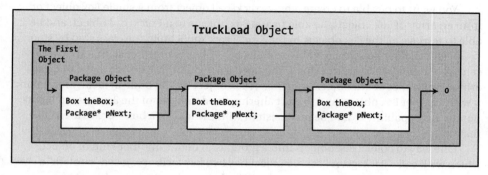

Figure 13-2. A linked list of three objects

Figure 13-2 shows a TruckLoad object that contains a list of Package objects; each Package object contains a Box object and a pointer to the next Package object. This TruckLoad object holds these three Package objects, but it could hold one object or a thousand. The TruckLoad object only needs to keep track of the first Package object in the list. By following the pNext pointer links in the Package objects, you can find any of the objects in the list by simply moving from one to the next.

In this elementary implementation, you'll only add Package objects at the end of the list. In this case, the constructor for the Package class needs to create an object that doesn't have a following Package object—that is, a Package object with a pNext member that is null.

To add a Package to the end of the list, define a function in the Package class that enables the pointer member, pNext, of the last object in the list to be updated with the address of the new object. The process that manages this is in the TruckLoad class, which represents the list.

NOTE *In a more advanced implementation, you'd find it relatively easy to implement a function that allows you to add Package objects at any point in the list. The standard library implementation of a linked list, list<>, that you'll meet in Chapter 20 supports this facility.*

Defining the Package Class

From the preceding discussion, when writing the Package class, your first instinct may be to design a class that has two data members: one of type Box and one of type *pointer to* Package:

```
class Package {
  public:
    Package(Box* pBox): theBox(*pBox), pNext(0){}  // Constructor

    Box getBox() const { return theBox; }           // Retrieve the Box object
    Package* getNext() const { return pNext; }      // Get next package address
    void setNext(Package* pPackage){ pNext = pPackage; }  // Add to end of list

  private:
    Box theBox;                                     // The Box object
    Package* pNext;                                 // Pointer to the next Package
};
```

Before you look into the other features of this class, seriously consider the consequences of implementing this class definition. When the Package constructor creates a Package object from a Box object, it initializes the data member theBox by dereferencing the pointer that's passed as an argument. Be aware of a very important issue here: the Package constructor creates a *duplicate* Box object.

Think about the physicality of this for a moment. The Package constructor creates a Package object by a copying a Box object (which already exists) and adding a *pointer to* Package. The first problem with this is the obvious waste of memory: why should a Package object have its own copy of a Box object, which already exists?

The second problem is a practical one that involves the copying procedure involved in this Package constructor. Every time you create a Package object, a Box object is copied, byte-by-byte, from its original location to the new object. The process of copying is generally a time-consuming one. If the objects being copied are large, or a large number of objects are copied within a single program, then your program is likely to be terribly inefficient. If you decide to increase the scale of your program in the future, then this could become a costly problem.

The third problem is also practical: if you have multiple copies of a single Box object, how can you be sure that they all carry the same values? Suppose, for some reason, the values of one Box object must be adjusted. How can you know that the object you've copied has been changed in some way? This is obviously not a very realistic proposition. Figure 13-3 illustrates what would happen if you tried to implement this version of the Package class.

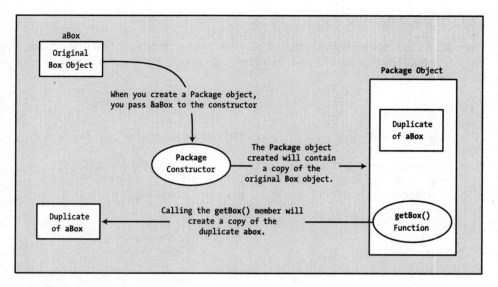

Figure 13-3. Copies of Box objects everywhere

As you can see, multiple copies of each Box object exist. The Package constructor generates one copy. Note that the getBox() member function (which makes the private Box data member available outside the Package class) also generates a copy of the Box data member, *each time it is called*. This is not only going to cause problems, it introduces considerable overhead in execution time and memory. To say this could get confusing is something of an understatement—it's clear that a Package class that contains a copy of an original Box object is not the way forward. You need to reconsider this aspect of the class design.

One solution is to design the Package class so that each Package object contains a pointer to the original Box object (rather than a copy of the Box object). The class definition then becomes

```
class Package {
  public:
    Package(Box* pNewBox):pBox(pNewBox), pNext(0){}       // Constructor
    Box* getBox() const { return pBox; }                  // Retrieve the Box pointer
    Package* getNext() const { return pNext; }            // Get next package address
    void setNext(Package* pPackage) { pNext = pPackage; } // Add to end of list

  private:
    Box* pBox;                                            // Pointer to the Box
    Package* pNext;                                       // Pointer to the next Package
};
```

This looks much more useful; at least you've eliminated the problems of your first attempt. Now you deal in pointers to Box objects throughout so that you don't duplicate Box objects. Figure 13-4 shows how the list looks with this definition for the Package class.

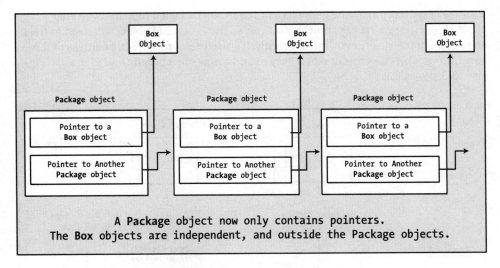

Figure 13-4. A list of packages containing only pointers

The getBox() function now allows access to the private Box* member of the Package class from outside the class. When you call the getNext() function for a particular Package object, it will return the address of the next Package object in the list (or the null pointer if the object is the last in the list).

The setNext() function updates the pointer to the next Package in the list. It stores the address that is passed as an argument to the function in the pNext pointer for the object. To add a new Package object to end of the list, simply pass its address to the setNext() function.

The Package class has enough capability for your needs at the moment. You can now use it to implement a list in the TruckLoad class.

 TIP *When developing container classes, such as this* TruckLoad *class, you'll need to consider carefully whether or not the data members of your class should be duplicates of the original objects. Sometimes it doesn't matter, but usually it does. Generally, when using containers, it is wise to avoid duplication if you can. Using pointers, as you've done here, is not the only solution. Later, you'll see how to use references to avoid copying objects.*

Defining the TruckLoad Class

A TruckLoad class represents a list of Package objects. The class must provide everything necessary to create and extend the list and also the means by which Box objects can be retrieved. If you store the address of the first Package object in the list as a data member of a TruckLoad object, then you can get to any of the other Package objects in the list by stepping through the chain of pNext pointers, using the getNext() function from the

Package class. Obviously, the getNext() function will be called repeatedly to step through the list one Package object at a time, so the TruckLoad object will need to track the object that was retrieved most recently. It's also useful to store the address of the last Package object, as this makes it easy to add a new object to the end of the list. Figure 13-5 shows this.

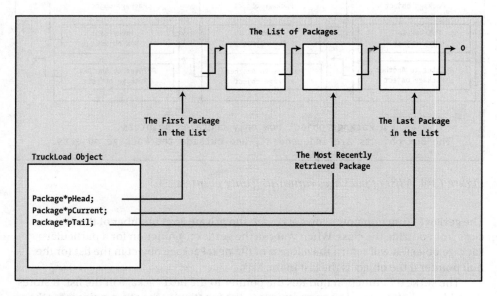

Figure 13-5. The information needed to work with the list

Think about how the process for retrieving Box objects from a TruckLoad object should work. The starting point is the first object in the list, so you'll need a function in the TruckLoad class to retrieve this. You could call it getFirstBox(). If you keep track of the Package that was retrieved most recently from a TruckLoad object, you can implement a getNextBox() function that will retrieve the Box object from the *next* Package object in the list and then update the record of the last Package object retrieved to reflect that. Another essential capability is the ability to add a Box to the list, so you'll also need a member function—addBox()—to do that.

Here's an initial definition for the TruckLoad class based on the ideas I've just discussed:

```
class TruckLoad {
  public:
    TruckLoad(Box* pBox = 0, int count = 1);    // Constructor

    Box* getFirstBox();                         // Retrieve the first Box
    Box* getNextBox();                          // Retrieve the next Box
    void addBox(Box* pBox);                     // Add a new Box to the list
```

```
    private:
       Package* pHead;                          // First in the list
       Package* pTail;                          // Last in the list
       Package* pCurrent;                       // Last retrieved from the list
};
```

Here you've declared all the data members as private, because you don't need any of them to be available outside the class. You've also declared one constructor for the class, but with the default values you've defined for the parameters, it serves as three. If you omit both arguments to the constructor, then it acts as a default constructor and creates an empty list. Omitting just the count argument creates a list containing a single Box object because count defaults to 1. Specifying both arguments creates a list containing the given number (count) of Box objects from the array pBox. You'll see how these are implemented in the definition for the TruckLoad constructor in a moment.

The member functions getFirstBox() and getNextBox() represent the mechanism for retrieving Box objects. Each of these needs to modify the pCurrent pointer, so you can't declare them as const member functions. The addBox() function also changes the list so you can't declare that as const either.

All of the member functions of the class require external definitions, so let's see how you'd put those together.

Implementing the TruckLoad Class

You can start with the constructor. This either creates a list of one or more Package objects from an array of Box objects, or it creates an empty list:

```
TruckLoad::TruckLoad(Box* pBox, int count) {
  pHead = pTail = pCurrent = 0;

  if((count > 0) && (pBox != 0))
    for(int i = 0 ; i<count ; i++)
      addBox(pBox+i);
}
```

This sets the data members of the class to 0 so that you start out with an empty list. If you have objects to add, then pBox will be non-null, and count will be positive, so check for this in the if condition. If both conditions are true, add the Box objects using the addBox() function member, which I'll get to in a moment. Each call of addBox() creates a Package object containing the Box object pointed to by the argument and adds this Package object to the list. Thus, in the for loop, add to the list the Box object pointed to by pBox, then pBox+1, then pBox+2, and so on.

 NOTE *Remember that incrementing a pointer by 1 increments it to point to the next object, so the address contained by* pBox *will be incremented by* sizeof(Box).

Defining the Member Functions

Let's define the addBox() function first, because we call that in the constructor:

```
void TruckLoad::addBox(Box* pBox) {
  Package* pPackage = new Package(pBox);   // Create a Package

  if(pHead)                                // Check list is not empty
    pTail->setNext(pPackage);              // Add the new object to the tail
  else                                     // List is empty
    pHead = pPackage;                      // so new object is the head
  pTail = pPackage;                        // Store its address as tail
}
```

The function creates a new Package object in the free store and stores its address in the local variable pPackage.

NOTE *It's possible that the operator* new *won't be able to allocate the memory required, but you'll ignore that problem here. You'll see how to deal with this when I discuss exception handling in Chapter 17.*

When you add an object to the list, consider whether or not the list is empty. If pHead is non-null, then the list is not empty, in which case you can add the new object to the end of the list by storing its address in the pNext member of the current tail **pTail**. If pHead is null, then the list is empty, so you can just store the address of the new object as the first member of the list. In this example, the new Package object is always added to the end of the list, so the data member pTail is updated to reflect this.

The getFirstBox() function definition is a piece of cake:

```
Box* TruckLoad::getFirstBox() {
  pCurrent = pHead;
  return pCurrent->getBox();
}
```

The address of the first Package object in the list is stored in pHead, and so you store that address in pCurrent. Then you call the getBox() function for the Package object to obtain the address of the Box object, which you return.

The getNextBox() function can access the *next* Package object via the getNext() function of the most recent Package object that was retrieved, but you must allow for the possibility that pCurrent may be null. The code defining getNextBox() is as follows:

```
Box* TruckLoad::getNextBox() {
  if(pCurrent)
    pCurrent = pCurrent->getNext();      // pCurrent is not null so set to next
  else                                   // pCurrent is null
    pCurrent = pHead;                    //  so set to the first list element

  return pCurrent ? pCurrent->getBox() : 0;
}
```

In the normal course of events, when pCurrent contains the valid address of a Package object, you call the getNext() function of the current Package object to obtain the address of the next one. If pCurrent is null, then you simply go back to the beginning of the list. All this is handled in the if-else statement. Of course, it is possible that you have run off the end of the list, and in this case, you have to set pCurrent to null; in this case you use a conditional statement to return 0. If you attempt to call the function getBox() with a null value in pCurrent, then the program fails. (You have not yet considered deleting elements from the list, but when you do, you'll also be able to end up with an empty list.) The null value returned enables you to detect when you have reached the end of a list: you simply check the pointer returned from the getNextBox() function.

Although you seem to have assembled all the bits and pieces that you need to create and use your list, you'll soon discover that you still have a serious problem with using the TruckLoad class. However, let's throw caution to the wind, try it out in an example, and then come back to the outstanding problem afterward.

Try It Out: Using a Linked List

You can put together a complete definition for the Box class in the header file, Box.h:

```
// Box.h - Definition of the Box class
#ifndef BOX_H
#define BOX_H
class Box {
  public:
    Box(double aLength = 1.0, double aWidth = 1.0,
                             double aHeight = 1.0);  // Constructor

    double volume() const;                           // Calculate Box volume

    double getLength()  const;
    double getWidth() const;
    double getHeight()  const;

    int compareVolume(const Box& otherBox) const;   // Compare volumes of boxes

  private:
    double length;
    double width;
    double height;
};
#endif
```

You have added functions to access the dimensions of a Box object, as you'll need them in your example.

(Continued)

You'll define the constructor and member functions in a separate .cpp file for this class, Box.cpp:

```
// Box.cpp Implementation of the Box class
#include "Box.h"

// Constructor
Box::Box(double aLength, double aWidth, double aHeight) {
    length = aLength > 0.0 ? aLength : 1.0;
    width = aWidth > 0.0 ? aWidth : 1.0;
    height = aHeight > 0.0 ? aHeight : 1.0;
}

// Calculate Box volume
double Box::volume() const{ return length*width*height; }

// getXXX() functions
double Box::getLength()  const { return length; }
double Box::getWidth() const { return width; }
double Box::getHeight()  const { return height; }

// Function to compare two Box objects
// If the current Box is greater than the argument, 1 is returned
// If they are equal, 0 is returned
// If the current Box is less than the argument -1 is returned
int Box::compareVolume(const Box& otherBox) const {
    double vol1 = volume();                      // Get current Box volume
    double vol2 = otherBox.volume();             // Get argument volume
    return vol1>vol2 ? 1 : (vol1<vol2 ? -1 : 0);
}
```

You can put the definitions for the two classes that implement a linked list in the same header file, List.h. To be consistent, rearrange the Package class definition so that the constructor and functions are defined in List.cpp. The file contents will be as follows:

```
// List.h classes supporting a linked list
#ifndef LIST_H
#define LIST_H

#include "Box.h"

// Class defining a list element
class Package {
  public:
    Package(Box* pNewBox);                       // Constructor
    Box* getBox() const;                         // Retrieve the Box pointer
    Package* getNext() const;                    // Get next package address
    void setNext(Package* pPackage);             // Add package to end of list
```

```
  private:
    Box* pBox;                              // Pointer to the Box
    Package* pNext;                         // Pointer to the next Package
};


// Class defining a TruckLoad - implements the list
class TruckLoad {
  public:
    TruckLoad(Box* pBox = 0, int count = 1);   // Constructor

    Box* getFirstBox();                     // Retrieve the first Box
    Box* getNextBox();                      // Retrieve the next Box
    void addBox(Box* pBox);                 // Add a new Box to the list

  private:
    Package* pHead;                         // First in the list
    Package* pTail;                         // Last in the list
    Package* pCurrent;                      // Last retrieved from the list
};
#endif
```

Note that the definition for the Package class precedes that of the TruckLoad class. If the order were reversed, then the code wouldn't compile, because the TruckLoad class refers to the Package type.

 NOTE *Sometimes you can find a situation with two classes, A and B, where each class definition contains references to the other class. In such a scenario, the name, A, must be declared as a class before class B is defined. The definition for class A can then follow that of class B. The declaration of class A is made with the following statement:*

```
class A;      // The name A is a class
```

This tells the compiler that A is a class, so it can go ahead and compile class B. The compiler then knows about class B so that it can compile the definition of class A.

The member function definitions can go in a file with the name List.cpp:

```
// List.cpp
#include "Box.h"
#include "List.h"

// Package class definitions
// Package constructor
Package::Package(Box* pNewBox):pBox(pNewBox), pNext(0){}
```

(Continued)

```cpp
// Retrieve the Box pointer
Box* Package::getBox() const { return pBox; }

// Get next package address
Package* Package::getNext() const { return pNext; }

// Add package to end of list
void Package::setNext(Package* pPackage) { pNext = pPackage; }

// TruckLoad class member definitions
// TruckLoad constructor
TruckLoad::TruckLoad(Box* pBox, int count) {
  pHead = pTail = pCurrent = 0;

  if((count > 0) && (pBox != 0))
    for(int i = 0 ; i<count ; i++)
      addBox(pBox+i);
}

// Retrieve the first Box
Box* TruckLoad::getFirstBox() {
  pCurrent = pHead;
  return pCurrent->getBox();
}

// Retrieve the next Box
Box* TruckLoad::getNextBox() {
  if(pCurrent)
    pCurrent = pCurrent->getNext();        // pCurrent is not null so set to next
  else                                     // pCurrent is null
    pCurrent = pHead;                      //  so set to the first list element

  return pCurrent ? pCurrent->getBox() : 0;
}

// Add a new Box to the list
void TruckLoad::addBox(Box* pBox) {
  Package* pPackage = new Package(pBox);   // Create a Package

  if(pHead)                                // Check list is not empty
    pTail->setNext(pPackage);              // Add the new object to the tail
  else                                     // List is empty
    pHead = pPackage;                      // so new object is the head
  pTail = pPackage;                        // Store its address as tail
}
```

CAUTION *Member functions declared as* const *in the class definition must be declared as* const *when you define them. The function signature includes* const, *which means that if you forget to specify them as* const *in the function definitions, the compiler thinks that they are different functions from those that appear in the class definition.*

Notice that the file List.h *contains an* #include *directive for the definition of the* Box *class. In fact you have, a number of* #include *directives for header files. In particular, the file* List.cpp *contains* #include *directives for* Box.h *and* List.h. *The* #ifndef/#endif *preprocessing directives in each header file—which I introduced in Chapter 10—prevent any definitions from appearing in a source file more than once. Without them, the file* List.cpp *won't compile, because it would include the definitions of* Box.h *twice: once directly, and once indirectly, by including* List.h.

You can define main() in the file prog13_01.cpp to create some Box objects and then organize them in a linked list. You'll generate two lists: one by that contains a single Box object and then adds further objects, and the other from an array of Box objects. You can use a version of the random() function that you wrote in Chapter 10 to generate Box dimensions. To exercise the lists, search each of them for the largest Box object. Here's the code:

```
// Program 13.1 Exercising a linked list of Box objects    File: prog13_01.cpp
#include <iostream>
#include <cstdlib>              // For random number generator
#include <ctime>               // For time function

using std::cout;
using std::endl;

#include "Box.h"
#include "List.h"

// Function to generate a random integer 1 to count
inline int random(int count) {
  return 1 + static_cast<int>
          (count*static_cast<double>(std::rand())/(RAND_MAX+1.0));
}


int main() {
  const int dimLimit = 100;            // Upper limit on Box dimensions
  std::srand((unsigned)std::time(0)); // Initialize the random number generator

  // Create an empty list
  TruckLoad load1;
```

(Continued)

```
// Add 10 random sized Box objects to the list
for(int i = 0 ; i < 10 ; i++)
  load1.addBox(new Box(random(dimLimit), random(dimLimit), random(dimLimit)));

// Find the largest Box in the list
Box* pBox = load1.getFirstBox();
Box* pNextBox;
while(pNextBox = load1.getNextBox())  // Assign & then test pointer to next Box
  if(pBox->compareVolume(*pNextBox) < 0)
    pBox = pNextBox;

cout << endl
     << "The largest box in the first list is "
     << pBox->getLength() << " by "
     << pBox->getWidth() << " by "
     << pBox->getHeight() << endl;

const int boxCount = 20;            // Number of elements in Box array
Box boxes[boxCount];                // Array of Box objects

for(int i = 0 ; i < boxCount ; i++)
  boxes[i] = Box(random(dimLimit), random(dimLimit), random(dimLimit));

TruckLoad load2(boxes, boxCount);

// Find the largest Box in the list
pBox = load2.getFirstBox();
while(pNextBox = load2.getNextBox())
  if(pBox->compareVolume(*pNextBox) < 0)
    pBox = pNextBox;

cout << endl
     << "The largest box in the second list is "
     << pBox->getLength() << " by "
     << pBox->getWidth() << " by "
     << pBox->getHeight() << endl;

// Delete the Box objects in the first list
pNextBox = load1.getFirstBox();
while(pNextBox) {
  delete pNextBox;
  pNextBox = load1.getNextBox();
}
return 0;
}
```

When I ran this example, I obtained this output:

```
The largest box in the first list is 94 by 68 by 55

The largest box in the second list is 80 by 73 by 78
```

You'll almost certainly get something different from this, because of the random numbers generated for the dimensions of the Box objects. You'll recall (from Chapter 10) that the random number generator is seeded from your computer's clock.

HOW IT WORKS

The function main() creates two lists of Box objects. In the absence of any real Box objects, you generate some randomly sized ones whose dimensions are pseudo-random integer values between 1 and 100. The random dimensions are generated by the function defined as follows:

```cpp
inline int random(int count) {
  return 1 + static_cast<int>
          (count*static_cast<double>(std::rand())/(RAND_MAX+1.0));
}
```

This calls the standard library function rand(), which as we have already seen, produces pseudo-random integers between 0 and RAND_MAX. You initialize this process by calling the standard library function srand() with a seed value that you specify as the current clock time because this provides a different seed each time a program executes. You scale the value returned by the function rand() to produce values between 0 and count-1 and than add 1 so that numbers between 1 and count are returned by random(). You cast the value returned by rand() to type double to ensure that the multiplication is done with double values. Otherwise you could get a value that exceeds the capacity of int.

You use the default version of the constructor for TruckLoad to create an empty list:

```cpp
TruckLoad load1;
```

You then use a for loop to add ten Box objects with random dimensions to the list load1:

```cpp
for(int i = 0 ; i < 10 ; i++)
  load1.addBox(new Box(random(dimLimit), random(dimLimit), random(dimLimit)));
```

On each loop iteration, you create a Box object in the free store, and add it to the list using the addBox() function. You don't need to keep track of any of these objects because their addresses are stored in the list.

(Continued)

You scan the list to find the Box object with the largest volume like this:

```
Box* pBox = load1.getFirstBox();
Box* pNextBox;
while(pNextBox = load1.getNextBox()) // Assign & then test pointer to next Box
  if(pBox->compareVolume(*pNextBox) < 0)
    pBox = pNextBox;
```

In this part of the program, the pointer pBox is used to store the address of the *largest* object. To begin, pBox is arbitrarily set to the first object in the list. The while loop is controlled by the address returned by the getNextBox() function for load1. It's important to notice that the while loop condition contains an assignment (=) rather than the comparison (==); hence, the expression tested in the while loop is the resulting pNextBox *after* the assignment has been made. The comment in the code indicates this; if it didn't, another programmer might misinterpret the code. Your compiler may also issue a warning message because using an assignment in this way is often an error. When the value of pNextBox is zero, this indicates that you've reached the end of the list, and so the loop terminates.

Within the loop, use the compareVolume() function in the Box class to compare the volumes of the Box pointed to by pBox and the Box object at the current position in the list, which is pointed to by pNextBox. You must use the ->> operator to call compareVolume() because you're calling it through a pointer, pBox. The function requires the argument to be an object of type Box, so you have to dereference the pNextBox pointer. If the return value is negative, then the argument is greater than the object pointed to by pBox, so you store its address in pBox as the new largest object. When the loop ends, pBox will contain the address of the Box object in the list with the largest volume.

You then display the dimension of this Box object, with this statement:

```
cout << endl
     << "The largest box in the first list is "
     << pBox->getLength() << " by "
     << pBox->getWidth() << " by "
     << pBox->getHeight() << endl;
```

You repeat the same process with a second list, load2, which you create from an array of Box objects.

Note that the Box objects in the first list were created in the free store, whereas the Box objects in the array are local objects. Therefore you need to delete the Box objects in the first list when you're done.

Well, everything seems to work OK, and you get the right answers, so what's wrong with the TruckLoad class? In fact, you need to look into three problems:

1. The least significant problem is that the Package class is accessible to all, even though you only want to use this class in the context of the TruckLoad class.

2. A somewhat more serious problem (although it's not evident in this particular example) concerns the duplication of a TruckLoad object. Suppose you take a TruckLoad object load1, and create a direct copy of it, load2. The result is that load2 is *not* independent of load1, because not only do both lists contain pointers to the same Box objects, but they also contain pointers to the same Package objects. If you deleted load2, the objects that belonged to the load1 list would cease to exist because they'd be deleted as a part of load2.

3. The third problem is one of memory management. Look again at how you create Package objects in the TruckLoad class. They're created in the free store, and yet no provision has been made for deleting them. Every time you add a new Box to a list, a new Package object will be created that is never deleted, even when the TruckLoad object goes out of scope. This is a very serious memory leak that you shouldn't ever overlook.

Let's look at how to deal with each of these problems, starting with the first.

Controlling Access to a Class

The need to limit the accessibility of a class arises quite often in practice. You designed the Package class to be used specifically with the TruckLoad class, and therefore you should really make sure that Package objects can only be created by functions in the TruckLoad class. What you really need is a mechanism by which you can declare Package objects as public to the Truckload class but private to the rest of the world. The best way to do this is by using the concept of a nested class.

Nested Classes

A **nested class** is a class that has its definition inside the definition of another class. The name of the nested class is within the scope of the enclosing class. We could put the definition of the Package class inside the definition of the TruckLoad class, like this:

```
class TruckLoad {
  public:
    TruckLoad(Box* pBox = 0, int count = 1);   // Constructor

    Box* getFirstBox();                        // Retrieve the first Box
    Box* getNextBox();                         // Retrieve the next Box
    void addBox(Box* pBox);                    // Add a new Box to the list

  private:
    // Class defining a list element
    class Package {
      public:
        Box* pBox;                             // Pointer to the Box
        Package* pNext;                        // Pointer to the next Package
```

```
        void setNext(Package* pPackage);              // Add package to end of list
        Package(Box* pNewBox);                        // Constructor
    };

    Package* pHead;                                   // First in the list
    Package* pTail;                                   // Last in the list
    Package* pCurrent;                                // Last retrieved from the list
};
```

The Package type is now local to the scope of the TruckLoad class definition. Because you've put the definition of the Package class in the private section of the TruckLoad class, it is not possible to create Package objects from outside the TruckLoad class.

Because the Package class is entirely private to the TruckLoad class, you can make the Package members public. Hence, they're directly accessible to function members of a TruckLoad object, so you can dispense with the Package member functions getBox() and getNext(). All of the Package members will be inaccessible outside the class.

You also need to modify the definitions of the member functions of the TruckLoad class. The addBox() function can add a new object to the end of the list by accessing the pNext member of the last object directly:

```
void TruckLoad::addBox(Box* pBox) {
  Package* pPackage = new Package(pBox);    // Create a Package

  if(pHead)                                 // Check list is not empty
    pTail->pNext = pPackage;                // Add the new object to the tail
  else                                      // List is empty
    pHead = pPackage;                       // so new object is the head
  pTail = pPackage;                         // Store its address as tail
}
```

The function to retrieve the first Box object no longer requires a function to get at the pointer to the Box object, so the definition now becomes

```
Box* TruckLoad::getFirstBox() {
  pCurrent = pHead;
  return pCurrent->pBox;
}
```

The function to obtain the address of the next Box object in the list can now be defined as:

```
Box* TruckLoad::getNextBox() {
  if(pCurrent)
    pCurrent = pCurrent->pNext;            // pCurrent is not null so set to next
  else                                     // pCurrent is null
    pCurrent = pHead;                      //  so set to the first list element

  return pCurrent ? pCurrent->pBox : 0;
}
```

NOTE *Nesting the* Package *class inside the* TruckLoad *class simply defines the* Package *type. Objects of type* TruckLoad *aren't affected in any way—they'll have exactly the same members as before.*

Function members of a nested class can directly reference static members of the enclosing class, as well as any other types or enumerators defined in the enclosing class. Other members of the enclosing class can only be accessed from the nested class in the normal ways: via a class object, or a pointer, or a reference to a class object.

Nested Classes with Public Access Specifiers

Of course, you could put the Package class definition in the public section of the TruckLoad class. This would mean that the Package class definition was part of the public interface so it *would* be possible to create Package objects externally. Because the Package class name is within the scope of the TruckLoad class, you can't use it by itself. You must qualify the Package class name with the name of the class in which it is nested. Here's an example:

```
TruckLoad::Package aPackage(aBox);       // Define a variable of type Package
```

Of course, making the type Package public in your example would rather defeat the rationale for making it a nested class in the first place! Of course, you'll find yourself in other circumstances where you want a nested class to be public.

Friend Classes

It's also possible to control access to members of a class by using the friend class facility. You could declare all the members of the Package class as private, for instance, and then declare the class to be a friend of the Truckload class by including the following statement in the Package class definition:

```
friend class Truckload;
```

This declaration makes all the members of Package objects available to objects of the Truckload class, even if they're private. The private members of the Package class would be otherwise inaccessible outside of the class.

 NOTE *In subsequent examples in this chapter, we'll employ the concept of nested classes. This concept reinforces the idea that* Package *class is not an independent entity and only has a role in the context of* Truckload *objects.*

The Importance of the Copy Constructor

You use a copy constructor to create a new object that is identical to an existing object. In the context of Program 12.5, I mentioned that the compiler supplies a default copy constructor if you don't include one in the class definition. The default copy constructor works by copying the values of the data members of the original object into the corresponding data members of the newly created object.

Simply copying the values of data members when creating a duplicate object can cause problems in some circumstances, and it certainly does so in the case of the TruckLoad class. Suppose that you want to duplicate a TruckLoad object—say, if you were to repeat the same delivery schedule on two different days. When you duplicate a TruckLoad class object, the default copy constructor simply copies the addresses stored in the data members pHead, pTail, and pCurrent to the new object. The result is that both TruckLoad objects share the same chain of Package objects, as shown in Figure 13-6.

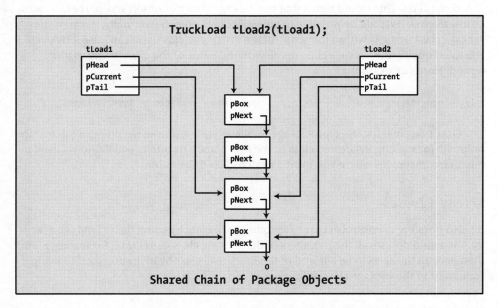

Figure 13-6. Duplicating an object using the default copy constructor

You don't really have two lists here at all, just one. However, you do have two different ways to access the list; this is where the danger lies. A modification to the list using tLoad1, say, affects the chain of Package objects, but this change won't be reflected in the data members of tLoad2. In particular, if you add to the list tLoad1, then the pTail member of tLoad2 points to a Package object that is no longer the last in the list.

In fact, there is a further subtlety. You are likely to experience similar problems if you create a function that takes a TruckLoad argument. Remember that the copy constructor is called when a function receives an argument via the pass-by-value mechanism. Therefore, the function call uses the TruckLoad copy constructor to create a duplicate of the original TruckLoad object. Then the function that is being called only needs to add an object to the list to invalidate the original TruckLoad object.

Implementing the Copy Constructor

The copy constructor for an object must accept an argument of the same class type and create a duplicate in an appropriate manner. This poses an immediate problem that you must overcome; you can see it clearly if you try to write the copy constructor for the TruckLoad class as follows:

```
TruckLoad::TruckLoad(TruckLoad Load) {
  // Code to create a duplicate of the object Load
}
```

This looks OK at first, but consider what happens when the constructor is called. The argument is passed *by value*, so the compiler arranges to call the copy constructor to make a copy of the argument. Of course, the argument to the copy constructor is passed by value, so another call to the copy constructor is required, and so on. In short, you've set up a recursive call to the copy constructor.

In fact, your compiler won't allow this code to compile. The solution is to specify the parameter as a reference.

Reference Parameters

The copy constructor should be defined, with a const reference parameter, as follows:

```
TruckLoad::TruckLoad(const TruckLoad& Load) {
  // Code to create a duplicate of the object Load
}
```

Now the argument is no longer passed by value, so the recursive calls to the copy constructor are avoided. Instead, the compiler simply initializes the parameter with the object that is passed to it by reference. The parameter should be const because a copy constructor is only in the business of creating duplicates; it should not modify the original. You can conclude from this that the parameter type for a copy constructor is *always* a const reference to an object of the same class. In other words, the form of the copy constructor is the same for any class:

```
Type::Type(const Type& object) {
  // Code to produce a duplicate of object
}
```

In this general form of the copy constructor, Type is the class type name.

So, how should you implement the copy constructor for your TruckLoad class? You must create a chain of duplicate Package objects for the new TruckLoad object that you're creating. You could do this with the following code for the TruckLoad class that has the Package class nested within it:

```
// TruckLoad copy constructor
TruckLoad::TruckLoad(const TruckLoad& load) {
  pHead = pTail = pCurrent = 0;
  if(load.pHead == 0)
    return;

  Package* pTemp = load.pHead;        // Saves addresses for new chain
  do {
    addBox(pTemp->pBox);
  }while(pTemp = pTemp->pNext);        // Assign and then test pointer to next Box
}
```

If pHead for the load object is null, the list is empty, so you're done. If it isn't null, you execute the loop. The loop steps through the list of Package objects in the original list that is stored in the load object. The pTemp pointer starts out pointing to the first in this list, and the loop condition assigns the address of the next in the list as well as testing it for null. You create a new Package object that corresponds to each Package object in the original list by calling addBox() and passing the address of the Box object pointed to in the original Package object. You get the address of the Box object by using pTemp to access the pBox pointer in the original Package object. The addBox() function automatically takes care of updating the pNext pointer in previous the Package object in the new list with the address of the new object in the chain.

Let's see if your version works.

Try It Out: Using a Copy Constructor

You'll need the files Box.h and Box.cpp just as in Program 13.1. You'll use the nested TruckLoad/Package class discussed earlier, and add the copy constructor, so that List.h contains the following class definition:

```
class TruckLoad {
  public:
    TruckLoad(Box* pBox = 0, int count = 1);   // Constructor
    TruckLoad(const TruckLoad& load);          // Copy constructor

    Box* getFirstBox();                        // Retrieve the first Box
    Box* getNextBox();                         // Retrieve the next Box
    void addBox(Box* pBox);                    // Add a new Box to the list

  private:
    // Class defining a list element
    class Package {
```

```
    public:
        Box* pBox;                          // Pointer to the Box
        Package* pNext;                     // Pointer to the next Package

        void setNext(Package* pPackage);    // Add package to end of list
        Package(Box* pNewBox);              // Constructor
    };

    Package* pHead;                         // First in the list
    Package* pTail;                         // Last in the list
    Package* pCurrent;                      // Last retrieved from the list
};
```

The prototype for the TruckLoad copy constructor has been added here, as a public member of the class. The file List.cpp must be updated to contain its definition; you must also update the definitions of the TruckLoad member functions addBox(), getFirstBox(), and getNextBox(), and remove the definitions of Package member functions getBox() and getNext(). The final amendment to List.cpp is to update the qualifications of the other Package member definitions so the file contents will be as follows:

```
// List.cpp
#include "Box.h"
#include "List.h"

// Package class definitions
// Package constructor
TruckLoad::Package::Package(Box* pNewBox):pBox(pNewBox), pNext(0){}

// Add package to end of list
void TruckLoad::Package::setNext(Package* pPackage) { pNext = pPackage; }


// TruckLoad class member definitions
// TruckLoad constructor
TruckLoad::TruckLoad(Box* pBox, int count) {
  pHead = pTail = pCurrent = 0;

  if((count > 0) && (pBox != 0))
    for(int i = 0 ; i<count ; i++)
      addBox(pBox+i);
}

// TruckLoad copy constructor
TruckLoad::TruckLoad(const TruckLoad& load) {
  pHead = pTail = pCurrent = 0;
  if(load.pHead == 0)
    return;
```

(Continued)

```
        Package* pTemp = load.pHead;        // Saves addresses for new chain
        do   {
          addBox(pTemp->pBox);
        }while(pTemp = pTemp->pNext);        // Assign and then test pointer to next Box

    }

    // Retrieve the first Box
    Box* TruckLoad::getFirstBox() {
      pCurrent = pHead;
      return pCurrent->pBox;
    }

    // Retrieve the next Box
    Box* TruckLoad::getNextBox() {
      if(pCurrent)
        pCurrent = pCurrent->pNext;    // pCurrent is not null so set to next
      else                             // pCurrent is null
        pCurrent = pHead;              //   so set to the first list element

      return pCurrent ? pCurrent->pBox : 0;
    }

    // Add a new Box to the list
    void TruckLoad::addBox(Box* pBox) {
      Package* pPackage = new Package(pBox);   // Create a Package

      if(pHead)                                // Check list is not empty
        pTail->pNext = pPackage;               // Add the new object to the tail
      else                                     // List is empty
        pHead = pPackage;                      // so new object is the head
      pTail = pPackage;                        // Store its address as tail
    }
```

You'll create a TruckLoad object with just three box objects this time. You can use the copy constructor to copy the existing TruckLoad object, and then extend it. Because you'll want to find the Box object with the largest volume from several lists, it will be better if you put the code to do that into a separate function. Here's the code:

```
// Program 13.2 Exercising the copy constructor     File: prog13_02.cpp
#include <iostream>
#include <cstdlib>                 // For random number generator
#include <ctime>                   // For time function

using std::cout;
using std::endl;

#include "Box.h"
#include "List.h"
```

```
// Function to generate a random integer 1 to count
inline int random(int count) {
  return 1+static_cast<int>
            (count*static_cast<double>(std::rand())/(RAND_MAX+1.0));
}

// Find the Box in the list with the largest volume
Box* maxBox(TruckLoad& Load) {
  Box* pBox = Load.getFirstBox();
  Box* pNextBox;
  while(pNextBox = Load.getNextBox())  // Assign & then test pointer to next Box
    if(pBox->compareVolume(*pNextBox) < 0)
      pBox = pNextBox;
  return pBox;
}

int main() {
  const int dimLimit = 100;            // Upper limit on Box dimensions
  std::srand((unsigned)std::time(0));  // Initialize the random number generator

  // Create a list
  TruckLoad load1;

  // Add 3 Boxes to the list
  for(int i = 0 ; i < 3 ; i++)
    load1.addBox(new Box(random(dimLimit), random(dimLimit), random(dimLimit)));

  Box* pBox = maxBox(load1);           // Find the largest Box in the first list

  cout << endl
       << "The largest box in the first list is "
       << pBox->getLength()  << " by "
       << pBox->getWidth() << " by "
       << pBox->getHeight()  << endl;

  TruckLoad load2(load1);              // Create a copy of the first list

  pBox = maxBox(load2);               // Find the largest Box in the second list

  cout << endl                        // Display it
       << "The largest box in the second list is "
       << pBox->getLength()  << " by "
       << pBox->getWidth() << " by "
       << pBox->getHeight()  << endl;

  // Add 5 more boxes to the second list
  for(int i = 0; i<5; i++)
    load2.addBox(new Box(random(dimLimit), random(dimLimit), random(dimLimit)));

  pBox = maxBox(load2);              // Find the largest Box in the extended list
  cout << endl                       // Display it
```

```
                << "The largest box in the extended second list is "
                << pBox->getLength()  << " by "
                << pBox->getWidth() << " by "
                << pBox->getHeight()  << endl;

    // Count the number of boxes in the first list and display the count
    Box* pNextBox = load1.getFirstBox();
    int count = 0;                          // Box count
    while(pNextBox) {                       // While there is a box
      count++;                              // Increment the count
      pNextBox = load1.getNextBox();        // and get the next box
    }
    cout << endl << "First list still contains "
        << count << " Box objects."<< endl;

    // Delete the Box objects in the free store
    pNextBox = load2.getFirstBox();
    while(pNextBox) {
      delete pNextBox;
      pNextBox = load2.getNextBox();
    }
    return 0;
}
```

When I ran this, it produced the following output:

```
The largest box in the first list is 44 by 92 by 87

The largest box in the second list is 44 by 92 by 87

The largest box in the extended second list is 55 by 83 by 85

First list still contains 3 Box objects.
```

You'll certainly get something different, and you may have to run the example a few times to get the largest box in the extended list to be different from that in the first list.

HOW IT WORKS

Your new function, maxBox(), accepts a TruckLoad object as its argument. It returns a pointer to the Box object in this truckload that has the greatest volume. The code for this function is taken from the body of the main() function of Program 13.1. Note that the parameter is a reference so that you don't incur the overhead of copying what might be a substantial list.

To demonstrate that the TruckLoad class copy constructor works as it should, you first create an empty TruckLoad object, load1:

```
  TruckLoad load1;
```

You then add Box objects to the list, as you did in Program 13.1. Each Box object is created in the free store:

```
for(int i = 0 ; i < 3 ; i++)
   load1.addBox(new Box(random(dimLimit), random(dimLimit), random(dimLimit)));
```

For checking purposes, you obtain the most voluminous Box object in the list by calling the maxBox() function:

```
Box* pBox = maxBox(load1);            // Find the largest Box in the first list
```

After displaying the dimensions of this Box object, you create a copy of load1 using the TruckLoad class copy constructor:

```
TruckLoad load2(load1);               // Create a copy of the first list
```

You use maxBox() again to obtain the largest Box object contained in load2, and display its dimensions. This indicates that load2 is the same as the original. Then you add a further five Box objects to the list load2:

```
for(int i = 0; i<5; i++)
   load2.addBox(new Box(random(dimLimit), random(dimLimit), random(dimLimit)));
```

Next, you use the maxBox() function again with load2 to find the largest of all eight boxes in the list, and display its dimensions.

```
pBox = maxBox(load2);            // Find the largest Box in the extended list
cout << endl                     // Display it
     << "The largest box in the extended second list is "
     << pBox->getLength() << " by "
     << pBox->getWidth() << " by "
     << pBox->getHeight() << endl;
```

To demonstrate that load1 has not been modified as a result of your additions to load2, you count the number of Box objects contained in load1:

```
Box* pNextBox = load1.getFirstBox();
int count = 0;                      // Box count
while(pNextBox) {                   // While there is a box
   count++;                         // Increment the count
   pNextBox = load1.getNextBox();   // and get the next box
}
```

The loop is controlled by the pointer pNextBox. To begin with, it contains the address of the first Box object. As long as pNext is not null, you increment count and move pNext to the next in the list. When you reach the end of the list, getNextBox() returns null, so the loop ends.

Finally, after displaying the value of count, you delete all the Box objects in load2 from the free store. Of course, this includes the objects contained in load1, so you don't need to delete them explicitly.

(Continued)

Your TruckLoad class is put together on the assumption that the user takes responsibility for the Box objects stored. The user could create them in the free store, as you did in the example, or they could be automatic objects—your class works just as well. Giving the user of your class responsibility for Box objects means that he or she has the power to invalidate a TruckLoad object by deleting a Box object from the free store. One way to do this would be to duplicate and then delete a TruckLoad object. You can prevent the user from doing this, quite simply, by declaring the TruckLoad copy constructor as a private member of the class. This prevents its use outside the class and inhibits the compiler from generating a default version. Because it could not be used in that case, you wouldn't need to provide a definition for it.

Dynamic Memory Allocation Within an Object

Let's move on to the third of the problems with the TruckLoad class that I identified earlier. It's another serious problem—a memory leak—and it arises because the TruckLoad class constructors (including the copy constructor) and the addBox() function allocate memory dynamically.

Members that are created dynamically are allocated memory in the free store. Because your code allocated the memory, your code is responsible for freeing it. You must always release the free store memory for an object before you lose track of the address of the object. Without the address of where the object is located in the free store, you have no way to release the memory subsequently. If you repeatedly fail to release free store memory (in a loop for instance) and you succeed in filling the free store, then your program fails.

 NOTE *Of course, the memory will always be reclaimed by the operating system when your program finishes, but that's not much help to your program while it is executing.*

This is different from creating a new object dynamically. When you create an object in the free store, the new operator allocates the space for it and the constructor is called to create the object. It is not the constructor that allocates the space, but the code that causes the constructor to be called. When you no longer need the object, you can release the memory it occupies by using the delete operator in the way you've seen because the code that created the object still has its address. Here you're allocating space in the free store for objects that are tracked internally to the TruckLoad object. The class constructors and the addBox() function are causing free store memory to be allocated and the addresses are stored in members of the object. The only way this memory can be released is by explicitly using the delete operator with these addresses to release it. To do this, you must be able execute the code that is necessary to release the memory at the point when a TruckLoad object is destroyed.

What Is a Destructor?

In fact, there is another kind of class member that will help you release memory when necessary called a **destructor**. The compiler always supplies a destructor by default, and the destructor is *always* called when an object is destroyed. You'll almost never need to call a destructor explicitly, but you'll often need to define one.

The default destructor doesn't release free store memory that you have allocated within a class object because that's your responsibility. In fact, the default destructor does nothing. However, you can always replace the default constructor with your own version.

Defining the Destructor

The destructor for a class always has the same form. It is a `public` member function with the same name as the class, preceded by a tilde ~. The class destructor doesn't have any parameters, and it doesn't return a value. Whereas a class can have several constructors, it can only ever have one destructor. For the `TruckLoad` class, the class destructor would be defined like this:

```
TruckLoad::~TruckLoad() {
  // Code to destroy the object
}
```

 CAUTION *It's an error to specify a return type or parameters for a destructor.*

The Default Destructor

Just like the default constructor, the compiler generates the default destructor in the absence of any explicit destructor being provided with a class. If you don't define a destructor for a class, the compiler always supplies one that is `public` and `inline`.

Each of the objects that you've used up to now has caused its default destructor to be called when it was explicitly deleted from the free store or when it went out of scope if it was an automatic variable. You can see this happening by adding an explicit destructor to each of the classes in the previous example.

Try It Out: The Destructor in Action

You can modify Program 13.2 by adding a definition of a destructor to each of the classes. You need to amend the Box class definition by adding the following destructor definition to the file Box.cpp:

```
// Box destructor
Box::~Box() {
  cout << "Box destructor called." << endl;
}
```

Don't forget the #include directive for <iostream> and using declarations for cout and endl.

You also need to add the destructor prototype to the public section of the Box class definition, in Box.h:

```
class Box {
  public:
    ~Box();        // Box destructor

    // Rest of the class as before....
};
```

You can add destructor definitions for the Package and TruckLoad classes to List.cpp in a similar way:

```
// TruckLoad destructor
TruckLoad::~TruckLoad() {
  cout << "TruckLoad destructor called." << endl;
}

// Package destructor
TruckLoad::Package::~Package() {
  cout << "Package destructor called." << endl;
}
```

Of course, you need to add the prototypes to the class definition in the List.h header file:

```
class TruckLoad {
  public:
    ~TruckLoad();          // TruckLoad destructor

    // other TruckLoad public member declarations

  private:
    class Package {
      public:
        ~Package();        // Destructor
```

```
        // Rest of Package class definition...
    };

    // Rest of TruckLoad class definition...
};
```

For each `.cpp` file, you'll also need to include the standard header file `<iostream>`, and add using declarations for `cout` and `endl`.

You'll use the same `main()` function code that you used in Program 13.2.

// Program 13.3 Exercising and tracing the destructor   File:prog13_03.cpp

```
// Code as Program 13.2 ...
```

If you compile and run this example, you'll get a trace of all the destructor calls that occur during program execution.

HOW IT WORKS

Let's go through the output to see what is happening in the program. You may find some of what is going on surprising. The first part of the output is something like the following:

```
The largest box in the first list is 52 by 83 by 93

The largest box in the second list is 52 by 83 by 93

The largest box in the extended second list is 52 by 83 by 93

First list still contains 3 Box objects.
```

Nothing should surprise you so far. Next, you have a record of eight Box destructor calls, followed by two `TruckLoad` destructors call:

```
Box destructor called.
Box destructor called.
Box destructor called.
Box destructor called.
Box destructor called.
Box destructor called.
Box destructor called.
Box destructor called.
TruckLoad destructor called.
TruckLoad destructor called.
```

(Continued)

The eight Box destructor calls occur because you explicitly delete the Box objects that you allocated in the free store for the first list, load1:

```
pNextBox = load2.getFirstBox();
while(pNextBox) {
  delete pNextBox;
  pNextBox = load2.getNextBox();
}
```

Without this code, the memory wouldn't be released until after the program was terminated. When return is executed in main(), the two TruckLoad objects go out of scope, which causes the TruckLoad class destructor calls just listed.

Notice that no Package destructor calls exist. This means that all those Package objects were created, but they were never deleted. The memory for all the Package objects was allocated dynamically, so it is your responsibility to delete these objects. Because you didn't, their destructors are never called. This is a serious defect. Let's fix it now.

Implementing a Destructor

The responsibility for deleting the Package objects should lie with the object that created them. Because Package objects are created by TruckLoad objects, you can address the problem by implementing a suitable destructor for the TruckLoad class. When a TruckLoad object is destroyed, it needs to delete each Package object in its list. You can implement this within the TruckLoad class destructor. Replace the destructor definition in the List.cpp file with the following:

```
TruckLoad::~TruckLoad() {
  cout << "TruckLoad destructor called." << endl;
  while(pCurrent = pHead->pNext) {
    delete pHead;                    // Delete the previous
    pHead = pCurrent;                // Store address of next
  }
  delete pHead;                      // Delete the last
}
```

If you run the example with this version of the TruckLoad destructor, you'll get the following output:

```
The largest box in the first list is 98 by 79 by 78

The largest box in the second list is 93 by 68 by 99

The largest box in the extended second list is 89 by 98 by 78

First list still contains 3 Box objects.
```

```
Box destructor called.
Box destructor called.
Box destructor called.
Box destructor called.
Box destructor called.
Box destructor called.
Box destructor called.
Box destructor called.
TruckLoad destructor called.
Package destructor called.
Package destructor called.
Package destructor called.
Package destructor called.
Package destructor called.
Package destructor called.
Package destructor called.
Package destructor called.
TruckLoad destructor called.
Package destructor called.
Package destructor called.
Package destructor called.
```

After each `TruckLoad` destructor call, call the `Package` destructor the appropriate number of times—once for each `Package` object that was created. This is due entirely to the code that you've just added to the destructor for the `TruckLoad` class. Because there were three objects in the first list and eight in the second, it's clear from the output that the `TruckLoad` objects are being destroyed in the reverse order from which they were created.

Out of all this comes a golden rule:

GOLDEN RULE *If you allocate memory dynamically within an object, you must implement a destructor for the class.*

References in Classes

You've seen how being able to use a reference as a function parameter type is fundamental to writing a copy constructor—it's the only way it can be done. You'll encounter lots of other situations where using a reference parameter is highly advantageous, because it avoids the copying implicit in the pass-by-value mechanism. In the next chapter, you'll see that returning a reference from a member function can be important too.

You may also use a reference as a data member of a class. This does not come up very often, but you need to take a closer look at this, because references require special consideration in this context.

References As Members of a Class

To demonstrate how to declare a data member as a reference, use a reference to a Box object (instead of a *pointer to* Box) as a data member of the Package class. The basic definition of the amended Package class within the TruckLoad class will be as follows:

```
class Package {
    public:
        Box& rBox;                          // Reference to the Box
        Package* pNext;                     // Pointer to the next Package

        ~Package();                         // Destructor

        void setNext(Package* pPackage);    // Add package to end of list
        Package(Box& rNewBox);              // Constructor
};
```

The definition of the constructor, in List.cpp, should be changed to this:

```
TruckLoad::Package::Package(Box& rNewBox):rBox(rNewBox), pNext(0){}
```

You know that you should always initialize ordinary data members in the initializer list where you can because it's more efficient, but with reference data members, you don't have a choice. A reference is an alias for another name, so you can't initialize it in an assignment within a constructor—you *must* use the initializer list.

Consider how storing a reference to a Box object affects the function members of the TruckLoad class. You'll look at the addBox() member first. You can change the parameter to a reference and pass the reference to the Package class constructor:

```
void TruckLoad::addBox(Box& rBox) {
  Package* pPackage = new Package(rBox);  // Create a Package

  if(pHead)                               // Check list is not empty
    pTail->pNext = pPackage;              // Add the new object to the tail
  else                                    // List is empty
    pHead = pPackage;                     // so new object is the head
  pTail = pPackage;                       // Store its address as tail
}
```

You should also adjust the function prototype appropriately. This changes the way that the addBox() function is used. It now requires an object as an argument, not as a pointer. A disadvantage of this is that the function call doesn't provide any clues that tell you that the argument is passed by reference. You must also change the parameter in the declaration of this function within the definition of the TruckLoad class.

You'll still want the possibility of passing an array to the TruckLoad class constructor so that you could leave the parameter list as it is, but you must now pass the array to the addBox() function as a reference:

```
TruckLoad::TruckLoad(Box* pBox, int count) {
  pHead = pTail = pCurrent = 0;

  if((count > 0) && (pBox != 0))
    for(int i = 0 ; i<count ; i++)
      addBox(*(pBox+i));
}
```

The only change is to dereference the pointer pBox+i so that you pass an object to addBox() rather than an address.

The copy constructor calls the addBox() member, so you must change the definition of that, too:

```
TruckLoad::TruckLoad(const TruckLoad& load) {
  pHead = pTail = pCurrent = 0;
  if(load.pHead == 0)
    return;

  Package* pTemp = load.pHead;        // Saves addresses for new chain
  do  {
    addBox(pTemp->rBox);
  } while(pTemp = pTemp->pNext);      // Assign and then test pointer to next Box
}
```

The getFirstBox() and getNextBox() currently return pointers. Should you change these so that they return a reference? You can decide on the answer to this question by considering how you use the return value. You access successive Box objects in a list by successive calls to the getNextBox() function in the TruckLoad class, and you detect the end of a list by a null return value. You can't do this with a reference return type because a null reference doesn't exist. Therefore, these functions should continue to return a *pointer to* Box.

You must make the following adjustment to the definition of getFirstBox():

```
Box* TruckLoad::getFirstBox() {
  pCurrent = pHead;
  return &pCurrent->rBox;
}
```

You just return the address of the reference to the Box object in the Package object. You don't need parentheses in the expression that does this, because the -> operator is of higher precedence than the address-of operator.

The definition of getNextBox() should be changed to the following:

```
Box* TruckLoad::getNextBox() {
  if(pCurrent)
    pCurrent = pCurrent->pNext;       // pCurrent is not null so set to next
  else                                // pCurrent is null
    pCurrent = pHead;                 // so set to the first list element

  return pCurrent ? &pCurrent->rBox : 0;
}
```

The constructor for the TruckLoad class is unaffected so you have completed all the changes necessary to use a reference in the Package class.

If you want to run the last version of main() with this version of the classes, you must alter the argument passed to addBox() in main() to an object—you just need to dereference the address returned by the operator new in both instances. You must change the first of these statements to the following:

```
load1.addBox(*(new Box(random(dimLimit), random(dimLimit), random(dimLimit))));
```

 NOTE *Also, don't forget that you've changed the function signature for the* addBox() *function, so you'll need to reflect that change in the function prototype!*

Changing your classes to use references has demonstrated some of the implications of using a reference as a class member, but it doesn't improve the classes. The solution using pointers is preferable. When you use references to dynamic objects, you always risk the object being deleted, so the reference becomes an alias for a nonexistent object.

Summary

In this chapter, you've learned about the basic set of parts you can put together in implementing your own classes. What you need to implement in a particular class is up to you. You need to decide the nature and scope of the facilities that each of your classes should provide. Always keep in mind that you are defining a data type—a coherent entity—and that your class needs to reflect its nature and characteristics.

The important points you've seen in this chapter include the following:

- You can only initialize class members that are references through the constructor's initializer list. A reference can't be initialized with an assignment statement.

- A copy constructor is called whenever you pass an object by value to a function. The consequence of this is that the parameter to the copy constructor for a class must be a reference.

- If you allocate memory dynamically within a member function of a class, always implement a destructor to release memory, a copy constructor, and the copy assignment operator.

- You can limit access to a class by declaring all its members as private. Then, only friend classes can create objects of the class type.

- A nested class is a class that has its definition inside that of another class. The nested class name is within the scope of the enclosing class. To refer to the nested class type from outside the enclosing class, the type name must be qualified by the name of the enclosing class.

- If a nested class definition is placed in the `private` section of the enclosing class, objects of the nested class type can't be created outside the enclosing class.

Exercises

The following exercises enable you to try out what you've learned in this chapter. If you get stuck, look back over the chapter for help. If you're still stuck after that, you can download the solutions from the Apress website (`http://www.apress.com/book/download.html`), but that really should be a last resort.

Exercise 13-1. Write a class called Sequence to store an ascending, incremental sequence of integer values in the free store. The length and starting value of a sequence are specified as arguments of the constructor. Ensure that a sequence always has at least two values and make the default a sequence of ten values starting at zero (0, 1, 2, 3, 4, 5, 6, 7, 8, 9). You'll need to allocate enough memory to hold the sequence and then fill the memory with the requisite values.

Provide a show() function to list the sequence so that you can be sure Sequence objects are being created correctly.

Make sure that any memory that you allocate to hold the sequence is freed when Sequence objects are destroyed. (Note: be certain that you release *all* the memory!) Demonstrate the operation of the class by creating and outputting five sequences of random length (limited!) and a default sequence.

Exercise 13-2. Write a function to compare two sequences for equality. Sequence objects are different if they're different lengths or if they're the same length but their corresponding values differ. They're equal when they're of the same length and their corresponding values are the same. Write this function as a member of the Sequence class.

Exercise 13-3. Rewrite the comparison function to be a friend of the Sequence class. How will you have to change the arguments and the way in which you call it? Which technique do you think is better?

Exercise 13-4a. Although the standard library includes a string class, creating your own class to encapsulate strings provides a very good introduction to the issues involved in designing and writing a "real" C++ class. You can write one using the basic char data type, and you'll see as you progress how it's possible to hide much of the complexity involved in using C-style strings.

Start by creating a header file for a MyString class, putting it into its own namespace. Give the class two private data members: an integer length, and a char* that points to the string that the object is managing. Why is it useful to store the length as a data member of the class?

Exercise 13-4b. Create an implementation (.cpp) file for your class, and provide constructors so that MyString objects can be constructed from the following data types:

- A string literal (e.g., of type const char*), so that you can write:

  ```
  MyString s1("hello");
  ```

- A single character repeated a number of times. The default repeat value should be one. An example of using this constructor would be

  ```
  MyString s2('c', 5);
  ```

- An integer value, so that MyString s3(10) would store the string "10".

Do you think that these constructors ought to be explicit or not?

Make sure that the constructors provide error handling wherever necessary.

Exercise 13-4c. The constructors allocate memory to hold the string. Provide a destructor so that the memory is properly released when the object is destroyed.

Exercise 13-4d. Write a copy constructor for the class so that your MyString objects can be created and initialized from other strings.

Exercise 13-4e. Add some member functions to the class that

- Return the length of the string

- Output the string

- Find the zero-based position of a character or substring within the string, returning –1 if it isn't found

Now you can write a test program to create and manipulate MyString objects in various ways. Satisfy yourself that everything works the way it should.

CHAPTER 14

Operator Overloading

IN THIS CHAPTER, you'll be exploring how to add support for operators (such as add and subtract) to your classes so that they can be applied to objects of a class type. This will make the types that you define behave more like C++'s fundamental data types.

You've already seen how your classes can have member functions that operate on the data members of an object, but you can do much more than that. With operator overloading, you can write functions that enable the C++ basic operators so that they can be applied to your class objects.

In this chapter you will learn the following:

- What C++ operators you can implement for your own data types

- How to implement functions in your classes that overload operators

- How to implement operator functions as class members and as ordinary functions

- When you must implement the assignment operator

- How to define type conversions as operator functions

- What smart pointers are

Implementing Operators for Your Classes

Your Box class that you developed in Chapters 12 and 13 was designed so that it could be applied in an application that is primarily concerned with the volume of a box. For such an application, you obviously need the ability to compare box volumes so that you can determine the relative sizes of the boxes. In Chapter 12, you implemented the compareVolume() function in the Box class to compare the volume of two objects, but wouldn't it be nice if you could write the following:

```
if(Box1 < Box2)
  // Do something...
```

instead of this rather clumsy looking call:

```
if(Box1.compareVolume(Box2) < 0)
  // Do something...
```

You might also like to add the volumes of two Box objects with an expression such as Box1 + Box2, or even select the third Box in a list of Box objects with an expression like load1[2]. Well, it's quite possible to do all of this and more by implementing functions that overload the basic operators for a class.

Operator Overloading

Operator overloading enables you to apply standard operators (such as +, -, *, <, and so on) to objects of your own data types. To do this, you write a function that redefines each operator that you want to use with your class objects so that it performs a particular action every time it is applied to objects of your class.

For example, in order to use the < operator with Box objects, you could write a member function in the Box class that defines the operator's behavior. In this case, you're interested in the volume of a Box object, so you could define the function to return true if the volume of the first Box object is smaller than that of the second. The name of such a function in this case would be operator<().

In general, the name of a function that overloads a given operator is composed of the keyword operator, followed by the operator that you are overloading. In the case of operators that use alphabetic characters, such as new and delete, you must place at least one space between the keyword and the operator itself. For other operators, the space is optional.

Operators That Can Be Overloaded

Operator overloading doesn't allow you to invent new operators. Also, you can't change the precedence of an operator or the number of operands, so your overloaded version of an operator will have the same priority in the sequence of evaluating an expression as the original base operator. You can find a table showing the precedence of all the operators in Appendix D.

Although you can't overload all the operators, the restrictions aren't particularly oppressive. Table 14-1 lists the operators that you *can't* overload.

Table 14-1. Operators You Can't Overload

Operator	Symbol
The scope resolution operator	::
The conditional operator	?:
The direct member access operator	.
The dereference pointer to class member operator	.*
The sizeof operator	sizeof

NOTE *You haven't met the pointer to class member operator yet, but you will in Chapter 16.*

Also, you can't overload the preprocessor directive symbol, #, or the token pasting symbol, ##. Anything else is fair game, which gives you quite a bit of scope. As you'll see, a function that overloads an operator for a particular class doesn't necessarily have to be a member of the class; it can be an ordinary function. I'll show you examples of both.

NOTE *Obviously, it's a good idea to ensure that your version of a standard operator is reasonably consistent with its normal usage, or at least reasonably intuitive in its meaning and operation in the context of your class. It wouldn't be very sensible to produce an overloaded + operator for a class that performed the equivalent of a multiply on class objects.*

The best way to understand how operator overloading works is to step through an example, so let's implement what I just referred to—the less-than operator (<) for the Box class.

Implementing an Overloaded Operator

To overload an operator for a class, you just have to write an operator function. A binary operator implemented as a member of a class has one parameter, which I'll explain in a moment, and you can add the following prototype for the function to overload the < operator to the Box class definition:

```
class Box {
  public:
    bool operator<(const Box& aBox) const;    // Overloaded 'less-than' operator

    // The rest of the Box class
};
```

Because you're implementing a comparison here, the return type is bool. Your operator function operator<() will be called as a result of an expression comparing two Box objects using <. When it is called, the argument to the function will be the right operand of the < operator and the left operand will correspond to the current object that is pointed to by this. Because the function doesn't change either operand, you've specified the parameter and the function as const.

To see how this works, consider the following `if` statement:

```
if(box1 < box2)
    cout << "box1 is less than box2" << endl;
```

The test expression between the parentheses will result in your operator function being called. The expression is equivalent to the function call `box1.operator<(box2)`. Indeed, if you were so inclined, you could write it like this in the `if` statement:

```
if(box1.operator<(box2))
    cout << "box1 is less than box2" << endl;
```

You can see that being able to use the `<` operator with the `Box` object will make the code much more readable.

Now that you know how the operands in the expression `box1 < box2` map to the function call, you can implement the overloaded operator quite easily. The definition of the member function to overload the `<` operator is shown in Figure 14-1.

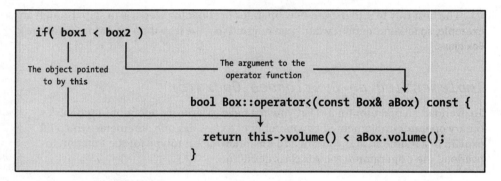

```
if( box1 < box2 )
```

The object pointed to by this

The argument to the operator function

```
bool Box::operator<(const Box& aBox) const {
    return this->volume() < aBox.volume();
}
```

Figure 14-1. Overloading the less than operator

Here you use a reference parameter to the function to avoid unnecessary copying of the argument when the function is called. The `return` expression uses the member function `volume()` to calculate the volume of the `Box` object pointed to by `this` and compares the result (using the basic `<` operator) with the volume of the `aBox` object. Thus, the Boolean value `true` is returned if the `Box` object pointed to by the `this` pointer has a smaller volume than the `aBox` object passed as a reference argument—and `false` is returned otherwise.

NOTE *Here, I have used the* this *pointer just to show the association with the first operand. It isn't necessary to use* this *explicitly.*

Let's see if this works.

....

Try It Out: Using an Overloaded < Operator

You can exercise the overloaded less than operator for Box objects with an example. As in the previous chapter, the definition of the Box class is contained in the header file Box.h, and you'll add the definition of the overloaded operator function operator<() to what you had in the class previously:

```cpp
// Box.h - Definition of the Box class
#ifndef BOX_H
#define BOX_H

class Box {
  public:
    // Constructor
    Box(double aLength = 1.0, double aWidth = 1.0, double aHeight = 1.0);

    double volume() const;                        // Calculate Box volume

    double getLength()  const;
    double getWidth() const;
    double getHeight()  const;

    bool operator<(const Box& aBox) const {       // Overloaded 'less-than' operator
      return volume() < aBox.volume();            // Defined inline
    }

  private:
    double length;
    double width;
    double height;
};
#endif
```

Notice that you've defined the overloaded operator as an inline function, it will be more efficient if it is compiled as such. The definitions for the other member functions will be contained in Box.cpp as follows:

```cpp
// Box.cpp
#include "Box.h"

// Box constructor
Box::Box(double aLength, double aWidth, double aHeight):
        length(aLength), width(aWidth), height(aHeight) {}

// Calculate Box volume
double Box::volume() const {
  return length*width*height;
}

// getXXX() functions
double Box::getLength()  const { return length; }
double Box::getWidth() const { return width; }
double Box::getHeight()  const { return height; }
```

(Continued)

Overloading the comparison operators makes the compareVolume() member superfluous so you can dispense with it.

Let's exercise the overloaded < operator by finding the largest element in an array of Box objects. Here's the code to do that:

```cpp
// Program 14.1 Exercising the overloaded 'less-than' operator  File: prog14_01.cpp
#include <iostream>
#include <cstdlib>              // For random number generator
#include <ctime>               // For time function
using std::cout;
using std::endl;

#include "Box.h"

// Function to generate random integers from 1 to count
inline int random(int count) {
  return 1+static_cast<int>
            (count*static_cast<double>(std::rand())/(RAND_MAX+1.0));
}

int main() {
  const int dimLimit = 100;             // Upper limit on Box dimensions
  std::srand((unsigned)std::time(0)); // Initialize the random number generator

  const int boxCount = 20;              // Number of elements in Box array
  Box boxes[boxCount];                  // Array of Box objects

  for(int i = 0 ; i < boxCount ; i++)
    boxes[i] = Box(random(dimLimit), random(dimLimit), random(dimLimit));

  // Find the largest Box object in the array
  Box* pLargest = &boxes[0];

  for(int i = 1 ; i < boxCount ; i++)
    if(*pLargest < boxes[i])
      pLargest = &boxes[i];

  cout << endl
       << "The box with the largest volume has dimensions: "
       << pLargest->getLength()  << " by "
       << pLargest->getWidth() << " by "
       << pLargest->getHeight()  << endl;
  return 0;
}
```

When I ran this example, it produced the following output:

```
The box with the largest volume has dimensions: 76 by 92 by 90
```

Random numbers being what they are, you'll most probably get a different result.

HOW IT WORKS

The function `main()` first creates an array of `Box` objects. You arbitrarily assume that the first array element is the largest, and store its address with this statement:

```
Box* pLargest = &boxes[0];
```

Then you compare the `Box` object at the address contained in the pointer `pLargest` with each of the succeeding array elements:

```
for(int i = 1 ; i < boxCount ; i++)
  if(*pLargest < boxes[i])
    pLargest = &boxes[i];
```

The comparison in the `if` results in your `operator<()` function being called. The argument to the function is `boxes[i]`, and the `this` pointer points to the `Box` object pointed to by `pLargest`. If `boxes[i]` has a larger volume than the `Box` object pointed to by `pLargest`, then the result of the comparison is `true`, so you save the address of `boxes[i]` as the new largest `Box` object. You use a pointer here because it's much more efficient than the alternative:

```
Box largest = boxes[0];
for(int i = 1 ; i < boxCount ; i++)
  if(largest < boxes[i])
    largest = boxes[i];          // Copies the object from the array
```

You have more overhead in this code than in the original. Every time a `Box` object is stored in the variable `largest` within the loop, the object in the `boxes` array has to be copied to the `largest` object, member by member. Exactly how much time this requires depends on the size and complexity of the objects, but it'll certainly be more than when you use a pointer, because then only the address is copied. A further overhead arises with this code because each time you store a new copy of a `Box` object in `largest`, the old object that was stored must be destroyed so the destructor will be called.

When you exit the loop, the pointer `pLargest` contains the address of the largest `Box` object in the array, so you output the dimensions of the largest object using the pointer:

```
cout << endl
     << "The box with the largest volume has dimensions: "
     << pLargest->getLength()  << " by "
     << pLargest->getWidth() << " by "
     << pLargest->getHeight()  << endl;
```

Global Operator Functions

The volume() function is a public member of the Box class, so you could implement the overloaded < operator as an ordinary function—a **global operator function**—outside of the class. In this case, the definition of the function would be

```
inline bool operator<(const Box& Box1, const Box& Box2) {
  return Box1.Volume()<Box2.Volume();
}
```

Here, you've declared operator<() to be an inline function, because you want it to be compiled as such if possible. With the operator defined in this fashion, the code in main() in the previous example would work in exactly the same way. Of course, you must not declare this version of the operator function as const; const can only be applied to functions that are members of a class.

NOTE *When you specify a member function as* const, *you are saying it doesn't modify the object for which it's called, so in this context,* const *applies specifically to the object to which the function belongs.*

Even if an operator function needed access to private members of the class, it would still be possible to implement it as an ordinary function by declaring it as a friend function of the class. Generally, though, if a function must access private members of a class, then it is better practice to define it as a class member.

Implementing Full Support for an Operator

Implementing an operator such as < for a class creates an expectation. You can write expressions like Box1 < Box2, but what about Box1 < 25.0, or 10 < Box2? Your operator function, operator<(), won't handle either of these. When you start to implement an overloaded operator for a class, you need to consider the likely range of circumstances in which the operator might be used.

NOTE *When you use the basic < operator, to compare a* float *value with a value of type* int *for example, the compiler automatically converts one of the operands to the same type as the other before implementing the comparison. This is because the basic < operator can only compare two numerical values of the same type. The situation in the context of* Box *objects is a little different. You need to overload the < operator so that the meaning of comparisons in which a* Box *object is involved makes sense. Here you're comparing volumes (which implies each operand is a volume)—either a value that is a volume or the volume of a* Box *object.*

You can quite easily support the various possibilities you have for comparing Box volumes. Let's first add a function that compares the volume of a Box object that is the first operand with a second operand of type double. You'll define it as an inline function with the definition outside the class in this instance, just to see how it's done. You need to add the following prototype to the public section of Box class definition:

```
bool operator<(double aValue) const;    // Compare Box volume < double value
```

The Box object will be passed to the function as the implicit pointer this, and the double value is passed as an argument. Implementing this function is as easy as the first operator function—there's just one statement in the body of the function:

```
// Function to compare volume of a Box object with a constant
inline bool Box::operator<(double aValue) const {
  return volume() < aValue;
}
```

This definition should follow the class declaration in Box.h. An inline function shouldn't be defined in a separate .cpp file, because the definition of an inline function must appear in every source file that uses it. Putting it together with the class definition ensures this will always be so.

Dealing with an expression like 10 < box2 isn't any harder; it's just different. A *member* operator function always provides the this pointer as the left operand. Because, in this case, the left operand is of type double, you can't implement the operator as a member function. That leaves you with two choices: to implement the function as an ordinary global operator function, or to implement it as a friend function. Because you don't need to access any private members of the class, you can implement it as an ordinary function:

```
// Function comparing a constant with volume of a Box object
inline bool operator<(const double aValue, const Box& aBox) {
  return aValue < aBox.volume();
}
```

You now have three overloaded versions of the < operator for Box objects, so as well as expressions like box1 < box2, you can handle things such as box1 < 2.5 * box2.volume(), or even 0.5 * (box1.Volume() + box2.Volume()) < box3. Either operand for the < operator can be any expression that results in a value of type double, or a Box object. Let's see that in action.

....

Try It Out: Complete Overloading of the < Operator

In this example, in addition to the operator function, you'll add a function to the Box class that will display the dimensions of an object. This makes the code in main() more compact. To update the Box.h file from Program 14.1, first remove the old operator<() function definition, and then add the prototypes to the public section of the class definition:

```
bool operator<(const Box& aBox) const;        // Compare Box < Box
bool operator<(const double aValue) const;     // Compare Box < double value
```

Then add the following inline member function definitions to Box.h following the class definition:

```
// Function comparing Box object < Box object
inline bool Box::operator<(const Box& aBox) const {
  return volume() < aBox.volume();
}

// Function comparing Box object < double value
inline bool Box::operator<(const double aValue) const {
  return volume() < aValue;
}
```

Finally, add the global operator function definition to the end of Box.h:

```
// Function comparing double value < Box object
inline bool operator<(const double aValue, const Box& aBox) {
  return aValue < aBox.volume();
}
```

You should place these three operator function definitions between the end of the Box class definition and the #endif directive. You've included the definition for all the operator functions in the header file, Box.h, because they're all inline. Only definitions for member functions that are not inline should go in a .cpp file. Therefore, the Box.cpp file is unchanged from Program 14.1.

You can apply the new operators to finding all the Box objects in an array that have a volume between specified limits. Here's the code to do that:

```
// Program 14.2 Exercising the overloaded 'less-than' operators File: prog14_02.cpp
#include <iostream>
#include <cstdlib>                // For random number generator
#include <ctime>                  // For time function
using std::cout;
using std::endl;

#include "Box.h"
```

```
// Function to generate random integers from 1 to count
inline int random(int count) {
  return 1+static_cast<int>
                 (count* static_cast<double>(std::rand())/(RAND_MAX+1.0));
}

// Display box dimensions
void show(const Box& aBox) {
  cout << endl
       << aBox.getLength() << " by " << aBox.getWidth() << " by " <<
aBox.getHeight();
}

int main() {
  const int dimLimit = 100;            // Upper limit on Box dimensions
  std::srand((unsigned)std::time(0));  // Initialize the random number generator

  const int boxCount = 20;             // Number of elements in Box array
  Box boxes[boxCount];                 // Array of Box objects

  for(int i = 0 ; i < boxCount ; i++)
    boxes[i] = Box(random(dimLimit), random(dimLimit), random(dimLimit));

  // Find the largest Box object in the array
  Box* pLargest = &boxes[0];

  for(int i = 1 ; i < boxCount ; i++)
    if(*pLargest < boxes[i])
      pLargest = &boxes[i];

  cout << endl
       << "The largest box in the array has dimensions:";
  show(*pLargest);

  int volMin = 100000.0;               // Lower Box volume limit
  int volMax = 500000.0;               // Upper Box volume limit
  // Display details of Box objects between the limits
  cout << endl << endl
       << "Boxes with volumes between "
       << volMin << " and " << volMax << " are:";
  for(int i = 0 ; i < boxCount ; i++)
    if(volMin < boxes[i] && boxes[i] < volMax)
      show(boxes[i]);

  cout << endl;
  return 0;
}
```

(Continued)

When I ran the example, I got the following output:

```
The largest box in the array has dimensions:
100 by 79 by 99

Boxes with volumes between 100000 and 500000 are:
92 by 38 by 46
76 by 83 by 44
83 by 78 by 18
31 by 87 by 83
93 by 15 by 90
62 by 64 by 88
```

HOW IT WORKS

The function show() displays the dimensions of the Box object that is passed as an argument. This is just a convenient function that you'll use in main().

The first part of main() creates an array of Box objects and finds the Box with the largest volume, as before. This exercises the original version of operator<() that you defined as a member of the Box class. You try out the two new operator functions that you've added in the code that lists all Box objects with volumes between volMin and volMax. These are found in the following loop:

```
for(int i = 0 ; i < boxCount ; i++)
  if(volMin < boxes[i] && boxes[i] < volMax)
    show(boxes[i]);
```

The if expression calls both new versions of the operator. The subexpression volMin < boxes[i] is equivalent to operator<(volMin, boxes[i]) and the expression boxes[i] < volMax is equivalent to calling the member function with the expression boxes[i].operator < (volMax). To display the dimensions of a Box object that meets the criteria, simply pass it to the show() function.

 NOTE Any *comparison operator can be implemented in much the same way as you've implemented the less than operator. They would only differ in the minor details; the general approach to implementing them would be exactly the same.*

Operator Function Idioms

All the binary operators that can be overloaded always have operator functions of the form that you've seen in the previous section. When an operator X is being overloaded, and the left operand is an object of the class for which X is being overloaded, the *member* function defining the overload is of the following form:

```
Return_Type operator X(Type RightOperand);
```

The Return_Type depends on what the operator does. For comparison and logical operators, it is typically bool (although you could use int). Operators such as + and * need to return an object in some form, as you'll see.

When you implement a binary operator using a *non-member* function, it is of the form:

```
Return_Type operator X(Class_Type LeftOperand, Type RightOperand);
```

Here, Class_Type is the class for which you are overloading the operator X. If the left operand, of type Type, for a binary operator is not implemented as a member of the class Type, then it must be implemented as a *global* operator function that is of this form:

```
Return_Type operator X(Type LeftOperand, Class_Type RightOperand);
```

When you implement unary operators as member functions of a class, they don't require a parameter in general, although the increment and decrement operators are exceptions to this, as you'll see. For example, the general form of a unary operator function for the operation Op as a member of the class Class_Type looks like this:

```
Class_Type& operator Op();
```

Unary operators implemented as *global* operator functions have a single parameter that is the operand. As a non-member function, the operator function for the unary operator Op could be declared as follows:

```
Class_Type& operator Op(Class_Type&);
```

Note that for all operator functions—either as member functions or as global operator functions—you have no flexibility in the number of parameters. You must use the number of parameters specified for the particular operator.

I won't go through examples of overloading every operator, as most of them are similar to the ones you've already seen. However, I *will* give you a closer look at those operators that have particular idiosyncrasies when you overload them.

Overloading the Assignment Operator

The assignment operator is the operator =, and is referred to as such to distinguish it from the operators +=, *=, and so on. The implementation of the assignment operator for a class copies from an object of a given type (on the right of an assignment) to another of the same type (on the left). You call the assignment operator when you write the following:

```
Box box1;
Box box2(10, 10, 10);
box1 = box2;          // Call the assignment operator
```

If you don't provide an overloaded assignment operator function to copy objects of your class, the compiler provides a default version: operator=().

It's interesting to note what happens if you define an extremely simple class, such as a class with just a single data member:

```
class Data {
  public:
    int value;
};
```

Depending on how you use it, what you may actually be getting, courtesy of your compiler, is this:

```
class Data {
  public:
    int value;

    Data(){}                                    // Default constructor
    ~Data(){}                                   // Destructor

    Data(const Data& aData) : Value(aData.value) {}   // Copy constructor

    Data& operator=(const Data& aData) {        // Assignment operator
      value = aData.value;
      return *this;
    }
};
```

The default version of the assignment operator simply provides a member-by-member copying process, similar to that of the default copy constructor.

CAUTION *Don't confuse the copy constructor with the assignment operator function; they are definitely not the same. The copy constructor is called when a class object is created and initialized with an existing object of the same class, or when an object is passed to a function by value. The assignment operator function is called when the left side and the right side of an assignment statement are objects of the same class type.*

For your Box class, the default assignment operator works with no problem, but for any class that has members allocated dynamically, you need to look carefully at the requirements placed on it. Your program may not work correctly if you don't implement an assignment operator under these circumstances. The problems are similar to those that I discussed when I covered the copy constructor. If you apply the default assignment operator to objects with dynamic memory allocation, you'll end up with two objects sharing objects in the free store so that the two objects become interdependent. A change to one object can render the other invalid.

Your TruckLoad class, from Chapter 13, is a case in point. Member-wise copying of one TruckLoad to another results in both objects sharing the same list; that was the problem you had to overcome in Chapter 13. The solution is simple: implement the assignment operator so that the parts of an object created dynamically are duplicated properly. This is not all that it needs to do though, as you'll see.

 NOTE *In fact, any class that has problems with the default copy constructor will also have problems with the default assignment operator. If you need to implement one, you also need to implement the other—and the destructor too.*

Implementing the Assignment Operator

Let's look at what the function has to do. An assignment has two operands: the right operand is the object being copied, whereas the left operand is the destination for the assignment, which ends up as a copy of the right operand. You'll do all the copying within the operator function, so what should the return type be? Do you actually need to return anything?

Take a look at how your function is applied in practice. With normal usage of the assignment operator, you'd be able to write this:

```
load1 = load2 = load3;
```

These are three variables of type TruckLoad, and you're making load1 and load2 copies of load3. Because the assignment operator is right associative, this is equivalent to

```
load1 = (load2 = load3);
```

Because the result of the rightmost assignment is evidently the right operand for the leftmost assignment operation, you definitely need to return something. In terms of the member function `operator=()`, this statement is equivalent to

```
load1.operator=(load2.operator=(load3));
```

It is clear from this that whatever you return from `operator=()` can end up as the argument to another `operator=()` call. Because the parameter for `operator=()` is a reference to an object, you can conclude that the function must return the object that is the left operand. Further, if you are to avoid unnecessary copying, the return type must be a reference to this object.

The process for duplicating the right operand is the same as the one you used for the copy constructor, and because you now know what the return type should be, you can have a first stab at defining the = operator function for the `TruckLoad` class. Take a moment to consider the following, and then we'll discuss what's wrong with it:

```
TruckLoad& TruckLoad::operator=(const TruckLoad& load) {
  pHead = pTail = pCurrent = 0;
  if(load.pHead == 0)
    return;

  Package* pTemp = load.pHead;      // Saves addresses for new chain
  do {
    addBox(pTemp->pBox);
  }while(pTemp = pTemp->pNext);

  return *this;                     // Return the left operand
}
```

The `this` pointer contains the address of the left argument, so returning `*this` returns the object. Apart from that, this code is the same as what you had for the copy constructor. The function looks OK, and it appears to work most of the time, but there are two problems with it.

The first problem is with the left operand. It is a `TruckLoad` object that potentially contains a list. By setting its data member pHead to 0, you cast adrift any `Package` objects owned by the `TruckLoad` object. You must first delete any `Package` objects owned by the left operand, so let's add code to do that to the function definition:

```
TruckLoad& TruckLoad::operator=(const TruckLoad& load) {
  while(pCurrent = pHead) {      // Copy and check pointer for null
    pHead = pHead->pNext;        // Move pHead to the address of the next object
    delete pCurrent;             // Delete current object
  }

  pHead = pTail = pCurrent = 0;
  if(load.pHead == 0)
    return;
```

```
    Package* pTemp = load.pHead;   // Saves addresses for new chain
    do {
      addBox(pTemp->pBox);
    }while(pTemp = pTemp->pNext);

    return *this;                  // Return the left operand
}
```

If the left operand contains a list, pHead will be non-null. The while loop saves the pointer to the first Package object in the list and checks it for null. If it is not null, the body of the loop executes, which moves pHead to the address of the next Package object in this list and then deletes the current head of the list. In this way, you progress down the list, repeatedly deleting the object at the head until you reach a null pointer.

That takes care of the left operand, but you've still got a problem. Suppose someone were to write this:

```
    load1 = load1;
```

This doesn't look like a very sensible assignment, but the situation could arise as a consequence of a more complex statement, where it is not obvious that this will be the outcome. In this situation, because of your fix for the first problem, you'll delete the list contained in the object and then attempt to copy the now nonexistent list. You need to check for the possibility of both operands being the same. To do this, modify the function to

```
TruckLoad& TruckLoad::operator=(const TruckLoad& load) {
  if(this == &load)                 // Compare operand addresses
    return *this;                   // if equal return the 1st operand

  while(pCurrent = pHead) {    // Copy and check pointer for null
    pHead = pHead->pNext;      // Move pHead to the address of the next object
    delete pCurrent;           // Delete current object
  }

  pHead = pTail = pCurrent = 0;
  if(load.pHead == 0)
    return;

  Package* pTemp = load.pHead;      // Saves addresses for new chain
  do {
    addBox(pTemp->pBox);
  }while(pTemp = pTemp->pNext);

  return *this;                     // Return the left operand
}
```

If both operands are the same object, they'll have the same address, so comparing this with the address of the argument passed to operator=() does the trick.

CAUTION *Whenever you write an assignment operator, you should always check for the possibility of both operands being the same object.*

You can now extend the golden rule for classes—the one that allocates memory dynamically—that you started to develop at the end of Chapter 13.

GOLDEN RULE *If your class functions allocate memory in the free store, always implement a copy constructor, an assignment operator, and a destructor.*

You're not limited to overloading the copy assignment operator just to copy an object. In general, you can have several overloaded versions of the assignment operator for a class. Additional versions of the assignment operator would have a parameter type that was different from the class type, so they would effectively be conversions. In any event, the return type should be a reference to the left operand. Of course, you can also overload the other operators of the form op= if you want.

In many cases, it is likely that you specifically *don't* want to allow certain assignment operations on the objects of your class. If this is the case, you can prevent them by declaring the assignment operator as a private member of the class.

Try It Out: Implementing the Assignment Operator

Let's put together a simple working example that illustrates how class objects behave, with and without an assignment operator defined. Therefore it should explain exactly why overloading the assignment operator is so important. You can define a class ErrorMessage to represent an error message with a copy constructor, an assignment operator, and a destructor in the first instance:

```
// ErrorMessage.h
#ifndef ERRORMESSAGE_H
#define ERRORMESSAGE_H
#include <iostream>
using namespace std;

class ErrorMessage {
  public:
    ErrorMessage(const char* pText = "Error");            // Constructor
    ~ErrorMessage();                                      // Destructor
    void resetMessage();                                  // Change the message
    ErrorMessage& operator=(const ErrorMessage& Message); // Assignment operator

    char* what() const{ return pMessage; }                // Display the message
```

```
  private:
    char* pMessage;
};
#endif
```

Of course, this class must define a copy constructor, a copy assignment operator, and a destructor because it allocates memory dynamically. By removing the assignment operator function from the class, you'll be able to see what happens when you forget to implement it.

The definitions for the constructor, destructor, and other member functions can go in ErrorMessage.cpp:

```
// ErrorMessage.cpp ErrorMessage class implementation
#include <cstring>
#include "ErrorMessage.h"
using std::cout;
using std::endl;

// Constructor
ErrorMessage::ErrorMessage(const char* pText) {
  pMessage = new char[ strlen(pText) + 1 ];          // Get space for message
  std::strcpy(pMessage, pText);                      // Copy to new memory
}

// Destructor to free memory allocated by new
ErrorMessage::~ErrorMessage() {
  cout << endl << "Destructor called." << endl;
  delete[] pMessage;                                 // Free memory for message
}

// Change the message
void ErrorMessage::resetMessage() {
  // Replace message text with asterisks
  for(char* temp = pMessage ; *temp != '\0' ; *(temp++) = '*')
    ;
}

// Assignment operator
ErrorMessage& ErrorMessage::operator=(const ErrorMessage& message) {
  if(this == &message)                               // Compare addresses, if equal
    return *this;                                     // return left operand

  delete[] pMessage;                                 // Release memory for left operand
  pMessage = new char[ strlen(message.pMessage) + 1];

  // Copy right operand string to left operand
  std::strcpy(this->pMessage, message.pMessage);

  return *this;                                      // Return left operand
}
```

(Continued)

You can put this version of the error message class through its paces with the following source file:

```cpp
// Program 14.3 Overloading the copy assignment operator  File: prog14_03.cpp
#include <iostream>
#include <cstring>
using std::cout;
using std::endl;

#include "ErrorMessage.h"

int main() {
  ErrorMessage warning("There is a serious problem here");
  ErrorMessage standard;

  cout << endl << "warning contains - " << warning.what();
  cout << endl << "standard contains - " << standard.what();

  standard = warning;                         // Use assignment operator

  cout << endl << "After assigning the value of warning, standard contains - "
       << endl << standard.what();

  cout << endl << "Resetting warning, not standard" << endl;
  warning.resetMessage();                     // Reset the Warning message

  cout << endl << "warning now contains - " << warning.what();
  cout << endl << "standard now contains - " << standard.what();
  cout << endl;

  return 0;
}
```

If you compile and run this as it is, you'll get the following output:

```
warning contains - There is a serious problem here
standard contains - Error
After assigning the value of warning, standard contains -
There is a serious problem here
Resetting warning, not standard

warning now contains - ******************************
standard now contains - There is a serious problem here

Destructor called.

Destructor called.
```

As you can see, everything works as it should. You're able to reset the message contained in the first `ErrorMessage` object without affecting the object that was copied.

Now remove or comment out the declaration of the assignment operator in the class definition and its definition in `ErrorMessage.cpp`. When you recompile the program and run it again, you'll produce this output:

```
warning contains - There is a serious problem here
standard contains - Error
After assigning the value of warning, standard contains -
There is a serious problem here
Resetting warning, not standard

warning now contains - ******************************
standard now contains - ******************************

Destructor called.

Destructor called.
```

You may well get other error messages because, as it stands, the program attempts to release memory in the free store twice for the same object.

HOW IT WORKS

The interesting aspect of this example is its peculiar operation without the assignment operator. In the `main()` function, you create an object, `warning`, which contains a specific text string with the following statement:

```
ErrorMessage warning("There is a serious problem here");
```

This calls the `ErrorMessage` constructor with the string passed as an argument. Next you create an `ErrorMessage` object using the default message string:

```
ErrorMessage standard;
```

After displaying both objects' messages, you call the assignment operator for the `ErrorMessage` class with this statement:

```
standard = warning;                           // Use assignment operator
```

The second time you ran the program, this was the *default* assignment operator provided by the compiler, so both objects' `pMessage` members contained the same address. As a consequence, when you modified the `warning` object with this statement:

```
warning.resetMessage();                       // Reset the Warning message
```

(Continued)

you were modifying the string common to both objects. The output clearly showed the standard string to be the same as the warning string.

At the end of the program the two ErrorMessage objects go out of scope and their destructors are called, as indicated by the output. The first destructor call deletes the string pointed to by pMessage from the free store. In the defective version, when the second destructor call occurs, it attempts to delete the same string again. Because the pMessage members of both ErrorMessage objects contain the same address, your system may produce a warning of its own. And all because you didn't define an assignment operator!

The first time you ran the program using the ErrorMessage class with the assignment operator implemented, an independent copy of the right operand was created and standard was not affected by the modification of warning. The pMessage pointers in the two objects now point to separate strings, so no problem arises with the destructors.

Overloading the Arithmetic Operators

Let's look at how you can overload the addition operator for your Box class. This is an interesting case, because addition is a binary operation that involves creating and returning a new object. The new object will be the sum (whatever you define that to mean) of the two Box objects that are its operands.

What do you want the sum to mean? You have a number of possibilities to consider, but because the primary purpose of a box is to hold something, and its volumetric capacity is of primary interest, you might reasonably expect that the sum of two boxes was a box that could hold as much as both together. Using this assumption, let's define the sum of two Box objects to be a Box object that's large enough to contain the two original boxes stacked on top of each other. This is consistent with the notion that your class might be used for packaging, because adding a number of Box objects together results in a Box object that can contain them.

You can implement the addition operator in a simple-minded way, as follows. The new object has a length member that is the larger of the length members of the objects being summed; and a width member derived in a similar way. The height member is the sum of the height members of the two operands, so that the resultant Box object can contain the other two Box objects. By altering the constructor, you'll also arrange that the length member of a Box object is always greater than or equal to the width member.

Figure 14-2 illustrates the Box object that will be produced by adding two Box objects together.

Because the result of this addition is a new Box object, the function implementing addition must return a Box object. If the function that overloads the + operator is to be a member function, then the declaration of the function in the Box class definition can be

```
Box operator+(const Box& aBox) const;        // Adding two Box objects
```

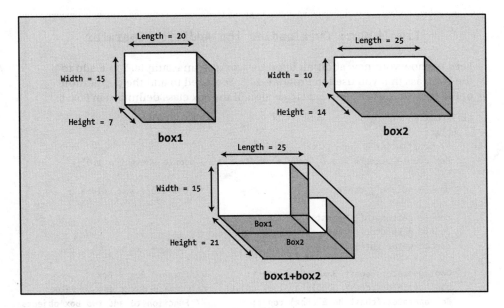

Figure 14-2. The result of adding two Box *objects*

You can define the *parameter* as const, because the function won't modify it. By specifying it to be a reference, you avoid unnecessary copying of the right operand when the function is called. You can declare the *function* as const because it doesn't alter the left operand. The definition of the member function will be

```
// Function to add two Box objects
inline Box Box::operator+(const Box& aBox) const {
    // New object has larger length and width, and sum of heights
    return Box( length > aBox.length ? length : aBox.length,
                width > aBox.width ? width : aBox.width,
                height + aBox.height );
}
```

Notice particularly that you don't create a Box object in the free store to return to the caller. This would be a very poor way of implementing the function, because it is hard to see how you could ensure that the memory was released. Returning a pointer would also affect how other operators, such as operator=(), are written. The way the function is written, a local Box object is created and a copy is returned to the calling program. Because these are automatic variables, the memory management is taken care of automatically.

Try It Out: Overloading the Addition Operator

Let's see how your new addition operator works in an example. You'll add to the Box class that you used in Program 14.3. You need to add the declaration of the operator function to public section of the Box class definition in Box.h:

```
class Box {
  public:
    // Constructor
    Box(double aLength = 1.0, double aWidth = 1.0, double aHeight = 1.0);

    double volume() const;                      // Calculate Box volume

    double getLength()  const;
    double getWidth() const;
    double getHeight()  const;

    bool operator<(const Box& aBox) const;      // Compare Box < Box
    bool operator<(const double aValue) const;  // Compare Box < double value
    Box operator+(const Box& aBox) const;       // Function to add two Box objects
  private:
    double length;
    double width;
    double height;
};
```

You need to add the inline definition of the operator+() function that you saw just now (it was following the class definition in the header file).

You'll modify the definition of the constructor in Box.cpp to

```
Box::Box(double aLength, double aWidth, double aHeight) {
  double maxSide = aLength > aWidth ? aLength : aWidth;
  double minSide = aLength < aWidth ? aLength : aWidth;
  length = maxSide > 0.0 ? maxSide : 1.0;
  width = minSide > 0.0 ? minSide : 1.0;
  height = aHeight > 0.0 ? aHeight : 1.0;
}
```

Now the constructor ensures that the length member always contains the longer of the length and width of a Box object. This presents the objects in a consistent orientation, although your addition operator may produce some very tall narrow boxes.

Let's exercise the addition operator together with the < operator by finding the pair of Box objects from an array that has the least volume when they are added together. With an array of 20 Box objects, this involves checking 380 pairs of objects. Here's the code to do that:

```
// Program 14.4 Adding Box objects   File: prog14_04.cpp
#include <iostream>
#include <cstdlib>                  // For random number generator
#include <ctime>                    // For time function
using std::cout;
using std::endl;

#include "Box.h"

// Function to generate random integers from 1 to count
inline int random(int count) {
  return 1+static_cast<int>
         (count* static_cast<double>(std::rand())/(RAND_MAX+1.0));
}

// Display box dimensions
void show(const Box& aBox) {
  cout << endl
       << aBox.getLength() << " by " << aBox.getWidth()
       << " by " << aBox.getHeight();
}

int main() {
  const int dimLimit = 100;          // Upper limit on Box dimensions
  std::srand((unsigned)std::time(0)); // Initialize the random number generator

  const int boxCount = 20;           // Number of elements in Box array
  Box boxes[boxCount];               // Array of Box objects

  // Create 20 Box objects
  for(int i = 0 ; i < boxCount ; i++)
    boxes[i] = Box(random(dimLimit), random(dimLimit), random(dimLimit));

  int first = 0;                     // Index of first Box object of pair
  int second = 1;                    // Index of second Box object of pair
  double minVolume = (boxes[first] + boxes[second]).volume();

  for(int i = 0 ; i < boxCount - 1 ; i++)
    for(int j = i + 1 ; j < boxCount ; j++)
      if(boxes[i] + boxes[j] < minVolume)          {
        first = i;
        second = j;
        minVolume = (boxes[i] + boxes[j]).volume();
      }

  cout << "The objects that sum to the smallest volume are:";
  cout << endl << "boxes[" << first << "] ";
  show(boxes[first]);
  cout << endl << "boxes[" << second << "] ";
  show(boxes[second]);
  cout << endl << "Volume of the sum is " << minVolume << endl;

  return 0;
}
```

(Continued)

I got the following output:

```
The objects that sum to the smallest volume are:
boxes[8]
15 by 15 by 23
boxes[16]
21 by 15 by 41
Volume of the sum is 20160
```

You should get a different result each time you run the program.

HOW IT WORKS

You record the pair of elements of the array, whose Box objects give the smallest volume when summed, by storing the index values in the variables first and second. You arbitrarily set the first two array elements as the initial pair and store their combined volume with this statement:

```
double minVolume = (boxes[first] + boxes[second]).volume();
```

Because operator+() returns a Box object, you can call the volume() function for the Box object that results from adding boxes[first] and boxes[second]. The parentheses around the sum of the two Box objects are essential, as the precedence of the member access operator is higher than that of +. Of course, if you had wanted to *save* the combined Box object, you could have written this:

```
Box combined = boxes[first] + boxes[second];  // Assigns sum to new Box object
double minVolume = combined.volume();
```

The pair that combines to form the smallest Box object is found in the nested loop:

```
for(int i = 0 ; i < boxCount - 1 ; i++)
  for(int j = i + 1 ; j < boxCount ; j++)
    if(boxes[i] + boxes[j] < minVolume) {
      first = i;
      second = j;
      minVolume = (boxes[i] + boxes[j]).volume();
    }
```

The outer loop, controlled by i, iterates through the array elements from the first to the last-but-one. The inner loop, controlled by j, combines the Box object selected by i with each of the following objects in the array in turn. For each pair of Box objects, the volume of the sum is compared with minVolume using the overloaded operator < in the if expression. This expression is equivalent to

```
(boxes[i].operator+(boxes[j])).operator<(minVolume)
```

The operator+() function returns a Box object whose operator<() function is then called. If the operator<() function returns true, you record the current index values in first and second and store the volume of the sum of the Box objects in minVolume.

Finally, you use the show() function to output the results for the Box objects you have found with these statements:

```
cout << "The objects that sum to the smallest volume are:";
cout << endl << "boxes[" << first << "] ";
show(boxes[first]);
cout << endl << "boxes[" << second << "] ";
show(boxes[second]);
cout << endl << "Volume of the sum is " << minVolume << endl;
```

Of course, you can use your overloaded addition operator in more complex expressions to sum Box objects. For example, you could write this:

```
Box box4 = box1 + box2 + box3;
```

The result is a Box object box4 that can contain the other three Box objects stacked on top of each other.

You could equally well have implemented the addition operation for the class as a normal (that is, non-member) function, because the dimensions of a Box object are accessible through public member functions. Here is the prototype of such a function:

```
Box operator+(const Box& aBox, const Box& bBox);
```

If the values of the data members aren't accessible in this way, you can still write it as a normal function that you declared as a friend function within the Box class. Of these choices, the friend function is always the least desirable, so always take the alternative to a friend function if you have one. Operator functions are quite a fundamental class capability, so I generally prefer to implement them as class members—which represents that the operation really is an integral part of the type.

Implementing One Operator in Terms of Another

One thing always leads to another. If you implement the addition operator for a class, you inevitably create the expectation that the += operator will work too. Of course, in practice there's no connection between + and +=, but if you are going to implement both, it's worth noting that you can implement + in terms of += very economically.

First, let's define the function to implement += for the Box class. Because assignment is involved, it needs to return a reference. If you use the same idea of addition that you used when you implemented the addition operator function for the Box class, you might come up with the following definition for a function to implement +=:

```
// Overloaded += operator
inline Box& Box::operator+=(const Box& right) {
  length =  length  > right.length  ? length  : right.length;
  width = width > right.width ? width : right.width;
  height += right.height;
  return *this;
}
```

This is very straightforward. You simply modify the left operand, which is *this, by effectively adding the right operand according to your definition for addition of Box objects. Once again, the resulting object can contain the original objects placed one on top of the other.

You can now implement operator+() using operator+=(), so the definition of the operator function simplifies to

```
// Function to add two Box objects
inline Box Box::operator+(const Box& aBox) const {
  return Box(*this) += aBox;
}
```

Here, the expression Box(*this) calls the copy constructor to create a copy of the left operand to use in the addition. The operator+=() function is then called to add the right operand object, right, to the new Box object. This object is then returned.

You could apply the same ideas to implement overloaded versions of -=, *=, and so on for a class. While I am on the topic of defining one operator in terms of another, let me mention that you can do the same sort of thing with comparisons. Because you've defined the operator<() function, you can define a function to overload >= using operator<():

```
inline bool Box::operator>=(const Box& aBox) const {
  return !(*this<(aBox));
}
```

The negation of *less than* is *greater than or equal to*, so that's why you can define the function like this.

Overloading the Subscript Operator

The subscript operator [] provides very interesting possibilities for certain kinds of classes. Clearly, this operator is aimed primarily at selecting one of a number of objects that you can interpret as an array; but in fact, the objects could be contained in any one of a number of different containers. You can overload the subscript operator to access the elements of a sparse array (where many of the elements are empty), or an associative array, or even a linked list. The data might even be stored in a file, and you could use the subscript operator to hide the complications of file input and output operations. Because you control what goes on inside the operator function, you could even improve on the way the standard subscript operator works—for instance, by checking that a given index value is legal.

Your TruckLoad class, from Chapter 13, is an example of a class that would support an implementation of the subscript operator. Each TruckLoad object contains an ordered set of objects, so rather than making users write their own code to iterate through the Box objects in the list, you could provide them with a means of accessing these objects through an index value. An index of 0 would return the first object in the list; an index of 1 would return the second; and so on. The inner workings of the subscript operator would take care of iterating through the list to find the object required.

Let's think about how the operator[]() function might work in this case. It needs to accept an index value that is interpreted as a position in the list and return the Box object at that position. You must return an object (not a pointer) if you're to be consistent with the normal meaning of an expression such as load[3], which ought to refer to the fourth object in the list represented by the object load. Therefore, the declaration for the function in the TruckLoad class might be

```
class TruckLoad {
  public:
    Box operator[](int index) const;        // Overloaded subscript operator
    // Rest of the class as before...
};
```

You could implement the function as follows:

```
// Subscript operator
Box TruckLoad::operator[](int index) const {
  if(index<0) {                             // Check for negative index
    cout << endl << "Negative index";
    exit(1);
  }

  Package* pPackage = pHead;                // Address of first Package
  int count = 0;                            // Package count
  do   {
    if(index == count++)                    // Up to index yet?
      return *pPackage->pBox;               // If so return the Box
  } while(pPackage = pPackage->pNext);

  cout << endl << "Out of range index";     // If we get to here index is too high
  exit(1);
}
```

CAUTION *Some older compilers may not support this use of* exit(); *they may complain that no value is returned from the function. If you have this problem, try replacing each of the two statements* exit(1); *with* return *pTail->pBox;. *This defeats the purpose of testing the index value but your code should at least compile successfully.*

If the value of index is negative, you display a message and terminate the program by calling the exit() function. In the do-while loop, you traverse the list, incrementing count as you go. When the value of count is the same as index, the loop has reached the Package object that you're looking for, so you return the Box object that corresponds to that Package object. If you traverse the entire list without count reaching the value of index, then index must be out of range, so you terminate the program after issuing a message.

NOTE *Just terminating the program here is not a good way of handling this kind of problem. You really want to allow the program to continue if possible, while also signaling that an error has occurred. C++ provides exceptions to handle exactly this kind of situation; I'll discuss these in Chapter 17.*

Let's see how this pans out in practice by trying another example.

Try It Out: Overloading the Subscript Operator

In this example, you'll use the Box class as defined for Program 14.4. You can extend the TruckLoad class definition in List.h to include your overloaded subscript operator function:

```
// List.h classes supporting a linked list
#ifndef LIST_H
#define LIST_H

#include "Box.h"

class TruckLoad {
public:
    // Constructors
    TruckLoad(Box* pBox = 0, int count = 1);      // Constructor
    TruckLoad::TruckLoad(const TruckLoad& Load); // Copy constructor

    ~TruckLoad();                                 // Destructor

    Box* getFirstBox();                           // Retrieve the first Box
    Box* getNextBox();                            // Retrieve the next Box
```

```
    void addBox(Box* pBox);                    // Add a new Box to the list
    Box operator[](int index) const;           // Overloaded subscript operator

  private:
   class Package {
      public:
         Box* pBox;                             // Pointer to the Box
         Package* pNext;                        // Pointer to the next Package

         Package(Box* pNewBox);                 // Constructor
};

    Package* pHead;                             // First in the list
    Package* pTail;                             // Last in the list
    Package* pCurrent;                          // Last retrieved from the list
};

#endif
```

The implementation of the function will go in the List.cpp file. Just to make sure you have it all, the complete file contents appear here:

```
// List.cpp Implementations for the Package and TruckLoad classes
#include <iostream>
#include "Box.h"
#include "List.h"
using std::cout;
using std::endl;

// Package class functions
// Package constructor
TruckLoad::Package::Package(Box* pNewBox):pBox(pNewBox), pNext(0){}

// TruckLoad class functions
// Constructor
TruckLoad::TruckLoad(Box* pBox, int count) {
  pHead = pTail = pCurrent = 0;

  if(count > 0 && pBox != 0)
  for(int i = 0 ; i<count ; i++)
    addBox(pBox+i);
  return;
}

// Copy constructor
TruckLoad::TruckLoad(const TruckLoad& Load) {
  pHead = pTail = pCurrent = 0;
  if(Load.pHead == 0)
    return;
```

(Continued)

```
      Package* pTemp = Load.pHead;                  // Saves addresses for new chain
      do {
        addBox(pTemp->pBox);
      }while(pTemp = pTemp->pNext);
    }


    // Destructor
    TruckLoad::~TruckLoad() {
      while(pCurrent = pHead->pNext) {
        delete pHead;                                // Delete the previous
        pHead = pCurrent;                            // Store address of next
      }
        delete pHead;                                // Delete the last
    }

    // Get the first Box in the list
    Box* TruckLoad::getFirstBox() {
      pCurrent = pHead;
      return pCurrent->pBox;
    }

    // Get the next Box in the list
    Box* TruckLoad::getNextBox() {
      if(pCurrent)
        pCurrent = pCurrent->pNext;                  // pCurrent is not null so set to next
      else
        pCurrent = pHead;                            //  pCurrent is null
                                                     //   so set to the first list element

      return pCurrent ? pCurrent->pBox : 0;
    }

    // Add a list element
    void TruckLoad::addBox(Box* pBox) {
      Package* pPackage = new Package(pBox);         // Create a Package

      if(pHead)                                      // Check list is not empty
        pTail->pNext = pPackage;                     // Add the new object to the tail
      else                                           // List is empty
        pHead = pPackage;                            // so new object is the head
      pTail = pPackage;                              // Store its address as tail
    }

    // Subscript operator
    Box TruckLoad::operator[](int index) const {
      if(index<0) {                                  // Check for negative index
        cout << endl << "Negative index";
        exit(1);
      }

      Package* pPackage = pHead;                     // Address of first Package
      int count = 0;                                 // Package count
```

```
  do {
    if(index == count++)                    // Up to index yet?
      return *pPackage->pBox;               // If so return the Box
  } while(pPackage = pPackage->pNext);

  cout << endl << "Out of range index";     // If we get to here index is too high
  exit(1);
}
```

Note that the output from the destructor for the TruckLoad class has been removed because you no longer need it.

To try out your subscript operator, you create a linked list of Box objects (as you did in Program 13.1), and then use the subscript operator to find the largest:

```cpp
// Program 14.5 Using the overloaded subscript operator  File: prog14_05.cpp
#include <iostream>
#include <cstdlib>                 // For random number generator
#include <ctime>                   // For time function
using std::cout;
using std::endl;

#include "Box.h"
#include "List.h"

// Function to generate random integers from 1 to count
inline int random(int count) {
  return 1+static_cast<int>
            (count*static_cast<double>(std::rand())/(RAND_MAX+1.0));
}

// Display box dimensions
void show(const Box& aBox) {
  cout << endl
       << aBox.getLength() << " by " << aBox.getWidth()
                           << " by " << aBox.getHeight();
}

int main() {
  const int dimLimit = 100;                 // Upper limit on Box dimensions
  std::srand((unsigned)std::time(0));       // Initialize the random number generator

  const int boxCount = 20;                  // Number of elements in Box array
  Box boxes[boxCount];                      // Array of Box objects

  // Create 20 Box objects
  for(int i = 0 ; i < boxCount ; i++)
    boxes[i] = Box(random(dimLimit), random(dimLimit), random(dimLimit));

  TruckLoad load = TruckLoad(boxes, boxCount);
```

(Continued)

```
   // Find the largest Box in the list
   Box maxBox = load[0];

   for(int i = 1 ; i < boxCount ; i++)
     if(maxBox < load[i])
       maxBox = load[i];

   cout << endl
        << "The largest box in the list is ";
   show(maxBox);
   cout << endl;
   return 0;
}
```

When I ran this example, it produced the following output:

```
The largest box in the list is
90 by 79 by 77
```

HOW IT WORKS

The main() function now uses the subscript operator to retrieve Box objects from the linked list. The first Box object in the list is retrieved with this statement:

```
Box maxBox = load[0];
```

This statement is equivalent to

```
Box maxBox = load.operator[](0);
```

Using the subscript operator that you've defined for Box objects, you use an index to iterate through the remaining objects in the list to find the largest:

```
for(int i = 1 ; i < boxCount ; i++)
  if(maxBox < load[i])
    maxBox = load[i];
```

You also use the overloaded < operator to compare the current largest object, maxBox, with the object at index position i in the list, load[i]. This is not a particularly efficient process because your overloaded subscript operator has to iterate through the list every time you refer to an object in the list. The process could be improved if you kept track of the index position of the last recorded element, and used it to get to subsequent elements. However, it is always going to be slower than iterating through the list as you did previously. Looks neat though, doesn't it?

Lvalues and the Overloaded Subscript Operator

You'll encounter circumstances under which you might want to overload the subscript operator and use the object returned from it as an lvalue—that is, on the left of an assignment statement. With your present implementation, your program compiles but won't necessarily work correctly if you write this:

```
load[0] = load[1];
```

The problem is the return value from operator[](). The object that is returned is a temporary copy of an object that is created by the compiler, which could cause you problems if you use it on the left of an assignment. The assignment will work, but you are not changing the first object in the list, just a copy of it that won't be around for very long. Of course, the next time you use the expression long[0], you'll get a *different* copy of the first object in the list. However, you can fix the problem by redefining the operator so that it returns a reference, and that *can* be used as an lvalue (obviously, you must not return a reference to a local object in this situation). You can change the definition of the subscript operator to

```
Box& TruckLoad::operator[](int index) const {
  if(index<0) {                         // Check for negative index
    cout << endl << "Negative index";
    exit(1);
  }

  Package* pPackage = pHead;            // Address of first Package
  int count = 0;                        // Package count
  do {
    if(index == count++)                // Up to index yet?
      return *pPackage->pBox;           // If so return the Box
  } while(pPackage = pPackage->pNext);

  cout << endl << "Out of range index"; // If we get to here index is too high
  exit(1);
}
```

None of the code in the body of the function needs to be changed—just the header line. Of course, the declaration within the TruckLoad class definition must also return a reference. Now you can use statements such as the following:

```
load[0] = load[1] + load[2];
```

Just to be sure you understand what is really happening here, let's see what this translates to in terms of function calls. The statement will be equivalent to

```
load.operator[](0) = (load.operator[](1)).operator+(load.operator[](2));
```

If you had overloaded the assignment operator for the Box class, this would have broken down further to

```
load.operator[](0).operator=((load.operator[](1)).operator+(load.operator[](2)));
```

Overloading on const

In some circumstances, you may not want to allow Box objects to be used as modifiable lvalues. On the other hand, sometimes you do. How can you differentiate between the two situations?

One way is to use a TruckLoad object that is const when you don't want to allow modification of the Box objects it contains, and a non-const object when you do. You can overload a member function that is non-const with another that is const, so you can have two versions of your subscript operator. The const version will be called for const TruckLoad objects, and the non-const version otherwise; this is what const implies when it's applied to a member function. The non-const version would be defined as in the previous example. Here's how you could define the const version:

```
const Box& TruckLoad::operator[](int index) const {
  // Body of the function the same as before...
}
```

The body of the function is exactly the same, but the return type is const, so the reference can't be used on the left of an assignment. The effect is that Box objects that are returned by the operator[]() function for a const TruckLoad object can't be used on the left of an assignment.

Overloading Type Conversions

You can define an operator function to convert from one class type to another type. The type you're converting to can be a basic type or a class type. Operator functions that are conversions for objects of an arbitrary class, Object, are of this form:

```
class Object {
  public:
    operator Type();                // Conversion from Object to Type
  // Rest of Object class definition ...
};
```

Here, Type is the destination type for the objects of the class. Note that no return type is specified. The target type is always implicit, so here the function must return an object of type Type.

As an example, you might want to define an operator function to convert from type TruckLoad to type Box*—which is a pointer to an array of Boxes. The declaration of the function within the TruckLoad class would be as follows:

```
class TruckLoad {
  public:
    operator Box*() const;
  // Rest of TruckLoad class definition ...
};
```

The return type—Box*—is implicit in the name of the operator function, so you don't need to specify it. Implementing this particular function has its complications. You'd need to create the array in the free store, so the caller would need to assume responsibility for deleting it, all of which is asking for memory leaks.

Another possibility might be to define a conversion from type Box to type double. For application reasons, you might decide that this conversion would result in the volume of the Box being converted. You could define this as follows:

```
class Box {
  public:
    operator double() const
      { return volume(); }
  // Rest of Box class definition ...
};
```

Then, given a Box object named theBox, the operator function would be called if you wrote this statement:

```
double boxVolume = theBox;
```

You could also cause the operator function to be called explicitly with a statement that induced the cast explicitly:

```
double total = 10 + static_cast<double>(theBox);
```

> **NOTE** *You can also invoke this kind of conversion with the old-style casts by writing an expression such as* (double)TheBox.

Ambiguities with Conversions

When you implement conversion operators for your classes, you need to be conscious that you might create ambiguities that will cause compiler errors. As I have said, constructors can also effectively implement a conversion, so you can implement a conversion from type Type1 to type Type2 by including a constructor in class Type2 with this declaration:

```
Type2(const Type1& theObject);       // Constructor converting Type1 to Type2
```

If you now implement a conversion operator in class Type2 to do the same as this constructor, you'd declare the conversion operator function in the class as follows:

```
operator Type1();                    // Conversion from type Type1 to Type2
```

Now the compiler may not be able to decide which function to use when a conversion is required—the constructor or the conversion operator function. To remove the ambiguity, declare the constructor as explicit, as I discussed in Chapter 12. This will prohibit the use of the constructor for implicit conversions, so the conversion operator will be selected by the compiler.

CAUTION *An obvious consequence of the potential for ambiguity between constructors and conversion operators functions is that you need to be very careful when implementing conversion operators for a class.*

Overloading the Increment and Decrement Operators

The ++ and -- operators present a new problem for the functions that implement overloading them for a class type, as they behave differently depending on whether or not they prefix their operand. Therefore, you need two functions for each operator: one to be called in the prefix case and the other to be called for postfix case.

The postfix form of the operator function is distinguished from the prefix form by the presence of a parameter of type int. This parameter only serves to distinguish the two cases and is not otherwise used. The declarations for the functions to overload ++ for an arbitrary class, Object, will be

```
class Object {
  public:
    Object& operator++();            // Overloaded prefix increment operator
    const Object operator++(int);    // Overloaded postfix increment operator
  // Rest of Object class definition ...
};
```

The return type for the prefix form normally needs to be a reference to the current object after the increment operation has been applied to it.

For the postfix form of the operator, you must create a copy of the object in its original form before you modify it; then return the *copy* of the original after the increment operation has been performed on the object. The return value for the postfix operator is declared as const to prevent expressions such as theObject++++ from compiling. Such expressions are inelegant, confusing, and inconsistent with the normal behavior of the operator. However, if you don't declare the return type as const, such usage is possible.

NOTE *For any class implementation that overloads the increment and decrement operators, the return type for the prefix form will always be a reference to the current object, and the return type for the postfix form will always be a new object that is a copy of the original before it has been incremented.*

Smart Pointers

Because you have the ability to overload the dereference operator, *, and the operator, ->, you can define a type that represents a **smart pointer**—something that behaves like a pointer but is really a class object. The standard library makes extensive use of one form of smart pointers—referred to as **class iterators** as you'll see in Chapter 20—but what exactly are smart pointers used for?

A smart pointer is an object that can act as an intelligent pointer to objects that may be organized in a complicated way. It can hide the complication in the organization of the objects it points to by allowing you to move from one object to the next or previous object, simply by incrementing or decrementing the smart pointer. A smart pointer can simply return the object that it currently points to when it is dereferenced, or it can access its members through the -> operator, just like an ordinary pointer.

Each smart pointer class is designed to suit the context in which it is to be applied. For example, the objects you want to refer to may be stored in a container class of some kind, which stores objects in a complex structure such as a tree or a list. Or, you might want to use a smart pointer to access and step through such objects without worrying about their internal organization. In addition, the objects that you access through a smart pointer may not even be all in one place. In fact, in a very complex application context, you might have objects stored in files or databases across multiple systems on a network, but within your program you want a smart pointer object to take care of sorting out how to retrieve the objects when you iterate through them. From the perspective of your program code, local objects look just the same as remote objects. All of the complexity of accessing the objects pointed to by a smart pointer is buried inside the class that defines it. Externally, you'd expect to use a smart pointer in the same way as you would an ordinary pointer.

You could create a class that defines a smart pointer that you could use with the TruckLoad class to access the Box objects it contains. This would provide you with an opportunity to see a simple implementation of a smart pointer and see some more examples of overloaded operators. You can also include a practical demonstration of overloading the increment operator.

Defining a Smart Pointer Class for Box Objects

Your smart pointer should work like a regular Box pointer, except that it would point to Box objects within a TruckLoad object. You can call the class type for your smart pointer BoxPtr. You could create a BoxPtr object from a reference to a TruckLoad object and have it automatically point to the first Box in the linked list. This implies that the BoxPtr object needs to keep track of the current Box object pointed to in the TruckLoad object and the TruckLoad object itself. You can put these in an outline definition for the BoxPtr class that you'll put in the header file BoxPtr.h:

```
#ifndef BOXPTR_H
#define BOXPTR_H
#include "List.h"

class BoxPtr {
  public:
    BoxPtr(TruckLoad& load);                   // Constructor

  private:
    Box* pBox;                                 // Points to current Box in rLoad
    TruckLoad& rLoad;

    // Not accessible so not implemented
    BoxPtr();                                  // Default constructor
    BoxPtr(BoxPtr&);                           // Copy constructor
    BoxPtr& operator=(const BoxPtr&);          // Assignment operator
};
#endif
```

By only allowing a BoxPtr object to be created from a TruckLoad object, you can be reasonably sure that the TruckLoad object exists when a function for a BoxPtr object is being executed—although it might be empty. You don't want to allow BoxPtr objects to be created using a default constructor, so you declare it as a private member of the class. Having copies of BoxPtr objects also complicates things, but you can avoid that too by declaring the copy constructor and the assignment operator in the private section of the class.

You won't need to modify the TruckLoad or Box classes at all. You can use the versions that you employed in Program 14.5. What else do you need in your BoxPtr class? You certainly need to implement the * and -> operators if a BoxPtr object is going to behave like a pointer, so let's add those to the definition:

```
class BoxPtr {
  public:
    BoxPtr(TruckLoad& load);                   // Constructor
    Box& operator*() const;                    // * overload
    Box* operator->() const;                   // -> overload

  private:
    Box* pBox;                                 // Points to current Box in rLoad
    TruckLoad& rLoad;

    // Not accessible so not implemented
    BoxPtr();                                  // Default constructor
    BoxPtr(BoxPtr&);                           // Copy constructor
    BoxPtr& operator=(const BoxPtr&);          // Assignment operator
};
```

Because it is to behave like a Box* pointer, dereferencing a BoxPtr object should return a reference to a Box object, and that's why the return type is Box&. The * operator is a unary operator, so the function has no parameters.

The operator->() function is a little odd, so let's first see how it works when it is used. It will be called in situations like this:

```
BoxPtr pLoadBox(aTruckLoad);
double boxVol = pLoadBox->volume();
```

Here, aTruckLoad is a TruckLoad object. Because the pLoadBox initially represents a pointer to the first Box object in aTruckLoad, the second statement should call the volume() member of that object. The second statement will actually be equivalent to

```
double boxVol = (pLoadBox.operator->())->volume();
```

An extra -> operator gets inserted to access the member, volume(), so the operator->() function must return a pointer of type Box*.

You want to be able to increment a BoxPtr object so that an expression such as ++pLoadBox should point to the next Box object in the TruckLoad object. You can add both the prefix and the postfix forms to the BoxPtr class:

```
class BoxPtr {
  public:
    BoxPtr(TruckLoad& load);            // Constructor
    Box& operator*() const;             // * overload
    Box* operator->() const;            // -> overload
    Box* operator++();                  // Prefix increment
    const Box* operator++(int);         // Postfix increment

  private:
    Box* pBox;                          // Points to current Box in rLoad
    TruckLoad& rLoad;

    // Not accessible so not implemented
    BoxPtr();                           // Default constructor
    BoxPtr(BoxPtr&);                    // Copy constructor
    BoxPtr& operator=(const BoxPtr&);   // Assignment operator
};
```

Of course, because you're incrementing a stand-in for a pointer, each of these functions returns type Box*. The postfix form returns a const object to prevent repeated applications of the operator, such as pLoadBox++++.

Do you need anything else? You most certainly do. You'll want to be able use a BoxPtr object as a test condition in statements such as the following:

```
if(pLoadBox) {
  // Do something...
}
```

You need the object to behave like a normal pointer here and have it automatically translated into something that is a valid if test expression. One way to do this is to implement a conversion to bool for objects of type BoxPtr. If you do that, the compiler automatically inserts the conversion operator when you use a BoxPtr as a logical expression where a result of type bool is required. You can add a declaration for that to the BoxPtr class:

```
class BoxPtr {
  public:
    BoxPtr(TruckLoad& load);            // Constructor
    Box& operator*() const;             // * overload
    Box* operator->() const;            // -> overload
    Box* operator++();                  // Prefix increment
    const Box* operator++(int);         // Postfix increment
    operator bool();                    // Conversion to bool

  private:
    Box* pBox;                          // Points to current Box in rLoad
    TruckLoad& rLoad;

    // Not accessible so not implemented
    BoxPtr();                           // Default constructor
    BoxPtr(BoxPtr&);                    // Copy constructor
    BoxPtr& operator=(const BoxPtr&);   // Assignment operator
};
```

Note that no return type is required or allowed here, as it is implicit in the nature of the conversion operator function. You'll come across other ways to make objects work as an if test expression in the context of the standard library classes for stream input/output, that you'll explore in Chapter 19.

That's enough for our purposes, so let's see how you can put together the definitions for the member functions of your BoxPtr class.

Implementing the Smart Pointer Class

The constructor is very easy. All you have to do is to initialize the member that is a reference to a TruckLoad object, and store the address of the first Box object that it contains. You can put the definition in a source file, BoxPtr.cpp:

```
// BoxPtr.cpp
#include <iostream>
#include "List.h"
#include "BoxPtr.h"
using std::cout;
using std::endl;

BoxPtr::BoxPtr(TruckLoad& load):rLoad(load) {
  pBox = rLoad.getFirstBox();
}
```

The rLoad member must be initialized in the initialization list for the constructor; this is the only way you can initialize a member that is a reference. To get the address of the first Box object, you just call the getFirstBox() member of the object passed as an argument. The #include directive for <iostream> and the using declarations are there for the next function definition that you'll add to the file.

The dereference operator function should return the object that is pointed to by the pBox member of the BoxPtr object, but you have to consider the possibility that one might not exist. You can define the function as follows:

```
Box& BoxPtr::operator*() const {
  if(pBox)
    return *pBox;
  else   {
    cout << endl << "Dereferencing null BoxPtr";
    exit(1);
  }
}
```

If pBox is null, you can't return an object in the normal way at all. Dereferencing a null pointer is a disaster situation, so you display a message and end the program, but you know that this is not a good way to deal with this. You'll learn about a better way to handle this kind of error in Chapter 17.

NOTE *If you find that your compiler doesn't support this use of* exit(), *try replacing the statement* exit(1); *with the statement* return *pBox;—*just as a short term fix.*

The indirect member selection operator is much simpler. You just need to return the pBox member:

```
Box* BoxPtr::operator->() const {
  return pBox;
}
```

This function returns whatever address is contained in pBox, so when pBox is null, the return value will be null. The user of your class will need to verify that the smart pointer is not null before using it—just like using a regular pointer.

The prefix increment operator for BoxPtr objects also returns a pointer, just like when you increment an ordinary pointer:

```
Box* BoxPtr::operator++() {
  return pBox = rLoad.getNextBox();
}
```

Remember that the prefix operator increments its operand *before* it is used in an expression, so you just return the address of the next pointer in the TruckLoad object, which you obtain with the getNextBox() member. The getNextBox() function returns null if you increment beyond the end of the last Box object.

The postfix version of the increment operator must increment the smart pointer *after* using the current value in the expression. This sounds difficult but it isn't. You can implement it as follows:

```
const Box* BoxPtr::operator++(int) {
  Box* pTemp = pBox;
  pBox = rLoad.getNextBox();
  return pTemp;
}
```

You save a copy of the current address in pBox, then increment pBox to point to the next Box object before returning the original. Easy, isn't it?

The last member function you must define is the conversion operator. This is as close to being trivial as it gets:

```
BoxPtr::operator bool() {
  return pBox != 0;
}
```

You want to return true if pBox is not null, and the expression in the return statement does exactly that.

Let's make sure all this works by running another example.

Try It Out: Using a Smart Pointer

You can try out your smart pointer class by creating a TruckLoad object that contains a set of random Box objects as you've done before. You can then try out most of your operator functions. Here's the code:

```
// Program 14.6 Using a smart pointer
#include <iostream>
#include <cstdlib>                 // For random number generator
#include <ctime>                   // For time function
using std::cout;
using std::endl;

#include "Box.h"
#include "List.h"
#include "BoxPtr.h"
```

```
// Function to generate random integers from 1 to count
inline int random(int count) {
  return 1+static_cast<int>
          (count*static_cast<double>(std::rand())/(RAND_MAX+1.0));
}

int main() {
  const int dimLimit = 100;             // Upper limit on Box dimensions
  std::srand((unsigned)std::time(0));   // Initialize the random number generator

  const int boxCount = 20;              // Number of elements in Box array
  Box boxes[boxCount];                  // Array of Box objects

  // Create 20 Box objects
  for(int i = 0 ; i < boxCount ; i++)
    boxes[i] = Box(random(dimLimit), random(dimLimit), random(dimLimit));

  TruckLoad load = TruckLoad(boxes, boxCount);

  // Find the largest Box in the list
  BoxPtr pLoadBox(load);                // Create smart pointer

  Box maxBox = *pLoadBox;               // Intialize maxBox object using * operator
  if(pLoadBox)                          // Try the bool conversion
    cout << endl << "Volume of first Box is " << pLoadBox->volume(); // and ->

  while(++pLoadBox)                     // Prefix increment smart pointer
    if(maxBox < *pLoadBox)
      maxBox = *pLoadBox;

  cout << endl
       << "The largest box in the list is "
       << maxBox.getLength() << " by "
       << maxBox.getWidth() << " by "
       << maxBox.getHeight() << " with volume "
       << maxBox.volume()   << endl;
  return 0;
}
```

This example produces the following output:

```
Volume of first Box is 110880
The largest box in the list is 100 by 74 by 91 with volume 673400
```

(Continued)

Let's walk through how the operator functions are applied in this example. After setting up a TruckLoad object to contain 20 Box objects, you create a smart pointer with this statement:

```
BoxPtr pLoadBox(load);              // Create smart pointer
```

When it is created, the pLoadBox object is a surrogate for a pointer to the first Box object in the TruckLoad object, load. Therefore, you can dereference it to initialize the maxBox object:

```
Box maxBox = *pLoadBox;             // Intialize maxBox object using * operator
```

This statement calls the default constructor for the Box class to create maxBox. It then calls the operator*() function for the pLoadBox object and uses the reference to the Box object that is returned as the argument to the operator=() function for the Box object maxBox.

Next, the if statement calls two member functions of the BoxPtr class:

```
if(pLoadBox)                        // Try the bool conversion
  cout << endl << "Volume of first Box is " << pLoadBox->volume(); // and ->
```

The if expression implicitly calls the operator bool() function, and the output statement calls the operator->() function that returns the address of the current Box object.

The while loop uses the prefix increment operator in the loop control expression:

```
while(++pLoadBox)                   // Prefix increment smart pointer
  if(maxBox < *pLoadBox)
    maxBox = *pLoadBox;
```

The operator++() function returns the pointer to the next Box object. If it is not null, you use the operator*() function to dereference it and then use the operator<() member of the maxBox object to compare volumes. If the latest Box object has a greater volume, you store it in maxBox—using operator*() for the pLoadBox object class and operator=() for the maxBox object.

At the end of the loop, pLoadBox represents a null pointer, so you can no longer use it. You finally output information about the maxBox object in the usual way.

Overloading Operators new and delete

You can overload the operators new and delete for a particular class, and if you implement new, you should implement delete. The usual reason for overloading these operators is to make memory allocation and deallocation faster and more economical for a particular class of objects. This can arise when you need to allocate space for very large numbers of objects that each requires a small amount of memory. Allocating space for small objects one at a time can carry a considerable penalty in terms of overhead in the actual amount of memory allocated to each object and the time it takes to allocate and release the memory.

The standard approach to implementing new is to allocate a big chunk of memory using the default new operator, and then farm this out in small chunks of the size required. Obviously, the class delete operation must then be implemented to handle the release of the small chunks of memory. Typical declarations for class-specific new and delete operators are

```
class Data {
  public:
    void* operator new(size_t Size);
    void operator delete(void* Object, size_t size);
  // Rest of Data class definition ...
};
```

To call the global operators from within class-specific operator functions, just use the scope resolution operator, ::. For example, to call the global new from within the class-specific new operator, write something like this:

```
void* operator new(size_t size) {
  // ...
  pSpace = ::new char(size);     // size bytes allocated by global new
  // ...
}
```

Implementing these operators is not for the faint-hearted, as managing out-of-memory and other error conditions can get a little complicated. You shouldn't attempt it unless it is absolutely essential. Because overloading these operators is a rare necessity, I won't dwell on it further.

Summary

In this chapter, you learned about how to add function to make objects of your own data types work with the basic operators in C++. What you need to implement in a particular class is up to you. You need to decide the nature and scope of the facilities each of your classes should provide. Always keep in mind that you are defining a data type— a coherent entity—and that your class needs to reflect its nature and characteristics. You should also make sure that your implementation of an overloaded operator doesn't conflict with what the operator does in its standard form.

The important points you've seen in this chapter include the following:

- You can overload any operator within a class to provide class-specific behavior—except for the scope resolution operator(::), the conditional operator (?:), the member access operator (.), the dereference pointer to class member operator (.*), and the sizeof operator.

- Operator functions can be defined as members of a class or as global operator functions.

- For a unary operator defined as a class member function, the operand is the class object.

- For a unary operator defined as a global operator function, the operand is the function parameter.

- For a binary operator function declared as a member of a class, the left operand is the class object and the right operand is the function parameter.

- For a binary operator defined as a global operator function, the first parameter specifies the left operand, and the second parameter specifies the right operand.

- To overload the increment operator, you need two functions to provide for the prefix and postfix forms of the operators. The function to implement a postfix operator has an extra parameter of type int that serves only to distinguish the function from the prefix version. The same is true of the decrement operator.

- Functions that implement the overloading of the += operator can be used in the implementation of the + function. This is true for all op= operators.

- A smart pointer is an object that behaves like a pointer. One form of smart pointer is used to iterate through a complex collection of objects of a given type, in much the same way that you use an ordinary pointer. The standard template library uses smart pointers extensively.

Exercises

The following exercises enable you to try out what you've learned in this chapter. If you get stuck, look back over the chapter for help. If you're still stuck after that, you can download the solutions from the Apress website (http://www.apress.com/book/download.html), but that really should be a last resort.

NOTE *These exercises are going to build on the exercises from the previous chapter that involved creating the* MyString *class, so I hope you completed them!*

Exercise 14-1. Provide an overloaded assignment operator for your MyString class. Make sure that you guard against self-assignment! Test that your operator works correctly with the following statements, where s1, s2, and s3 are mystring objects:

```
s1 = s2;

s1 = s1;

s1 = s2 = s3;
```

Exercise 14-2. Overload the + operator to provide string concatenation. Test that s1 = s2 + s3; works correctly. Provide the += operator; what should this operator return?

Exercise 14-3. Overload [ ] to provide access to individual characters in the string so that s1[4] returns the fifth character of s1. How will you ensure that this can be used on either side of an assignment?

Exercise 14-4. Provide overloads for the ==, !=, > and < operators, which can be used to compare your mystring objects. What types should these Boolean operators return? Check that expressions such as if (s1 == s2) work correctly.

Exercise 14-5. (Harder) Overload the () operator to return a substring from a mystring object so that s1(2, 3) returns the three characters starting at s1[2].

CHAPTER 15

Inheritance

IN THIS CHAPTER, you're going to look into a topic that lies at the heart of object-oriented programming: **inheritance**. Inheritance is the means by which you can create new classes by reusing and expanding on existing class definitions.

Inheritance is also fundamental to making **polymorphism** possible, and polymorphism lies at the very heart of object-oriented programming. I discuss polymorphism in the next chapter, so you should also consider what you investigate there to be an integral part of what inheritance is all about.

In this chapter you'll learn about

- How inheritance fits into the idea of object-oriented programming

- What base classes and derived classes are, and how they're related

- How to define a new class in terms of an existing class

- The use of the keyword protected to define a new access specification for class members

- How constructors behave in a derived class and what happens when they're called

- What happens with destructors when using a derived class

- Multiple inheritance and how it works

- Conversions between class types in a class hierarchy

Classes and Object-Oriented Programming

Let's start by reviewing what you've learned so far about classes and see how that leads to the ideas you'll explore in this chapter.

In Chapter 12, I introduced the concept of a class and you learned that a class is a data type that you define to suit your own application requirements. When you use object-oriented programming to solve a problem, your first step is to identify the types of entities to which your problem relates and to determine the characteristics for each type and the operations you'll need in the solution to the problem. Then you must code these types by writing class definitions. Finally, you program the solution to your problem in terms of objects that will be instances of the classes that you've defined and using the operations that apply directly to those objects.

Any type of entity can be represented by a class—from the completely abstract (such as the mathematical concept of a complex number) to something as decidedly physical as a tree or a truck. Your class definition should characterize a *set* of entities, which are identified by a common set of properties. So, as well as being a data type, a class can also be a definition of a real-world object (or, at least, an approximation that is useful for solving a given problem).

In many real-world problems, the *types* of the entities involved are related. For example, a dog is a special kind of animal, which has all the properties of an animal plus a few more. Consequently, your class definitions of Animal and Dog should be related in some way. After all, a dog is a kind of animal so you would expect the class definitions to be able to reflect this in some way. A different case is illustrated by the idea that an automobile has an engine. There should really be some way of using your Engine class when defining the Automobile class, but an engine is certainly not an automobile so you would expect a different kind of relationship from that between the Animal and Dog classes. In this chapter you'll see how these two fundamentally different relationships are implemented in C++.

Hierarchies

In previous chapters, you've used the Box class to describe a rectangular box—your definition of a Box object consisted of just the three orthogonal dimensions. You can apply this basic definition to the many different kinds of rectangular boxes that you find in the real world: cardboard cartons, wooden crates, candy boxes, cereal boxes, and so on. Each of these objects has three orthogonal dimensions, and in this way they're just like your generic Box objects. In addition, each of them has other properties—for example, the things they're designed to hold or the materials from which they're made. In fact, you could describe them as specialized kinds of Box objects.

For example, you might describe a Carton class, which has the same properties as a Box object—namely the three dimensions—plus the additional property of its composite material. You might then specialize even further by using the Carton definition to describe a class called FoodCarton—this will be a special kind of Carton that is designed to hold food. It will have all the properties of a Carton object and an additional member to model the intended contents.

The relationship between classes in such a hierarchy is shown in Figure 15-1.

The Carton class is an extension of the Box class—you might say that the Carton class is *derived* from the specification of the Box class. In a similar way, the FoodCarton class has been derived from the Carton class. It's common to indicate this relationship diagrammatically by using an arrow pointing toward the more general class in the hierarchy. I've used this convention in Figure 15-1.

In this process of specifying one class in terms of another, you're developing a hierarchy of interrelated classes. In the hierarchy, one class is derived from another by adding extra properties—in other words, by specialization—making the new class a specialized version of the more general class. In Figure 15-1, each class in the hierarchy has *all* the properties of the Box class, which illustrates precisely the mechanism of class inheritance in C++. You could define the Box, Carton, and FoodCarton classes quite independently of each other, but by defining them as related classes, you gain a tremendous amount. Let's look at how this works in practice.

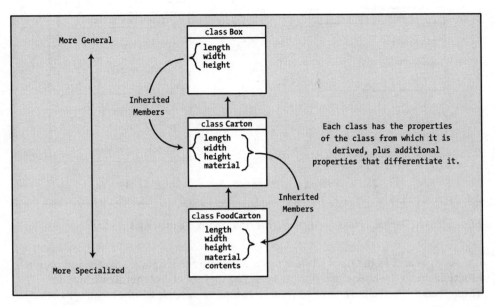

Figure 15-1. Classes in a hierarchy

Inheritance in Classes

To begin with, let's establish the terminology that you'll use for related classes. Given a class A, suppose that you create a new class B that is a specialized version of A. Class A is called the **base class**, and class B is called the **derived class**. You might think of A as being the "parent" and B as being the "child." The derived class automatically contains all of the data members of the base class, and (with some restrictions that I discuss) all the function members. The derived class is said to **inherit** the data members and function members of the base class.

If class B is a derived class defined *directly* in terms of class A, then you say that class A is a **direct base class** of B. You also say that B is **derived from** A. In the preceding example, the class Carton is a direct base class of FoodCarton. Because Carton is itself defined in terms of the class Box, you can say that the class Box is an **indirect base class** of the class FoodCarton. An object of the FoodCarton class will have inherited members from Carton, including the members that the Carton class inherits from the Box class.

The way in which a derived class inherits members from a base class is illustrated in Figure 15-2.

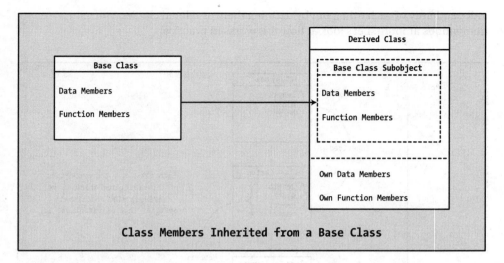

Figure 15-1. Derived class members inherited from a base class

As you can see, the derived class has a complete set of data members and member functions from the base class, plus its own data members and member functions. Thus, each derived class object contains a complete base class subobject, plus other members.

Inheritance vs. Aggregation

The process of class inheritance isn't merely a means of getting members of one class to appear in another. There's a very important idea that underpins the whole concept: derived class objects should represent sensible base class objects.

To illustrate what I mean, there are a number of simple tests that you can employ. The first is the *is a kind of* test: any derived class object *is a kind of* base class object. In other words, a derived class should describe a subset of the objects that are represented by the base class. For example, a class Dog might be derived from a class Animal. This makes sense because a dog *is a kind of* animal; rather, a Dog object is a reasonable representation of a particular kind of Animal object. On the other hand, a Table class shouldn't be derived from the Dog class. Although Table objects and Dog objects share a common attribute in that they both usually have four legs, a Table object can't really be considered to be a Dog in any way or vice versa.

The *is a kind of* test is an excellent first check, but it's not infallible. For example, suppose that you defined a class, Bird, that, among other things, reflected the fact that most birds can fly. Now, an ostrich *is a kind of* bird, but it's nonsense to derive a class Ostrich from the Bird class, because ostriches can't fly! If your classes pass the *is a kind of* test, then you should double-check by asking the following question: Is there anything I can say about (or demand of) the base class that's inapplicable to the derived class? If there is, then the derivation probably isn't safe. Thus, deriving Dog from Animal is sensible, but deriving Ostrich from Bird, as you've described it, isn't. Instead, you would probably need to define Bird in a more general way and derive the classes Flighted_Birds and Flightless_Birds from that.

If your classes fail the *is a kind of* test, then you almost certainly shouldn't use class derivation. In this case, you could instead implement the *has a* test. A class object passes the *has a* test if it contains an instance of another class. You can accommodate this situation by including an object of the second class as a data member of the first. This type of dependence is called **aggregation**.

For example, consider once again an Automobile class. This class is likely to contain major automobile components as its class members. Clearly, an automobile *has an* engine, *has a* transmission, *has a* body, and *has* suspension, so it makes sense for the Automobile class to contain objects of type Engine, Transmission, Body, and Suspension. Clearly, it's not true to say that an engine or any of the other components is a kind of automobile. Hence, these classes fail the *is a kind of* test, so deriving Engine from Automobile would be nonsensical.

Here's a summary of the three tests:

- The *is a kind of* test is a first-stop test to check whether inheritance is an appropriate way to implement your classes.

- If the classes pass the *is a kind of* test, then double-check by asking the following question: Is there anything I can say about (or demand of) the base class that's inapplicable to the derived class? If the answer is no, then inheritance is usually appropriate.

- If the classes fail the *is a kind of* test, then try the *has a* test. If they pass the *has a* test, then aggregation is usually the answer.

Of course, what is appropriate in the implementation of a class is dependent on your application, and these rules are a guide rather than gospel. Sometimes, class derivation is used simply to assemble a set of capabilities, so that the derived class is an envelope for packaging a given set of functions. Even then, the derived class generally represents a set of functions that are related in some way.

It's time to see what the code looks like when you derive one class from another.

Deriving Classes from a Base Class

Let's go back to a simplified version of the Box class, which has three private data members and a public constructor:

```
// Box.h - defines Box class
#ifndef BOX_H
#define BOX_H
class Box {
  public:
    Box(double lv=1.0, double wv=1.0, double hv=1.0);

  private:
    double length;
```

```
      double width;
      double height;
   };
   #endif
```

Because you've specified default values for the parameters in the constructor, it will also serve as the default constructor. You can save this definition in a header file Box.h, and add it to the example with a #include directive. To be consistent, the definition for the Box constructor is contained in the file Box.cpp:

```
// Box.cpp
#include "box.h"

// Constructor
Box::Box(double lv, double wv, double hv) : length(lv), width(wv), height(hv)
{}
```

Now, let's define another class called Carton. A Carton object will be much as described earlier—similar to a Box object, but with an extra data member that indicates the composite material of the object. You can declare the new data member to be a null-terminated string that describes the sort of material the box is made of. (In practice, you may prefer to use a string object for this, but by using a null-terminated string you can demonstrate some of the implications of dynamic memory allocation). You'll define Carton as a derived class, using the Box class as the base class:

```
// Carton.h - defines the Carton class with the Box class as base
#ifndef CARTON_H
#define CARTON_H
#include "Box.h"                                // For Box class definition

class Carton : public Box {
  public:
    Carton(const char* pStr = "Cardboard");     // Constructor

    ~Carton();                                   // Destructor

  private:
    char* pMaterial;
};
#endif
```

You must #include the Box class definition into this file because it is the base class for Carton. The definitions are out of line and contained in the file Carton.cpp:

```
// Carton.cpp
#include "Carton.h"
#include <cstring>

// Constructor
```

```
Carton::Carton(const char* pStr) {
  pMaterial = new char[strlen(pStr)+1];    // Allocate space for the string
  std::strcpy( pMaterial, pStr);            // Copy it
}

// Destructor
Carton::~Carton() {
  delete[] pMaterial;
}
```

The first line of the Carton class definition indicates that Carton is derived directly from Box:

```
class Carton : public Box
```

The keyword public is the base class access specifier, and it indicates how the members of Box are to be accessed within the Carton class. I'll discuss this further in a moment.

In all other respects, the Carton class definition looks like any other. It contains a new member, pMaterial, which is a pointer to a null-terminated string. It is initialized, by the class constructor, to the address of a string that is created in the free store. This will ensure the object has its own string describing the material. You must also supply a destructor to release the memory for the string object that pMaterial points to. Notice that the constructor includes a default value for the string describing the contents of a Carton object, so that this is also the default constructor for the Carton class. Objects of the class Carton contain all the data members of the base class, Box, plus the additional data member, pMaterial.

Let's see how this operates in a working example.

....

Try It Out: Using a Derived Class

Here's the code for your first example using a derived class:

```
// Program 15.1 Defining and using a derived class
#include <iostream>
#include "Box.h"              // For the Box class
#include "Carton.h"           // For the Carton class
using std::cout;
using std::endl;

int main() {
  // Create a Box and two Carton objects
  Box myBox(40.0, 30.0, 20.0);
  Carton myCarton;
  Carton candyCarton("Thin cardboard");
```

(Continued)

```
    // Check them out - sizes first of all
    cout << endl
        << "myBox occupies "      << sizeof myBox       << " bytes" << endl;
    cout << "myCarton occupies "  << sizeof myCarton    << " bytes" << endl;
    cout << "candyCarton occupies " << sizeof candyCarton << " bytes" << endl;

//  myBox.length = 10.0;          // uncomment this for an error
//  candyCarton.length = 10.0;    // uncomment this for an error

    return 0;
}
```

On my machine I get the following output:

```
myBox occupies 24 bytes
myCarton occupies 32 bytes
candyCarton occupies 32 bytes
```

HOW IT WORKS

First, you have #include directives for the header files that contain the definitions for the Box and Carton classes. Of course, the file containing the definition of the Carton class also includes Box.h, but the #ifndef/#endif preprocessing directives will prevent the Box class definition from being duplicated.

You declare a Box object and two Carton objects in main(), and then output the number of bytes occupied by each object. The output shows what you would expect—that a Carton object is larger than a Box object. A Box object has three data members of type double; each of these occupies 8 bytes on my machine, so that's 24 bytes in all. Both of your Carton objects are the same size: 32 bytes. The additional memory occupied by each Carton object is down to the data member pMaterial. The length of the string doesn't affect the size of a Carton object, because pMaterial is a pointer. The space to store the string itself will be allocated in the free store.

If you uncomment either of the next two statements, the program will no longer compile. The first of these statements is

```
//  myBox.length = 10.0;          // uncomment this for an error
```

Of course, you would expect this statement to cause an error. The length member of the Box object myBox was declared as a private data member, and so it's not accessible to this output statement. By uncommenting the next statement, you'll see that you can't access the length member of the Carton object either:

```
//  candyCarton.length = 10.0;    // uncomment this for an error
```

The compiler will generate a message to the effect that the length member from the base class isn't accessible. This is perhaps a little unexpected—after all, when you defined the Carton class, didn't you inherit the Box class members as public?

The reason for the error is that length is a private data member in the base class. In the derived class Carton, the length member is a publicly inherited private data member. The compiler interprets this by making length a private member of Carton. Consequently, when you attempt to access the member candyCarton.length, the compiler immediately flags up this as an error.

 NOTE *If you really want to access these* private *data members, then you could use a* public *function member such as* getLength(), *as discussed in Chapter 12.*

Thus, access to the inherited members of a derived class object is determined by *both* the access specifier of the data member in the base class and the access specifier of the base class in the derived class.

The whole question of the access of inherited members in a derived class needs to be looked at more closely. A third access specifier, protected, will come into play shortly. First, I'll discuss some more examples, and later on, I'll present a summary of how base class access specifiers affect the access level of inherited class members.

Access Control Under Inheritance

The private data members of a base class are also members of the derived class, but they remain private to the *base* class within the derived class. This means that the inherited data members are accessible to the inherited function members from the base class, but they are *not* accessible to the member functions declared within the derived class definition.

For example, let's add a function volume() to the derived class Carton. The file Carton.h would update to this:

```
// Carton.h - defines the Carton class with the Box class as base
#ifndef CARTON_H
#define CARTON_H
#include "Box.h"                          // For Box class definition

class Carton : public Box {
  public:
    Carton(const char* pStr = "Cardboard");   // Constructor

    ~Carton();                              // Destructor

    double volume() const;                  // Error - members not accessible
```

```
  private:
    char* pMaterial;
};
#endif
```

and the file `Carton.cpp` would update to this:

```
// Carton.cpp
#include "Carton.h"
#include <cstring>

// Constructor
Carton::Carton(const char* pStr) {
  pMaterial = new char[strlen(pStr)+1];     // Allocate space for the string
  std::strcpy( pMaterial, pStr);            // Copy it
}

// Destructor
Carton::~Carton() {
  delete[] pMaterial;
}

// Function to calculate the volume of a Carton object
double Carton::volume() const {
  return length*width*height;
}
```

Any program that uses this class together with the Box class from Program 15.1 won't compile. The function `volume()` in the `Carton` class attempts to access the private members of the base class, which isn't legal—even though they'll be inherited members of the derived class.

However, it *is* legal to use the `volume()` function if it's a base class member. So if you move the definition of the function `volume()` to the `public` section of the base class Box, then not only will the program compile, but also you can use the function to obtain the volume of a `Carton` object. Let's see that working.

Try It Out: Base Class Member Functions

First change the class definition in `Box.h` to this:

```
class Box {
  public:
    Box(double lv=1.0, double wv=1.0, double hv=1.0);

// Function to calculate the volume of a Box object
    double volume() const;
```

```
private:
   double length;
   double width;
   double height;
};
```

You can declare the volume() function as const because it doesn't alter any data members of the class—it just uses them to calculate the volume of an object. Add the function definition to the file Box.cpp:

```
// Box.cpp
#include "box.h"

// Constructor
Box::Box(double lv, double wv, double hv) : length(lv), width(wv), height(hv)
{}

// Function to calculate the volume of a Box object
double Box::volume() const {
   return length*width*height;
}
```

For this program, you use the files Carton.h and Carton.cpp, which you used in Program 15.1. Thus, the Carton class inherits the Box class publicly and also has a constructor, a destructor, and a private data member pMaterial.

You can now calculate the volumes of the Box and Carton objects that you created in Program 15.1 to see how using a base class function in a derived class works out:

```
// Program 15.2 Using a function inherited from a base class File: prog15_02.cpp
#include <iostream>
#include "Box.h"                              // For the Box class
#include "Carton.h"                           // For the Carton class
using std::cout;
using std::endl;

int main() {
   // Create a Box and two Carton objects
   Box myBox(40.0, 30.0, 20.0);
   Carton myCarton;
   Carton candyCarton("Thin cardboard");

   cout << endl;
   cout << "myBox volume is "        << myBox.volume()        << endl;
   cout << "myCarton volume is "     << myCarton.volume()     << endl;
   cout << "candyCarton volume is " << candyCarton.volume() << endl;
   return 0;
}
```

(Continued)

I get the following output:

```
myBox volume is 24000
myCarton volume is 1
candyCarton volume is 1
```

This demonstrates that the volume() function defined in the Box class works equally well for objects of the Carton class. It's able to access the base class data members, even though they're private and not accessible from derived class functions. The volume of both Carton objects is 1, so evidently you have the default dimensions that are set in the base class constructor.

The Carton class constructor is called when you create an object of the class, but clearly the base class constructor must also be called somehow, because the derived class constructor offers no provision (and indeed no possibility) for initializing the data members inherited from the base class. You can confirm that the base class constructor is called for a Carton object by adding output statements to trace when each constructor is called. For Box you could add the following statement to the body of the constructor:

```
cout << "Box constructor" << endl;
```

You could put a similar statement in the Carton class constructor. Don't forget to include the iostream header file and to add using declarations for cout and endl in each .cpp file. If you run the program again you'll get the following output:

```
Box constructor
Box constructor
Carton constructor
Box constructor
Carton constructor

myBox volume is 24000
myCarton volume is 1
candyCarton volume is 1
```

The first line of output is due to the creation of the Box object, myBox. The next two lines are generated by the creation of the Carton object, myCarton. You can see that to create a Carton object, there's an automatic call of the Box class constructor (in fact, the default constructor) before the Carton class constructor is executed, and it is this that initializes the base class members.

Later in this chapter, you'll have a closer look at base class constructors, and in particular, how you can have more control over how base class data members are initialized.

Declaring Members of a Class As protected

The private members of a base class are only accessible to member functions of the base class, but this isn't always convenient. There will doubtless be many occasions when you want the members of a base class to be *accessible* from within the derived class, but nonetheless *protected* from outside interference. As you'll surely have anticipated by now, C++ provides a way to do this.

In addition to the public and private access specifiers for members of a class, you can also declare members of a class as protected. Within the class, the keyword protected has exactly the same effect as the keyword private. Members of a class that are protected can only be accessed by member functions of the class, friend classes, and friend functions of the class. These protected class members can't be accessed from outside the class, so they behave like private class members.

The difference between protected and private members only becomes apparent in a derived class. Members of a base class that are declared as protected are freely accessible in function members of a derived class, whereas the private members of the base class are not.

You could redefine your Box class to have protected data members as follows:

```
class Box {
  public:
    Box(double lv=1.0, double wv=1.0, double hv=1.0);

  protected:
    double length;
    double width;
    double height;
};
```

Now the data members of Box are still effectively private, in that they can't be accessed by ordinary global functions, but they're now accessible within member functions of a derived class. Let's go through an example to demonstrate.

....

Try It Out: Using Inherited protected Members

You can use this version of the Box class to derive a new version of the Carton class that accesses the members of the base class through its own member function, volume().

You first need to remove the volume() function prototype from the Box class definition (as previously) and also remove the volume() function definition from Box.cpp. Then you'll add the volume() function prototype to the Carton class definition, and you'll add the volume() function definition to Carton.cpp. You'll also declare the data member of the Carton class as protected, so that it will have the same specification as the data members inherited from Box. Here's the Carton class definition:

(Continued)

```
class Carton : public Box {
```

```
    public:
      Carton(const char* pStr = "Cardboard");       // Constructor

      ~Carton();                                     // Destructor

      // Function to calculate the volume of a Carton object
      double volume() const;

    protected:
      char* pMaterial;
};
```

Here's the function definition to be added to Carton.cpp:

```
// Function to calculate the volume of a Carton object
double Carton::volume() const {
  return length*width*height;
}
```

You can try out the new Carton class with the following program:

```
// Program 15.3 Using inherited protected members in a derived class
// File: prog15_03.cpp
#include <iostream>
#include "Box.h"                                     // For the Box class
#include "Carton.h"                                  // For the Carton class
using std::cout;
using std::endl;

int main() {
  // Create a Box and two Carton objects
  Box myBox(40.0, 30.0, 20.0);
  Carton myCarton;

  cout << endl;
  cout << "myCarton volume is " << myCarton.volume()  << endl;
// Uncomment either of the following two statement for error
//cout << "myBox volume is "    << myBox.volume()      << endl;
//cout << "myCarton length is " << myCarton.length     << endl;

  return 0;
}
```

The comments are for demonstrating aspects of your new versions of the Box and Carton classes. This program as it stands displays the following output:

```
Box constructor
Box constructor
Carton constructor

myCarton volume is 1
```

If you uncomment the output statement that purports to calculate the volume of myBox, then the program won't compile:

```
//cout << "myBox volume is "    << myBox.volume()    << endl;
```

This is because the Box class now has no function volume() defined. You can only calculate the volume of Carton objects.

The volume of the Carton object, myCarton, is calculated by invoking the volume() function that is defined in the derived class:

```
cout << "myCarton volume is " << myCarton.volume()  << endl;
```

This function accesses the inherited members length, width, and height to produce the result. These members were declared as protected in the base class and remain protected in the derived class. The output shows that the volume is being calculated properly for myCarton. Its volume turns out to be 1, because default values are assigned to the members inherited from Box.

NOTE *Because you specified* pMaterial *in the* Carton *class as* protected, *all the data members of this class will now be* protected, *and therefore they all could be accessed in another class derived from* Carton.

You can demonstrate that the protected members of the base class remain protected in the derived class by uncommenting the following statement:

```
//cout << "myCarton length is " << myCarton.length    << endl;
```

If you do this, you'll get an error message from the compiler to the effect that the member length is protected, and so it can't be accessed from outside the derived class.

The Access Level of Inherited Class Members

As you've seen, when you derive a class from a base class, you must choose the base class access specifier. There are three possibilities: public, protected, or private.

NOTE *In fact, the* default *base class access specifier is* private. *So if you omit the specifier altogether—for example, by writing* class Carton : Box *at the top of the* Carton *class definition in Program 15.1—then the* private *access specifier is assumed.*

You also know that the access specifiers for the data members of the base class come in three flavors—again, the choice is public, protected, or private.

By using the base class to create a derived class, the base class access specifier affects the access status of the inherited members. There are nine different combinations; you've seen some of them in the examples in this chapter. I cover all of the possible circumstances in the following paragraphs, although the usefulness of some of these will only become apparent in the next chapter when I move on to discuss polymorphism.

First, let's consider how private members of a base class are inherited into a derived class. Regardless of the base class access specifier (public, protected, or private), a private base class member always remains private to the base class. There are two consequences of this. First, inherited private members are private members of the derived class (so they're inaccessible outside the derived class). Second, they're also inaccessible to member functions of the derived class (because they're private to the base class).

Now, let's look at how public and protected base class members are inherited. In all of the remaining cases, the inherited members can be accessed by member functions of the derived class. Let's see how the members are inherited.

1. The most common form of inheritance is public inheritance. In this case, the access status of the inherited members is unchanged. Thus, inherited public members are public, and inherited protected members are protected.

2. When the inheritance of the base class is protected, inherited public members become protected in the derived class. The protected inherited members retain their original access level in the derived class.

3. Finally, when the inheritance of the base class is private, inherited public and protected members become private to the derived class—so they're accessible by member functions of the derived class but can't be accessed if they're inherited in another derived class.

This is summarized in Figure 15-3.

Being able to change the access level of inherited members in a derived class gives you a degree of flexibility, but remember that you can only make the access level more stringent—you can't relax the access level specified in the base class.

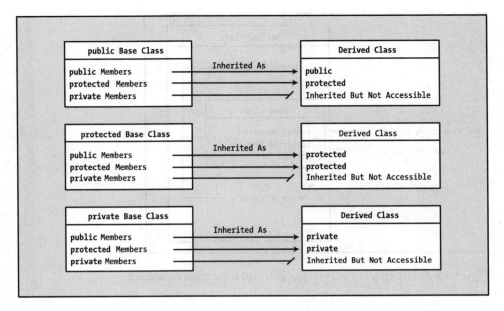

Figure 15-3. The effect of the base class specifier on inherited members

Using Access Specifiers in Class Hierarchies

As you've just seen, you have two aspects to consider when defining a hierarchy of classes: the class member access specifiers and the base class access specifier. As I said in Chapter 12, the public members of a class define the external interface to the class and this shouldn't normally include data members. Class members that aren't part of the class interface shouldn't be directly accessible from outside the class, and this means that they should be private or protected. Which access specification you choose for a particular member will depend on whether or not you want to allow access in a derived class. If you do, use protected; otherwise, use private. It's generally wise to keep things as locked away as possible.

As Figure 15-4 shows, the accessibility of inherited members is only affected by the access specifiers of these members in the base class definition. Within the derived class, the public and protected base class members are always accessible, and the private base class members are never accessible. From outside the derived class, only public base class members may be accessed—and this is only the case when the base class is declared as public.

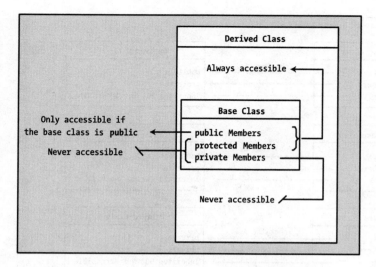

Figure 15-4. The effect of access specifiers on base class members

If the base class access specifier is public, then the access status of inherited members remains unchanged. By using the protected and private base class access specifiers, you are able to do two things:

1. You can prevent access to public base class members from outside the derived class—either specifier will do this. If the base class has public function members then this is a serious step because the class interface for the base class is being removed from public view in the derived class.

2. You can affect how the inherited members of the derived class are inherited in another class, which uses the derived class as its base.

As Figure 15-5 shows, the public and protected members of a base class can be handed on as protected members of another derived class. Members of a privately inherited base class won't be accessible in any further derived class.

In the majority of instances, as the examples reflect, you'll find that the public base class access specifier is most appropriate, with the base class data members declared as either private or protected. By using either the protected or private base class access specifiers, the base class subobject is internal to the derived class object and is therefore not part of the public interface to a derived class object. In practice, because the derived class object *is a kind of* base class object, you'll want the base class interface to be inherited in the derived class, and this implies that the base class must be specified as public.

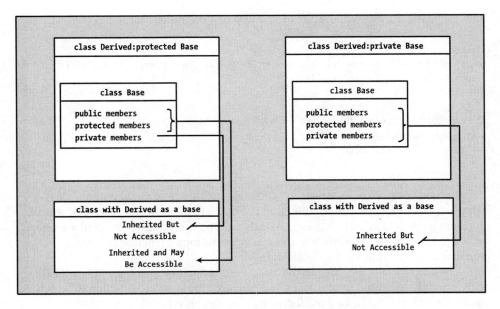

Figure 15-5. Affecting the access specification of inherited members

Changing the Access Specification of Inherited Members

You might want to exempt a particular base class member from the effects of a protected or private base class access specifier. Let's take an example. Suppose you define the Box class with a public member function, volume():

```
class Box {
  public:
    // Constructor
    Box(double lv=1.0, double wv=1.0, double hv=1.0);

    // Function to calculate the volume of a Box object
    double volume() const;

  protected:
    double length;
    double width;
    double height;
};
```

Just for the record, here are the out-of-line function definitions for this class:

```
}// Constructor
Box::Box(double lv, double wv, double hv) : length(lv), width(wv), height(hv) {
  cout << "Box constructor" << endl;
}

// Function to calculate the volume of a Box object
double Box::volume() const {
  return length*width*height;
}
```

You now want to derive a new class, Package, using Box as a private base class—but you'd really like the volume() function to be public in the derived class. Of course, the default result of private inheritance is that all the public and protected members will be private in the derived class. You can alter this for a particular inherited member by employing a using declaration.

This is essentially the same as the using declaration that you saw in Chapter 10, when you learned about namespaces. You can force the volume() function to be public in the derived class by writing the following class definition:

```
class Package : private Box {
  public:
    using Box::volume;                  // Inherit as public

  // Rest of the class definition
};
```

The class definition defines a scope, and the using declaration within the class definition introduces a name into that class scope. The using declaration here overrides the private base class access specifier just for the base class member function, volume(). The function will be inherited as public in the Package class, not as private.

There are two points of syntax to note here. First, when you apply a using declaration to the name of a member of a base class, you must qualify the name with the base class name as you have done previously, because the class name specifies the context for the member name. Second, note that you don't supply a parameter list or a return type here—just the qualified name of the member function.

NOTE *Here, you've used a* using *declaration to override the effect of the base class specifier on an inherited member function, but the same technique also works for inherited data members. Simply use the base class name and the scope resolution operator before the member name.*

It's also possible to use a `using` declaration to override an original `public` or `protected` base class access specifier. Hence, you can use this technique to allow a base class member more accessibility, or less accessibility, in the derived class. For example, if the `volume()` function was `protected` in the `Box` base class, then you could make it `public` in the derived class, `Package`, with the same `using` declaration that you used previously.

Note that you can't apply a `using` declaration in this way to a `private` member of a base class, because `private` members can't be accessed in a derived class.

Now that you know how you can hide members of a base class and still access them in a derived class, let's return to the question of constructors.

Constructor Operation in a Derived Class

Although in Programs 15.2 and 15.3 the default base class constructor was called automatically, this doesn't have to be the case. You can arrange to call a particular base class constructor from the derived class constructor. This will enable you to initialize the base class data members with a constructor other than the default. It will also allow you to choose one or other base class constructor, depending on the data supplied to the derived class constructor.

....

Try It Out: Calling Base Class Constructors

You can demonstrate this by using a modified version of Program 15.3. You'll keep the trace statements in the existing class constructors. To show how you can call a base class constructor explicitly, you'll add a second constructor for the `Carton` class that allows you to specify the dimensions of the object. You need to alter the `Carton` class definition in `Carton.h` to this:

```
class Carton : public Box {
  public:
    // Constructor which can also act as default constructor -
    //   calls default base constructor automatically
    Carton(const char* pStr = "Cardboard");

    // Constructor explicitly calling the base constructor
    Carton(double lv, double wv, double hv, const char* pStr = "Cardboard");

    ~Carton();                                    // Destructor

    // Function to calculate the volume of a Carton object
    double volume() const;

  protected:
    char* pMaterial;
};
```

(Continued)

As ever, the out-of-line function definitions will be contained in `Carton.cpp`:

```cpp
// Carton.cpp
#include "Carton.h"
#include <cstring>
#include <iostream>
using std::cout;
using std::endl;

// Constructor which can also act as default constructor -
//             calls default base constructor automatically
Carton::Carton(const char* pStr) {
  pMaterial = new char[strlen(pStr)+1];     // Allocate space for the string
  std::strcpy( pMaterial, pStr);            // Copy it
  cout << "Carton constructor 1" << endl;
}

// Constructor explicitly calling the base constructor
Carton::Carton(double lv, double wv, double hv, const char* pStr):
                                                 Box(lv, wv, hv) {
  pMaterial = new char[strlen(pStr)+1];     // Allocate space for the string
  std::strcpy(pMaterial, pStr);             // Copy it
  cout << "Carton constructor 2" << endl;
}

// Destructor
Carton::~Carton() {
  delete[] pMaterial;
}

// Function to calculate the volume of a Carton object
double Carton::volume() const {
  return length*width*height;
}
```

You'll modify the definition to provide a separate default constructor so that you can track when the default constructor in the Box class is called:

```cpp
class Box {
  public:
    Box();                               // Default constructor
    Box(double lv, double wv, double hv);   // Constructor

  protected:
    double length;
    double width;
    double height;
};
```

Again, you will put the out-of-line definitions into the file Box.cpp:

```cpp
// Box.cpp
#include "box.h"
#include <iostream>
using std::cout;
using std::endl;

// Default constructor
Box::Box() : length(1.0), width(1.0), height(1.0) {
  cout << "Default Box constructor" << endl;
}

// Constructor
Box::Box(double lv, double wv, double hv) : length(lv), width(wv), height(hv) {
  cout << "Box constructor" << endl;
}
```

Now you just need a version of main() that will call both Carton class constructors:

```cpp
// Program 15.4 Calling a base class constructor
//                     from a derived class constructor
// File prog15_04.cpp
#include <iostream>
#include "Box.h"                          // For the Box class
#include "Carton.h"                       // For the Carton class
using std::cout;
using std::endl;

int main() {
  // Create two Carton objects
  Carton myCarton;
  Carton candyCarton(50.0, 30.0, 20.0, "Thin cardboard");

  cout << endl << "myCarton volume is "    << myCarton.volume();
  cout << endl << "candyCarton volume is " << candyCarton.volume()
       << endl;

  return 0;
}
```

Compiling and running this version of the program produces this output:

```
Default Box constructor
Carton constructor 1
Box constructor
Carton constructor 2

myCarton volume is 1
candyCarton volume is 30000
```

(Continued)

HOW IT WORKS

The output statement in each constructor provides you with a clear understanding of the sequence of events. For the Carton object myCarton, the compiler first calls the default Box constructor, followed by the first Carton constructor. The default Box constructor call is the automatic call that you've seen before.

For the second Carton object, the Box constructor is called as a result of an explicit constructor call, in the header of the second Carton constructor:

```
Carton::Carton(double lv, double wv, double hv, const char* pStr):
                                              Box(lv, wv, hv)
```

The explicit call of the constructor for the Box class appears after a colon in the header of the derived class constructor. The call appears only in the constructor definition, not in the prototype. The parameters of the Carton constructor are passed to the base class constructor as arguments.

 NOTE *You may have noticed that the notation for calling the base class constructor is exactly the same as that used for initializing data members in a constructor. You've used this notation in the constructors for the Box class. This is perfectly consistent with what you're doing here, because essentially you're initializing the Box subobject of the Carton object using the arguments passed to the Carton constructor.*

The following table explains what each of the constructors calls recorded in the output is responsible for:

Program Output	Object Being Constructed
Default Box constructor	Box subobject of myCarton
Carton constructor 1	Remainder of myCarton object
Box constructor	Box subobject of candyCarton
Carton constructor 2	Remainder of candyCarton object

When a derived class object is created, the base class constructor must be called *before* the derived class constructor. This is a general rule. When several levels of inheritance are involved, the class constructor of the *most general* base class is called first; subsequent constructor calls are made in order of derivation, until finally the derived class constructor is called.

Although base class data members that aren't private to the base class can be *accessed* from the derived class, they can't be *initialized* in the initialization list for the derived class constructor. For example, try replacing the second Carton class constructor with the following (you'll only need to change the file Carton.cpp):

```
// Constructor that won't compile!
Carton::Carton(double lv, double wv, double hv, const char* pStr):
                                    length(lv), width(wv), height(hv) {
```

```
    pMaterial = new char[strlen(pStr)+1];      // Allocate space for the string
    strcpy(pMaterial, pStr);                    // Copy it
    cout << "Carton constructor 2" << endl;
}
```

At first sight, you might expect this to work, because length, width, and height are protected base class members that are inherited publicly, so the Carton class constructor should be able to access them. However, the compiler complains that length, width, and height are *not* members of the Carton class. So what's really happening here?

The answer is that the derived class constructor *can* refer to protected base class members, but not in the initialization list, because at that stage, they still don't exist. The initialization list is processed before the base class constructor is called and before the base part of the object has been created. If you want to initialize the inherited data members explicitly, you must do it in the body of the constructor. You could, instead, use the following constructor definition in the file Carton.cpp:

```
// This constructor doesn't cause a compiler error
Carton::Carton(double lv, double wv, double hv, const char* pStr) {
    length = lv;
    width = wv;
    height = hv;
    pMaterial = new char[strlen(pStr)+1];      // Allocate space for the string
    strcpy(pMaterial, pStr);                    // Copy it
    cout << "Carton constructor 2" << endl;
}
```

By the time the body of the constructor is executed, the base part of the object has been created. In this case, base part of the Carton object is created by an automatic call of the default base class constructor. You can subsequently refer to the names of the non-private base class members without a problem.

The Copy Constructor in a Derived Class

You saw previously what happens when an object of a user-defined class is declared and initialized with another object of the same class. Let's briefly look at this again. Consider these statements:

```
Box myBox(2.0, 3.0, 4.0);                        // Calls constructor
Box copyBox(myBox);                              // Calls copy constructor
```

You declare a Box object, myBox, but the second statement, in which the copy object, copyBox, is declared and initialized, is the key statement here. You saw in Chapter 13 how the copy constructor is called automatically by the compiler for such an initialization. In Program 12.5 you also saw that the compiler will supply a default copy constructor that creates the new object by copying the original object member by member if you haven't defined your own version for a class.

Now, let's exercise the copy constructors in a derived class situation. To do this, you will add to the class definitions that you used in Program 15.4. First, you'll add a copy constructor to the base class, Box, by inserting the following code into Box.cpp:

```
// Copy constructor
Box::Box(const Box& aBox) :
              length(aBox.length), width(aBox.width), height(aBox.height) {
  cout << "Box copy constructor called" << endl;
}
```

> **NOTE** *You saw in Chapter 13 that you must always specify the parameter for the copy constructor as a reference.*

This copy constructor implementation initializes the data members by copying the original values and generates some output so that you can track when the Box copy constructor is being called. You must also add the copy constructor declaration to the public section of the Box class declaration in Box.h:

```
    Box(const Box& aBox);                    // Copy constructor
```

For the Carton class, you also add your own copy constructor. For a first effort, you'll try adding the following definition to Carton.cpp:

```
// Copy constructor
Carton::Carton(const Carton& aCarton) {
  pMaterial = new char[strlen(aCarton.pMaterial)+1]; // Allocate space for string
  strcpy(pMaterial, aCarton.pMaterial);              // Copy it
  cout << "Carton copy constructor" << endl;
}
```

Of course, you also need to add the prototype to the class definition in Carton.h:

```
    Carton(const Carton& aCarton);           // Copy constructor
```

> **NOTE** *In fact, the copy constructor for the Carton class is important because the class contains a data member, pMaterial, which is a pointer. Your copy constructor must duplicate the string pointed to by pMaterial, rather than just copying the pointer. Otherwise, the original and copy objects would each contain a pointer that points to the same string, and when one of the objects is deleted, the string is also deleted, and the pointer in the remaining object would be useless.*

Let's see if this works.

....

Try It Out: The Copy Constructor in Derived Classes

You can try to exercise the copy constructors that you've just defined in the Box and Carton classes by creating a Carton object and then creating a duplicate of it:

```cpp
// Program 15.5 Using a derived class copy constructor  File: prog15_05.cpp
#include <iostream>
#include "Box.h"                               // For the Box class
#include "Carton.h"                            // For the Carton class
using std::cout;
using std::endl;

int main() {
    // Declare and initialize a Carton object
    Carton candyCarton(20.0, 30.0, 40.0, "Glassine board");

    Carton copyCarton(candyCarton);            // Use copy constructor

    cout << endl
        << "Volume of candyCarton is " << candyCarton.volume()
        << endl
        << "Volume of copyCarton is " << copyCarton.volume()
        << endl;

    return 0;
}
```

This produces the following output:

```
Box constructor
Carton constructor 2
Default Box constructor
Carton copy constructor

Volume of candyCarton is 24000
Volume of copyCarton is 1
```

HOW IT WORKS (OR WHY IT DOESN'T WORK)

A cursory inspection of the output will show that all is not as it should be. Clearly the volume of copyCarton isn't the same as candyCarton, which is strange, because one is supposed to be a copy of the other. The output also shows the reason for this.

(Continued)

In order to copy the candyCarton object, you call the copy constructor for the Carton class. As part of the copy process, the Carton copy constructor must make a copy of the Box subobject of candyCarton, and to do this it should call the Box copy constructor. However, the output clearly shows that the *default* Box constructor is being called instead.

The Carton copy constructor doesn't call the Box copy constructor, simply because you didn't tell it to. The compiler knows that it has to create a Box subobject for the object copyCarton, but you didn't specify how it should be done, and the compiler can't second-guess your intentions. The best it can do is create a default base object.

 CAUTION *When you write a constructor for an object of a derived class, you must remember that you're responsible for ensuring that the members of the derived class object are properly initialized. This includes all the directly inherited data members, as well as the data members that are specific to the derived class.*

The fix for this is to call the Box copy constructor in the initialization list of the Carton copy constructor. Simply change the copy constructor definition in Carton.cpp to this:

```
// Copy constructor
Carton::Carton(const Carton& aCarton) : Box(aCarton) {
  pMaterial = new char[strlen(aCarton.pMaterial)+1]; // Allocate space for string
  strcpy(pMaterial, aCarton.pMaterial);              // Copy it
  cout << "Carton copy constructor" << endl;
}
```

Now, the Box class copy constructor is called with the aCarton object as an argument. The object aCarton is of type Carton, but the parameter for the Box class copy constructor is a reference to a Box object. The compiler will insert a conversion for aCarton—from type Carton to type Box—and this will result in only the base part of aCarton being passed to the Box class copy constructor. Now, if you compile and run the example again, the output will be as follows:

```
Box constructor
Carton constructor 2
Box copy constructor called
Carton copy constructor

Volume of candyCarton is 24000
Volume of copyCarton is 24000
```

The output shows that the constructors are called in the correct order. In particular, the Box copy constructor (for the Box subobject of copyCarton) is called before the Carton copy constructor. By way of a check, you can see that the volumes of the candyCarton and copyCarton objects are now identical.

To summarize, here's another golden rule to remember.

GOLDEN RULE *When you write your own definition of a constructor for a derived class, you're responsible for ensuring that all members of the derived class object are properly initialized, including all its directly inherited members.*

Destructors Under Inheritance

Destroying a derived class object, either when it goes out of scope or, in the case of an object in the free store, when you delete it, involves both the derived class destructor *and* the base class destructor.

You can demonstrate this by employing statements in the Box and Carton destructor definitions that will allow you to trace exactly when they're called. You can amend the class definitions that you used in Program 15.5 to do this. Add the destructor definition to the file Box.cpp:

```
// Destructor
Box::~Box() {
  cout << "Box destructor" << endl;
}
```

Don't forget to add the prototype to the class definition in Box.h:

```
~Box();                          // Destructor
```

The Carton class already has a destructor, so you just need to add the trace statement to the destructor definition. Add the following line to Carton.cpp:

```
// Destructor
Carton::~Carton() {
  cout << "Carton destructor. Material = " << pMaterial << endl;
  delete[] pMaterial;
}
```

The trace output displays the composite material so you'll be able to tell which Carton object is being destroyed by assigning a different composite material to each one. Let's see how these classes behave in practice.

Try It Out: Destructors in a Class Hierarchy

You can see how class destructors behave with objects of a derived class with the following version of main():

```cpp
// Program 15.6 Destructors in a class hierarchy File: prog15_06.cpp
#include <iostream>
#include "Box.h"                                    // For the Box class
#include "Carton.h"                                 // For the Carton class
using std::cout;
using std::endl;

int main() {
  Carton myCarton;
  Carton candyCarton(50.0, 30.0, 20.0, "Thin cardboard");

  cout << endl << "myCarton volume is "    << myCarton.volume();
  cout << endl << "candyCarton volume is " << candyCarton.volume()
       << endl << endl;

  return 0;
}
```

If you recompile the program with the changes to the header files containing the class definitions, you'll get the following output:

```
Default Box constructor
Carton constructor 1
Box constructor
Carton constructor 2

myCarton volume is 1
candyCarton volume is 30000

Carton destructor. Material = Thin cardboard
Box destructor
Carton destructor. Material = Cardboard
Box destructor
```

HOW IT WORKS

You create two Carton objects here: the first is an object with default dimensions, and the second has explicit dimensions and a material description. Then you output the volume of each object, for no particular reason.

The point of the exercise is to see how the destructors behave. The output from the destructor calls indicates two aspects of how the objects are destroyed. First, you can see the order in which destructors are called for a particular object, and second, you can see the order in which the objects are destroyed.

The destructor calls recorded by the output correspond to the following actions:

Destructor Output	Object Destroyed
Carton destructor Material = Thin cardboard	candyCarton object
Box destructor	Box subobject of candyCarton
Carton destructor Material = Cardboard	myCarton object
Box destructor	Box subobject of myCarton

You can see from this that the objects that make up a derived class object are destroyed in the *reverse* order from which they were created. The object myCarton was created first and destroyed last; the candyCarton object was created last and destroyed first.

This order is chosen to ensure that you never end up with an object in an illegal state. An object can only be used after it has been declared—this means that any given object can only contain pointers (or references) that point (or refer) to objects that have already been created. By destroying a given object *before* any objects that it might point (or refer) to, you ensure that the execution of a destructor can't result in any invalid pointers or references.

The Order in Which Destructors Are Called

For a particular derived class object, the order of destructor calls is the reverse of the constructor call sequence for the object. The derived class destructor is called first, and then the base class destructor, just as in the example. The case of a three-level class hierarchy is illustrated in Figure 15-6.

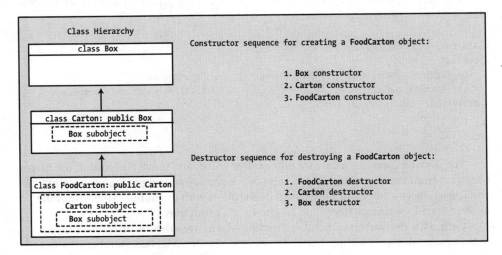

Figure 15-6. The order of destructor calls

For an object with several levels of base class, this order of destructor calls runs through the hierarchy of classes, starting with the derived class destructor and ending with the destructor for the most general base class.

Duplicate Member Names

It's possible that you could find a situation in which a base class and a derived class each have a data member with the same name. If you're really unlucky, you might even have names duplicated in the base class and in an indirect base.

Of course, this situation is confusing, and you should never deliberately set out to create such an arrangement in your own classes. However, circumstances may dictate that this is how things turn out. For example, if you're deriving your class from a base class designed by another programmer, you would almost certainly know nothing about the private data members of his class—you would only know about the base class interface. What happens if, by coincidence, the base and derived classes use the same data member names?

In fact, duplication of names is no bar to inheritance. Let's look at how to differentiate between identically named base and derived class members.

Suppose you have a class Base, defined as follows:

```
class Base {
  public:
    Base(int number = 10){ value = number; }      // Constructor
  protected:
    int value;
};
```

This just contains a single data member, value, and a constructor. You can derive a class Derived from Base as follows:

```
class Derived: public Base {
  public:
    Derived(int number = 20){ value = number; }    // Constructor
    int total() const;                              // Total value of data members
  protected:
    int value;
};
```

The derived class has a data member called value, and it will also inherit the member value from the base class. As you can see, it's already starting to look confusing! You'll see how you can distinguish the two members with the name value within the derived class by writing a definition for the total() function.

Within the derived class member function, the name value by itself refers to the data member declared within that scope—that is, the derived class member. The base class member is declared within a different scope, and to access it from the derived class member function you must qualify the member name (using the base class name and the scope resolution operator). Thus, you can write the implementation of the `total()` function as follows:

```
int Derived::total() const {
  return value + Base::value;
}
```

The expression `Base::value` specifies the base class data member, and the name value by itself refers to the member declared in the `Derived` class.

Duplicate Function Member Names

What happens when base class and derived class member functions share the same name? You can identify two situations that may arise in relation to a function in a derived class that has the same name as a base class member function.

In the first case, the functions have the same name but different parameter lists. Although the function signatures are different, this is *not* a case of function overloading. This is because overloaded functions must be defined within the same scope, and each class, base or derived, defines a separate scope.

In fact, scope is the key to the situation. The derived class function member will hide the inherited function member with the same name. Thus, when the base and inherited member functions have the same name, you must introduce the qualified name of the base class member function into the scope of the derived class with a using declaration. Either function can then be called for a derived class object, as illustrated in Figure 15-7.

```
class Base {
  public:
    void doThat(int arg);
    ...
};
```

By default the derived class function doThat() would hide the inherited function with the same name. The using declaration introduces the function name, doThat, from the base class into the derived class's scope, so the derived class scope includes both versions of the function.

```
Derived object;
object.doThat(2);        // Call inherited base function
object.doThat(2.5);      // Call derived function
```

```
class Derived: public Base
{
  public:
    void doThat(double arg);
    using Base::doThat;
    ...
};
```

Figure 15-7. Inheriting a function with the same name as an existing function

The second possibility is that the inherited functions are the same in all respects, so they even have the same function signature. You can still differentiate the inherited function from the derived class function by using the class name and the scope resolution operator to call the base class function:

```
Derived object;              // Object declaration
object.Base::doThat(3);      // Call base version of the function
```

However, there's a lot more to it than that—this subject is closely related to polymorphism, so I'll defer further discussion of this possibility until the next chapter.

Multiple Inheritance

So far, your derived classes have all been derived from a *single* direct base class. However, you're not limited to this structure. A derived class can have as many direct base classes as your application requires. This concept is referred to as **multiple inheritance** (as opposed to **single inheritance**, in which a single base class is used), and it opens vast new dimensions of potential complexity in inheritance.

Multiple inheritance is used much less frequently than single inheritance, so I won't explore it here in great depth. I'll just examine the basic ideas behind how multiple inheritance works and see where the complications come in.

Multiple Base Classes

Multiple inheritance involves two or more direct base classes being used to derive a new class, so things are immediately more complicated. The idea of a derived class being a specialization of its base leads in this case to the notion that the derived class defines an object that is a specialization of two or more different and independent class types concurrently.

In practice, multiple inheritance isn't often used in this way. More often, multiple base classes are used to add the features of the base classes together to form a composite object containing the capabilities of its base classes, sometimes referred to as "mix-in" programming. This is usually for convenience in the implementation rather than to reflect any particular relationships between objects. For example, you night consider a programming interface of some kind—for graphics programming, perhaps. A comprehensive interface could be packaged in a set of classes, each of which defines a self-contained interface that provides some specific capability, such as drawing two-dimensional shapes. You can then use several of these classes as bases to derive a new class that provides precisely the set of capabilities you need for your application.

To explore some of the implications of multiple inheritance, let's start with a hierarchy that includes the Box and Carton classes that you've been using. Suppose that you want to define a class that represents a package containing dry contents, such as a carton of cereal. It's possible to do this by using single inheritance, deriving a new class from the Carton class and adding a data member to represent contents, but you could also do it using the hierarchy illustrated in Figure 15-8.

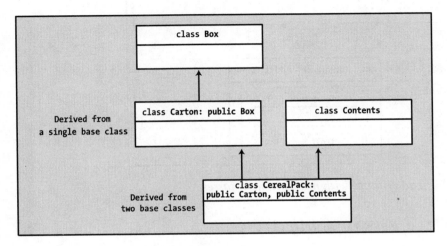

Figure 15-8. An example of multiple inheritance

The definition of the CerealPack class would look like this:

```
class CerealPack: public Carton, public Contents {
  // Details of the class...
};
```

Each base class is specified after the colon in the class header, and the classes are separated by commas. Each base class has its own access specifier and, as with single inheritance, if you omit the access specifier, the default private is assumed.

As Figure 15-9 shows, the CerealPack class will now inherit *all* the members of *both* base classes, so this will include the members of the indirect base, Box. As in the case of single inheritance, the access level of each inherited member is determined by two factors: the access specifier of the member in the base class and the base class access specifier. A CerealPack object contains two subobjects, a Contents subobject and a Carton subobject, which itself has a further subobject of type Box.

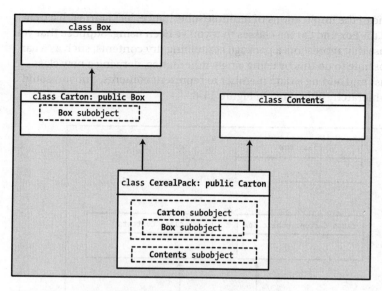

Figure 15-9. Inheritance with multiple base classes

Inherited Member Ambiguity

Let's put some flesh on the bones and define the classes in more detail. You can define the Box class in Box.h as follows:

```
// Box.h - defines Box class
#ifndef BOX_H
#define BOX_H
class Box {
  public:
    Box(double lv=1, double wv=1, double hv=1); // Constructor

    Box(const Box& aBox);                       // Copy constructor

    ~Box();                                     // Destructor

    // Function to calculate the volume of a Box object
    double volume() const;

  protected:
    double length;
    double width;
    double height;
};
#endif
```

The member function definitions are out of line and contained in the file Box.cpp:

```cpp
// Box.cpp
#include "box.h"
#include <iostream>
using std::cout;
using std::endl;

// Default constructor
Box::Box(double lv, double wv, double hv) : length(lv), width(wv), height(hv) {
  cout << "Box constructor" << endl;
}

// Copy constructor
Box::Box(const Box& aBox) :
             length(aBox.length), width(aBox.width), height(aBox.height) {
  cout << "Box copy constructor called" << endl;
}

// Destructor
Box::~Box() {
  cout << "Box destructor" << endl;
}

// Function to calculate the volume of a Box object
double Box::volume() const {
  return length*width*height;
}
```

This version of the Box class is very similar to previous versions. You have a single constructor, which also acts as the default constructor by supplying default parameter values. The volume() function is now back in the base class, where it should be.

Let's extend the Carton class definition slightly from the previous versions. The header file Carton.h should contain the following:

```cpp
// Carton.h - defines the Carton class with the Box class as base
#ifndef CARTON_H
#define CARTON_H
#include "Box.h"                        // For Box class definition

class Carton : public Box {
  public:
    // Constructor explicitly calling the base constructor
    Carton(double lv = 1, double wv = 1, double hv = 1,
        const char* pStr = "Cardboard",
        double dense = 0.125, double thick = 0.2);

    ~Carton();                          // Destructor
```

```
    double getWeight() const;            // "Get carton weight" function

  protected:
    char* pMaterial;                     // Carton material
    double thickness;                    // Material thickness inches
    double density;                      // Material density in pounds/cubic inch
};
#endif
```

There are two new data members that record the thickness and density of the material from which the Carton object is made. The constructor provides defaults for all the Carton class data members. There is a new function in the class, getWeight(), which uses the new data members to calculate the weight of an empty Carton object. The definitions, in Carton.cpp, are as follows:

```
// Carton.cpp
#include "Carton.h"
#include <cstring>
#include <iostream>
using std::cout;
using std::endl;

// Constructor
Carton::Carton(double lv, double wv, double hv,
               const char* pStr, double dense, double thick):
                      Box(lv, wv, hv), density(dense), thickness(thick) {
  pMaterial = new char[strlen(pStr)+1];    // Allocate space for the string
  strcpy( pMaterial, pStr);                // Copy it
  cout << "Carton constructor" << endl;
}

// Destructor
Carton::~Carton() {
  cout << "Carton destructor" << endl;
  delete[] pMaterial;
}

// "Get carton weight" function
double Carton::getWeight() const {
  return 2*(length*width + width*height + height*length)*thickness*density;
}
```

The Contents class will describe an amount of a dry product, such as breakfast cereal, which can then be contained in a carton. The Contents class has three data members: name, volume, and density (in pounds per cubic inch). In practice, you would probably want to include a set of possible cereal types, complete with their densities, so that you could validate the data in the constructor—but let's ignore such niceties in the interest of keeping things simple.

Here's the class definition along with the preprocessing directives that you need to put in the header file `Contents.h`:

```
// Contents.h - Dry contents
#ifndef CONTENTS_H
#define CONTENTS_H

class Contents {

  public:
    Contents(const char* pStr = "cereal", double weight =0.3, double vol = 0);
                                // Constructor

    ~Contents();                // Destructor

    double getWeight() const;   // "Get contents weight" function

  protected:
    char* pName;                // Contents type
    double volume;              // Cubic inches
    double unitweight;          // Pounds per cubic inch
};
#endif
```

In addition to the constructor and the destructor, you have a public function `getWeight()` to calculate the weight of the volume of the material. The definitions are contained in `Contents.cpp`:

```
// Contents.cpp
#include "contents.h"
#include <cstring>
#include <iostream>
using std::cout;
using std::endl;

// Constructor
Contents::Contents(const char* pStr, double weight, double vol):
                                unitweight(weight), volume(vol) {
  pName = new char[strlen(pStr)+1];
  std::strcpy(pName, pStr);
  cout << "Contents constructor" << endl;
}

// Destructor
Contents::~Contents() {
  delete[] pName;
  cout << "Contents destructor" << endl;
}

// "Get Contents weight" function
```

```
double Contents::getWeight() const {
  return volume*unitweight;
}
```

Now you can define the CerealPack class with the Carton and Contents classes as public base classes. Put the definition in a header file, CerealPack.h:

```
// Cerealpack.h - Class defining a carton of cereal
#ifndef CEREALPACK_H
#define CEREALPACK_H
#include "Carton.h"
#include "Contents.h"

class CerealPack: public Carton, public Contents {
  public:
    CerealPack(double length, double width, double height,
                                      const char* cerealType); // Constructor
    ~CerealPack();                                             // Destructor
};
#endif
```

Once again, the definitions go in the Cerealpack.cpp file:

```
// Cerealpack.cpp
#include <iostream>
#include "Carton.h"
#include "Contents.h"
#include "Cerealpack.h"
using std::cout;
using std::endl;

// Constructor
CerealPack::CerealPack(double length, double width, double height,
                                              const char* cerealType):
            Carton(length, width, height, "cardboard"), Contents(cerealType) {
  cout << "CerealPack constructor" << endl;
  Contents::volume = 0.9*Carton::volume();         // Set contents volume
}

// Destructor
CerealPack::~CerealPack() {
  cout << "CerealPack destructor" << endl;
}
```

This class inherits from both the Carton and Contents classes. The constructor requires only the external dimensions and the cereal type. The material for the Carton object is set in the Carton constructor call, in the initialization list.

The CerealPack object will contain two subobjects corresponding to the two base classes. Each subobject is initialized through constructor calls in the initialization list for the CerealPack class constructor. Note that the volume data member of the Contents class is zero by default so, in the body of the CerealPack constructor, you calculate the value for amount from the size of the carton. The reference to the volume data member inherited from the Contents class must be qualified here because it's the same as the name of the function inherited from Box via Carton. You'll be able to trace the order of constructor and destructor calls from the output statements here and in the other classes.

Try It Out: Using Multiple Inheritance

You could try creating a CerealPack object and calculate its volume and weight with the following very simple program:

```
// Program 15.7 Using multiple inheritance File: prog15_07.cpp
#include <iostream>
#include "CerealPack.h"            // For the CerealPack class
using std::cout;
using std::endl;

int main() {
  CerealPack packOfFlakes(8.0, 3.0, 10.0, "Cornflakes");

  cout << endl;
  cout << "packOfFlakes volume is " << packOfFlakes.volume() << endl;
  cout << "packOfFlakes weight is " << packOfFlakes.getWeight()
       << endl;

  return 0;
}
```

Unfortunately, you now run into a problem. This program won't compile. The difficulty is that you've rather foolishly used some nonunique function names in the base classes, so the name volume (inherited as a function from Box and as a data member from Contents) and the getWeight() function (inherited from Carton and from Contents) aren't unique in the CerealPack class. In short, you have an ambiguity problem.

Of course, when writing classes for use in inheritance, you should avoid duplicating member names in the first instance. The ideal solution to this problem is to rewrite your classes.

(Continued)

If you were unable to rewrite the classes—for example, if the base classes were taken from a library of some sort—then you would be forced to qualify the function names of your main() function. You could amend the program as follows:

```
// Program 15.7a Using multiple inheritance. Compilable version!
// File: prog15_07a.cpp
#include <iostream>
#include "CerealPack.h"                      // For the CerealPack class
using std::cout;
using std::endl;

int main() {
  CerealPack packOfFlakes(8.0, 3.0, 10.0, "Cornflakes");

cout << endl;
  cout << "packOfFlakes volume is " << packOfFlakes.Carton::volume() << endl;
  cout << "packOfFlakes weight is "
       << packOfFlakes.Carton::getWeight()+packOfFlakes.Contents::getWeight()
       << endl;

  return 0;
}
```

Now the program will compile, and when you run it, it will produce the following output:

```
Box constructor
Carton constructor
Contents constructor
CerealPack constructor

packOfFlakes volume is 240
packOfFlakes weight is 71.5
CerealPack destructor
Contents destructor
Carton destructor
Box destructor
```

HOW IT WORKS

You can see from the output that this cereal will give you a solid start to the day—a single packet weighs over 4 pounds. You can also see that the constructor and destructor call sequence follows the same pattern that you observed in the single inheritance context: the constructors run down the hierarchy from most base to most derived, and the destructors run in the opposite order.

The object of type CerealPack has subobjects from both legs of its inheritance chain, and all the constructors for these subobjects are involved in the creation of a CerealPack object.

Repeated Inheritance

The previous example demonstrated how ambiguities can occur when member names of base classes are duplicated. You also need to be conscious of another ambiguity that can arise in multiple inheritance: when a derived object contains multiple versions of a subobject of one of the base classes.

When using multiple inheritance, you must not use a class more than once as a direct base class. However, it's clearly still possible to end up with duplication of an *indirect* base class. Suppose that the Box and Contents classes were themselves derived from a class Common.

Figure 15-10 shows the class hierarchy created here.

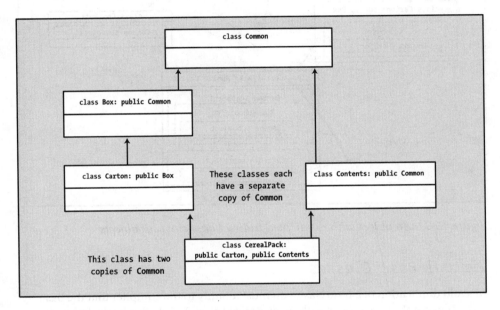

Figure 15-10. Duplicate base classes in a derived class

The CerealPack class inherits all the members of both the Contents class and the Carton class. The Carton class inherits all the members of the Box class, and both the Box and Contents classes inherit the members of the Common class. Thus, as Figure 15-10 shows, the Common class is duplicated in the CerealPack class. The effect of this on objects of type CerealPack is illustrated in Figure 15-11.

As Figure 15-11 shows, every CerealPack object will have two subobjects of type Common.

It is conceivable—just—that you actually want to *allow* the duplication of the Common class. In this case, you must qualify each reference to the Common class member so that the compiler can tell which inherited member you're referring to in any particular instance. In this case, you could do this by using the Carton and Contents class names as qualifiers because each of these classes contains a unique subobject of type Common. Of course, to call the Common class constructors when you're creating a

CerealPack object, you would also need qualifiers to specify which of the two base objects you were initializing.

More typically, though, you would want to *prevent* the duplication of a base class, so let's see how to do that.

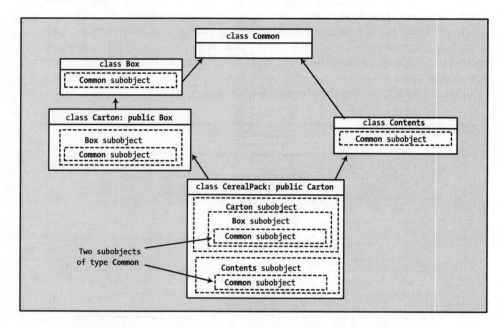

Figure 15-11. An object with duplicated indirect base class subobjects

Virtual Base Classes

To avoid duplication of a base class, you must identify to the compiler that the base class should only appear once within any derived class. You do this by declaring the class as a **virtual base class** using the keyword virtual. The Contents class would be defined as follows:

```
class Contents: public virtual Common {
  ...
};
```

The Box class would also be defined with a virtual base class:

```
class Box: public virtual Common {
  ...
};
```

Now, any class that uses the Contents and Box classes as direct or indirect bases will inherit the other members of the base classes as usual but will inherit only one instance of the Common class. So, in the preceding example, the derived CerealPack class would inherit only a single instance of the Common base class. Because there is no duplication of the members of Common in the CerealPack class, no qualification of the member names is needed when referring to them in the derived class.

Declaring the Common class as a virtual base class for the Contents and Box classes doesn't preclude the possibility of another class having Common as a nonvirtual base class and that class being a third base class for CerealPack, for example:

```
class Freebie: public Common {
  ...
};
```

The CerealPack class could be

```
class CerealPack: public Carton, public Contents, public Freebie {
  ...
};
```

Now the CerealPack class has two subobjects of type Common: one is inherited from the Carton and Contents classes, and the other is inherited from the Freebie class. In order to reference members of Common for a particular subobject, you would have to qualify the member name by the name of the direct base class from which it came. If you declared Common as a *virtual* base class of Freebie, then the CerealPack class would predictably inherit just one subobject of type Common.

Converting Between Related Class Types

Every derived class object has at least one base class object inside it waiting to get out. Conversions from a derived type to its base are always legal and automatic. Define a Carton object with the following declaration:

```
Carton aCarton(40, 50, 60, "fiberboard");
```

You can convert this object to a base class object of type Box and store the result with this statement:

```
Box aBox;
aBox = aCarton;
```

This statement converts the aCarton object to a new automatic object of type Box and stores a copy of it in the variable aBox. Of course, it's only the Box portion of aCarton that is used here—the Carton portion is sliced off and discarded. The assignment operator being used is the default assignment operator for the Box class. Remember that the preceding statements aren't equivalent to this:

```
Box aBox = aCarton;
```

The end result is the same, but in this case it involves the copy constructor for the Box class, rather than the assignment operator. The aCarton object is converted to a Box object, and that is passed to the copy constructor for Box.

As this example demonstrates, conversions up the class hierarchy (that is, toward the base class) are legal and automatic as long as there is no ambiguity. Ambiguity can arise when two base classes each have the same type of subobject. For example, if you use the definition of the CerealPack class that contains two Common subobjects (as you saw in the previous section), and you initialize an object packOfFlakes, of type CerealPack, then the following will be ambiguous:

```
Common commonObject = packOfFlakes;
```

The compiler will try to initialize the value of commonObject, but it won't be able to determine whether the conversion of packOfFlakes should be to the Common subobject of Carton or to the Common subobject of Contents.

You can't obtain automatic conversions for objects down the class hierarchy (that is, toward the more specialized classes). An object of type Box contains no information about any class type that may be derived from Box, so the conversion doesn't have a sensible interpretation.

Summary

In this chapter, you learned how to define a class based on one or more existing classes and how class inheritance determines the makeup of a derived class. Inheritance is a fundamental characteristic of object-oriented programming and it makes polymorphism possible. The important points to take from this chapter include the following:

- A class may be derived from one or more base classes, in which case the derived class inherits members from all of its bases.

- Single inheritance involves deriving a class from a single base class. Multiple inheritance involves deriving a class from two or more base classes.

- Access to the inherited members of a derived class is controlled by two factors: the access specifier of the member in the base class and the access specifier of the base class in the derived class declaration.

- A constructor for a derived class is responsible for initializing all members of the class, including the inherited members.

- Creation of a derived class object always involves the constructors of all of the direct and indirect base classes, which are called in sequence (from the most base through to the most direct) prior to the execution of the derived class constructor.

- A derived class constructor can explicitly call constructors for its direct bases in the initialization list for the constructor.

- A member name declared in a derived class, which is the same as an inherited member name, will hide the inherited member. To access the hidden member, use the scope resolution operator to qualify the member name with its class name.

- When a derived class with two or more direct base classes contains two or more inherited subobjects of the same class, the duplication can be prevented by declaring the duplicated class as a virtual base class.

Exercises

The following exercises enable you to try out what you've learned in this chapter. If you get stuck, look back over the chapter for help. If you're still stuck, you can download the solutions from the Downloads area of the Apress website (http://www.apress.com), but that really should be a last resort.

Exercise 15-1. Define a base class called Animal that contains two private data members: a string to store the name of the animal (e.g., "Fido" or "Yogi") and an integer member called weight that will contain the weight of the Animal in pounds. Also include a public member function, who(), that displays a message giving the name and weight of the Animal object. Derive two classes named Lion and Aardvark, using Animal as a public base class. Then, write a main() function to create Lion and Aardvark objects ("Leo" at 400 pounds and "Algernon" at 50 pounds, say). Demonstrate that the who() member is inherited in both derived classes by calling it for the derived class objects.

Exercise 15-2. Change the access specifier for the who() function in the Animal class to protected, but leave the rest of the class as before. Now modify the derived classes so that the original version of main() still works without alteration.

Exercise 15-3. In the solution to the previous exercise, change the access specifier for the who() member of the base class back to public, and implement the who() function as a member of each derived class so that the output message also identifies the name of the class. Now change the function main() to call the base class version of who() as well as the derived class version, for each of the derived class objects.

Exercise 15-4. Define a Person class containing data members for age, name, and gender. Derive a class called Employee from Person that adds a data member to store a personnel number. Derive a further class Executive from Employee. Each derived class should define a function that displays information about what it is. (Name and type will do—something like "Fred Smith is an Employee.") Write a main() function to generate an array of five executives and an array of five ordinary employees, and then display information about them. In addition, display the information on the executives by calling the member function inherited from the Employee class.

CHAPTER 16

Virtual Functions and Polymorphism

POLYMORPHISM IS SUCH A POWERFUL feature of object-oriented programming that you'll use it in the majority of your C++ programs. Polymorphism requires you to use derived classes, and the content of this chapter relies heavily on the concepts related to inheritance in derived classes that I introduced in the previous chapter.

In this chapter you will learn the following:

- What polymorphism is, and how you can get polymorphic behavior with your classes

- What a virtual function is

- When and why you need virtual destructors in a class hierarchy

- How default parameter values for virtual functions are used

- What a pure virtual function is, and how you declare a function as such

- What an abstract class is

- How you can cast between class types in a hierarchy

- How you can determine the type of a pointer to an object at runtime

- What pointers to members are, and how you can use them

Understanding Polymorphism

Polymorphism is a term that refers to a particular mechanism that you can obtain with a variety of object-oriented languages. Because of the way polymorphism is implemented in C++, it is often described by the term **virtual function call** in this context. As you'll see, polymorphism always involves the use of a pointer to an object or a reference to an object when you call a function. Also, polymorphism only operates within a class hierarchy between classes that share a common base class, so the ability to derive one class from another is fundamental to making polymorphism possible.

What exactly does polymorphism entail? You can get a rough idea of how it works by considering an example with more boxes, but first you need to understand the role of a pointer to a base class.

Using a Base Class Pointer

In the previous chapter, you saw how an object of a derived class type contains an object of the base class type. In other words, you can regard every derived class object as a base class object. Because of this, you can always use a *pointer to base class* to store the address of a derived class object; in fact, you can even use a pointer to any direct or indirect base class for this purpose.

Figure 16-1 shows how the Carton class is derived from the Box base class by single inheritance and the CerealPack class is derived by multiple inheritance from the Carton and Contents base classes. It also illustrates how pointers to base classes could be used to store addresses of the derived objects within such a class structure.

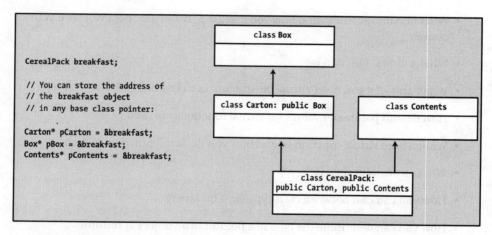

Figure 16-1. Storing the address of a derived class object in a base class pointer

The reverse of this is not true. For instance, you can't use a pointer of type CerealPack* to store the address of any (direct or indirect) base class object. This is logical, because the base classes don't describe a complete derived class object. A derived class object always contains a complete subobject of each of its bases, but each base class only represents a part of a derived class object.

Let's take a specific example. Suppose you were to derive two classes from your Box class featured in the previous chapter to represent different kinds of containers. If you did, the Carton class definition would be of the form:

```
class Carton: public Box {
   // Details of the class...
};
```

A new class called ToughPack has a similar definition:

```
class ToughPack: public Box {
    // Details of the class...
};
```

Now suppose that the volume of each of these derived types is calculated differently. For a Carton made of cardboard, you might just reduce the volume slightly to take the thickness of the material into account. For a ToughPack object, on the other hand, you might have to reduce the usable internal volume by a considerable amount to allow for protective packaging.

Given these class definitions, you can declare and initialize a pointer as follows:

```
Carton aCarton(10.0, 10.0, 5.0);
Box* pBox = &aCarton;
```

The pointer pBox, of type *pointer to* Box, has been initialized with the address of aCarton (which is of type Carton). This is possible because Carton is derived from Box, and therefore it contains a subobject of type Box. You could use the same pointer to store the address of a ToughPack object, as the ToughPack class is also derived from Box:

```
ToughPack hardcase(12.0, 8.0, 4.0);
pBox = &hardcase;
```

At any given time, the pointer pBox might contain the address of an object of any class that has Box as a base. The type of the pointer at the time of its declaration is called its **static type**—the static type of pBox is *pointer to* Box. Because pBox is a pointer to a base class, it also has a **dynamic type**, which varies according to the type of object to which it points. When pBox is pointing to a Carton object, its dynamic type is *pointer to* Carton. When pBox is pointing to a ToughPack object, its dynamic type is *pointer to* ToughPack. When pBox points to an object of type Box, its dynamic type is the same as its static type.

The magic of **polymorphism** springs from this. Under conditions that I'll get to shortly, you can use the pointer pBox to call a function that's defined in the base class and in each derived class. The function that is actually called will then be selected on the basis of the dynamic type of pBox. Consider this statement:

```
pBox->volume();
```

If pBox contains the address of a Carton object, then you can use this statement to call the volume() function for a Carton object. If pBox points to a ToughPack object, then this statement calls the volume() function for ToughPack. This would work just as well for other classes derived from Box, if you were to create them.

Thus, the expression pBox->volume() can result in different behavior depending on what pBox is pointing to. Perhaps more importantly, the behavior that is *appropriate* to the object that is pointed to by pBox will be selected automatically at runtime. It's as though the pointer has a built-in switch statement that tests for the type and selects the function to be called accordingly.

This is an extremely powerful mechanism. Situations often arise in which the specific type of object you'll be dealing with can't be determined in advance—not at design time or at compile time; only at runtime—and can be handled easily using polymorphism. Polymorphism is commonly used with interactive applications, where the type of input is up to the whim of the user.

For instance, a graphics application that allows different shapes to be drawn— circles, lines, curves, and so on—may define a derived class for each shape type, and these classes all have a common base class called Shape. The program stores the address of whichever object the user creates in a base class pointer pShape, of type *pointer to* Shape, and then draws the appropriate shape with a statement such as pShape->draw();. This calls the draw() function that corresponds to the particular shape being pointed to, and so this one expression is capable of drawing any kind of shape.

In order to operate in this way, the function being called must be a member of the base class. Let's take a more in-depth look at how inherited functions behave.

Calling Inherited Functions

Before I get to the specifics of polymorphism, you need to look more closely at the behavior of inherited member functions and the relationship that they have with derived class member functions. To help with this, you'll revise the Box class to include a function that calculates the volume of a Box object, and another function that displays the resulting volume. The new version of the class definition in Box.h and Box.cpp will be

```
// Box.h
#ifndef BOX_H
#define BOX_H

class Box {
  public:
    Box(double lengthValue = 1.0, double widthValue = 1.0,
                                   double heightValue = 1.0);

    // Function to show the volume of an object
    void showVolume() const;

    // Function to calculate the volume of a Box object
    double volume() const;

  protected:
    double length;
    double width;
    double height;
};
#endif
```

The definitions in `Box.cpp` will be

```cpp
// Box.cpp
#include "Box.h"
#include <iostream>
using std::cout;
using std::endl;

// Constructor
Box::Box(double lvalue, double wvalue, double hvalue) :
                    length(lvalue), width(wvalue), height(hvalue) {}

// Output the volume
void Box::showVolume() const {
  cout << "Box usable volume is " << volume() << endl;
}

// Calculate the voilume
double Box::volume() const {
  return length * width * height;
}
```

You no longer need to define the destructor as the default will do fine, and you don't
need the trace statement that was previously in the constructor. With the `Box` class
in this form, you can display the usable volume of a `Box` object just by calling the
`showVolume()` function for that object. You use the same data members (`length`, `width`,
and `height`), and they are specified as `protected` so that they'll be accessible to the
member functions of any derived class.

You'll also define the `ToughPack` class with `Box` as a base. A `ToughPack` object incorporates packing material to protect its contents, so its capacity is only 85 percent of the
capacity of a basic `Box` object. Therefore, you need a different `volume()` function in
the derived class to account for this:

```cpp
// ToughPack.h
#ifndef TOUGHPACK_H
#define TOUGHPACK_H

#include "Box.h"

class ToughPack : public Box {          // Derived class
  public:
    // Constructor
    ToughPack(double lengthValue, double widthValue, double heightValue);

    // Function to calculate volume of a ToughPack allowing 15% for packing
    double volume() const;
};
#endif
```

The .cpp file will contain the following definitions:

```
// ToughPack.cpp
#include "ToughPack.h"

ToughPack::ToughPack(double lVal, double wVal, double hVal) :
                                          Box(lVal, wVal, hVal) {}

double ToughPack::volume() const {
  return 0.85 * length * width * height;
}
```

Conceivably, you could have other additional members in this derived class, but for the moment, we'll keep it simple, concentrating on how the inherited functions work. The derived class constructor just calls the base class constructor in its initializer list to set the data member values. You don't need any statements in the body of the derived class constructor. You also have a new version of the volume() function to replace the version from the base class. The idea here is that you can get the inherited function showVolume() to call the derived class version of volume() when you call it for an object of the ToughPack class. Let's see if it works.

....

Try It Out: Using an Inherited Function

You can test your new derived class very simply by creating a Box object and a ToughPack object that have identical dimensions, and then verifying that the correct volumes are being calculated. The main() function to do this would be as follows:

```
// Program 16.1 Behavior of inherited functions in a derived class
// File: prog16_01.cpp
#include <iostream>
#include "Box.h"                          // For the Box class
#include "ToughPack.h"                    // For the ToughPack class
using std::cout;
using std::endl;

int main() {
  Box myBox(20.0, 30.0, 40.0);           // Declare a base box
  ToughPack hardcase(20.0, 30.0, 40.0);  // Declare derived box - same size

  cout << endl;
  myBox.showVolume();                    // Display volume of base box
  hardcase.showVolume();                 // Display volume of derived box

  return 0;
}
```

When I run the program, I get this rather disappointing output:

```
Box usable volume is 24000
Box usable volume is 24000
```

HOW IT WORKS

The derived class object is supposed to have a smaller capacity than the base class object, so your program is obviously not working as you intend it to. Let's try and establish what's going wrong. The second call to showVolume() is for an object of the derived class, ToughPack, but evidently this is not being taken into account. The volume of a ToughPack object should be 85 percent of that of a basic Box object with the same dimensions.

The trouble is that in this program, when the volume() function is called by the showVolume() function, the compiler sets it once and for all as the version of volume() defined in the base class. No matter *how* you call showVolume(), it will never call the ToughPack version of the volume() function.

When function calls are fixed in this way before the program is executed, it is called **static resolution** of the function call, or **static binding**. The term **early binding** is also commonly used. In this example, a particular volume() function is *bound* to the call from the function showVolume() during the compilation of the program. Every time showVolume() is called, it uses the base class volume() function that's bound to it.

NOTE *The same kind of resolution would occur in the derived class* ToughPack, *if you'd set the conditions appropriately. That is, if you add a function* showVolume() *(which called* volume()*) to the* ToughPack *class, the* volume() *call resolves statically to the derived class function.*

What if you call the volume() function for the ToughPack object directly? As a further experiment, let's add statements to call the volume() function of a ToughPack object directly and also through a pointer to the base class:

```
cout << "hardcase volume is " << hardcase.volume() << endl;
Box *pBox = &hardcase;
cout << "hardcase volume through pBox is " << pBox->volume() << endl;
```

(Continued)

721

Place these statements just before the return statement in main(). Now when you run the program, you'll get this output:

```
Box usable volume is 24000
Box usable volume is 24000
hardcase volume is 20400
hardcase volume through pBox is 24000
```

This is quite informative. You can see that a call to volume() for the derived class object, hardcase, calls the derived class volume() function, which is what you want. The call through the base class pointer pBox, however, is resolved to the base class version of volume(), even though pBox contains the address of hardcase. In other words, both calls are resolved statically. The compiler implements these calls as follows:

```
cout << "hardcase volume is " << hardcase.ToughPack::volume() << endl;
Box *pBox = &hardcase;
cout << "hardcase volume through pBox is " << pBox->Box::volume() << endl;
```

A static call of a function through a pointer is determined solely by the type of the pointer and not by the object to which it points. The pointer pBox is of type *pointer to* Box, so any static call using pBox can only call a function member of Box.

NOTE *Any call to a function through a base class pointer that is resolved statically calls a base class function.*

What you really want from your example is for the question of which volume() function to use in any given instance to be resolved when the program is executed. So, if you call showVolume() with a derived class object, you'd like it to determine that the derived class volume() function should be called, not the base class version. Similarly, if you call the volume() function through a base class pointer, then you want it to choose the volume() function that is appropriate to the object pointed to. This sort of operation is referred to as **dynamic binding**, or **late binding**.

The program doesn't achieve your aims yet because you have to tell the compiler that the volume() function in Box and the classes derived from Box are special, and that you want calls to it to be resolved dynamically. You need to specify that volume() is a **virtual function** because this will enable you to use a **virtual function call**.

Virtual Functions

When you declare a function as **virtual** in a base class, you indicate to the compiler that you want dynamic binding for the function in any class that's derived from this base class. A virtual function is declared in a base class by using the keyword `virtual`, as shown in Figure 16-2.

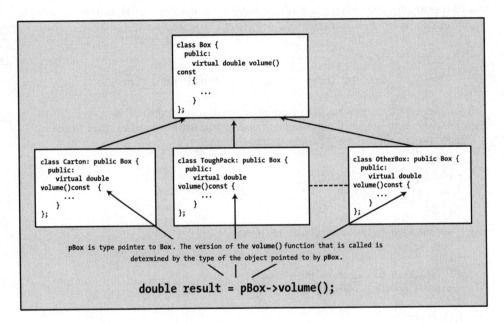

Figure 16-2. Calling a virtual function

A function that you declare as `virtual` in a base class will also be virtual in all classes that are directly or indirectly derived from the base. To obtain polymorphic behavior, each derived class may implement its own version of the virtual function (although it's not obliged to—we'll look into that later). You can make virtual function calls using a variable that is a pointer or a reference to a base class object. Figure 16-2 illustrates how a call to a virtual function through a pointer is resolved dynamically. The pointer to the base class type is used to store the address of an object with a type corresponding to one of the derived classes. It could point to an object of any of the three derived classes shown or, of course, to a base class object. The type of the object to which the pointer points when the call executes determines which `volume()` function is called.

NOTE *Describing a class as **polymorphic** means that it is a derived class that contains at least one virtual function.*

Before you read on, note that a call to a virtual function using an object is *always* resolved statically. You only get dynamic resolution of calls to virtual functions through a pointer or a reference. That said, let's give virtual functions a whirl.

Try It Out: Using a Virtual Function

To make the example work as I originally hoped, you need to make a very small change to the Box class. You just need to add the keyword virtual to the declaration of the volume() function in that class:

```
class Box {
  public:
    Box(double lengthValue = 1.0, double widthValue = 1.0,
                                    double heightValue = 1.0);

    // Function to show the volume of an object
    void showVolume() const;

    // Function to calculate the volume of a Box object
    virtual double volume() const;

  protected:
    double length;
    double width;
    double height;
};
```

CAUTION *Note that you don't need to add the* virtual *keyword to the function definition, and in fact, it would be an error to do so.*

To make it more interesting, let's implement the volume() function in a new class called Carton a little differently. Here is the class definition:

```
// Carton.h
#ifndef CARTON_H
#define CARTON_H

#include <string>
#include "Box.h"
using std::string;
```

```cpp
class Carton : public Box {
  public:
    // Constructor explicitly calling the base constructor
    Carton(double lv, double wv, double hv, string material = "Cardboard");

    // Copy constructor
    Carton(const Carton& aCarton);

    // Destructor
    ~Carton();

    // Function to calculate the volume of a Carton object
    double volume() const;

  private:
    string* pMaterial;
};

#endif
```

The definitions that go in the `.cpp` file will be as follows:

```cpp
// Carton.cpp
#include "Carton.h"

Carton::Carton(double lv, double wv, double hv, string material) : Box(lv, wv, hv) {
  pMaterial = new string(material);
}

Carton::Carton(const Carton& aCarton) {
  length = aCarton.length;
  width = aCarton.width;
  height = aCarton.height;
  pMaterial = new string(*aCarton.pMaterial);
}

Carton::~Carton() {
  delete pMaterial;
}

double Carton::volume() const {
  double vol = (length - 0.5) * (width - 0.5) * (height - 0.5);
  return vol > 0.0 ? vol : 0.0;
}
```

The `volume()` function for a `Carton` assumes the thickness of the material is 0.25, so 0.5 is subtracted from each dimension to account for the sides of the carton. If a `Carton` object has been created with any of its dimensions less than 0.5 for some reason, then this will result in a negative value for the volume, so in such a case, the carton's volume will be set to 0.

(Continued)

You'll also be using the ToughPack class as you defined it in Program 16.1. You can modify the main() function from the previous example to make use of a Carton object and also to call the showVolume() function using the pointer pBox:

```cpp
// Program 16.2 Using virtual functions   File: prog16_02.cpp
#include <iostream>
#include "Box.h"                         // For the Box class
#include "ToughPack.h"                   // For the ToughPack class
#include "Carton.h"                      // For the Carton class
using std::cout;
using std::endl;

int main() {
  Box myBox(20.0, 30.0, 40.0);          // Declare a base box
  ToughPack hardcase(20.0, 30.0, 40.0); // Declare derived box - same size
  Carton aCarton(20.0, 30.0, 40.0);     // A different kind of derived box

  cout << endl;
  myBox.showVolume();                   // Display volume of base box
  hardcase.showVolume();                // Display volume of derived box
  aCarton.showVolume();                 // Display volume of derived box
  cout << endl;

  // Now try using a base pointer for the Box object
  Box* pBox = &myBox;                         // Points to type Box
  cout << "myBox volume through pBox is " << pBox->volume() << endl;
  pBox->showVolume();
  cout << endl;

  // Now try using a base pointer for the ToughPack object
  pBox = &hardcase;                           // Points to type ToughPack
  cout << "hardcase volume through pBox is " << pBox->volume() << endl;
  pBox->showVolume();
  cout << endl;

  // Now try using a base pointer for the Carton object
  pBox = &aCarton;                            // Points to type Carton
  cout << "aCarton volume through pBox is " << pBox->volume() << endl;
  pBox->showVolume();

  return 0;
}
```

You can now recompile the example with these changes. When you run it, the output that is produced should be as follows:

```
Box usable volume is 24000
Box usable volume is 20400
Box usable volume is 22722.4
```

```
myBox volume through pBox is 24000
Box usable volume is 24000

hardcase volume through pBox is 20400
Box usable volume is 20400

aCarton volume through pBox is 22722.4
Box usable volume is 22722.4
```

HOW IT WORKS

The keyword virtual in the base class definition of the function volume() is sufficient to determine that *all* declarations of the function in derived classes will also be understood to be virtual. You can (optionally) use the virtual keyword for your derived class functions as well—this was illustrated in Figure 16-2.

TIP *In this example, I omitted the keyword* virtual *from the declarations of* volume() *to demonstrate that it is not necessary to use it. However, I recommend that you* do *use the keyword* virtual *with* all *declarations of virtual functions in derived classes, because it makes it clear to anyone reading the derived class definition that the functions are indeed virtual and that they will be linked to dynamically.*

The program is now clearly doing what you wanted in the first place. The first call to the function showVolume() with the Box object myBox is

```
myBox.showVolume();                    // Display volume of base box
```

This calls the base class version of volume(), because myBox is of type Box. The second call to showVolume() is with the ToughPack object, hardcase:

```
hardcase.showVolume();                 // Display volume of derived box
```

This statement calls the showVolume() function defined in the Box class; in fact, no other versions of showVolume() exist. The function is inherited as a public member of the ToughPack class, so you won't have a problem calling it in this way. However, the call to volume() in showVolume() is resolved to the version defined in the derived class, because volume() is a virtual function. Therefore you get the volume calculated appropriately for a ToughPack object.

The third call of showVolume() is for a Carton object:

```
aCarton.showVolume();                  // Display volume of derived box
```

(Continued)

The showVolume() function is inherited in Carton and the call to volume() is resolved to the Carton class version, so again you get the correct volume for the object.

Next, you use the pointer pBox to call the volume() function directly and also indirectly through the showVolume() function. The pointer first contains the address of the Box object myBox, then the addresses of the two derived class objects in turn. The resulting output for each object shows that the appropriate version of the volume() function is selected automatically in each case, so you have a clear demonstration of polymorphism in action.

Requirements for a Function to Be Virtual

For a function to behave "virtually," you must declare and define it in any derived class with the same name and parameter list as it has in the base class. Further, if you have declared the base class function as const, then you must declare the derived class function to const as well. Generally, the return type of the function in a derived class must also be the same as that in the base class, but an exception occurs when the return type in the base class is a pointer or a reference to a class type. In this case, the derived class version of a virtual function may return a pointer or a reference to a more specialized type than that of the base. I won't be going into this further, but in case you come across it elsewhere, the technical term used in relation to these return types is **covariance**.

From the rules for virtual function definitions, you can conclude that if you try to use different parameters for a virtual function in a derived class from those in the base class, then the virtual function mechanism won't work. The function in the derived class will operate with static binding that is established and fixed at compile time. This will be also the case if you forget to declare a derived class function as const when the base class function is const.

You can test this out by deleting the const keyword from the declaration of volume() in the Carton class and running Program 16.2 again. This action means that the volume() function in Carton no longer matches the virtual function declared in Box, and so the derived class volume() function is not virtual. Consequently, the resolution is static so that the function called for Carton objects through a base pointer, or even indirectly through the showVolume() function, is the base class version.

If the function name and parameter list of a function in a derived class are the same as those of a virtual function declared in the base class, then the return type *must* be consistent with the rules for a virtual function. If it isn't, the derived class function won't compile. Another restriction is that a virtual function can't be a template function (you learned about function templates in Chapter 9).

Virtual Functions and Class Hierarchies

If you want your function to be treated as virtual when it is called using a base class pointer, then you *must* declare it as virtual in the base class. You can declare as many virtual functions as you need in a base class, but not all virtual functions need to be declared within the most basic base class in a hierarchy of several levels. This is illustrated by the example shown in Figure 16-3.

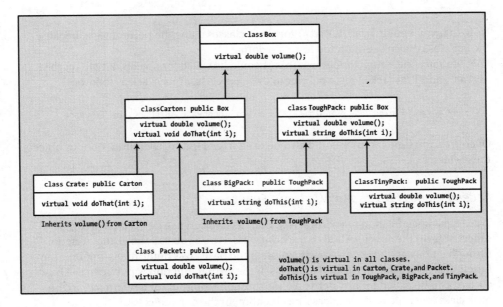

Figure 16-3. Virtual functions in a hierarchy

When you declare a function as virtual in one class, the function is virtual in all classes derived directly or indirectly from that class. For example, all of the classes derived from the Box class in Figure 16-3 inherit the virtual nature of the volume() function. You could call the volume() function for any of these classes through a pointer pBox of type Box*, because the pointer could contain the address of an object of any class in the hierarchy:

```
double result = pBox->volume();        // Call for any class in the hierarchy
```

The Crate class doesn't declare the virtual function volume(), so the version inherited from Carton would be called for Crate objects. It is inherited as a virtual function, and therefore it can be called polymorphically.

A pointer pCarton, of type Carton*, could also be used to call the volume() function, but only for objects of the Carton class and the two classes that have Carton as a base: Crate and Packet:

```
result = pCarton->volume();            // Call for Carton, Crate, or Packet
```

The Carton class and the classes derived from it also contain the virtual function doThat(). This function can also be called polymorphically using a pointer of type Carton*:

```
pCarton->doThat(12);                    // Call for Carton, Crate, or Packet
```

Note that you couldn't call doThat() for these classes using the pointer pBox, because the Box class doesn't contain the function doThat().

Similarly, the virtual function doThis() could be called for objects of type ToughPack, BigPack, and TinyPack using a pointer to the base class, pToughPack as follows:

```
string answer = pToughPack->doThis(3);  // For ToughPack, BigPack, or TinyPack
```

Of course, the same pointer could also be used to call the volume() function for objects these classes.

Access Specifiers and Virtual Functions

The access specification of a virtual function declaration in a derived class *can* be different from the specification in the base class. When you call the virtual function through a pointer, the access specification in the base class determines whether the function is accessible in the derived class. If the virtual function is public in the base class, it can be called for any derived class through a pointer (or a reference) to the base class, regardless of the access specification in the derived class.

You can demonstrate this by modifying the previous example.

....

Try It Out: The Effect of Access Specifiers on Virtual Functions

Modify the definition of the ToughPack class from the previous example to make the volume() function protected, and add the virtual keyword to its declaration:

```
class ToughPack : public Box {          // Derived class
  public:
    // Constructor
    ToughPack(double lengthValue, double widthValue, double heightValue);

  protected:
    // Function to calculate volume of a ToughPack allowing 15% for packing
    virtual double volume() const;
};
```

You must change the main() function just slightly:

```cpp
// Program 16.3 Access specifiers and virtual functions  File: prog16_03.cpp
#include <iostream>
#include "Box.h"                           // For the Box class
#include "ToughPack.h"                      // For the ToughPack class
#include "Carton.h"                         // For the Carton class
using std::cout;
using std::endl;

int main() {
  Box myBox(20.0, 30.0, 40.0);             // Declare a base box
  ToughPack hardcase(20.0, 30.0, 40.0);    // Declare derived box - same
size
  Carton aCarton(20.0, 30.0, 40.0);        // A different kind of derived
box

  cout << endl;
  myBox.showVolume();                       // Display volume of base box
  hardcase.showVolume();                    // Display volume of derived
box
  aCarton.showVolume();                     // Display volume of derived
box
  cout << endl;

// Uncomment the following statement for an error
//  cout << "hardcase volume is " << hardcase.volume() << endl;

  // Now try using a base pointer for the Box object
  Box *pBox = &myBox;                                  // Points to type Box
  cout << "myBox volume through pBox is " << pBox->volume() << endl;
  pBox->showVolume();
  cout << endl;

  // Now try using a base pointer for the ToughPack object
  pBox = &hardcase;                                    // Points to type ToughPack
  cout << "hardcase volume through pBox is " << pBox->volume() << endl;
  pBox->showVolume();
  cout << endl;

  // Now try using a base pointer for the Carton object
  pBox = &aCarton;                                     // Points to type Carton
  cout << "aCarton volume through pBox is " << pBox->volume() << endl;
  pBox->showVolume();

  return 0;
}
```

It should come as no surprise that this code produces exactly the same output as the last example.

(Continued)

Even though volume() is declared as protected in the ToughPack class, you can still call it for the hardcase object through the showVolume() function that is inherited from the Box class. You can also call it directly through a pointer to the base class, pBox. However, if you uncomment the line that calls the volume() function directly using the hardcase object, the code won't compile.

What matters here is whether the call is resolved dynamically or statically. When you use a class object, the call is determined statically (that is, by the compiler), and because the volume() function is protected in the ToughPack class, the call using the hardcase object won't compile. All the other calls are resolved when the program executes; they are polymorphic calls. In this case, the access specification for a virtual function in the base class is inherited in all the derived classes. This is regardless of the explicit specification in the derived class; the explicit specification will *only* affect calls that are resolved statically.

Default Argument Values in Virtual Functions

Because default values are dealt with at compile time, you can get unexpected results when you use default argument values with virtual function parameters. If the base class declaration of a virtual function has a default argument value and you call the function through a base pointer, you'll *always* get the default argument value from the base class version of the function. Any default argument values in derived class versions of the function will have no effect.

You can demonstrate this by altering the previous example to include a parameter with a default argument value for the volume() function.

Try It Out: Default Parameter Values

Modify the definition for the volume() function in the file Box.cpp from Program 16.3 to the following:

```
// Box.cpp
#include "Box.h"
#include <iostream>
using std::cout;
using std::endl;

// Constructor
Box::Box(double lvalue, double wvalue, double hvalue) :
                    length(lvalue), width(wvalue), height(hvalue) {}

// Output the volume
void Box::showVolume() const {
  cout << "Box usable volume is " << volume() << endl;
}
```

```
// Calculate the volume
double Box::volume(const int i) const {
  cout << "Parameter = " << i << endl;
  return length * width * height;
}
```

You'll also have to adjust the function member declaration in the Box class:

```
// Box.h
#ifndef BOX_H
#define BOX_H

class Box {
  public:
    Box(double lengthValue = 1.0, double widthValue = 1.0,
                                          double heightValue = 1.0);

    // Function to show the volume of an object
    void showVolume() const;

    // Function to calculate the volume of a Box object
    virtual double volume(const int i = 5) const;

  protected:
    double length;
    double width;
    double height;
};
#endif
```

The parameter serves no purpose here other than to demonstrate how default values are assigned.

Modify the Carton class in the same way, but make the default parameter value 50. The code in Carton.h should look like this:

```
// Carton.h
#ifndef CARTON_H
#define CARTON_H

#include <string>
#include "Box.h"
using std::string;

class Carton : public Box {
  public:
    // Constructor explicitly calling the base constructor
    Carton(double lv, double wv, double hv, string material = "Cardboard");
```

(Continued)

```
        // Copy constructor
        Carton(const Carton& aCarton);

        // Destructor
        ~Carton();

        // Function to calculate the volume of a Carton object
        virtual double volume(const int i = 50) const;
    private:
        string* pMaterial;
};

#endif
```

In the ToughPack class, you can make the default 500 and restore the public access specification for the volume() function. After these changes, the contents of ToughPack.h will be

```
// ToughPack.h
#ifndef TOUGHPACK_H
#define TOUGHPACK_H

#include "Box.h"

class ToughPack : public Box  {            // Derived class
    public:
        // Constructor
        ToughPack(double lengthValue, double widthValue, double heightValue);

        // Function to calculate volume of a ToughPack allowing 15% for packing
        virtual double volume(const int i = 500) const;
};
#endif
```

The contents of your ToughPack.cpp file should now be

```
// ToughPack.cpp
#include "ToughPack.h"
#include <iostream>
using std::cout;
using std::endl;

ToughPack::ToughPack(double lVal, double wVal, double hVal) :
                                              Box(lVal, wVal, hVal) {}

double ToughPack::volume(const int i) const {
    cout << "Parameter = " << i << endl;
    return 0.85 * length * width * height;
}
```

Once you've made these changes to the class definitions, you can try out the default parameter values with an amended main() function from the previous example, in which you simply uncomment the line that calls the volume() member for the hardcase object directly. Here's the code for that:

```cpp
// Program 16.4 Default parameter values in virtual functions
// File : prog16_04.cpp
#include <iostream>
#include "Box.h"                    // For the Box class
#include "ToughPack.h"              // For the ToughPack class
#include "Carton.h"                 // For the Carton class
using std::cout;
using std::endl;

int main() {
  Box myBox(20.0, 30.0, 40.0);          // Declare a base box
  ToughPack hardcase(20.0, 30.0, 40.0); // Declare derived box - same size
  Carton aCarton(20.0, 30.0, 40.0);     // A different kind of derived box

  cout << endl;
  myBox.showVolume();                   // Display volume of base box
  hardcase.showVolume();                // Display volume of derived box
  aCarton.showVolume();                 // Display volume of derived box
  cout << endl;

  cout << "hardcase volume is " << hardcase.volume() << endl;

  // Now try using a base pointer for the Box object
  Box* pBox = &myBox;                              // Points to type Box
  cout << "myBox volume through pBox is " << pBox->volume() << endl;
  pBox->showVolume();
  cout << endl;

  // Now try using a base pointer for the ToughPack object
  pBox = &hardcase;                               // Points to type ToughPack
  cout << "hardcase volume through pBox is " << pBox->volume() << endl;
  pBox->showVolume();
  cout << endl;

  // Now try using a base pointer for the Carton object
  pBox = &aCarton;                                // Points to type Carton
  cout << "aCarton volume through pBox is " << pBox->volume() << endl;
  pBox->showVolume();

  return 0;
}
```

(Continued)

You'll get this output:

```
Parameter = 5
Box usable volume is 24000
Parameter = 5
Box usable volume is 20400
Parameter = 5
Box usable volume is 22722.4

Parameter = 500
hardcase volume is 20400
Parameter = 5
myBox volume through pBox is 24000
Parameter = 5
Box usable volume is 24000

Parameter = 5
hardcase volume through pBox is 20400
Parameter = 5
Box usable volume is 20400

Parameter = 5
aCarton volume through pBox is 22722.4
Parameter = 5
Box usable volume is 22722.4
```

HOW IT WORKS

In every instance when you called the volume() function except one, the default value output is that for the base class function. The exception is when you call volume() using the hardcase object. This will be resolved statically, so the default parameter value for the ToughPack class is used. All the other calls are resolved dynamically, so the base class default argument value applies.

Using References to Call Virtual Functions

You can also call a virtual function through a reference; reference parameters are powerful aids to applying polymorphism. Calling a virtual function through a variable that is a reference doesn't have the same magic as calling through a pointer, because a reference variable is initialized once and only once, and therefore, it can only ever call the functions for that object. Calling a function using an argument corresponding to a reference parameter, however, is a different matter.

Suppose you define a function with a parameter that's a reference to a base class. You can then pass a *derived* class object to the function as an argument. Within the function, you can use the reference parameter to call a virtual function. When your function executes, the appropriate virtual function for the object that was passed is selected automatically. You can show this in action by modifying the function main() from Program 16.2 to call a function that has a parameter of type *reference to* Box.

Try It Out: Using References with Virtual Functions

In this example, you're going to add a new function called showVolume() as a separate global function that will output the volume of an object. You can pass it a reference argument and use that to call the showVolume() function for an object. The function definition will be as follows:

```cpp
void showVolume(const Box& rBox) {
  rBox.showVolume();
}
```

You can call this function from main() with some derived class arguments to see how it works. The only changes you need to make to the class definitions have to do with the volume() member functions, from which you should remove the i parameters and the lines that output i in their definitions.

You just need to alter the source file containing main() to the following:

```cpp
// Program 16.5 Using virtual functions through a reference to the base class
// File: prog16_05.cpp
#include <iostream>
#include "Box.h"                          // For the Box class
#include "ToughPack.h"                    // For the ToughPack class
#include "Carton.h"                       // For the Carton class
using std::cout;
using std::endl;

void showVolume(const Box& rBox);         // Prototype for global function

int main() {
  Box myBox(20.0, 30.0, 40.0);            // Declare a base box
  ToughPack hardcase(20.0, 30.0, 40.0);   // Declare derived box - same size
  Carton aCarton(20.0, 30.0, 40.0);       // A different kind of derived box

  cout << endl;
  showVolume(myBox);                      // Display volume of base box
  showVolume(hardcase);                   // Display volume of derived box
  showVolume(aCarton);                    // Display volume of derived box

  // Lines deleted

  return 0;
}

// Global function to display the volume of a box
void showVolume(const Box& rBox) {
  rBox.showVolume();
}
```

(Continued)

Running this program should produce this output:

```
Box usable volume is 24000
Box usable volume is 20400
Box usable volume is 22722.4
```

HOW IT WORKS

In the function main(), you create a base class object, myBox, and two different derived class objects, hardcase and aCarton. You then call the global showVolume() function with each of these objects as an argument. As you see from the output, the correct volume() function is being used in each case, confirming that polymorphism works through a reference parameter.

Each time the volume() function is called, a reference parameter is initialized with the object passed as an argument. Because the parameter is a reference to a base class, the compiler arranges for the binding to the virtual function volume() to occur at runtime. If you had specified the parameter as a reference to a derived class, the call would've been resolved statically, because it would've been completely determined. Only calls of a virtual function through a base class reference will result in dynamic binding.

Calling the Base Class Version of a Virtual Function

You've seen that it's easy to call the derived class version of a virtual function though a pointer or reference to a derived class object—the call is made dynamically. However, what do you do in the same situation, when you actually want to call the *base class* function for the derived class object?

Your Box class provides an opportunity to see why such a call might be required. It could be useful to calculate the loss of total volume in a Carton or ToughPack object; one way to do this would be to calculate the difference between the results returned from the base class and derived class versions of the volume() function.

You can force the virtual function for a base class to be called statically by using the class name, with the scope resolution operator, to specify the particular function you want. Suppose you have a pointer pBox that's defined as follows:

```
Carton aCarton(40.0, 30.0, 20.0);
Box* pBox = &aCarton;
```

You can now calculate the loss in total volume for a Carton object with this statement:

```
double difference = pBox->Box::volume() - pBox->volume();
```

The expression pBox->Box::volume() calls the *base* class version of the volume() function. The class name, together with the scope resolution operator, identifies a particular volume() function, so this will be a static call resolved at compile time.

 NOTE *You can call the base class implementation of any member function using the scope resolution operator, provided the access specifiers allow you access to the function.*

You can't use a class name qualifier to force the selection of a particular *derived* class function in a call through a pointer to a base class type. The expression pBox->Carton::volume() won't compile, because Carton::volume() is not a member of the Box class. A call of a function through a pointer is either a static call to a function member of the class type for the pointer, or it is a dynamic call to a virtual function.

Calling the base class version of a virtual function through an *object* of a derived class is also simple. You can use a **static cast** to convert the derived class object to the base class; then you can use the result to call the base class function. You can calculate the loss in volume for the aCarton object with this statement:

```
double difference = static_cast<Box>(aCarton).volume() - aCarton.volume();
```

Both calls in this statement are resolved statically. Casting aCarton to type Box results in an object of type Box, so the function call will be to the Box version of volume(). Calls to virtual functions using an object are always resolved statically.

Converting Between Pointers to Class Objects

If your program contains a pointer to a *derived* class, you can easily make an implicit conversion to a pointer to a *base* class, and you can do this for both direct and indirect base classes. For example, let's first declare a pointer to a Carton object as

```
Carton* pCarton = new Carton(30, 40, 10);
```

You can convert this pointer implicitly to a pointer to a direct base class of Carton (recall that Box is a direct base class of Carton):

```
Box* pBox = pCarton;
```

The result is a *pointer to* Box, which is initialized to point to the new Carton object. You could also implicitly convert a pointer to a derived class type into a pointer to an *indirect* base. Suppose you have the hierarchy shown in Figure 16-4.

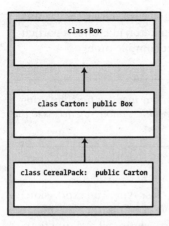

Figure 16-5. A class hierarchy

Here, Box is a direct base class of Carton, so it is an indirect base class of CerealPack. Therefore you can write the following:

```
Box* pBox = pCerealPack;
```

This statement converts the address in pCerealPack from type *pointer to* CerealPack to *type pointer to* Box. If you need to specify the conversion explicitly, you can use the static_cast<>() operator:

```
Box* pBox = static_cast<Box*>(pCerealPack);
```

The compiler can usually expedite this cast because it can determine that Box is a base class of CerealPack. Because a CerealPack object will contain a Box object, the cast is possible. The circumstances where it wouldn't be legal are if the Box class was inaccessible or if the Box class was a virtual base class, but the compiler should be able to spot these. Figure 16-5 shows the possible static casts for pointers up the hierarchy from the most derived class, CerealPack.

As you can see, the result in each case is a pointer to the subobject corresponding to the destination type. It is easy to get confused when you're thinking about casting pointers to class types. Don't forget that a pointer to a class type can only point to objects of that type, or to objects of a derived class type, and not the other way round. To be specific, the pointer pCarton could contain the address of an object of type Carton (which could be a subobject of a CerealPack object), or an object of type CerealPack. It *couldn't* contain the address of an object of type Box, because a CerealPack object is a specialized kind of Carton, but a Box object isn't.

Despite what you might think from the things you've seen so far, it's sometimes possible to make casts in the opposite direction. Casting a pointer *down* a hierarchy from a base class to a derived class is different because whether the cast works depends on what the base pointer is pointing to. For a static cast from a base class pointer such as pBox to a derived class pointer such as pCarton to be legal, the base class pointer must be pointing to a Box subobject of a Carton object. If that's not the case, the result of the cast is undefined.

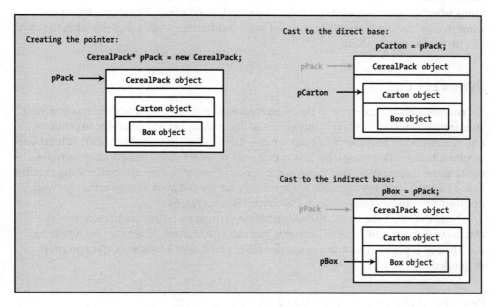

Figure 16-5. Casting pointers up a class hierarchy

Figure 16-6 shows static casts from a pointer, pBox, that contains the address of a Carton object. The cast to type Carton* will work because the object is of type Carton. The result of the cast to type CerealPack* on the other hand, is undefined because no object of this type exists.

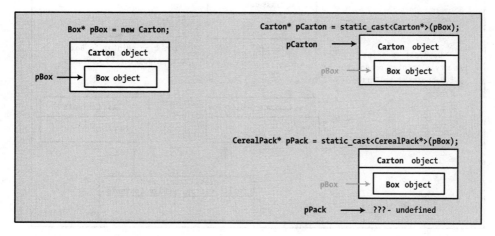

Figure 16-6. Casting pointers down a class hierarchy

If you're in any doubt about the legitimacy of a static cast, you shouldn't use it. The success of an attempt to cast a pointer down a class hierarchy depends on whether the pointer contains the address of an object of the destination type. A static cast doesn't check whether this is the case, so if you attempt it in circumstances where you don't know what the pointer points to, you risk an undefined result. Therefore, when you want to cast down a hierarchy, you need to do it differently—in a way in which the cast can be checked at runtime.

Dynamic Casts

A **dynamic cast** is a conversion that's performed at runtime. To specify a dynamic cast, you use the `dynamic_cast<>()` operator. You can *only* apply this operator to pointers and references to polymorphic class types—that is, class types that contain at least one virtual function. The reason for this is that only pointers to polymorphic class types contain the information that the `dynamic_cast<>()` operator needs to check the validity of the conversion. This operator is specifically for the purpose of converting between pointers or between references to class types in a hierarchy.

Note that the types you are casting between must be pointers or references to classes within the same class hierarchy. You can't use `dynamic_cast<>()` for anything else. To begin your exploration of the operator, you'll take a look at casting pointers dynamically.

Casting Pointers Dynamically

There are two basic kinds of dynamic cast. The first is a "cast down a hierarchy," *from* a pointer to a direct or indirect base type *to* a pointer to a derived type. This is referred to as a **downcast**. The second possibility is a cast *across* a hierarchy; this is referred to as a **crosscast**. Examples of both of these are illustrated in Figure 16-7.

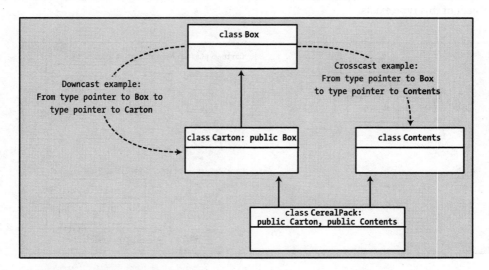

Figure 16-7. Downcasts and crosscasts

For a pointer pBox, of type *pointer to* Box, you could write the downcast shown in Figure 16-7 as

```
Carton* pCarton = dynamic_cast<Carton*>(pBox);
```

As you can see, the dynamic_cast<>() operator is written in the same way as the static_cast<>() operator. The destination type goes between the angled brackets following dynamic_cast, and the expression that you want to be converted to the new type goes between the parentheses. For this cast to be legal, the classes Box and Carton must contain virtual functions, either as declared or inherited members. For the cast to *work*, pBox must point to either a Carton object or a CerealPack object, because only objects of these types contain a Carton subobject. If the cast doesn't succeed, the pointer pCarton will be set to 0.

The crosscast shown in Figure 16-7 could be written as follows:

```
Contents* pContents = dynamic_cast<Contents*>(pBox);
```

As in the previous case, both the Contents class and the Box class must be polymorphic for the cast to be legal. The cast can only succeed if pBox contains the address of an object of type CerealPack, because this is the only type that contains a Contents object and can be referred to using a pointer of type Box*. Again, if the cast doesn't succeed, 0 will be stored in pContents.

Using dynamic_cast<>() to cast down a class hierarchy may fail, but in contrast to the static cast, the result will be a null pointer rather than just "undefined." This provides a clue as to how you can use this. Suppose you have some kind of object pointed to by a pointer to Box, and you want to call a non-virtual function member of the Carton class. A base class pointer only allows you to call the *virtual* functions of a derived class, but the dynamic_cast<>() operator can enable you to call a non-virtual function. Suppose that surface() is a non-virtual function member of the Carton class. You could call it with this statement:

```
dynamic_cast<Carton*>(pBox)->surface();
```

This is obviously hazardous. You still need to be sure that pBox is pointing to a Carton object, or to an object of a class that has the Carton class as a base. If it isn't, the dynamic_cast<>() operator returns null, and the call fails. To fix this, you can use the dynamic_cast<>() operator to determine whether what you intend to do is valid; for example:

```
if(Carton* pCarton = dynamic_cast<Carton*>(pBox))
  pCarton->surface();
```

Now you'll only attempt the function call if the result of the cast is not null.

Note that you can't remove const-ness with dynamic_cast<>(). If the pointer type you're casting from is const, then the pointer type you are casting to must also be const. If you want to cast from a const pointer to a non-const pointer, you must first cast to a non-const pointer of the same type as the original by using the const_cast<>() operator.

Converting References

You can also apply the dynamic_cast<>() operator to a reference parameter in a function, in order to cast down a class hierarchy to produce another reference. In the following example, the parameter to the function doThat() is a reference to a base class (Box) object. In the body of the function, you can cast the parameter to a reference to a derived type:

```
double doThat(Box& rBox) {
  ...
  Carton& rCarton = dynamic_cast<Carton&>(rBox);
  ...
}
```

This statement casts from *reference to* Box to *reference to* Carton. Of course, in general, the object passed as an argument may not be a Carton object, and if this is the case, the cast won't succeed. There is no such thing as a null reference, so this fails in a different way from a failed pointer cast: execution of the function stops, and an exception of type bad_cast is thrown. You haven't met exceptions yet, but you'll find out what this means in the next chapter.

The Cost of Polymorphism

As you know, there's no such thing as a free lunch—this tenet certainly applies to polymorphism. You have to pay for polymorphism in two ways: it requires more memory, and virtual function calls result in additional overhead. Each of these consequences arise because of the way that virtual function calls are typically implemented in practice.

For instance, suppose two classes, A and B, contain identical data members, but A contains virtual functions, whereas B's functions are non-virtual. In this case, an object of type A requires more memory than an object of type B.

 NOTE *You can create a simple program with two such class objects and use the* sizeof *operator to see the memory difference for yourself. Also, the* .exe *file of a program containing virtual functions will be larger than the equivalent program with non-virtual functions.*

The reason for the increase in memory requirements is that when you create an object of a polymorphic class type such as class A, a special pointer is created in the object. This pointer is then used to call any of the virtual functions in the object. The special pointer points to a table of function pointers that gets created for the class, and this table, usually called a **vtable**, has one entry for each virtual function in the class.

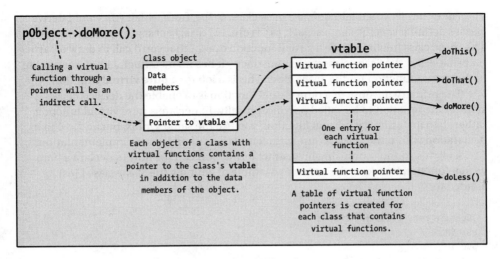

Figure 16-8. How a polymorphic function call works

When a function is called through a pointer to a base class object, the following sequence of events occurs:

1. First, the pointer to the vtable in the object being pointed to is used to find the beginning of the vtable for the class.

2. Then, the entry for the function to be called is found in the vtable for the class, usually by using an offset.

3. Finally, the function is called *indirectly* through the function pointer in the vtable. This indirect call is a little slower than a direct call of a non-virtual function, so each call of a virtual function carries some overhead in execution time.

However, this overhead is quite small, and shouldn't give you cause for concern. A few extra bytes per object and slightly slower function calls are small prices to pay for the power and flexibility that polymorphism offers. I offer this explanation then, just so you'll know why the size of an object that has virtual functions is larger than that of an equivalent object that doesn't.

Pure Virtual Functions

You might visualize a situation that demands a base class with a number of derived classes, and a virtual function that's redefined to suit each of your derived classes, but in which you can't give any meaningful definition to the function in the base class itself.

For example, you might define a base class, Shape, from which you would derive classes defining specific shapes, such as Circle, Ellipse, Rectangle, Curve, and so on. The Shape class might include a virtual function draw() that you'd call to draw a particular shape, but the Shape class itself is abstract—it has no meaningful implementation of the draw() function for the Shape class. This is a job for a **pure virtual function**.

The primary purpose of a pure virtual function is to enable the derived class versions of the function to be called polymorphically. To declare a pure virtual function rather than an "ordinary" virtual function, you use the same syntax, but add = 0 to its declaration within the class. A pure virtual function usually has no implementation.

If all this sounds confusing in abstract terms, you can see how to declare a pure virtual function by taking the concrete example of defining the Shape class I just alluded to:

```
// Generic base class for shapes
class Shape {
  public:
    // Pure virtual function to draw a shape
    virtual void draw() const = 0;

    // Pure virtual function to move a shape
    virtual void move(const Point& newPosition) = 0;

  protected:
    Point position;                          // Position of a shape

    Shape(const Point& shapePosition) : position(shapePosition) {}
};
```

The Shape class contains a data member of type Point (which is another class type) that stores the position of a shape. It's in the base class because every shape must have a position, and the constructor initializes it. The draw() function is *virtual* because you've used the keyword virtual, and *pure* because the = 0 (following the parameter list) specifies that the function isn't defined for this class. In other words, the draw() function is a *pure virtual* function. You can see that move() is also a pure virtual function.

A class that contains a pure virtual function is called an **abstract class**. In this case, the Shape class contains two pure virtual functions—draw() and move()—so it is most definitely an abstract class. Let's look a little more at exactly what this means.

Abstract Classes

Even though it has a data member and a constructor, the Shape class is an incomplete description of an object, because the draw() and move() functions are not defined. Therefore, you're not allowed to create instances of the Shape class; it exists purely for the purpose of defining classes derived from it. Because you can't create objects of an abstract class, you can't use it as a function parameter type, or as a return type. Note however that pointers or references to an abstract class *can* be used as parameter or return types.

This begs the question, "If you can't create an instance of an abstract class, then why does the abstract class contain a constructor?" The answer is that the constructor for an abstract class is there to initialize its data members. To allow this, the constructor for an abstract class can be called from the initializer list of a derived class constructor. If you try to call the constructor for an abstract class from anywhere else, you'll get an error message from the compiler.

Because the constructor for an abstract class can't be used generally, it's a good idea to declare it as a protected member of the class, as I have done for the Shape class. Note that the constructor for an abstract class must not call a pure virtual function; the effect of doing so is undefined.

Any class that derives from the Shape class must define both the draw() function and the move() function if it is not also to be an abstract class. More specifically, if any pure virtual function of an abstract base class *isn't* defined in the derived class, then the pure virtual function will be inherited as such, and the derived class will *also* be an abstract class.

To illustrate this, you could define a new class called Circle, which has the Shape class as a base:

```
// Class defining a circle
class Circle: public Shape {
  public:
    Circle(Point center, double circleRadius) : Shape(center),
                                        radius(circleRadius) {}

    virtual void draw() const {
      // Circle center is at point 'position', inherited from the base class
      cout << " Circle center " << position << " radius " << radius << endl;
    }

    virtual void move(const Point& newCenter) {position = newCenter;}

  private:
    double radius;                          // Radius of a circle
};
```

The draw() function and the move() function are defined, so this class is not abstract. If either function weren't defined here, then the Circle class would be abstract. The class includes a constructor, which initializes the base class subobject by calling the base class constructor.

NOTE *You can call the constructor of an abstract base class in the initializer list of a derived class constructor.*

Of course, an abstract class can also contain non-pure and non-virtual functions. It can also contain any number of pure virtual functions, as the example illustrates. The presence of at least *one* pure virtual function is what makes a given class abstract. A derived class must have definitions for every pure virtual function in its base; otherwise, it will also be an abstract class. Let's look at a working example of using an abstract class.

Try It Out: An Abstract Class

You could define a new version of the Box class with the volume() function declared as a pure virtual function:

```
class Box {
  public:
    Box(double lengthValue = 1.0, double widthValue = 1.0,
                                           double heightValue = 1.0);

    // Function to calculate the volume of a Box object
    virtual double volume() const = 0;

  protected:
    double length;
    double width;
    double height;
};
```

You no longer need the definition of volume() in the file Box.cpp, and you can get rid of the showVolume() function for this example as well. Because Box is now an abstract class, you can no longer create objects of this class. Both the Carton and ToughPack classes define the volume() function, so they aren't abstract, and you can use objects of these classes to confirm that the virtual volume() functions are still working as before:

```
// Program 16.6 Using an abstract base class  File: prog16_06.cpp
#include <iostream>
#include "Box.h"                  // For the Box class
#include "ToughPack.h"            // For the ToughPack class
#include "Carton.h"               // For the Carton class
using std::cout;
using std::endl;

int main() {
  cout << endl;

  ToughPack hardcase(20.0, 30.0, 40.0);
  Box* pBox = &hardcase;                    // Store address of ToughPack object
  cout << "Volume of hardcase is " << pBox->volume() << endl;
```

```
    Carton aCarton(20.0, 30.0, 40.0);
    pBox = &aCarton;                        // Store address of a Carton object
    cout << "Volume of aCarton is " << pBox->volume() << endl;

    return 0;
}
```

This generates the following output:

```
Volume of hardcase is 20400
Volume of aCarton is 22722.4
```

The pure virtual declaration of volume() in the Box class ensures that the volume() functions in the Carton and ToughPack classes are also virtual. Therefore you can call them through a pointer to the base class, and the call will be resolved dynamically. You define and initialize first a ToughPack object, and then the pointer pBox:

```
    ToughPack hardcase(20.0, 30.0, 40.0);
    Box* pBox = &hardcase;                  // Store address of ToughPack object
```

pBox now contains the address of the ToughPack object, hardcase. You use the pointer to the base class, Box, to call the ToughPack class version of the volume() function:

```
    cout << "Volume of hardcase is " << pBox->volume() << endl;
```

You can see from the output that the function call is resolved dynamically to the ToughPack version of the volume() function.

Next, you store the address of a Carton object in pBox:

```
    Carton aCarton(20.0, 30.0, 40.0);
    pBox = &aCarton;                        // Store address of a Carton object
```

The address of the ToughPack object contained in pBox is overwritten by the address of the Carton object. You then use pBox to display the volume of the Carton object:

```
    cout << "Volume of aCarton is " << pBox->volume() << endl;
```

Because pBox contains the address of the Carton object, the call is resolved dynamically to the volume() function in the Carton class.

Abstract Classes As Interfaces

Sometimes, an abstract class arises simply because a function has no sensible definition in the context of the class and only has a meaningful interpretation in a derived class. However, there is another way of using abstract classes.

An abstract class that contains *only* pure virtual functions can be used to define a **standard class interface**. It would typically represent a declaration of a set of related functions that supported a particular capability—a set of functions for communications through a modem, for example. As we've discussed, a class that derives from such an abstract base class must define an implementation for each virtual function, but the way in which each virtual function is implemented is specified by whoever is implementing the derived class. The abstract class fixes the interface, but the implementation (via the derived class) is flexible.

Indirect Abstract Base Classes

I briefly mentioned indirect inheritance earlier in this chapter. Given a base class and a derived class, it may be that the base itself is derived from a more general base class. In this situation, the most derived class inherits *indirectly* from the most base class. You can create as many levels of derivation as you need. A small extension of the last example demonstrates indirect inheritance involving an abstract class, and also illustrates the use of a virtual function across a second level of inheritance.

....

Try It Out: More Than One Level of Inheritance

You could define a Vessel class to represent a generic container that you could use as an abstract base class for the Box class. This would allow for classes representing other types of storage containers (Bottle or Can, for instance) to be derived from Vessel, so that you could deal with calculating volumes of these types of object polymorphically. You could put a definition for the Vessel class in a new header file called Vessel.h:

```
// Vessel.h - Abstract class defining a vessel
#ifndef VESSEL_H
#define VESSEL_H

class Vessel {
  public:
    virtual double volume() const = 0;
};
#endif
```

This is an abstract class because it contains the pure virtual function, volume(). You can now modify the Box class to define the Vessel class as a base:

```
// Box.h
#ifndef BOX_H
#define BOX_H
```

```
#include "Vessel.h"

class Box : public Vessel {
  public:
    Box(double lengthValue = 1.0, double widthValue = 1.0,
                                      double heightValue = 1.0);

    // Function to calculate the volume of a Box object
    virtual double volume() const;

  protected:
    double length;
    double width;
    double height;
};
#endif
```

In addition to including the header for the Vessel class and making Box derive from Vessel, you've returned the volume() function to its virtual (rather than pure virtual) status, so you can reinstate the function definition in Box.cpp:

```
double Box::volume() const {
  return length * width * height;
}
```

While you're about it, you can add another class derived from Vessel that defines a can, placing the definition in Can.h and the implementation in Can.cpp. Here is the class definition:

```
// Can.h Class defining a cylindrical can of a given height and diameter
#ifndef CAN_H
#define CAN_H

#include "Vessel.h"

class Can : public Vessel {
  public:
    Can(double canDiameter, double canHeight);
    virtual double volume() const;

  protected:
    double diameter;
    double height;
    static const double pi;
};
#endif
```

(Continued)

This class defines Can objects that represent regular cylindrical cans, such as a beer can. The class defines pi as a const static member because it's required within function members of the class. Static class members exist even if the constructor is never called, so you must initialize pi at global namespace scope. You can do this by placing the definition in Can.cpp, along with the definition of the volume() function. Here's what the .cpp file should contain:

```
// Can.cpp
#include "Can.h"

Can::Can(double canDiameter, double canHeight) :
                                diameter(canDiameter), height(canHeight) {}

// Function to calculate the volume of a Can object
double Can::volume() const {
  return pi * diameter * diameter * height / 4;
}


// Definitions for the Can class
const double Can::pi = 3.14159265;                    // Initialize static member
```

You could conceivably put the definition for pi in the header file after the class definition, but you'd need to ensure that the definition appeared between the #ifndef/#endif pair of directives, because there must be only one definition for each static data member in a program. It is generally much better to initialize static class members of a class in a .cpp file.

Believe it or not, you can exercise all the classes, new and old, with a very short main() function:

```
// Program 16.7 Using an indirect base class  File: prog16_07.cpp
#include <iostream>
#include "Box.h"                            // For the Box class
#include "ToughPack.h"                      // For the ToughPack class
#include "Carton.h"                         // For the Carton class
#include "Can.h"                            // for the Can class
using std::cout;
using std::endl;

int main() {
  Box aBox(40, 30, 20);
  Can aCan(10, 3);
  Carton aCarton(40, 30, 20);
  ToughPack hardcase(40, 30, 20);

  Vessel* pVessels[] = { &aBox, &aCan, &aCarton, &hardcase };

  cout << endl;
  for(int i = 0 ; i < sizeof pVessels / sizeof(pVessels[0]) ; i++)
    cout << "Volume is " << pVessels[i]->volume() << endl;

  return 0;
}
```

This generates the following output:

```
Volume is 24000
Volume is 235.619
Volume is 22722.4
Volume is 20400
```

HOW IT WORKS

You have a three-level class hierarchy in this example, as shown in Figure 16-9.

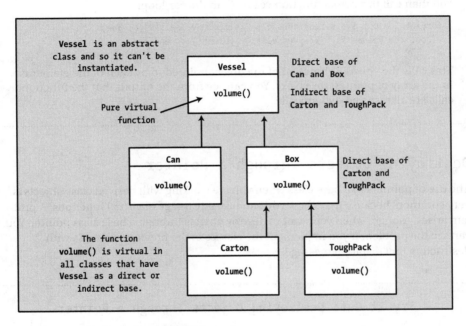

Figure 16-9. A three-level class hierarchy

The volume() function is virtual in all the classes that have Vessel as a direct or indirect base. If a derived class fails to define a function that's declared as a pure virtual function in the base class, then the function will be inherited as a pure virtual function, and this will make the derived class an abstract class. You can demonstrate this effect by removing the const declaration from either the Can or the Box class. This makes the function different from the pure virtual function in the base class, so the derived class inherits the base class version, and the program won't compile.

(Continued)

This time around, we use an array of pointers of type *pointer to* Vessel to exercise the virtual functions:

```
Box aBox(40, 30, 20);
Can aCan(10, 3);
Carton aCarton(40, 30, 20);
ToughPack hardcase(40, 30, 20);

Vessel* pVessels[] = { &aBox, &aCan, &aCarton, &hardcase };
```

The array elements are initialized with the addresses of the four different types of vessel you've defined; this declares and initializes an array with four elements. You then call the virtual function volume() in the for loop:

```
for(int i = 0 ; i < sizeof pVessels / sizeof(pVessels[0]) ; i++)
    cout << "Volume is " << pVessels[i]->volume() << endl;
```

This calls the volume() function of the object pointed to by each of the elements in the array of pointers, pVessels. You can see from the output that the function calls are all resolved dynamically.

Destroying Objects Through a Pointer

The use of pointers to a base class when you are working with derived class objects is very common, because that's how you can take advantage of virtual functions. A problem arises, though, when you want to destroy objects through a base class pointer. You can see the problem if you implement the classes in the previous example with destructors that display a message.

Try It Out: Destroying Objects Through a Pointer

To begin, add a destructor to the Vessel class that just displays a message when it gets called:

```
class Vessel {
  public:
    virtual double volume() const = 0;
    ~Vessel();
};
```

You'll need to create the Vessel.cpp file containing the following code:

```
// Vessel.cpp
#include <iostream>
#include "Vessel.h"
```

```
Vessel::~Vessel() {
  std::cout << "Vessel destructor" << std::endl;
}
```

Do the same for the Can, Box, and ToughPack classes, and add an output statement to the destructor for the Carton class. You'll need to include the <iostream> header into several of the .cpp files involved, as well.

You now need to modify main() from the previous example to initialize the pVessels array with the addresses of objects that are created in the free store. You also need to use the delete operator to release the memory when you're done.

```
// Program 16.8 Destroying objects through a pointer  File: prog16_08.cpp
#include <iostream>
#include "Box.h"             // For the Box class
#include "ToughPack.h"       // For the ToughPack class
#include "Carton.h"          // For the Carton class
#include "Can.h"             // for the Can class
using std::cout;
using std::endl;

int main() {
  Vessel* pVessels[] = { new Box(40, 30, 20),    new Can(10, 3),
                         new Carton(40, 30, 20), new ToughPack(40, 30, 20) };

  cout << endl;
  for(int i = 0 ; i < sizeof pVessels / sizeof(pVessels[0]) ; i++)
    cout << "Volume is " << pVessels[i]->volume() << endl;

  // Delete the objects from the free store
  for(int i = 0 ; i < sizeof pVessels/sizeof(pVessels[0]) ; i++)
    delete pVessels[i];

  return 0;
}
```

If you run this, you'll get the following output:

```
Volume is 24000
Volume is 235.619
Volume is 22722.4
Volume is 20400
Vessel destructor
Vessel destructor
Vessel destructor
Vessel destructor
```

(Continued)

Clearly you have yet another failure on your hands: the wrong destructors are being called in each case. Once again, the problem occurs because the binding to the destructor is being set at compile time, and because you're applying the `delete` operator to an object pointed to by a pointer to `Vessel`, the `Vessel` class destructor is called every time. To fix this, you need dynamic binding for the destructors.

Virtual Destructors

To ensure that the correct destructor is called for objects allocated in the free store, you need to employ **virtual class destructors**. To implement a virtual class destructor, you just add the keyword `virtual` to the destructor declaration in the class. This signals to the compiler that destructor calls through a pointer or a reference parameter should have dynamic binding, and so the destructor that is called will be selected at runtime. This works in spite of the fact that all the destructors have different names; destructors are treated as a special case for this purpose.

Try It Out: Calling Virtual Destructors

You can show this effect by modifying the last example— just add the keyword virtual to the destructor declaration in the base class, like this:

```
class Vessel {
  public:
    virtual double volume() const = 0;
    virtual ~Vessel();
};
```

The destructors of all the derived classes will automatically be virtual as a result of declaring a virtual base class destructor. If you run the example again, you'll get this output:

```
Volume is 24000
Volume is 235.619
Volume is 22722.4
Volume is 20400
Box destructor
Vessel destructor
Can destructor
Vessel destructor
Carton destructor
Box destructor
Vessel destructor
ToughPack destructor
Box destructor
Vessel destructor
```

HOW IT WORKS

What a difference one little keyword makes! The output shows that deleting the Box object results in two destructor calls, one for the Box destructor, and one for the Vessel destructor. Deleting the Can object also results in two destructor calls. Deleting the Carton and ToughPack objects results in three destructor calls for each, the class destructor for the object, then the destructor for the direct base class, and finally the destructor for the indirect base.

You saw earlier in the book that objects are *always* destroyed in this way, with destructor calls for each successive base class, until the "ultimate" base is reached. This is the reverse of the sequence of constructor calls when a derived class object is created.

GOLDEN RULE *When you are using inheritance and a class contains at least one virtual function, you should declare your base class destructor as* virtual *as a matter of course. A small overhead in the execution of the class destructors does exist, but you won't notice it in the majority of circumstances. Using virtual destructors ensures that your objects are properly destroyed and avoids potential problems that might otherwise occur.*

Identifying Types at Runtime

You know by now that a pointer to a base class can contain the address of an object of any derived type. This means that at a given moment in time, it may not necessarily be obvious what type of object the pointer is pointing to. The pointer may be passed as an argument or as a class member; in either case, the address is set elsewhere. The same is true for reference parameters—a parameter of type *reference to* Base may be used with an argument that is an object of any class type derived from Base.

In these situations, it helps to know the type of the pointer or reference—your course of action might depend on this knowledge. This may be particularly useful where there are two or more "limbs" in a hierarchy derived from a common base, such as the one you used earlier in Example 16.7 that contained the Can class in one limb and the Carton class in another.

The typeid() operator allows you to discover a type at runtime. To use the operator, you must include the standard header <typeinfo> into your source file; the header contains the definition of the type_info class. The typeid() operator returns an object of type type_info—or more strictly, of type const std::type_info. The type_info class implements the == operator, allowing you to compare one type_info object with another.

For a particular type, you get the type_info object by using the expression typeid(type). For example, the expression typeid(Box*) returns the type_info object that represents the type Box*. You could check whether a particular pointer, pVessel, is pointing to a derived class object of type Carton with this statement:

```
if(typeid(*pVessel) == typeid(Carton))
  cout << "Pointer is type Carton" << endl;
else
  cout << "Pointer is not type Carton" << endl;
```

In practice, you'll be using typeid() to perform rather more exciting actions than this; for example, you might be calling a non-virtual function for a particular class. A top-level const qualifier is ignored here, just as it is with parameter types in function over-loading, so that type const Carton results in the same type_info object as type Carton.

When you apply typeid() to determining dynamic types, you'll usually need to dereference a pointer to a base class in order to test the type of the object pointed to, as in the preceding code snippet. Of course, with reference parameters you just use the parameter name to get the type_info object for the type of the argument. Here's an example:

```
void Box::doThat(Vessel& rVessel) {
  ...

  if(typeid(rVessel) == typeid(Carton))
    cout << "Type Carton was passed" << endl;
  else
    cout << "Type Carton was not passed" << endl;

  ...
}
```

Here, doThat() is a hypothetical function, defined in the Box class, which accepts an object of any class derived from Vessel. The code determines whether the object that is passed as the argument to the function is of type Carton. Of course, you could test for any or all of the class types that have Vessel as a base.

NOTE *Don't forget that if you want to use the* typeid() *operator, you must include the* <typeinfo> *header into your source file.*

You should find that you don't need to use typeid() extensively in your programs. If you're overusing typeid(), then you are probably not using polymorphism where you should. Using typeid() too often makes your program very inflexible: you inevitably introduce tests for specific class types into your program, and such tests need to be changed if you introduce new classes into your hierarchy.

By contrast, virtual functions are very flexible: you can add new classes to your hierarchy without the need to change any existing code that calls virtual functions in the hierarchy. Consequently, any new class type that implements existing virtual functions will be accommodated automatically.

Pointers to Class Members

You've seen how to define a pointer to a variable of any type. You've also seen how to define pointers to functions. You can even use a pointer to store the address of a data member of a given class object (assuming it is accessible). However, you *can't* use a pointer to a function to store the address of a member function, even when the pointer type reflects the same function signature as the member function. This is because a member function uses the class type as part of its type, so the type of a member function is always different from the type of an ordinary function with the same parameter list.

You can, however, define pointers to members of a *class*, and such pointers can point to data members or member functions.

Pointers to class members provide an additional level of generalization in your programs. A pointer to a class member can point to any of several compatible members, and can be used to access the member it points to for *any* object of that class. Let's look at pointers to data members first, as they are simpler than pointers to member functions.

Pointers to Data Members

A *regular* pointer contains the address of a specific variable. It could be an ordinary variable or a data member of a class object, but in either case, the pointer contains the address of a specific location in memory.

A pointer to a data member of a class works differently. It can store the address of any data member of a class with a given *type*, and *only* refers to a particular location in memory when it is combined with a class object. To illustrate what that means, you can return to the code you had in Program 16.5 and modify the Box class to see how pointers to data members work. Let's alter the access specification for the data members to public. (This is for demonstration only; they'll revert to protected access again shortly.) The class definition will be

```
class Box {
  public:
    Box(double lengthValue = 1.0, double widthValue = 1.0,
                                      double heightValue = 1.0);

    // Function to show the volume of an object
    void showVolume() const;

    // Function to calculate the volume of a Box object
    virtual double volume() const;

  public:
    double length;
    double width;
    double height;
};
```

Because the three data members are all of type double, you can declare a pointer to a data member that could be used to refer to any of them. The pointer type will be double Box::*, and the declaration will be as follows:

```
double Box::* pData;
```

> **NOTE** *For a clumsy-looking type name like* double Box::*, *it wouldn't be a bad idea to use* typedef *to create a synonym. You could use this statement:*
>
> ```
> typedef double Box::* pBoxMember;
> ```
>
> *This create a synonym,* pBoxMember, *that you could then use in place of* double Box::*.

Now you could assign the address of the width member of the class to this pointer with this statement:

```
pData = &Box::width;
```

Of course, pData doesn't point to a specific item of data because it isn't a pointer to a data member of a class object. It is a pointer to a class member *in general*. It only refers to a particular location in memory when you combine it with an object of type Box.

A pointer to a data member is most useful when your class contains several data members of the same type. If your class only has one such class member, then you might as well refer to it directly. To make use of a pointer to a data member of a class, you need to look at some new operators.

Pointer to Member Selection Operators

So far, you've set up a pointer to a data member of a class. As I mentioned, though, you can only use it to access members of a particular *object*. You'll always use pointers such as this in conjunction with an object, a reference to an object, or a pointer to an object. Let's declare and define an object of type Box:

```
Box myBox(20.0, 30.0, 40.0);                    // Declare a box
```

Given that pData is still defined as in the previous section, you can now use it to refer to the width member of the myBox object. First, we'll work with the myBox object name directly. You can refer to the width member of myBox by using the expression myBox.*pData. You could use this expression to display the value of the width data member of myBox in the statement:

```
std::cout << "Data member value is " << myBox.*pData << std::endl;
```

This uses the ***direct pointer to member* selection operator**, .*. You can see that this is a combination of the member selection operator (.) and the dereference operator (*), applied to the pointer to data member. The .* operator is always is used to select a member of a class object by combining a class object (or a reference to a class object) with a pointer to a member. Here, the pointer pData is dereferenced to access the width member of the Box class, and the member selection operator applies this to the myBox object, so you effectively get myBox.width.

Next, you can see how this can be used with a pointer to myBox. To do so, you need to declare and initialize a *pointer to* Box with the declaration:

```
Box* pBox = &myBox;
```

You'll access the data member of myBox via this pointer, with the help of a pointer to data member, pData. To do this, you must use the ***indirect pointer to member* selection operator**, ->*, as follows:

```
cout << "Data member value is " << pBox->*pData << endl;
```

This is a combination of the arrow operator, ->, and the dereference operator, *. Let's see how all this fits together within a working example.

··

Try It Out: Using a Pointer to a Data Member

With the data members of the Box class declared as public as we discussed earlier, you can try out a pointer to a data member with the following program, which is based on Program 16.5:

```
// Program 16.9 Using a pointer to a data member  File: prog16_09.cpp
#include <iostream>
#include "Box.h"                        // For the Box class
#include "ToughPack.h"                  // For the ToughPack class
#include "Carton.h"                     // For the Carton class
using std::cout;
using std::endl;

typedef double Box::* pBoxMember;       // Define pointer to data member type

int main() {
  Box myBox(20.0, 30.0, 40.0);          // Declare a base box
  ToughPack hardcase(35.0, 45.0, 55.0); // Declare a derived box
  Carton aCarton(48.0, 58.0, 68.0);     // A different kind of derived box

  pBoxMember pData = &Box::length;      // Define pointer to Box data member

  cout << endl;
```

(Continued)

```
// Using a pointer to class data member with class objects
cout << "length member of myBox is " << myBox.*pData << endl;
pData = &Box::width;

cout << "width member of myBox is " << myBox.*pData << endl;
pData = &Box::height;

cout << "height member of myBox is " << myBox.*pData << endl;
cout << "height member of hardcase is " << hardcase.*pData << endl;
cout << "height member of aCarton is " << aCarton.*pData << endl;

Box* pBox = &myBox;                        // Define pointer to Box

// Using a pointer to class data member with a pointer to the base class
cout << "height member of myBox is " << pBox->*pData << endl;
pBox = &hardcase;
cout << "height member of hardcase is " << pBox->*pData << endl;

cout << endl;
return 0;
}
```

If you compile and run this, you will get this output:

```
length member of myBox is 20
width member of myBox is 30
height member of myBox is 40
height member of hardcase is 55
height member of aCarton is 68
height member of myBox is 40
height member of hardcase is 55
```

HOW IT WORKS

Prior to the definition of main(), you define the type pBoxMember with the statement:

```
typedef double Box::* pBoxMember;          // Define pointer to data member type
```

This defines pBoxMember as a synonym for the type *pointer to a* double *member of* Box.

After defining objects of each of the classes Box, Carton, and ToughPack, you declare and initialize a pointer to a double member of the Box class with this declaration:

```
pBoxMember pData = &Box::length;           // Define pointer to Box data member
```

pData now points to the length member of the Box class, so you can use it to refer to the length member of any Box object. You display the length member of myBox with this statement:

```
cout << "length member of myBox is " << myBox.*pData << endl;
```

Because pData is a pointer, you can reassign it to point to a different member of the Box class:

```
pData = &Box::width;
```

Now pData points to the width member of the class. Remember that pData can only store the address of a data member of type double. If there was a data member of a different type, string say, you'd have to declare a different pointer to class data member to store the address.

You're now able to display the value of the width member of myBox with a very similar statement to the earlier one:

```
cout << "width member of myBox is " << myBox.*pData << endl;
```

Just to prove that it wasn't a fluke, you store the address of the height member of Box and display the value of that member for the myBox object with these statements:

```
pData = &Box::height;
cout << "height member of myBox is " << myBox.*pData << endl;
```

Of course, every object of a class derived from Box contains a Box subobject, so you're also able to use the pointer to data member with Carton and ToughPack objects.

After declaring and initializing pBox, use the indirect pointer to member selection operator to display the value of the height member of myBox:

```
Box* pBox = &myBox;
cout << "height member of myBox is " << pBox->*pData << endl;
```

Of course, this also works when the pointer to the base class contains the address of a derived class object:

```
pBox = &hardcase;
cout << "height member of hardcase is " << pBox->*pData << endl;
```

This displays the value of the height member of the object pointed to by pBox, so you effectively get the value of hardcase.height.

Pointers to Member Functions

The type of a *pointer to a member function of a class* involves the class type as well as the function parameter list and return type. This means that such a pointer is specific to a class, and can't be used to store addresses of function members of any other class. Apart from that, such pointers follow the same principles as the pointers to functions that we discussed in Chapter 9. The declaration of a pointer to a member function gets a little messy, so let's get down to a specific instance.

Let's reset the Box class data members to be protected, and add public functions to retrieve the values of the data members:

```
class Box {
  public:
    Box(double lengthValue = 1.0, double widthValue = 1.0,
                                  double heightValue = 1.0);

    // Function to show the volume of an object
    void showVolume() const;

    // Function to calculate the volume of a Box object
    virtual double volume() const;

    // Get values of data members
    double getLength() const { return length; }
    double getWidth() const { return width; }
    double getHeight() const { return height; }

  protected:
    double length;
    double width;
    double height;
};
```

You can now declare a pointer to member function of Box, which you can use to store the address of any of the three functions you've added. The pointer is declared as follows:

```
double(Box::*pGet)() const;
```

This declares the pointer pGet. As with the pointer to data member, this points to a function member of the class, and only translates to a specific function when it is combined with a class object. The class name qualifies the pointer name within the parentheses and identifies the pointer with the class. In general, to declare a pointer to a function for a given class, class_type, you would write this:

```
return_type(class_type::*pointer_name)(parameter_type_list);
```

This is a complicated declaration. It starts with the return type for member functions that can be pointed to. The first pair of parentheses encloses the specification for the pointer name, pointer_name, and the second pair of parentheses encloses the parameter list that will be common to member functions that can be pointed to. Because this isn't simple and multiple occurrences of this won't enhance the readability of the code, such types are very often declared using a typedef within a program file. Instead of the declaration you just saw, you can begin again by defining a synonym for the type of the pointer pGet with this statement:

```
typedef double(Box::*pBoxFunction)() const;
```

Now you can use the type pBoxFunction to declare a pointer:

```
pBoxFunction pGet = &Box::getLength;
```

As well as declaring the pointer pGet, this statement also initializes pGet with the address of the function getLength(). Of course, pGet can only point to functions that are members of the Box class that have the return type and parameter list as specified in the typedef statement. This also means that pGet can only point to const member functions.

Here is the general form for declaring a synonym for a pointer to a member function type:

```
typedef return_type(class_type::*ptr_typename)(parameter_type_list);
```

This defines the type ptr_typename. Pointers of this type can store the address of any member function of the class class_type that has a return type return_type, and the parameter types listed in parameter_type_list.

You use pointers to member functions in combination with a class object, a reference to an object, or a pointer, and use the same operators you saw in the context of pointers to class data members. Let's give pointer to member functions a whirl in another example.

Try It Out: Pointers to Member Functions

With the Box class defined as you have just seen and the other classes the same
as in the previous example, you can call members of the Box class through a
pointer to the member function with the following code:

```cpp
// Program 16.10 Using a pointer to a function member    File: prog16_10.cpp
#include <iostream>
#include "Box.h"                        // For the Box class
#include "ToughPack.h"                  // For the ToughPack class
#include "Carton.h"                     // For the Carton class
using std::cout;
using std::endl;

typedef double (Box::*pBoxFunction)() const;  // Pointer to member function type

int main() {
  Box myBox(20.0, 30.0, 40.0);          // Declare a base box
  ToughPack hardcase(35.0, 45.0, 55.0); // Declare a derived box
  Carton aCarton(48.0, 58.0, 68.0);     // A different kind of derived box

  pBoxFunction pGet = &Box::getLength;  // Pointer to member function

  cout << endl;

  // Call member function for an object through the pointer
  cout << "length member of myBox is " << (myBox.*pGet)() << endl;

  pGet = &Box::getWidth;
  cout << "width member of myBox is " << (myBox.*pGet)() << endl;

  pGet = &Box::getHeight;
  cout << "height member of myBox is " << (myBox.*pGet)() << endl;

  // It works for derived class objects too
  cout << "height member of hardcase is " << (hardcase.*pGet)() << endl;
  cout << "height member of aCarton is " << (aCarton.*pGet)() << endl;

  Box* pBox = &myBox;                    // Pointer to the base class

  // Calling a function with a pointer to a class object
  cout << "height member of myBox is " << (pBox->*pGet)() << endl;

  pBox = &hardcase;
  cout << "height member of hardcase is " << (pBox->*pGet)() << endl;

  cout << endl;
  return 0;
}
```

This program generates the following output:

```
length member of myBox is 20
width member of myBox is 30
height member of myBox is 40
height member of hardcase is 55
height member of aCarton is 68
height member of myBox is 40
height member of hardcase is 55
```

HOW IT WORKS

The typedef defines a synonym for a pointer to Box member function type:

```
typedef double(Box::*pBoxFunction)() const;  // Pointer to member function type
```

Pointers of this type can only point to function members of the Box class that have no arguments, return a value of type double, *and* are const. Another function member that differs in *any* respect requires a different pointer type.

You use the type that you've defined in main() to declare the pointer pGet:

```
pBoxFunction pGet = &Box::getLength;    // Pointer to member function
```

You can use pGet to store the address of any of the three functions in Box that retrieve the values of the data members, because they all have the same signature and return type. Here, it is initialized with the address of the getLength() function member.

To call the getLength() function for the myBox object, you just use the direct pointer member selection operator:

```
cout << "length member of myBox is " << (myBox.*pGet)() << endl;
```

The parentheses around the expression myBox.*pGet are mandatory—without them, the statement won't compile. This is because the precedence of the function call operator, (), is higher than the precedence of the operator .*. Without the parentheses, the expression would be equivalent to myBox.*(pGet()). In this case, you'd be trying to apply the direct member selection operator to the value return by a function called pGet() in the global namespace. The same applies later in the program, when you use the indirect member selection operator to call a function member through a pointer to a class object:

```
cout << "height member of myBox is " << (pBox->*pGet)() << endl;
```

Once again, the function call operator is of a higher precedence than the indirect member selection operator, and so you must include the parentheses. As you can see from the output from the rest of the code in the example, you can call functions for derived class objects through the pointer pGet in the same way as you did for a pointer to a class data member.

Passing Pointers to Members to a Function

The parameters of member functions can be *pointer to a member*. They can be pointers to data members, or pointers to function members. Let's look at an example of the latter.

By applying the proverbial sledgehammer to crack a nut, you could write a function to calculate the area of any side of a Box object as a function member of the Box class with two parameters that are pointers to member functions:

```
class Box {
  public:
    double sideArea(double (Box::*pGetSide1)() const,
                                    double (Box::*pGetSide2)() const) {
      return (this->*pGetSide1)() * (this->*pGetSide2)();
    }

  // Rest of the class as before ...
};
```

This code shows the parameter types in their full glory, although you can make the same code look much simpler by first defining the type, pBoxFunction, from the previous example using typedef:

```
typedef double (Box::*pBoxFunction)() const;   // Pointer to member function type
```

Now the function definition in the class becomes

```
class Box {
  public:
    double sideArea(pBoxFunction pGetSide1, pBoxFunction pGetSide2) {
      return (this->*pGetSide1)() * (this->*pGetSide2)();
    }

  // Rest of the class as before ...
};
```

Given a Box object myBox, you could obtain the area of a side with a statement such as this:

```
std::cout << "Side area is "
          << myBox.sideArea(&Box::getHeight, &Box::getLength)
          << std::endl;
```

This passes the addresses of the member functions getHeight() and getLength() as arguments to the sideArea() function, so these will be used to obtain the values for the side lengths in the area calculation.

You could equally well call this function for a derived class object, because the function will be inherited. Of course, you could also call it through a base class pointer for a Box object, or an object of the Carton or ToughPack classes.

Summary

In this chapter, I've covered the principal ideas involved in using inheritance. The fundamentals that you should keep in mind are these:

- Polymorphism involves calling a function through a pointer or a reference and having the call resolved dynamically—that is, the function to be called is determined when the program is executing.

- A function in a base class may be declared as virtual. This forces all occurrences of the function in classes that are derived from the base to be virtual as well. When you call a virtual function through a pointer or a reference, the function call is resolved dynamically and the type of object for which the function call is made will determine the particular function that is used.

- A call of a virtual function using an object and the direct member selection operator is resolved statically—that is, at compile time.

- If a base class contains a virtual function, then you should always declare the base class destructor as virtual. This will ensure correct selection of a destructor for dynamically created derived class objects.

- A pure virtual function has no definition. A virtual function in a base class can be specified as pure by placing = 0 at the end of the function declaration.

- A class with one or more pure virtual functions is called an abstract class, for which no objects can be created. In any derived class, all the inherited pure virtual functions must be defined. If they're not, it too becomes an abstract class, and no objects of the class can be created.

- Default argument values for parameters in virtual functions are assigned statically, so if default values for a base version of a virtual function exist, default values specified in a derived class will be ignored for dynamically resolved function calls.

- You can declare pointers to class members. These can be pointers to data members or pointers to function members. You can use such a pointer in conjunction with an object, a reference, or a pointer to an object, to refer to the class member of the object defined by the pointer to member.

Exercises

The following exercises enable you to try out what you've learned in this chapter. If you get stuck, look back over the chapter for help. If you're still stuck after that, you can download the solutions from the Apress website (http://www.apress.com/book/download.html), but that really should be a last resort.

Exercise 16-1. As in last chapter's exercises, define a base class called Animal that contains two private data members: a string member to store the name of the animal (e.g., "Fido"), and an integer member, weight, that will contain the weight of the Animal in pounds. Also include a virtual public member function, who(), that returns a string object containing the name and weight of the Animal object, and a pure virtual function called sound() that in a derived class should return a string representing the sound the animal makes. Derive at least three classes—Sheep, Dog, and Cow—with the class Animal as a public base, and implement the sound() function appropriately in each class.

Define a class called Zoo that can store up to 50 animals of various types in an array (use an array of pointers). Write a main() function to create a random sequence of a given number of derived class objects and store pointers to them in a Zoo object. Use a member function of the Zoo object to output information about each animal in the Zoo, and the sound that it makes.

Exercise 16-2. Define a class called BaseLength that stores a length as an integral number of millimeters, and which has a member function length() that returns a double value specifying the length. Derive classes called Inches, Meters, Yards, and Perches from the BaseLength class that override the base class length() function to return the length as a double value in the appropriate units. (1 inch is 25.4 millimeters; 1 meter is 1000 millimeters; 1 yard is 36 inches; 1 perch [US] is 5.5 yards.). Define a main() function to read a series of lengths in various units and create the appropriate derived class objects, storing their addresses in an array of type BaseLength*. Output each of the lengths in millimeters as well as the original units.

Exercise 16-3. Define conversion operator functions to convert each of the derived types in the previous example to any other derived type. For example, in the Inches class, define members operator Meters(), operator Perches() and operator Yards(). Add code to main() to output each measurement in the four different units. (Remember that conversion operators don't need to have a return type specified because it is implicit in their name.)

Exercise 16-4. Repeat the previous exercise using constructors for the conversions instead of conversion operators.

CHAPTER 17

Program Errors and Exception Handling

EXCEPTIONS ALLOW YOU to signal errors or unexpected conditions in your C++ programs. Using exceptions to signal errors is not mandatory, and you'll sometimes find it more convenient to handle them in other ways. However, it is important to understand how exceptions work, because they can arise out of the use of standard language features such as the operators new and dynamic_cast, and they're used extensively within the standard library.

In this chapter you will learn the following:

- What an exception is

- How you can use exceptions to signal error conditions in your program

- How you handle exceptions

- What exceptions are defined within the standard library

- How you can limit the types of exceptions that a function can throw

- How to deal with exceptions that are thrown in a constructor

- How an exception being thrown can affect a destructor for a class

Handling Errors

Error handling is a fundamental element of successful programming. You need to equip your program to deal with potential errors and abnormal events, and this can take more effort than writing the code that executes when things work the way they should. The quality of the error-handling code that you write determines how robust your program is, and it is usually a major factor in making a program user-friendly. It also has a substantial impact on how easy it is to correct errors in the code or to add functionality to your application.

Not all errors are equal though, and the nature of the error determines how it is best dealt with in your program. In many cases, you'll want to deal with errors directly where they occur. For example, consider the task of reading input from the keyboard. Typing mistakes can result in erroneous input, but this isn't really a serious problem. It's usually quite easy to detect an input error, and the most appropriate course of action is often simply to discard the input and prompt the user to enter the data again.

In this case, the error-handling code is integrated with the code that handles the overall input process.

More serious errors are often recoverable and can be dealt with in a manner that doesn't prejudice other activity within a program. When an error is discovered within a function, it's often convenient to return an error code of some kind to tell the caller about the error so that the caller can decide how best to proceed.

Exceptions provide you with an *additional* approach to handling errors—they don't replace the kinds of mechanisms I have just described. The primary advantage of using exceptions to signal errors is that the error-handling code is separated completely from the code that caused the error.

Understanding Exceptions

An **exception** is a temporary object, of any type, that is used to signal an error. An exception could be a basic type of object, such as int or char*, but it's usually an object of a class that you define specially for the purpose. An exception object is intended to carry information from the point at which the error occurred to the code that is to handle the error, and because usually more than one piece of information is involved, this is best done with an object of a class.

When you identify an error in your code, you can signal the error by **throwing** an exception. The term throwing effectively indicates what happens. The exception is tossed to another block of code that catches the exception and deals with it. Code that may throw exceptions must be enclosed within a special block bounded by braces, called a try **block**. If a statement not within a try block throws an exception, your program terminates. I'll discuss this a little further in a moment.

A try block is followed by one or more catch **blocks**. Each catch block contains the code to handle a particular kind of exception; for this reason, a catch block is sometimes referred to as a **handler**. Thus, if you throw exceptions when errors occur, all the code that deals with the errors is within catch blocks, completely separate from the code that is executed when nothing is wrong. The code to handle normal events is completely separated from the code that handles exceptional events.

As Figure 17-1 shows, a try block is a normal block between braces preceded by the keyword try. Each time the try block executes, it may throw any one of several different kinds of exception. Therefore, it may be followed by a number of different catch blocks, each of which is intended to handle a different type of exception. The type of exception that a handler deals with is identified by a single parameter between parentheses. You place the catch keyword followed by the parentheses enclosing the parameter immediately before the braces for the catch block that contains the code to handle the exception.

A catch block is only executed when an exception of a matching type is thrown. If a try block doesn't throw an exception, then none of the corresponding catch blocks is executed. You can't branch into a try block, by using a goto, for instance. The only way to execute a try block is to start from the beginning, with the first statement following the opening brace.

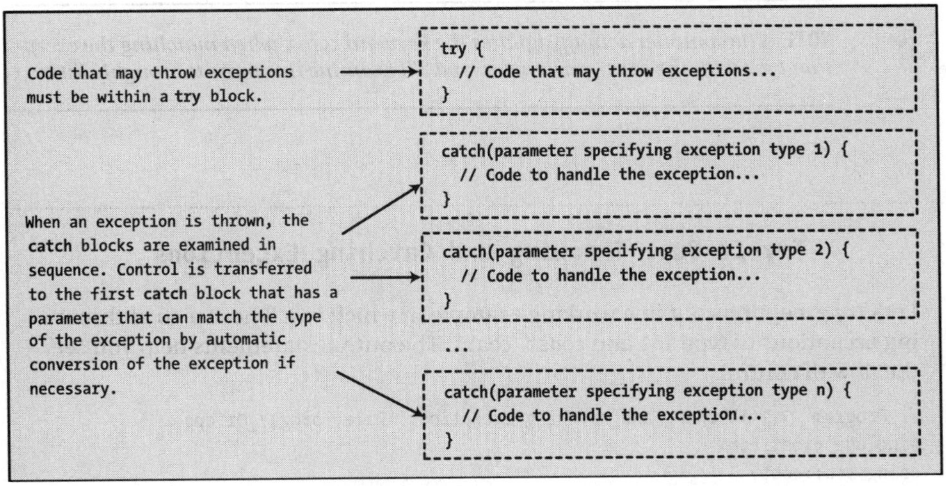

Figure 17-1. A try block and its catch blocks

Throwing an Exception

It's high time you threw an exception to find out what happens when you do. Although you should always use class objects for exceptions (as you'll do later in the chapter), you can begin by using basic types, because doing so will keep the code very simple while you explore what's going on.

You throw an exception using a **throw expression**, which you write using the keyword throw. Here's an example of how to throw an exception:

```
try {
  // Code that may throw exceptions...

  if(test > 5)
    throw "test is greater than 5";              // Throws an exception

  // This code executes if the exception is not thrown
}
catch(const char* message) {
  // Code to handle the exception...
  // This code executes if an exception of type 'char*' or 'const char*' is thrown
  cout << message << endl;
}
```

If the value of test is greater than 5, the throw statement throws an exception. In this case, the exception is, "test is greater than 5". Control is immediately transferred out of the try block, to the first handler for the type of the exception being thrown: const char*. You have just the one handler here, which happens to catch exceptions of type const char*, so the statement in the catch block executes, and this displays the exception.

NOTE *The compiler actually ignores the keyword* const *when matching the exception type with the* catch *parameter type. I'll examine this more thoroughly later.*

Try It Out: Throwing and Catching Exceptions

Let's try exceptions out in a working example in which you'll have a go at throwing exceptions of type int and const char*. The output statements help you see the flow of control:

```cpp
// Program 17.1 Throwing and catching exceptions  File: prog17_01.cpp
#include <iostream>
using std::cout;
using std::endl;

int main() {
  cout << endl;
  for(int i = 0 ; i < 7 ; i++) {
    try {
      if(i < 3)
        throw i;
      cout << " i not thrown - value is " << i << endl;

      if(i > 5)
        throw "Here is another!";
      cout << " End of the try block." << endl;
    }
    catch(const int i) {          // Catch exceptions of type int
      cout << " i caught - value is " << i << endl;
    }
    catch(const char* pmessage) { // Catch exceptions of type char*
      cout << "  \"" << pmessage << "\" caught" << endl;
    }

    cout << "End of the for loop body (after the catch blocks) - i is "
        << i << endl;
  }

  return 0;
}
```

This example produces the following output:

```
  i caught - value is 0
End of the for loop body (after the catch blocks) - i is 0
  i caught - value is 1
End of the for loop body (after the catch blocks) - i is 1
  i caught - value is 2
End of the for loop body (after the catch blocks) - i is 2
  i not thrown - value is 3
  End of the try block.
End of the for loop body (after the catch blocks) - i is 3
  i not thrown - value is 4
  End of the try block.
End of the for loop body (after the catch blocks) - i is 4
  i not thrown - value is 5
  End of the try block.
End of the for loop body (after the catch blocks) - i is 5
  i not thrown - value is 6
  "Here is another!" caught
End of the for loop body (after the catch blocks) - i is 6
```

HOW IT WORKS

Within the for loop, you have a try block containing code that will throw an exception of type int if i (the loop counter) is less than 3, and an exception of type const char* if i is greater than 5:

```
try {
  if(i < 3)
    throw i;
  cout << "  i not thrown - value is " << i << endl;

  if(i > 5)
    throw "Here is another!";
  cout << "  End of the try block." << endl;
}
```

Throwing an exception *immediately* transfers control out of the try block, so the output statement at the end of the try block only executes if no exception is thrown. You can see from the output that this is the case. You only get output from the last statement when i has the value 3, 4, or 5. For all other values of i, an exception is thrown, so the output line is not executed.

The first catch block immediately follows the try block:

```
catch(const int i) {          // Catch exceptions of type int
  cout << "  i caught - value is " << i << endl;
}
```

(Continued)

The exception handlers for a try block must immediately follow the try block. If you place any code between the try block and the first catch block, or between successive catch blocks for a try block, then the program won't compile. This catch block handles exceptions of type int, and you can see from the output that it executes when the first throw statement is executed. You can also see that the next catch block is *not* executed in this case. After this handler executes, control passes directly to the last statement at the end of the loop.

The second handler deals with exceptions of type char*:

```
catch(const char* pmessage) { // Catch exceptions of type char*
  cout << " \"" << pmessage << "\" caught" << endl;
}
```

When you throw the exception "Here is another!", control passes from the throw statement directly to this handler, skipping the previous catch block. If no exception is thrown, then neither of the catch blocks is executed. You could put this catch block before the previous handler, and the program would work just as well. On this occasion, the sequence of the handlers doesn't matter, but that is not always the case. You'll see examples of when the order of the handlers is important later in this chapter.

Here is the statement that marks the end of an iteration of the loop:

```
cout << "End of the for loop (after the catch blocks) - i is "
    << i << endl;
```

This code is executed whether or not a handler is executed. As you can see, throwing an exception doesn't end the program—unless you want it to, of course. If you can fix the problem that caused the exception within the handler, then your program can continue.

The Exception Handling Process

Having seen the example, you should have a fairly clear idea of the sequence of events when an exception is thrown. Some other things happen in the background, though, and you might be able to guess some of them if you think about how control is transferred from the try block to the catch block. The throw/catch sequence of events is illustrated conceptually in Figure 17-2.

Of course, a try block is a statement block, and you know already that a statement block always defines a scope. Throwing an exception leaves the try block immediately, and at that point, all the automatic objects that have been declared within the try block (up to the point when the exception is thrown) are destroyed. The fact that none of the automatic objects created in the try block exists by the time the handler code is executed is most important—it implies that you must not throw an exception object that's a pointer to an object that is local to the try block. It is also the reason why the exception object is copied.

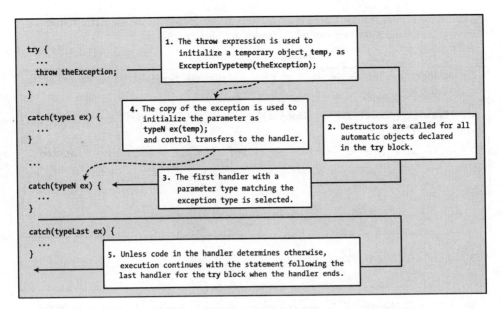

Figure 17-2. The mechanism behind throwing and catching an exception

 CAUTION *An exception object must be of a type that can be copied. An object of a class that has a private copy constructor* can't *be used as an exception.*

Because the throw expression is used to initialize a temporary object—and therefore creates a copy of the exception—you *can* throw objects that are local to the try block. The copy of the object that is thrown will then be used to initialize the parameter for the catch block when the handler has been selected.

The catch block is *also* a statement block, so when the catch block has finished executing, all automatic objects that are local to it (including the parameter) will be destroyed. Unless you use a goto or a return statement to transfer control out of the catch block, execution continues with the statement immediately following the last catch block for this try block.

Once a handler has been selected for an exception and control has been passed to it, the exception is considered handled. This is true even if you leave the catch block empty and it does nothing.

Unhandled Exceptions

If an exception thrown in a try block is not handled by any of its catch blocks, then (subject to the possibility of nested try blocks, which I'll discuss shortly) the standard library function terminate() is called. This function is declared in the <exception> header and calls a predefined **default terminate handler function**, which in turn calls the standard library function abort() declared in the <cstdlib> header. The sequence of events for an uncaught exception is shown in Figure 17-3.

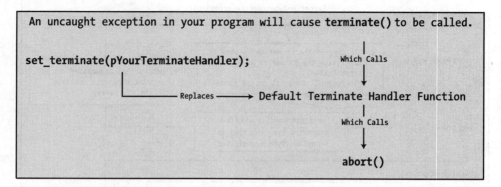

Figure 17-3. Uncaught exceptions

 NOTE *The* abort() *function terminates the entire program immediately. Unlike* exit(), *it doesn't call destructors for any constructed static objects.*

The default action provided by the default terminate handler could be disastrous in some situations—for example, it may leave your files in an unsatisfactory state, or a connection to a telephone line may be left open. In such cases, you'd want to make sure that things are tidied up properly. You can do this by replacing the default terminate handler function with your own version by calling the standard library function set_terminate(), as illustrated in Figure 17-3. The set_terminate() function accepts an argument of type terminate_handler, and returns a value of the same type. This type is defined in the exception header file as follows:

```
typedef void (*terminate_handler)();
```

terminate_handler is a pointer to a function that has no parameters and doesn't return a value, so your replacement function must be of this form. You can do what you want within your version of the terminate handler, but it *must not* return—it must ultimately terminate the program. Your definition of the function could take this form:

```
void myHandler() {
  // Do necessary clean-up to leave things in an orderly state...
  exit(1);
}
```

Calling the exit() standard library function is a more satisfactory way of terminating your program than calling abort(). Calling exit() ensures that destructors for global objects are called, and any open input/output streams are flushed if necessary and closed. Any temporary files that were created using standard library functions will be deleted. The integer argument that you pass to the exit() function is returned to the operating system as a status code. A non-zero value indicates abnormal program termination.

To set up the myHandler() function as the terminate handler, you could write this:

```
terminate_handler pOldHandler = set_terminate(myHandler);
```

The return value is a pointer to the previous handler that was set, so by saving it, you'll be able to restore it later if necessary. The first time you call set_terminate(), the return value will be a pointer to the default handler. Each subsequent call to instate a new handler will return a pointer to whatever handler is in effect. This means that you can have your handler in effect for a particular part of your program, and then restore the default handler when your handler no longer applies.

Of course, you can set different terminate handlers at various points in your program to provide shutdown actions that suit the particular conditions that apply at any given time. For example, when your program is involved in database operations, you might need to make sure that the database shuts down in an orderly fashion when a fatal error occurs. You would define a terminate handler to take care of this. Another part of your program might involve managing communications using a modem, in which case you'll probably want your terminate handler to close the communications link. Different terminate handlers accommodating different shutdown requirements can be used whenever you need them.

Code That Causes an Exception to Be Thrown

I said at beginning of this discussion that try blocks enclose code that may throw an exception. However, this doesn't mean that the code that throws the exception must be *physically* between the braces bounding the try block. It only needs to be *logically* within the try block. This means that if a function is called from within a try block, any exception thrown from within that function can be caught by one of the try block's catch blocks. An example of this is illustrated in Figure 17-4.

Two function calls are shown within the try block: fun1() and fun2(). Exceptions of type exceptionType that arise within either function can be caught by the catch block following the try block. An exception that is thrown but not caught within a function may be passed on to the calling function the next level up. If it isn't caught there, it can be passed on up to the next level; this is illustrated in Figure 17-4 by the exception thrown in fun3(). If an exception reaches a level where no further catch handlers exist and it is still uncaught, then the terminate handler is called to end the program.

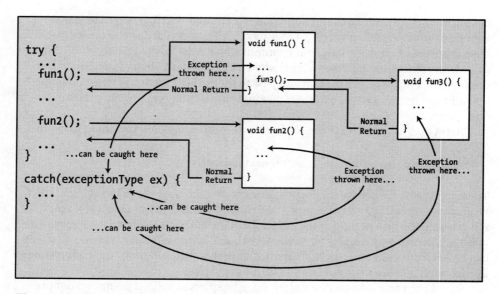

Figure 17-4. Exception thrown by functions called within a try block

Of course, if the same function is called from different points in a program, the exceptions that the code in the body of the function may throw could be handled by different catch blocks at different times. You can see an example of this situation in Figure 17-5.

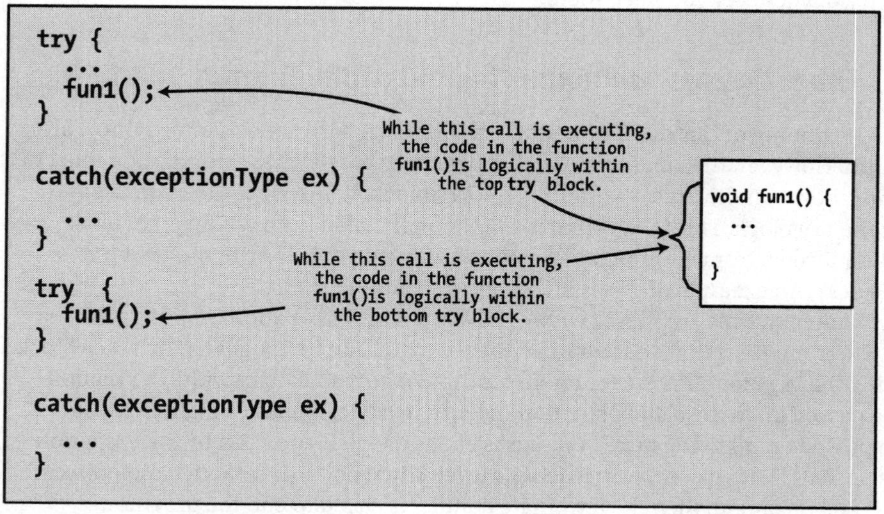

Figure 17-5. Calling the same function from within different try blocks

While the function is executing, as a consequence of the call in the first try block, the catch block for that try block handles any exceptions of type exceptionType thrown by fun1(). When it is called from within the second try block, the catch handler for that try block deals with any exception of type exceptionType that is thrown.

From this, you should be able to see that you can choose to handle exceptions at the level that is most convenient to your program structure and operation. If it suited you, in an extreme case, you could catch all the exceptions that arose anywhere in a program in main() just by enclosing the code in main() in a try block and appending a suitable variety of catch blocks.

Nested try Blocks

You can nest a try block inside another try block. Each of these has its own set of catch blocks to handle the exceptions that may be thrown within it, and the catch blocks for a try block are *only* invoked for exceptions thrown within the corresponding try block. This process is shown in Figure 17-6.

```
try {              // outer try block
  ...
  try {            // inner try block
  {
    ...
  }
  catch(exceptionType ex)  {◄─────────── This handler can catch exceptions
    ...                                    thrown in the inner try block.
  }
  ...
}
catch(exceptionType ex) { ◄───────────── This handler can catch exceptions thrown
  ...                                      anywhere in the outertry block, as well as
}                                          uncaught exceptions from the inner try block.
```

Figure 17-6. Nested try blocks

Figure 17-6 shows one handler for each try block, but in general there may be several. When the code within an inner try block throws an exception, its handlers get the first chance to deal with it. Each of its handlers is checked for a matching exception type, and if none match, the handlers for the outer try block have a chance to catch the exception. You can nest try blocks in this way to whatever depth is appropriate for your application.

When an exception is thrown by the code in the outer try block, that block's catch handlers handle it, even if the statement originating the exception precedes the inner try block. The catch handlers for the inner try block can never be involved in dealing with exceptions thrown by code within the outer try block.

Naturally, the code within both try blocks may call functions, in which case, while the function is executing, the code within the body of the function is logically within the try block that called it. Any or all of the code within the body of the function could also be within its own try block, in which case this try block would be nested within the try block that called the function.

Try It Out: Nested try Blocks

That all sounds rather complicated in words, but it's much easier in practice. You can put together a simple example in which you throw an exception and then see where it ends up. Once again, you're going for explanation rather than gritty realism at this stage, so you'll throw exceptions of type int and type long. The code for this program demonstrates both nested try blocks and throwing an exception within a function:

```cpp
// Program 17.2 Throwing exceptions in nested try blocks  File: prog17_02.cpp
#include <iostream>
using std::cout;
using std::endl;

void throwIt(int i) {
  throw i;                              // Throws the parameter value
}

int main() {
  for(int i = 0 ; i <= 5 ; i++)   {
    try {
      cout << endl << "outer try: ";
      if(i == 0)
        throw i;                        // Throw int exception

      if(i == 1)
        throwIt(i);                     // Call the function that throws int

      try {                             // Nested try block
        cout << endl << " inner try: ";
        if(i == 2)
          throw static_cast<long>(i);   // Throw long exception

        if(i == 3)
          throwIt(i);                   // Call the function that throws int
      }                                 // End nested try block
      catch(int n) {
        cout << endl << "Catch int for inner try. "
             << "Exception " << n;
      }

      cout << endl << "  outer try: ";
```

```
      if(i == 4)
        throw i;                     // Throw int
      throwIt(i);                    // Call the function that throws int
    }
    catch(int n) {
      cout << endl << "Catch int for outer try. "
           << "Exception " << n;
    }
    catch(long n) {
      cout << endl << "Catch long for outer try. "
           << "Exception " << n;
    }
  }

  cout << endl;
  return 0;
}
```

This produces the following output:

```
outer try:
Catch int for outer try. Exception 0
outer try:
Catch int for outer try. Exception 1
outer try:
 inner try:
Catch long for outer try. Exception 2
outer try:
 inner try:
Catch int for inner try. Exception 3
  outer try:
Catch int for outer try. Exception 3
outer try:
 inner try:
  outer try:
Catch int for outer try. Exception 4
outer try:
 inner try:
  outer try:
Catch int for outer try. Exception 5
```

The throwIt() function throws its parameter value. If you were to call this function from outside a try block, it would immediately cause the program to end, because the exception would go uncaught and the default terminate handler would be called.

(Continued)

All the exceptions are thrown within the for loop. Within the loop, you determine when to throw an exception and what kind of exception to throw by testing the value of the loop variable, i, in successive if statements. At least one exception is thrown on each iteration. Entry to each try block is recorded in the output, and because each exception has a unique value, you can easily see where each exception is thrown and caught.

The first exception is thrown from the outer try block when the loop variable, i, is 0:

```
if(i == 0)
   throw i;                       // Throw int exception
```

You can see from the output that the catch block for exceptions of type int that follows the outer try block catches the exception thrown here. The catch block for the inner try block has no relevance in this case, as it can only catch exceptions thrown in the inner try block.

The next exception is thrown in the outer try block as a result of calling throwIt():

```
if(i == 1)
   throwIt(i);                    // Call the function that throws int
```

This is also caught by the catch block for int exceptions that follows the outer try block. The next two exceptions, however, are thrown in the inner try block:

```
if(i == 2)
   throw static_cast<long>(i);    // Throw long exception

if(i == 3)
   throwIt(i);                    // Call the function that throws int
```

The first of these is an exception of type long. No catch block for the inner try block for this type of exception exists, so it propagates to the outer try block. Here, the catch block for type long handles it, as you can see from the output. The second exception is of type int and is thrown in the body of the throwIt() function. No try block exists in this function, so the exception propagates to the point where the function was called in the inner try block. The exception is then caught by the catch block for exceptions of type int that follows the inner try block.

When one of the handlers for the inner try block catches an exception, execution continues with the remainder of the outer try block. Thus, when i is 3, you get output from the catch block for the inner try block, *plus* output from the handler for int exceptions for the outer try block. The latter exception is thrown as a result of the throwIt() function call at the end of the inner try block.

Finally, you throw two more exceptions in the outer try block:

```
if(i == 4)
   throw i;                       // Throw int
   throwIt(i);                    // Call the function that throws int
```

The handler for int exceptions for the outer try block catches both of these exceptions. The second exception here is thrown within the body of the function throwIt(), and because it is called in the outer try block, the catch block following the outer try block handles it.

Although none of these was a realistic exception—exceptions in real programs are invariably class objects—they did show the mechanics of throwing and catching exceptions and what happens with nested try blocks. Let's move on to take a closer look at exceptions that *are* objects.

Class Objects As Exceptions

You can throw any kind of class object as an exception. However, you should bear in mind that the idea of an exception object is to communicate information to the handler about what went wrong. Therefore, it's usually appropriate to define a specific exception class that is designed to represent a particular kind of problem. This is likely to be application-specific, but your exception class objects almost invariably contain a message of some kind explaining the problem, and possibly some sort of error code as well. You could also arrange for an exception object to provide additional information about the source of the error in whatever form was appropriate.

You could define a simple exception class of your own. Put it in a header file with a fairly generic name, such as MyTroubles.h, because you'll be adding to this file later:

```
// MyTroubles.h Exception class definition
#ifndef MYTROUBLES_H
#define MYTROUBLES_H

class Trouble {
  public:
    Trouble(const char* pStr = "There's a problem") : pMessage(pStr) {}
    const char* what() const {return pMessage;}

  private:
    const char* pMessage;
};

#endif
```

This class just defines an object representing an exception that stores a message indicating a problem. A default message is defined in the parameter list for the constructor, so you can use the default constructor to get an object that contains the default message. The what() member function returns the current message. Because you don't allocate memory in the free store, the default copy constructor is satisfactory in this case. To keep the logic of exception handling manageable, you need to ensure that the member functions of an exception class don't throw exceptions. Later in this chapter, you'll see how you can explicitly prevent a member function from doing so.

Let's find out what happens when a class object is thrown by trying to throw a few. As in the previous examples, you won't bother to create errors most of the time. You'll just throw exception objects so that you can follow what happens to them under various circumstances. Let's first make sure you know how to throw an object.

Try It Out: Throwing an Exception Object

You can exercise your exception class with a very simple example that throws some exception objects in a loop:

```cpp
// Program 17.3 Throw an exception object  File: prog17_03.cpp
#include <iostream>
#include "MyTroubles.h"
using std::cout;
using std::endl;

int main() {
  for(int i = 0 ; i < 2 ; i++) {
    try    {
      if(i == 0)
        throw Trouble();
      else
        throw Trouble("Nobody knows the trouble I've seen...");
    }
    catch(const Trouble& t) {
      cout << endl << "Exception: " << t.what();
    }
  }
  return 0;
}
```

This will produce the following output:

```
Exception: There's a problem
Exception: Nobody knows the trouble I've seen...
```

HOW IT WORKS

You throw two exception objects in the for loop. The first object thrown is created by the default constructor for the Trouble class, and contains the default message string. The second exception object is thrown in the else clause of the if statement and contains a message that you pass as an argument to the constructor. The catch block catches both of these exception objects.

Remember that an exception object is *always* copied when it is thrown, so if you don't specify the parameter in the catch block as a reference, it'll be copied a second time—quite unnecessarily. The sequence of events when an exception object is thrown is that first the object is copied (to create a temporary object), and then the original is destroyed because the try block is exited and the object goes out of scope. The copy is then passed to the catch handler—by reference, if the parameter is a reference. If you want to observe these events taking place, just add a copy constructor and a destructor containing some output statements to the Trouble class.

Matching a Catch Handler to an Exception

I said earlier that the handlers following a try block are examined in the sequence in which they appear in your code, and that the first handler whose parameter type matches the type of the exception will be executed. With exceptions that are basic types (rather than class types), an exact type match with the parameter in the catch block is necessary. With exceptions that are class objects, on the other hand, automatic conversions may be applied to match the exception type with the parameter type of a handler.

When you're matching the parameter (caught) type to the exception (thrown) type, the following are considered to be a match:

- The parameter type is the same as the exception type, ignoring const.

- The type of the parameter is a direct or indirect base class of the exception class type, or a reference to a direct or indirect base class of the exception class, ignoring const.

- The exception and the parameter are pointers, and the exception type can be converted automatically to the parameter type, ignoring const.

The possible type conversions listed here have implications for how you sequence the handlers for a try block. If you have several handlers for exception types within the same class hierarchy, then the most *derived* class type must appear first and the most *base* class type last. If a handler for a base type appears before a handler for a type derived from that base, then the base type is always selected to handle the derived class exceptions. In other words, the handler for the derived type is never executed.

Let's add a couple more exception classes to the header containing the Trouble class, and use Trouble as a base class for them. Here's how the contents of the header file MyTroubles.h will look with the extra classes defined:

```
// MyTroubles.h Exception class definition
#ifndef MYTROUBLES_H
#define MYTROUBLES_H

// Base exception class
class Trouble {
  public:
    Trouble(const char* pStr = "There's a problem");
```

```
    virtual ~Trouble();
    virtual const char* what() const;

  private:
    const char* pMessage;
};

// Derived exception class
class MoreTrouble : public Trouble {
  public:
    MoreTrouble(const char* pStr = "There's more trouble");
};

// Derived exception class
class BigTrouble : public MoreTrouble {
  public:
    BigTrouble(const char* pStr = "Really big trouble");
};

#endif
```

Note that the what() member and the destructor of the base class have been declared as virtual. Therefore, the what() function is also virtual in the classes derived from Trouble. It doesn't make much of a difference here, but remembering to declare a virtual destructor in a base class is a good habit to get into.

Other than different default strings for the message, the derived classes don't add anything to the base class. Often, just having a different class name can be used to differentiate one kind of problem from another. You just throw an exception of a particular type when that kind of problem arises; the internals of the classes don't have to be different. Using a different catch block to catch each class type provides the means to distinguish one kind of problem from another.

You can put the definitions of the member functions of the three classes in MyTroubles.cpp:

```
// MyTroubles.cpp
#include "MyTroubles.h"

// Constructor for Trouble
Trouble::Trouble(const char* pStr) : pMessage(pStr) {}

// Destructor for Trouble
Trouble::~Trouble() {}

// Returns the message
const char* Trouble::what() const {
  return pMessage;
}
```

```
// Constructor for MoreTrouble
MoreTrouble::MoreTrouble(const char* pStr) : Trouble(pStr) {}

// Constructor for BigTrouble
BigTrouble::BigTrouble(const char* pStr) : MoreTrouble(pStr) {}
```

You can now try this out in an example.

Try It Out: Throwing Exception Types That Are in a Hierarchy

Here's the code to throw exceptions of the Trouble, MoreTrouble, and BigTrouble types, and the handlers to catch them:

```
// Program 17.4 Throwing and Catching Objects in a Hierarchy File: prog17_04.cpp
#include <iostream>
#include "MyTroubles.h"
using std::cout;
using std::endl;

int main() {
  Trouble trouble;
  MoreTrouble moreTrouble;
  BigTrouble bigTrouble;

  cout << endl;
  for(int i = 0 ; i < 7 ; i++) {
    try {
      if(i < 3)
        throw trouble;
      if(i < 5)
        throw moreTrouble;
      else
        throw bigTrouble;
    }
    catch(BigTrouble& rT) {
      cout << "  BigTrouble object caught: " << rT.what() << endl;
    }
    catch(MoreTrouble& rT) {
      cout << " MoreTrouble object caught: " << rT.what() << endl;
    }
    catch(Trouble& rT) {
      cout << "Trouble object caught: " << rT.what() << endl;
    }

    cout << "End of the for loop (after the catch blocks) - i is " << i << endl;
  }
  cout << endl;
  return 0;
}
```

(Continued)

This produces the following output:

```
Trouble object caught: There's a problem
End of the for loop (after the catch blocks) - i is 0
Trouble object caught: There's a problem
End of the for loop (after the catch blocks) - i is 1
Trouble object caught: There's a problem
End of the for loop (after the catch blocks) - i is 2
 MoreTrouble object caught: There's more trouble
End of the for loop (after the catch blocks) - i is 3
 MoreTrouble object caught: There's more trouble
End of the for loop (after the catch blocks) - i is 4
  BigTrouble object caught: Really big trouble
End of the for loop (after the catch blocks) - i is 5
  BigTrouble object caught: Really big trouble
End of the for loop (after the catch blocks) - i is 6
```

HOW IT WORKS

After creating one object of each class type, you have a for loop that contains the following try block:

```
try {
  if(i < 3)
    throw trouble;
  if(i < 5)
    throw moreTrouble;
  else
    throw bigTrouble;
}
```

For values of the loop variable i that are less than 3, you throw an exception of type Trouble. When i is equal to 3 or 4, you throw an exception of type MoreTrouble. When i is 5 or greater, you throw an exception of type BigTrouble.

You have a handler for each class type, starting with exceptions of type BigTrouble:

```
catch(BigTrouble& rT) {
  cout << "  BigTrouble object caught: " << rT.what() << endl;
}
```

The other handlers are essentially the same, although they do contain slightly different messages. In the handlers for the two derived types, the inherited what() function still returns the message. Note that the parameter type for each of the catch blocks is a reference here, as in the previous example. One reason for using a reference is to avoid making *another* copy of the exception object. In the next example, you'll see another good reason why you should *always* use a reference parameter in a handler.

Each handler displays the message contained in the object thrown, and you can see from the output that each handler is called to correspond with the type of the exception thrown. The ordering of the handlers is important because of the way the exception is matched to a handler, and because the types of your exception classes are related. Let's explore that in a little more depth.

Catching Derived Class Exceptions with a Base Class Handler

Because exceptions of derived class types are automatically converted to a base class type for the purpose of matching the handler parameter, you could catch all the exceptions thrown in the previous example with a single handler. Let's modify the previous example to see this happening.

Try It Out: Using a Base Class Handler

All you need to do is delete (or comment out) the two derived class handlers from the previous example.

```
// Program 17.5 Catching exceptions with a base class handler   File: prog17_05.cpp
#include <iostream>
#include "MyTroubles.h"
using std::cout;
using std::endl;

int main() {
  Trouble trouble;
  MoreTrouble moreTrouble;
  BigTrouble bigTrouble;

  cout << endl;
  for(int i = 0 ; i < 7 ; i++) {
    try {
      if(i < 3)
        throw trouble;
      if(i < 5)
        throw moreTrouble;
      else
        throw bigTrouble;
    }
    catch(Trouble& rT) {                        // Base class handler only
      cout << "Trouble object caught: " << rT.what() << endl;
    }
```

(Continued)

```
    cout << "End of the for loop (after the catch blocks) - i is " << i << endl;
  }

  cout << endl;
  return 0;
}
```

The program now produces this output:

```
Trouble object caught: There's a problem
End of the for loop (after the catch blocks) - i is 0
Trouble object caught: There's a problem
End of the for loop (after the catch blocks) - i is 1
Trouble object caught: There's a problem
End of the for loop (after the catch blocks) - i is 2
Trouble object caught: There's more trouble
End of the for loop (after the catch blocks) - i is 3
Trouble object caught: There's more trouble
End of the for loop (after the catch blocks) - i is 4
Trouble object caught: Really big trouble
End of the for loop (after the catch blocks) - i is 5
Trouble object caught: Really big trouble
End of the for loop (after the catch blocks) - i is 6
```

HOW IT WORKS

The Trouble& handler now catches all the exceptions. If the parameter in a catch block is a reference to a base class, then it matches any derived class exception. So, although the output proclaims "Trouble object caught" for each exception, the last four catches actually correspond to objects *derived* from Trouble.

Because the dynamic type is retained when the exception is passed by reference, you could also get the dynamic type and display it using the typeid() operator. Just modify the code for the handler to

```
catch(Trouble& rT) {
  cout << typeid(rT).name() << " object caught: " << rT.what() << endl;
}
```

Some compilers don't enable runtime type identification by default, so if this doesn't work, check for a compiler option to switch it on. With this modification to the code, the output shows that the derived class exceptions still retain their dynamic types, even though a reference to the base class is being used. Remember, the typeid() operator returns an object of the type_info class; the name() member of the class returns the class name as const char*.

For the record, the output from this version of the program should look like this:

```
class Trouble object caught: There's a problem
End of the for loop (after the catch blocks) - i is 0
class Trouble object caught: There's a problem
End of the for loop (after the catch blocks) - i is 1
class Trouble object caught: There's a problem
End of the for loop (after the catch blocks) - i is 2
class MoreTrouble object caught: There's more trouble
End of the for loop (after the catch blocks) - i is 3
class MoreTrouble object caught: There's more trouble
End of the for loop (after the catch blocks) - i is 4
class BigTrouble object caught: Really big trouble
End of the for loop (after the catch blocks) - i is 5
class BigTrouble object caught: Really big trouble
End of the for loop (after the catch blocks) - i is 6
```

Now, you can try changing the parameter type for the handler to `Trouble` so that the exception is passed by value rather than by reference:

```
catch(Trouble t) {
    cout << typeid(t).name() << " object caught: " << t.what() << endl;
}
```

When you run *this* version of the program, you'll get the following output:

```
class Trouble object caught: There's a problem
End of the for loop (after the catch blocks) - i is 0
class Trouble object caught: There's a problem
End of the for loop (after the catch blocks) - i is 1
class Trouble object caught: There's a problem
End of the for loop (after the catch blocks) - i is 2
class Trouble object caught: There's more trouble
End of the for loop (after the catch blocks) - i is 3
class Trouble object caught: There's more trouble
End of the for loop (after the catch blocks) - i is 4
class Trouble object caught: Really big trouble
End of the for loop (after the catch blocks) - i is 5
class Trouble object caught: Really big trouble
End of the for loop (after the catch blocks) - i is 6
```

Here, the `Trouble` handler is still selected for the derived class objects, but the dynamic type is not preserved. This is because the parameter is initialized using the base class copy constructor, so any properties associated with the derived class are lost.

(Continued)

In this situation, only the base class subobject of the original derived class object is retained. All derived class members are removed from the object. This is an example of **object slicing**, which results because the base class copy constructor knows nothing about derived objects. Object slicing is a common source of error when passing objects by value, and it can happen with ordinary functions as well as with exception handlers. That leads us to another golden rule:

GOLDEN RULE *You should* always *use reference parameters in your* catch *blocks.*

Rethrowing an Exception

When a handler catches an exception, it can **rethrow** it to allow a handler for an outer try block to catch it. You can rethrow the current exception with a statement consisting of just the keyword throw, with no throw expression:

```
throw;                   // Rethrow the exception
```

This rethrows the existing exception object without copying it. You might rethrow an exception if the handler discovers that the nature of the exception requires it to be passed on to another level of try block. You might also want to register the point in the program where an exception was thrown, and then rethrow it for handling in some central location in the program, such as in main().

Note that rethrowing an exception from the inner try block doesn't make the exception available to other handlers for the inner try block. When a handler is executing, any exception that is thrown (including the current exception) needs to be caught by a handler for a try block that encloses the current handler, as illustrated in Figure 17-7.

The fact that a rethrown exception is *not* copied is important, especially when the exception is a derived class object that initialized a base class reference parameter. Let's demonstrate this with an example.

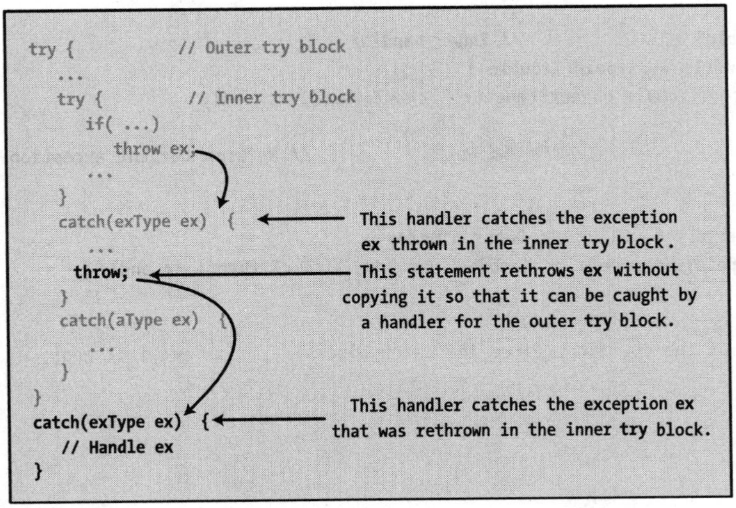

```
try {          // Outer try block
  ...
  try {          // Inner try block
    if( ...)
      throw ex;
    ...
  }
  catch(exType ex) {  ◄──────── This handler catches the exception
    ...                         ex thrown in the inner try block.
    throw;  ◄─────────────────── This statement rethrows ex without
  }                              copying it so that it can be caught by
  catch(aType ex) {             a handler for the outer try block.
    ...
  }
}
catch(exType ex) {  ◄────────── This handler catches the exception ex
  // Handle ex                   that was rethrown in the inner try block.
}
```

Figure 17-7. Rethrowing an exception

Try It Out: Rethrowing an Exception

You can throw some `Trouble`, `MoreTrouble`, and `BigTrouble` exception objects and then rethrow some of them to see how the mechanism works. This is a modification of the previous example:

```cpp
// Program 17.6 Rethrowing exceptions   File: prog17_06.cpp
#include <iostream>
#include "MyTroubles.h"
using std::cout;
using std::endl;

int main() {
  Trouble trouble;
  MoreTrouble moreTrouble;
  BigTrouble bigTrouble;

  cout << endl;
  for(int i = 0 ; i < 7 ; i++) {
    try {
      try {
        if(i < 3)
          throw trouble;
        if(i < 5)
          throw moreTrouble;
        else
          throw bigTrouble;
```

(Continued)

```
    }
        catch(Trouble& rT) {          // Inner handler
          if(typeid(rT) == typeid(Trouble))
            cout << "Trouble object caught: " << rT.what() << endl;
          else
            throw;                                          // Rethrow current exception
        }
      }
      catch(Trouble& rT) {          // Outer handler
        cout << typeid(rT).name() << " object caught: " << rT.what() << endl;
      }

      cout << "End of the for loop (after the catch blocks) - i is " << i << endl;
    }

    cout << endl;
    return 0;
  }
```

This example displays the following output:

```
Trouble object caught: There's a problem
End of the for loop (after the catch blocks) - i is 0
Trouble object caught: There's a problem
End of the for loop (after the catch blocks) - i is 1
Trouble object caught: There's a problem
End of the for loop (after the catch blocks) - i is 2
class MoreTrouble object caught: There's more trouble
End of the for loop (after the catch blocks) - i is 3
class MoreTrouble object caught: There's more trouble
End of the for loop (after the catch blocks) - i is 4
class BigTrouble object caught: Really big trouble
End of the for loop (after the catch blocks) - i is 5
class BigTrouble object caught: Really big trouble
End of the for loop (after the catch blocks) - i is 6
```

HOW IT WORKS

The for loop works as in the previous program, but this time you have one try block
nested inside another. The exception objects are thrown in the inner try block:

```
    try {
      if(i < 3)
        throw trouble;
      if(i < 5)
        throw moreTrouble;
      else
        throw bigTrouble;
    }
```

This throws the same sequence of objects as the previous examples. The handler catches them all because its parameter is a reference to the base class:

```
catch(Trouble& rT) {            // Inner handler
  if(typeid(rT) == typeid(Trouble))
    cout << "Trouble object caught: " << rT.what() << endl;
  else
    throw;                      // Rethrow current exception
}
```

This handler catches `Trouble` objects and any objects of the classes derived from `Trouble`. The `if` statement here tests the class type of the object passed and executes the output statement if it is of type `Trouble`. For any other type of exception, the exception is rethrown. You can distinguish the output from this `catch` block because it doesn't start with the word `class`.

The rethrown exception is available to be caught by the handler for the outer `try` block:

```
catch(Trouble& rT) {            // Outer handler
  cout << typeid(rT).name() << " object caught: " << rT.what() << endl;
}
```

The parameter here is also a reference to `Trouble`, so it catches all the derived class objects. You can see from the output that it catches the rethrown objects, and they're still in pristine condition.

You might imagine that the `throw` statement in the handler for the inner `try` block is equivalent to the following statement:

```
throw rT;                       // Rethrow current exception
```

After all, you're just rethrowing the exception, aren't you? The answer is no; in fact, there's a major difference. Make this modification to the program code and run it again. You'll get this output:

```
Trouble object caught: There's a problem
End of the for loop (after the catch blocks) - i is 0
Trouble object caught: There's a problem
End of the for loop (after the catch blocks) - i is 1
Trouble object caught: There's a problem
End of the for loop (after the catch blocks) - i is 2
class Trouble object caught: There's more trouble
End of the for loop (after the catch blocks) - i is 3
class Trouble object caught: There's more trouble
End of the for loop (after the catch blocks) - i is 4
class Trouble object caught: Really big trouble
End of the for loop (after the catch blocks) - i is 5
class Trouble object caught: Really big trouble
End of the for loop (after the catch blocks) - i is 6
```

(Continued)

Throwing the exception in this manner results in the exception being *copied*, using the copy constructor for the Trouble class. You have the object slicing problem again. The derived portion of each object is sliced off, so you are left with just the base class subobject in each case. You can see from the output that the typeid() operator identifies all the exceptions as type Trouble.

Catching All Exceptions

You can use an ellipsis (...) as the parameter specification for a catch block to indicate that the block should handle any exception:

```
catch(...) {
  // Code to handle any exception...
}
```

This catch block handles an exception of any type, so a handler like this must always be last in the sequence of handlers for a try block. Of course, you have no idea what the exception is, but at least you can prevent your program from terminating because of an uncaught exception. Note that even though you don't know anything about it, you can rethrow the exception as you did in the previous example.

Try It Out: Catching Any Exception

You can modify the last example to catch all the exceptions for the inner try block by using an ellipsis in place of the parameter:

```
// Program 17.7 Catching any exception  File: prog17_07.cpp
#include <iostream>
#include "MyTroubles.h"
using std::cout;
using std::endl;

int main() {
  Trouble trouble;
  MoreTrouble moreTrouble;
  BigTrouble bigTrouble;

  cout << endl;
  for(int i = 0 ; i < 7 ; i++) {
    try {
      try {
        if(i < 3)
```

```
          throw trouble;
        if(i < 5)
          throw moreTrouble;
        else
          throw bigTrouble;
      }
      catch(...) {           // Inner handler
        cout << "We caught something! Let's rethrow it." << endl;
        throw;                                // Rethrow current exception
      }
    }
    catch(Trouble& rT) { // Outer handler
      cout << typeid(rT).name() << " object caught: " << rT.what() << endl;
    }

    cout << "End of the for loop (after the catch blocks) - i is " << i << endl;
  }

  cout << endl;
  return 0;
}
```

This produces the following output:

```
We caught something! Let's rethrow it.
class Trouble object caught: There's a problem
End of the for loop (after the catch blocks) - i is 0
We caught something! Let's rethrow it.
class Trouble object caught: There's a problem
End of the for loop (after the catch blocks) - i is 1
We caught something! Let's rethrow it.
class Trouble object caught: There's a problem
End of the for loop (after the catch blocks) - i is 2
We caught something! Let's rethrow it.
class MoreTrouble object caught: There's more trouble
End of the for loop (after the catch blocks) - i is 3
We caught something! Let's rethrow it.
class MoreTrouble object caught: There's more trouble
End of the for loop (after the catch blocks) - i is 4
We caught something! Let's rethrow it.
class BigTrouble object caught: Really big trouble
End of the for loop (after the catch blocks) - i is 5
We caught something! Let's rethrow it.
class BigTrouble object caught: Really big trouble
End of the for loop (after the catch blocks) - i is 6
```

(Continued)

The only changes from the previous example are shown in bold. The `catch` block for the inner `try` block has been changed to

```
catch(...) {            // Inner handler
  cout << "We caught something! Let's rethrow it." << endl;
  throw;                                // Rethrow current exception
}
```

This is a genuine catch-all that can catch anything you throw at it. Every time an exception is caught, a message displays and the exception is rethrown to be caught by the `catch` block for the outer `try` block. There, its type is properly identified and the string returned by its `what()` member is displayed.

Functions That Throw Exceptions

A function can throw an exception that will be caught in the calling function, as you saw in Program 17.2. For this to occur, you need an exception to be *thrown* within the function and not caught there. Of course, if you don't want to have the program terminated, the exception needs to be caught *somewhere*, and for that to happen, the function call must be enclosed within a `try` block. The handlers for this `try` block should then catch the exception.

Of course, a function body can contain its own `try` blocks to handle its own exceptions. Any that are uncaught propagate to the point at which the function was called. It is sometimes convenient to make the whole body of a function a try block with its own set of handlers; you can do this by using a **function** try **block**.

Function try Blocks

You define a function `try` block by putting the keyword `try` before the opening brace of the body of the function. You then put the handlers for the function `try` block after the closing brace of the function body. Here's an example:

```
void doThat(int argument)
try {
  // Code for the function...
}
catch(BigTrouble& ex) {
  // Handler code for BigTrouble exceptions...
}
catch(MoreTrouble& ex) {
  // Handler code for MoreTrouble exceptions...
}
catch(Trouble& ex) {
  // Handler code for Trouble exceptions...
}
```

The entire body of the function is now a try block, whereas the catch blocks follow the closing brace for the function body.

Of course, a function that throws exceptions doesn't *need* to have a function try block, or indeed any try block at all. However, any *call* of a function that throws exceptions should be enclosed by a try block, otherwise the uncaught exception ends the program. It's a good idea to indicate in such cases that the function might throw exceptions.

Specifying the Exceptions That a Function May Throw

By default, a function can throw any type of exception. This is not particularly helpful, because if you want to be certain of catching all exceptions, you have to use catch-all catch blocks with ellipses for *every* try block that calls such a function. Also, you'll encounter situations in which throwing *any* exception is a serious inconvenience, and you may want to ensure that (and enforce) a function throws no exceptions.

You can specify the set of exceptions that a function might throw by adding an **exception specification** to the function header. The three options for the exception specification for a function appear in Table 17-1.

Table 17-1. Exception Specification Options

Exception Specification	Possible Exceptions
No exception specification	Your function allows exceptions of any type to be thrown.
throw()	No exceptions may be thrown.
throw(exception_type_list)	Exceptions of the types specified between the parentheses, separated by commas, may be thrown.

The exception specification limits the types of exception that a function can throw. If a function has an exception specification, it must appear in any function declaration as well as in the function definition.

Here's an example of a function definition that includes an exception specification:

```
void doThat(int argument) throw(Trouble, MoreTrouble)
try {
  // Code for the function...
}
catch(BigTrouble& ex) {
  // Handler code for BigTrouble exceptions...
}
```

This function handles any BigTrouble exceptions that may be thrown, but Trouble and MoreTrouble exceptions must be caught by the calling function. The declaration for the function also needs to include this exception specification:

```
void doThat(int argument) throw(Trouble, MoreTrouble);
```

If you declare a pointer to a function that includes an exception specification, then you must also include the exception specification. Here's an example:

```
void (*pFunction)(int) throw(Trouble, MoreTrouble); // Pointer to fctn declaration
pFunction = doThat;                                 // Store function address
```

If you use a typedef to define the pointer to function type, then you must *not* include the exception specification, because the exception specification is not part of the type. However, you must include it when you use the type in the declaration of the pointer, like this:

```
typedef void (*FunctionPtrType)(int);                 // Define pointer to function type
FunctionPtrType pFunction throw(Trouble, MoreTrouble); // Pointer to fctn declrtn
```

The first statement defines the type, which is then used in the second statement. You only include the exception specification in the pointer declaration.

Unexpected Exceptions

A function should only throw exceptions of the types allowed by its exception specification, but the compiler has no way to verify that this is the case. A function with an exception specification limiting the types of exceptions that it can throw can quite legitimately call other functions without exception specifications. Any of these could throw exceptions that aren't within the set of types specified by the exception specification. This possibility is recognized in C++ through the notion of an **unexpected exception**.

If a function does throw an exception that is not one of the types specified within its exception specification, it isn't propagated outside the function, as this renders the exception specification ineffective. Instead, the exception initiates a chain of events starting with the standard library function unexpected() being called. The complete chain is illustrated in Figure 17-8.

The purpose of this sequence of calls is to provide you with an opportunity to deal with unexpected exceptions a little more gracefully than by just bringing the program to an abrupt halt. The unexpected() function calls a handler function, the default action of which is to call the standard library function terminate(),which as you've seen, is called for uncaught exceptions. As you saw earlier, terminate() then calls a default terminate handler function, which calls abort() to end the program.

You can replace the default handler function to be called by unexpected() with your own version. The technique for doing so is similar to the one you use to replace the default terminate handler called by terminate(). You just call the set_unexpected() function with the address of your handler function as an argument. The parameter type for the set_unexpected() function is defined as follows:

```
typedef void (*unexpected_handler)();
```

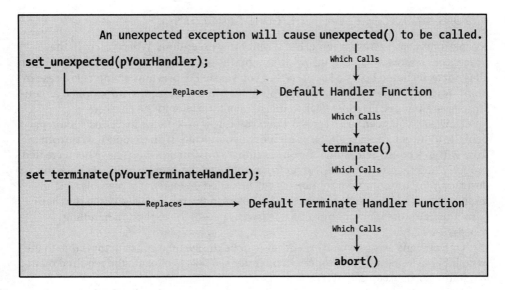

Figure 17-8. Handling unexpected exceptions

From the definition of the unexpected_handler type, you can see that your function must have no parameters and must not return a value. Within your unexpected handler function, you can do whatever you want, but you must end the function in one of the following ways:

- By throwing an exception that conforms to the exception specification for the function that threw the unexpected exception.

- By throwing an exception of type bad_exception—this is a standard type, which is defined in the <exception> header.

- By calling terminate(), exit(), or abort().

Just as with the terminate handler, you can have different handlers to suit different situations, and this gives you the freedom to deal with unexpected exceptions in your own way. The idea behind the std::bad_exception type is that you can always include a handler for this type to deal with unexpected exceptions. All functions that have an exception specification would then need to include this type as a permitted exception. In this way, you control how unexpected exceptions are dealt with, rather than accepting the rather crude handling provided by the default action of calling terminate(), which then calls abort(). However, if your unexpected handler function throws a bad_exception exception, and this type is not in the exception specification for the function, then the function terminate() will be called anyway.

Throwing Exceptions in Constructors

A constructor can't return a value, but it *can* throw exceptions. When you're in the process of creating an object, throwing exceptions provides a way for you to signal that all is not as it should be. The Box class that you've used in previous chapters is a case in point. You might want to throw an exception if invalid dimensions are supplied as constructor arguments. I'll come back to this point a little later in the chapter.

However, you need to be careful when you throw exceptions in a constructor, particularly if the constructor allocates memory dynamically. If an exception is thrown from within a constructor, then the object under construction won't have been created properly, and therefore the destructor for the object will never be called. At best, the destructor for any complete subobjects will be called. At worst, it is possible that any memory allocated in the free store is not released in the normal way. When that happens, the free store memory must be released as part of the exception handling process.

One obvious way in which exceptions can be thrown in a constructor is due to the default behavior of the operator new. If operator new fails to allocate the required memory, it throws an exception of type bad_alloc.

A constructor is a function, so it can have a function try block. What's more, the try block in a constructor can include the initialization list so that exceptions thrown by constructors for subobjects can also be caught. If your constructor might throw an exception, a good way to deal with it is to provide the constructor with a function try block, and add handlers to clean up when bad things happen. A class constructor to do this could be of the following form:

```
Example::Example(int count) throw(bad_alloc)
try : BaseClass(count) {
  // Allocate some memory...
  // Rest of the constructor...
}
catch(...) {
  // Release memory as necessary...
}
```

Here, the constructor for the Example class calls a constructor for a base class, BaseClass, in the initialization list. This call and the body of the constructor are within the function try block, so the handler will be invoked for any exception thrown by the base class constructor or the constructor for the current object. Note that you don't need to rethrow the exception in the catch block here. Exceptions thrown in a constructor try block are rethrown automatically.

Exceptions and Destructors

Because automatic objects are destroyed when an exception is thrown, some class destructors may be called before the handler for the exception is executed. Within a destructor, it can be important to know that the destructor is being called because an exception was thrown (rather than for an object going out of scope, for example).

When this is the case, *any* exception thrown within the destructor causes terminate() to be called, which ends the program immediately. This prevents the catch block for the original exception from ever being reached, which could be disastrous in many circumstances. In this situation, you need to be sure that no exceptions are thrown from the destructor in order to allow the handler for the original exception to execute.

As a general rule, your destructors shouldn't throw exceptions, but if they must, you can call a function to detect when a destructor is being called because an exception was thrown. The function uncaught_exception() returns true if an exception was thrown and the corresponding catch block hasn't been executed, so this allows a suitable course of action within your destructor. Of course, to prevent exceptions from escaping beyond the bounds of a destructor, you can enclose the code in a try block and use a handler that catches any exception.

Standard Library Exceptions

Several exception types are defined in the standard library. They're all derived from the standard class std::exception, which is defined in the <exception> header. The exception class includes a default constructor and copy constructor, the copy assignment operator, and a virtual function what(), which returns a null-terminated string that describes the exception. None of these functions will throw an exception. The standard exception classes derived from exception are shown in Figure 17-9.

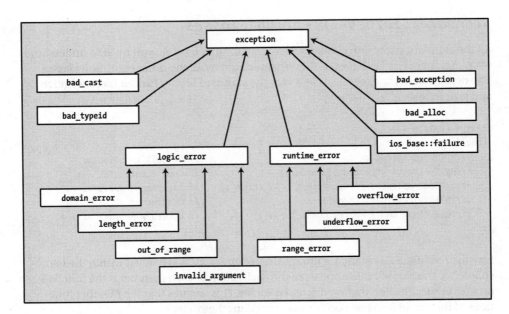

Figure 17-9. Standard exception class types

You've already seen the bad_cast exception that can be thrown by the dynamic_cast<>() operator; I referred to the bad_alloc exception when I discussed the operator new in Chapter 7; and you saw the bad_exception class a little earlier in this chapter. A bad_typeid exception is thrown if you use the typeid() operator with a null pointer. The ios_base::failure exception is thrown by functions in the standard library that support stream input-output. I'll discuss streams in Chapter 19.

The other types of exceptions fall into two groups, with each group having a base class that is derived from the exception class. These classes are all defined in the header <stdexcept>. The types that have logic_error as a base are exceptions thrown for errors that could (at least in principle) have been detected before the program executed because they are caused by defects in the program logic. The other group, derived from runtime_error, is for errors that are generally data dependent and can only be detected at runtime. The exception types thrown by standard library functions indicate errors of various kinds. For instance, if you access characters in a string object using the at() member function, and the index value is outside the legal range for the object, an exception of type out_of_range is thrown.

Because a catch block with a base class parameter matches any derived class exception, you can catch any of the standard exceptions by using a parameter of type exception&. Of course, you can also a parameter of type logic_error& or runtime_error& to catch any exceptions of types that are derived from these types, and that are thrown by standard library functions.

Standard Library Exception Classes

All the standard exception classes have exception as a base, so you need to understand what members this class has, as they are inherited by all the other exception classes. The definition of the exception class is in the standard library header file, exception, and is as follows:

```
class exception {
  public:
    exception() throw();                          // Default constructor
    exception(const exception&) throw();          // Copy constructor
    exception& operator=(const exception&) throw();  // Assignment operator
    virtual ~exception() throw();                 // Destructor
    virtual const char* what() const throw();     // Return a message string
};
```

Like the rest of the C++ standard library, the exception class is defined within the namespace std. The throw() that appears in the declaration of each member is the function exception specification that we discussed earlier. This ensures that the member functions of the exception class don't throw exceptions themselves.

Notice that there are no data members. The null-terminated string returned by the member what() is defined within the body of the function definition, and is implementation dependent. This function is declared as virtual, so it will also be virtual in any classes derived from exception. If you have a virtual function that can deliver a message that corresponds to each exception type, you can use it to provide a basic, economical way to record any exception that's thrown. You can provide your main() function with a function try block, plus a catch block for exceptions of type exception:

```
int main()
try {
  // Code for main...
}
catch(exception& rEx) {
  cout << endl << typeid(rEx).name() << " caught in main: " << rEx.what();
}
```

The catch block catches all exceptions that have the exception class as a base and displays the class type and the message returned by the what() function. Thus, this simple mechanism gives you information about any exception that is thrown anywhere in the program but is not caught. If your program uses exception classes that are *not* derived from exception, an additional catch block with ellipses in place of a parameter type catches all other exceptions, but in this case, you'll have no information as to what they are.

Although this is a handy catch-all mechanism, more local try blocks provide a direct way to localize the source code that is the origin of an exception when it is thrown.

Using Standard Exceptions

There is no reason why you shouldn't use the exception classes defined in the standard library, and several very good reasons why you should. You can use the standard library exceptions in two ways: you can throw exceptions of standard types in your own programs, and you can use the standard exception classes as a base for your own exception classes.

Obviously, if you are going to throw standard exceptions, you need to throw them in circumstances consistent with their purpose. This means that you shouldn't be throwing bad_cast exceptions, for instance, because these have a very specific role already. However, you'll find that you can use some of the exception classes derived from logic_error and runtime_error directly in your programs. To use a familiar example, you might throw the range_error exception in a Box class constructor when invalid dimensions are supplied as arguments:

```
Box::Box(double lv, double wv, double hv) throw(std::range_error) {
  if(lv <= 0.0 || wv <= 0.0 || hv <= 0.0)
    throw std::range_error();

  length = lv;
  width = wv;
  height = hv;
}
```

Of course, the source file would need to include the `<stdexcept>` header that defines the range_error class. The body of the constructor throws a range_error exception if any of the arguments are zero or negative. The constructor definition includes an exception specification restricting the exceptions thrown to range_error exceptions alone. Don't forget that the class definition must also include the same exception specification for the constructor.

Deriving Your Own Exception Classes

A major point in favor of always deriving your own classes from one of the standard exception classes is that your classes become part of the same family as the standard exceptions. This makes it possible for you to catch standard exceptions as well as your own exceptions within the same catch blocks. For instance, if your exception class is derived from logic_error, then a catch block with a parameter type of logic_error& catches your exceptions as well as the standard exceptions with that base. A catch block with exception& as its parameter type always catches standard exceptions— including yours, as long as your classes have exception as a base.

You can incorporate your Trouble exception class (and the exception classes derived from it) quite simply, by deriving it from the exception class. You just need to modify the class definition as follows:

```
class Trouble : public std::exception {
  public:
    Trouble(const char* pStr = "There's a problem") throw();
    virtual ~Trouble() throw();
    virtual const char* what() const throw();

  private:
    const char* pMessage;
};
```

This provides its own implementation of the virtual what() member defined in the base class. Your version displays the message from the class object, as before. With your new knowledge of the exception specification for functions, you've added an exception specification to each member function so that no exceptions are thrown from within them. You also need to update the member functions of the classes MoreTrouble and BigTrouble that are derived from Trouble in a similar fashion. Each of the definitions for the member functions must include the same exception specification that appears for the function in the class definition.

Summary

Exceptions are an integral part of C++. Several operators throw exceptions, and you've seen that they're used within the standard library to signal errors. Therefore it's important that you have a good grasp of how they work, even if you don't plan to use your own exception classes. The important points that I've covered in this chapter are as follows:

- Exceptions are objects used to signal errors in a program.

- Code that may throw exceptions is usually contained within a try block.

- The code to handle exceptions of various types that may be thrown in a try block is placed in one or more catch blocks following the try block.

- A try block, along with its catch blocks, can be nested inside another try block.

- A handler with a parameter of a base class type can catch an exception of a derived class type.

- If an exception isn't caught by any catch block, then the terminate() function is called, and this calls abort().

- The standard library defines a range of standard exceptions.

- An exception specification limits the types of exceptions that a function can throw.

- If an exception is thrown within a function that isn't permitted by the exception specification for the function, the unexpected() function is called.

- You can change the default behavior of the unexpected() function by implementing your own unexpected handler, and you can establish it by passing a pointer to your function to the set_unexpected() function.

- A function try block for a constructor can enclose the initialization list as well as the body of the constructor.

- The uncaught_exception() function allows you to detect when a destructor was called as a result of an exception being thrown.

Exercises

The following exercises enable you to try out what you've learned in this chapter. If you get stuck, look back over the chapter for help. If you're still stuck after that, you can download the solutions from the Apress website (http://www.apress.com/book/download.html), but that really should be a last resort.

Exercise 17-1. Derive your own exception class called CurveBall from the standard exception class to represent an arbitrary error, and write a function that throws this exception approximately 25 percent of the time. (One way to do this is to generate a random number between 1 and 20, and if the number is 5 or less, throw the exception.) Define the function main() to call this function 1,000 times and
to record and display the number of times an exception was thrown.

Exercise 17-2. Define another exception class called TooManyExceptions. Then throw an exception of this type from the catch block for CurveBall exceptions in the previous exercise when the number of exceptions caught exceeds 10.

Exercise 17-3. Implement your terminate handler in the code for the previous example so that a message is displayed when the TooManyExceptions exception is thrown.

Exercise 17-4. A **sparse array** is one in which most of the element values are zero or empty. Define a class for a one-dimensional sparse array of elements of type pointer to string such that only the non-zero elements are stored. The potential number of elements should be specified as a constructor argument, so a sparse array to store up to 100 string objects could be declared with this statement:

    SparseArray words(100);

Implement the subscript operator for the SparseArray class so that you can use the array notation to retrieve or store elements. Throw exceptions if the legal index range is exceeded in the subscript operator functions. (Hint: use a linked list internally so that each node stores an element along with its subscript.)

CHAPTER 18

Using Class Templates To Create Families of Classes

CLASS TEMPLATES PROVIDE you with a powerful mechanism for generating new class types automatically. A significant portion of the standard library is built entirely on the ability to define templates, so it's important that you understand the techniques involved.

By the end of this chapter, you will have learned the following:

- What a class template is and how it is defined

- What an instance of a class template is, and how one is created

- How to define templates for member functions of a class template outside the body of the class template definition

- How type parameters differ from non-type parameters

- How static members of a class template are initialized

- What a partial specialization of a class is and how it is defined

- How a class template can be nested inside another class template

Understanding Class Templates

Class templates are based on the same idea as the function templates that you saw back in Chapter 9. A class template is a **parameterized type**—that is, a recipe for creating a family of classes, using one or more parameters, where the argument that corresponds to each parameter is typically (but not always) a type. When you declare a variable using a class template, the compiler uses the template to produce a definition for a class corresponding to the template arguments that you use in your declaration. You can use a class template in this way to generate any number of different classes.

A class template has a name, just like an ordinary class, and a set of parameters. The name of a class template must be unique within a namespace, so you can't have another class or another template with the same name in the namespace in which the template is declared. A class *definition* is generated from a class template when you supply an argument for each of the template's parameters. This is illustrated in Figure 18-1.

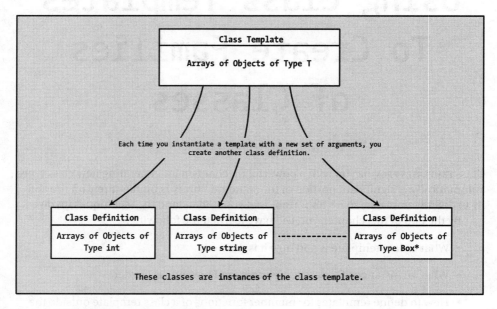

Figure 18-1. Instantiating a template

Each class generated from a template by the compiler is called an **instance** of the template. As you'll see, when you declare a variable using a template type, you create an instance of the template, but you can also declare instances of a class template explicitly, without declaring a variable at the same time. Classes instantiated from a template won't be duplicated, so once a given template instance has been created, it'll be used for any subsequent declarations of variables of its type.

Applications of Class Templates

Although many applications for class templates exist, they are perhaps most commonly used to define **container classes**. These are classes that can contain sets of objects of a given type, organized in a particular way. This might simply mean an array, for example, or a pushdown stack, or a linked list of objects; the important point is that the storage method used is independent of the type of objects being stored.

A class template provides exactly the tool you need to define a container that can store any kind of object. You can use the template parameter to specify the kinds of objects that the container will store. The Standard Template Library, which comes as part of a standard C++ implementation, has many templates that define containers of various kinds. You'll get to see how you can use some of those in Chapter 20.

Let's consider a specific situation in which a class template can help. Suppose that you are unhappy with the fact that arrays in C++ don't check whether the index value you supply is a legal value because this allows you inadvertently to overwrite memory locations that aren't within the bounds of the array. Of course, one solution is for you to write your own Array class that checks to see if an index value is within legal limits. All you have to do is define the operator[]() function for the class so that it checks the array index value and perhaps throws an exception if it isn't legal.

But what *kind* of array would your Array class represent? In one situation you might need an array of type double, and another time you might need an array of string objects—or indeed, an array of any type of object. You'd need a separate class to be defined for each type of array that you use, even though the classes would be very similar. Having to write several, essentially identical classes seems rather tedious and unnecessary, and indeed it is. Not only that, but in such a case, each of your classes also needs a different name, so you could end up with a range of classes with names like ArrayOfDouble, ArrayOfString, ArrayOfBox, and so on.

This is where a class template comes riding to the rescue because it can be used to generate an Array class to suit any type that you require. Once you have Array available as a class template, you can create new Array classes that manage any kind of object automatically. In fact, you don't have to define an Array template yourself. The standard library provides such a template with all the functionality I've described and more.

Defining Class Templates

When you first see class template definitions, they tend to look more complicated than they really are, largely because of the appearance of the notation used to define them and the parameters sprinkled around the code in the definition. Basically, class template definitions are very similar to those of ordinary classes, but like so many things, the devil is in the details.

You define a class template with the keyword template, and you place the parameters for the template between angled brackets following this keyword. The template class definition appears next and consists of the keyword class followed by the class template name with the body of the definition between braces. Just like a regular class, the whole definition ends with a semicolon. Thus, the general form of a class template looks like this:

```
template <template parameter list> class ClassName {
  // Template class definition...
};
```

In this conceptual definition, ClassName is the name of the *template*. You write the code for the body of the template just as you'd write the body of an ordinary class, except that some of the member declarations and definitions will be in terms of the template parameters that appear between the angled brackets separated by commas. To create a class from a template, you must specify arguments for each of the parameters in the list.

Template Parameters

A template parameter list can contain two kinds of parameters—**type parameters** and **non-type parameters**—and any number of parameters can be in the list. The argument corresponding to a type parameter is a type, such as int, or string, or Box, whereas the argument for a non-type parameter is either a value of a given type, such as 200, or a variable of a given type, such as ivalue. Type parameters in templates are much more common than non-type parameters, so I'll defer further discussion of non-type parameters until later in this chapter.

Type parameters are usually written using the keyword class followed by the parameter name (class T in Figure 18-2), but you can also use the keyword typename instead of class, so typename T would be just as good here. T is often used as a type parameter name (or T1, T2, and so on when there are several type parameters for a template), but you can use whatever name you want.

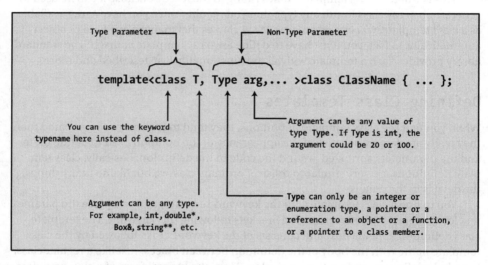

Figure 18-2. Class template parameters

 NOTE *Although the keyword* class *seems to imply that the argument for a type parameter has to be a class type, you can actually supply any type as an argument, so you can use the keyword* typename *if it makes it clearer in this context.*

You can see what the reality of class templates is like by looking at how a simple template with a single type parameter works in practice.

A Simple Class Template

Let's take the example that I introduced earlier in this chapter and define a class template for arrays that will do bounds checking on index values to make sure that they are legal. Although the standard library provides you with a comprehensive implementation of an array template, building your own limited array template is an effective basis from which you can learn about how templates work. You already have clear idea of how arrays work so you can concentrate on the template specifics. This will also make working with the Array template from the standard library that you'll see in Chapter 20 that much easier.

Your array template just has a single type parameter, so in outline, its definition will be

```
template <typename T> class Array {
  // Definition of the template...
};
```

The Array template has just one type parameter, T. You can tell that it's a type parameter because it's preceded by the keyword typename. Whatever is "plugged in" for this parameter when you instantiate the template—int, double*, string, or whatever—determines the type of the elements stored in an object of the resultant class. The definition in the body of the template will be much the same as a class definition, with data members and member functions that you can declare as public, protected, or private, and it will typically have constructors and a destructor. You can use T to declare variables or to specify the parameters or return types for member functions, either by itself or in types such as T* (*pointer to type* T). Furthermore, you can use the template name—Array, in this case—as a type name, as well as in the declaration of constructors and the destructor.

The very least you'll need by way of a class interface is a constructor; a copy constructor, because you'll be allocating the space for the array dynamically; an assignment operator, because the compiler will supply one if you don't; an overloaded subscript operator; and finally a destructor. With this in mind, you can write the initial definition of the template as follows:

```
template <typename T> class Array {
  private:
    T* elements;                              // Array of type T
    size_t size;                              // Number of elements in the array

  public:
    explicit Array<T>(size_t arraySize);      // Constructor
    Array<T>(const Array<T>& theArray);       // Copy Constructor
    ~Array<T>();                              // Destructor
    T& operator[](size_t index);             // Subscript operator
    const T& operator[](size_t index) const; // Subscript operator-const arrays
    Array<T>& operator=(const Array<T>& rhs); // Assignment operator
};
```

The body of the template looks much like a regular class definition, except it's sprinkled with T in various places. For example, it has a data member, elements, which is of type *pointer to* T (equivalent to *array of* T). When the class template is instantiated to produce a specific class definition, T is replaced by the actual type used to instantiate the template. If you create an instance of the template for type double, elements will be of type *array of* double.

You use type size_t for the size member that stores the number of elements in the array. This is a standard integer type defined in the standard header <cstddef>, and it corresponds to the type of value returned by the sizeof operator. It is the preferred type for specifying array dimensions.

Notice the way the first constructor is declared as explicit. Because this function takes a single integer argument, you have two ways to write a constructor call:

```
Array<int> data(5);        // explicit constructor notation
Array<int> numbers = 5;    // assignment-like notation
```

By declaring the constructor as explicit, you prohibit the second and rather unintuitive form of syntax. This also prevents you from passing integers to functions expecting an argument of an Array<int> type. Without the explicit declaration of the constructor, the compiler would insert a constructor call to convert the integer argument to type Array<int> in such cases.

The subscript operator has been overloaded on const. You learned about overloading functions with const and non-const parameters in Chapter 9. The non-const version of the subscript operator applies to non-const array objects and can return a non-const reference to an element of the array. Thus this version can appear on the left of an assignment. The const version is called for const objects and returns a const reference to an element. Obviously this can't appear on the left of an assignment.

In the assignment operator function declaration, you use the type Array<T>&. This type is *reference to* Array<T>. When a class is synthesized from the template—when T is type double, for example—this is a reference to the class name for that particular class, which is Array<double>, in this case. More generally, the class name for a specific instance of a template is formed from the template name followed by the actual type argument between angled brackets. The template name followed by the list of parameter names between angled brackets is called the **template ID**.

You don't need to use the full template ID within the template definition. Within the body of your class template, Array by itself will be taken to mean Array<T>, whereas Array& will be interpreted as Array<T>&, so you could simplify the class template definition to

```
template <typename T> class Array {
  private:
    T* elements;                          // Array of type T
    size_t size;                          // Number of elements in the array

  public:
    explicit Array(size_t arraySize);     // Constructor
    Array(const Array& theArray);         // Copy Constructor
```

```
    ~Array();                            // Destructor
    T& operator[](size_t index);         // Subscript operator
    const T& operator[](size_t index) const;  // Subscript operator-const arrays
    Array& operator=(const Array& rhs);  // Assignment operator
};
```

 CAUTION *If you need to identify the template outside the body of the template, you must use the template ID. You'll see this situation when you're defining class template member functions later in the chapter.*

The assignment operator allows you to assign one array object to another, which is something you can't do with ordinary arrays in C++. If you wanted to inhibit this capability for some reason, you still need to declare the operator=() function as a member of the template. If you don't, the compiler will create a public default assignment operator when necessary for any template instance. To inhibit use of the assignment operator, just declare it as a private member of the class; then it can't be accessed. Of course, you don't need an implementation for the member function in this case, because C++ doesn't require you to implement a member function unless it is used, and this one will never be used.

Defining Member Functions of a Class Template

If you include the definitions for the member functions of the class template within its body, they will be implicitly inline in any instance of the template, just like in an ordinary class. However, you'll want to define members outside of the template body from time to time, especially if they involve a lot of code. When you do so, the syntax is a little different; it appears rather daunting at first sight, so let's take a look at it.

The clue to understanding the syntax is that external definitions for the member functions of a template class are themselves templates. The parameter list for the template that defines a member function must be identical to that of the class template. If that sounds a little confusing, it helps to get down to specifics. You can write definitions for the member functions of your Array template, starting with the constructor.

When you're defining a constructor outside the class template definition, its name must be qualified by the class template name in a similar way to an ordinary class member function. However, this isn't a function definition, it's a *template* for a function definition, so that has to be expressed as well. Here's the definition of the constructor:

```
template <typename T>                 // This is a template with parameter T
Array<T>::Array(size_t arraySize) : size(arraySize) {
  elements = new T[size];
}
```

The first line identifies this as a template and also specifies the template parameter as T. Splitting the template function declaration into two lines, as you're doing here, is only for illustrative purposes, and isn't necessary if the whole construct fits on one line.

The template parameter, Array<T>, is essential in the qualification of the constructor name because it ties the function definition to the class template. Note that you *don't* use the typename keyword here; it's only used in the template parameter list. You don't need a parameter list after the constructor name itself. When the constructor is instantiated for an instance of the class template—for type double for example—the type name replaces T in the constructor qualifier, so the qualified constructor name for the class Array<double> is Array<double>::Array().

In the constructor, you must allocate memory in the free store for an elements array that contains size elements of type T. If T is a class type, a public default constructor must exist in the class T. If it doesn't, the instance of this constructor won't compile. The operator new throws a bad_alloc exception if the memory can't be allocated for any reason, so the Array constructor should usually be used within a try block.

The destructor must release the memory for the elements array, so its definition will be as follows:

```
template <typename T> Array<T>::~Array() {
  delete[] elements;
}
```

You're releasing memory allocated for an array so you must use the delete[] form of the operator here.

The copy constructor has to create an array for the object being created that's the same size as that of its argument, and then copy the latter's data members to the former. You can define the code for this as follows:

```
template <typename T> Array<T>::Array(const Array& theArray) {
  size = theArray.size;
  elements = new T[size];
  for(int i = 0 ; i < size ; i++)
    elements[i] = theArray.elements[i];
}
```

This assumes that the assignment operator works for type T. You can see how important it is to define the assignment operator for classes that allocate memory dynamically. If the class T doesn't define it, the default copy constructor for T is used, with undesirable side effects for classes that allocate memory dynamically, as I discussed back in Chapter 13. Without looking at the code for the template before you use it, you may not realize the dependency on the assignment operator.

The operator[]() function is quite straightforward, but you should ensure illegal index values can't be used. For an index value that is out of range, you can throw an exception:

```
template <typename T> T& Array<T>::operator[](size_y index) {
  if(index < 0 || index >= size)
    throw std::out_of_range(index < 0 ? "Negative index" : "Index too large");

  return elements[index];
}
```

You could define your own exception class to use here, but it's easier to borrow the out_of_range class that's already defined in the standard library in the <stdexcept> header. This is thrown if you index a string object with an out of range index value, for example, so your usage is consistent with that. You throw an exception of type out_of_range if the value of index is not between 0 and size-1. The argument to the constructor is a string object that describes the error. A null-terminated string (type const char*) corresponding to the string object is returned by the what() member of the exception object. The argument that you pass to the out_of_range constructor is a simple message in each case, but you could contrive to include information in the string object about the index value and the size of the array to make tracking down the source of the problem a little easier.

The const version of the subscript operator function will be almost identical to the non-const version:

```
template <typename T> const T& Array<T>::operator[](size_t index) const {
  if(index < 0 || index >= size)
    throw std::out_of_range(index < 0 ? "Negative index" : "Index too large");

  return elements[index];
}
```

The last template you need to define is for the assignment operator. This needs to release any memory allocated in the destination object and then do what the copy constructor did, after checking that the objects are not identical of course. Here's the definition:

```
template <typename T> Array<T>& Array<T>::operator=(const Array& rhs) {
  if(&rhs == this)                        // If lhs == rhs
    return *this;                         //   just return lhs

  if(elements)                            // If lhs array exists
    delete[]elements;                     // release the free store memory

  size = rhs.size;
  elements = new T[rhs.size];
  for(int i = 0 ; i < size ; i++)
    elements[i] = rhs.elements[i];
}
```

Checking to make sure that the left operand is identical to the right is essential here, otherwise you'd free the memory for the common elements member, then attempt to copy it when it no longer exists. With different operands you release any memory for the left operand before creating a copy of the right operand.

All the definitions that you've written here are templates and they are inextricably bound to the class template. They aren't function definitions, they're templates to be used by the compiler when the code for one of the member functions of the class template needs to be generated, so they need to be available in any source file that uses the template. For this reason, you'd normally put all the definitions of the member functions for a class template in the header file that contains the class template itself.

Even though you may define the member functions of a template as separate templates, they can still be inline functions. To request that the compiler should consider them as candidates for inline implementation, you just add the keyword inline to the beginning of the definition immediately following template<>, like this:

```
template <typename T> inline const T& Array<T>::operator[](size_t index) const {
  if(index < 0 || index >= size)
    throw out_of_range(index < 0 ? "Negative index" : "Index too large");

  return elements[index];
}
```

Instantiating a Class Template

The compiler instantiates a class template as a result of a declaration of an object that has a type produced by the template. Here's an example:

```
Array<int> data(40);
```

To compile this statement, two things need to happen: the type Array<int> must be declared so that the type is identified, and the constructor must exist because it will be called to create the object. Therefore, this statement results in an instance of your class template being created, which is the class Array<int>, and an instance of the constructor for that class. This is all that the compiler needs to create the object data, so it is all that it provides at this point.

The class definition that'll be included in your program is generated by substituting int in place of T in the template definition, but you'll run into one complication. The compiler only compiles the member functions that your program uses, not necessarily the entire class produced from a simple substitution for the template parameter. On the basis of the declaration for the object, data, it is equivalent to

```
class Array<int> {
  private:
    int* elements;          // Array of type int
    size_t size;            // Number of elements in the array

  public:
    Array(size_t arraySize);      // Constructor
};
```

You can see that, apart from the constructor, the member functions of the class are missing here. The compiler won't create instances of anything that isn't required to create the object, and it won't include parts of the template that aren't needed in your program. This implies that you could have coding errors in a class template, and your program may still compile, link, and run successfully. If the errors are in parts of the template that aren't required by your program, they may not be detected by the compiler because they won't be included in the code that is compiled. Obviously, you are almost certain to have other statements in a program besides the declaration of an object that use other member functions—for instance, you'll always need the destructor to destroy the object in any event—so the final version of the class in the program will include more than that shown in the preceding code. The point is that what is finally in the class generated from the template will be precisely those parts that are actually used in the program.

The instantiation of a class template from a declaration is referred to as an **implicit instantiation** of the template, because it arises as a by-product of declaring an object. This terminology is also to distinguish it from an **explicit instantiation** of a template, which I'll come to in a moment and which behaves a little differently.

As I said, the declaration of data also causes the class constructor, Array<int>::Array(), to be called, so the compiler uses the function template that defines the constructor to create a definition for the constructor for the class:

```
Array<int>::Array(long arraySize) : size(arraySize) {
  elements = new int[size];
}
```

Each time you use a class template with a different type argument to declare a variable, a new class is defined and included in your program. Because creating the class object requires a constructor to be called, the definition of the appropriate class constructor is also generated. Of course, creating an object of a type that you've created before doesn't necessitate any new template instances. The compiler just uses any previously created template instances as required.

When you use the member functions of a particular instance of the class template—by calling functions on the object that you defined using the template, for example—the code for each member function that you use is generated. If you have member functions that you don't use, no instances of their templates are created. The creation of each function definition is an implicit template instantiation because it arises out of the use of the function. The template itself isn't part of your executable code. All it does is enable the compiler to generate the code that you need automatically. This process is illustrated in Figure 18-3.

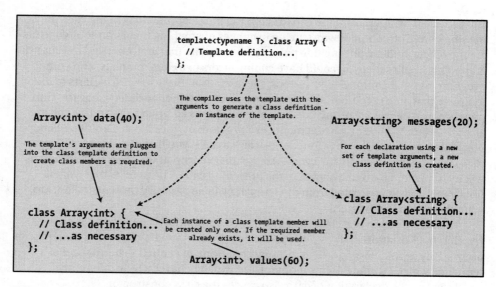

Figure 18-3. Implicit instantiation of a class template

Note that a class template is only implicitly instantiated when an object type needs to be created. Declaring a pointer to an object type won't cause an instance of the template to be created. Here's an example:

```
Array<string>* pObject;
```

This declares pObject to be of type *pointer to type* Array<string>. No object of type Array<string> is created as a result of this statement, and so no template instance is created either. Contrast this with the following declaration:

```
Array<string*> pMessages(10);
```

This results in an instance of the class template being created by the compiler. This declares an object of type Array<string*>, so each element of pMessages can store a pointer to a string object. An instance of the template defining the class constructor is also generated.

Let's try out your Array template in a working example.

Try It Out: Using a Class Template

You can put the class template and the templates defining the member functions of the template all together in a header file Array.h:

```
// Array class template definition
#ifndef ARRAY_H
#define ARRAY_H
#include <stdexcept>                        // For the exception classes

template <typename T> class Array {
  private:
    T* elements;                            // Array of type T
    size_t size;                            // Number of elements in the array

  public:
    explicit Array(size_t arraySize);       // Constructor
    Array(const Array& theArray);           // Copy Constructor
    ~Array();                               // Destructor
    T& operator[](size_t index);            // Subscript operator
    const T& operator[](size_y index) const; // Subscript operator
    Array& operator=(const Array& rhs);     // Assignment operator
};

// Constructor
template <typename T>                       // This is a template with parameter T
Array<T>::Array(size_t arraySize) : size(arraySize) {
  elements = new T[size];
}

// Copy Constructor
template <typename T>
Array<T>::Array(const Array& theArray) {
  size = theArray.size;
  elements = new T[size];
  for(int i = 0 ; i < size ; i++)
    elements[i] = theArray.elements[i];
}

// Destructor
template <typename T>
Array<T>::~Array() {
  delete[] elements;
}
```

(Continued)

```
    // Subscript operator
    template <typename T>
    T& Array<T>::operator[](size_t index) {
      if(index < 0 || index >= size)
        throw std::out_of_range(index < 0 ? "Negative index" : "Index too large");

      return elements[index];
    }

    // Subscript operator for const objects
    template <typename T>
    const T& Array<T>::operator[](size_t index) const {
      if(index < 0 || index >= size)
        throw std::out_of_range(index < 0 ? "Negative index" : "Index too large");

      return elements[index];
    }

    // Assignment operator
    template <typename T>
    Array<T>& Array<T>::operator=(const Array& rhs) {
      if(&rhs == this)                       // If lhs == rhs
        return *this;                        //  just return lhs

      if(elements)                           // If lhs array exists
        delete[]elements;                    // release the free store memory

      size = rhs.size;
      elements = new T[rhs.size];
      for(int i = 0 ; i < size ; i++)
        elements[i] = rhs.elements[i];
    }
    #endif
```

To use the template, you just need a program that'll declare some arrays using the template and try them out. In Program 18.1, I'll endeavor to use some out-of-range index values just to see that it works:

```
// Program 18.1 Using a class template  File: prog18_01.cpp
#include "Box.h"
#include "Array.h"
#include <iostream>
#include <iomanip>
using std::cout;
using std::endl;

int main() {
  const int doubleCount = 50;
  Array<double> values(doubleCount);        // Class constructor instance created
```

```
try   {
  for(int i = 0 ; i < doubleCount ; i++)
    values[i] = i + 1;                        // Member function instance created

  cout << endl << "Sums of pairs of elements:";
  int lines = 0;
  for(int i = doubleCount - 1 ; i >= 0 ; i--)
    cout << (lines++ % 5 == 0 ? "\n" : "")
         << std::setw(5) << values[i] + values[i-1];
}
catch(const std::out_of_range& ex) {
  cout << endl <<"out_of_range exception object caught! " << ex.what();
}

try {
  const int boxCount = 10;
  Array<Box> boxes(boxCount);                 // Template instance created
  for(int i = 0 ; i <= boxCount ; i++)    // Member instance created in loop
    cout << endl << "Box volume is " << boxes[i].volume();
}
catch(const std::out_of_range& ex) {
  cout << endl << "out_of_range exception object caught! " << ex.what();
}

cout << endl;
return 0;
}
```

The header file Box.h contains the definition of the Box class from Chapter 16, and you'll need to have Box.cpp containing the definitions for the Box class member functions as part of this program too.

This example will produce the following output:

```
Sums of pairs of elements:
   99   97   95   93   91
   89   87   85   83   81
   79   77   75   73   71
   69   67   65   63   61
   59   57   55   53   51
   49   47   45   43   41
   39   37   35   33   31
   29   27   25   23   21
   19   17   15   13   11
    9    7    5    3
out_of_range exception object caught! Negative index
Box volume is 1
Box volume is 1
Box volume is 1
```

(Continued)

```
Box volume is 1
Box volume is 1
Box volume is 1
Box volume is 1
Box volume is 1
Box volume is 1
Box volume is 1
out_of_range exception object caught! Index too large
```

HOW IT WORKS

At the beginning of main(), you create an object of type Array<double> using your class template with a parameter type of double:

```
Array<double> values(doubleCount);                // Template instance created
```

This statement declares values as type Array<double>, and the number of elements in the array is specified as doubleCount. When the compiler processes this statement, it creates a definition for the class Array<double> from the class template. To create the object, values, a constructor call is necessary (Array<double>::Array(doubleCount)), so the compiler uses the function template for the constructor to create the definition for the constructor in your program.

Within the try block, you initialize the elements of values with values from 1 to doubleCount in a for loop:

```
for(int i = 0 ; i < doubleCount ; i++)
    values[i] = i + 1;                    // Member function instance created
```

The expression values[i] results in an instance of the subscript operator function being created. This instance is called implicitly by this expression as values.operator[](i). Because values is not const, the non-const version is called.

You use a second for loop in the try block to output the sums of successive pairs of elements, starting at the end of the array:

```
for(int i = doubleCount - 1 ; i >= 0 ; i--)
  cout << (lines++ % 5 == 0 ? "\n" : "")
       << std::setw(5) << values[i] + values[i-1];
```

This also calls the subscript operator function, but the instance of the function template has already been created, so no new instance is generated. Clearly, the expression values[i - 1] has an illegal index value when i is 0, so this causes an exception to be thrown by the operator[]() function. The handler catches this:

```
catch(const std::out_of_range& ex) {
  cout << endl <<"out_of_range exception object caught! " << ex.what();
}
```

The what() function for the out_of_range exception returns a null-terminated string that corresponds to the string object passed to the constructor when the exception object was created. You can see from the output that a Negative index was thrown by the overloaded operator function.

When the exception is thrown by the subscript operator function, control is passed immediately to the handler, so the illegal element reference is not used, and nothing is stored at the location indicated by the illegal index. Of course, the loop also ends immediately at this point.

In the next try block, you define an object that can store an array of Box objects:

```
Array<Box> boxes(boxCount);          // Template instance created
```

This time, the compiler generates an instance of the class template, Array<Box>, which stores an array of Box objects, because the template hasn't been instantiated for Box objects previously. The statement also calls the constructor for this class to create the object boxes, so an instance of the function template for the constructor is created. The constructor for the Array<Box> class calls the default constructor for the Box class when the elements member of the class is created in the free store. Of course, all the Box objects in the elements array have the default dimensions of $1 \times 1 \times 1$.

You display the volume of each Box object in a for loop:

```
for(int i = 0 ; i <= boxCount ; i++)      // Member instance created in loop
    cout << endl << "Box volume is " << boxes[i].volume();
```

The expression boxes[i] calls the overloaded subscript operator, so again the compiler uses an instance of the template to produce a definition of this function. When i has the value boxCount, the subscript operator function throws an exception because boxCount is beyond the end of the elements array. The catch block following the try block catches the exception:

```
catch(const std::out_of_range& ex)  {
    cout << endl <<"out_of_range exception object caught! " << ex.what();
}
```

Because the try block is exited, all locally declared objects will be destroyed, including the boxes object. The values object still exists at this point, because it wasn't created within the previous try block, and it is still in scope.

Exporting Templates

A disadvantage of placing the code for member functions of a class template in a header file is that all this code has to be processed by the compiler in every source file into which it is included. This can represent a substantial processing overhead in a large program that makes extensive use of templates. An alternative approach allows you to place templates for member functions in a separate source file and make them available in any other source file that requires access to them. All you need to do is export the function template definitions by using the keyword export with each template. Here's an example:

```
// ArrayTemplate.cpp file
#include <stdexcept>                    // For the exception classes
#include "Array.h"

// Constructor
export template <typename T>            // This is a template with parameter T
Array<T>::Array(size_t arraySize) : size(arraySize) {
  elements = new T[size];
}

// Copy Constructor
export template <typename T>
Array<T>::Array(const Array& theArray) {
  size = theArray.size;
  elements = new T[size];
  for(int i = 0 ; i < size ; i++)
    elements[i] = theArray.elements[i];
}

// Plus templates for other member functions as before, but with export keyword...
```

You can now compile this file separately and use the object file produced as part of any program that uses the class template.

The header file, Array.h, contains the class template as before, but only declarations for the function templates are necessary:

```
// Array class template definition
#ifndef ARRAY_H
#define ARRAY_H

// Class template definition as before
template <typename T> class Array {
  private:
    T* elements;                            // Array of type T
    size_t size;                            // Number of elements in the array

  public:
    explicit Array(size_t arraySize);       // Constructor
    Array(const Array& theArray);           // Copy Constructor
    ~Array();                               // Destructor
    T& operator[](size_t index);            // Subscript operator
    const T& operator[](size_t index) const; // Subscript operator
    Array& operator=(const Array& rhs);     // Assignment operator
};

#endif
```

Now any program that wants to use the class template just needs to include the shorter version of Array.h into any source file that requires it and have Array.cpp available as a source file, or have access to the object files produced from Array.cpp when the program is linked.

Only function templates that are not inline can be exported. If you use the keyword export with an inline function template, it will be ignored. If you *do* export a template definition, you must not repeat the definition anywhere else in the program. Only declarations of an exported template can appear in other source files. You can't export a template that you've defined in an unnamed namespace.

You can also apply the export keyword to your class template. In this case, all the non-inline function members and function member templates of the template are considered to be exported and you are free to define them in a separate source file. Applying the export keyword to a class template also exports any static data members of the class template, as well as any member classes and member class templates so you can also put the definitions for these in separate files.

Static Members of a Class Template

A class template can have static members, just as an ordinary class can. Static member functions of a template class are quite straightforward. Each instance of a class template instantiates the static member function of the class as needed. Such a member function has no this pointer and therefore can't refer to non-static members of the class. The rules for defining static member functions of a class template are the same as those for a class, and a static member function of a class template behaves in each instance of the template just as if it were in an ordinary class.

A static data member is a little more interesting because it needs to be initialized outside the template definition. Suppose your Array template contained a static data member. The declaration of the member, and the template to initialize it, are shown here:

```
template <typename T> class Array {
  private:
    static T value;                        // Static data member
    T* elements;                           // Array of type T
    size_t size;                           // Number of elements in the array

  public:
    explicit Array(size_t arraySize);      // Constructor
    Array(const Array& theArray);          // Copy Constructor
    ~Array();                              // Destructor
    T& operator[](size_t index);           // Subscript operator
    const T& operator[](size_t index) const; // Subscript operator
    Array& operator=(const Array& rhs);    // Assignment operator};
};

template < typename T > T Array<T>::value;  // Initialize static data member
```

The initialization is accomplished through a template. A static data member is always dependent on the parameters of the template of which it is a member, so you must initialize value as a template with parameter T. The static variable name must also be qualified with the type name Array<T> so that it's identified with the instance of the class template. You can't use Array by itself here, as this definition is outside the body of the template, and the template ID is Array<T>.

As I indicated in the previous section, if you apply the export keyword to the class template, then you can place the definitions for the static data members of the class template in a separate file.

Non-Type Class Template Parameters

A non-type parameter looks like a function parameter—a type name followed by the name of the parameter. Therefore, the argument for a non-type parameter is a value of the given type. However, you can't use just any type for a non-type parameter in a class template. Non-type parameters are intended to be used to define values that might be useful in specifying a container, such as array dimensions or other size specification, or possibly as upper and lower limits for index values.

A non-type can only be an integral type, such as int or long; an enumeration type; a pointer or a reference to an object, such as string* or Box&; a pointer or a reference to a function; or a pointer to a member of a class. You can conclude from this that a non-type parameter *can't* be a floating point type or any class type, so types double, Box, and string are not allowed, and neither is string**. Remember that the primary rationale for non-type parameters is to allow sizes and range limits for containers to be specified. Of course, the argument corresponding to a non-type parameter *can* be an object of a class type, as long as the parameter type is a reference. For a parameter of type Box&, for example, you could use any object of type Box as an argument.

A non-type parameter is written just like a function parameter, with a type name followed by a parameter name. Here's an example:

```
template <typename T, size_t size> class ClassName {
  // Definition using T and size...
};
```

This template has a type parameter, T, and a non-type parameter, size. The definition is expressed in terms of these two parameters and the template name. If you need it, the *name* of a type parameter can also be the *type* of a non-type parameter:

```
template <typename T,      // T is the name of the type parameter
          size_t size,
          T value>         // T is also the type of this non-type parameter
class ClassName{
  // Definition using T, size, and value...
};
```

This template has a non-type parameter, value, of type T. The parameter T must appear before its use in the parameter list, so value couldn't precede the type parameter T here. Note that using the same symbol with the type and non-type parameters implicitly restricts the possible arguments for the typename parameter to the types permitted for a non-type argument (in other words, T must be an integral type).

To show how you could use non-type parameters, suppose you defined the class template for arrays as follows:

```
template <typename T, int arraySize, T value> class Array {
  // Definition using T, size, and value...
};
```

You could now use the non-type parameter, value, to initialize each element of the array in the constructor:

```
template <typename T, int arraySize, T value>
Array<T, size, value>::Array(size_t arraySize) : size(arraySize) {
  elements = new T[arraySize];
  for(int i = 0 ; i < arraySize, i++)
    elements[i] = value;
}
```

Because a non-type parameter can only be an integral type, a pointer, or a reference, you can't create Array objects to store double values, so the usefulness of the template is somewhat restricted.

Non-Type Parameter Example

As a more tangible example, you could consider adding a non-type parameter to the Array template to allow a bit more flexibility in indexing the array:

```
template <typename T, long startIndex> class Array {
  private:
    T* elements;                    // Array of type T
    size_t size;                    // Number of elements in the array

  public:
    explicit Array(size_t arraySize);       // Constructor
    Array(const Array& theArray);           // Copy Constructor
    ~Array();                               // Destructor
    T& operator[](size_t index);            // Subscript operator
    const T& operator[](size_t index) const; // Subscript operator
    Array& operator=(const Array& rhs);     // Assignment operator
};
```

This adds a non-type parameter, startIndex of type long. The idea is that you can specify that you want to use index values that vary over a given range—for example, from -10 to +10, in which case, you'd declare the array with the non-type parameter value as –10 and the argument to the constructor as 21, since the array would need 21 elements.

Because the class template now has two parameters, the templates defining the member functions of the class template must have the same two parameters. This is necessary even if some of the functions aren't going to use the non-type parameters. The parameters are part of the identification for the template, so to match the class template, they must have the same parameter list.

There are some serious disadvantages to what you've done here. A consequence of adding the new startIndex template parameter is that different values for the argument generate different template instances. This means that an array of double values indexed from 0 will be a different type from an array of double values indexed from 1. If you use both in a program, two independent class definitions will be created from the template, each with whatever member functions you use. This has at least two undesirable consequences: first, you'll get a lot more compiled code in your program than you might have anticipated (a condition often known as **code bloat**); second (and worse), you won't be able to intermix elements of the two types in an expression. You'd be much better off if you provided flexibility for the range of index values by adding a parameter to the constructor rather than using a non-type template parameter. Here's an example:

```
template <typename T> class Array {
  private:
    T* elements;                                   // Array of type T
    size_t size;                                   // Number of array elements
    long start;                                    // Starting index value

  public:
    explicit Array(size_t arraySize, long startIndex = 0); // Constructor
    Array(const Array& theArray);                  // Copy Constructor
    ~Array();                                      // Destructor
    T& operator[](long index);                     // Subscript operator
    const T& operator[](long index) const;         // Subscript operator for const
    Array& operator=(const Array& rhs);            // Assignment operator
};
```

The extra member, start, is intended to store the starting index for the array specified by the second constructor argument. The default value for the startIndex parameter is zero, so normal indexing is obtained by default.

However, in the interest of seeing how the member functions are defined when you have a non-template parameter, let's complete the set of function templates that you need for the Array class template.

Templates for Member Functions

Because you've added a non-type parameter to the class template definition, the code for the template for the constructor and the templates for the other member functions will also need to be changed. The template for the constructor will be

```
template <typename T, long startIndex>
Array<T, startIndex>::Array(size_t arraySize) : size(arraySize) {
  elements = new T[size];
}
```

The template ID is now Array<T, startIndex>, so this is used to qualify the constructor name. This is the only change apart from adding the new template parameter to the template.

For the copy constructor, you need to make similar changes to the template:

```
template <typename T, long startIndex>
Array<T, startIndex>::Array(const Array& theArray) {
  size = theArray.size;
  elements = new T[size];
  for(int i = 0 ; i < size ; i++)
    elements[i] = theArray.elements[i];
}
```

Of course, the external indexing of the array doesn't affect how you manage things internally.

The destructor also only needs to have the extra template parameter added:

```
template <typename T, long startIndex>
Array<T, startIndex>::~Array() {
  delete[] elements;
}
```

You need to change the template definition for the non-const subscript operator function to the following:

```
template <typename T, long startIndex>
T& Array<T, startIndex>::operator[](long index) {
  if(index < startIndex || index > startIndex + static_cast<long>(size) - 1)
    throw out_of_range(
                    index < startIndex ? "Index too small" : "Index too large");

  return elements[index - startIndex];
}
```

Significant changes have been made here. The index parameter is now of type long to allow negative values. The validity checks on the index value now verify that it's between the limits determined by the non-type template parameter and the number of elements in the array. Index values can only be from startIndex to startIndex+size-1. Because size_t is usually an unsigned integer type, you need to explicitly cast it to long, otherwise the other values will be converted automatically to size_t, and this will produce a wrong result if they are negative. The choice of message for the exception and the expression selecting it has also been changed.

You need to change the const version in a similar fashion:

```
template <typename T, long startIndex>
const T& Array<T, startIndex>::operator[](long index) const {
  if(index < startIndex || index > startIndex + static_cast<long>(size) -1)
    throw out_of_range(
                        index < startIndex ? "Index too small" : "Index too large");

  return elements[index - startIndex];
}
```

Finally, you need to alter the template for the assignment operator, but only the template parameter list and the template ID qualifying the operator name need to be modified here:

```
template <typename T, long startIndex>
Array<T, startIndex>& Array<T, startIndex>::operator=(const Array& rhs) {
  if(&rhs == this)                          // If lhs == rhs
    return *this;                           //  just return lhs

  if(elements)                              // If lhs array exists
    delete[]elements;                       // then release the free store memory

  size = rhs.size;
  elements = new T[rhs.size];
  for(int i = 0 ; i < size ; i++)
    elements[i] = rhs.elements[i];
}
```

You'll encounter restrictions on how you use a non-type parameter within a template. In particular, you must not modify the value of a parameter within the template definition. Thus, a non-type parameter can't be used on the left of an assignment or have the increment or decrement operator applied to it—in other words, it's treated as a constant.

Back in Chapter 9, you saw how the template arguments to function templates could be deduced from the function arguments. This isn't the case with class templates. All parameters in a class template must always be specified, unless there are default values for parameters. We will discuss the use of default argument values for class template parameters later in the chapter.

Arguments for Non-Type Parameters

An argument for a non-type parameter that is not a reference or a pointer must be a compile-time constant expression. This means that you can't use an expression containing a non-const integer variable as an argument, which is a slight disadvantage, but the compiler can validate the argument, which is a compensating plus. For example, the following statements won't compile:

```
long start = -10;
Array<double, start> values(21);     // Won't compile
```

The compiler will generate a message to the effect that the second argument here is invalid. Here are correct versions of these two statements:

```
const long start = -10;
Array<double, start> values(21);
```

Now that start has been declared as const, the compiler can rely on its value, and both template arguments are now legal.

The compiler also provides standard conversions on arguments if they are necessary to match the parameter type. For example, if you had a non-type parameter declared as type const size_t, the compiler converts an integer literal such as 10 to the required argument type.

Pointers and Arrays As Non-Type Parameters

The argument for a non-type parameter that is a pointer must be an address, but it can't be any old address. It must be the address of an object or function with external linkage; so for example, you can't use addresses of array elements or addresses of non-static class members as arguments. This also means that if your non-type parameter is of type const char*, you can't use a string literal as an argument when you instantiate the template. If you want to use a string literal as an argument in this case, you must initialize a pointer variable with the address of the string literal, and pass the pointer as the template argument.

Because a pointer is a legal non-type template parameter, you can specify an array as a parameter, but an array and a pointer are not always interchangeable when supplying arguments to a template. For example, you could define a template as follows:

```
template <long* pNumber> class MyClass {
  // Template definition...
};
```

You can now create instances of this template with the following code:

```
long data[10];              // Global
long* pData = data;         // Global

MyClass<pData> values;
MyClass<data> values;
```

Either an array name or a pointer of the appropriate type can be used as an argument corresponding to a parameter that is a pointer. However, the converse is not the case. Imagine that you've defined a template as follows:

```
template <long number[10]> class AnotherClass {
  // Template definition...
};
```

The parameter here is an array with 10 elements, and the argument must be of the same type. In this case, using the data array that you declared earlier, you can write this:

```
AnotherClass<data> numbers;              // OK
```

However, you *can't* use a pointer, so the following won't compile:

```
AnotherClass<pData> numbers;             // Not allowed!
```

In spite of the shortcomings of your Array template, let's see non-type parameters in action in a working example.

Try It Out: Using Non-Type Parameters

You just need to plug the changes we discussed earlier into the header file containing the Array template definition. You can then exercise the new features with the following example:

```
// Program 18.2 Using non-type parameters in a class template  File: prog18_02.cpp
#include "Box.h"
#include "Array.h"
#include <iostream>
#include <iomanip>
using std::cout;
using std::endl;

int main() {
  try {
    const int size = 21;                 // Number of array elements
    const int start = -10;               // Index for first element
    const int end = start+size-1;        // Index for last element

    Array<double, start> values(size);   // Declare array for double values

    for(int i = start;  i<= end ; i++)   // Initialize the elements
      values[i] = i - start + 1;

    cout << endl<< "Sums of pairs of elements: ";
    int lines = 0;
```

```
    for( int i = end ; i >= start ; i--)
      cout << (lines++ % 5 == 0 ? "\n" : "")
          << std::setw(5) << values[i] + values[i-1];
  }
  catch(const std::out_of_range& ex)    {
    cout << endl << "out_of_range exception object caught! " << ex.what();
  }
  catch(const std::exception& ex) {
    cout << endl << ex.what();
  }

  try {
    const int start = 0;
    const int size = 11;

    Array<Box, start - 5> boxes(size);

    for(int i = start - 5 ; i <= start + size - 5 ; i++)
        cout << endl << "Box volume is " << boxes[i].volume();
  }
  catch(const std::exception& ex) {
    cout << endl << typeid(ex).name() << " exception caught! "<< ex.what();
  }

  cout << endl;
  return 0;
}
```

This display the following output:

```
Sums of pairs of elements:
   41   39   37   35   33
   31   29   27   25   23
   21   19   17   15   13
   11    9    7    5    3
out_of_range exception object caught! Index too small
Box volume is 1
Box volume is 1
Box volume is 1
Box volume is 1
Box volume is 1
Box volume is 1
Box volume is 1
Box volume is 1
Box volume is 1
Box volume is 1
Box volume is 1
class std::out_of_range exception caught! Index too large
```

(Continued)

```
                        HOW IT WORKS
```

In the first try block, you start by defining some constants that specify the range of index values and the size of the array:

```
const int size = 21;                 // Number of array elements
const int start = -10;               // Index for first element
const int end = start+size-1;        // Index for last element
```

Then you create an instance of your template to store 21 values of type double:

```
Array<double, start> values(size);       // Declare array for double values
```

The second argument corresponds to the non-type parameter for the template and specifies the lower limit for the index values of the array. The size of the array is specified as the constructor argument.

You assign values to the elements of the values object within the for loop:

```
for(int i = start;  i<= end ; i++)       // Initialize the elements
  values[i] = i - start + 1;
```

The index value, i, runs from the lower limit start, which will be –10, to the upper limit end, which will be +10. Within the loop, you define the initial values for the array elements so that they run from 1 to 21.

With the array initialized, you output sums of pairs of successive elements, starting at the end of the array and counting down.

```
int lines = 0;
for( i = end ; i >= start ; i--)
  cout << (lines++ % 5 == 0 ? "\n" : "")
        << std::setw(5) << values[i] + values[i - 1];
```

The lines variable is just to enable you to output the sums five to a line. As in the earlier example, your sloppy control of the index value results in the expression values[i –1] causing an out_of_range exception to be thrown. The first handler for the try block catches it:

```
catch(const std::out_of_range& ex)    {
  cout << endl << "out_of_range exception object caught! " << ex.what();
}
```

This displays the message you see in the output. You also have a second handler for the try block:

```
catch(const std::exception& ex) {
  cout << endl << ex.what();
}
```

This actually catches *any* exception of type exception, or indeed of any type that has exception as a base, so all of the standard exceptions are caught by this. Therefore, it catches a bad_alloc exception if one is thrown by the Array<double> constructor. Remember that the parameter must be a reference here, otherwise derived class exceptions are converted to the base class type, and you get the object slicing problem that I discussed in the last chapter.

Because out_of_range also has the exception class as a base, you could have caught either exception with a single handler. For example, you could use the same handler that you used for the third try block:

```
catch(const std::exception& ex) {
  cout << endl << typeid(ex).name() << " exception caught! "<< ex.what();
}
```

In fact, as you learned in the previous chapter, you could have used the same handler with all three try blocks, reducing the source code and the size of the executable module. You'd still get full information about what exception was thrown. I wish I'd thought of it sooner!

In any case, the next try block creates an array to store Box objects:

```
Array<Box, start-5 > boxes(size);
```

You can see from this that expressions are acceptable as argument values for non-type parameters in a template instantiation. Such an expression must either evaluate to the type of the corresponding parameter, or it must be possible to convert the result to the appropriate type by means of a standard , conversion. You need to take care if the expression includes the > symbol. Here's an example:

```
Array<Box, start > 5 ? start : 5> boxes;      // Will not compile!
```

The intent of the expression for the second argument using the conditional operator is to supply a value of at least 5, but as it stands, this won't compile. The > in the expression is paired with the opening angled bracket, and closes the parameter list. You need to use parentheses to make the statement valid:

```
Array<Box, (start > 5 ? start : 5)> boxes;
```

 CAUTION *The same fix applies to expressions involving the arrow operator (->), or the shift right operator (>>).*

The next for loop throws another exception, just like the previous example, and the handler catches it.

Try It Out: The Better Solution

You must always keep in mind that non-type parameter arguments in a class template are part of the type that corresponds to an instance of the template. Every unique combination of template arguments produces another class type. As I indicated earlier, in the case of your Array<T, long> template, this is particularly inefficient, and the usefulness of the template is restricted. You can't assign one array of doubles, say, to another array of doubles, if the starting indexes for the arrays are different—the arrays will be of different types. The class template with an extra data member and an extra constructor parameter is much more effective. Here's the preferred version of the template that you saw earlier. The bold code shows the differences from the original template class:

```
template <typename T> class Array {
  private:
    T* elements;                              // Array of type T
    size_t size;                              // Number of elements in the array
    long start;                               // Starting index value

  public:
    explicit Array(size_t arraySize, long startIndex = 0); // Constructor
    Array(const Array& theArray);             // Copy Constructor
    ~Array();                                 // Destructor
    T& operator[](long index);                // Subscript operator
    const T& operator[](long index) const;    // Subscript operator for const
    Array& operator=(const Array& rhs);       // Assignment operator
};
```

The constructor has been changed slightly from the original version to initialize the new data member:

```
template <typename T>
Array<T>::Array(size_t arraySize, long startIndex) :
                                   size(arraySize), start(startIndex) {
  elements = new T[size];
}
```

The copy constructor also has to take care of the extra data member:

```
template <typename T>
Array<T>::Array(const Array& theArray) {
  size = theArray.size;
  start = theArray.start;
  elements = new T[size];
  for(int i = 0 ; i < size ; i++)
    elements[i] = theArray.elements[i];
}
```

This is also the case for the assignment operator:

```cpp
template <typename T>
Array<T>& Array<T>::operator=(const Array& rhs) {
  if(&rhs == this)                       // If lhs == rhs
    return *this;                        //  just return lhs

  if(elements)                           // If lhs array exists
    delete[]elements;                    // then release the free store memory

  size = rhs.size;
  start = rhs.start;
  elements = new T[rhs.size];
  for(int i = 0 ; i < size ; i++)
    elements[i] = rhs.elements[i];
}
```

Both subscript operator functions need to be changed in the same way; here's the non-const version as an example:

```cpp
template <typename T>
T& Array<T>::operator[](long index) {
  if(index < start || index > static_cast<long>(size) + start - 1)
    throw std::out_of_range(
                          index < start ? "Index too small" : "Index too large");

  return elements[index - start];
}
```

You could try this out with the following program:

```cpp
// Program 18.3 A better Array class template  File: prog18_03.cpp
#include "Box.h"
#include "Array.h"
#include <iostream>
#include <iomanip>
using std::cout;
using std::endl;

int main() {
  try  {
    const int size = 21;                     // Number of array elements
    const int startValues = -10;             // Index for first element
    const int endValues = startValues + size - 1; // Index for last element

    Array<double> values(size, startValues); // values[-10] to values[10]

    for(int i = startValues; i <= endValues ; i++) // Initialize the elements
      values[i] = i - startValues + 1;
    const int startData = startValues+5;          // Index for first element
```
(Continued)

```
        const int endData = endValues+5;                    // Index for last element

        Array<double> data(size, startData);                // Data[-5] to Data[15]

        // Initialize the array
        for(int j = startData, i = startValues ; i <= endValues ; i++, j++)
          data[j] = values[i];

        cout << endl << "Sums of pairs of elements: ";
        int lines = 0;
        for(int i = endData ; i >= startData ; i--)
          cout << (lines++ % 5 == 0 ? "\n" : "")
               << std::setw(5) << data[i] + data[i - 1];
      }
      catch(const std::exception& ex) {
        cout << endl << typeid(ex).name() << " exception caught! "<< ex.what();
      }

      cout << endl;
      return 0;
    }
```

This program displays the following output:

```
Sums of pairs of elements:
   41    39    37    35    33
   31    29    27    25    23
   21    19    17    15    13
   11     9     7     5     3
class std::out_of_range exception caught! Index too small
```

HOW IT WORKS

Because you set the start index by means of a constructor parameter rather than a class template parameter, you can work with arrays that use different index ranges, as long as they store values of the same type. Because the constructor has a default of 0 for the start index for the array, the template can be used in exactly the same way as the original when you want to use arrays indexed from zero.

The code in main() creates an object, values, that can be indexed from –10 to +10, and an object, data, that can be indexed from –15 to +10. Both objects store values of type double. You initialize the elements of the data object using elements of the values object, thus demonstrating that you can mix them in an expression. This would've been impossible with the class template with a non-type parameter because the non-type parameter would've resulted in the objects being of different types.

This suggests that you should always think twice about using non-type parameters in a class template to be sure that they're really necessary. Often you'll be able to use an alternative approach that can provide you with more flexible templates and more efficient code.

Default Template Argument Values

You can supply default argument values for both type and non-type parameters in a class template. If a given class template parameter has a default argument value, then all subsequent parameters in the list must also have default argument values specified. If you omit an argument for a class template parameter that has a default value specified, the default is used, just like with default parameter values in a function. Similarly, when you omit the argument for a given parameter in the list, then all subsequent arguments must also be omitted.

The default argument values for class template parameters are written in the same way as defaults for function parameters—following an = after the parameter name. You could supply defaults for both the parameters in the version of the Array template with a non-type parameter. Here's an example:

```
template < typename T = int, long startIndex = 0> class Array {
  // Template definition as before...
};
```

Of course, the same default values would also have to appear in the templates for the member functions. You could omit all the template arguments to declare an array of elements of type int indexed from 0.

```
Array<> numbers(101);
```

The legal index values run from 0 to 100, as determined by the default value for the non-type template parameter and the argument to the constructor. You must still supply the angled brackets, even though no arguments are necessary in the case. The other possibilities open to you are to omit the second argument or to supply them all, as shown here:

```
Array<string, -100> messages(200);    // Array of 200 string objects
Array<Box> boxes(101);                // Array of 101 Box objects
```

 CAUTION *You can't omit just the first argument. In general, all the template arguments that would have appeared to the right of the first one to be left out must also be omitted.*

If a class template has default values for any of its parameters, they're only specified in the first declaration of the template in a source file (which, of course, can also be the definition of the template).

Explicit Template Instantiation

So far, you've created instances of a class template *implicitly*, as a result of declaring a variable of a template type. You can also *explicitly* instantiate class templates and function templates. The effect of an explicit instantiation of a template is that the compiler will create the instance determined by the parameter values that you specify.

You have already seen how to explicitly instantiate *function* templates back in Chapter 9. To instantiate a class template, just use the keyword `template` followed by the template class name and the template arguments that you want to use. You could explicitly create an instance of the `Array` template with the following declaration:

```
template class Array<double, 1>;
```

This creates an instance of the template that can store values of type `double`, indexed from 1. Explicitly instantiating a class template generates the class type definition and it instantiates all of the member functions of the class from their templates.

Friends of Class Templates

Because a class can have friends, you won't be surprised to learn that a class template can also have friends that can be classes, functions, or other templates. If a class is a friend of a template, then all its member functions are friends of every instance of the template. A function that is a friend of a template is a friend of any instance of the template, as shown in Figure 18-4.

Templates that are friends of a template are a little different. Because they have parameters, the parameter list for the template class usually contains all the parameters to define the friend template. This is necessary to identify the instance of the friend template that is the friend of the particular instance of the original class template. However, the function template for the friend is only instantiated when you use it in your code. In the Figure 18-5, `getBest()` is a function template.

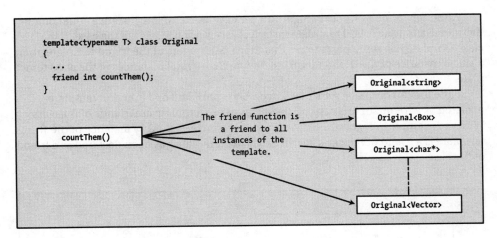

Figure 18-4. A friend function of a class template

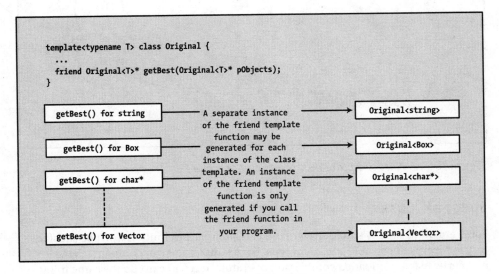

Figure 18-5. A function template that is a friend of a class template

Although in the example in Figure 18-5 each class template instance could potentially have a unique friend template instance, this is not necessarily the case. If the class template has some parameters that aren't parameters of the friend template, then a single instance of the friend template may service several instances of the class template.

Note that an ordinary class may have a class template or a function template declared as a friend. In this case, all instances of the template are friends of the class. With the example in Figure 18-6, every member function of every instance of the Thing template is a friend of the class Box, because the template has been declared as a friend of the class.

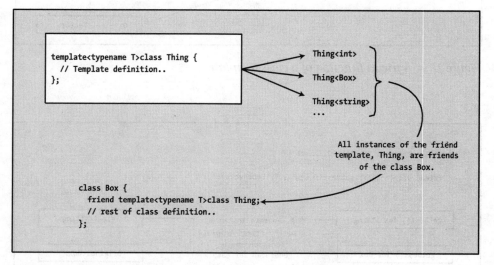

Figure 18-6. A class template that is a friend of a class

Special Cases

You'll encounter many situations where a class template definition won't be satisfactory for every conceivable argument type. For example, you can compare string objects by using overloaded comparison operators, but you can't do the same thing with null-terminated strings. If your template compares objects using the comparison operators, it will work for type string but not for type char*. To compare objects of type char*, you'll need to use the comparison functions declared in the <cstring> header.

To deal with this sort of problem, you can define a **class template specialization**. This provides a class definition that is specific to a given set of arguments for the template parameters. Note that this is a class definition, not a class template. Instead of using the template to generate the class for a particular type, char* say, the compiler uses your specialization instead. Thus a class template specialization provides a way for you to define specific versions of a class to be used by the compiler for specific class template argument values.

Suppose that you wanted to create a specialization of the first version of your Array template for type char*. Further suppose that it includes member functions for comparing objects of a template type; these might work by comparing the elements members of the two objects involved, element by element, but the detail of this is unimportant. You'd write the specialization of the class template definition as follows:

```
template <> class Array<char*> {
  // Definition of a class to suit type char*...
};
```

This definition of the specialization of the Array template for type char* must be preceded by the original template definition, or by a declaration for the original template. Because all the parameters are specified in the specialization here, it is called a **complete specialization** of the template, and that's why the first set of angle brackets are empty. Because you're taking care of specifying all the arguments, there's no room for any template arguments. You have no flexibility in this case—for type char* as the Array template argument, the compiler uses the specialization rather than apply the argument to the template.

It may be that just one or two member functions in a class template need to have code specific to a particular type. If the member functions are defined by separate function templates, rather than within the body of the class template, you can just provide specializations for the function templates.

Partial Template Specialization

If you were specializing the version of the template with two parameters, you'd only want to specify the type parameter for the specialization, leaving the non-type parameter open. You could do this with a **partial specialization** of the Array template that you could define as follows:

```
template <long start> class Array<char*, start> {
  // Definition to suit type char*...
};
```

The parameter list following the template keyword indicates the parameters that need to be specified for an instance of this template specialization—just one in this case. The first parameter is omitted because it is now fixed. The angled brackets following the template name specify how the parameters in the original template definition are specialized. The list here must have the same number of parameters as appear in the original, unspecialized template. The first parameter for this specialization is char*. The other parameter is specified as the corresponding parameter name in this template, and is therefore not specialized in any way.

Apart from the special considerations you might need to give to a template instance produced by using char* for a type parameter, it may well be that pointers in general are a specialized subset that need to be treated differently from objects and references. In order to obtain a suitable comparison when your template is instantiated using a pointer type, you'll need to dereference the variables before comparing them, otherwise you'll be just comparing addresses, and not the objects or values stored at those addresses.

For this situation, you can define another partial specialization of the template. The first parameter is not completely fixed in this case, but it must fit within a particular pattern that you can specify in the list following the template name. For example, a partial specialization of the Array template for pointers would look like this:

```
template <typename T, long start> class Array<T*, start> {
  // Definition to suit pointer types other than char*...
};
```

The first parameter is still T, but the T* between angled brackets following the template name indicates that this definition is to be used for instances where T is specified as a pointer type. The other two parameters are still completely variable, so this specialization will apply to any instance that corresponds to the first argument being a pointer.

Selecting from Multiple Partial Specializations

Suppose you had created both of the partial specializations of the Array template that we just discussed—the one for type char*, and the one for any pointer type. How can you be sure that the version for type char* is selected by the compiler when this is appropriate for any particular instantiation? For example, consider this declaration:

```
Array<Box*, -5> boxes(11);
```

Clearly, this only fits with the specialization for pointers in general, but both partial specializations fit the declaration if you write this:

```
Array<char*, 1> messages(100);
```

In this case, the compiler determines that the char* partial specialization is a better fit because it is more specialized than the alternative. The partially specialized template for char* is determined to be more specialized than the specialization for pointers in general because although anything that selects the char* specialization—which happens to be just char*— also selects the T* specialization, the reverse is not the case. A given specialization is more specialized than another when every argument that matches the given specialization matches the other, but the reverse is not true. Thus you can consider a set of specializations for a template to be ordered from most specialized to least specialized. When several template specializations may fit a given declaration, the compiler will select and apply the most specialized specialization from these.

Class Templates with Nested Classes

A class template definition can contain a nested class or a **nested class template**. A nested class template is independently parameterized, so you have a two-dimensional ability to generate classes. Dealing with this is outside the scope of this book, but you can explore some aspects of a class template with a nested class.

Let's take a particular example. Suppose you want to implement a stack, which is a "last in, first out" storage mechanism (illustrated in Figure 18-7). A **push operation** stores an item at the top of a stack, whereas a **pop operation** takes the item at the top of the stack off. You want a stack to be able to hold objects of any given kind, so this is a natural for a template.

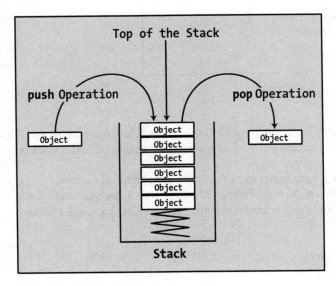

Figure 18-7. The concept of a stack

The template parameter for a Stack template is a type parameter that specifies the type of objects in the stack, so the initial template definition is going to be

```
template <typename T> class Stack {
  // Detail of the Stack definition...
};
```

If you want the stack's capacity to grow automatically, you can't use fixed storage for objects within the stack. One way of providing the ability to automatically grow and shrink the stack as objects are pushed onto or popped off of it, is to implement the stack as a linked list. The nodes in the linked list can be created in the free store, and the stack only needs to remember the node at the top of the stack. This is illustrated in Figure 18-8.

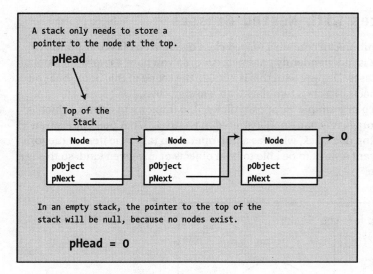

Figure 18-8. A stack as a linked list

When you create an empty stack, the pointer to the head of the list is null, so you can use the fact that it doesn't contain any Node objects as an indicator that the stack is empty.

You need a nested class in each instance of the Stack template that defines nodes in the list, and because a node must hold an object of type T, the Stack template parameter type, you can define it as a nested template. You can add this to your initial outline of the Stack template:

```
template <typename T> class Stack {
  private:
    class Node {
      public:
        T* pItem;                              // Pointer to object stored
        Node* pNext;                           // Pointer to next node

        Node(T& rItem) : pItem(&rItem), pNext(0) {} // Create node from an object
        Node() : pItem(0), pNext(0) {}         // Create an empty node
    };

  // Rest of the Stack definition...
};
```

Because the Node class is declared as private, you can afford to declare all the members as public so that they're directly accessible from member functions of the Stack template. You assume that objects of type T are the responsibility of the user, so you just store a pointer to an object of type T in a Node object. You further assume that the user of the Stack is entirely responsible for destroying the stored objects. The Node constructor with no parameters just sets both data members to null, so it is used to create a

Node in an empty stack. The other constructor is used when an object is pushed onto the stack. The parameter to this constructor is a reference to an object of type T.

You can now fill out the rest of the Stack class template to support the linked list of Node objects shown in the previous diagram:

```
template <typename T> class Stack {
  private:
    class Node {
      public:
        T* pItem;                                // Pointer to object stored
        Node* pNext;                             // Pointer to next node

        Node(T& rItem) : pItem(&rItem), pNext(0) {} // Create node from an object
        Node() : pItem(0), pNext(0) {}           // Create an empty node
    };

    Node* pHead;                                 // Points to top of the stack

  public:
    Stack():pHead(0){}                           // Default constructor
    Stack(const Stack& aStack);                  // Copy constructor
    ~Stack();                                    // Destructor
    Stack& operator=(const Stack& aStack);       // Assignment operator

    void push(T& rItem);                         // Push an object onto the stack
    T& pop();                                    // Pop an object off the stack
    bool isEmpty() {return pHead == 0;}          // Empty test
};
```

As I explained earlier, a stack only needs to "remember" the top node, so it has only one data member, pHead, of type Node. You have a default constructor, plus a copy constructor, a destructor, and the assignment operator, because nodes will be created dynamically. You also have the push() and pop() members to transfer objects to and from the stack, and the isEmpty() function that returns true if the stack is empty.

To complete the implementation of your stack, you just need the templates for the member functions of the Stack template.

Defining Function Templates for Members

The default constructor is defined within the template because all it has to do is initialize pHead to 0. The copy constructor must replicate the Stack<T> object being copied, and you can do this by walking through the nodes, copying them as you go:

```
template <typename T> Stack<T>::Stack(const Stack& aStack) {
  pHead = 0;
  if(aStack.pHead) {
    pHead = new Node(*aStack.pHead);    // Copy the top node of the original
    Node* pOldNode = aStack.pHead;      // Points to the top node of the original
```

```
        Node* pNewNode = pHead;              // Points to the node in the new stack

     while(pOldNode = pOldNode->pNext) { // If it is null, it is the last node
       pNewNode->pNext = new Node(*pOldNode);  // Duplicate it
       pNewNode = pNewNode->pNext;          // Move to the node just created
     }
   }
 }
```

The assignment operator is very similar to the copy constructor, but you must arrange for two extra things to be done. First, you must check to see whether or not the objects involved are identical. Second, you must release memory for nodes in the object on the left of the assignment. Here's the template to define the assignment operator so that it works in this way:

```
template <typename T> Stack<T>& Stack<T>::operator=(const Stack& aStack) {
  if(this == &aStack)                     // If objects are identical
    return *this;                         // return the left object

  // Release memory for nodes in the left object
  Node* pTemp;
  while(pHead) {                          // While current pointer is not null
    pTemp = pHead->pNext;                 // Get the pointer to the next
    delete pHead;                         // Delete the current
    pHead = pTemp;                        // Make the next current
  }

  if(aStack.pHead) {
    pHead = new Node(*aStack.pHead);      // Copy the top node of the original
    Node* pOldNode = aStack.pHead;        // Points to the top node of the original
    Node* pNewNode = pHead;               // Points to the node in the new stack

    while(pOldNode = pOldNode->pNext) {        // If it is null, it is the last node
      pNewNode->pNext = new Node(*pOldNode); // Duplicate it
      pNewNode = pNewNode->pNext;          // Move to the node just created
    }
  }
  return *this;                           // Return the left object
}
```

If the objects in the assignment are the same, you just dereference the this pointer to get the left-hand object, and return the object. If the objects are different, the first step is to delete all the nodes for the left-hand object before you replace them with copies of the nodes from the right-hand object. Having done that, just copy the right-hand object with code identical to the copy constructor. The code to do the copying is common to both the copy constructor and the assignment operator, so you can put it in a separate member function.

The code to delete nodes in the destructor is exactly the same as the code in the assignment operator function:

```
template <typename T> Stack<T>::~Stack() {
  Node* pTemp;
  while(pHead) {
    pTemp = pHead->pNext;
    delete pHead;
    pHead = pTemp;
  }
}
```

> **NOTE** *As with the copying code, you can put this code in a separate helper function that is private to the* Stack *class template, and then just call it when the capability is required. This reduces the size of the executable.*

The template for the push() operation is very easy:

```
template <typename T> void Stack<T>::push(T& rItem) {
  Node* pNode = new Node(rItem);      // Create the new node
  pNode->pNext = pHead;               // Point to the old top node
  pHead = pNode;                      // Make the new node the top
}
```

To create the node, you pass a reference to the object to the Node constructor. The pNext member of this node needs to point to the node that was previously at the top. You then make the new node the top of the stack.

The pop() operation is slightly more work because you must delete the top node:

```
template <typename T> T& Stack<T>::pop() {
  T* pItem = pHead->pItem;                    // Get pointer to the top node object
  if(!pItem)                                  // If it is empty
    throw std::logic_error("Stack empty");    // Pop is not valid so throw exception

  Node* pTemp = pHead;                        // Save address of top node
  pHead = pHead->pNext;                       // Make next node the top
  delete pTemp;                               // Delete the previous top node
  return *pItem;                              // Return the top object
}
```

It is possible that someone could attempt a pop operation on an empty stack. Because you return a reference, you can't signal an error through the return value, so you have to throw an exception in this case.

Once you've retrieved the pointer to the object in the top node, delete the top node, promote the next node to the top, and return the object. Now you've completed all the templates you need to define the stack, you can exercise your nested templates in a working example.

Try It Out: Using Nested Class Templates

You need to gather all the templates into a header file, Stacks.h. Here's how it looks with the helper functions that I mentioned in the text:

```
// Stacks.h Templates to define stacks
#ifndef STACKS_H
#define STACKS_H
#include <stdexcept>

template <typename T> class Stack {
  private:
    class Node {
      public:
        T* pItem;                          // Pointer to object stored
        Node* pNext;                       // Pointer to next node

        Node(T& rItem) : pItem(&rItem), pNext(0) {} // Create node from an object
        Node() : pItem(0), pNext(0) {}     // Create an empty node
    };

    Node* pHead;                           // Points to the top of the stack
    void copy(const Stack& aStack);        // Helper to copy a stack
    void freeMemory();                     // Helper to release free store memory

  public:
    Stack():pHead(0){}                     // Default constructor
    Stack(const Stack& aStack);            // Copy constructor
    ~Stack();                              // Destructor
    Stack& operator=(const Stack& aStack); // Assignment operator

    void push(T& rItem);                   // Push an object onto the stack
    T& pop();                              // Pop an object off the stack
    bool isEmpty() {return pHead == 0;}    // Empty test
};

// Copy constructor
template <typename T> Stack<T>::Stack(const Stack& aStack) {
  copy(aStack);
}

// Helper to copy a stack
template <typename T> void Stack<T>::copy(const Stack& aStack) {
  pHead = 0;
```

```
    if(aStack.pHead) {
      pHead = new Node(*aStack.pHead);      // Copy the top node of the original
      Node* pOldNode = aStack.pHead;        // Points to top node of the original
      Node* pNewNode = pHead;               // Points to the node in the new stack

      while(pOldNode = pOldNode->pNext) {   // If it is null, it is the last node
        pNewNode->pNext = new Node(*pOldNode);// Duplicate it
        pNewNode = pNewNode->pNext;         // Move to the node just created
      }
    }
}

// Assignment operator
template <typename T> Stack<T>& Stack<T>::operator=(const Stack& aStack) {
  if(this == &aStack)                       // If objects are identical
    return *this;                           // return the left object

  freeMemory();                             // Release memory for nodes in lhs
  copy(aStack);                             // Copy rhs to lhs

  return *this                              // Return the left object
}

// Helper to release memory for a stack
template <typename T> void Stack<T>::freeMemory() {
  Node* pTemp;
  while(pHead) {                            // While current pointer is not null
    pTemp = pHead->pNext;                   // Get the pointer to the next
    delete pHead;                           // Delete the current
    pHead = pTemp;                          // Make the next current
  }
}

// Destructor
template <typename T> Stack<T>::~Stack() {
  freeMemory();
}

// Push an object onto the stack
template <typename T> void Stack<T>::push(T& rItem) {
  Node* pNode = new Node(rItem);            // Create the new node
  pNode->pNext = pHead;                     // Point to the old top node
  pHead = pNode;                            // Make the new node the top
}

// Pop an object off the stack
template <typename T> T& Stack<T>::pop() {
  T* pItem = pHead->pItem;                  // Get pointer to the top node object
  if(!pItem)                                // If it is empty
    throw std::logic_error("Stack empty"); // Pop is not valid: throw exception
```

(Continued)

```
    Node* pTemp = pHead;                    // Save address of top node
    pHead = pHead->pNext;                   // Make next node the top
    delete pTemp;                           // Delete the previous top node
    return *pItem;                          // Return the top object
}
#endif
```

You can then use them in the following program that juggles strings around using stacks:

```
// Program 18.4 Using a stack defined by nested class templates  File prog18_04.cpp
#include "Stacks.h"
#include <iostream>
#include <string>
using std::cout;
using std::cin;
using std::endl;
using std::string;

int main() {
  const char* words[] = {"The", "quick", "brown", "fox", "jumps"};
  Stack<const char*> wordStack;                 // A stack of null terminated strings

  for(int i = 0 ; i < 5 ; i++)
    wordStack.push(words[i]);

  Stack<const char*> newStack(wordStack);   // Create a copy of the stack

  // Display the words in reverse order
  while(!newStack.isEmpty())
    cout << newStack.pop() << " ";
  cout << endl;

  // Reverse wordStack onto newStack
  while(!wordStack.isEmpty())
    newStack.push(wordStack.pop());

  // Display the words in original order
  while(!newStack.isEmpty())
    cout << newStack.pop() << " ";
  cout << endl;

  cout << endl << "Enter a line of text:" << endl;
  string text;
  getline(cin, text);                       // Read a line into the string object

  Stack<const char> characters;         // A stack for characters

  for(size_t i = 0 ; i < text.length() ; i++)
    characters.push(text[i]);               // Push the string characters onto the stack
```

```
cout << endl;
while(!characters.isEmpty())
   cout << characters.pop();          // Pop the characters off the stack

cout << endl;
return 0;
}
```

This example produces output something like the following:

```
jumps fox brown quick The
The quick brown fox jumps

Enter a line of text:
A nod is as good as a wink to a blind horse

esroh dnilb a ot kniw a sa doog sa si don A
```

HOW IT WORKS

You first define an array of five objects that are null-terminated strings, initialized with the words shown. Then you declare a stack object to store const char* objects with this statement:

```
Stack<const char*> wordStack;          // A stack of null terminated strings
```

This creates an instance of the Stack template and an instance of the constructor for Stack<const char*>. You push the array elements onto the stack in the for loop:

```
for(size_t i = 0 ; i < 5 ; i++)
   wordStack.push(words[i]);
```

The stack has the first word at the bottom of the wordStack stack and the last word at the top. You then create a copy of the stack with the statement:

```
Stack<const char*> newStack(wordStack);    // Create a copy of the stack
```

This calls the copy constructor, so an instance of the function template for this is created. newStack is a duplicate of wordStack. In the next while loop, you display the words in reverse order by popping them off the stack and outputting them:

```
while(!newStack.isEmpty())
   cout << newStack.pop() << " ";
```

This uses isEmpty() to continue popping objects off the stack until you reach the end; the function returns false as long as the stack is not empty. Using the isEmpty() function is a safe way of getting the complete contents of a stack. The newStack is empty by the end of the loop, but you still have the original in wordStack.

(Continued)

In the next while loop, you retrieve the words from wordStack and pop them onto newStack:

```
while(!wordStack.isEmpty())
  newStack.push(wordStack.pop());
```

The pop and push operations are combined in a single statement, where the object returned by pop() for wordStack is the argument for push() for newStack(). At the end of this loop, wordStack is empty and newStack contains the words in their original sequence—with the first word at the top of the stack. You then output the words by popping them off newStack, so at the end of this loop, both stacks are empty:

```
while(!newStack.isEmpty())
  cout << newStack.pop() << " ";
```

The next part of the program reads a line of text into a string object using the getline() function:

```
cout << endl << endl << "Enter a line of text:" << endl;
string text;
getline(cin, text);                    // Read a line into the string object
```

This reads the input into the string object, text. You then create a stack to hold characters:

```
Stack<const char> characters;          // A stack for characters
```

This creates a new instance of the Stack template, Stack<const char>, and a new instance of the constructor for this type of stack. At this point, the program contains two classes from the Stack template each with a nested Node class.

You peel off the characters from text and push them onto your new stack in a for loop:

```
for(size_t i = 0 ; i < text.length() ; i++)
  characters.push(text[i]);           // Push the string characters onto the stack
```

The length() function of the text object is used to determine when the loop ends; you can now display the input string in reverse by popping the characters off the stack:

```
cout << endl;
while(!characters.isEmpty())
  cout << characters.pop();           // Pop the characters off the stack
```

You can see from the output that my input was not even slightly palindromic, but you could try, "Ned, I am a maiden" or even "Are we not drawn onward, we few, drawn onward to new era."

More Advanced Class Templates

More advanced aspects of applying class templates are outside the scope of this book; a full discussion of this could be the topic for a complete book, but I'll just mention a couple of capabilities without going into more detail.

As you would expect, a class template can have base classes, and these can be ordinary classes or class templates themselves. For example, you might want a template that was derived from the Stack template in order to provide some additional capabilities not available in the basic Stack template. You could define the template like this:

```
template <typename T> class SpecialStack: public Stack<T> {
  public:
    SpecialStack();
    ~SpecialStack();
    SpecialStack(const SpecialStack& aStack);

    int ObjectCount();                    // Count the objects
};
```

This is a trivial example that just adds a function to determine how many objects are in the stack, but it illustrates that specifying a template as a base to a template is quite straightforward. An instance of this template derives from the Stack<T> instance, so it works in the same way as for ordinary derived classes.

Note also that a type parameter in a template can itself be a template, so you could define a template like this:

```
template <typename T1, template <typename T2> Array> class ClassName {
  // Template definition...
};
```

The first template parameter, T1, is a type parameter, the second parameter is also a type parameter but this time it is a template. The parameter T2 determines a specific instance of the Array template that is used as the second argument for the ClassName template.

Summary

You need to understand how class templates are defined and used in order to understand how to apply the capabilities of the Standard Template Library that I'll discuss in Chapter 20. The ability to define class templates is also a powerful augmentation of the basic language facilities for defining classes. The essential points I've discussed in this chapter include the following:

- A class template defines a family of class types.

- An instance of a class template is a class definition produced from the template by a given set of template arguments.

- An implicit instantiation of a class template arises out of a declaration for an object of a class template type.

- An explicit instantiation of a class template defines a class for a given set of arguments for the template parameters.

- An argument corresponding to a type parameter in a class template is a type that can be a basic type, a class type, a pointer type, or a reference type.

- The type of a non-type parameter can be an integral or enumeration type, a pointer type, or a reference type.

- A partial specialization of a class template defines a new template that is to be used for a specific, restricted subset of the possible arguments for the original class template.

- A complete specialization of a class template defines a new template for a specific, complete set of parameter arguments for the original class template.

- A friend of a class template can be a function, a class, a function template, or a class template.

- An ordinary class can declare a class template or a function template as a friend.

Exercises

The following exercises enable you to try out what you've learned in this chapter. If you get stuck, look back over the chapter for help. If you're still stuck after that, you can download the solutions from the Apress website (http://www.apress.com/book/download.html), but that really should be a last resort.

Exercise 18-1. You created a sparse array class in the exercises at the end of the previous chapter. This time, define a *template* for one-dimensional sparse arrays that will store objects of any type so that only the elements stored in the array occupy memory. The potential number of elements that can be stored by an instance of the template should be unlimited. The template might be used to define a sparse array containing pointers to elements of type double with the following statement:

    SparseArray<double> values;

Define the subscript operator for the template so that element values can be retrieved and set just like in a normal array. If an element doesn't exist at an index position, the subscript operator should return an object created by the default constructor for the object class. Exercise the template with a main() function that stores 20 random element values of type int within the range 32 to 212 at random positions in a sparse array with an index range from 0 to 499, and output the non-zero element values along with their index positions.

Exercise 18-2. Define a template for a linked list that allows the list to be traversed backward, from the end of the list, as well as forward from the beginning. (Each node needs a pointer to the previous node as well as a pointer to the next.) Apply the template in a program to store individual words from some arbitrary prose or poetry as string objects, and then to display them five to a line in reverse order.

Exercise 18-3. Use the linked list and sparse array templates to produce a program that stores words from a prose or poetry sample in a sparse array of up to 26 linked lists, where each list contains words that have the same initial letter. Output the words, starting each group with a given initial letter on a new line. (Remember to leave a space between successive > characters when specifying template arguments—otherwise, >> will be interpreted as a shift right operator.)

Exercise 18-4. Add an insert() function to the SparseArray template that adds an element following the last element in the array. Use this function and a SparseArray instance that has elements that are SparseArray objects storing string objects to perform the same task as the previous exercise.

CHAPTER 19

Input and Output Operations

THE C++ LANGUAGE itself has no provision for input and output. The subject of this chapter is the input and output capabilities that are available in the standard library, which provides you with support for device-independent input and output operations in your programs. You've used elements of these facilities to read from the keyboard and write to the screen in all the book's examples so far, and here you'll expand on that and look at how you can read and write disk files. By the end of this chapter, you'll have learned

- What a stream is

- What the standard streams are

- How binary streams differ from text streams

- How to create and use file streams

- How errors in stream operations are recorded, and how you can manage them

- How to use unformatted stream operations

- How to write numerical data to a file as binary data

- How objects can be written to and read from a stream

- How to overload the insertion and extraction operators for your classes

- How to implement stream support for template classes

- How to create string streams

Input and Output in C++

You'll need many different kinds of input and output capabilities in your C++ programs. Your application might need to store and retrieve data in a database, to create and display graphics on the screen, to communicate over a telephone line through a modem, or to communicate over a network. All of these examples have one thing in common. They're totally outside the remit of the C++ language and library facilities.

This implies that in the majority of situations, you'll use input/output (I/O) facilities that aren't part of the C++ standard, although they may well be provided as part of your C++ development environment. It may also be the case that some of the facilities provided by C++ aren't consistent with the environment in which your program is to execute. Your computer's operating system controls communication with the screen and the keyboard, and it could be that reading from cin and writing to cout isn't possible. This is the case if you're programming for Microsoft Windows on a PC, for example, although the facility is emulated in many C++ development systems for Windows and provides the ability to read and write as console operations on the command line.

Of course, the capabilities that are defined within C++ are still very important, as they represent a substantial standard library facility with extensive functionality. Not only do they provide you with file I/O capability, but they also include facilities for data formatting using string-based I/O.

Understanding Streams

The I/O functionality provided by the standard library involves using streams. A **stream** is an abstract representation of an input device or an output device that is a source or destination for data in your program. You can visualize a stream as a sequence of bytes flowing between an external device and the main memory of your computer. You can write data to an **output stream** and read data from an **input stream**, and some streams can provide the capability for both input and output of data. Fundamentally, all input and output is a sequence of bytes being read from, or written to, some external device.

When you're reading data from an external device, it's up to you to interpret the data correctly. When you read bytes from an external source, the bytes could be a sequence of 8-bit characters, a sequence of UCS characters, binary values of various types, or a mixture of all of them. There's no way to tell from the data itself what it is. You have to know the structure and type of data in advance, and read and interpret it accordingly.

Data Transfer Modes

There are two modes for transferring data to and from streams: **text mode** and **binary mode**. In text mode, the data is interpreted as a sequence of characters that is organized as one or more lines terminated by the newline character, '\n'. In text mode, the stream may transform newline characters as they're read from or written to the physical device. Whether this occurs, and how characters are changed, is system dependent. On some systems such as Microsoft Windows, a single newline character written to a stream will be replaced by *two* characters: a carriage return and a line feed. When a carriage return and a line feed are read from a stream, they're mapped into a single character, '\n'. On other systems such as Unix, the newline will remain a single character. In binary mode, such transformations of characters in the stream don't occur. The original bytes are transferred to or from the stream without conversion.

Stream Read and Write Operations

There are two ways in which you can read from and write to a stream. First, you can read and write various types of data using the extraction and insertion operators, as you've been doing throughout the book when you read from the keyboard or write to the screen. These are **formatted input/output operations** that occur in text mode. Binary numerical data in your program, such as integers and floating-point values, are converted to a character representation before they're written to the stream, and the inverse process occurs when data values are read from the stream. All the operations for writing to cout and reading from cin that you've performed so far in the examples were formatted I/O operations in text mode.

The second way of working with a stream is to read or write bytes. A read or write operation can be for just a single byte, a given number of bytes, or a sequence of bytes terminated by a delimiter of some kind, but the most significant point about this method is that you only read or write *bytes*. There's no specific provision for writing or reading any other type of data. These are referred to as **unformatted input/output operations**, and you would use these operations with a stream in binary mode. The data that you write to the stream may actually be made up of character strings as well as binary numerical values of various kinds, but whatever they are it's the bytes that make up the data values in memory that are written directly to the stream.

One important point to keep in mind with binary streams is that if the source or destination of the data is a different system, complications can arise. The way in which binary values are represented in memory can differ between one system and another, so you need to take this into account when you're reading binary data that originated on a different computer. If you aren't familiar with these kinds of problems, you can find more details of the differences that occur in Appendix E.

Advantages of Using Streams

The primary reason for using streams as the basis for I/O operations in C++ is to make your source code for these operations independent of the physical device involved. This has a couple of advantages. First, you don't have to worry about the detailed mechanics of each device, as that is all taken care of behind the scenes. Second, your program will work with a variety of disparate I/O devices without necessitating any changes to the source code.

The physical reality of an output stream—in other words, where the data goes when you write to it—can be any device to which a sequence of bytes can be transferred. It will typically be the screen, a file on your hard disk, or possibly your printer. The standard library defines three output streams, cout, cerr, and clog, all of which are typically associated with your display screen. cout is the standard output stream. cerr and clog are both connected to the **standard error stream**, which is used for error reporting from your program. The difference between the last two streams is that cerr is unbuffered (so data is written immediately to the output device), whereas clog is buffered (so data will only be written when the buffer is full). Figure 19-1 shows some devices and the kinds of streams that they would represent.

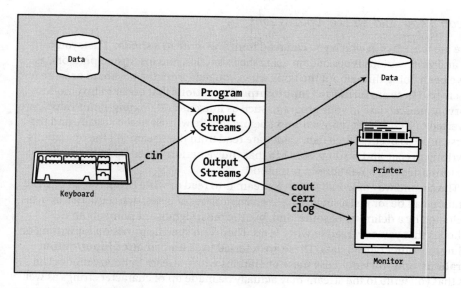

Figure 19-1. I/O devices and streams

In principle, an **input stream** can also be any serial source of data, but it's typically a disk file or the keyboard. The standard library defines a standard input stream, cin, which is usually associated with the keyboard.

As you might have guessed by now, streams in C++ are objects of classes, and the standard streams are predefined objects that are already associated with specific external devices on your system. When you've been reading objects from cin using the extraction operator, >>, or writing objects to cout using the insertion operator, <<, you've been using overloaded versions of the operator<<() and operator>>() functions for these objects. As far as the standard streams are concerned, everything is set up and ready to go. However, when you want to use something other than the standard streams—for *file* input and output, or instance—you must create the stream objects that you need and associate them with the physical source or destination for the data. To set you on your way, let's take a look at the classes that define streams.

Stream Classes

There are quite a few classes involved in stream I/O, but the main ones that you're interested in and the relationships between them are illustrated in Figure 19-2.

Figure 19-2 is a simplified representation, but it's all you need to understand the principles. ios_base is an "ordinary" class, and the others are instances of templates. The istream class, for example, is an instance of the basic_istream template, and the ios class is an instance of the basic_ios template. However, you're interested in the classes rather than their templates, because you'll be using the classes in your programs. The stream classes share a common base, ios, which inherits flags that record the state of a stream and the formatting modes in effect from the ios_base class. Thus, all the stream classes that provide the I/O operations that you'll be using share a common set of status and formatting flags, and the functions to query and set them.

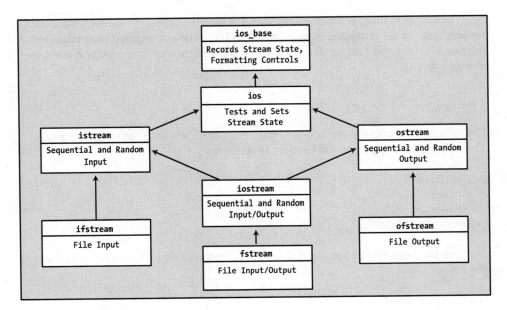

Figure 19-2. The main stream classes

The standard input stream cin is an object of type istream, and the standard output streams cout, cerr, and clog are ostream objects. You can see that the stream classes for file handling, ifstream, fstream, and ofstream, all have istream, ostream, or both as base classes, so the facilities that you've been using with the standard streams cin and cout are going to be available with file streams too.

The template classes generally have type parameters that specify the character sets for a particular stream, and the classes identified in the diagram apply to streams that deal with characters of type char. There are instances of these templates that define streams that can handle characters of type wchar_t, called wistream, wostream, wiostream, wifstream, wofstream, and wfstream. I won't discuss these wide-character stream classes specifically in this chapter, but they work in the same way as the byte stream classes.

Because you'll sometimes see references to the original templates rather than to the abbreviated class type names that appear in Figure 19-2, you need to be aware of the template names. The stream classes are defined using typedefs as follows:

```
typedef basic_ios<char>       ios;
typedef basic_istream<char>   istream;
typedef basic_ostream<char>   ostream;
typedef basic_iostream<char>  iostream;
typedef basic_ifstream<char>  ifstream;
typedef basic_ofstream<char>  ofstream;
typedef basic_fstream<char>   fstream;
```

The corresponding wide-character streams just have `wchar_t` as the type parameter argument to the template, in place of `char`. I'll use the abbreviated class names in the rest of this chapter rather than the full template names, as they involve considerably less typing!

Standard Streams

The standard streams are defined as stream class objects within the `std` namespace. These definitions appear in the header file `iostream`:

```
extern istream cin;
extern ostream cout;
extern ostream cerr;
extern ostream clog;
```

The `iostream` header file also defines the corresponding wide-character stream objects as follows:

```
extern wistream wcin;
extern wostream wcout;
extern wostream wcerr;
extern wostream wclog;
```

You've already made extensive use of the standard input stream `cin` and the standard output stream `cout`. The `cerr` and `clog` streams are used in exactly the same way as `cout`. I won't repeat in this chapter what I covered in previous chapters about how reading from and writing to the standard streams is handled. Instead, you'll concentrate on understanding more of the background of how they work, and how the same techniques and mechanisms apply to other stream types.

To begin with, you'll revisit the formatted stream operations you're already familiar with, and you'll explore how you can use them for files as well as for the standard streams. You'll then look into how unformatted stream operations work, and how and when you can use those to your advantage.

Stream Insertion and Extraction Operations

The insertion and extraction operators that you've been using with standard stream objects work just the same with other types of stream objects. All the standard streams operate in text mode, because this mode ensures that the data is presented correctly on output.

The insertion and extraction operators are principally concerned with converting between internal binary representations of data values and their external character representations. When you use these operators with streams other than the standard streams, you'll still usually want to use them in text mode, because they're geared to working with a text-based representation of the data. Text mode is concerned with ensuring that the visual presentation of the data is correct.

Stream Extraction Operations

The function operator>>() is implemented as a set of overloaded members of the istream class to support reading basic types of data from any input stream. There will be an overloaded version of this operator for each of the basic data types in C++. Let's look at how the code you've been writing connects to these operator functions by considering what happens when you write statements such as these:

```
int i = 0;
double x = 0.0;
std::cin >> i >> x;
```

Remember that cin is an object of type istream. The last statement, which reads the two variables from the standard stream, cin, translates to this:

```
(std::cin.operator>>(i)).operator>>(x);
```

As you might expect, the operator>>() function is called once for each time you use the extraction operator. The operator>>() function for streams returns a reference to the stream object for which it was called (in this case cin), so the return value is used to call the next operator function. The parameter to the operator>>() function has to be a reference, to allow the function to store the data value read from the stream in the variable that is passed as an argument.

A whitespace character is always regarded as a delimiter between values, so you can't read whitespace characters into your program using the operator>>() members of the istream class. Excess whitespace characters are generally ignored. You'll recall that you had to use the getline() function for cin when you wanted to read a line of text from the keyboard.

The operator>>() function is implemented as an overloaded set of members of the istream class for the following basic types:

short	int	long
unsigned short	unsigned int	unsigned long
float	double	long double
bool	void*	

The function that supports the last of these types, void*, enables you to read address values into a pointer of any type, *except* for a pointer to type char, which refers to a null-terminated string and is treated as a special case. A pointer of any type can be passed as an argument to a function with a parameter of type *reference to void**, but there are non-member versions of operator>>() that accept arguments that are pointers to null-terminated strings. They have the following prototypes:

```
istream& operator>>(istream& in, signed char* pStr);
istream& operator>>(istream& in, unsigned char* pStr);
```

One of these functions will always be selected when you use a pointer to a null-terminated string with the extraction operator. If you want to read an address and store it in a pointer of type char*, you must read it as type void*, and then cast the address to type char* to store it.

Reading a single character using the extraction operator is also supported through operator>>() functions that aren't members of the istream class, because they can be implemented using the get() function defined for istream objects. There are three versions, corresponding to reading a single character as type char, signed char, and unsigned char. I'll come back to the get() function later in the chapter.

Stream Insertion Operations

The operator<<() function is overloaded in the ostream class for formatted stream output of data values of the basic types. Output to cout works analogously to input with cin. You could write the data values i and x to cout with this statement:

```
std::cout << i << ' ' << x;
```

This statement translates to three calls of operator<<() functions:

```
operator<<(std::cout.operator<<(i), ' ').operator<<(x);
```

All versions of the operator<<() function return a reference to the stream object for which they're called, so the return value can always be used to call the next operator<<() function. As I've explained, the operator<<() functions that write single characters and null-terminated strings to the stream are implemented as non-member functions. That's why the operator function call to write i to the stream appears as the first argument to the operator function call to write the space. The non-member function returns the stream object, and that's used to call the member function that writes the value of x.

The operator<<() function is overloaded in the ostream class for the same set of types as the operator>>() functions in the istream class listed previously. In addition, outputting of a single character or a null-terminated string is catered for by non-member versions of operator<<(). The functions that output a single character to an output stream have the following prototypes:

```
ostream& operator<<(ostream& out, char ch);
ostream& operator<<(ostream& out, signed char ch);
ostream& operator<<(ostream& out, unsigned char ch);
```

There are similar functions defined that will output null-terminated strings:

```
ostream& operator<<(ostream& out, const char* pStr);
ostream& operator<<(ostream& out, const signed char* pStr);
ostream& operator<<(ostream& out, const unsigned char* pStr);
```

You can see now why you can output a string using a pointer, when pointers to other types are always written to a stream as an address. Because these functions exist, sending a variable of type const char* to an output stream writes the string to which the pointer points to the stream, rather than the address stored in the pointer variable. If for some reason you want the address contained in the pointer to be output rather than the string, you must explicitly cast it to type void*. Then, the member function of ostream that has a parameter of that type will be called, and the address will be sent to the stream. Thus, if you have the statements

```
const char* pMessage = "More is less and less is more.";
cout << pMessage;
```

you'll display the message. To output the address contained in pMessage, you must write the output statement as

```
cout << static_cast<void*>(pMessage);
```

Stream Manipulators

You've already made extensive use of manipulators to control formatting of a stream. In particular, the basic manipulators shown in Table 19-1 can be inserted into a stream.

Table 19-1. Basic Stream Manipulators

Manipulator	Effect
dec	Sets the default radix for integers to decimal
oct	Sets the default radix for integers to octal
hex	Sets the default radix for integers to hexadecimal
fixed	Outputs floating-point values in fixed-point notation without an exponent
scientific	Outputs floating-point values in scientific notation with an exponent
boolalpha	Represents bool values as alphabetic; true and false in English
noboolalpha	Represents bool values as 1 and 0
showbase	Indicates the base for octal (0 prefix) and hexadecimal (0x prefix) integers
noshowbase	Omits the base indication for octal and hexadecimal integers
showpoint	Always outputs floating-point values to the stream with a decimal point
noshowpoint	Outputs integral floating-point values without a decimal point
showpos	Displays a + prefix for positive integers
noshowpos	Does not display a + prefix for positive integers
skipws	Skips whitespace on input
noskipws	Does not skip whitespace on input
uppercase	Uses uppercase for hexadecimal digits A to F, and E for an exponent
nouppercase	Uses lowercase for hexadecimal digits a to f, and e for an exponent

(Continued)

Table 19-1. Basic Stream Manipulators (Continued)

Manipulator	Effect
internal	Inserts "fill characters" to pad the output to the field width
left	Aligns values left in an output field
right	Aligns values right in an output field
endl	Writes a newline character to the stream buffer and writes the contents of the buffer to the stream
flush	Writes data from the stream buffer to the stream

All of the manipulators in Table 19-1 can be placed directly into the stream, for example:

```
int i = 1000;
std::cout << std::hex << std::uppercase << i;
```

This will output the value of the integer, i, as a hexadecimal value, using uppercase hexadecimal digits. In other words, you'd see 3E8 on the screen.

It's interesting to see how this works. You know that using an insertion operator results in a version of operator<<() being called, but none of the versions you've seen so far can be involved here, because they only deal with values being output to the stream. The effect of these manipulators doesn't involve sending data to a stream, so they can't be data values. In fact, all of the manipulators in Table 19-1 are pointers to functions of the same type. When you use one of these manipulators, a special version of operator<<() that accepts a pointer to a function is called, and the manipulator is passed as an argument.

To make this clearer, the manipulator hex is the name of this function:

```
ios_base& hex(ios_base& str);
```

You might use this manipulator in a statement such as

```
std::cout << std::hex << i;
```

which translates to

```
(std::cout.operator<<(std::hex)).operator<<(i);
```

The first call of operator<<() has the pointer to function, hex, as an argument. Within the operator function, the function hex() will be called to set the output formatting to transfer the value of i to the stream in hexadecimal format.

The ios_base class that cropped up in the prototype for hex() is the base class of the ios class, as you saw at the beginning of this chapter. Because this is inherited by all of the stream classes, the type ios_base& can reference any stream object. All of the manipulators are pointers to functions that have a parameter and a return type of type *reference to ios_base*, so they all result in the same version of operator<<() being called, which will call the function pointed to by the argument. ios_base defines flags that control the stream, and the function that is called when you use a manipulator modifies the appropriate flags to produce the desired result. You can modify these flags directly using the functions setf() and unsetf() for a stream object, but it's much easier to use the manipulators.

Manipulators with Arguments

There are some manipulators that accept an argument when you use them. To access these, you must #include the <iomanip> header into your source file, because it contains their declarations. You use these manipulator functions in the same way as the other manipulators, by effectively inserting a function call into the stream. Table 19-2 shows these manipulators.

Table 19-2. Manipulators That Accept an Argument

Manipulator	Effect
setprecision(int n)	Sets the precision for floating-point output to n digits. This remains in effect until you change it.
setw(int n)	Sets the field width for the next output value to n characters. This will reset on each output to the default setting, which outputs a value in a field width that is just sufficient to accommodate the value.
setfill(char ch)	Sets the fill character to be used as padding within the output field to ch. This is modal, so it remains in effect until you change it again.
setbase(int base)	Sets the output representation for integers to octal, decimal, or hexadecimal, corresponding to values for the argument of 8, 10, or 16. Any other values will leave the number base unchanged.

The return type for each of the manipulators in Table 19-2 is implementation defined. An example of using them is as follows:

```
std::cout << std::endl << std::setw(10) << std::setfill('*') << std::left << i;
```

This statement outputs the value i left-justified in a field that's ten characters wide. The field will be padded with '*' in any unused character positions to the right of the value. The fill character will be in effect for any following output values, but you must set the field width explicitly prior to each output value.

 CAUTION *It's an error to include parentheses for the manipulators that are function pointers (such as* left*), so don't mix them up with the four discussed here.*

The <iomanip> header also declares the functions setiosflags() and resetiosflags() that you can use to set or reset the flags controlling stream formatting by specifying a mask. You construct the mask that you pass as an argument by using the bitwise OR operator to combine the flags that are defined in the ios_base class. The name of each flag is the same as the name of the manipulator that sets it, so you could set the flags for left-justified, hexadecimal output as follows:

```
std::cout << std::endl << std::setw(10)
          << std::setiosflags(std::ios::left | std::ios::hex) << i;
```

This will output i as a left-justified, hexadecimal value in a field that's ten characters wide. You can use ios as the qualifier for the flag names here, because the flags are inherited in the ios class from ios_base.

File Streams

There are three types of stream class objects that you can use for working with files: ifstream, ofstream, and fstream. As you saw earlier, these have istream, ostream, and iostream as base classes, respectively. An istream object represents a file stream you can only read from, an ofstream object represents a file output stream that you can only write to, and fstream is a file stream that you can read from or write to.

You can associate a file stream object with a physical file on disk when you create it. Alternatively, you can create a file stream object that isn't associated with a particular file, and then use a member function to establish the connection with the physical file later on. In order to read or write a physical file, you must "open" the file, attaching it to your program via the operating system with a set of permissions that describe how you are going to use it. If you create a file stream object with an initial association to a particular file, the file is opened and available for use in your program immediately. Note that it's possible to change the physical file that a file stream object is associated with, so you could use a single ofstream object to write to different files at different times.

A file stream has some important properties. It has a **length**, which corresponds to the number of characters in the stream; it has a **beginning**, which is the first character in the stream; and it has an **end**, which is the position *after* the last character in the stream. It also has a **current position**, which is the index position of the character in the stream where the next read or write operation will start. The first character in a file stream is at position 0. These properties provide a way for you to move around a file to read the particular parts that you're interested in or to overwrite selected areas of the file.

Writing to a File

To begin investigating file streams, let's look at how you can write to a file output stream. An output file will be represented by an ofstream object, which you can create like this:

```
ofstream outFile("filename");
```

The file called filename will automatically be opened for writing, so you can write to it immediately in the default mode, text mode. If the file called filename doesn't exist, it will be created. If it already exists, any data that was in the file is discarded, and the data that you write to the file will form its new contents. Even if you *don't* write to the file after opening it, the original contents will be discarded and you'll have an empty file. The object outFile has an ostream subobject, so all of the stream operations I've been discussing in the context of the standard stream, cout, apply equally well to outFile. You can exercise this with a version of the example back in Chapter 7 that generated primes, Program 7.6.

Try It Out: Writing to a File

You can write the primes to a file instead of to the screen. All you need to do is define an ostream object for a file and use that in place of cout in the example. Here's the modified code, with the altered lines in bold:

```cpp
// Program 19.1 Writing primes to a file   File: prog19_01.cpp
#include <fstream>                              // For file streams
#include <iomanip>

int main() {
    const int max = 100;                        // Number of primes required
    long primes[max] = {2, 3, 5};               // First three primes defined
    int count = 3;                              // Count of primes found
    long trial = 5;                            // Candidate prime
    bool isprime = true;                       // Indicates when a prime is found

    do {
        trial += 2;                             // Next value for checking
        int i = 0;                             // Index to primes array

        // Try dividing the candidate by all the primes we have
        do {
            isprime = trial % *(primes + i) > 0;   // False for exact division
        } while(++i < count && isprime);

        if(isprime)                             // We got one...
            *(primes + count++) = trial;        // ...so save it in primes array
    } while(count < max);

    std::ofstream outFile("c:\\JunkData\\primes.txt"); // Define file stream object

    // Output primes 5 to a line
    for(int i = 0 ; i < max ; i++) {
        if(i % 5 == 0)                          // New line after every 5th prime
            outFile << std::endl;
        outFile << std::setw(10) << *(primes + i);
    }
    return 0;
}
```

(Continued)

This program doesn't send any output to the screen. The only output is the file that gets written. Note that if you use the path specified in the program, you must create the JunkData directory before you run it. The program only creates the file, not the directory, so you must create the directory before you run the program. You should be able to view the contents of the file using any text editor.

HOW IT WORKS

First of all, you have a #include directive for the <fstream> header that defines the file stream classes:

```
#include <fstream>                              // For file streams
```

You no longer need the <iostream> header, because you don't use any of the standard streams in this example. All of the calculations are the same as in Chapter 7, so the first change to main() is the addition of a declaration for the file output stream object:

```
std::ofstream outFile("C:\\JunkData\\primes.txt"); // Define file stream object
```

This defines an ofstream object, outFile, and associates it with the file called primes.txt in the JunkData directory on your C: drive. This code uses MS-DOS notation for the path, so you should use a file path and name to suit your environment here. Remember that you need to use \\ for a single backslash in the path, because a single \ starts an escape sequence. On this occasion, I've used the extension .txt in the file name because I'm writing the file in text mode, and it should therefore be viewable by applications that handle .txt files. I haven't added checks for success in this program, but I'll cover those possibilities later.

If you don't specify a path, the file will be assumed to be in the current directory. If it doesn't already exist there, it will be created in that directory. If you want to err on the side of caution, you could do as I've done and set aside a directory somewhere that you'll use to experiment with file operations. As long as you use fully qualified file names in all your programs, there is then no risk of corrupting important files by accident.

The final modification to the original program is to make it write to the file in exactly the same way as you originally wrote to cout, by using the insertion operator <<:

```
for(int i = 0 ; i < max ; i++) {
  if(i % 5 == 0)                            // New line after every 5th prime
    outFile << std::endl;
  outFile << std::setw(10) << *(primes + i);
}
```

When the program is done, you should find the file primes.txt in the C:\JunkData directory (or whatever path you specified). If you view the contents using a text editor, you'll see that the file contains the same data as was displayed by the original version of the program.

Of course, if you just want to use the file as a medium for intermediate storage and you don't want to look at the contents directly, you can dispense with the newline characters. You still need whitespace between one value and the next if you want to read them back using the extraction operator, but you can reduce this to a single space. In that case, the output statement could be as follows:

```
for(int i = 0 ; i < max ; i++)
    outFile << ' ' << *(primes + i);
```

Notice that you didn't have to do anything to close the file. When an `ostream` object is destroyed, the file that it's associated with is closed automatically, so your file will be closed when the `outFile` object goes out of scope. If you want to close the file explicitly, you can call the `close()` function for the object, so this statement will close the file represented by your `outFile` object:

```
outFile.close();
```

On my system, an `ostream` object overwrites any existing file contents. You can verify that this is the case for your system by running the program again with a different value for the number of primes and taking another look at the file contents.

NOTE *You don't always have to overwrite the file each time; that just happens to be the default setting. You'll look at how to control the way a file is written a little later in the chapter.*

Reading from a File

To read from a file, you can create an object of type `ifstream` and associate it with the file on your disk, for example:

```
const char* filename = "C:\\JunkData\\primes.txt";
std::ifstream inFile(filename);
```

This defines the object `inFile`, associates it with the file `primes.txt` in the `JunkData` directory on the `C:` drive, and opens the file. If you're going to read a file, it must already exist, but we all know that things don't always go as planned. What happens if you try to read from a file that you haven't prepared earlier?

As far as this definition is concerned, the answer is absolutely nothing: you just have a file stream object that won't work. To find out if everything is as it should be, you must test the status of the file, and there are several ways to do this. One possibility is for you to call the `is_open()` member of the `ifstream` object, which returns `true` if the file is open and `false` if it isn't. Another option is to call the `fail()` function that is inherited in the file stream classes from the `ios` class, which returns `true` if any file error occurred.

Alternatively, you can use the ! operator with the file stream object. This operator is overloaded in the ios class to check the stream status indicators that are defined in that class. When applied to the stream object, it returns true if the stream isn't in a satisfactory state. Using the overloaded ! operator is equivalent to calling the fail() function, and so to make sure your stream object is in a satisfactory condition and ready for use, you could write this:

```
if(!inFile) {
  std::cout << std::endl << "Failed to open file " << filename;
  return 1;
}
```

You can test that an output file stream object is available for use in exactly the same way, as the ofstream class inherits the overloaded ! operator too. It also inherits the fail() function and implements the is_open() function. You'll look further into stream error states a little later in the chapter.

Reading a file in text mode is just like reading from cin—you use the extraction operator in exactly the same way. However, you don't necessarily know how many data values there are in a file, so how do you know when you've reached the end? The eof() function that is inherited from basic_ios in the ofstream class provides a neat solution. It returns true when the end of file is reached, so you can just continue to read data until that happens.

Try It Out: Reading a File

You now have enough knowledge about how input file streams work to have a go at reading back the file that you wrote in the previous example. You'll just read the file and output the values to the screen. Here's the code:

```cpp
// Program 19.2 Reading the primes file  File: prog19_02.cpp
#include <fstream>
#include <iostream>
#include <iomanip>
using std::cout;
using std::endl;


int main() {
  const char* filename = "C:\\JunkData\\primes.txt";  // Name of the file to read
  std::ifstream inFile(filename);                      // Create input stream object

  // Make sure the file stream is good
  if(!inFile) {
    cout << endl << "Failed to open file " << filename;
    return 1;
  }
```

```
  long aprime = 0;
  int count = 0;
  while(!inFile.eof()) {                          // Continue until EOF is found
    inFile >> aprime;                             // Read a value from the file
    cout << (count++ % 5 == 0 ? "\n" : "") << std::setw(10) << aprime;
  }
  cout << endl;
  return 0;
}
```

I get the following output from this example:

2	3	5	7	11
13	17	19	23	29
31	37	41	43	47
53	59	61	67	71
73	79	83	89	97
101	103	107	109	113
127	131	137	139	149
151	157	163	167	173
179	181	191	193	197
199	211	223	227	229
233	239	241	251	257
263	269	271	277	281
283	293	307	311	313
317	331	337	347	349
353	359	367	373	379
383	389	397	401	409
419	421	431	433	439
443	449	457	461	463
467	479	487	491	499
503	509	521	523	541

HOW IT WORKS

You create the file stream object from the file name with these statements:

```
const char* filename = "C:\\JunkData\\primes.txt"; // Name of the file to read
std::ifstream inFile(filename);                    // Create input stream object
```

Before you use the file, you check that it has been opened successfully:

```
if(!inFile) {
  cout << endl << "Failed to open file " << filename;
  return 1;
}
```

(Continued)

The operator!() function for the object inFile that is inherited from the base class, ios, will return true if the constructor wasn't able to create the stream object properly and open the file. This will be the case if the file doesn't exist, for instance. If something has gone wrong, you display an error message and end the program.

Once you're sure the file is open, it's just a question of reading values from the file and outputting them to the standard stream, cout:

```
long aprime = 0;
int count = 0;
while(!inFile.eof()) {                                    // Continue until EOF is found
  inFile >> aprime;                                       // Read a value from the file
  cout << (count++ % 5 == 0 ? "\n" : "") << setw(10) << aprime;
}
```

The while loop continues until the value returned from the eof() member of inFile is true. Within the loop, you read a value from the inFile stream into aprime, and you output the value to cout. The conditional operator outputs a newline character after every five values. After the last value has been read from the file, the eof() member will return true because the current file position will be at the end of file.

Setting the File Open Mode

The file **open mode** for an ifstream or ofstream object determines what you can do with a file. It's determined by a combination of bit mask values that are defined in the ios_base class and inherited in the ios class as values of type openmode. The mask values that can be set are shown in Table 19-3.

Table 19-3. File Stream Bit Mask Values

Value	Meaning
ios::app	Moves to the end of the file before each write (**app**end). This ensures that you can only add to what is already in a file; you can't overwrite it.
ios::ate	Moves to the end of the file after opening it (**at e**nd). You can move the current position to elsewhere in the file subsequently.
ios::binary	Sets binary mode rather than text mode. In binary mode, all characters are unchanged when they're transferred to or from the file.
ios::in	Opens the file for reading.
ios::out	Opens the file for writing.
ios::trunc	Truncates the existing file to zero length.

Because these are bit masks, you generate a specification for the open mode by bitwise-ORing combinations of these values. For a file that is to be opened for writing in binary mode, such that data can only be added at the end of the file, you would specify the mode by using the expression ios::out | ios::app | ios::binary.

You can also open a file for reading *and* writing by specifying both ios::in and ios::out; for this, you must use an object of type fstream, as you'll see shortly.

You set the file open mode by specifying it as a second argument to the file stream class constructor. Both the ifstream and ofstream constructors have a second parameter of type openmode that has a default value specified. The default value for the file open mode for an ifstream object is ios::in, which just opens the file for input. The default for an ofstream object is ios::out | ios::trunc, which specifies that the file is to be opened for output. If it already exists, its length is set to 0, thus ensuring that any existing contents are overwritten.

Suppose that you want to specify the file open mode for a file output stream such that you can append data to the file rather than overwrite the contents. You could do this with the following statement:

```
const char* filename = "C:\\JunkData\\primes.txt";
std::ofstream outFile(filename, std::ios::out|std::ios::app);
```

If you explicitly close a file stream by calling the close() function for the stream object, you can open the file again with a new open mode by calling the stream object's open() function. The open() function accepts two arguments, the first being the file name, and the second being the open mode mask. The default values for the second parameter to the open() member of a file stream class are the same as for the class constructor. You could close the outFile stream and reopen it with a different open mode setting with the following statements:

```
outFile.close();
outFile.open(filename);
```

This reopens the file to overwrite the original contents, as ios::out | ios::trunc is the default value for the second parameter.

....

Try It Out: Specifying the File Open Mode

You could amend the prime numbers example once again, so that it will generate and display the number of primes that you specify, but so that the primes are stored in a file for reuse in the future. That way, the program will only need generate primes in excess of those already in the file. Any that are already in the file can be displayed immediately. Here's the code to do that:

```
// Program 19.3 Reading and writing the primes file  File: prog19_03.cpp
#include <fstream>
#include <iostream>
#include <iomanip>
#include <cmath>
#include <string>
using std::ios;
```

(Continued)

```
using std::cout;
using std::cin;
using std::endl;
using std::string;

// Function to find the prime after lastprime
long nextprime(long lastprime, const char* filename);

int main() {
  const char* filename = "C:\\JunkData\\primes.txt";
  int nprimes = 0;                          // Number of primes required
  int count = 0;                            // Count of primes found
  long lastprime = 0;                       // Last prime found

  // Get number of primes required
  int tries = 0;                            // Number of input tries
  cout << "How many primes would you like (at least 3)?: ";
  do {
    if(tries)
      cout << endl << " You must request at least 3, try again: ";
    cin >> nprimes;

    if(++tries == 5) {                      // Five tries is generous
      cout << endl << " I give up!" << endl;
      return 1;
    }
  } while(nprimes < 3);

  std::ifstream inFile;                     // Create input file stream object
  inFile.open(filename);                    // Open the file as an input stream

  cout << endl;
  if(!inFile.fail()) {
    do {
      inFile >> lastprime;
      cout << (count++ % 5 == 0 ? "\n" : "") << std::setw(10) << lastprime;
    } while(count < nprimes && !inFile.eof());
    inFile.close();
  }
  inFile.clear();                           // Clear any errors

  try {
    std::ofstream outFile;
    if(count == 0) {
      outFile.open(filename);               // Open file to create it
      if(!outFile.is_open())
        throw ios::failure(string("Error opening output file ") +
                           string(filename) +
                           string(" in main()"));
      outFile << " 2 3 5";
      outFile.close();
```

```
        cout << std::setw(10) << 2 << std::setw(10) << 3 << std::setw(10) << 5;
        lastprime = 5;
        count = 3;
      }

      while(count < nprimes) {
        lastprime = nextprime(lastprime, filename);
        outFile.open(filename, ios::out|ios::app);      // Open file to append data
        if(!outFile.is_open())
          throw ios::failure(string("Error opening output file ") +
                                    string(filename) +
                                    string(" in main()"));
        outFile << " " << lastprime;
        outFile.close();
        cout << (count++ % 5 == 0 ? "\n" : "") << std::setw(10) << lastprime;
      }
      cout << endl;
      return 0;
    }
    catch(std::exception& ex) {
      cout << endl << typeid(ex).name() << ": " << ex.what();
      return 1;
    }
}
```

This uses the nextprime() function, which returns the next prime after the first argument value. The second argument is the name of the file containing the primes found so far. The definition of this function is as follows:

```
// Find the next prime after the argument
long nextprime(long lastprime, const char* filename) {
  bool isprime = false;                    // Indicator that we have a prime
  long aprime = 0;                         // Stores primes from the file
  std::ifstream inFile;                    // Local input stream object

  // Find the next prime
  for( ; ; ) {
    lastprime += 2;                        // Next value for checking
    long limit = static_cast<long>(std::sqrt(static_cast<double>(lastprime)));

    // Try dividing the candidate by all the primes up to limit
    inFile.open(filename);                 // Open the primes file
    if(!inFile.is_open())
      throw ios::failure(string("Error opening input file ") +
                      string(filename) +
                      string(" in nextprime()"));
    do {
      inFile >> aprime;
    } while(aprime <= limit && !inFile.eof() &&
                        (isprime = lastprime % aprime > 0));
```

(Continued)

```
    inFile.close();
    if(isprime)                           // We got one...
      return lastprime;                   // ...so return it
  }
}
```

This program will output the number of primes that you request and write them to the file `primes.txt`.

HOW IT WORKS

The program is now structured a little differently. Because you'll keep all the primes in a file, you no longer need to store them in memory. Primes are now found by the `nextprime()` function, but before exploring that, let's look at how the code in `main()` works.

After getting the number of primes required from the user, you open the `primes.txt` file as an input stream with these statements:

```
std::ifstream inFile;                // Create input file stream object
inFile.open(filename);               // Open the file as an input stream
```

The `ifstream` object, `inFile`, is created using the default constructor. The object will not be associated with a particular file at this point. To use the stream object to open the `primes.txt` file, you call the `open()` function with the file name as the argument. The function will accept a second argument—the open file mode—but because you didn't specify it, the default value of `ios::in` will be used.

Of course, it could be that the file doesn't yet exist, so you must verify that the file stream is in a good state before you try to read it. You test the file stream object using its `fail()` function:

```
if(!inFile.fail()) {
  do       {
    inFile >> lastprime;
    cout << (count++ % 5 == 0 ? "\n" : "") << std::setw(10) << lastprime;
  } while(count < nprimes && !inFile.eof());
  inFile.close();
}
```

You only read the file if `fail()` returns `false`. Within the `if` block, you read up to nprimes numbers from the file in the do-while loop. You check for end-of-file in the loop condition by calling the `eof()` function for `inFile`. The complement of the bool value returned is ANDed with the comparison of count and nprimes, and so the loop ends either when you've read the required number of primes from the file or when you reach the end of file.

After the `if` statement, there could be errors set for the file stream object—either because the file doesn't exist or because the end of file was reached. These are not reset when you close the file, so because you may want to use the object again, you reset any error flags by calling the `clear()` function for the stream object:

```
inFile.clear();                          // Clear any errors
```

I'll discuss what else you can do with the `clear()` function a little later in the chapter.

The remainder of the code in `main()` comes within a `try` block, because you'll throw exceptions if you encounter problems with opening files. The `catch` block will catch any exception type that has `exception` as a base, and it gives you a convenient way to handle errors of the same type in the same place.

At this point, you can use the value of `count` as an indicator of whether any primes were read from the file. If not, then you can write the file from scratch with the first three primes. You do this with the following code:

```
std::ofstream outFile;
if(count == 0) {
  outFile.open(filename);                // Open file to create it
  if(!outFile.is_open())
    throw ios::failure(string("Error opening output file ") +
                       string(filename) +
                       string(" in main()"));
  outFile << " 2 3 5";
  outFile.close();
  cout << std::setw(10) << 2 << std::setw(10) << 3 << std::setw(10) << 5;
  lastprime = 5;
  count = 3;
}
```

You create an output file stream object named `outFile`, and then call its `open()` function to open the `primes.txt` file. This will open the file with the open mode specified as `ios::out | ios::trunc`, so any previous contents of the file will be erased and you'll write the file from the beginning. In the code, you call the `is_open()` function member of `outFile` in an `if` statement to verify that the file is open and ready to be written. If nothing went wrong, you write the first three primes to the file and close it. You then write the same three primes to `cout`, and set the `lastprime` value and the count of the number of primes appropriately. If you can't open the file to write it for some reason, you throw an exception of type `ios::failure`. This exception class is actually defined in the `ios_base` class and is therefore inherited in `ios` and all the stream classes. Of course, being a standard exception class, it has the `exception` class as a base. The constructor accepts an argument of type `string`, and whatever you pass to the constructor will be returned by the `what()` member function of the object, so you can use that to identify the exception in a `catch` block, as you do in `main()`.

(Continued)

Chapter 19

At this point, you may need to calculate more primes, if the number of primes from the file is lower than the number requested. This is taken care of in the while loop that continues until count is equal to nprimes:

```
while(count < nprimes) {
  lastprime = nextprime(lastprime, filename);
  outFile.open(filename, ios::out|ios::app); // Open file to append data
  if(!outFile.is_open())
    throw ios::failure(string("Error opening output file ") +
                       string(filename) +
                       string(" in main()"));
  outFile << " " << lastprime;
  outFile.close();
  cout << (count++ % 5 == 0 ? "\n" : "") << std::setw(10) << lastprime;
}
```

The nextprime() function calculates the next prime number after the value of the first argument. The second argument specifies the name of the file from which to retrieve existing primes for use in the calculation. The file is then opened for output, but this time the file open mode determines that whatever you write to the file will always be appended to the end. Again, if you have a problem opening the file, you throw an exception.

After writing the prime returned from nextprime(), you close the file. This is necessary because on the next iteration, nextprime() will need to open the file again to read it. On each iteration, the prime number found is also written to cout. The loop continues until nprimes numbers have been displayed, and after the loop the file will contain at least the same set of primes as it contained at the start, because any new primes will just have been added to it.

Finding a new prime in the nextprime() function involves using the primes from the file as divisors, so a local ifstream object is created. The process for finding the next prime is in the indefinite for loop. The first value to be checked is obtained by incrementing lastprime by 2:

```
lastprime += 2;                          // Next value for checking
```

The value passed to the function as lastprime will be the last prime number found, so you don't need to check that it is odd. To check whether the value is a prime number, you must try dividing by all the primes up to the square root of the value, so you calculate this as the integer value limit with this statement:

```
long limit = static_cast<long>(sqrt(static_cast<double>(lastprime)));
```

This statement uses the standard library sqrt() function that's declared in the <cmath> header. You have to cast the argument to double to enable the compiler to select which overloaded version of the function is to be used, and you cast the double result from the sqrt() function back to long.

You open the file stream and verify that the file was opened successfully with these statements:

```
inFile.open(filename);                          // Open the primes file
if(!inFile.is_open())
   throw ios::failure(string("Error opening input file ") +
                      string(filename) +
                      string(" in nextprime()"));
```

If opening the file fails, you throw the same type of exception that you threw in main() for a file problem. Here you have a slightly different argument to the constructor, so you'll be able to identify where the problem occurred in the program. The exception will be caught by the catch block in main(), so all file problems will be handled in the same place.

After opening the input file stream, the candidate prime is checked in the do-while loop:

```
do {
   inFile >> aprime;
} while(aprime <= limit && !inFile.eof() &&
                          (isprime = lastprime % aprime > 0));
```

A prime is read from the file within the loop, but all the rest of the work is done in the loop condition. This has three logical expressions ANDed together, so if any of the three is false, the loop ends.

The first condition is that the divisor is less than limit, the square root of the candidate value. If it isn't, you've checked all divisors up to this value without finding an exact division, so you must have a prime. The second condition is that you haven't reached the end of file, and this should never occur. If it does, there is a serious defect in the program somewhere, or with the file. The third condition checks the remainder after the division. If it's 0, you have an exact division, so lastprime isn't prime and you need to try another candidate.

When the loop ends, you close the file so that you can open it again at the beginning of the next iteration:

```
inFile.close();
```

Whether or not you've found a prime is indicated by isprime, set in the loop condition. If it's true, you have a prime and you can return the value. If it isn't true, you just go around the for loop again.

```
if(isprime)                    // We got one...
   return lastprime;           // ...so return it
```

The program works, but this process of opening and closing the file every time you go around the loop is very inefficient. It would be much better if you could just read the file from the beginning each time, so let's see how you could do that.

Managing the Current Stream Position

You control the current stream position using functions defined in the `istream` and `ostream` classes, but they don't apply to the standard streams, because the standard streams don't relate to physical devices for which a stream position would be meaningful. They *do* apply, however, to objects of the file stream classes that are associated with a physical file. The functions in `istream` and `ostream` are inherited in `ifstream` and `ofstream`, respectively, and both sets of functions will be inherited by the `fstream` class via `iostream`.

Basically, there are two things that you can do in relation to the stream position: you can obtain and record the current position in the stream, and you can change the current position. The current position is returned by the `tellg()` function for input stream objects and by the `tellp()` function for output stream objects. The *g* in `tellg()` is for "get" and the *p* in `tellp()` is for "put," so this indicates whether you get data from the stream the function relates to or you put data into it. Both functions return a value of type `pos_type`, which represents an absolute position in a stream.

For example, you might obtain the current position in an input file stream object called `inFile` with the following statement:

```
pos_type here = inFile.tellg();              // Record current file position
```

You can define a new position in a stream by passing a position that you earlier recorded using `tellg()` or `tellp()` to the `seekg()` member function for an input stream object, or to the `seekp()` member function for an output stream object. You just call the function corresponding to the stream type with a previously recorded stream position. For example, you could reset the stream position for `inFile` back to `here` with this statement:

```
inFile.seekg(here);                          // Set current position to here
```

The `pos_type` value, `here`, is an integral value that corresponds to a character index position in the stream, where the first character is at index position 0. It's therefore possible to use numerical values to move to specific positions in a stream. This can be hazardous in text mode because the number of bytes stored in the stream may be different from the number of characters written. However, seeking to position 0 is always going to move to the beginning of the stream, so you could have used that in the `nextprime()` function:

```
long nextprime(long lastprime, const char* filename) {
    bool isprime = false;                    // Indicator that we have a prime
    long aprime = 0;                         // Stores primes from the file
    std::ifstream inFile(filename);          // Local input stream object

    if(!inFile.is_open())
        throw ios::failure(string("Error opening input file ") +
                           string(filename) +
                           string(" in nextprime()"));
```

```
// Find the next prime
for( ; ; )   {
  lastprime += 2;                               // Next value for checking
  long limit = static_cast<long>(sqrt(static_cast<double>(lastprime)));

  // Try dividing the candidate by all the primes up to limit
  do     {
    inFile >> aprime;
  } while(aprime <= limit && !inFile.eof() &&
                              (isprime = lastprime % aprime > 0));

    if(isprime) {                         // We got one...
      inFile.close();                     // ...so close the file...
      return lastprime;                   // ...and return the prime
    }
    inFile.seekg(0);                      // Move to beginning of file
  }
}
```

With this version of the function, you open the file when you create the `ifstream` object and simply reset the file position to the first character in the file at the end of the `for` loop.

As an alternative to moving to a new position in a stream that you specify with a positive value of type `pos_type`, you can move by using an offset value relative to one of three specific positions in a stream. The offset can be positive or negative. You can define a new position relative to the first character in the stream (the offset must be positive), relative to the last character in the stream (the offset must be negative), or relative to the current position. In the latter case, the offset can be either positive or negative, as long as you're not at one of the ends. This is shown in Figure 19-3.

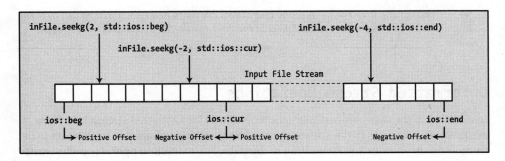

Figure 19-3. Defining a relative stream position

To set a relative position, you use versions of `seekg()` or `seekp()` that accept two arguments. The first argument is the offset, which is an integral value of type `off_type`, and the second argument must be one of the values in Table 19-4 that are defined in the `ios` class.

Table 19-4. File Stream Position Values

Value	Description
ios::beg	Offset is relative to the first character in the file.
ios::cur	Offset is relative to the current file position.
ios::end	Offset is relative to the last character in the file.

As I explained, the offset value must be positive relative to ios::beg and negative relative to ios::end. You can go in either direction relative to ios::cur by using positive or negative values for the offset. You can specify the offset as an explicit integer constant, or you can provide the value of the offset as an expression that evaluates to an integer.

The seekg() functions return a reference to the file stream object, so you can combine the seek operation with an input operation by using an extraction operator, for example:

```
inFile.seekg(10, std::ios::beg) >> value;
```

This statement will move the file position to an offset of ten characters from the beginning of the file and read from that point into value.

Similarly, you can use the seekp() function to move to a position where you want to start the next *output* operation, and the function arguments are exactly the same as for seekg(). The next write to the stream will overwrite characters, starting with the character at the new position.

Relative seek operations can be a dubious operation in text mode, particularly when you're writing characters to the stream. This is because the number of characters that are actually stored may be different from the number of characters that you wrote to the stream.

 NOTE *You aren't done with the operations I've discussed here. You'll return to them later in this chapter when I discuss random read/write operations on a stream.*

Unformatted Stream Operations

In addition to the insertion and extraction operators for formatted stream I/O, there are member functions in the stream classes for transferring character-based data to or from a stream without any formatting of the data. The extraction operator treats whitespace characters as delimiters, but otherwise ignores them. In general, the unformatted stream input functions don't skip whitespace characters—they're read and stored just like any other characters.

An important use of some of the unformatted I/O functions is reading and writing file streams in binary mode, as you'll see later. Although these functions only specifically provide a way to write character-based data, you can still use some of them to read and write binary numeric data. First of all, let's look at what the unformatted input functions can do for you.

Unformatted Stream Input

There is a wealth of unformatted input functions defined in the istream class, and they're inherited in the ifstream, iostream, and fstream classes. For a start, there are four varieties of the member function get(), the first two of which read a single character from a stream:

int_type get();: This version reads a single character from the stream and returns it as type int_type. The type int_type is implementation defined and will be an integral type capable of storing any character. It will usually correspond to type int. If the end of file is reached, the function returns the character EOF, which is defined in the iostream header file. If a character can't be read from the stream, for whatever reason, the error flag ios::failbit will be set. (I cover this and other error flags later in the chapter, when I discuss I/O errors.)

istream& get(char& ch);: This function also reads a single character from the stream, but this time the character read is stored in ch. The function returns a reference to the stream object, so you can combine calling this function with other member function calls. As with the previous function, if a character can't be read from the stream, the failbit error flag will be set, and EOF will be stored in ch.

There is another member function, called peek(), which is the equivalent of the previous first get() function in that it reads the next character from the stream, but the character is left *in* the stream, so you can read it again. peek() returns a character read from a stream as a value of type int_type, as described for the get() function.

You can write the last character read from the stream back to the stream using the member function unget(). This function returns a reference to the istream object for which it was called. It's typically used in combination with one of the get() functions that reads a single character, when you're parsing input from a stream. For example, you might need a function to skip nondigits in a file input stream in order to position the stream at the next digit:

```
void skipnondigits(std::ifstream& in) {
  int_type ch = 0;
  while((ch = in.get()) != EOF)    // Read while not EOF
    if(isdigit(ch)) {              // If a digit is read...
      in.unget();                  // ...put back the digit...
      return;                      // ...and return
    }
}
```

The putback() member function has a similar effect to unget(), but in this case you specify the character to put back in the stream as an argument. In the preceding example, instead of the statement calling unget(), you could have written this:

```
    in.putback(ch);               // ...put back the digit...
```

The character that you supply as the argument to putback() must be the same as the last character read; otherwise, the result is undefined. Both functions return a reference to the stream.

The other two get() functions read a sequence of characters as a null-terminated string:

istream& get(char* pArray, streamsize n);: This function reads up to n-1 characters from the stream and stores them in the array pArray, adding a null terminator at the end to make n characters in total. Characters are read until a newline character is read, the end of file is reached, or n-1 characters have been read and stored. If a newline character is reached, it isn't stored in the array, but a null byte is always appended at the end of the sequence of characters read. The effect of this function is to read a whole line of text without storing the '\n' character that marks the end of the line, but the string is stored with a terminating null character. It also leaves the '\n' character as the next character in the stream to be read. Because a total of n characters may be stored in the array, the array pointed to by pArray should have at least n elements. The ios::failbit is set if no characters are stored. The type streamsize for the second parameter is a signed integer type that is implementation defined, usually as long.

istream& get(char* pArray, streamsize n, char delim);: This works in the same way as the previous function, except that you can specify a delimiter, delim, that will be used in place of newline to end the input process. If the delimiter is found, it isn't stored in the array, and it's left in the stream.

In addition, there are two getline() function members that are almost equivalent to the two get() functions that read a line of text:

```
istream& getline(char* pArray, streamsize n);
istream& getline(char* pArray, streamsize n, char delim);
```

The difference between getline() and the corresponding get() function is that getline() removes the delimiter from the input stream, so the next character to be read is the character following the delimiter.

When you use one of these unformatted input functions, you can determine the number of characters actually read from the stream by calling the member function gcount(). This will return the count of characters read by the last unformatted input operation as a value of type streamsize.

It's also possible to read a specified number of characters from a stream, assuming they're available, with the read() member function:

```
istream& read(char* pArray, streamsize n);
```

This function reads n characters of any kind into pArray, including newlines and null characters. If the end of the file is reached before n characters have been read, ios::failbit is set in the input object.

You'll typically use the read() function when you expect that n characters *are* available in the stream. There's another member function that you might use when this isn't the case. The `readsome()` function operates similarly to `read()`, but it returns the count of the number of characters read:

```
streamsize readsome(char* pstr, streamsize n);
```

If fewer than n characters are available in the stream, the function sets the flag `ios::eofbit`.

You can skip over a number of characters in an input stream with this function:

```
istream& ignore(streamsize n, int_type delim);
```

Up to n characters are read from the stream and discarded. Reading a `delim` character or reading n characters ends the process. There are default values for the parameters n and `delim` of 1 and `EOF`, respectively. Thus, you can skip a single character with the following statement:

```
inFile.ignore();            // Skip one character
```

To skip 20 characters, you would write this:

```
inFile.ignore(20);          // Skip 20 characters up to the end of the file
```

Reading the end of file will stop the process in this case, but you could skip 20 characters in the current line with the following statement:

```
inFile.ignore(20, '\n');    // Skip 20 characters up to the end of the current line
```

Unformatted Stream Output

In stark contrast to the plethora of input functions, for unformatted output to a stream you have just two functions available: `put()` and `write()`. The `put()` function takes the following form:

```
ostream& put(char ch);
```

This writes the single character, ch, to the stream and returns a reference to the stream object. To write a sequence of characters to a stream, you use the `write()` function, which has this form:

```
ostream& write(const char* pArray, streamsize n);
```

This writes n characters to the stream from the array, pArray. Any kind of characters can be written, including null characters.

Generally, output to a stream will be buffered, and on occasion you'll want the contents of the stream buffer written to the stream regardless of whether the buffer is full. In such cases, you call the flush() member of ostream. This function will write the contents of the stream buffer to the stream and return a reference to the stream object.

Errors in Stream Input/Output

All the stream classes store the state of the stream in three flags that record different kinds of errors for a stream. These flags are defined as bit masks of type iostate in the base class ios. The meanings of these flags are shown in Table 19-5.

Table 19-5. Stream State Flags

Flag	Meaning
ios::badbit	Sets when a stream is in a state in which it can't be used further—if an I/O error occurred, for example. This isn't recoverable.
ios::eofbit	Sets when the end of file is reached.
ios::failbit	Sets if an input operation didn't read the characters expected or an output operation failed to write characters successfully. This is typically due to a conversion or formatting error. Any subsequent operations will fail while the bit is set, but the situation may be recoverable.

Thus, if EOF is read in a stream, the stream state will be ios::eofbit. If a serious error occurred while reading from a stream and no characters could be read from it, both the badbit and failbit flags would be set, so the stream state would be the result of ios::badbit | ios::failbit.

You can test the state of a stream by using a stream object in an if statement or a loop condition. The stream object by itself in these contexts calls the overloaded void*() operator, for example:

```
while(inFile) {
  // Read from inFile...
}
```

I haven't discussed overloading operator void*() previously because it's rather specialized. The operator function doesn't have a return type specified because it's implicit—as void*, of course. The operator void*() function for a stream object returns a pointer that is intended to be used as a Boolean test of the state of that object.

Because the object is used as the if test expression, the operator void*() member of inFile will be called automatically. This returns null if either failbit or badbit is set, and non-null otherwise. Note that the non-null pointer that's returned isn't intended to be dereferenced. You can use this kind of loop to read to the end of a file, because when the end of file is reached, the read operation will set failbit.

As I discussed earlier, you can also use the overloaded ! operator to test the state of the stream, as it returns true if either badbit or failbit is set.

The stream classes inherit function members that you can use to test their flags individually. As shown in Table 19-6, they each return a value of type bool.

Table 19-6. Functions for Testing Stream State Flags

Function	Action
bad()	Returns true if badbit is set in the stream object
eof()	Returns true if eofbit is set in the stream object
fail()	Returns true if failbit or badbit is set in the stream object
good()	Returns true if none of the bits is set in the stream object

Once a flag is set, it remains set unless you reset it. You'll sometimes want to reset the flags—when you reach the end of a file, for example—as a means of terminating reading from a file stream that you may subsequently want to read again. Calling the clear() function member for an object resets all three flags. In fact, clear() accepts an argument of type iostate that corresponds to all three flags bitwise ORed together, but it has a default of 0. (Actually, the default is ios::goodbit, which is defined as 0.) So, once you've read end-of-file for an input stream, inFile, you can reset the stream state with this statement:

```
inFile.clear();
```

The clear() function has a return type of void.

Input/Output Errors and Exceptions

When errors occur in stream input and output operations, exceptions may be thrown. The exceptions for stream errors are of type ios::failure and, as discussed earlier, this is a nested class of ios inherited from ios_base. A mask that is a member of a stream object determines whether an exception will be thrown when a particular stream state flag is set. You can set this mask by passing a mask to the exceptions() member of the stream object, with bits set to specify which flags you want to throw exceptions. For example, if you would like to have exceptions thrown when *any* of the flag bits is set for a stream called inFile, you could enable this with the following statement:

```
inFile.exceptions(ios::badbit | ios::eofbit | ios::failbit);
```

Now if anything goes wrong at all, even when the end of a file is reached, an exception of type ios::failure will be thrown.

Generally, it's better to test the error flags in one of the ways I've discussed, rather than to use exceptions for handling I/O errors, at least as far as the eofbit and failbit flags are concerned. Most of the time, you'll be involved in dealing with failbit and eofbit flags, because these are a part of the normal process of handling stream input and output. The default position in most development environments is that exceptions are *not* thrown for stream errors. You can check whether exceptions will be thrown by calling a version of exceptions() with no arguments that returns a value of type iostate. The value returned reflects which error flags will result in an exception being thrown, so you can test whether a given flag being set will throw exceptions as follows:

```
iostate willthrow = inFile.exceptions();
if(willthrow & std::ios::badbit)
  std::cout << "Setting badbit will throw an exception";
```

The result of ANDing ios::badbit with willthrow will be 0 unless ios::badbit is set to 1 in willthrow.

Using Binary Mode Stream Operations

There are situations in which text mode isn't appropriate or convenient, and it can sometimes cause you difficulties. The transformation of newline characters into two characters on some systems and not others makes relative seek operations unreliable for programs that are to run in both environments. By using **binary mode**, you avoid these complications and make your stream operations much simpler. You've already seen how to open a stream in binary mode: you just need to specify the open mode flags appropriately. Let's try this in an example.

....

Try It Out: Copying Files in Binary Mode

You can copy any file using the get() and put() functions that read and write a single character:

```
// Program 19.4 Copying files  File: prog19_04.cpp
#include <iostream>                  // For standard streams
#include <cctype>                    // For character functions
#include <fstream>                   // For file streams
#include <string>                    // For strings
#include <stdexcept>                 // For standard exceptions
using std::cout;
using std::cin;
using std::endl;
using std::string;
using std::ios;
using std::invalid_argument;

int main(int argc, char* argv[]) {
  try {
    // Verify correct number of arguments
    if(argc != 3)
      throw invalid_argument("Input and output file names required.");

    const string source = argv[1];
    const string target = argv[2];
```

```
  // Check for output file identical to input file
  if(source == target)
    throw invalid_argument(string("Cannot copy ") +
                           string(source) +
                           string(" to itself."));

  std::ifstream in(source.c_str(), ios::in | ios::binary);
  if(!in)                                    // Stream object OK?
    throw ios::failure(string("Input file ") +
                       string(source) +
                       string(" not found"));

  // Check if output file exists
  std::ifstream temp(target.c_str(), ios::in|ios::binary);
  char ch = 0;                               // Stores a character
  if(temp) { // If the file stream object is ok then the output file exists
    temp.close();                            // Close the stream
    cout << endl << target << " exists, do you want to overwrite it? (y or n): ";
    ch = cin.get();
    if(std::toupper(ch) != 'Y')
      return 0;
  }

  // Create output file stream
  std::ofstream out(target.c_str(), ios::out|ios::binary|ios::trunc);

  // Copy the file
  while(in.get(ch))
    out.put(ch);

  if(in.eof())
    cout << endl << source << " copied to " << target << " successfully.";
  else
    cout << endl << "Error copying file";
  return 0;
 }
 catch(std::exception& ex) {
   cout << endl << typeid(ex).name() << ": " << ex.what();
   return 1;
 }
}
```

This program requires the name of the input file and the name of the output file as command-line arguments. I applied it to copying the executable module for this program, so it produced the following output:

```
FileCopy.exe copied to FullCopy.exe successfully.
```

(Continued)

HOW IT WORKS

The array argv will have argc elements, the first of which will contain the program name. Thus, argv should have three elements, accommodating the program name plus the two file names, so you first verify that to be the case with these statements:

```
if(argc != 3)
  throw invalid_argument("Input and output file names required.");

const string source = argv[1];
const string target = argv[2];
```

If there are no command-line arguments, you throw a standard exception of type invalid_argument that will be caught by the catch block at the end of main(). Having checked the arguments, you then assign them to a pair of string objects that will make for easier manipulation and recognition in the remainder of the code.

You don't want to be copying a file to itself, so you check that the files aren't the same by comparing them. If they are the same, you don't continue—you throw another exception:

```
// Check for output file identical to input file
if(source == target)
  throw invalid_argument(string("Cannot copy ") +
                         source +
                         string(" to itself."));
```

Once you're past the validity checks on the command-line arguments, you're ready to create the file stream object corresponding to the input file:

```
std::ifstream in(source.c_str(), ios::in|ios::binary);
```

This uses the string::c_str() function, which returns the null-terminated string contained within the source object. The file is opened as a binary input file, specified by the second constructor argument. You must verify that the stream object was created properly before you try to use it:

```
if(!in)                                    // Stream object OK?
    throw ios::failure(string("Input file ") +
                       source +
                       string(" not found"));
```

This uses the overloaded ! operator for the stream object. The istream constructor will set failbit if the file can't be found and opened.

Next, you need to see whether the output file exists. If so, you should verify that it is to be overwritten:

```
std::ifstream temp(target.c_str(), ios::in | ios::binary);
char ch = 0;                        // Stores a character
if(temp) { // If the file stream object is ok then the output file exists
  temp.close();                     // Close the stream
  cout << endl << target << " exists, do you want to overwrite it? (y or n): ";
  ch = cin.get();
  if(std::toupper(ch) != 'Y')
    return 0;
}
```

When you create an `ifstream` object for a file, the file must exist. If the file can't be found and opened, the constructor will set `failbit`, so the `operator void*()` member that is called implicitly by using the stream object in the `if` condition will return null. Thus, the code in the `if` block will only be executed if the file exists. Once you've established that, you can close the file, because you have no intention of reading it. You just offer the option of not overwriting it.

You create the output file stream object next:

```
std::ofstream out(target.c_str(), ios::out|ios::binary|ios::trunc);
```

Now you can proceed with the copy, which is done in a very simple loop:

```
while(in.get(ch))
  out.put(ch);
```

In the loop condition, you read a character from `in` using the `get()` function. This returns EOF when the end of file is reached, which will cause the loop to end. On each iteration, the character that was stored in `ch` is written to the output file stream, `out`.

Finally, you verify that you did reach the end of the file, so that you're sure the entire file was copied properly:

```
if(in.eof())
  cout << endl << source << " copied to " << target << " successfully.";
else
  cout << endl << "Error copying file";
```

The `eof()` function returns `true` if `eofbit` is set in the file stream object, `in`.

Writing Numeric Data in Binary Form

When using binary mode, it's often more convenient to use unformatted stream I/O operations than the insertion and extraction operators. This provides the possibility of writing numerical values as binary values, with no conversion to a text string representation of a number. Doing this neatly avoids the errors that may be introduced when converting binary floating-point values to decimal representation, and it takes up less space in the file. Furthermore, you don't need to write whitespace to a file to separate one value from the next; this will also make the file shorter, and therefore faster to read. As long as you know what kind of data was written, you can read back exactly what you wrote.

Beware, however, that these benefits only apply if you're reading the data on the same sort of computer that wrote it. There is a whole range of potential disparities between binary data produced by different machines. The representation of characters can vary—IBM mainframes use EBCDIC, for example, whereas PCs use ASCII. Equally, there can be differences in the representations of binary floating-point values, and even binary integers can be stored differently on different machine architectures.

There are no stream functions in the standard library that will write numerical data values to a file in binary, or read them back, but you can write some of your own. You can use the read() and write() functions to implement a set of functions that will write any of the numerical types as binary data. The best way to see how this might work is, as ever, to consider an example.

Suppose you want to write values of type double to a file. You could implement your own write() function to do this as follows:

```
void write(std::ostream& out, double value) {
  out.write(reinterpret_cast<char*>(&value), sizeof(double));
}
```

To write a floating-point value to a file, you just want to write the succession of bytes that the value occupies in memory. This is illustrated in Figure 19-4, assuming that type double occupies 8 bytes.

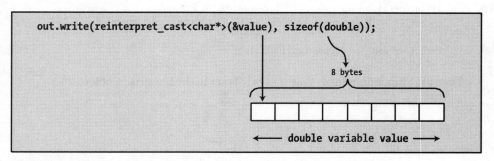

Figure 19-4. Writing a double value to a stream in binary mode

You force the conversion of the address of the first byte of the double value to char*, and then pass that to the write() member function of the stream object, out. The reinterpret_cast<>() operator just alters the *interpretation* of the pointer, without converting the value that it points to in any way. The sizeof operator provides the number of bytes to be written for type double, so you pass that value to the write() member of the stream object as the count of the number of bytes to be written.

Clearly, you can write any of the numeric types to a stream in exactly the same way, so you could consider defining a template that will generate these functions when required. However, such a template would also create functions for class types, creating the illusion that they would work with any class object. Unfortunately, this isn't the case. Any class object that contained a pointer data member wouldn't be valid when it was read back from a file, because the address in the pointer member would almost certainly be invalid. You should never violate encapsulation, and you should *only* use the copying capabilities provided by a class. Thus, you must write an overloaded function for each numeric type that you want to support and avoid the potential misuse that a function template would present.

Returning to the theme, a function to read a binary value back from the file is also easily implemented:

```
void read(std::istream& in, double& value) {
  in.read(reinterpret_cast<char*>(&value), sizeof(double));
}
```

This reads the number of bytes that a double variable occupies into the memory locations occupied by the double variable, value. The second argument here must be a reference, because you're going to store the data read from the file at this location.

Notice that you use a reference to an istream object as the first parameter type here, rather than a reference to an ifstream object. Similarly, with the write() function you use ostream& as the type for the stream parameter. Although you'll only want to use these functions with file streams, making the parameters references to file streams has a distinct disadvantage. The fstream class is derived from iostream, and so has istream and ostream as indirect base classes. It isn't derived from ifstream or ofstream at all. By using istream& and ostream& as the parameter types, you ensure that both functions will work with fstream as well as ifstream in the case of read(), or ofstream in the case of write().

Implementing functions to read and write *arrays* of values of the basic types is also not difficult, although you would need to pass a length as an argument to each function, as you can't deduce the length of an array passed to a function.

You can see some versions of the functions that I just discussed in action with an alternate version of Program 19.3 that works with binary files.

......

Try It Out: Writing Binary Numeric Data to a File

The only changes you need to make to the original program will be to create the file stream objects as binary streams and to replace the formatted I/O operations with your own read and write functions:

```cpp
// Program 19.5 Reading and writing a binary File: prog19_05.cpp
#include <fstream>
#include <iostream>
#include <iomanip>
#include <cmath>
#include <string>
using std::ios;
using std::cout;
using std::cin;
using std::endl;
using std::string;
// Find the prime after lastprime
long nextprime(long lastprime, const char* filename);

void write(std::ostream& out, long value);   // Write binary long value
void read(std::istream& in, long& value);    // Read binary long value

int main() {
  const char* filename = "C:\\JunkData\\primes.bin";
  int nprimes = 0;                              // Number of primes required
  int count = 0;                                // Count of primes found
  long lastprime = 0;                           // Last prime found

  // Get number of primes required
  int tries = 0;                                // Number of input tries
  cout << "How many primes would you like (at least 3)?: ";
  do
  {
    if(tries)
      cout << endl << " You must request at least 3, try again: ";
    cin >> nprimes;

    if(++tries == 5) {                          // Five tries is generous
      cout << endl << " I give up!" << endl;
      return 1;
    }
  } while(nprimes < 3);

  std::ifstream inFile;                         // Create input file stream object
  inFile.open(filename, ios::in|ios::binary);

  cout << endl;
  if(!inFile.fail()) {
    do {
```

```
      read(inFile, lastprime);
      cout << (count++ % 5 == 0 ? "\n" : "") << std::setw(10) << lastprime;
    } while(count < nprimes && !inFile.eof());
    inFile.close();
  }
  inFile.clear();                             // Clear any errors

  try {
    std::ofstream outFile;
    if(count == 0) {
      // Open file to create it
      outFile.open(filename, ios::out|ios::binary|ios::app);
      if(!outFile.is_open())
        throw ios::failure(string("Error opening output file ") +
                           string(filename) +
                           string(" in main()"));
      write(outFile, 2L);                     // Write 2 as binary long
      write(outFile, 3L);                     // Write 3 as binary long
      write(outFile, 5L);                     // Write 5 as binary long
      outFile.close();
      cout << std::setw(10) << 2 << std::setw(10) << 3 << std::setw(10) << 5;
      lastprime = 5;
      count = 3;
    }

    while(count < nprimes) {
      lastprime = nextprime(lastprime, filename);

      // Open file to append data
      outFile.open(filename, ios::out | ios::binary | ios::app);
      if(!outFile.is_open())
        throw ios::failure(string("Error opening output file ") +
                           string(filename) +
                           string(" in main()"));
      write(outFile, lastprime);              // Write prime as binary
      outFile.close();
      cout << (count++ % 5 == 0 ? "\n" : "") << std::setw(10) << lastprime;
    }
    cout << endl;
    return 0;
  }
  catch(std::exception& ex) {
    cout << endl << typeid(ex).name() << ": " << ex.what() << endl;
    return 1;
  }
}
```

(Continued)

You need to make very few changes to the definition of the nextprime() function:

```cpp
long nextprime(long lastprime, const char* filename) {
  bool isprime = false;                      // Indicator that we have a prime
  long aprime = 0;                           // Stores primes from the file
  std::ifstream inFile;                      // Local input stream object

  // Find the next prime
  for( ; ; ) {
    lastprime += 2;                          // Next value for checking
    long limit = static_cast<long>(std::sqrt(static_cast<double>(lastprime)));

    // Try dividing the candidate by all the primes up to limit
    inFile.open(filename, ios::in | ios::binary);  // Open the primes file
    if(!inFile.is_open())
      throw ios::failure(string("Error opening input file ") +
                         string(filename) +
                         string(" in nextprime()"));

    do {
      read(inFile, aprime);                  // Read prime as binary
    } while(aprime <= limit &&
                    !inFile.eof() && (isprime = lastprime % aprime > 0));

    inFile.close();
    if(isprime)                              // We got one...
      return lastprime;                      // ...so return it
  }
}
```

Of course, you must add definitions for the read() and write() functions to the source file:

```cpp
// Read a long value from a file as binary
void read(std::istream& in, long& value) {
  in.read(reinterpret_cast<char*>(&value), sizeof(value));
}

// Write a long value to a file as binary
void write(std::ostream& out, long value) {
  out.write(reinterpret_cast<char*>(&value), sizeof(value));
}
```

The program will output as many primes as you specify when you run it.

HOW IT WORKS

I'll only discuss the specifics of the file operations, as you've seen the other code before. First, you have the prototypes for the binary read() and write() functions:

```
void write(std::ostream& out, long value);    // Write binary long value
void read(std::istream& in, long& value);     // Read binary long value
```

The file name has a different extension to distinguish it from the primes.txt file that you created earlier:

```
const char* filename = "C:\\JunkData\\primes.bin";
```

If you were to read the text file as binary, it would create a significant amount of confusion in the program!

When you open the input file, you specify the open mode as binary:

```
inFile.open(filename, ios::in|ios::binary); // Open the file as an input stream
```

The second argument to the constructor is now explicit, rather than assuming the default value of an input file in text mode. If the file doesn't already exist, you open it as a binary output file to create it:

```
outFile.open(filename, ios::out|ios::binary|ios::app);
```

You then write the first three primes to the new file as binary values:

```
write(outFile, 2L);             // Write 2 as binary long
write(outFile, 3L);             // Write 3 as binary long
write(outFile, 5L);             // Write 5 as binary long
```

When you're adding primes to the file, you also open it as a binary output file:

```
// Open file to append data
outFile.open(filename, ios::out|ios::binary|ios::app);
```

Of course, writing to the file now uses your own write() function that will write the bytes:

```
write(outFile, lastprime);               // Write prime as binary
```

Within the nextprime() function definition, the file is opened as a binary input file, and you use your own version of read() to read each of the prime values. If type long occupies 4 bytes, then each value will only occupy four character positions (bytes) in the file, regardless of the actual value, and there are no spaces between one value and the next. Thus, any value greater than 999 will occupy less file space in your new regime, and if you were writing floating-point values to the file, the reduction in file space may be even greater. Binary files are in general more compact than text files and faster to read. There is no additional processing overhead due to formatting, either.

Read/Write Operations on a Stream

You can open a stream so that you can carry out both input and output operations. For general streams, the iostream class implements the capability, but you'll usually be using fstream class objects, because they specifically support I/O with files. As you saw early on in this chapter, fstream inherits from iostream, which in turn inherits from istream and ostream, so all the input and output functions discussed so far are available for an fstream object.

You can declare an fstream object with a file name as argument, just like an ifstream or ofstream object, for example:

```
const char* filename = "C:\\Junk Data\\primes.txt";
std::fstream bothways(filename);
```

The default open mode is ios::in | ios::out, so like the other streams it will be in text mode by default. If you want to specify it as a binary stream, just use the second parameter, exactly as you've done before, for example:

```
std::fstream bothways(filename, std::ios::in|std::ios::out|std::ios::binary);
```

This opens the file for both input and output operations in binary mode. If the file can't be opened for any reason, ios::failbit will be set. Note that you can't use ios::app with fstream objects, but you can use ios::trunc, which will discard any previous file contents. In fact, you can't use ios::app in combination with ios::in at all, so you can't use it for ifstream objects either. This isn't unreasonable, because ios::app implies that you'll *write* at the end of the file, which isn't particularly meaningful for a read operation.

The default constructor creates a stream object with no associated file. You can then open a particular physical file by using the open() member of the fstream object, for example:

```
std::fstream inout;
inout.open(filename, std::ios::in|std::ios::out|std::ios::binary|std::ios::trunc);
```

The first statement creates an fstream object without associating it with a particular file. The second statement will open the file specified by filename for both input and output in binary mode and discard any existing file contents. If you omit the second argument that specifies the open file mode, the default is the same as for the constructor: ios::in | ios::out.

If you're both writing and reading a file, then almost by definition you'll want to access the file at random positions within it, so let's look at how you do that.

Random Access to a Stream

Although you'll be exploring random access to a file in the context of fstream, you can apply the same techniques to reading an ifstream or (a less likely possibility) to writing an ofstream. Once you've opened a file stream for input and output, you can read from or write to any position in the stream. However, you do need to know where you are in the stream and where you want to go next. For a stream that was written using format-ted write operations with the insertion operator, this may be decidedly tricky.

The difficulty stems from the fact that unless you always set the width of the field when you're using a formatted write operation, you really don't know in general how many bytes will be written to the stream. If you write an integer to the stream, the number of bytes written will depend on the number of decimal digits and whether a sign is included. A width specification just sets a minimum, so unless you set it to a value that is at least as many characters as the maximum width that you're going to output, you still can't be sure. Text mode provides an added layer of complication in that there may be more bytes written on some systems than on others for a given out-put. For this reason, random access is easiest and safest in binary mode, using unfor-matted read and write operations. Let's see how you might access a binary file randomly.

Random Access to a Binary Stream

You could modify Program 19.5, which writes prime numbers to a binary file, to pro-vide the possibility of requesting a particular prime—the twenty-fifth or four-hundred-thirty-second prime, for instance. The idea is that if the prime is in the file, the program should just fetch it and display it. If it isn't, the program should calculate up to the prime required and add the new ones to the file.

This time, the file will be a little different. If you can keep track of how many primes are in the file, you can easily determine whether a requested prime is already there. An easy way to record this is to always write a count of the number of primes as the last data item in the file.

The input to the program will be the sequence number of the prime required: 3 for the third prime, 101 for the one-hundred-first prime, and so on. The basic logic of the program is shown in Figure 19-5.

Let's work through the logic of this one step at a time and put the code together piecemeal. Apart from some dialogue with the user, the first step is to open the file or, if it doesn't exist, to create it. You'll use an fstream object for the file. Because you can both read and write an fstream, once you've opened it at the beginning of the program, you can use it anywhere for input or output as necessary:

```
int main() {
  const char* filename = "C:\\JunkData\\nuprimes.bin";
  std::fstream primes;                        // Create file stream object
  primes.open(filename, ios::in|ios::out|ios::binary); // Open the file
  long count = 0;                             // Count of primes found

  // Rest of the code...
}
```

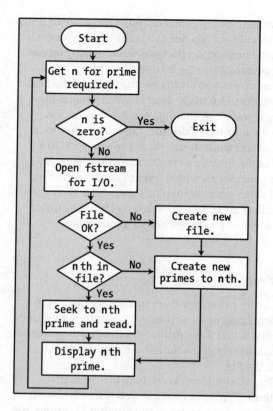

Figure 19-5. Logic of the program to read and write the primes file

You'll add a using declaration for ios so you've used the name unqualified here. Aside from the simple but important task of setting up a long variable to hold the number of primes found so far, this code opens the file in binary mode for both read and write operations. Because the open mode is specified as input as well as output, this will fail if the file doesn't exist, so you must check that the stream is good:

```
int main() {
  try {
    const char* filename = "C:\\JunkData\\nuprimes.bin";
    std::fstream primes;                     // Create file stream object
    primes.open(filename, ios::in|ios::out|ios::binary); // Open the file
    long count = 0;                          // Count of primes found

    if(!primes) {
      primes.clear();
      cout << endl << "File doesn't exist - creating..." << endl;
      primes.open(filename, ios::out|ios::binary); // Create binary file

      if(!primes)
        throw ios::failure(string("Failed to create output file ") +
                           string(filename) +
```

```
                         string(" in main()"));
    write(primes, 2L);                    // Write 2 as binary long
    write(primes, 3L);                    // Write 3 as binary long
    write(primes, 5L);                    // Write 5 as binary long
    write(primes, count = 3L);            // Write prime count
    primes.close();
    primes.open(filename, ios::in|ios::out|ios::binary);
  }

    // Rest of the code...
  }
  catch(std::exception& ex) {
    cout << endl << typeid(ex).name() << ": " << ex.what() << endl;
    return 1;
  }
}
```

If the file wasn't opened successfully, you clear the `ios` error flags and attempt to open the file again, but this time in binary mode for output only. This should create a new file, but you still check to make sure. If an error flag was set, you throw an `ios::failure` exception that contains a string explaining the error.

When you get past this check, you write the first three prime numbers and the count to the file. Then you close the stream, so that it can be reopened for both input and output. You're ready to start the process of finding the required prime.

First, you must read the sequence number of the prime required. If you put the whole process inside an indefinite `for` loop, you'll be able to repeat the cycle of finding specific primes as often as required, and you can use a zero or negative value entered as the signal to terminate the program:

```
int main() {
  try {
    // Code to open the file...

    long nprime = 0;                      // Sequence no. of prime required
    long lastprime = 0;                   // Last prime found
    for( ; ; ) {
      cout << "Which prime (e.g. enter 15 for the 15th prime, zero to end)?: ";
      cin >> nprime;
      if(nprime <= 0)                     // Zero or negative?
        return 0;                         // ...yes, so we are done

      // Rest of the code for finding the prime to follow...
    }
    cout << endl;
    return 0;
  }
  catch(std::exception& ex) {
    cout << endl << typeid(ex).name() << ": " << ex.what() << endl;
    return 1;
  }
}
```

The rest of the code will follow the existing code inside the for loop. To determine whether the requested prime is in the file, you need to obtain the count of the number of primes in the file:

```
// Go to start of last item
primes.seekg(-static_cast<int>(sizeof(long)), ios::end);
read(primes, count);                    // Read the last item
```

The count is the last item in the file. You might argue that placing it at the start would give you an easier ride, but this way you get to give some of the functions that you've seen a stiffer workout—you'll have to seek relative to the end of the file. The count value will be at a position that's sizeof(long) bytes back from the end of the file, but sizeof returns a value of size_t, which is usually defined as an unsigned integer, so you need to cast it to int before changing its sign. After seeking to that position, you read count using the version of read() from Program 19.5 that reads binary values of type long.

Now you must check whether nprime is less than this value—if it is, you can just read the prime from the appropriate position in the file:

```
if(nprime <= count)        {
    cout << endl << "Prime in file";
    primes.seekg((nprime-1)*sizeof(long), ios::beg); // Seek to position of nth
    read(primes, lastprime);                    // ...and read it
}
```

You can get to any prime number by seeking directly to its position in the file, relative to the beginning. The offset from ios::beg for the first prime is 0 bytes, for the second prime it's sizeof(long) bytes, for the third prime it's 2 * sizeof(long) bytes, and so on. Thus the one you're looking for will be (nprime-1) * sizeof(long) bytes from the beginning of the file. When you get there, you just read it using your binary read() function.

If nprime is greater than count, you must calculate new primes and continue to add them to the file until you have a total of nprime primes in it. You do this in the else part of the if:

```
if(nprime <= count)        {
    cout << endl << "Prime in file";
    primes.seekg((nprime-1)*sizeof(long), ios::beg); // Seek to position of nth
    read(primes, lastprime);                         // ...and read it
}
else
    while(count < nprime) {
        lastprime = nextprime(primes);
        primes.seekp(-static_cast<int>(sizeof(long)), ios::end); // Move to end
        write(primes, lastprime);            // Write prime as binary
        write(primes, ++count);              // Write prime as binary
    }
```

This uses a revised version of nextprime() that accepts a single argument: the file stream. This function will calculate and return the prime that follows the last prime in the file, but let's come back to how that works in a moment. When you *have* the next prime, you seek to the position of the count at the end of the file and overwrite it with the new prime. You then write the incremented count to the file. Note that you use seekp() here rather than seekg() because you're going to write to the file. This is essential because fstream has separate internal, synchronized buffers for input and output; seekg() applies to one and seekp() applies to the other.

The last step in the for loop is to display the prime required before going around for another choice. The following statement will do this:

```
cout << endl << "The " << nprime << " prime is " << lastprime << endl;
```

If you're a stickler for detail, you can use conditional operators to figure out here whether it should be "st", "nd", "rd", or "th" after the value of nprime in the output:

```
cout << endl    << "The "
     << nprime << ((nprime%10 == 1) && (nprime != 11) ? "st" :
                   (nprime%10 == 2) && (nprime != 12) ? "nd" :
                   (nprime%10 == 3) && (nprime != 13) ? "rd" : "th")
     << " prime is " << lastprime << endl;
```

You can implement the nextprime() function as follows:

```
long nextprime(std::fstream& primes) {
  bool isprime = false;                    // Indicator that we have a prime
  long aprime = 0;                         // Stores primes from the file
  long candidate = 0;                      // Value to be tested

  primes.seekg(-static_cast<int>(2*sizeof(long)), ios::end); // Go to last in file
  read(primes, candidate);                                   // ...and read it

  // Find the next prime
  for( ; ; ) {
    candidate += 2;                        // Next value for checking

    // Calculate upper limit for divisors
    long limit = std::sqrt(static_cast<double>(candidate));
    primes.seekg(0, ios::beg);             // Go to the start of the file

    // Try dividing the candidate by all the primes up to limit
    do {
      read(primes, aprime);                // Read prime as binary
    } while(aprime <= limit && (isprime = candidate % aprime > 0));

    if(isprime)                            // We got one...
      return candidate;                    // ...and return the prime
  }
}
```

The interesting parts here are the file access sections; the actual calculation is essentially as before. You first seek to where the last prime is in the file. Each item has sizeof(long) bytes, so you back off twice that number of bytes from the end of the file using seekg(). This takes account of that fact that the count of the number of primes in the file is the last item stored in the file and is also of type long. You then store the last prime in candidate using your own binary read() function.

To check the candidate, you seek to the beginning of the file, which corresponds to an offset of 0 bytes relative to ios::beg, and read consecutive prime divisors from the file. You use these to test the candidate in the loop condition. The limit check ensures you never reach the end of the file, so no ios flags for the stream should ever be set.

Try It Out: Randomly Accessing a File

You can package all the code that you've seen together and give it a whirl. The complete version of main() is as follows:

```cpp
// Program 19.6 Reading and writing binary primes file File: prog19_06.cpp
#include <fstream>
#include <iostream>
#include <cmath>
#include <string>
using std::cout;
using std::cin;
using std::endl;
using std::string;
using std::ios;

long nextprime(std::fstream& primes);        // Find the prime after lastprime
void write(std::ostream& out, long value);   // Write binary long value
void read(std::istream& in, long& value);    // Read binary long value

int main() {
  try {
    const char* filename = "C:\\JunkData\\nuprimes.bin";
    std::fstream primes;                      // Create file stream object
    primes.open(filename, ios::in|ios::out|ios::binary); // Open the file
    long count = 0;                           // Count of primes found

    if(!primes)  {
      primes.clear();
      cout << endl << "File doesn't exist - creating..." << endl;
      primes.open(filename, ios::out|ios::binary); // Create binary file

      if(!primes)
        throw ios::failure(string("Failed to create output file ") +
                           string(filename) +
                           string(" in main()"));
      write(primes, 2L);                      // Write 2 as binary long
```

```cpp
    write(primes, 3L);                    // Write 3 as binary long
    write(primes, 5L);                    // Write 5 as binary long
    write(primes, count = 3L);            // Write prime count
    primes.close();
    primes.open(filename, ios::in|ios::out|ios::binary);
  }

  long nprime = 0;                        // Sequence no. of prime required
  long lastprime = 0;                     // Last prime found
  for( ; ; ) {
    cout << "Which prime (e.g. enter 15 for the 15th prime, zero to end)?: ";
    cin >> nprime;
    if(nprime <= 0)                       // Zero or negative?
      return 0;                           //  ...yes, so we are done

    primes.seekg(-static_cast<int>(sizeof(long)), ios::end); // Go to last
    read(primes, count);                                     // Read the last

    if(nprime <= count) {
      cout << endl << "Prime in file";
      primes.seekg((nprime - 1) * sizeof(long), ios::beg); // Seek to nth
      read(primes, lastprime);                             //  ...and read it
    }
    else
      while(count < nprime) {
        lastprime = nextprime(primes);
        primes.seekp(-static_cast<int>(sizeof(long)), ios::end); // Move to end
        write(primes, lastprime);         // Write prime as binary
        write(primes, ++count);           // Write count as binary
      }

    cout << endl   << "The "
         << nprime << ((nprime%10 == 1) && (nprime != 11) ? "st" :
                       (nprime%10 == 2) && (nprime != 12) ? "nd" :
                       (nprime%10 == 3) && (nprime != 13) ? "rd" : "th")
         << " prime is " << lastprime << endl;
  }
  cout << endl;
  return 0;
}
catch(std::exception& ex) {
  cout << endl << typeid(ex).name() << ": " << ex.what() << endl;
  return 1;
}
}
```

(Continued)

You need to add the definition for nextprime() from the previous section and definitions for the read() and write() functions from the previous example, Program 19.5. A sample of the sort of output you can get is as follows:

```
File doesn't exist - creating...
Which prime (e.g. enter 15 for the 15th prime, zero to end)?: 9

The 9th prime is 23
Which prime (e.g. enter 15 for the 15th prime, zero to end)?: 99

The 99th prime is 523
Which prime (e.g. enter 15 for the 15th prime, zero to end)?: 1001

The 1001st prime is 7927
Which prime (e.g. enter 15 for the 15th prime, zero to end)?: 5000

The 5000th prime is 48611
Which prime (e.g. enter 15 for the 15th prime, zero to end)?: 3456

Prime in file
The 3456th prime is 32213
Which prime (e.g. enter 15 for the 15th prime, zero to end)?: 0
```

HOW IT WORKS

You covered all the details of developing the code. All input and output operations are carried out with the same file stream object, and you seek directly to the position that you require. Because you're using unformatted I/O operations in binary mode, this is a snap, as you always know how many bytes each item in the file occupies. Even with various kinds of data in the file, as long as you know what data items were written, and what the sequence was, you can figure out where things are in an unformatted binary file.

String Streams

There are three **string stream classes** that connect a stream to a string object: istringstream, ostringstream, and stringstream, which have istream, ostream, and iostream as base classes, respectively. Operations on these classes are essentially the same as for the file streams, except of course that the input and output operations are to string objects.

Although they can use any of the I/O functions that are inherited from their corresponding base class, string streams are used most often with the insertion and extraction operators. The reason for this is that their primary application is formatting data in memory, or analyzing input. For example, you might have an application in which the format of the input isn't known in advance. In such a case, you could read the data as a sequence of characters into a string object, and then use the stream input operations with an istringstream object attached to your string object to carry out formatted read operations on it. This provides the possibility to read the input as many times as necessary to figure out its format.

Suppose you read a line of input from cin with these statements:

```
string buffer;
getline(std::cin, buffer);
```

Having read the input into buffer, you can create an istringstream object with the following statement:

```
std::istringstream inStr(buffer);
```

You can now read from buffer via the stream inStr just like any other stream and make use of the conversion capability from character representation to binary:

```
long value = 0;
double data = 0.0;
inStr >> value >> data;
```

You can use an ostringstream object to format data into a string. For instance, you could create a string object and an output string stream with these statements:

```
string outBuffer;
std::ostringstream outStr(outBuffer);
```

You can now use the insertion operators to write to outBuffer via outStr:

```
double number = 2.5;
outStr << "number = " << (number/2.0);
```

As a result of the write to the string stream, outBuffer will contain "number = 1.25". The string outBuffer will automatically expand to accommodate however many characters you write to the stream, so it is a very flexible way of forming strings or complex output messages.

The string parameter to the string stream constructors is a reference in each case, so write operations for the ostringstream and stringstream objects act directly on the string object. There is also a default constructor for each of the string stream classes. When you use these, the string stream object will maintain a string object internally, and you can obtain a copy of this using the str() member, for example:

```
std::ostringstream outStr;
double number = 2.5;
outStr << "number = " << (3 * number / 2);
string output = outStr.str();
```

After these statements have been executed, output will contain the string "number = 3.75".

Objects and Streams

So far I've talked primarily about transferring basic data types to and from a stream. However, in previous chapters I've been telling you how great object-oriented programming is, so what about writing objects to a file? I just knew that question would come up.

As far as the C++ standard library is concerned, you're on your own. Although this is inconvenient, it's not altogether surprising—by nature, a class is completely open ended, and therefore by definition it's an unknown quantity. Input and output operations are going to be class specific, whether you like it or not. In spite of the difficulties implicit in this, some C++ development systems do provide a framework of support for reading and writing objects, sometimes at the small expense of having to use a particular base class. However, if yours doesn't provide anything, don't worry—you *can* do it yourself. What's more, you don't need to go to the trouble of deriving your own stream classes to do it.

Ideally, you want to be able to read and write objects of your classes using the same extraction and insertion operators that you use for the basic data types. All that's required is for you to supply functions to overload these operators for your class types. How easy or difficult this will be depends on the complexity of your classes. Once you know how to do it for formatted I/O, you should have little trouble implementing unformatted operations for use in binary mode. First of all, then, let's see how you might implement formatted I/O for class objects in a simple case.

Overloading the Insertion Operator for Class Objects

You can implement an overloaded version of operator<<() that will write objects of a given class to a stream as a friend of the class. Let's take a version of the Box class that you've used from time to time in this book and enable Box objects to be written to a stream.

To start with, you need to declare the function as a friend of the Box class, so that it has access to its data members:

```
// Box.h
#ifndef BOX_H
#define BOX_H
#include <iostream>

class Box {
  public:
    Box(double lv = 1, double wv = 1, double hv = 1);   // Constructor

    virtual ~Box();                  // Virtual Destructor
    void showVolume() const;         // Show the volume of an object
    virtual double volume() const;   // Calculate the volume of a Box object

    // Friend insertion operator
    friend std::ostream& operator<<(std::ostream& out, const Box& rBox);
```

```
  protected:
    double length;
    double width;
    double height;
};
#endif
```

Because the operator<<() function returns a reference to the stream object, you'll be able to use it to write Box objects to a stream in the same way as any of the basic data types. This applies to a file stream just as well as it does to cout. You can implement the function using the overloaded insertion operations for standard types:

```
std::ostream& operator<<(std::ostream& out, const Box& rBox) {
  return out << ' ' << rBox.length << ' ' << rBox.width << ' ' << rBox.height;
}
```

This just writes the three data members to the stream, with each preceded by a space, and returns the stream object that was passed to it, out. If you only intend the operator to be used to output objects to cout, then you might want to embellish the output with more descriptive information, such as the member names. However, if you intend to use it for writing to a file, such formatting would make reading objects back rather messy, so it's better to keep it simple in this case.

If the class contains query functions that retrieve the values of the data members (such as getLength(), etc. that you've used in other chapters), then the operator<<() function doesn't need to be a friend of the class—you could implement it using the public query functions. For now, though, let's see how to work with what you've got.

....

Try It Out: Writing Objects to a Stream

Box.h, which contains the friend declaration for operator<<(), is listed previously. You'll also need to define the function in Box.cpp, which looks like this:

```
// Box.cpp
#include <iostream>
#include "Box.h"
using std::cout;
using std::endl;

// Constructor
Box::Box(double lv, double wv, double hv) :
                                    length(lv), width(wv), height(hv){}


// Destructor
Box::~Box() {}
```

(Continued)

```cpp
// Function to show the volume of an object
void Box::showVolume() const {
  cout << endl << "Box usable volume is " << volume();
}

// Function to calculate the volume of a Box object
double Box::volume() const {
  return length * width * height;
}

// Friend operator function for Box
std::ostream& operator<<(std::ostream& out, const Box& rBox) {
  return out << ' ' << rBox.length << ' ' << rBox.width << ' ' << rBox.height;
}
```

In main(), you'll just create a couple of Box objects and output them:

```cpp
// Program 19.7 Writing Box object to cout   File: prog19_07.cpp
#include <iostream>
#include "Box.h"
using std::cout;
using std::endl;

int main() {
  Box bigBox(50, 60, 70);
  Box smallBox(2, 3, 4);
  cout << endl << "bigBox is " << bigBox;
  cout << endl << "smallBox is " << smallBox;
  cout << endl;
  return 0;
}
```

This example produces the following output:

```
bigBox is   50 60 70
smallBox is  2 3 4
```

HOW IT WORKS

After declaring the two Box objects, you output them with the following statements:

```cpp
cout << endl << "bigBox is " << bigBox;
cout << endl << "smallBox is " << smallBox;
```

The first of these is equivalent to this statement:

```
operator<<((cout.operator<<(endl)).operator<<("bigBox is "), bigBox);
```

In other words, you're calling the friend version of operator<<() with (cout.operator<<(endl)).operator<<("bigBox is ") as the first argument and bigBox as the second argument. The expression for the first argument calls the member function for cout to output the newline, followed by the member function to output the string. This latter call returns the stream object, out, which is passed as the first argument to your friend function. The second statement works in exactly the same way. Easy, isn't it?

Overloading the Extraction Operator for Class Objects

Reading objects from a stream just requires an implementation of operator>>() for your class, which will need to be a friend if the data members are private or protected. Of course, you can avoid the requirement for a friend function if you implement public member functions to set the data members' values, but I'm trying to keep the class as small as possible for the purposes of this discussion. It goes without saying that the insertion and extraction operators for a class object have to be implemented consistently, with the members' values being read in the same order in which they're written. You could implement the operator for the Box class as follows:

```
std::istream& operator>>(std::istream& in, Box& rBox) {
  return in >> rBox.length >> rBox.width >> rBox.height;
}
```

Because you're modifying the members of rBox, the second parameter can't be const. This is a very simple-minded implementation that takes no account of input errors. In practice, not only would you want to deal with errors such as the end of file occurring before you've read all the values you need, but also you would want to do some validity checking on the values themselves to ensure you end up with a valid Box object. However, this simple version will be sufficient to show the mechanics. Let's try it out, along with the insertion operator.

Try It Out: Reading and Writing Objects

Of course, you could just read a Box object from the keyboard, but let's be more adventurous and try writing Box objects to a file and then reading them back. You need to add a friend declaration for operator>>() to the Box class definition in Box.h:

```
class Box {
    ...

    // Friend insertion and extraction operators
    friend std::ostream& operator<<(std::ostream& out, const Box& rBox);
    friend std::istream& operator>>(std::istream& in, Box& rBox);

    ...
};
```

You must also add the definition of the operator>>() function, as shown in the previous section, to Box.cpp. The program to use your new operator function will be this:

```
// Program 19.8 Writing Box objects to a file  File: prog19_08.cpp
#include <fstream>
#include <iostream>
#include <string>
using std::cout;
using std::endl;
using std::string;
using std::ios;

#include "Box.h"

int main() {
  try {
    const string filename = "C:\\JunkData\\boxes.txt";

    std::ofstream out(filename.c_str());
    if(!out)
      throw(ios::failure(string("Failed to open output file ") + filename));

    Box bigBox(50, 60, 70);
    Box smallBox(2,3,4);

    out << bigBox << smallBox;
    out.close();

    cout << endl << "Wrote two Box objects to the file:";
    cout << endl << "bigBox is " << bigBox;
    cout << endl << "smallBox is " << smallBox;
    cout << endl;
```

```
    std::ifstream in(filename.c_str());
    if(!in)
      throw(ios::failure(string("Failed to open input file ") + filename));

    cout << endl << "Reading objects from the file:";
    Box newBox;                                    // Default Box object

    in >> newBox;
    cout << endl << "First Box read is " << newBox;
    in >> newBox;
    cout << endl << "Second Box read is " << newBox;
    cout << endl;
    return 0;
  }
  catch(std::exception& ex) {
    cout << endl << typeid(ex).name() << ": " << ex.what() << endl;
    return 0;
  }
}
```

This produces the following output:

```
Wrote two Box objects to the file:
bigBox is   50 60 70
smallBox is   2 3 4

Reading objects from the file:
First Box read is   50 60 70
Second Box read is   2 3 4
```

HOW IT WORKS

There is really very little to say about this code, because it works in the same way
as reading and writing the basic types. You use a new file to hold Box objects:

```
    const string filename = "C:\\JunkData\\boxes.txt";
```

After creating two Box objects, you write them to the file with this statement:

```
    out << bigBox << smallBox;
```

This is equivalent to the following statement:

```
    operator<<(operator<<(out, bigBox), smallBox);
```

(Continued)

Because ofstream has ostream as a base class, returning the ofstream object out as type ostream& in the first argument to the outer operator<<() call works perfectly well. Having written the file, you then close it and use your operator<<() function with the standard stream, cout:

```
cout << endl << "bigBox is " << bigBox;
cout << endl << "smallBox is " << smallBox;
```

This outputs the two Box objects to the screen, just as it did in the last example. To prove that there's no sleight of hand going on, you can now read a Box object back from the file into a new Box object, newBox, with the following statement:

```
in >> newBox;
```

This is making use of your new extraction operator to retrieve a Box object from the file stream, in. The statement is equivalent to this:

```
operator>>(in, newBox);
```

The use of separate input statements isn't significant—you could equally well have read both Box objects from the file into separate Box objects in memory with a single statement. Last of all, each Box object is read from the file and displayed on cout to show that the program has worked correctly.

More Complex Objects in Streams

With the Box object, I deliberately chose a simple case. Handling derived class objects is a little more complicated because your operator>>() and operator<<() functions aren't class members and therefore can't be virtual. You really do *need* a virtual input and output mechanism to ensure that derived class objects are handled properly when they're referred to using a base pointer or a reference to a base class, but there's no way you can make the operator functions class members.

The insertion and extraction operators are binary operators, and binary operator functions that are members of a class can only have one parameter. You would have no way to pass the stream object *and* the right operand to the function. The operator functions *could* call a virtual class member, though, and that provides a way to deal with the difficulty. For your Box class, you could implement it like this:

```
class Box {
  public:
    // Constructor
    Box(double lv = 1, double wv = 1, double hv = 1);

    // Virtual Destructor
    virtual ~Box();

    // Function to show the volume of an object
    void showVolume() const;
```

```
// Function to calculate the volume of a Box object
virtual double volume() const;

// Member stream I/O functions
virtual std::ostream& put(std::ostream& out) const;
virtual std::istream& get(std::istream& in);

protected:
  double length;
  double width;
  double height;
};

// Insertion and extraction operators
std::ostream& operator<<(std::ostream& out, const Box& rBox);
std::istream& operator>>(std::istream& in, Box& rBox);
```

You've added two virtual members to the class that will perform the stream I/O operations, and because your insertion and extraction operators will now call functions in the class's public interface, they no longer need to be friend functions. All you have to do is implement the operator functions to make use of the new members. You can define the put() member function like this:

```
std::ostream& Box::put(std::ostream& out) const {
  return out << ' ' << length << ' ' << width << ' ' << height;
}
```

This does exactly the same thing as the earlier version of the operator<<() function, which you can now implement as follows:

```
std::ostream& operator<<(std::ostream& out, const Box& rBox) {
  return rBox.put(out);
}
```

This just calls the virtual function put() to perform the output operation and returns the stream object. Similarly, the get() function definition will be this:

```
std::istream& Box::get(std::istream& in) {
  return in >> length >> width >> height;
}
```

Once again, you can use this in the implementation of the friend function operator>>():

```
std::istream& operator>>(std::istream& in, Box& rBox) {
  return rBox.get(in);
}
```

To provide stream support for a derived class of Box, such as Carton, you just need to define member functions that override the virtual get() and put() functions in the base class. The derived class member functions can call the corresponding base class versions where necessary.

You'll remember the Carton class inherited from Box, implementing a different volume() function and adding a string* data member that held a pointer to a string containing the name of the material from which the Carton was made. The prototypes of the get() and put() member functions for this class would be as follows:

```
class Carton: public Box {
  public:
    virtual std::ostream& put(std::ostream& out) const;
    virtual std::istream& get(std::istream& in);

  // Rest of the class definition...
};
```

The put() function could be implemented as follows:

```
std::ostream& Carton::put(std::ostream& out) const {
  out << ' ' << *pMaterial;
  return Box::put(out);
}
```

You could implement the get() function as follows:

```
std::istream& Carton::get(std::istream& in) {
  pMaterial = new string;                // Allocate for new string
  in >> *pMaterial;                      // Read the string
  return Box::get(in);
}
```

Now, whether you output an object of the base class, Box, or of the derived class, Carton, the base class operator<<() will select the appropriate virtual put() function for the object, even when the object is referenced by a base class reference. This will work for any class that has Box as a base, as long as the get() and put() members are implemented for the class.

Classes that contain pointers to objects of other classes add a further complication. One fundamental prerequisite is that the class type of the object being pointed to has overloaded operators to do the business. You can then use these to write or retrieve the objects pointed to. Another prerequisite is that there has to be a way of constructing the object from the data read from the stream. One way to do this requires that the class pointed to must have a default constructor. You can then use this when you're reading objects from a stream, to synthesize objects in the free store, and then initialize them with data from the stream. Another possibility is to provide a class constructor that accepts an input stream as an argument and constructs an object using data from the stream.

As bad as that sounds, it can get even trickier if the object pointed to by a member of a class *also* has pointers to class objects. You could explore some of the ramifications of this with an example, so in the next example you'll really stick your neck out and try to implement a modicum of stream support for a version of the Stack template defined in the previous chapter. You won't do a comprehensive job on this, but you'll see enough to cover the principles involved. It will give you some experience of stream operations with templates, as well as classes that contain pointers to other class objects.

Stream Support for Template Classes

Let's first think about how output of a Stack<T> object to a stream is going to work. The only data member of a template instance is the pointer pHead, which will contain the address of the first node if there is one and 0 otherwise. You'll have to write the Node object to which pHead points to the file, and you could consider a friend function to the inner class Node for this, but this class is private to Stack, and it would be better to keep it so. An alternative approach would be to declare a helper function, writeNodes(), as a member of the Stack template that would write all the Node objects to the file. The principle of how this is going to work is illustrated in Figure 19-6.

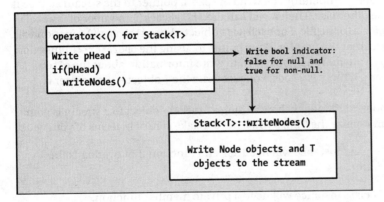

Figure 19-6. A helper function for writing a Stack object to a file

There is no point in writing addresses contained in pointers to a stream, as they'll be invalid when they're read back. What's important about a pointer in this situation is whether or not it's null, because this will tell you whether there's an object in the file that the pointer used to point to. You can easily write this information about a pointer to the stream as a bool value.

The writeNodes() function will also need to take care of the object pointed to by the Node data member, pItem, because no one else is going to! The object pointed to is of type T, and because you have to write it to the stream, you'll assume that there's an implementation of the insertion operator for objects of class T. Clearly, this has to be the case if your function is going to work.

You now have a clearer idea of how a Stack<T> object with an arbitrary number of nodes is going to get written to a stream. The mechanism is illustrated in Figure 19-7.

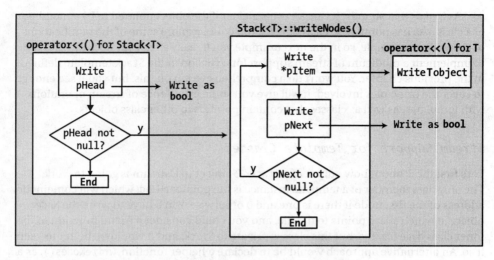

Figure 19-7. Writing a complete Stack<T> object to a stream

The Stack<T> insertion operator will write the pHead pointer to the stream as true if it isn't null and false otherwise. Then it will call the writeNodes() member of Stack<T> to write the Node objects to the file. For each Node object, the writeNodes() function will also write the T object that the pointer pItem points to, using the operator<<() function for objects of type T. Note that you *don't* need to write information about the pItem member to the stream. If there is a Node, you just write the T object—the pointer is never null.

So, you now understand roughly how writing a Stack<T> object to a stream is going to work, and you can itemize the things you'll need to take care of in terms of your code:

- Each Stack<T> class instance will need a friend function that overloads the insertion operator.

- Each Stack<T> class instance will need a private member function, writeNodes(), that writes all Node objects to the stream.

- The friend function for insertion of Stack<T> objects and the writeNodes() member function will need to be defined by templates.

Implementing Insertion for the Stack Class Template

First of all, you can add the friend declaration for operator<<() template and the declaration for the writeNode() member function to the Stack template. Because you're adding a function template as a friend of your class template, you must also declare the function template as such, prior to the class template definition. Further, because the function template refers to the Stack name before it has been defined, you must also declare Stack as a template:

```
template<typename T> class Stack;        // Class template declaration

// Prototype for friend function template
template<typename T>
 std::ostream& operator << (std::ostream& out, const Stack<T>& rStack);


template <typename T> class Stack {
  public:
    Stack():pHead(0){}                    // Default constructor
    Stack(const Stack& aStack);           // Copy constructor
    ~Stack();                             // Destructor
    Stack& operator=(const Stack& aStack); // Assignment operator

    void push(T& rItem);                  // Push an object onto the stack
    T& pop();                             // Pop an object off the stack
    bool isEmpty() {return pHead == 0;}   // Empty test

  friend std::ostream& operator<< <T>(std::ostream& out, const Stack& rStack);

  private:
    class Node {
      public:
        T* pItem;                         // Pointer to object stored
        Node* pNext;                      // Pointer to next node

      // Construct a node from an object
      Node(T& rItem) : pItem(&rItem), pNext(0) {}
      Node() : pItem(0), pNext(0) {}      // Construct an empty node
    };

    Node* pHead;                          // Points to the top of the stack
    void copy(const Stack& aStack);       // Helper to copy a stack
    void freeMemory();                    // Helper to release free store memory

    // Write Node objects to a stream
    std::ostream& writeNodes(std::ostream& out, Node* pNode) const;
};
```

The form of the friend function is similar to previous non-member implementations you've seen, but you have the template parameter specification, <T>, following the function template name. This is to indicate that the template parameter for the function template is the same as that of the class template. Note that the space following the function template name is essential for the code to compile.

The first argument to operator<< <T>() is a reference to the ostream object, and the second argument is a const reference to the object to be written. The return value must be a reference to the ostream object if you're to be able to use it in a succession of << operations in a single statement. Note that this function isn't a member function and that the use of Stack& as the type of the second parameter implies Stack<T>&, so this is a function template that is a friend of the class template.

The writeNodes() function has two parameters. The first is a reference to a stream, and the second is a pointer to the Node object. A pointer will be easier to work with here, because a Node object is always referenced through a pointer. For convenience, the function returns a reference to the stream object.

You can add a function template for the operator<<() function to the Stack.h file:

```
template <typename T>
std::ostream& operator<<(std::ostream& out, const Stack<T>& rStack) {
  out << ' ' << (rStack.pHead != 0);
  return rStack.writeNodes(out, rStack.pHead);
}
```

This function writes a bool value to the stream that will be true if the pHead member of rStack isn't null and then passes the same pointer to the writeNodes() function to write the Node objects to the stream. Not too difficult, is it?

You need to bear in mind that data items need whitespace separating them if they're to be read from a stream by an extraction operator. You can make sure that this is the case by always outputting a space before each item, as you've done here with the bool data.

The template defining the writeNodes() member function will also go in Stack.h:

```
template <typename T>
std::ostream& Stack<T>::writeNodes(std::ostream& out, Node* pNode) const {
  while(pNode) {
    out << ' ' << *(pNode->pItem);
    out << ' ' << (pNode->pNext != 0);
    pNode = pNode->pNext;
  }
  return out;
}
```

The pointer pNode determines whether a Node object is written. You first write the T object pointed to by pItem to the stream and then the bool indicator for the pNext pointer. You then store the pNext pointer for the current node in pNode for the next iteration.

It might have sounded difficult to begin with, but that's all you need to write Stack<T> objects to a stream. Let's see if you can figure out how to read them back.

Understanding Extraction for the Stack Class Template

A good place to start is to look at exactly what ends up in a stream when the functions for which you've just created templates write a Stack object to it. A Stack<T> object with four nodes is illustrated in Figure 19-8.

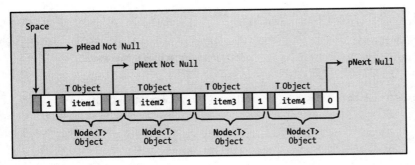

Figure 19-8. A stream containing a Stack<T> object with four nodes

The first value in the stream is a space, followed by the bool value for pHead, which will be true if there's a following Node object. Each Node<T> object is just the T object to which its pItem member points, followed by a bool value that's true if there's a "next" Node object. The last Node object will have the bool indicator for pNext set to false, because there's no next node in that case.

The friend operator>>() function in Stack<T> can read the pHead indicator and then call a private helper function named readNodes() if the indicator is true, so the input process will be a mirror of the output process.

When you read a Node object from a stream, you'll need to create the object that the data member pItem points to. This raises some serious complications that you must consider very carefully. Because *you're* now creating these objects of type T, you must take responsibility for deleting them. This implies you must use a different strategy for dealing with objects in the stack. If you provide the capability to write a Stack object to a stream, you should always create objects in the free store, even when they're pushed on the stack. You can then return a copy rather than a reference and delete the object from the free store when it's popped from the stack or when a node is destroyed.

Managing Objects in the Stack

You must add the Node class destructor to the template and modify the constructor to accept a pointer argument rather than a reference. You also need to alter the pop() member function to return an object rather than a reference:

```
template<typename T> class Stack;        // Class template declaration

// Prototype for friend function template
template<typename T>
 std::ostream& operator << (std::ostream& out, const Stack<T>& rStack);

template <typename T> class Stack {
public:
    Stack():pHead(0){}                    // Default constructor
    Stack(const Stack& aStack);           // Copy constructor
    ~Stack();                             // Destructor
```

```
    Stack& operator=(const Stack& aStack);  // Assignment operator

    void push(T& rItem);                     // Push an object onto the stack
    T pop();                                 // Pop an object off the stack
    bool isEmpty() {return pHead == 0;}      // Empty test

  friend std::ostream& operator<< <T>(std::ostream& out, const Stack& rStack);

  private:
    class Node {
      public:
        T* pItem;                            // Pointer to object stored
        Node* pNext;                         // Pointer to next node

        // Construct a node from an object
        Node(T* pNew) : pItem(pNew), pNext(0) {}
        Node() : pItem(0), pNext(0) {}       // Construct an empty node
        ~Node() {delete pItem;}
};

    Node* pHead;                             // Points to the top of the stack
    void copy(const Stack& aStack);          // Helper to copy a stack
    void freeMemory();                       // Helper to release free store memory

    // Write a Node object to a stream
    std::ostream& writeNodes(std::ostream& out, Node* pNode) const;
};
```

The destructor just deletes the object pointed to by pItem. You don't need to test pItem for null—it should never be so, and calling delete on a null pointer is always safe anyway. In the Stack template, you've changed the return type of the pop() member to T, so that you'll return a copy of the object in the stack.

You have to alter the implementations of push() and pop() for the Stack template. Let's deal with push() first. You must modify the Stack<T>::push() template definition to create a T object in the free store that's a *copy* of the object passed as a reference, rather than just storing the address of the original object:

```
template <typename T> void Stack<T>::push(T& rItem) {
  Node* pNode = new Node(new T(rItem));    // Create node from object copy
  pNode->pNext = pHead;                    // Point to the old top node
  pHead = pNode;                           // Make the new node the top
}
```

The Stack<T>::pop() template must now make a local copy of the free store object, and then delete the free store object:

```
template <typename T> T Stack<T>::pop() {
  if(!pHead)                               // If it is empty
    throw std::logic_error("Stack empty"); // Pop is not valid so throw exception
```

```
    T item(*pHead->pItem);          // Local copy of top object
    Node* pTemp = pHead;            // Save address of top node
    pHead = pHead->pNext;           // Make next node the top
    delete pTemp;                   // Delete the previous top node
    return item;                    // Return copy of top object
}
```

Of course, the return mechanism will also make a copy of the object, item, before the local object is destroyed. Your Stack template is now self-contained, because it creates and manages copies of all the objects in the stack in the free store, regardless of whether they were pushed onto the stack or created from a stream.

Implementing Extraction for the Stack Class Template

You can add a friend declaration for the operator>>() function and the declaration of readNodes() to the Stack<T> template:

```
template<typename T> class Stack;      // Class template declaration

// Prototypes for friend function templates
template<typename T>
 std::ostream& operator<< (std::ostream& out, const Stack<T>& rStack);
template<typename T>
std::istream& operator>> (std::istream& in, Stack& rStack);

template <typename T> class Stack {
  public:
    Stack():pHead(0){}                   // Default constructor
    Stack(const Stack& aStack);          // Copy constructor
    ~Stack();                            // Destructor
    Stack& operator=(const Stack& aStack);  // Assignment operator

    void push(T& rItem);                 // Push an object onto the stack
    T pop();                             // Pop an object off the stack
    bool isEmpty() {return pHead == 0;}  // Empty test

    friend std::ostream& operator<< <T>(std::ostream& out, const Stack& rStack);
    friend std::istream& operator>> <T>(std::istream& in, Stack& rStack);

  private:
    class Node {
      public:
        T* pItem;                        // Pointer to object stored
        Node* pNext;                     // Pointer to next node

        // Construct a node from an object
        Node(T* pNew) : pItem(pNew), pNext(0) {}
        Node() : pItem(0), pNext(0) {}   // Construct an empty node
        ~Node() {delete pItem;}
    };
```

```
    Node* pHead;                          // Points to the top of the stack
    void copy(const Stack& aStack);       // Helper to copy a stack
    void freeMemory();                    // Helper to release free store memory

    // Write Node objects to a stream
    std::ostream& writeNodes(std::ostream& out, Node* pNode) const;
    Node* readNodes(std::istream& in);    // Read Node objects from stream
};
```

The readNodes() function returns a pointer to the first Node read, so that it can be stored in pHead in the operator>>() function. You can define the function template for the extraction operator for Stack<T> objects as follows:

```
template <typename T>
std::istream& operator>>(std::istream& in, Stack<T>& rStack) {
  bool notEmpty;
  in >> notEmpty;
  if(notEmpty)
    rStack.pHead = rStack.readNodes(in);
  else
    rStack.pHead = 0;
  return in;
}
```

The first bool value from the stream is stored in the variable notEmpty. It this is true, you know that a Node object follows, so you call readNodes() to read the Node objects from the stream. If it's false, you just set pHead to null.

You can implement the template for the readNodes() function like this:

```
template <typename T>
typename Stack<T>::Node* Stack<T>::readNodes(std::istream& in) {
  Node* pNode = new Node;           // Create a Node object
  pNode->pItem = new T;             // Create the T object and store its address
  in >> *pNode->pItem;              // Read the T object from the stream

  bool isNext;
  in >> isNext;
  if(isNext)
    pNode->pNext = readNodes(in);
  else pNode->pNext = 0;
  return pNode;
}
```

The return type is a pointer to the Node type that's defined within the template. Because the Node class appears within the template definition, it's referred to as a dependent type. The compiler needs a little help in this case, so you have to prefix the return type specification of a dependent type with the typename keyword to tell the compiler that this is a type rather than some other name.

As long as you make sure you read from the stream in the same order as you write to it, all the objects just fall into place. You create the new Node object and the new object of type T, and store the address of the T object in the pItem pointer of the Node that you've just created. You then read the bool indicator for the pNext pointer. If that is true, it indicates there's another Node object to be read, so you read that from the stream by calling readNodes() and storing the pointer returned in the pNext member of the Node object. This will continue until a Node object is read that has the pNext indicator as false, when the sequence of function calls will unwind.

....

Try It Out: Stream Operations with Template Class Instances

You can try out the modified template class with a set of Box objects. The version of the Box class that you used earlier in this chapter has a default constructor. You also implemented the insertion and extraction operators for Box objects, and the default copy constructor will be fine, so the class is fully equipped for stream operations in a stack. Here's the code to test it:

```cpp
// Program 19.9 Writing a stack to a stream  File:prog19_09.cpp
#include <fstream>
#include <iostream>
#include <string>
using std::cout;
using std::endl;
using std::string;

#include "Stack.h"
#include "Box.h"

int main() {
  Box Boxes[10];                          // 10 default boxes

  for(int i = 0 ; i < 10 ; i++)           // Create different objects
    Boxes[i] = Box(10*(i + 1), 10*(i + 2), 10*(i + 3));

  Stack<Box> boxStack;                    // A stack for Box objects

  // Push all Box objects onto the stack
  for(int i = 0 ; i < 10 ; i++)
    boxStack.push(Boxes[i]);

  const string boxFileName = "C:\\JunkData\\boxes.txt"; // Stack file
  std::ofstream outBoxFile(boxFileName.c_str());

  outBoxFile << boxStack;                 // Write the stack
  outBoxFile.close();                     // Close the stream
```

(Continued)

```
// Display volumes for original set
while(!boxStack.isEmpty())
  cout << endl << "Volume = " << boxStack.pop().volume();

Stack<Box> copyBoxStack;                    // New stack for Box objects

std::ifstream inBoxFile(boxFileName.c_str());
inBoxFile >> copyBoxStack;                  // Read the stack

// Output volumes of Box objects off the stack from the stream
int i = 0;
while(!copyBoxStack.isEmpty())
  cout << endl << "Volume of Box[" << (i++) << "] is "
       << copyBoxStack.pop().volume();

cout << endl;
return 0;
}
```

This should produce the following output:

```
Volume = 1.32e+006
Volume = 990000
Volume = 720000
Volume = 504000
Volume = 336000
Volume = 210000
Volume = 120000
Volume = 60000
Volume = 24000
Volume = 6000
Volume of Box[0] is 1.32e+006
Volume of Box[1] is 990000
Volume of Box[2] is 720000
Volume of Box[3] is 504000
Volume of Box[4] is 336000
Volume of Box[5] is 210000
Volume of Box[6] is 120000
Volume of Box[7] is 60000
Volume of Box[8] is 24000
Volume of Box[9] is 6000
```

HOW IT WORKS

You can see from the output that the Box objects popped from the stack that's read from the file have exactly the same volumes as the original objects. In main(), you create an array of default Box objects:

```
Box Boxes[10];                              // 10 default boxes
```

You set the array elements to different Box objects in a loop:

```
for(int i = 0 ; i < 10 ; i++)               // Create different objects
  Boxes[i] = Box(10 * (i + 1), 10 * (i + 2), 10 * (i + 3));
```

The first object will have dimensions (10, 20, 30), the next will have (20, 30, 40), and so on. You then create an empty stack that can store Box objects with this statement:

```
Stack<Box> boxStack;                         // A stack for Box objects
```

Next, you push the elements of the Boxes array onto the stack in a for loop:

```
for(int i = 0 ; i < 10 ; i++)
  boxStack.push(Boxes[i]);
```

The push() member of boxStack will make a copy of the object passed as a reference argument and use that internally to the stack. The next step is to write boxStack to a file stream:

```
const string boxFileName = "C:\\JunkData\\boxes.txt"; // Stack file
std::ofstream outBoxFile(boxFileName.c_str());

outBoxFile << boxStack;                      // Write the stack
outBoxFile.close();                          // Close the stream
```

This uses the << operator that you implemented as a friend function template of the Stack template. After writing the Stack<Box> object, you close the file. For reference, you pop the Box objects off the original stack and display their volumes:

```
while(!boxStack.isEmpty())
  cout << endl << "Volume = " << boxStack.pop().volume();
```

Of course, you're working with copies of the Box objects that are internal to the stack here. The pop() member will delete the node corresponding to the popped Box object, and the destructor for Node<Box> will delete the Box object from the free store.

You now want to read the stack back from the stream, so you create another stack to store Box objects and an input file stream for the file that you just wrote:

```
Stack<Box> copyBoxStack;                     // New stack for Box objects
std::ifstream inBoxFile(boxFileName.c_str());
```

To read the stack, you use the extraction operator:

```
inBoxFile >> copyBoxStack;                   // Read the stack
```

(Continued)

The last step is to pop the objects off the stack and display the volumes to show they're the same as the originals:

```
int i = 0;
while(!copyBoxStack.isEmpty())
  cout << endl << "Volume of Box[" << (i++) << "] is "
       << copyBoxStack.pop().volume();
```

As I'm sure you've gathered, implementing stream operations is quite a tricky business on the whole, so if your C++ implementation provides its own support for this, it will save you a lot of work!

Summary

In this chapter, you've covered the basics of stream operations and how you can apply them to using files in your C++ programs. The important elements that you've explored in this chapter include the following:

- The standard library supports input/output (I/O) operations on character streams, binary (byte) streams, and string streams.

- The standard streams for input and output are cin and cout. There are also error streams called cerr and clog.

- The extraction and insertion operators provide formatted stream input-output operations.

- A file stream can be associated with a file on disk for input, for output, or for both.

- The file open mode determines whether you can read from a stream or write to a stream.

- If you create a file output stream and associate it with a file name for which no file exists, a file will be created.

- A file has a beginning, an end, and a current position.

- You can alter the current position in a file stream to a position that was recorded previously. This can be a position that is a positive offset from the beginning of the stream, a position that is a negative offset from the end of a stream, or a position that is a positive or negative offset from the current position.

- To support stream operations for your class objects, you can overload the insertion and extraction operators with operator functions that are friends of your class.

- The string stream classes provide stream I/O operations to or from string objects.

Exercises

The following exercises enable you to try out what you've learned in this chapter. If you get stuck, look back over the chapter for help. If you're still stuck, you can download the solutions from the Downloads area of the Apress website (http://www.apress.com), but that really should be a last resort.

Exercise 19-1. Write a `Time` class that stores hours, minutes, and seconds as integers. Provide an overloaded insertion operator (`<<`) that will print the time in the format `hh:mm:ss` to any output stream.

Exercise 19-2. Provide a simple extraction operator (`operator>>()`) for the `Time` class that will read time values in the form `hh:mm:ss`. How are you going to cope with the `:` characters? (Hint: What sort of variable would you use to hold a `:`?)

Exercise 19-3. Write a program to log time values to a file. Write a matching program to read a file of time values and output them to the screen.

Exercise 19-4. Write a program that reads lines of text from standard input and writes them to standard output, removing all leading whitespace and converting multiple spaces to single spaces. Test it on input from the keyboard and on characters read from a file. Write a second program that converts lowercase characters to uppercase, and test that too.

CHAPTER 20

Introducing the Standard Template Library

As you already know, C++ provides an extensive standard library that simplifies many programming tasks. In addition to what you have seen up to now, this library also provides a range of templates that provide a much higher level of capability. You can use these templates to create standard **containers**, **algorithms**, and **functions** for your data types whenever you need such facilities in your programs. Collectively these templates are often referred to as the **Standard Template Library (STL)**. This chapter introduces the basic STL **containers** and the **algorithms** that work alongside these containers.

In this chapter you will learn the following:

- The basic architecture of the STL

- How to create and use the **sequence containers** vector<> and list<>, and the **associative containers** map<> and multimap<>

- What **iterators** are and how you use them

- What algorithms are and why iterators are important in this context

- How iterators bridge containers with plain old-fashioned standard C++ arrays

- How you can create and use stream iterators

- How you can define your own iterator classes

- How to create and use the associative containers map<> and multimap<>

An Introduction to the STL Architecture

The STL provides you with a generic set of tools that you can adapt to work with your class objects. For instance, using the STL you can create a class that defines a linked list for any of your data types. If you need a linked list to store Box objects or FootballPlayer objects, it's no problem with the STL; in fact, it can do more. The STL also provides you with standard ways to process your objects. If you need to sort your Box objects in ascending order, then the STL can generate a sort function that will do this for you. In fact, the STL can generate a function that will sort data of any data type that defines comparison operator functions for objects of that type. Whatever types of objects your program uses, if you need a standard way to organize or analyze them, chances are the STL can help.

The STL has a vast range of facilities; far more than I can possibly detail here. I'd need a whole book to cover the details of how you use the STL adequately. The aim of this chapter is to provide you with sufficient insight into the way the STL works so that you'll be able to explore it further on your own. My approach will be to give you a feel for the scope of what the STL has to offer, and then to demonstrate how to apply the most frequently used facilities through working examples.

STL Components

You get three main categories of tools with the STL: **containers**, **iterators**, and **algorithms**. These plug together in the fashion illustrated in Figure 20-1.

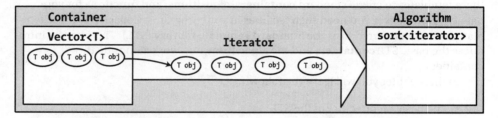

Figure 20-1. A container connected to an algorithm by an iterator

Containers are class objects that store other objects in various ways. A linked list is one example of a container. The STL provides a range of containers with different characteristics, and your choice of which container to use in a particular application will depend on how you want to access the contents of the container.

An iterator is a form of smart pointer, like the BoxPtr object that you used with the TruckLoad container in Chapter 14. You use an iterator to access the contents of a container when you want to process the objects in some way.

An algorithm is a function that processes elements from a source, such as a container, in a particular way. Some algorithms sort and search the contents of a container, for instance, whereas others process data numerically. You use an iterator to extract the objects from a container and supply them to an algorithm for processing.

Before I get into the details of writing code that uses the STL, I'll first give you an overview of the facilities that it provides in a bit more depth. I'll first look at the various container types and their capabilities. This will enable you to see how each container type is designed to suit a particular way of working with the contents. I'll then show you what various kinds of iterators can do and their role in relation to containers. Finally I'll outline the functions you have available within the STL algorithms.

STL Containers

Containers are the most interesting of the STL capabilities because you'll almost certainly use them most frequently. Having said that, if you use a container you'll also be using iterators, so you'll need a good understanding of those too. The STL provides two main categories of container: the **sequence containers** store objects in a linear organization, and the **associative containers** store objects together with associated keys. You can retrieve an object from an associative container by supplying its associated key. You can also retrieve the objects in an associative container through an iterator.

It's important to appreciate that all the STL containers store *copies* of the objects that you put into them. This means that if you add an object to a container and modify the original, the original and the object in the container are now different. Similarly, when you retrieve an object from a container, you get a copy of the object in the container. If you want to change an object in a container, you must replace it with a new version. The copies are created using the copy constructor for the type of object stored. For some objects, copying can be a process that carries a lot of overhead. In this case, it may be better to store pointers to objects in the container and keep the original objects externally.

Sequence Containers

Three basic types of **sequence container** correspond to the templates: vector<T>, deque<T>, and list<T>. These all store a set of objects of a specified type, T, organized in a linear sequential fashion, but each provides access to the contents optimized in a different way. Thus, which sequence container you choose in a particular instance depends on how you want to work with the entities that you store in it. The type of entity that you store can be of a fundamental type such as int or double, a class type, or a pointer to a fundamental type or a class type.

A vector<T> container stores objects of type T much like an ordinary array, except that its capacity adjusts to accommodate as many objects as you need to store. You would choose to use a vector<T> container when you want to work with the objects as you would with an array. You can use the subscript operator, [ ], to access an existing element in a vector, just like in an array. The **size** of a vector is the number of elements occupied, whereas its **capacity** is the current maximum number of elements that it can accommodate. When you first create a vector object with a specified capacity, the size and capacity will be the same. For instance, you could create a vector with a capacity for ten elements of type int like this:

```
std::vector<int> a(10);    // A vector with 10 elements
```

The elements of a vector that you create in this way are initialized using the default constructor for the type that you specify as the template parameter. In this case, the element type is int so the elements are set to zero. Because the elements have all been initialized, the size and the capacity are both 10.

If you add one or more elements to a vector, the size increases by some factor to accommodate the new elements so that the capacity may be greater than (but never less than) the size. You can obtain the size and capacity for a vector container by calling its `size()` and `capacity()` members respectively. Both values are returned as a value of type `size_type`, which is defined by a `typedef` as an unsigned integral type that is usually the same as `size_t`. A vector with the name a that stores values of type `int` is illustrated in Figure 20-2.

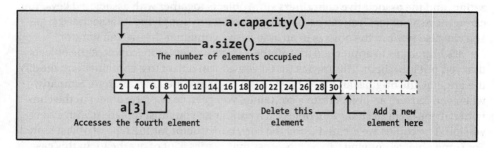

Figure 20-2. An example of a vector container

A `vector` is most efficient when you only add or delete elements at the end of the sequence. Of course, the vector grows automatically if you exceed the capacity. You *can* insert elements at the beginning or in the interior of a vector, but this is a relatively inefficient process because it involves moving all the elements that follow the insertion position and may involve allocating new space in the free store. Deleting elements from the beginning or from the interior of a vector is also slow because elements are moved in this instance too. If you expect to be adding or deleting elements in the interior of a sequence container, you probably shouldn't be using a vector. You can use a `list` container instead.

A `deque<T>` is a container that is organized as a queue of elements of type T. deque is an abbreviation of "**d**ouble-**e**nded **que**ue," which indicates its primary characteristic. It has the advantage over a vector container in that you can add or delete objects efficiently at the beginning of the sequence as well as at the end so you choose this type of container when you need this capability. You can create a `deque` object with a given size in essentially the same way as you do a vector:

```
std::deque<int> b(10);    // A deque object with 10 elements.
```

A deque container with the name b that stores elements of type `int` is illustrated in Figure 20-3.

A deque container is similar to a vector in that you can access the elements using the subscript operator. However, elements are organized internally in a different, more complicated way than they are in a vector. This makes it so the size of a deque container is always equal to its capacity. For this reason, no `capacity()` member function is defined for a deque container, but it still has a `size()` member that returns the current size as type `size_type`. Because of its different internal organization, a deque is a little slower to use than a vector. As with a vector, you can add or delete elements in the interior of a deque sequence, but the process is relatively slow because it always results in existing elements being copied.

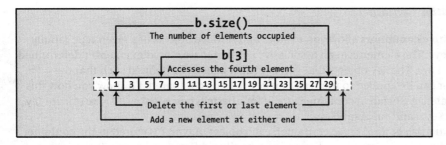

Figure 20-3. An example of a deque container

A list<T> container stores elements of type T in a linked list. You use a list container when you want to store elements in a sequence and be able to insert or delete elements in the interior of the sequence. A list<T> container is conceptually like the linked list that you developed in Chapter 14, but considerably more sophisticated. For one thing, a list<T> container maintains forward and backward pointers for the list elements so that the list can be traversed in either direction. A possible organization for elements in a list container is shown in Figure 20-4.

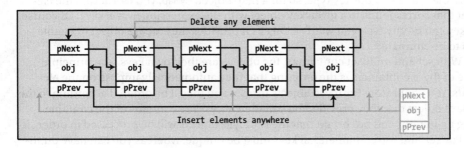

Figure 20-4. An example of a list

When you're using a list, you can efficiently insert an element at any point in the sequence—no moving of existing elements is necessary. All that has to happen is that the pNext and pPrev pointers shown in Figure 20-4 for the elements on either side of the insertion position for your new element need to be set to point to the new element. Deleting any element from a list is also a fast operation. The major limitation of a list container is that accessing elements at random is slow because it involves finding each element that you want by stepping through the list starting from the first or the last element. The general STL sort() algorithm can't be applied to a list because it requires an iterator that provides random access to the elements. However, you can still sort the contents of a list container by using the sort() function that is built in to it.

Container adapters are templates that take a sequence container template as a parameter to create templates for modified versions of a basic sequence container. The container adapters provide you with templates for stack container classes, which provide first-in last-out storage; queue container classes, which provide first-in first-out storage; and priority_queue containers, which provide storage where the next object to be retrieved is always the largest in the container. You also have a specialization of the vector template defined in the STL that is optimized to store elements of type bool.

Associative Containers

Associative containers allow you to store and retrieve objects of a given type rapidly using keys. The elements in an associative container are stored in an order determined by their keys. The Key objects that you use must at least be defined such that the < operator can be applied to them so that keys can be compared. I'll show you how this works later. Associative containers are of four basic types: map<Key, T>, multimap<Key, T>, set<Key>, and multiset<Key>.

With a map or a multimap container, each object of type T is stored in the container along with its associated key object of potentially a different type, Key. To retrieve an object from a container, you just need to supply its key. For example, you could store Employee objects in an associative container using personnel numbers, say, of type long, as keys for the objects. You could use a map<Employee, long> container instance to do this. You can then retrieve any Employee object from the container by supplying the appropriate personnel number as the key. The Employee objects that you store in the container will be ordered in ascending sequence of their personnel numbers.

A very useful characteristic of a map container is that you can use it as an **associative array**. An associative array is an array that permits access to its elements through an index that can be any kind of object. A map implements the subscript operator, [ ], where the index is of the key type, so for a map object, mymap, you can access the element that corresponds to a given key object with the expression mymap[key]. Of course, the key can be any type you want as long as it provides the Compare object to enable keys to be compared.

With set and multiset containers, the objects are their own keys. The principle value of these containers is the ordering that they automatically impose on the elements. You could store Employee objects in a set and they'll be ordered according to the Compare object that they provide. You can then access the contents of the container using an iterator and be certain that the Employee objects will be processed in order.

For set and map containers, all keys must be unique, whereas you can have duplicate keys in the multiset and multimap containers. You also have a bitset container template that creates classes for storing and operating on sequences of bits that are of a fixed size.

STL Iterators

As I've already said, an **iterator** is a form of smart pointer. You use iterators to access the elements that you've stored in a container when you are processing them in some way, and in particular when you are applying an STL algorithm to them. You can obtain an iterator object from a container that'll allow you to step through the elements that you've stored in the container by applying the increment operator to the iterator so that you can move from one object to the next. You may be able to use other operations with an iterator, but this will depend on what kind of container you are using.

You'll also come across iterators in the STL that you can use to transfer objects to or from a stream. The STL algorithms expect to receive input from an iterator. Therefore you can apply the algorithms to objects that are available from any source that is accessible through an iterator. This means, for instance, that algorithms can be applied directly to objects from a stream as well as to objects from a container. They can also be applied in any context in which you can provide an acceptable iterator; later in this chapter you'll see what such an iterator involves.

There are four categories of iterators with different levels of capability. I'll show these categories ordered from the simplest to the most complex:

1. **Input and output iterators** are used to read or write a sequence of objects and are single use only. If you need to read or write a sequence a second time, then you must create a new input or output iterator. The operations that you can apply to these iterators are ++iter or iter++, iter1==iter2 and iter1!= iter2, and *iter, but only read access in the case of input iterators, and only write access in the case of output iterators. You can use iter->member for input iterators only.

2. **Forward iterators** combine the capabilities of both the input and output iterators. You can also reuse a forward iterator to read or write a sequence of objects more than once.

3. **Bidirectional iterators** provide the same capabilities as forward iterators but allow traversal backward and forward through a sequence of objects. Therefore you can apply --iter and iter-- operators to these iterators.

4. **Random access iterators** provide the same capabilities as bidirectional iterators but also allow elements to be read or written at random. In addition to the operations permitted for bidirectional iterators, these iterators support the following operations: iter+n or iter-n; iter[n], which is equivalent to *(iter+n); iter += n or iter -+ n; iter1-iter2; and iter1<iter2, iter1>iter2, iter1<=iter2, or iter1>=iter2.

The capabilities of the iterators in this list are cumulative, with each category of iterator adding to the capabilities of its predecessor. Thus, the input and output iterators are the least capable and the random access iterators are the most capable. If an algorithm requires an iterator of a given type, then you can't use an inferior iterator. However, you can always use a superior iterator if you wish. The forward, bidirectional, and random access iterators can also be **mutable** or **constant**, depending on whether dereferencing the iterator produces a reference or a reference to a constant. You can't place the result of dereferencing a constant iterator on the left of an assignment.

The characteristics of the iterator that you obtain from a container depend on the type of the container. A random access iterator is supplied by vector and deque containers. The list, map, multimap, set, and multiset containers supply bidirectional iterators.

STL Algorithms

Algorithms provide computational and analysis functions for sets of objects that you access using iterators. Because they access data elements through iterators, you can apply algorithms to the contents of a container, but you can also apply them to any sequence that can be accessed through an iterator, so you can also apply them to streams.

The algorithms are the largest collection of tools in the STL. A relatively small proportion of these are relevant to a large number of applications though, and some of them are quite specialized in their use. I won't cover the STL algorithms comprehensively in this chapter, but I'll apply some of them in the examples.

Three broad categories of algorithms exist:

1. **Non-modifying sequence operations** don't change the sequence to which they are applied in any way. Operations in this category include find(), find_end(), find_first(), adjacent_find(), count(), mismatch(), search(), and equal().

2. **Mutating sequence operations** do change the elements in a sequence. Operations in this category include swap(), copy(), transform(), replace(), remove(), reverse(), rotate(), fill(), and random_shuffle().

3. **Sorting, merging, and related operations** may in some instances change the order of the sequences to which they are applied. Operations in this category include sort(), stable_sort(), binary_search(), merge(), min(), max(), and lexicographical_compare().

Note that the examples that are mentioned in these categories don't represent an exhaustive list of what is available.

Some of these operations, such as transform(), need **function objects** to work. Function objects are class objects that overload the function call operator, operator()(), and are specifically designed to pass a function as an argument more efficiently than using a raw function pointer.

Numerical Algorithms

The <numeric> header declares function templates for algorithms for numerical processing. Although these are not part of the STL, they can be used with containers because they work with iterators.

Table 20-1 shows the templates for functions that carry out numerical algorithms declared in the <numeric> header.

Table 20-1. Templates for Numerical Algorithms

Template	Description
accumulate<>	Functions generated by this template compute the sum of elements in a range that is specified by iterators.
adjacent_difference<>	Functions generated by this template compute successive differences between adjacent elements in the specified range and output the results to another specified range.
inner_product<>	Functions generated by this template compute the inner product of two ranges and add it to a specified initial value.
partial_sum<>	Functions generated by this template compute successive sums from the first to the nth element in a specified range and output the results to another specified range.

These may not be particular meaningful to you if you aren't familiar with the sorts of problems in which these algorithms are important, in which case you can ignore them.

STL Headers

Table 20-2 shows the headers in which the containers that are provided by the STL are declared.

Table 20-2. Headers for STL Containers

File	Description
`<vector>`	Single-ended array container
`<deque>`	Double-ended array container
`<list>`	Bidirectional linked list container
`<map>`	Map and multimap associative array container
`<set>`	Set and multiset ordered set container
`<bitset>`	Objects representing sequences of bits
`<queue>`	Double-ended queue (container adapter)
`<stack>`	Stack (container adapter)

The declarations you need for iterator support are in the `<iterator>` header, but the headers that provide the container declarations also include this header. Thus, you only need to include the `<iterator>` header into your source file if you aren't using a container. The `<utility>` header contains the declarations you need to define and manage key/value pairs that are used by the map and multimap containers, so this header is automatically included by the `<map>` header.

The declarations for algorithms that you can apply to containers and other sequences accessible through an iterator are in the `<algorithm>` header. Support for function objects is provided by declarations that are in the `<functional>` header.

The library of algorithms for numerical processing is not strictly part of the STL, but these algorithms are compatible with the STL because they work through iterators. The declarations required for the numerical algorithms are in the `<numeric>` header. Two other headers provide useful capabilities in the numerical processing context. The `<complex>` header provides support for complex numbers and the `<valarray>` header supports arrays of numerical values.

In addition, some iterators declared in the family of stream headers—`<iostream>`, `<istream>`, `<ostream>`, and `<sstream>`—work with STL to support input and output based on the fundamental STL algorithms.

Using the vector Container

As you've seen, the vector container mimics an ordinary C++ array. In fact, you can use this container almost anywhere you might use a C++ array. However, a vector is much easier to use than a C++ array. With an array, you must take on the responsibility of managing the size and capacity of the array yourself, but with a vector, all of this is automated within the container. An ordinary array is fixed in size but a vector container automatically expands its capacity as required. Once you get used to using vector containers, you may decide never to use a plain array again.

Creating a vector Container

You can create an empty vector that stores elements of type int with the statement:

```
std::vector<int> numbers;
```

This calls the default constructor for the container class that is created using the template parameter argument, int, and the default constructor creates a container with an initial capacity and size of zero. As we said earlier, the capacity is the number of elements that can be stored in a container at any given time, and the size is the number of elements actually stored. This isn't a very useful way of creating a vector. Each time you add a new element, the capacity needs to be extended and this involves copying existing elements to a new enlarged area of memory. In general, you should try to create your vector container with a capacity that approximates to what you'll need. For example, here's how you could create a vector with ten elements of type int:

```
std::vector<int> samples(10);
```

This vector will have ten elements initialized with zero.

Of course, you could also create a vector to hold your Box objects:

```
std::vector<Box> boxes(20);
```

This creates a vector of 20 Box objects where each element is initialized with a Box object created by calling the default Box class constructor.

This does imply that the Box class must have a default constructor for this to work. This raises the question of what exactly the requirements are for a type T to be acceptable in a container. The bare minimum for type T looks like this:

```
class T{
  public:
    T();                        // default constructor
    T(const T& t);              // Copy constructor
    ~T();                       // Destructor
    T& operator=(const T& t);   // Assignment operator
};
```

Note that operator<() is not strictly required and therefore hasn't been included in the above definition for T. However, it's best to provide a definition for ordering your elements whenever it makes sense. If you don't, your element class will be unusable as keys in any of the associative containers such as map and set, and your element sequences won't work with any of the ordering algorithms. Considering that the compiler provides default implementations for all of these in many circumstances, most class types should qualify for use in a container.

Note that you can change the size (*not* the capacity) of a vector container by calling its resize() function with the argument specifying a new value for the number of elements. If the new size is less than the old, elements are deleted from the end of the sequence. If the new size is greater than the old, elements are added at the end of the sequence with the new elements being created by the default constructor for the type of element stored. For fundamental types, this is the type equivalent of zero. You can set a minimum for the capacity of a vector by calling its reserve() member with a number of elements as the argument. If the value that you pass to reserve() is less than the current capacity, the capacity is left unchanged.

You can't initialize a vector container directly with a set of static initializers. Instead, you can use a C++ array to declare the set of initializers that you want to use to initialize the contents of a container:

```
int values[] = { 99, 136, 247, 459, 679, 871, 928, 1045, 1300, 1302 };
```

You can now copy these to the vector of int elements like this:

```
for(int i = 0 ; i<sizeof values/sizeof values[0] ; i++)
  samples[i] = values[i];
```

This uses the subscript operator with the container to store each element value in exactly the same way as you access the elements in the ordinary array, values.

Another possibility is to use a constructor that accepts a range of initializing values specified as an interval in some external source of elements:

```
std::vector<int> samples(values, values+sizeof values/sizeof values[0]);
```

This constructor requires the interval to be specified by two arguments that are iterators, but because a pointer is a perfectly good iterator, you can use pointers to elements of the array here. The two arguments specify the range of values as a **semi-open interval**. A semi-open interval is one where one of the range limits is included in the set of values—in this case, the first—but the other is not.

A further possibility for creating a vector is to initialize all of the elements to a given value. Here's how you can create a vector of 50 elements of type double that are each initialized with the value 3.14159:

```
std::vector<double>(50, 3.14159);
```

The first argument is the number of elements in the container and they'll all be initialized with the value specified by the second argument.

Let's jump right in and use a vector container in an example.

Try It Out: Comparing vector<> with the C++ Array

In this example, you'll take a look at an int array and a vector of elements of type int and compare the way that they function.

```cpp
// Program 20.1 A quick comparison of array and vector  File: prog20_01.cpp
#include <iostream>
#include <vector>
using std::cout;
using std::endl;
using std::vector;

int main() {
  int a[10];                      // C++ array declaration
  vector<int> v(10);              // Equivalent STL vector declaration

  cout << "size of 10 element array:  " << sizeof a << endl;
  cout << "size of 10 element vector: " << sizeof v << endl;

  for (int i = 0; i < 10; ++i)
    a[i] = v[i] = i;

  int a_sum = 0, v_sum = 0;
  for (int i = 0; i < 10; ++i) {
    a_sum += a[i];
    v_sum += v[i];
  }

  cout << "sum of 10 array  elements: " << a_sum << endl;
  cout << "sum of 10 vector elements: " << v_sum << endl;

  vector<int> vnew(a, a+sizeof a/sizeof a[0]);  // Initialized from an interval
  int vnew_sum = 0;
  for (int i = 0; i < vnew.size(); ++i)
   vnew_sum += vnew[i];
    cout << "sum of 10 new vector elements: " << v_sum << endl;

  return 0;
}
```

When you run this program, it produces this output:

```
size of 10 element array:   40
size of 10 element vector: 16
sum of 10 array  elements: -8
sum of 10 vector elements: -8
sum of 10 new vector elements: -8
```

All STL objects are part of the standard library and are therefore defined within the namespace std. Of course, you must include the appropriate headers for the STL facilities you need *before* you use them, and if you don't want to use names qualified with std, you can provide a using declaration for each of the names you are using, as I've done here.

The only difference between using an array and a vector in your code is in the following declarations:

```
int a[10];                    // C++ array declaration
vector<int> v(10);            // Equivalent STL vector declaration
```

The C++ array is a built-in language type declared with [ ] syntax. The vector is a STL type implemented as a **class template**. The template parameter specifies the type of objects that the vector contains. In this case, you declare a vector to hold objects of type int.

In this example, the array a and the vector v are both automatic variables. For the array, this means that storage for 10 integers is created in automatic storage. On my machine, a variable of type int takes up 4 bytes of memory so the array a occupies 40 bytes, as you can see from the output.

Although the vector object, v, is automatic, it internally allocates space on the free store to hold the elements. Initially, it obtains at least enough storage for the number of elements specified. The vector's internal mechanism handles all the problems of storage allocation, and obtaining enough free store memory to hold whatever you put into it (subject to the size of your free store).

The size obtained for the vector object using the sizeof operator doesn't include the space needed to store the elements. For this reason, this kind of object is often called a **handle**. It only contains enough memory to allow the vector to manage the storage of its elements. You can see that the vector object, v, occupies only 16 bytes. The *real* contents of v—the space needed to contain the values or objects that it stores—are allocated dynamically and take up another 40 bytes in the free store.

Clearly, the array object uses less storage than the vector container. However, the overhead for a vector object is very low. A drawback of the array object is that it's allocated on the program stack and the space and number of elements are fixed at compile time. The compensation for the small overhead of vector is twofold: first, your memory management is performed automatically, and second, you can add more elements to the vector as and when you need them.

The last output shows that using the constructor that accepts initial values specified by a semi-open interval works as described. The sum of the elements for the vector vnew is the same as for the array a and the vector v.

Accessing Elements in a vector Container

You can access elements in a vector container in a variety of ways. You can use the subscript operator as you've already seen or you can use an iterator (a smart pointer); with either mechanism elements can be accessed sequentially or at random. You can also access particular elements through function members of the container. This is illustrated in Figure 20-4.

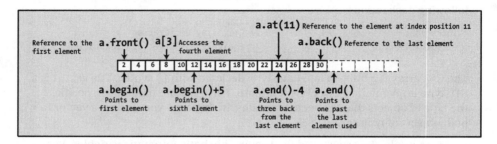

Figure 20-5. Accessing elements in a vector

Figure 20-5 shows a vector, a, that stores elements of type int. The container is in a state where values have been stored in the first 15 elements and the capacity is 20. The begin() member of a vector object returns an object of type iterator that points to the first element. The iterator type is defined within the vector object to be a pointer to the type of object stored. The end() member returns an iterator that points one beyond the last element of the vector. You can use these iterators to run through the elements of a vector if you wish—just increment the iterator returned by begin() until it equals the iterator returned by end(). Here is an example:

```
std::vector<double> pies(20, 3.141259);  // Vector with 20 elements
double sum_pies = 0.0;
for(std::vector<double>::iterator iter = pies.begin()
                              ; iter != pies.end() ; iter++)
  sum_pies += *iter;                // Add the object pointed to by iter
```

This sums the elements of the pies vector that you've created using the iterator returned by the begin() member function. The variable, iter, that you use to store this is of type std::vector<double>::iterator, which is the iterator type defined within your container class. You increment the iterator in the for loop until it is equal to the iterator returned by the end() member function. To access an element to add it to sum_pies, you just dereference the iterator in exactly the way you would dereference an ordinary pointer.

Of course, you could also use the subscript operator, [ ], to implement the previous loop:

```
for(int i = 0 ; i<pies.size() ; i++)
  sum_pies += pies[i];
```

You can apply arithmetic operations to the iterators that you get from a vector container, and the effect is the same as with an ordinary pointer. Adding 5 to the iterator returned by the begin() function results in a pointer to the element that is five positions further along. You can also apply the increment and decrement operators to iterators in the same way that you can to ordinary pointers. To access an element, you can use the subscript operator. In Figure 20-5, a[4] accesses the fifth element in the vector. The expression *(a.begin()+4) would also access the fifth element in the vector because the begin() member of a returns an iterator that initially points to the first element in the vector.

The front(), back(), and at() member functions return references to elements; you use these or the subscript operator when you want to work directly with the elements. To demonstrate these, I could rewrite the loop summing the elements of pies as follows:

```
double sum_pies = pies.front();
for(int i = 1 ; i<pies.size() ; i++)
  sum_pies += pies.at(i);
```

Reverse Iterators

The vector container can also supply **reverse iterators** that are designed to iterate through the elements backward, from last to first. The member rbegin() returns an iterator of type reverse_iterator that points to the last element in the vector; incrementing this iterator moves the pointer to the previous element. The rend() member function returns an iterator that points to the position preceding the first element in the vector. You could rewrite the pies loop to use reverse iterators:

```
for(std::vector<double>::reverse_iterator iter = pies.rbegin()
                               ; iter != pies.rend() ; iter++)
  sum_pies += *iter;              // Add the object pointed to by iter
```

This looks very similar to what you had previously, but the process is quite different. The elements are summed starting with the last and working back to the first.

Basic Operations on a vector Container

Working with a vector is far more flexible than working with a regular array. As I've said, you can add new elements at the end of a vector or delete the last element, and the space needed to accommodate the number of elements in the vector will always be taken care of automatically. You can also insert or delete elements in the interior of the vector if you are prepared to accept the overhead. The basic vector operations to add or remove elements are listed in Table 20-3.

Table 20-3. Operations for Adding or Removing Elements

Operation	Description
push_back()	Adds the object that is passed as an argument to the end of the vector.
pop_back()	Removes the object that is at the end of the vector.
erase()	Erases one or more elements.
clear()	Erases all elements.
insert()	Inserts one or more objects. This capability is provide through two member functions plus a function template. The function template enables you to insert elements from another container into a vector. In order for a single object to be inserted, the first argument needs to be an iterator that specifies the insertion position, and the second argument needs to be the object to be inserted. As I noted earlier, it's best to avoid this operation when you're using vector containers.

The empty() member function provides you with the means to avoid attempting to access elements in a vector that is empty. The function returns true if the vector contains no elements.

To understand how some of these operations work, try them out in the following example.

Try It Out: Exercising a vector Container

This program runs through the simple vector operations that I've just introduced. You'll try adding and removing some elements from a vector object and exercise various ways of inspecting the vector's contents.

In this example, the function show_sequence() has been written to demonstrate the use of the copy() algorithm in conjunction with a stream iterator to produce output. The inspect_vector() function that you use to output the contents of a vector at various points calls the show_sequence() function with iterator arguments.

```cpp
// Program 20.2 Manipulations of the vector<> container  File: prog20_02.cpp
#include <iostream>
#include <vector>                          // For the vector container
#include <algorithm>                       // For the copy() function
using std::cout;
using std::endl;
using std::vector;

// Display a sequence of elements
void show_sequence(vector<int>::const_iterator first,
                        vector<int>::const_iterator last) {
  cout << "{ ";
  std::copy(first, last, std::ostream_iterator<int>(cout, " "));
  cout << "}" << endl;
}

// Display the contents of a vector
```

```
void inspect_vector(const vector<int>& v) {
  cout << "  vector has " << v.size() << " elements: ";
  show_sequence(v.begin(), v.end());
}

int main() {
  vector<int> v;                        // Create empty vector
  cout << "new vector created" << endl;
  inspect_vector(v);

  cout << "filling vector from array" << endl;
  int values[] = {1, 3, 7, 5};
  v.insert(v.end(), values+1, values+3);    // Insert two elements
  inspect_vector(v);

  cout << "appending value 5" << endl;
  v.push_back(5);                       // Add an element at the end
  inspect_vector(v);

  cout << "erasing element at offset 1" << endl;
  v.erase(&v[1]);                       // Remove the second element
  inspect_vector(v);

  cout << "inserting element 4 at offset 1" << endl;
  v.insert (v.begin()+1, 4);            // Insert an element
  inspect_vector(v);

  cout << "clearing all elements" << endl;
  v.clear();                            // Delete all elements
  inspect_vector(v);

  return 0;
}
```

The output summarizes the contents of the vector object after each vector operation:

```
new vector created
  vector has 0 elements: { }
filling vector from array
  vector has 2 elements: { 3 7 }
appending value 5
  vector has 3 elements: { 3 7 5 }
erasing element at offset 1
  vector has 2 elements: { 3 5 }
inserting element 4 at offset 1
  vector has 3 elements: { 3 4 5 }
clearing all elements
  vector has 0 elements: { }
```

(Continued)

You can see that the vector container is good at keeping track of what it contains. With an array, you'd have to shovel all these elements around the hard way.

HOW IT WORKS

The code begins with #include directives for two of the STL headers:

```
#include <vector>                    // For the vector container
#include <algorithm>                 // For the copy() function
```

The <vector> header defines the vector container and all of its built-in operations. The <algorithm> header provides the operations that you can apply to a container, and here you'll be using the copy() function.

Next, you define the function show_sequence() that displays a sequence of elements:

```
void show_sequence(vector<int>::const_iterator first,
                        vector<int>::const_iterator last) {
  cout << "{ ";
  std::copy(first, last, std::ostream_iterator<int>(cout, " "));
  cout << "}" << endl;
}
```

The values are passed to the function as a semi-open interval defined by two iterators of type vector<int>const_iterator. This type is a const iterator type for the elements in your vector. If the parameter to your inspect_vector() function hadn't been declared as const, you could use the type vector<int>iterator for the parameters to your show_sequence() function. The iterator type is defined inside the vector<T> template by a typedef as an iterator that points to an object of type T. The const_iterator type is similarly defined as an iterator type that points to const T.

The show_sequence() function uses the STL algorithm, copy(), to output to cout an interval of values referenced through a pair of pointers. The first two arguments of copy() are iterators that define the source interval in the container from which the elements are being copied. Copying begins with first and proceeds up to, but doesn't include, last. The copy() function accepts any iterators for its first two arguments.

The third argument to the copy() function is an iterator that specifies the destination position for the elements that are being copied. In this example, you supply an output iterator that is created by the expression ostream_iterator<int>(cout, " ") for the destination position. The first argument, cout, is the stream to which this iterator applies. The second argument is the delimiter to be used to separate the elements that are transferred. The copy() algorithm assigns each source element into your destination object without knowing exactly what kind of destination object it's dealing with. The copy() function just passes the objects to be copied to the iterator specified by the third argument and assumes that the iterator knows where to put them. This makes the copy() function independent of the source and destination of the objects it is copying. In this case, the destination object transfers each value that is copied to the standard output stream, cout.

The inspect_vector() function outputs the entire contents of a vector by calling the show_sequence() function:

```
void inspect_vector(const vector<int>& v) {
  cout << "  vector has " << v.size() << " elements: ";
  show_sequence(v.begin(), v.end());
}
```

Notice that you're passing a vector object as a single argument. You don't need to pass a second argument that indicates how many elements the vector contains because you can always obtain the number of elements in a vector by calling its size() member. The value that the size() function returns is of type size_type, which is an unsigned integer type.

You obtain iterators to the first and last elements in your vector object by calling its begin() and end() members, and you pass these to the show_sequence() function.

As you've already seen, v.begin() points to the first element of the sequence. You can access the first element of the sequence by writing the expression *v.begin(), or v[0], or simply v.front(). Generally, you'll choose the expression to suit the particular context in which you're working.

Of course, you can't access the element pointed to by the iterator that is returned by end() because it points to the address one step *past* the last element in the container. However, the expression *(v.end()-1) is a legal and useful way to gain access to the very last value of a sequence. You can also access the last element of a sequence by using the expression *(v.begin()+v.size()-1), or v[v.size()-1], or simply v.back().

Before you attempt to access an element, be sure that the container has elements. You can check this with the v.empty() member, which returns true when the vector v contains no elements at all.

Your program uses the vector instance vector<int>, so you get a vector container that stores int values:

```
vector<int> v;                    // Create empty vector
```

Here you declare v as an instance of a class template vector<int> by calling the default constructor. You can see from the program output that your new vector starts life in the empty state.

(Continued)

You have many ways in which you can put values into your new vector. One of the most powerful ways of adding several elements to a vector is to use the insert() member function. You've used this in the example to copy an entire sequence into v:

```
cout << "filling vector from array" << endl;
int values[] = {1, 3, 7, 5};
v.insert(v.end(), values+1, values+3);        // Insert two elements
inspect_vector(v);
```

Here you can see again that the STL likes to define a sequence as an interval delimited by a pair of iterators. The first argument to the insert() function, v.end(), is a pointer to the location where you want the new elements to be inserted. Note that you're using the past-the-end value here—it's legitimate to use this address when you're adding to the end of a vector.

The second and third arguments to insert(), the expressions values+1 and values+3, together specify the extent of the source sequence to be inserted. This demonstrates that you can use ordinary pointers in place of iterators. Your source sequence is the array, and you copy only the second and third elements—that is, beginning at values+1 and ending at the element preceding the position, values+3. Intervals are typically specified like this in the STL. As you saw earlier, an interval that includes the first position but excludes the last is referred to as a semi-open interval. You'll sometimes see them written as [begin, end), where the square bracket indicates that the interval is closed at the left end and the parenthesis indicates that it's open at the right end. Thus, the interval includes the position begin but not the position end.

 CAUTION *When you specify* [begin, end) *intervals, such as with the expressions* values+1 *and* values+3, *make certain that the end expression is larger than the begin expression and that both iterators or both pointers are associated with the same source object. These are common mistakes you may make when specifying intervals using iterators.*

Let's return to the discussion of Program 20.2. Now you add an element using the push_back() member of the vector:

```
v.push_back(5);                         // Add an element at the end
```

This adds the value 5 as a new element, tacked on to the end of the vector v.

Next, you exercise the erase() operation:

```
v.erase(&v[1]);                         // Remove the second element
```

This statement removes the second element from the vector v by passing the address of the element to be removed to the erase() function. It uses the simplest form of erase(), which takes a single iterator argument that specifies a single element to be removed from v. Typically, you can use a pointer argument instead of an iterator, and the expression &v[1] is the address of the second element of v. As a result of this statement, the second element, whose value is 7, is eliminated from v.

Next, insert a new element with this statement:

```
v.insert (v.begin()+1, 4);          // Insert an element
```

You've already used insert() previously, with two iterator arguments. In this form of insert(), the two arguments are an iterator and an integer. You specify an interior position in the container using the expression v.begin()+1 and insert the new element—the value 4—at this destination position. The element that is currently occupying the destination position and all the following elements must be moved so that the new arrival can be inserted. Once again, the vector object allocates new space and copies elements as necessary to keep things organized.

 NOTE *All this automatic copying is very convenient. However, your programs certainly slow to a crawl if the vector is large and insertions and erasures near the front are frequent.*

You use clear() to erase all the elements from the vector explicitly:

```
v.clear();                          // Delete all elements
```

However, this is not a necessity here. When the vector instance v goes out of scope (at the end of the enclosing block), v and the contents of v are all cleaned up automatically by the destructor for v. In fact, v.clear() is equivalent to the expression v.erase(v.begin(), v.end()).

....

Using vector Containers with Array Operations

Let's return for a moment to an example that you first encountered when we discussed functions back in Chapter 8. This is the average() function from Program 8.5, and it is interesting because it takes an array[] argument:

```
// Function to compute an average
double average(double array[], int count) {
  double sum = 0.0;                 // Accumulate total in here
  for(int i = 0 ; i < count ; i++)
    sum += array[i];                // Sum array elements

  return sum/count;                 // Return average
}
```

Before the STL came on the scene, all C and C++ programs were written in this style. In spite of everything you've waded through since Chapter 8, you can probably still recall that double array[] and double* array in this context mean exactly the same thing, so the first argument to average() is a pointer. Because an array doesn't know how many elements it contains, you always need to pass an extra argument indicating this. (If the array wasn't fully occupied and the function was to add elements to the array, you'd need to pass the size of the array and the number of elements occupied to the function.)

Now let's look again at your show_sequence() function, from Program 20.2. This function *also* takes a pointer in the form of an iterator as its first argument, but it uses a very different idiom. The second argument is also a pointer:

```
void show_sequence(vector<int>::const_iterator first,
                   vector<int>::const_iterator last) {
  cout << "{ ";
  copy(first, last, ostream_iterator<int>(cout, " "));
  cout << "}" << endl;
}
```

The interval between first and last is a semi-open interval—first is contained in the interval, but last is not. This is significantly different from using a pair of index values. An index value simply denotes a position, whereas an iterator encapsulates the type of the object pointed to as well as its position.

Although using an interval to specify a subset of the elements in a vector is different from having an array and a variable count indicating the number of elements, it is still very easy to find out how many elements you're working with:

```
int count = last - first;
```

So why does the STL work with intervals rather than arrays and counts? There are several reasons. First, when you're doing a lot of work with arrays, working with pointers is usually more convenient. Second, using pointers can be a lot more efficient than using indexes. Third, and perhaps most important, an iterator encapsulates the type of the object as well as its position, so you can write algorithms to use iterators so that they can be applied to objects of any type from virtually any source.

Computing Averages Using Iterators

You could define a template for the average() function that uses iterators instead of arrays. The code for the template in this case would be

```
template <typename Iter>
double average (Iter begin, Iter end) {
  double sum = 0.0;
  int count = end-begin;
  for(begin != end)
    sum += *begin++;
  return sum/(count == 0.0 ? 1.0 : count);
}
```

Notice how few operations we perform on the parameter, begin. Table 20-4 lists these.

Table 20-4. Operations Performed on the begin *Parameter*

Operation	Function
end-begin	Calculates the difference, which is the object count
begin != end	Checks for last value
*begin	Obtains the current value
begin++	Advances to the next value

In the preceding code, the last two were combined into the single expression *begin++. The way the template is coded implies that the operations * and postfix ++ must work for the type Iter, and that this is the case for either pointer types or iterators. Using iterators has simplified the code quite a bit. Let's take it for a run.

....

Try It Out: Computing Averages with Template Iterators

Here's a program that calculates averages using your template:

```cpp
// Program 20.3 Computing the average function with template iterators
//  File: prog20_03.cpp
#include <iostream>
#include <vector>
using std::cout;
using std::endl;
using std::vector;

template <typename Iter>
double average (Iter begin, Iter end) {
  double sum = 0.0;
  int count = end-begin;
  while(begin != end)
    sum += *begin++;
  return sum/(count == 0.0 ? 1.0 : count);
}

int main() {
  double temperature[] = { 10.5, 20.0, 8.5 };
  cout << "array average = "
       << average(temperature,
                     temperature+sizeof temperature/sizeof temperature[0])
       << endl;

  vector<int> sunny;
  sunny.push_back(7);
  sunny.push_back(12);
  sunny.push_back(15);
```

(Continued)

```
    cout << sunny.size() << " months on record" << endl;
    cout << "average number of sunny days: ";
    cout << average(sunny.begin(), sunny.end()) << endl;

    return 0;
}
```

The output from this program is as follows:

```
array average = 13
3 months on record
average number of sunny days: 11.3333
```

HOW IT WORKS

The great thing about templates is that you get as many versions as you want for the price of one. This example generates two instances of the function template average.

The first instantiation of average is for values stored in a regular C++ array:

```
double temperature[] = { 10.5, 20.0, 8.5 };
cout << "array average = "
    << average(temperature,
                    temperature+sizeof temperature/sizeof temperature[0])
    << endl;
```

The instance is created as a result of the output statement. The type for the template instance is determined implicitly from the function arguments. The second argument must be a pointer to the element *after* the last element you want to include; you calculate this by adding the number of elements in the array to the pointer, temperature.

The second instantiation of average is for values stored in a vector container of values of type int. First you declare the vector<int> object, sunny:

```
vector<int> sunny;
```

Then the instantiation of the function template is generated by the following statement:

```
cout << average(sunny.begin(), sunny.end()) << endl;
```

The values returned by sunny.begin() and sunny.end() are of type vector<int>::iterator and this type is used to instantiate the second version of the template. Consequently, the two instantiations of the template function average() have the following prototypes:

```
double average<double*>(double* begin, double* end);
double average<vector<int>::iterator>(vector<int>::iterator begin,
                                        vector<int>::iterator end);
```

As you can see from the output, the calculation of the averages proceeds as expected. Your function works just as well with elements in a `vector` container as it does with an ordinary array.

Although this version of the average template works well in most situations, it won't work with stream iterators because the number of objects available from the stream is not known in advance, and therefore can't be computed as end-begin. In this case, you must accumulate the total in `count` within the loop. This would work equally well here of course.

The Template Array Alternative

In Program 20.3, you used the interval convention for your template. Of course, you could still have used iterators with the template using the array idiom.

Try It Out: Computing Averages with Template Arrays

Here's an alternative version of Program 20.3:

```cpp
// Program 20.4 Computing an average with template arrays  File: prog20_04.cpp
#include <iostream>
#include <vector>
using std::cout;
using std::endl;
using std::vector;

template <typename Array>
double average(Array a, long count) { // Array can be a pointer or an iterator
  double sum = 0.0;
  for (long i = 0L; i<count; ++i)
    sum += a[i];
  return sum/(count==0.0 ? 1.0 : count);
}

int main() {
  double temperature[] = { 10.5, 20.0, 8.5 };

  // second argument is now the count
  cout << "array average = "
       << average(temperature, sizeof temperature/sizeof temperature[0])
       << endl;

  vector<int> sunny;
  sunny.push_back(7);
  sunny.push_back(12);
  sunny.push_back(15);
```

(Continued)

```
    cout << sunny.size() << " months on record" << endl;
    cout << "average number of sunny days: ";
    cout << average(sunny.begin(), sunny.end() - sunny.begin()) << endl;
    return 0;
}
```

The output for this program is the same as Program 20.3, but the code looks simpler. Note how you now only need one operation on the element a, namely a.operator[](long). You can see from this notation that the subscript operator takes an argument of type long to represent the index value. However, in this version, you also have to create the loop variable i here—and you have to increment and compare it with count on each iteration. With the previous version that was unnecessary.

Using an Input Stream Iterator

The next example shows how you can combine template algorithms with unusual kinds of iterators. You've seen ostream_iterator in action already—this time you use its complement, istream_iterator, to obtain data from an input stream. Both stream iterators are defined in the <iostream> header.

Try It Out: Using the istream_iterator<>

In the Programs 20.3 and 20.4, you used your average() function on values that already existed in an array or container. This time, the average() function obtains values directly from an input stream just by using another instance of the function template. You'll use a variation of the average() function template from Program 20.3:

```
// Program 20.5 Taking the average of values from a stream  File: prog20_05.cpp
#include <iostream>
#include <iterator>                 // For the istream_iterator<> template
using std::cout;
using std::endl;
using std::cin;
using std::istream_iterator;

template <typename Iter>
double average (Iter begin, Iter end) {
  double sum = 0.0;
  int count = 0;
  for(;begin != end; count++)
    sum += *begin++;
  return sum/(count == 0.0 ? 1.0 : count);
}
```

```
int main() {
    cout << "Enter some real numbers separated by whitespace - spaces, " << endl
         << "tabs or newline. Then press the special key sequence " << endl
         << "that marks the end-of-file (Ctrl-Z on a PC)" << endl;

    double av = average(istream_iterator<double>(cin), istream_iterator<double>());
    cout << "The average value is " << av << endl;
    return 0;
}
```

 CAUTION *When you run the example, take care to use the right convention for closing the input stream. In the PC world, the magic keystroke for this purpose is Ctrl+Z and in the Unix world it is Ctrl+D. You may then need to press Enter. One popular programming environment comes from a company that needs to hear everything twice, so if at first you don't succeed in closing the stream, try pressing Ctrl+Z a few times on separate lines.*

Here's what the program output can look like:

```
Enter some real numbers separated by whitespace - spaces,
tabs or newline. Then press the special key sequence
that marks the end-of-file (Ctrl-Z on a PC)
  3.6
  4.5
  5.7
  ^Z
The average value is 4.6
```

Your system may display something slightly different.

HOW IT WORKS

The following statement generates an instance of your template:

```
double av = average(istream_iterator<double>(cin), istream_iterator<double>());
```

You're now passing some really strange-looking expressions into your average function. Let's write this another way so that you can take a closer look at it:

```
istream_iterator<double> begin(cin);
istream_iterator<double> end;
double av = average(begin, end);
```

(Continued)

The object begin is an instance of the template class istream_iterator<double>. The stream object cin is passed into the constructor so that the iterator reads from the standard input stream.

The object end is also an instance of istream_iterator<double>. You create end using the default constructor for the istream_iterator<double> class. The variable end, when created in this way, behaves like a past-the-end value that corresponds to end-of-file.

Your new versions of begin and end definitely aren't pointers, they're class objects, so why does this work? The obvious answer is that these class objects are iterators, which means that they can behave like pointers. They still provide the three operators that you're depending upon in your average() function, namely those in Table 20-5.

Table 20-5. Operators Required by the average() *Function*

Operator	Purpose
bool Iter::operator!=(Iter end_value);	Comparison
double Iter::operator*();	Dereference
Iter Iter::operator++(int);	Increment

This time, I have presented these as class functions because they really *are* class functions. They are overloaded operators functions in the class istream_iterator<double>. Remember that operator++(int) doesn't really take an int argument—that's just how you remind the compiler that you're specifying the postfix version of the increment operator. Any object of type istream_iterator<double> allows you to perform these operations.

Of course, you couldn't use the mechanism to calculate count that was in the version of the average template in Program 20.3. The number of input values is unknown when the template function is called, so the difference between the begin and end iterators can't be computed at this time. In fact, such an operation won't compile because the iterator has no operator-() function that will work with these iterators. Here you must determine count by incrementing its value in the loop. Although this version involves a little more work in the function, it will work equally well in Program 20.3, so this version is a little more general.

istream_iterator *Iterators with Functionality*

The istream_iterator objects in the previous example are pretending to be pointers, just as your BoxPtr class objects were in Program 14.6. However, these objects do much more. They provide you with the functionality of something as complex as stream I/O operators as well as acting as pointers. This is a fundamental concept that helps make the STL such a powerful library. Once you combine template functions and iterators, you can capture your intervals from *any* source and process them. You can't do that using the old array notation.

Try It Out: More istream_iterator<> Capability

To emphasize the general nature of iterators, I'll show you one final example. This time you'll exercise your semi-open interval around values contained in a string that you'll access as a stream using an iterator.

```cpp
// Program 20.6 Taking the average of values from a string stream.
// File: prog20_06.cpp
#include <iostream>
#include <iterator>
#include <string>
#include <sstream>                  // For the istringstream class
using std::cout;
using std::endl;
using std::istream_iterator;
using std::istringstream;
using std::string;

template <typename Iter>
double average(Iter begin, Iter end) {
  double sum = 0.0;
  int count = 0;
  for( ; begin != end ; ++count)
    sum += *begin++;
  return sum/(count == 0 ? 1 :count);
}

int main() {
  string stock_ticker = "4.5 6.75 8.25 7.5 5.75";
  istringstream ticker(stock_ticker);
  istream_iterator<double> begin(ticker);
  istream_iterator<double> end;

  cout << "Readings: " << stock_ticker
       << "Today's average is "
       << average (begin, end) << endl;
  return 0;
}
```

The program produces this output:

```
Readings: 4.5 6.75 8.25 7.5 5.75
Today's average is 6.55
```

(Continued)

If you look closely, you'll see that this is almost identical to Program 20.5, which read from the stream cin. The difference is that you've created your own stream, ticker, as a replacement for cin using the istringstream class:

```
string stock_ticker = "4.5 6.75 8.25";
istringstream ticker(stock_ticker);
```

You initialize your input stream, ticker, so that it takes its values directly from the string, stock_ticker. You then pass your stream object to the istream_iterator<double> constructor:

```
istream_iterator<double> begin(ticker);
```

The nice thing about your new stream ticker is that you can use it in most places where you might have put cin instead; istream_iterator isn't too fussy. It is happy taking your istringstream object ticker, or taking any stream that is a source of characters. Everything else remains essentially the same, including your average() template.

The Iterator Advantage

The most recent version of your template function average() is very flexible. If you used the same definition in the examples 20.3 through 20.6, you'd only create three unique instances of the template:

```
double average<double*>(double*, double*);
double average<int*>(int*, int*);
double average<istream_iterator<double>>
                    (istream_iterator<double>, istream_iterator<double>);
```

You can see that the first two instances deal with simple pointers, whereas the third deals with istream_iterator, which is a class object. In Program 20.3, for example, you passed elements from a vector<int> container into the average<int*> version. You got extra mileage from the use of istream_iterator; in Programs 20.5 and 20.6, it allowed you to read numeric values from the console and directly from a string. The pointer versions cover both basic C++ arrays and vectors, whereas the istream_iterator version covers both files and strings. And you've still barely scratched the surface, where iterators are concerned.

The iterator class object still looks rather mysterious, so let's dig a little deeper into how iterator class objects really work. You'll soon see that it's not that difficult to create iterator classes of your own.

Creating Your Own Iterators

You have some experience with a very simple iterator—from the BoxPtr class in Chapter 14—but you'll find that iterators are more complicated when the STL is involved. You can understand how the STL iterators work by building one of your own from the ground up. You'll start off with the simplest possible iterator and extend it until you get to where you want to be—a full member of the STL iterator fraternity with the maximum iterator functionality. That enables you to use your own iterators with the STL.

....

Try It Out: Creating Your Own Iterator

You'll start with a simple iterator that iterates over the integers. Here's the code for the definition of the Integer class:

```
// Integer.h Integer class definition
#ifndef INTEGER_H
#define INTEGER_H
#include <iostream>
using std::cout;
using std::endl;

class Integer {
  public:
    Integer (int arg = 0) : x(arg) {}

    bool operator!=(const Integer& arg) const {   // Comparison !=
      if (x == arg.x)                             // Debugging output...
        cout << endl
             << "operator!= returns false"
             << endl;                             // ...just to show that we are here
      return x != arg.x;
    }

    int operator*() const { return x; }      // De-reference operator

    Integer& operator++() {                  // Prefix increment operator
      ++x;
      return *this;
    }

  private:
    int x;
};
#endif  // INTEGER_H
```

(Continued)

Here's the code for a program to exercise objects of type Integer:

```
// Program 20.7 Using the Integer iterator class  File: prog20_07.cpp
#include <iostream>
using std::cout;
using std::endl;

int main() {
  Integer begin(3);
  Integer end(7);
  cout << "Today's integers are: ";
  for( ; begin != end ; ++begin)
    cout << *begin << " ";
  cout << endl;
  return 0;
}
```

When you run this program, it produces this exciting output:

```
Today's integers are: 3 4 5 6
operator!= returns false
```

HOW IT WORKS

The program works as if you had declared begin and end to be plain integers and assigned them the same values. One major difference is that your Integer objects output a message when the overloaded != operator returns false. You define the constructor for the Integer class as follows:

```
Integer (int arg = 0) : x(arg) {}
```

The Integer class has a data member, x, that stores the current value. If you fail to initialize an Integer object when you declare it, then the data member x defaults to zero.

The class defines an operator function for !=:

```
bool operator!=(const Integer& arg) const { // Comparison !=
  if (x == arg.x)                            // Debugging output
    cout << endl
         << "operator!= returns false"
         << endl;                            // Just to show that we are here
  return x != arg.x;
}
```

The function takes an Integer object as the right argument and returns a Boolean value. You can see from the program output that as soon as begin is equal to end, the != operator returns false and your loop terminates.

The dereference operator is defined as follows:

```
int operator*() const { return x; }      // Dereference operator
```

This returns the data member x for the current Integer object, effectively dereferencing the Integer object. This function and operator!=() are declared as const because they leave the internal state of the Integer object unchanged.

You've defined the prefix increment operator as follows:

```
Integer& operator++() {                   // Prefix increment operator
  ++x;
  return *this;
}
```

NOTE *For the* average() *algorithm in the preceding examples, you used the expression* *begin++, *which involved the postfix increment operator,* operator++(int), *instead.*

Your Integer class now has four simple functions. In fact, that's all you need to make it behave sufficiently like a pointer to allow you to do a few things. In the function main(), you use this statement:

```
for( ; begin != end ; ++begin)
  cout << *begin << " ";
```

This sort of statement should look pretty familiar by now. You used something very similar in the average() algorithm, but there you used the expression *begin++. In fact, replacing *begin with *begin++ in the output statement won't work here, because you haven't defined the operator++(int) function that supports the postfix increment notation for the Integer class. Instead, you use *begin in the output line and ++begin in the loop control.

In fact, you can write this:

```
for( ; begin != end ; )
  cout << *++begin << " ";
```

Here, the loop outputs the values 4 through 7 instead. The return value from *++begin is the value of the data member begin.x *after* the increment has taken place.

Passing Iterators to an Algorithm

Ideally you want to use your `Integer` type to define an iterator that you can pass to an algorithm such as that provided by your average template. Instances of the average template require the postfix increment operator to be implemented for the iterators that are passed to it. The definition for the operator function for the class looks like this:

```
const Integer operator++(int) {          // Postfix ++ operator
  Integer temp(*this);                   // save our current value
  ++x;                                   // change to new value
  return temp;                           // return unchanged saved value
}
```

This is a straightforward implementation for this operator that is along the lines you've seen before. This should be enough for `Integer` objects to be usable with an instance of the average template so let's see if it works.

···

Try It Out: Passing an Integer Object to average<>

Here's the new improved version of the `Integer` class:

```
// Integer.h Integer class definition
#ifndef INTEGER_H
#define INTEGER_H
#include <iostream>
using std::cout;
using std::endl;

class Integer {
  public:
    Integer (int arg = 0) : x(arg) {}

    bool operator!=(const Integer& arg) const {  // Comparison !=
      return x != arg.x;
    }

    int operator*() const { return x; }     // Dereference operator

    Integer& operator++() {                  // Prefix increment operator
      ++x;
      return *this;
    }

      const Integer operator++(int) {        // Postfix ++ operator
      Integer temp(*this);                   // save our current value
      ++x;                                   // change to new value
      return temp;                           // return unchanged saved value
    }
```

```
  private:
    int x;
};
#endif  // INTEGER_H
```

The program to exercise this version of the Integer class is as follows:

```
// Program 20.8 Averaging values from Integer  File: prog20_08.cpp
#include <iostream>
#include "Integer.h"
using std::cout;
using std::endl;

template <typename Iter>
double average(Iter a, Iter end) {
  double sum = 0.0;
  int count = 0;
  for( ; a != end ; ++count)
    sum += *a++;
  return sum/count;                    // Lets bad things happen when count==0
}

int main() {
  Integer first(1);
  Integer last(11);
  cout << "The average of the integers from " << *first << " to " << *last-1;
  cout << " is " << average(first, last) << endl;
  return 0;
}
```

This program produces the following output:

```
The average of the integers from 1 to 10 is 5.5
```

HOW IT WORKS

You didn't change much in the Integer class. Apart from removing the debugging statements from operator!=(), you just added the postfix version of operator++().

You know that to implement the postfix increment operator, you have to create a copy of the current object—something you don't have to do with the prefix form. Of course, this creates extra work because it calls the copy constructor for the current object type. For this reason, most of the examples that follow use the prefix form ++iter wherever possible, because it's more efficient. It doesn't make much difference for your simple class, Integer, but when working through template algorithms you can't be sure just how expensive it might be to create the copy of the object that the expression iter++ involves.

(Continued)

You can apply your Integer class in these statements:

```
Integer first(1);
Integer last(11);
cout << "The average of the integers from " << *first << " to " << *last-1;
cout << " is " << average(first, last) << endl;
```

Once again, last is a past-the-end value. You have to subtract one to get the inclusive range.

If you stop to think about it, you've done something very different by calling average() with your new Integer iterator. In all the other examples, the values you averaged were associated with a source—they lived in arrays, they lived in vectors, or they lived in streams. In this example, the values don't exist anywhere. They're computed inside the Integer class as the average() algorithm invokes the operator!=(), operator*() and operator++() functions.

STL Iterator Type Requirements

So far your example class Integer has served adequately as an iterator for your simple purposes. However, the STL places a number of specific requirements on objects that purport to be iterators. This is to ensure that all the algorithms that accept iterators will work as expected. Different algorithms require iterators of different capabilities and each iterator has different sets of requirements for each of its different categories: input and output, forward, bidirectional, and random access. Because you can always use a more capable iterator where a less capable one is required, let's go the whole hog and make your Integer class into a random access iterator.

One problem with template programming in general and with the STL in particular is that you don't always know all the types that you need to use before you use them. Consider the following example:

```
template <typename Iter>
void swap(Iter& a, Iter& b) {
  tmp = *a;  // error -- variable tmp undeclared
  *a = *b;
  *b = tmp;
  }
```

This template function is intended to swap two objects that are identified by the iterators, a and b. What type should tmp be? You have no way of knowing—you know that it's the type pointed to by the iterator, but you have no idea what that might be because that will be determined at runtime. How do you declare a variable whose type you don't know?

A simple solution would be to ensure that every iterator contains a public type definition for the type value_type so that it corresponds to the type of object to which the iterator relates. This could be used in the swap function template like this:

```
template <typename Iter>
void swap (Iter& a, Iter& b) {
  typename Iter::value_type tmp = *a; // Much better - but still not good enough
  *a = *b;
  *b = tmp;
}
```

This works fine with *most* of the STL iterators. However, if Iter is an ordinary pointer type such as int*—as is often the case—then this approach is not viable. The problem is that you can't simply write int*::value_type in this case because pointers are built-in language types that don't contain internal type definitions.

The STL solves this problem and other related problems very elegantly through the iterator_traits template. This involves using **iterator tags** and a set of required **iterator types**. If you were to apply this in the swap template, it would look like this:

```
template <typename Iter>
void swap (Iter& a, Iter& b) {
  // Cumbersome, but always works
  typename iterator_traits<Iter>::value_type tmp = *a;
  *a = *b;
  *b = tmp;
}
```

This specifies the type for tmp as the value_type defined by the iterator_traits template instantiated with the parameter type, Iter. The way the iterators_traits template works depends on whether or not the parameter type, Iter, is a pointer. The template allows the argument to be an ordinary pointer or an iterator by defining a specialization of the iterators_traits template for pointers. If Iter is a pointer to type T, then the specialization of the template applies and something of the form iterator_traits<T*>::value_type is equivalent to the object type, T. This is the case simply because that is how it's defined in the template specialization. If Iter is an iterator that is a class object of type T, then the standard template applies. In this case, something of the form iterator_traits<T>::value_type is equivalent to T::value_type, which is the definition of value_type in the iterator object.

Therefore, to make your Integer iterator work with iterator_traits, it must contain an internal public type definition for value_type. The easiest way of doing this is to use the iterator template that the STL provides as a base for your Integer class. This involves definitions for some other types too, so let's look into that a little further.

Using the iterator Template

The STL defines the iterator template as a template for a struct that has five parameters like this:

```
template<class Category, class T, class Distance = ptrdiff_t,
                              class Pointer = T*, class Reference = T&>
struct iterator {
typedef T value_type;
typedef Distance difference_type;
typedef Pointer pointer;
typedef Reference reference;
typedef Category iterator_category
};
```

You'll recall that a struct is essentially the same as a class except that its members are public by default. This template defines all of the types that STL requires a custom iterator to define. For example, if you have an unknown template parameter Iter, you can write Iter::pointer when you need to declare a pointer to the type that the iterator provides when it is dereferenced. Table 20-6 lists the meaning for each of these types.

Table 20-6. Types Defined by the iterator<> *Template*

Iterator Types for Iter to T	Meaning
value_type	The type of the object pointed to
difference_type	The difference between two iterators
pointer	T*, a pointer to the object type
reference	T&, a reference to the object type
iterator_category	Input, output, forward, bidirectional, or random access

The value of iterator_category must be one of a fixed set of category tags and specifies what sort iterator it is. This determines what classes of algorithms the iterator is capable of working with. Table 20-7 lists the possible iterator tag values.

Table 20-7. Iterator Tag Values

Iterator Type	Required Category Tag
input	input_iterator_tag
output	output_iterator_tag
forward	forward_iterator_tag
bidirectional	bidirectional_iterator_tag
random access	random_access_iterator_tag

A random access iterator has the full functionality of a C++ pointer. The other iterator categories are more restricted. Shortly I'll show you a list container that provides bidirectional iterators. This kind of iterator can move forward or backward in single steps, but it can't be used with the subscript operator[ ] to perform random access.

You can make your `Integer` class meet the STL requirements for type definitions by introducing an instance of the `iterator` template as a base for your class:

```
class Integer : public iterator<random_access_iterator_tag, int, int, int*, int>
```

This takes care of defining all the types that are required by the STL for an iterator. The first argument to the template specifies the type of your iterator as a full random access iterator. The second argument is the type of object pointed to by your iterator, `int`. The third argument is the type for a difference between two of your iterators, which is also `int`. The fourth template argument is the type of a pointer to an object so that you have `int*`. Finally the last template argument specifies the type for a reference, which is also type `int`.

The STL Iterator Member Function Requirements

The STL also defines a set of member functions that each type of iterator must support. Because you're interested in implementing a random access iterator, I'll show you the full set. It helps if you collect them into groups.

The first group is the **constructors**. This includes some very important functions that all complex classes need to have: the **default constructor**, the **copy constructor**, and the **assignment operator**. As a rule of thumb, if you write any of these functions for an iterator, then you should also write an explicit **destructor**. For your Integer class you don't need to define one. Because a destructor does nothing for Integer, the default destructor is fine. The full set of functions in this group is as follows:

```
Integer(int n=0);                       // Default constructor
Integer(const Integer& y);              // Copy constructor
~Integer();                             // Destructor
Integer& operator=(const Integer& y);   // Assignment operator
```

You can get the default constructor in the `Integer` class through the default value for your constructor parameter. The STL uses the default constructor when it creates new elements in your containers, so it is essential that it is defined.

The STL requires that you implement a full set of **equality** and **relational** operators for a random access iterator class. In fact, you can get away with just the following by using some other templates provided by the standard library:

```
bool operator==(const Integer& y) const;
bool operator<(const Integer& y)  const;
```

This assumes that you have the following #include directive for the `<utility>` header and a using directive for the `std::relops` namespace:

```
#include <utility>
using namespace std::rel_ops;
```

If you provide operator==() and operator<() for your class type, then the rel_ops namespace declared within the std namespace contains function templates that automatically generate operator functions for !=, >, >=, and <=, for your class type. So activating rel_ops with the using directive saves you the work of defining these four operators explicitly. If you provide any of the operator functions that would be generated by the templates in the std::rel_ops namespace, your implementations take precedence over the ones that the template in the rel_ops namespace might create on your behalf.

The operator<() function is special. It is called the **ordering relation**. It is important in searching and comparison algorithms. Given a definition for operator<(), a template in the rel_ops namespace automatically creates an operator>() function.

The operator==() function is used to test for when two containers or objects have identical contents. There is an interesting aspect to how this works. You might think that for any pair of operands, x and y, the expression (x<y || y<x || x==y) must always return true and exactly one of the three component expressions must be true. In fact, it doesn't necessarily have to work that way. It's clear that if (x==y) is true, then neither (x<y) nor (y<x) can be true. One thing you can be certain about is that equal elements can't be different.

However, if (x!=y) you *must not* assume that one of (x<y) or (y<x) is true—when (!(x<y)) && (!(y<x)) is true, the elements x and y are said to be *inequivalent*, which simply means you don't have a preference when sorting. A common example of this occurs when you're sorting strings, but ignoring case. On a case-insensitive basis, the strings "A123" and "a123" are inequivalent (neither belongs first), but they're not the same, nor are they equal.

The STL also requires the **access** operators to be implemented for a random access iterator:

```
int operator*() const;
int operator[](int n) const;
```

These are used to return values from within the sequence. The operator function operator[]() is only found in iterators that belong to the random_access category.

The bidirectional operators that a bidirectional iterator must implement must also be supported by a random access iterator:

```
Integer& operator++();
Integer& operator--();
Integer& operator++(int);
Integer& operator--(int);
```

These allow you to step forward or backward one element at a time. Forward iterators don't go backward, and so they don't provide either of the two decrement forms.

Here are the operators needed to support **random access**:

```
Integer operator+(int n) const;
Integer operator-(int n) const;
```

These are found whenever operator[ ]() is present in a sequence container. They allow you to access any element in the sequence directly from any iterator position simply by applying the appropriate offset to the iterator.

If you put all that lot together for your Integer class, you should be in business so far as the STL is concerned.

Try It Out: A Fully Fledged Iterator

You'll now add all the bells and whistles to the Integer class that the STL requires of a random access iterator.

```
// Integer.h Integer class definition
#ifndef INTEGER_H
#define INTEGER_H
#include <iostream>
using std::cout;
using std::endl;
using std::iterator;
#include <utility>
using namespace std::rel_ops;   // Access to templates for relational ops

class Integer :
      public iterator<std::random_access_iterator_tag, int, int, int*, int> {
   public:
     Integer(int n=0) : x(n) {}              // Default constructor
     Integer(const Integer& y) : x(y.x) {}   // Copy constructor
     ~Integer() {}                           // Destructor

     Integer& operator=(const Integer& y) {  // Assignment operator
       x = y.x;
       return *this;
     }

     // Relational operators
     bool operator==(const Integer& y) const { return x == y.x; }
     bool operator!=(const Integer& y) const { return !(*this == y); }
     bool operator<(const Integer& y)  const { return x < y.x; }

     int operator*() const { return x; }
     int operator[](int n) const { return x+n; }

     // Bidirectional operators
     Integer& operator++() {
       ++x;
       return *this;
     }
```

(Continued)

```cpp
    Integer& operator--() {
      --x;
      return *this;
    }

    Integer& operator++(int) {
      Integer temp(*this);
      ++x;
      return temp;
    }

    Integer& operator--(int) {
      Integer temp(*this);
      --x;
      return temp;
    }

    // Random access operators
    Integer operator+(int n) const { return Integer (x+n); }
    Integer operator-(int n) const { return Integer (x-n); }

  private:
    int x;
};
#endif  // INTEGER_H
```

Here is the program to exercise this version of the Integer class:

```cpp
// Program 20.09 Full "random access" Integer iterator  File: prog20_09.cpp
#include <iostream>
#include <algorithm>
#include "Integer.h"
using std::cout;
using std::endl;

int main() {
  Integer F1(-1);
  Integer L1(10);
  cout << "The values [-1..10) in forward order: " << endl;
  copy (F1, L1, std::ostream_iterator<int>(cout, " "));
  cout << endl;

  typedef std::reverse_iterator<Integer> CountDown;
  CountDown F2(10);
  CountDown L2(-1);
  cout << "the values (10..-1] in reverse order: " << endl;
  copy (F2, L2, std::ostream_iterator<int>(cout, " "));
  cout << endl;

  return 0;
}
```

Your tiny `Integer` class isn't so tiny any more. It now has everything a full-blown STL iterator requires.

When you run this example, you should see this output:

```
The values [-1..10) in forward order:
-1 0 1 2 3 4 5 6 7 8 9
The values (10..-1] in reverse order:
9 8 7 6 5 4 3 2 1 0 -1
```

HOW IT WORKS

You have implemented everything that I described in the previous section for your Integer class. You've provided operator==() and operator<() for the class type, so the function templates in the rel_ops namespace automatically generate the other operator functions that you need. In this example, you did provide your own operator!=() implementation for the Integer class so this won't be created by the template in the rel_ops namespace.

The creation of the iterator class `CountDown` in `main()` is a good demonstration that you have a fully-fledged STL iterator with your `Integer` class implementation:

```
typedef reverse_iterator<Integer> CountDown;
CountDown F2(10), L2(-1);
cout << "the values (10..-1] in reverse order: " << endl;
copy (F2, L2, ostream_iterator<int>(cout, " "));
```

CountDown is a new class that you've created from your Integer class using a STL adapter class. The reverse_iterator type is a template class that takes an iterator as its parameter and creates a new iterator. The new iterator is exactly like the iterator you started with, but with everything working in reverse. Thus you can use your CountDown objects to output the integers in the interval (10, -1], which is open at the front rather than the back. The reverse_iterator template only works with bidirectional or random access iterators, so you're certain that Integer is at least the former and you can be reasonably confident that it is also the latter.

Insert Iterators

As I said right at the beginning, **input iterators** can only be used to read values and **output iterators** can only be used to write values. These iterator categories don't support random access or stepping backward. In fact, with these iterators you can read or write only once at each position. The primary use of these iterators is to allow the STL algorithms, such as copy(), to act on streams. You've already used both ostream_iterator and istream_iterator in this chapter.

I'll refer to another very useful kind of output_iterator as the **insert iterator family**. You can use iterators in this family when you want to insert elements into a container using an algorithm such as copy(). For example, the back_inserter() function template creates an iterator that can add elements to the end of a container. You could use it to define a template function append() like this:

```
template <typename Container, class Iter>
void append(Container& C, Iter src, Iter src_end) {
  copy(src, src_end, back_inserter(C));
}
```

This defines a template for a function that appends elements to a container of the type specified by the first template parameter, where the source of the elements to be appended is an iterator of a type specified by the second template parameter. Thus, this function can append elements from any source that can be defined by iterators to any container.

The destination to which the elements should be copied is determined by the first argument to the append() function. The elements to be copied to the container are specified by the second and third arguments, which are iterators of type Iter. The back_inserter() function takes a container as its argument and returns an output_iterator that appends each value that is received to the target container. If you copied to C.end() directly, the copy operation would function in **overwrite mode**, and you'd violate the vector bounds by writing into areas of the vector that aren't available for writing. The output iterator produced by the back_inserter() function operates in **insert mode**, so it grows the container as necessary.

The front_inserter() complements back_inserter() and enables you to insert elements at the beginning of a container. Note that you can't use front_inserter() with a vector container, because front_inserter() relies on the push_front() member of the container to insert elements at the beginning, and vector containers don't declare this member function.

Finally, the inserter() function generates an output iterator that can insert elements at any given position. For example:

```
copy(src, src_end, inserter(C, any_iterator_position_within_C));
```

This inserter inserts each element and then advances to the next position. The elements are inserted as a group in forward order starting at the insert position specified, so the container is expanded by the number of elements that are inserted.

Try It Out: Using an Inserter

You can try out front_inserter(). Because you can't use it with a vector container, you'll try it out on a list container instead. Here is the code:

```cpp
// Program 20.10 - Using an inserter  File: 20_10.cpp
#include <iostream>
#include <iterator>
#include <algorithm>
#include <list>
using std::cout;
using std::cout;
using std::endl;
using std::front_inserter;
using std::ostream_iterator;

// Front insert
template <typename Container, class Iter>
void pre_insert(Container& C, Iter src, Iter src_end) {
  std::copy(src, src_end, front_inserter(C));
}

int main() {
  int values[] = { 1, 9, 7, 5, 15 };
  std::list<int> numbers;                  // Create a list container of integers

  // Append elements of values array to the front of the numbers list
  pre_insert(numbers, values, values+sizeof values/sizeof values[0]);

   // Copy the list to the output stream
  std::copy(numbers.begin(), numbers.end(), ostream_iterator<int>(cout," "));
  cout << endl;
  return 0;
}
```

The output of this program displays the inserted values in reverse order:

```
15 5 7 9 1
```

HOW IT WORKS

The values from the array are reversed because you used front_inserter() in your append() function template. The values are inserted successively at the beginning of the list<int> container, L, starting with the first element in the array and ending with the last, so the last element of the array ends up as the first element in the container. As I said, you can't apply front_inserter to a vector container, but you can apply back_inserter() to both vector and list containers.

Let's explore list containers in a little more depth.

The list Container

Of paramount concern for the designers of the STL was providing efficient mechanisms for any task that might arise. The vector serves well in any situation where a C++ array might be used, and it is a very useful, general-purpose container. However, if frequent insertions or deletions within the sequence of elements are necessary, the vector container is a poor performer. The primary advantage of a list container is that all insertions and deletions take constant time. The disadvantage is that you lose the ability to access elements at random.

A list container supports bidirectional iterators. This means that you can move forward and backward from one element to the next efficiently, but you can't make big jumps. Most algorithms can be performed efficiently on lists, even without the random access capability that operator[] provides. Let's look at some of the facilities that a list container provides.

Creating list Containers

You have a similar range of constructors for list containers to the one available for vector containers. You could create an empty list container to store values of type double with this statement:

```
std::list<double> data;
```

If you want to specify the number of elements in the list you can write the following:

```
std::list<double> values(20);
```

This creates a list of 20 elements each initialized to 0.0. If the template argument is a class type, the default constructor for the class is called to create the initial value for each element.

You could set the values for the elements in this list with these statements:

```
std::list<double>::iterator first = values.begin();
double x = 1.0;
while(first != values.end())
  *first++ = x++;
```

This sets the elements in the list to the values from 1.0 to 20.0.

You can initialize all the elements in the list that you create with a specific value:

```
std::list<double> data(20, 3.14159);
```

All 20 elements in this list will be set to 3.14159.

You can construct a list from an interval specified by two iterators. For example, you can construct a new list from elements in the values list that you initialized to the values from 1.0 to 20.0:

```
std::list<double>::iterator begin = ++values.begin();   // Begin()+1
std::list<double>::iterator end = begin++;               // end = begin, begin += 1
for(int i = 0 ; i<7 ; i++, ++end);                       // end += 6
std::list<double> some_data(begin, end);
```

You create two iterators, begin and end, that point to the third and ninth elements in the values list. You use the increment operator and a loop to set these iterators to these positions. These contortions to set the positions of the iterators are because you can only increment these iterators one step at a time. You use them to create a new list from the elements from values in the interval [begin, end) so that the some_data list contains elements with the value 3, 4, 5, 6, 7, and 8.

The number of elements in a list is returned by the size() function. You can change the number of elements by calling its resize() function with an argument that specifies the new size for the list. If the new size for the list is greater than the old, new elements are added using the default constructor for the objects in the list. If the new size is less that the old, elements are deleted from the end of the list.

Accessing Elements in a List

For processing the elements in a list in sequence, you have two options. You've already seen how you can use begin() and end() to obtain iterators you can use to access the elements in sequence. You also have rbegin() and rend() functions that return reverse iterators you can use to step through the elements in reverse order. All these iterators are bidirectional, so you can only increment or decrement them by one.

The front() and back() members return references to the first and last elements respectively.

Operations on Lists

The push_front() and push_back() member functions insert an element at the beginning or the end of a list, respectively. The pop_front() and pop_back() functions delete the first or the last element. You use the insert() member function to insert one or more elements in a list at a position specified by an iterator. The insert() function comes in three versions:

```
iterator insert(iterator position, const T& x);      // Insert a single element
void insert(iterator position, size_type n  const T& x); // Insert n copies
template<class InputIterator>                         // Insert from another source
        void insert(iterator position, InputIterator first, InputIterator last);
```

The first version inserts *x* at the position specified by the first argument and returns an iterator pointing to the same position. The second version inserts *n* copies of *x* at the specified position in the list. The template version inserts elements from an interval that is specified by the second and third arguments at the position specified by the first argument. Because the iterators specifying the semi-open interval are of type InputIterator, they can be from any external source that provides iterators of this type.

You can remove elements using the erase() member function. One version accepts a single iterator specifying the element to be erased. The other version accepts two iterator arguments specifying a semi-open interval of elements to be removed. Both versions return an iterator that points to the element following the element or elements that were removed. You can also remove an element with a given value using the remove() function. The argument is the value to be removed. To remove all the elements in a list, you just call its clear() function. You can test for an empty list by calling its empty() function.

The list container also has a special function, splice(), that removes elements from one list and grafts them into another list of the same type. This saves you from having to combine separate insert and erase steps to accomplish the same thing. This function doesn't move any list elements; it just changes the pointers to the next and previous elements for the first and last of the elements to be spliced so that they are part of the new list, and alters the pointers for the elements on either side of the insertion position so that they point to the first and last of the inserted elements. The splice() function has three versions, and the first has one argument that is always the position in the current list where elements are to be inserted. In the version with two arguments, the second argument is a list to be inserted, in its entirety, into the current list. With the version with three arguments, the second argument is a list that is the source of the elements to be inserted, and the third argument is an iterator that points to the first of these elements. All elements from this iterator position to the end are transferred to the current list. With the third version, the last two arguments are iterators specifying a semi-open interval of elements that are to be transferred from the list identified by the third argument.

The general purpose sort() algorithm that is declared in the algorithm header doesn't work with a list<> container because it requires a random access iterator. However, a list<> container does provide a special sort() function member that you can use to sort the elements in a list.

Try It Out: Using the list Container

You took a long look at the list data structure in Chapter 13 when you developed the Package class for storing boxes by the truckload. Now you can see how an implementation of the TruckLoad class looks with the full power of the STL list container at your disposal.

First you can define the Box class like this:

```cpp
// Box.h definition of the Box class
#ifndef BOX_H
#define BOX_H
#include <iostream>
using std::cout;
using std::ostream;

class Box {
  public:
    Box(double lv = 1.0, double wv = 1.0, double hv = 1.0) :
                                  length(lv), width(bv), height(hv) {}

    double volume() const { return length*width* height; }
    bool operator<(const Box& x) const { return volume() < x.volume(); }

    friend ostream& operator<<(ostream& out, const Box& box) {
      out << "(" << box.length << "," << box.width << "," << box.height << ")";
      return out;
    }

  private:
    double length;
    double width;
    double height;
};
#endif
```

You can define the TruckLoad class in the header file TruckLoad.h like this:

```cpp
// TruckLoad.h definition of the TruckLoad class
#ifndef TRUCKLOAD_H
#define TRUCKLOAD _H
#include <list>
#include "Box.h"

class TruckLoad {
    typedef std::list<Box> Contents;

  public:
    typedef Contents::const_iterator const_iterator;
    TruckLoad() {}
    TruckLoad(const Box& one_box) : load (1, one_box) {}

    template<typename FwdIter>
    TruckLoad(FwdIter first, FwdIter last) : Load (first, last) {}

    void add_box(const Box& new_box) { load.push_back (new_box); }
```

(Continued)

```
        const_iterator begin() const { return load.begin(); }
        const_iterator end() const { return load.end(); }

    private:
        Contents load;
};
#endif
```

Here is the program that tries out the new TruckLoad and Box classes:

```
// Program 20.11 A TruckLoad container implemented using an STL list container
// Recapitulates Program 13.1
#include <iostream>
#include <algorithm>
using std::cout;
using std::endl;

// Random number generation 1 to count
inline int random(int count) {
  return 1 + static_cast<int>
                (count*static_cast<double>(rand())/(RAND_MAX+1.0));
}

// Create a Box with random dimensions in a range
inline Box random_box(int range) {
  return Box(random(range),random(range),random(range));
}

int main() {
  TruckLoad rig1(Box(30,30,30));
  for(int i = 0; i < 8; ++i)
    rig1.add_box(random_box(100));

  cout << "Contents of rig1" << endl;
  std::copy(rig1.begin(), rig1.end(), std::ostream_iterator<Box> (cout, "\n"));
  cout << endl;

  typedef TruckLoad::const_iterator BoxIter;
  BoxIter big_one = max_element(rig1.begin(), rig1.end());

  cout << "The biggest box in rig1 is " << *big_one
       << " with volume " << big_one->volume() << endl;
  cout << endl;

  cout << "Copying all boxes starting at big box to rig2" << endl;
  TruckLoad rig2(big_one, rig1.end());
  cout << "Contents of rig2" << endl;
  std::copy(rig2.begin(), rig2.end(), std::ostream_iterator<Box> (cout, "\n"));
  cout << endl;

  return 0;
}
```

When you run this program, it produces the following output:

```
Contents of rig1
(30,30,30)
(20,57,1)
(48,59,81)
(83,90,36)
(86,18,75)
(31,52,72)
(37,10,2)
(99,17,15)
(1,12,45)

The biggest box in rig1 is (83,90,36) with volume 268920

Copying all boxes starting at big box to rig2
Contents of rig2
(83,90,36)
(86,18,75)
(31,52,72)
(37,10,2)
(99,17,15)
(1,12,45)
```

HOW IT WORKS

Before you look at what happens in main(), let's cover the groundwork. You are already familiar with class Box and how it is used. This version of the Box class supplies two operator functions. Here is the first:

```
bool operator<(const Box& x) const { return volume() < x.volume(); }
```

By providing operator<(), you can compare pairs of boxes; this is necessary when you use the max_element() function from the STL.

You also overload the insertion operator in the Box class for a stream:

```
friend ostream& operator<<(ostream& out, const Box& box) {
  out << "(" << box.length << "," << box.width << "," << box.height << ")";
  return out;
```

Defining operator<<() for use with an ostream object makes it easy to write a Box object to an output stream. Remember that a friend function to a class is *not* a member function, so it doesn't receive a this pointer. The box object that is output by this function is passed to the operator<<() function explicitly as the second argument. The return type for the function is ostream&. This makes your function more convenient to use in compound statements because it makes it possible to use the function in a series of successive writes to a stream.

(Continued)

Your definition of the TruckLoad class is very simple, and in outline, it is like this:

```
class TruckLoad {
  typedef list<Box> Contents;

  // public members ...

  private:
    Contents load;
};
```

This definition provides you with your own interface, on top of what the list container gives you for free. The contents of the TruckLoad are contained in the data member load, which is a list of Box objects. Almost every function that you define is implemented using an equivalent function provided by the load object. You use the typedef for Contents as a convenience for simplifying the declarations for other class functions; this is pretty much a standard approach when you're working with the STL. The declaration of the load member is exactly the same as if you had written this:

```
  private:
    list<Box> Load;
```

You have three constructors in the TruckLoad class:

```
  TruckLoad() {}
  TruckLoad(const Box& one_box) : load (1, one_box) {}

  template<typename FwdIter>
  TruckLoad(FwdIter first, FwdIter last) : load (first, last) {}
```

The first constructor is a default constructor. The second constructor initializes the TruckLoad object to contain a single Box element. This is achieved by initializing the load object, which is of type list<Box>, by calling the list<Box> constructor that takes a count of the number of elements to be inserted as the first argument and the object that is to be inserted the specified number of times as the second argument.

The third constructor is provided by a constructor template. You can pass iterators to this constructor, to initialize your TruckLoad with a copy of any **sequence** of Box objects that you have already created. The iterators are declared using a class template, so the type of the iterator is very flexible—they could be pointers to an array of boxes, iterators into a vector<>- or list<>-based collection of boxes, or even iterators into the contents of another TruckLoad object.

This is easy for you to implement. The load object is a list, so it already provides you with a template constructor for a sequence. All you have to do is pass along the first and last arguments just as you received them, and the load constructor does the rest.

The add_box() function adds a Box object to a TruckLoad object. This is defined as follows:

```
void add_box(const Box& new_box) { load.push_back (new_box); }
```

You could have used push_front() to put the new Box object at the front of the load list. Trucks aren't usually loaded that way, so you use push_back() and add your new Box to the end of the list.

You have another typedef in the public section of the class definition:

```
typedef Contents::const_iterator const_iterator;
```

You have defined Contents as a synonym for the type list<Box>, so Contents::const_iterator is a synonym for list<Box>::const_iterator. This is a useful shorthand if you can remember what all the synonyms mean.

You make it possible for clients of the TruckLoad class to gain access to iterators to the truck's contents with the begin() and end() members:

```
const_iterator begin() const { return load.begin(); }
const_iterator end() const { return load.end(); }
```

These are constant iterators. You don't want your clients changing the contents of your TruckLoad behind your back just before you attempt to clear customs.

Your two functions, begin() and end(), return the load iterators directly. It's not a perfect design because you're exposing part of your implementation—the fact that you're using a list internally to track the contents. However, it is very convenient, and if your clients are well behaved, they won't take advantage of any special knowledge that they gain by knowing that these iterators point to a list rather than some other kind of container.

Because you're returning iterators, your TruckLoad behaves a lot like a container. That's not a bad thing, because your TruckLoad is conceptually a lot like a container to begin with.

The program uses the global functions random() and random_box(), which provide an easy way to create random boxes for use in the example program:

```
inline int random(int count) {
  return 1 + static_cast<int>(count*static_cast<double>(rand())/(RAND_MAX+1.0));
}

inline Box random_box(int range) {
  return Box(random(range),random(range),random(range));
}
```

You saw this same definition of random in the previous TruckLoad example—the details of how it works are covered in Chapter 13.

(Continued)

Now you can look at some of the more interesting parts of the function `main()`. Consider these statements:

```
cout << "Contents of rig1" << endl;
std::copy(rig1.begin(), rig1.end(), std::ostream_iterator<Box>(cout, "\n"));
cout << endl;
```

The first two arguments to the `copy()` algorithm are the range of boxes to copy, which, in this example, is the entire `TruckLoad` from `begin()` to `end()`. The third argument in the `copy()` function uses the `ostream_iterator` in the way you've seen previously, except that here the separator between output values is a new-line character, `"\n"`.

The code is very concise and typical of how STL objects work together. Note that `ostream_iterator` is making use of your `Box::operator<<(ostream,Box)` to control how the `Box` object is written to the stream `cout`. It all fits together to provide a very compact way of saying, "output all the boxes."

You have a `typedef` statement defining `BoxIter` based on the `const_iterator` type defined in the public section of the `TruckLoad` class.

```
typedef TruckLoad::const_iterator BoxIter;
```

You use this synonym to declare a constant iterator, `big_one`:

```
BoxIter big_one = max_element(rig1.begin(), rig1.end());
```

Remember that `TruckLoad::const_iterator` is a synonym for `list<Box>::const_iterator`, but this time there is an important difference: the client doesn't know that these are synonyms, and doesn't need to. As far as the client is concerned, `const_iterator` is an anonymous type provided by the public interface of `TruckLoad` that is used for any iterators received from `TruckLoad::begin()` and `TruckLoad::end()`.

You have used another STL algorithm, `max_element()`, here. Its arguments define a range that it searches, returning an iterator to the largest value found within the range. If the range is empty, the return iterator will be at, or beyond, `rig1.end()`, where there are no elements.

 NOTE *A key feature of working with the STL is the ability to work with types defined by objects within your programs. In this example, you can see that* `BoxIter` *is some kind of iterator provided by the* `TruckLoad` *class, but at this level, you don't know that this is actually an iterator from the STL* `list` *container. Only* `TruckLoad` *knows that kind of internal detail.*

To copy *part* of the TruckLoad, starting with the biggest box found, use these statements:

```
cout << "Copying all boxes starting at big box to rig2" << endl;
TruckLoad rig2(big_one, rig1.end());
```

You use the copy constructor, which takes an iterator range to make this copy. This shows that the iterator returned from the algorithm, max_element(), works in the same way as any other iterator does. Therefore, you can use the iterator to refer to positions within the TruckLoad sequence of Box elements.

The Associative Containers

So far, you've only tried the vector<> and list<> containers, which are sequence containers. The order of elements in a sequence container is established by the method that you choose to insert the elements. **Associative containers** work differently. Each object is stored with an associated key (which may be the object itself) and the objects are stored internally in a sequence sorted by key. When you insert a new element, the key is automatically used to place the element in the container in the position that maintains the sorted order.

You also access elements in an associative container by key. The data type for a key *must* provide an ordering relation. The ordering relation can be provided via the operator<() function, or by a function object, Compare, which returns true if the first object is less than the second, and false otherwise. You haven't met function objects before, so I'll introduce you to more detail on these a little later in this chapter. Although you can't use objects that don't provide such an ordering relation as keys in an associative container, no other restrictions exist on the data types used for keys, so your associated values can be of any convenient data type that has a well-defined order.

As you saw in the beginning of this chapter, four varieties of associative containers exist: map, set, multimap, and multiset. The map and set containers are suitable when you're sure that keys are unique, whereas you use the multimap and multiset containers when duplicate keys are required. An additional factor that you must consider when deciding which associative container to use is that the keys of the map and multimap containers have associated values (which are typically objects), whereas in the set and multiset containers, the objects are their own keys.

Let me illustrate what this means in practical terms. For example, you might use a map or a multimap to store names and phone numbers. Each of these containers stores a collection of elements that associate a *key* with an *object*; in this case, the name would be the key, and the phone number would be the associated object. Which should you use? If you use a map, then the key must be unique. This means that not only can you not accommodate entries for two people with a common name, such as Jeremiah Hackenbush, for instance, but each person can only have one phone number. Because many people have the same name, and many also have more than one phone number, you really need to be able to have duplicate "person" keys. This leads you to your only choice in this instance—the multimap container.

 NOTE *In some ways, the* multimap *is the most general of the associative containers. However, using the* multimap *isn't necessarily the default choice. When you opt for the more general* multimap, *you give up the convenience of the subscript operator that a* map *container provides, so you lose the associative array capability.*

Because the set and multiset containers don't have separate keys, they're simpler than map containers. The automatic ordering of the elements is the main advantage of set and multiset containers.

Using a map Container

The map template is defined with four template parameters, but normally you'll only need to specify the first two. The first is the type for the keys, and the second is the type for the objects to be stored. The third and fourth template parameters define the type of **function object** used to compare keys and the type of object used to allocate memory within the map respectively. Both have defaults assigned that are satisfactory in most instances. Occasionally, you may want to define a different type of object for comparing keys; you'll see an example of how to do this a little later in the section "Understanding Function Objects."

The default constructor for a map creates an empty map. For example, you could create a map container that stored the Person object with keys of type string like this:

```
std::map<std::string, Person>  personnel;
```

The first template argument specifies the type for the key as string, and the second template argument specifies the object type associated with the key as Person. Here, the keys might be personnel numbers expressed as strings. Of course, either or both of the first two template parameters can also be fundamental types.

Each element in a map is stored as an object that encapsulates the key and the object associated with the key. The element type is a template type specified by the fourth map<> template parameter. With the default type for this in effect, elements in the personnel map are of type pair<string, Person>. This template type is not exclusively for use in this context. You can use it yourself if it is convenient when you need to package two objects together as a single object.

Apart from the copy constructor that duplicates an existing map, the only other option you have for creating a map is to create it from a set of elements from another map<> container. You specify the elements by a semi-open interval that you define by two iterators. If you think you have populated the personnel container with elements, you can create a new container with a subset of these elements with the following statement:

```
std::map<std::string, Person>  department(iter1, iter2);
```

The iterators `iter1` and `iter2` specify a semi-open interval of keys, [iter1, iter2), to elements in the `personnel` map. This statement constructs an empty map and then inserts the elements from the interval into the new map.

Accessing Elements in a Map

The subscript operator is implemented by a `map`, so you can use a key as an index to retrieve the associated object. Here's an example:

```
Person chosen_one = personnel["666"];
```

This retrieves the `Person` object that corresponds to the personnel number `"666"` that you've supplied as the key. Note that using the subscript isn't simply a retrieval mechanism. If no `Person` object corresponds to `"666"`, then a `Person` object is created using the default `Person` class constructor, and that is then inserted into the map with the key `"666"`. Therefore, this is only a sensible retrieval mechanism when you're sure the key actually exists in the map. For this reason, you'd typically use the subscript operator when you're updating elements in the map or inserting them if they aren't already present. The other major use for the subscript operator is on the left of an assignment to change an existing entry.

When you use the subscript operator with a map to store or modify the object stored in an entry, you put the key between the square brackets to identify the entry and put the associated object as the right operand of the assignment, as shown here:

```
personnel["999"] = chief_exec;    // Store the Person chief_exec
```

This stores the `Person` object `chief_exec` in the `personnel` map with the personnel number `"999"` as the key.

One way to check whether an entry exists for a key is to use the `find()` method. This method returns either an iterator that points to the position of the entry in the map, or an iterator that points to one beyond the end of the map if the entry doesn't exist. Therefore, you could check for the presence of an element in the `personnel` map that you defined like this:

```
if(personnel.find("666") 1= personnel.end())
    std::cout << "Number 666 is in there!" << std::endl;
```

Another possibility is to use the `count()` method for the map. This method returns the number of elements in the map that correspond to the key that you pass as the argument. For a map container, this can only be 0 or 1, but for a `multimap` container, you may have several entries for a given key value. You could check for number `"666"` like this:

```
if(personnel.count("666"))
    std::cout << "Number 666 is in there!" << std::endl;
```

The return value of 1 will be cast to the bool value, true, so in this case, the output statement will be executed.

In addition to using the subscript operator, you can also access elements in a map through an iterator. A map also has begin(), end(), rbegin(), and rend() functions that return bidirectional iterators as type iterator, which is a type defined within a map<> class. For the personnel map, you'd specify the iterator type as map<string, Person>::iterator. You can use these iterators to step through the elements in the map in the same way you did for a list container. Dereferencing the iterator results in the object that is stored. The objects in a map are ordered by their keys, so stepping through from begin() to end() provides access to the objects in ascending key order, which is determined by the ordering relation that must be available for the keys. The ordering relation can be provided either by the operator<() function or a Compare function object.

A map iterator actually points to an element of type pair<>. Although dereferencing the iterator directly provides you with access to the object in the key/object pair, you can also obtain the key for the element. For instance, here's how you could list the keys in the personnel map:

```
map<string, Person>:: iterator iter = personnel.begin();
while(iter != personnel.end())
  std::cout << iter->second << std::endl;
```

The second member of the pair<> object that an iterator point to stores the key. Unsurprisingly, the object associated with the key is stored in the first member.

Try It Out: Using Maps to Collect Collocations

A common form of collocation involves counting how often each word occurs in a text. You can do this using a map container:

```
// Program 20.12 A simple word collocation  File: prog20_12.cpp
#include <iostream>
#include <iomanip>
#include <string>
#include <sstream>
#include <map>
using std::cout;
using std::endl;
using std::string;

const string twister =
  "How much wood would a woodchuck chuck if a woodchuck "
  "could chuck wood?  A woodchuck would chuck as much wood "
  "as a woodchuck could chuck if a woodchuck could chuck wood.";

int main() {
  typedef std::map<string, int> Collocation;     // Type for our map
  typedef Collocation::const_iterator WordIter; // Iterator type for our map
```

```
Collocation words;              // Map to store words and word counts

std::istringstream text(twister);          // Text string as a stream
std::istream_iterator<string> begin(text); // Stream iterator
std::istream_iterator<string> end;         // End stream iterator

for( ; begin != end ; ++begin)       // Iterate over the words in the stream
  words[*begin]++;                   // Store and increment word count

// Ouput the words and their counts
for(WordIter iter = words.begin() ; iter != words.end() ; ++iter)
  cout << std::setw(6) << iter->second << " " << iter->first << endl;

  return 0;
}
```

This program produces the following output:

```
     1 A
     1 How
     4 a
     2 as
     5 chuck
     3 could
     2 if
     2 much
     2 wood
     1 wood.
     1 wood?
     5 woodchuck
     2 would
```

HOW IT WORKS

You have an #include directive for the header, <map>:

```
#include <map>
```

Both the map and multimap containers are declared in the header <map>. You don't want to type out map<string,int>::const_iterator in full very often. It's better to take advantage of typedef:

```
typedef std::map<string, int> Collocation;      // Type for our map
typedef Collocation::const_iterator WordIter;   // Iterator type for our map
```

(Continued)

Here you supply two parameters to the map<> template. The first is the data type of the key, and the second is the data type of the associated object. In this program, your keys are objects of type string that represent words found in your sample text. The associated value for each string is a value of type int that you use to count the number of occurrences of the key. You use an iterator of type WordIter to display the contents of your collocation.

The definition of the map container for the collocation is now very simple:

```
Collocation words;              // Map to store words and word counts
```

Next, you create a string stream object from your string object and create some iterators for the stream:

```
std::istringstream text(twister);              // Text string as a stream
std::istream_iterator<string> begin(text);     // Stream iterator
std::istream_iterator<string> end;             // End stream iterator
```

You've used istringstream before. You create an istream_iterator object, begin, that initially points to the beginning of the text stream that was initialized with your tongue twister. The default constructor for istream_iterator creates an end-of-stream iterator, so end marks the end of text. You can use these to iterate over each lexeme in your text. I say *lexeme*, rather than *word*, because istream_iterator isn't very intelligent; it simply breaks out sequences of printable characters embedded between stretches of white space, as the output shows.

Inserting and counting within the collocation is so easy that you might have missed it. It's all performed within the single statement in the body of the for loop:

```
for( ; begin != end ; ++begin)     // Iterate over the words in the stream
    words[*begin]++;               // Store and increment word count
```

The expression *begin returns a string that contains one of the lexemes peeled out of your tongue twister. The container words is subscripted with a key of type string. Elements in associative containers are accessed *associatively*—this means that when the map is given a key, it returns the associated value of type int, which is then incremented.

For a map container, operator[]() is actually a shorthand for insert(). This means that you have to be a bit careful sometimes. Consider this statement:

```
if(words["brawn"] > 0)
    cout << "too much muscle" << endl;
```

This looks like a test to see if the string "brawn" has a positive count, but beware! Because of the way operator[]() is defined for maps, this statement inserts a new entry, "brawn", if it doesn't already exist in the container. Of course, this works to your advantage in your loop. When elements are inserted in this way, the value part is initialized with the default constructor. For an integer value, this means that value is initialized by the expression int(). As with all initializers for built-in types, int() returns the default value for type int, which is zero. So any new keys inserted in this way start life with a count of zero.

If you want to check for the existence of a key, you can use the count() function:

```
if (words.count("brawn"))
   cout << "too much brawn" << endl;
```

The expression words.count() returns 1 if the key "brawn" is present, and 0 otherwise. Hence, this expression determines whether you have too much brawn *without* the side effect of creating a new entry in the map if it didn't already exist.

Once you have the collocation filled out in the for loop, displaying it involves a simple loop using map iterators.

```
for(WordIter iter = words.begin() ; iter != words.end() ; ++iter)
   cout << std::setw(6) << iter->second << " " << iter->first << endl;
```

Using a Multimap

A **multimap container** is a map that allows entries with duplicate keys. In all other respects, it's the same as a map container and has a similar set of operations. The potential for duplicate keys means that the subscript operator can't be used with a multimap. To add elements to a multimap, you can use the insert() member function. This requires an argument that is a pair<Key, T> object that is appropriate for the container instance.

Of course, once you have duplicate keys, you have the problem of determining which elements correspond to a given key. The find() function member of a multimap returns an iterator that corresponds to the first element with a given key. The upper_bound() function member returns an iterator to the first member with a key that is greater than the key passed as the argument. Therefore, you can use these functions in combination to define the semi-open interval that contains all the elements with a given key. Here's an example:

```
iter1 = mymultimap.find(aKey);
iter2 = mymultimap.upper_bound(aKey);
while(iter1 != iter2)                    // List objects for aKey
   std::cout << *iter1++ << std::endl;
```

You can try getting the collocation from the previous example in descending sequence of the number of occurrences of a word by using a multimap. This will also provide an opportunity for you to extract a key from an iterator. Because it involves specifying the third template parameter for the multimap as a function object type to obtain a different ordering of the elements within the multimap, you'd better get a rough idea of how function objects work first.

Understanding Function Objects

A **function object** is an object of a type that overloads the function call operator, (). The sole purpose of a function object is to encapsulate a function so that is can be passed to another function as an argument, and do this more efficiently than it could using a function pointer. This is particularly important for functions that are going to be called very frequently, such as functions that perform comparisons.

A typical class template that defines function object types looks something like this:

```
template<class T>
struct less : public binary_function <T, T, bool> {
  bool operator() ( const T& left, const T& right) const {
    return left<right;
  }
}
```

This happens to be the template that is used to define the default value for the third map and multimap template parameter as less<Key> where Key is the type for keys. The function call operator looks a little weird because the function name is operator() because the operator is (). The result is that the function is of the form operator() (). The base class for the less type, binary_function, simply defines some types using typedefs that can be used to refer to the argument types and return type for a binary function. These types are inherited in any instance of the less template.

The overloaded function call operator function that appears in the less<> class template obviously defines a less-than comparison operation for objects of type T, as long as type T supports the < operator. Because the less<> template overloads the function call operator, objects of type less<T> can be used directly to perform comparisons. The template can be used to instantiate an object like this:

```
less<Box> compare_boxes;   // Function object for comparing Box objects
```

To compare Box objects, you can now write the following:

```
if(compare_boxes(box1, box2))
  std::cout << "box1 is less than box2";
```

Because the compare_boxes object contains an overloaded function call operator, you can use the object just as though it was a function. The expression compare_boxes(box1, box2) is equivalent to compare_boxes.operator()(box1, box2). Using this operation is much faster than using a function pointer because no dereferencing is necessary here. This is a regular call of a function member of an object. The function object concept can be used for any operation, not just comparisons.

The STL defines a large number of standard function object types in the <functional> header. These include function object types in the categories in Table 20-7.

Table 20-7. Categories of Function Objects

Category	Function Objects
arithmetic operations	`plus<T>`, `minus<T>`, `multiplies<T>`, `divides<T>`, `modulus<T>`, `negates<T>`
comparisons	`equal_to<T>`, `not_equal_to<T>`, `greater<T>`, `less<T>`, `greater_equal<T>`, `less_equal<T>`
logical operations	`logical_and<T>`, `logical_or<T>`, `logical_not<T>`

Many other function object types are defined in this header and you should find details of these in your compiler documentation.

The STL uses function objects very widely in the algorithms and in the associative containers. It should be apparent that if you don't like the ordering you get in a map container due to the default function object type `less<T>`, you can change it by specifying a suitable value for the third map template parameter. Let's try this.

....

Try It Out: Inverting the Collocation with a multimap Container

You can extend Program 20.12 to use the `multimap` container like this:

```cpp
// Program 20.13 An inverted word collocation   File: prog20_13.cpp
#include <iostream>
#include <iomanip>
#include <string>
#include <sstream>
#include <map>
using std::cout;
using std::endl;
using std::string;
const string twister =
  "How much wood would a woodchuck chuck if a woodchuck "
  "could chuck wood?  A woodchuck would chuck as much wood "
  "as a woodchuck could chuck if a woodchuck could chuck wood.";

int main() {
  typedef std::map<string, int> Collocation;     // Type for our map
  typedef Collocation::const_iterator WordIter;  // Iterator type for our map

  Collocation words;              // Map to store words and word counts

  std::istringstream text(twister);          // Text string as a stream
  std::istream_iterator<string> begin(text); // Stream iterator
  std::istream_iterator<string> end;         // End stream iterator

  for( ; begin != end ; ++begin)    // Iterate over the words in the stream
    words[*begin]++;                // Store and increment word count
```

(Continued)

```
typedef std::multimap<int,string, std::greater<int> > WordRank;
typedef WordRank::const_iterator RankIter;

WordRank rank;

for(WordIter iter = words.begin() ; iter != words.end() ; ++iter)
  rank.insert(std::make_pair(iter->second,iter->first));

for(RankIter iter = rank.begin() ; iter != rank.end() ; ++iter)
  cout << std::setw(6) << iter->first << " " << iter->second << endl;

  return 0;
}
```

This program produces the following output:

```
     5 chuck
     5 woodchuck
     4 a
     3 could
     2 as
     2 if
     2 much
     2 wood
     2 would
     1 A
     1 How
     1 wood.
     1 wood?
```

HOW IT WORKS

You still assemble the initial collocation in a map container. You need to do this because the unique key requirement of a map ensures that you only have one entry for each lexeme string in the text.

Once you've created the collocation in your words map, you have two more typedefs:

```
typedef std::multimap<int,string, std::greater<int> > WordRank;
typedef WordRank::const_iterator RankIter;
```

The first statement defines a multimap type. Note that you've reversed the order of the template parameter arguments that appeared in the map template instantiation. Here the keys are of type int and the objects are of type string. You also specify your own comparison criteria in the third template argument.

greater<> is one of the standard STL function object types that are defined in the <functional> header, and this header is automatically included into the

`<map>` header. By using greater`<int>`, rather than the default less`<int>`, you'll see that your rankings in the multimap will be in descending order rather than ascending. Of course, you could have iterated the WordRank table in reverse order just by using rbegin() and rend(), but you've already seen these in action elsewhere.

The second typedef defines a convenience type for iterators in your multimap.

After creating the multimap instance, rank, you insert elements into it using the insert() function:

```
for(WordIter iter = words.begin() ; iter != words.end() ; ++iter)
  rank.insert(std::make_pair(iter->second,iter->first));
```

When you use the map container to assemble the collocation, you're able to insert elements using operator[](). You can't do that here because multimap doesn't even *have* an operator[](). This is because the subscript operator doesn't make sense in the context of a multimap container because the keys may be duplicated. The insert() function requires the argument to be an object of the element type, combining both the key and the object. In your case, this is an object of type pair`<int, string>`, and you create this from the element iterator for the map by calling the make_pair() function. This is a convenience function for creating pair`<>` objects that is defined in the`<utility>` header. This header also defines the pair`<>` template that defines the type for map elements and will be automatically included by the map header. The make_pair() function returns a pair`<>` object that it creates using the first argument as a key and the second argument as the associated object. Obviously the type parameters for the pair`<>` template correspond to the types of arguments that you pass to the make_pair() function. You extract these from the element that you've extracted from the map by using the iterator to select the second and first members of the pair`<>` object.

In your program, you could replace the make_pair() call with the following statement:

```
for(WordIter iter = words.begin() ; iter != words.end() ; ++iter)
  rank.insert(std::pair<int, string>(iter->second, iter->first));
```

Here, you're using a constructor from an instance of the pair`<>` template. I'll leave it up to you to decide whether you prefer this approach over using the make_pair() function.

Take a closer look at the statements inside the two for loops:

```
for(WordIter iter = words.begin() ; iter != words.end() ; ++iter)
  rank.insert(std::make_pair(iter->second,iter->first));
```

```
for(RankIter iter = rank.begin() ; iter != rank.end() ; ++iter)
  cout << std::setw(6) << iter->first << " " << iter->second << endl;
```

(Continued)

The first involves the Collocation iterator and the second involves the WordRank iterator. Remember that the WordRank map is a *reversal* of the Collocation with the key and object types switched, so you have a very nasty and dangerous state of affairs here. In the first line, iter->first is the lexeme, but in the second line, iter->second is the lexeme, so there is plenty of scope for confusion. It seems easy enough to keep the two straight in this example, but in a big program with many interrelated maps, first and second can become tiresome in a big hurry. In such a case, you probably want to add a few careful comments to your code to indicate exactly what's going on and use different names for the iterators involved to make it clear that they aren't the same.

Performance and Specialization

The library of numerical algorithms includes functions that perform relatively trivial tasks that you could code very easily for yourself, so you should explore the reasoning behind why they are there at all. At the beginning of this chapter, when you first encountered iterators and algorithms, you saw many examples of how the function average() might be written. Here is a representative implementation of average(), using a pointer interface, which is simple and efficient:

```
// Simple average function written without using any STL algorithms
double average(float* first, float* last) {
  double sum = 0.0;
  for ( ; first != last ; ++first)
    sum += *first;
  return sum/(last-first);
}
```

Alternatively, you can use the built-in STL template algorithm accumulate():

```
// An average function based on the STL accumulate algorithm
template <typename RndIter>
double average(RndIter first, RndIter last) {
  return std::accumulate(first, last, 0)/(last-first);
}
```

As you've seen, the accumulate() function is an algorithm defined in the <numeric> header. Here it just computes the sum of all the elements in the range first to last. The code here is very simple, but what do you really gain by digging up a library function to replace three simple lines of code?

To answer this, let's take a look at something that you might find in an aggressive implementation of the STL:

```
// Possible specialization of template accumulate<> for float* iterators
#include <numeric>
```

```
template<> float std::accumulate(float* first, float* last, float init) {
  double s0 = 0.0;
  double s1 = 0.0;
  double s2 = 0.0
  double s3 = 0.0;
  int burst_blocks = (last - first) / 4;
  float* burst = first + 4 * burst_blocks;

  for( ; first < burst ; first+=4) {
    s0 += first[0];
    s1 += first[1];
    s2 += first[2];
    s3 += first[3];
  }

  for( ; burst<last ; ++burst) {
    s0 += *burst;          // Capture up to three tail elements
  }

  return init + (s0 + s1 + s2 + s3);
}
```

This is an example of template specialization. This particular specialization is targeted at summing a sequence of floating-point values that are referenced through pointers. It looks much more complicated than your simple loop, yet it computes the same result:

```
template<> float accumulate<float*>(float* first, float* last, float init)
```

The key to this specialization and the reason for including it at all is the block of four statements:

```
    s0 += first[0];
    s1 += first[1];
    s2 += first[2];
    s3 += first[3];
```

The idea of this is to create more parallelism in the computation. Instead of directing all the sums into a single variable, which can become a bottleneck, this version keeps four separate subtotals going in parallel. A fast processor with pipelining and multiple floating-point arithmetic units might have all four of these additions going at the same time.

How does this specialization perform compared to the simple loop? Well, that depends on your compiler, your implementation of the STL, the size of your vectors, and the capability of your processor. The specialization might not be any faster, but it could be up to four times as fast. Of course, if the computation involved takes a few milliseconds, then the potential advantages are likely to be irrelevant. However, if a lot of data is involved and the execution time is minutes or hours, then the potential savings will be well worth having.

It is interesting to note that the specialization also offers greater precision. When you first encountered the floating-point data type, in Chapter 2, you observed that summing sequences of floating-point values is an inherently risky operation. If you're unlucky, the result can have very poor accuracy due to rounding errors accumulated during the summation. This specialization uses the more precise double type for internal calculations, so it is also more accurate than the simple loop. A really good specialization—one that is more sophisticated than this example—can employ techniques to eliminate almost all of the rounding errors and still maintain high performance. It's very difficult to write such code yourself.

Even the simplest algorithms can be written in surprising and clever ways. Implementations of the STL are always improving. If performance is important, use the STL algorithms whenever the opportunity arises. They're likely to be more sophisticated than anything you might write yourself.

Summary

This has been a relatively short stroll through new territory; I've pointed out the interesting sights as we went. I've barely scratched the surface of the potential for the STL here, but you should have enough of an idea to be capable of conducting and interested in a bit of exploration on your own.

Some of the fundamental points you've investigated are the following:

- The STL provides functionality through three broad classifications of templates: containers, iterators, and algorithms.

- Containers provide various ways of storing and organizing objects of an arbitrary type, providing that the types of objects that are to be stored meet the basic requirement for an element.

- Iterators are objects that can behave like pointers. Iterators are examples of smart pointers.

- Iterators are used to access objects in a container or to retrieve objects from a stream.

- Iterators are used in pairs to define a set of objects in a semi-open interval within a sequence. The first object is included in the interval, and the last object isn't.

- Algorithms are generalized standard functions that can be used with sets of objects that are specified by iterators.

- The algorithms are independent of the containers but can be applied to objects in virtually any container through iterators.

Exercises

The following exercises enable you to try out what you've learned in this chapter. If you get stuck, look back over the chapter for help. If you're still stuck after that, you can download the solutions from the Apress website (http://www.apress.com/book/ download.html), but that really should be a last resort.

Exercise 20-1. Write a program that uses a vector to store an arbitrary number of cities read from the keyboard as string objects and then lists them.

Exercise 20-2. Add code to the previous example to use the sort() algorithm to sort the cities in ascending order before listing them.

Exercise 20-3. Write a program to read an arbitrary number of names and associated telephone numbers from the keyboard (in the form "Laurel, Stan" 5431234, for example), and store them in a map container so that given a name, the number can be retrieved. The program should allow an arbitrary number of random retrievals from the map after a series of names and numbers has been entered.

Exercise 20-4. Using your code from the previous exercise, use an iterator to list the contents of the map.

Exercise 20-5. Change your solution to Exercise 20-4 to use a multimap container instead of a map, and arrange for all numbers for a given name to be listed in response to a query.

APPENDIX A

ASCII Codes

THE FIRST 32 AMERICAN STANDARD CODE for Information Interchange (ASCII) characters in Table A-1 provide control functions. Many of these haven't been referenced in this book but are included here for completeness. In Table A-1, only the first 128 characters have been included. The remaining 128 characters include further special symbols and letters for national character sets.

Table A-1. The First 128 ASCII Characters

Decimal	Hexadecimal	Character	Control
000	00	null	NUL
001	01	☺	SOH
002	02	●	STX
003	03	♥	ETX
004	04	♦	EOT
005	05	♣	ENQ
006	06	♠	ACK
007	07	•	BEL (Audible bell)
008	08		Backspace
009	09		HT
010	0A		LF (Line feed)
011	0B		VT (Vertical tab)
012	0C		FF (Form feed)
013	0D		CR (Carriage return)
014	0E		SO
015	0F		SI
016	10		DLE
017	11		DC1
018	12		DC2
019	13		DC3
020	14		DC4
021	15		NAK
022	16		SYN
023	17		ETB
024	18		CAN
025	19		EM

(Continued)

Table A-1. The First 128 ASCII Characters (Continued)

Decimal	Hexadecimal	Character	Control
026	1A	→	SUB
027	1B	←	ESC (Escape)
028	1C	∟	FS
029	1D		GS
030	1E		RS
031	1F		US
032	20		space
033	21	!	
034	22	"	
035	23	#	
036	24	$	
037	25	%	
038	26	&	
039	27	'	
040	28	(	
041	29	)	
042	2A•		
043	2B	+	
044	2C	,	
045	2D	-	
046	2E	.	
047	2F	/	
048	30	0	
049	31	1	
050	32	2	
051	33	3	
052	34	4	
053	35	5	
054	36	6	
055	37	7	
056	38	8	
057	39	9	
058	3A	:	
059	3B	;	
060	3C	<	
061	3D	=	
062	3E	>	
063	3F	?	

(Continued)

Table A-1. The First 128 ASCII Characters (Continued)

Decimal	Hexadecimal	Character	Control
064	40	@	
065	41	A	
066	42	B	
067	43	C	
068	44	D	
069	45	E	
070	46	F	
071	47	G	
072	48	H	
073	49	I	
074	4A	J	
075	4B	K	
076	4C	L	
077	4D	M	
078	4E	N	
079	4F	O	
080	50	P	
081	51	Q	
082	52	R	
083	53	S	
084	54	T	
085	55	U	
086	56	V	
087	57	W	
088	58	X	
089	59	Y	
090	5A	Z	
091	5B	[	
092	5C	\	
093	5D	]	
094	5E	^	
095	5F	_	
096	60	'	
097	61	a	
098	62	b	
099	63	c	
100	64	d	
101	65	e	

(Continued)

Table A-1. The First 128 ASCII Characters (Continued)

Decimal	Hexadecimal	Character	Control
102	66	f	
103	67	g	
104	68	h	
105	69	i	
106	6A	j	
107	6B	k	
108	6C	l	
109	6D	m	
110	6E	n	
111	6F	o	
112	70	p	
113	71	q	
114	72	r	
115	73	s	
116	74	t	
117	75	u	
118	76	v	
119	77	w	
120	78	x	
121	79	y	
122	7A	z	
123	7B	{	
124	7C			
125	7D	}	
126	7E	~	
127	7F	DEL (delete)	

APPENDIX B

C++ Keywords

KEYWORDS ARE WORDS that have been assigned special significance within the C++ language, so you must not use them as names within your programs. The following keywords are defined:

asm	false	sizeof
auto	float	static
bool	for	static_cast
break	friend	struct
case	goto	switch
catch	if	template
char	inline	this
class	int	throw
const	long	true
const_cast	mutable	try
continue	namespace	typedef
default	new	typeid
delete	operator	typename
do	private	union
double	protected	unsigned
dynamic_cast	public	using
else	register	virtual
enum	reinterpret_cast	void
explicit	return	volatile
export	short	wchar_t
extern	signed	while

You'll also encounter words called digraphs that are reserved for use as alternatives to the bitwise and logical operators in C++, so you must not use these for other purposes. These reserved words are as follows:

and	compl	or_eq
and_eq	not	xor
bitand	not_eq	xor_eq
bitor	or	

APPENDIX C

Standard Library Headers

ALL THE HEADERS for the C++ standard library have names without an extension. The contents of the C++ standard library are defined in a total of 50 standard header files, 18 of which provide Standard C library facilities. Standard header names that are of the form <*cname*> (with the exception of <complex>) have essentially the same contents as header files of the form *name*.h that are included with ISO-standard C but have been adapted in some instances to accommodate the more extensive language capability in C++. Within the headers of the form <*cname*>, names that correspond to macros are defined at global scope and all other names are declared within the std namespace. You can also use the Standard C library header file names of the form *name*.h in a C++ program because they're available within Standard C++ for compatibility with Standard C. In this case, the contents are the equivalent of the corresponding <*cname*> header but with all the names available at global scope.

The contents of the C++ standard library can be subdivided into these ten categories:

- Language Support

- Input/Output

- Diagnostics

- General Utilities

- Strings

- Containers

- Iterator Support

- Algorithms

- Numerical Operations

- Localization

Each of these categories spans a substantial range of functionality with the necessary definitions and declaration spread over several header files in some instances.

Language Support

The headers that relate to standard library support for the language capability are shown in Table C-1.

Table C-1. Headers Related to Standard Library Support for the Language

Header	Description
`<cstddef>`	Defines the macros NULL and offsetof, and additional standard types size_t and ptrdiff_t. Deviations from the corresponding Standard C header file are that NULL is an implementation-defined C++ null pointer constant and the macro offsetof accepts structure or union type arguments as long as they have no non-static members of type pointer-to-member.
`<limits>`	Provides definitions relating to the basic data types. For example, for each numeric data type, it defines the maximum and minimum values that can be represented and the number of binary digits. We use these library facilities in Chapter 3.
`<climits>`	Provides C-style definitions relating to the basic integer data types. The same information is provided in C++ style in `<limits>`.
`<cfloat>`	Provides C-style definitions relating to the basic floating point data types. The same information is provided in C++ style in `<limits>`.
`<cstdlib>`	Provides macros and functions supporting program start-up and termination. This header also declares a number of other functions of a miscellaneous nature such as searching and sorting functions and conversions from string to numeric values, for example. It deviates from the equivalent Standard C header file, stdlib.h, in that it defines abort(void). The abort() function also has additional behavior in that it doesn't call destructors for static or automatic objects and doesn't call functions passed to the atexit() function. It also defines additional behavior for the exit() function in that it destroys static objects, calls functions registered with atexit() in the reverse order of their registration, flushes and closes all open C streams, and returns control to the host environment.
`<new>`	Supports dynamic memory allocation.
`<typeinfo>`	Supports runtime type identification of a variable.
`<exception>`	Supports exception handling—which is a way of handling error conditions that may arise in your program.
`<cstdarg>`	Supports functions that accept a variable number of arguments—that is, functions to which you can transfer a variable number of data items when you call the function. It defines macros va_arg, va_end, and va_start and the va_list type.
`<csetjmp>`	Provides functions for C-style non-local jumps. These aren't usually used in C++ programs.
`<csignal>`	Provides C-style support for interrupt handling.

Input/Output

The headers in Table C-2 provide support for stream input and output.

Table C-2. Headers supporting stream I/O

Header File	Description
<iostream>	Supports input and output for the standard streams, cin, cout, cerr, and clog. It also supports the wide character standard streams, wcin, wcout, wcerr, and wclog.
<iomanip>	Provides manipulators that enable you to modify the state of a stream—to alter the formatting of output, for example.
<ios>	Defines the base classes for iostream.
<istream>	Defines template classes for managing input from an input stream buffer.
<ostream>	Defines template classes for managing input from an output stream buffer.
<sstream>	Supports stream input and output for strings.
<fstream>	Supports file stream input and output.
<iosfwd>	Provides for forward declarations for input and output objects.
<streambuf>	Supports buffering of stream input and output.
<cstdio>	Supports C-style input and output for standard streams.
<cwchar>	Supports C-style input and output of wide characters.

Diagnostics

The C++ diagnostics capability is defined in the three headers described in Table C-3.

Table C-3. Diagnostic Headers

Header File	Description
<stdexcept>	Defines standard exceptions. Exceptions are the way error conditions are handled.
<cassert>	Defines the assert macro that you can use for checking runtime conditions.
<cerrno>	Supports C-style error information.

General Utilities

The group of headers listed in Table C-4 defines utility functions used by other components of the C++ library. You can also use these utility functions in your programs.

Table C-4. Headers Defining Utility Functions

Header File	Description
<utility>	Defines overloaded relational operators to simplify the writing of your own relational operators and the pair type, which is simply a templated type that holds a pair of values. These features are used elsewhere in the library.
<functional>	Defines a number of functional object types and features that support functional objects. A functional object is any object that supports operator() (), the function call operator.
<memory>	Defines the standard memory allocator for containers, functions for managing memory, and the auto_ptr template class.
<ctime>	Supports system clock functions.

Strings

The headers listed in Table C-5 provide the capability to manipulate string objects and C-style strings.

Table C-5. Headers Providing Support for String Manipulation

Header File	Description
<string>	Provides support and definitions for string types, including string for narrow character strings (i.e., strings composed of char) and wstring for wide character strings (i.e., strings composed of wchar_t).
<cctype>	Provides classification functions for narrow characters.
<cwctype>	Provides classification function for wide characters.
<cstring>	Provides functions for manipulating null-terminated byte sequences and blocks of memory. This differs from the corresponding Standard C library header in that several of the original C library functions for C-style string operations are replaced by pairs of functions with const and non-const return values.
<cwchar>	Provides functions for manipulating, performing I/O, and converting wide character sequences. This differs from the corresponding Standard C library header in that several of the original C library functions for wide C-style string operations are replaced by pairs of functions with const and non-const return values.
<cstdlib>	Provides functions for converting narrow character strings to numerics and converting between wide characters and multibyte strings.

Containers

Headers in Table C-6 define templates that you use to create container classes.

Table C-6. Headers Defining Templates for Container Classes

Header File	Description
<vector>	Defines the vector sequence template, which is a resizable array type that is safer and more flexible than plain arrays.
<list>	Defines the list sequence template, which is a linked list for sequences that often have elements inserted and removed from arbitrary positions.
<deque>	Defines the deque sequence template, which supports efficient insertion and removal at each end.
<queue>	Defines sequence adaptors, queue and priority_queue, for queue (*first in, first out*) data structures.
<stack>	Defines a sequence adaptor, stack, for stack (*last in, first out*) data structures.
<map>	A map is an associative container type that allows values to be searched by a key value where the key values are unique and held in ascending order. A multimap is similar to a map, except that keys need not be unique.
<set>	A set is an associative container type for holding unique values in ascending order. A multiset is similar to a set, except that the values need not be unique.
<bitset>	Defines the bitset template for fixed-length sequences of bits, which can be treated as a packed fixed-length array of bool.

Iterator Support

Only one header file supports the definition of iterators, as shown in Table C-7.

Table C-7. Header for Iterator Support

Header File	Description
<iterator>	Provides definitions and support for iterators.

General Purpose Algorithms

Table C-8 lists the two header files for algorithms.

Table C-8. Header Files for Algorithms

Header File	Description
`<algorithm>`	Provides a range of algorithm-based functions including **permuting**, sorting, merging, and searching.
`<cstdlib>`	Declares C standard library functions `bsearch()` and `qsort()` for searching and sorting.
`<ciso646>`	Allows you to use and instead of &&, and so on, in your code.

Numerical Operations

This group includes capability for operations with complex numbers as well as mathematical functions. Table C-9 lists these five header files.

Table C-9. Header Files for Numerical Operations

Header File	Description
`<complex>`	Supports the definition of, and operations on complex numbers.
`<valarray>`	Supports operations on numerical vectors.
`<numeric>`	Defines a set of general mathematical operations on sequences of numbers, such as `accumulate` and `inner_product`.
`<cmath>`	Is the C math library with additional overloads to support C++ conventions.
`<cstdlib>`	Provides functions for taking the absolute value of an integer and performing remainder division on integers.

Localization

Localization provides facilities for dealing with things that vary regionally, such as currency symbols, date representation, and sort sequences. The two header files that relate to this are listed in Table C-10.

Table C-10. Header Files for Localization

Header File	Description
`<locale>`	Provides for localization including character classification, sort sequences, and monetary and date representation.
`<clocale>`	Provides C-style support for localization.

APPENDIX D

Operator Precedence and Associativity

THE SEQUENCE IN WHICH different operators in an expression are executed is largely determined by the **precedence** of the operators, although for some expressions, the sequence of execution is undefined. The ISO/ANSI standard for C++ doesn't define operator precedence explicitly, but it can be deduced from the syntax rules. Because operator precedence is an easy way for you to work out the sequence of execution for most expressions, the precedence of each operator is shown in Table D-1. Operators with a higher precedence are executed before operators with a lower precedence. In this table, operators are grouped in descending order of precedence, so those with the highest precedence are at the top. Operators within the same group in the table are of equal precedence.

Table D-1. Operator Precedence

Group	Description	Operator
1	scope resolution	`::`
2	direct member selection	`.`
	indirect member selection	`->`
	subscript	`[]`
	function call	`()`
	postfix increment	`++`
	postfix decrement	
3	unary plus	`+`
	unary minus	`-`
	prefix increment	`++`
	prefix decrement	
	logical negation—not	`!`
	bitwise complement	`~`
	address-of	`&`
	dereference	`*`
	explicit cast (old style)	`(type)`
	size of object or type	`sizeof`
	allocate memory	`new`
	deallocate memory	`delete`

(Continued)

Table D-1. Operator Precedence (Continued)

Group	Description	Operator
3	compile-time checked cast	static_cast
	run-time checked cast	dynamic_cast
	cast away const	const_cast
	unchecked cast	reinterpret_cast
	type identification	typeid
4	direct pointer-to-member selection	.*
	indirect pointer-to-member selection	->*
5	multiply	*
	divide	/
	modulus	%
6	binary addition	+
	binary subtraction	-
7	shift left	<<
	shift right	>>
8	less than	<
	less than or equal to	<=
	greater than	>
	greater than or equal to	>=
9	equal to	==
	not equal to	!=
10	bitwise AND	&
11	bitwise exclusive OR	^
12	bitwise OR	|
13	logical AND	&&
14	logical OR	||
15	assignment	=
	apply operator and then assign	*= /= %= += -= &= ^= |= <<= >>=
16	conditional operator	?:
17	throw exception	throw
18	comma	,

The associativity of an operator determines how it groups with its operands in an expression. All unary operators and all assignment operators are right associative. All other operators are left associative.

The right associativity of the assignment operator means that a statement such as this:

```
x = y = z = t;
```

is evaluated as though it were written as follows:

```
x = ( y = ( z = t));
```

Thus the assignment z = t is done first. The value of that assignment expression, which will be the same as the value of t, is assigned to y, and the value of that is assigned to x.

The left associativity of the binary addition operator implies that a statement such as this:

```
result = x + y + z + t;
```

is evaluated as though it were written as follows:

```
result = ((x + y) + z) + t;
```

Thus x and y are added, then that result is added to z, then that result is added to t.

Note that precedence and associativity doesn't fully determine the order of evaluation in an expression. Where it is not determined, the order depends on your compiler. For example, in the expression (x*y)-(z*t), the order in which the parenthesized expressions will be evaluated is not specified and may vary from one compiler to another. Therefore it is important that you don't write expressions where the result depends on the order of execution of parenthesized expressions.

Understanding Binary and Hexadecimal Numbers

Your computer stores numbers in binary form and operates on them using binary arithmetic. You use hexadecimal number representation as a convenient and compact way of representing binary values in your program code, so an understanding of both binary and hexadecimal numbers is important to a full understanding of C++.

Binary Numbers

First, let's consider exactly what you intend when you write a common, everyday decimal number, such as 324, or 911. Obviously, what you mean is "three hundred and twenty-four," or "nine hundred and eleven." Put more precisely, you mean the following:

324 is $3 \times 10^2 + 2 \times 10^1 + 4 \times 10^0$, which is $3 \times 10 \times 10 + 2 \times 10 + 4$

911 is $9 \times 10^2 + 1 \times 10^1 + 1 \times 10^0$, which is $9 \times 10 \times 10 + 1 \times 10 + 1$

You call it decimal notation because it is built around powers of ten (derived from the Latin *decimalis* meaning "of tithes," which was a tax of 10 percent—ah, those were the days. . .).

Representing numbers in this way is very handy for people with ten fingers and/or ten toes, or indeed ten of any kind of appendage. However, your PC is rather less handy, being built mainly of switches that are either on or off. It's OK for counting up to two, but not spectacular at counting to ten. I'm sure you're aware that this is the primary reason your computer represents numbers using base 2, rather than base 10. Representing numbers using base 2 is called the binary system of counting. With numbers expressed using base 10, digits can be from 0 to 9 inclusive, whereas with binary numbers digits can only be 0 or 1, which is ideal when you only have on/off switches to represent them. In an exact analogy to your system of counting in base 10, the binary number 1101, for example, breaks down like this:

$1 \times 2^3 + 1 \times 2^2 + 0 \times 2^1 + 1 \times 2^0$, which is $1 \times 2 \times 2 \times 2 + 1 \times 2 \times 2 + 0 \times 2 + 1$

This amounts to 13 in the decimal system. In Table E-1, you can see the decimal equivalents of all the possible numbers you can represent using 8 binary digits (a **binary digit** is more commonly known as a **bit**).

Table E-1. Decimal Equivalents for Binary Values

Binary	Decimal
0000 0000	0
0000 0001	1
0000 0010	2
...	...
0001 0000	16
0001 0001	17
...	...
0111 1100	124
0111 1101	125
0111 1110	126
0111 1111	127
1000 0000	128
1000 0001	129
1000 0010	130
...	...
1001 0000	144
1001 0001	145
...	...
1111 1100	252
1111 1101	253
1111 1110	254
1111 1111	255

Notice that using the first 7 bits, you can represent numbers from 0 to 127, which is a total of 2^7 numbers, and that when you use all 8 bits, you get 256, or 2^8 numbers. In general, if you have n bits, you can represent 2^n integers, with values from 0 to 2^n-1.

Adding binary numbers inside your computer is a piece of cake, because the "carry" from adding corresponding digits can only be 0 or 1, and very simple circuitry can handle the process. Figure E-1 shows how the addition of two 8-bit binary values would work.

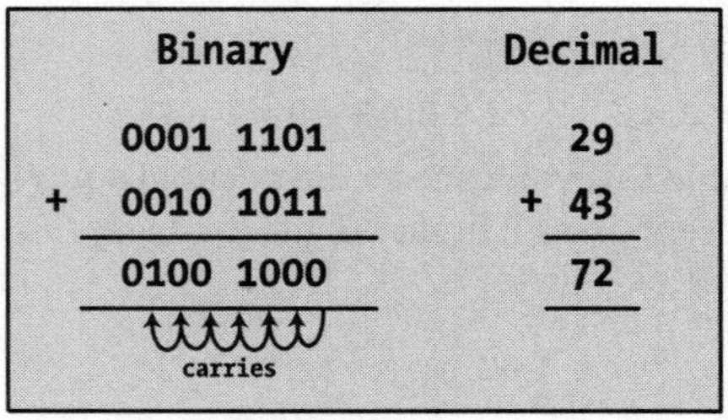

Figure E-1. Adding binary values

Hexadecimal Numbers

When you start dealing with larger binary numbers, a small problem arises. Look at this one:

1111 0101 1011 1001 1110 0001

Here, binary notation starts to be more than a little cumbersome for practical use, particularly when you consider that if you work out what this is in decimal, it's only 16,103,905—a miserable 8 decimal digits. You can sit more angels on a pinhead than that! Clearly, you need a more economical way of writing this, but decimal is not always appropriate. Sometimes (as you can see in Chapter 3), you might need to be able to specify that the 10th and 24th bits from the right are set to 1, but without the overhead of writing out all the bits in binary notation. To figure out the decimal integer required to do this sort of thing is hard work and there's a good chance you'll get it wrong anyway. A much easier solution is to use hexadecimal notation, where the numbers are represented using base 16.

Arithmetic to base 16 is a much more convenient option, and it fits rather well with binary. Each hexadecimal digit can have values from 0 to 15 (the digits from 10 to 15 are represented by letters A to F, as shown in the Table E-2), and values from 0 to 15 correspond nicely with the range of values that four binary digits can represent.

Table E-2. Hexadecimal Digits As Binary Values

Hexadecimal	Decimal	Binary
0	0	0000
1	1	0001
2	2	0010
3	3	0011
4	4	0100
5	5	0101
6	6	0110
7	7	0111
8	8	1000
9	9	1001
A	10	1010
B	11	1011
C	12	1100
D	13	1101
E	14	1110
F	15	1111

Because a hexadecimal digit corresponds to four binary digits, you can represent your large binary number as a hexadecimal number simply by taking groups of four binary digits, starting from the right, and writing the equivalent hexadecimal digit for each group. Look at the following binary number:

1111 0101 1011 1001 1110 0001

If you take each group of four bits in turn and replace it with the corresponding hexadecimal digit from the table, this number expressed in hexadecimal notation will come out as follows:

F 5 B 9 E 1

Now you have six hexadecimal digits that correspond to the six groups of four binary digits. Just to prove that it all works out with no cheating, you can convert this number directly from hexadecimal to decimal by again using the analogy with the meaning of a decimal number.

The value of this hexadecimal number therefore works out as follows. F5B9E1 as a decimal value is given by

$$15 \times 16^5 + 5 \times 16^4 + 11 \times 16^3 + 9 \times 16^2 + 14 \times 16^1 + 1 \times 16^0$$

which turns out to be

15,728,640 + 327,680 + 45,056 + 2,304 + 224 + 1

Thankfully, this adds up to the same number you got when you converted the equivalent binary number to a decimal value—16,103,905.

Negative Binary Numbers

You also need to understand another aspect of binary arithmetic: negative numbers. So far, you've assumed that everything is positive—the optimist's view, if you will—and so your glass is still half full. But you can't avoid the negative side of life—the pessimist's perspective that your glass is already half empty. How can a negative number be represented inside a computer? Well, you only have binary digits at your disposal, so the solution has to be to use one of those to indicate whether the number is negative or positive.

For numbers that you want to allow to have negative values (referred to as **signed numbers**), you must first decide on a fixed length (in other words, the number of binary digits) and then designate the leftmost binary digit as a **sign bit**. You have to fix the length in order to avoid any confusion about which bit is the sign bit.

Because your computer's memory consists of 8-bit bytes, your binary numbers are going to be stored in some multiple (usually a power of two) of 8 bits. Thus you can have some numbers with 8 bits, some with 16 bits, and some with 32 bits (or whatever), and as long as you know what the length is in each case, you can find the sign bit—it's just the leftmost bit. If the sign bit is 0, the number is positive, and if it is 1, the number is negative.

This seems to solve your problem, and in some computers it actually does. Each number consists of a sign bit that is zero for positive values and 1 for negative, plus a given number of bits that specify the absolute value of the number—unsigned, in other words. Changing +6 to –6 just involves flipping the sign bit from 0 to 1. Unfortunately, this representation carries a lot of overhead with it in terms of the complexity of the circuits you need to perform arithmetic with this number representation. For this reason, most computers take a different approach.

Ideally, when two integers are added, you don't want the computer to be messing about checking whether either or both of the numbers are negative. You just want to use simple "add" circuitry regardless of the signs of the operands. The add operation combines corresponding binary digits to produce the appropriate bit as a result—with a 1 carried over to the next digit along where this is necessary. If you add –8 in binary to +12, you'd really like to get the answer +4 using the same circuitry that would apply if you were adding +3 and +8.

If you try this with your simplistic solution, which just involves setting the sign bit of the positive value to 1 to make it negative, and then perform the arithmetic with conventional carries, you'll find that it doesn't quite work:

12 in binary is 0000 1100.

You assume –8 in binary is 1000 1000.

If you now add these together, you get 1001 0100.

This seems to be –20, which is not what you wanted at all. It's definitely not +4, which you know is 0000 0100. "Ah," I hear you say, "I can't treat a sign just like another digit." But that is just what you *do* want to do.

Let's see how the computer would like us to represent –8—by trying to subtract +12 from +4—because that should give you the right answer:

+4 in binary is 0000 0100.

+12 in binary is 0000 1100.

Subtract the latter from the former, and you get 1111 1000.

For each digit from the fourth from the right onward, you had to "borrow" 1 to do the subtraction, just as you would if you were performing ordinary decimal arithmetic. This result is supposed to be –8, and even though it doesn't look like it, that's exactly what it is. Just try adding it to +12 or +15 in binary, and you'll see that it works!
Of course, if you want to produce –8, you can always do so by subtracting +8 from 0.

What *exactly* did you get when you subtracted 12 from 4, or +8 from 0, for that matter? It turns out that what you have here is called the **two's complement** representation of a negative binary number, and you can produce this from any positive binary number by a simple procedure that you can perform in your head. At this point, I need to ask for a little faith on your part and avoid getting into explanations of *why* it works. I'll just show you how the two's complement form of a negative number can be constructed from a positive binary value, and you can prove to yourself that it does work.

Let's return to the previous example, where you need the two's complement representation of –8. You start with +8 in binary:

0000 1000

Now "flip" each binary digit, changing zeros to ones, and vice versa:

1111 0111

This is called the **one's complement** form, and if you add 1 to this, you'll get the two's complement form:

1111 1000

This is exactly the same as the representation of –8 you got by subtracting +12 from +4. Just to make absolutely sure, try the original sum of adding –8 to +12:

+12 in binary is 0000 1100.

Your version of –8 is 1111 1000.

If you add *these* together, you get 0000 0100.

The answer is 4—magic. It works! The "carry" propagates through all the leftmost 1s, setting them back to zero. One fell off the end, but you shouldn't worry about that—it's probably compensating for the one you borrowed off the end in the subtraction sum you did to get –8! In fact, what's happening is that you're making an assumption that the sign bit, 1 or 0, repeats forever to the left. Try a few examples of your own; you'll find it always works, automatically. The really great thing about using two's complement representation of negative numbers is that it makes arithmetic very easy (and fast) for your computer.

Big-Endian and Little-Endian Systems

As we have discussed, generally integers are stored in memory as binary values in a contiguous sequence of bytes, commonly in groups of two, four, or eight bytes. The question of the sequence in which the bytes can be very important; it's one of those things that doesn't matter until it matters—then it really matters!

Let's consider the decimal value 262657 stored as a 4-byte binary value. I chose this value because in binary it happens to be

 0000 0000 0000 0100 0000 0010 0000 0001

so each byte has a pattern of bits that is easily distinguished from the others. If you are using an Intel PC, the number will be stored as follows:

Byte Address:	00	01	02	03
Data bits:	0000 0001	0000 0010	0000 0100	0000 0000

As you can see, the most significant 8 bits of the value—the ones that are all zeros—are stored in the byte with the highest address—in other words, last. The least significant 8 bits are stored in the byte with the lowest address, which is the leftmost byte. This arrangement is described as **little endian**.

If you're using a mainframe computer, a risc workstation, or a Mac machine based on a Motorola processor, the same data is likely to be arranged in memory like this:

Byte Address:	00	01	02	03
Data bits:	0000 0000	0000 0100	0000 0010	0000 0001

Now the bytes are in reverse sequence with the most significant 8 bits stored in the leftmost byte, which is the one with the lowest address. This arrangement is described as **big endian**.

NOTE *Regardless of whether the byte order is big endian or little endian, within each byte, the bits are arranged with the most significant bit on the left and the least significant bit on the right.*

"This is all very interesting," you may say, "but why should it matter?" Most of the time, it doesn't. More often than not you can happily write your C++ program without knowing whether the computer on which the code will execute is big endian or little endian. It *does* matter, however, when you are processing binary data that comes from another machine. Binary data is written to a file or transmitted over a network as a sequence of bytes. It is up to you to interpret it. If the source of the data is a machine with a different endian-ness from the machine on which your code is running, you must reverse the order of the bytes in each binary value. If you don't, you have garbage.

NOTE *For those of you who collect curious background information, the terms big endian and little endian are drawn from* Gulliver's Travels *by Jonathan Swift. The emperor of Lilliput commanded all his subjects to always crack their eggs at the smaller end. This was a consequence of the emperor's son having cut his finger following the traditional approach of cracking his egg at the big end. Ordinary law-abiding Lilliputian subjects who did so were described as Little Endians. The Big Endians were a rebellious group of traditionalists in the Lilliputian kingdom who insisted on continuing to crack their eggs at the big end. Many were put to death as a result.*

Example Project

YOU'VE READ THE BOOK. You've digested the text. Now it's time to apply your newfound knowledge to a small, but perfectly formed project. In this appendix I'll set up the problem, and give some hints on how to solve it.

NOTE *You'll find the model answer source code on the Apress website* (http://www.apress.com).

Outline

The aim of the example project is to create an object-oriented program that keeps track of information about teachers and students in an educational establishment. This information will be held as a series of Teacher and Student records, both of which will contain the common attributes listed in Table F-1.

Table F-1. Common Attributes for Example Project

Attribute	Type	Max. Length	Restrictions/Comments
First Name	Alphabetic	20 chars	
Surname	Alphabetic	20 chars	
Address1	Mixed	30 chars	First line of street address
Address2	Mixed	30 chars	Second line
Address3	Mixed	30 chars	Last line
City	Alphabetic	20 chars	
State	Alphabetic	3 chars	
Zip Code	Numeric	6 chars	
Phone Number	Numeric	8 chars	Must be of the form ###-####

All Student records will have the additional attributes listed in Table F-2.

Table F-2. Additional Attributes for Student Records

Attribute	Type	Max. Length	Restrictions/Comments
Student ID	Mixed	6 chars	
Grade (or GPA)	Number		Must be between 0 and 100

All Teacher records will have the additional attributes listed in Table F-3.

Table F-3. Additional Attributes for Teacher Records

Attribute	Type	Max. Length	Restrictions/Comments
Teaching experience(in years)	Number		Must be positive integer
Salary	Number		Must be positive integer

The program should be menu driven and the user should be allowed to perform the following operations:

- Add records

- Delete records

- Search the records

- Display the records

- Clear all records

- Save the records to a database file

- Retrieve the set of records from a database file

When the program is adding a record, all the attributes of the Student or Teacher record should be properly entered by the user. The street address can consist of up to three lines; if it is less than three lines, you can terminate input by entering a period (.) on a line by itself.

When a user goes to deletes a record, they should be prompted to enter the surname of the Teacher or Student record they wish to delete. Once deleted, a record can't be searched for or displayed.

When a user searches for a record, they should be prompted to enter the surname of the record they wish to find. The program should then display all the attributes of the record containing the desired surname (i.e., if the record refers to a Student, then the GPA and Student ID fields should be displayed). A deleted record can't be searched for.

When displaying records, the user should be given the following options:

- Display all Student records and their attributes.

- Display all Teacher records and their attributes.

- Display all Teacher AND Student records and their attributes.

The program should save records to a plain text file in a suitable format. When the user initiates a save operation, they should be prompted for the name of a file and the program should verify that this file can be created before continuing.

When reading a file, the program should prompt the user for a file name and verify that it can be opened. Records should be read from the file, validated, and added to the current record set.

Improving the Project Specification

Now that I have stated the problem, you should be able to see some potential gray areas in the specification:

- You're searching the data by surname, so you're effectively using the surname field as the search key. You might want to think about how you'd handle duplicate names—for instance, if you have two Smiths in the database, how are you going to handle a search for Smith?

- Just about everyone is going to have an address, but what happens if the person doesn't have a phone?

Developer's Notes

Here are some suggestions on how you might implement the program.

The overall design of this project is based on these simple rules:

- Have the objects take care of themselves.

- Use a container class to organize the objects.

- Use the main() function as a simple "traffic cop." It directs program execution but has no effect on the individual objects, apart from adding and deleting objects in the container.

The Person class is at the heart of the project. It implements the very basic functionality of all objects in the project. It's the base class of the other classes found in this project, namely the Student class and the Teacher class. All objects within this program are of type Teacher or Student, and these derived classes implement only specific functionality according to their type. For example, the Teacher class includes a member variable unique to teachers that denotes the "number of years experience."

Each class performs its own validation. The class member functions are designed to validate user input because, as a rule, objects need to be responsible for the integrity of their own data. If validation was to occur somewhere outside the class, then you're placing objects at the mercy of an external entity and code maintenance becomes very cumbersome, in addition to violating one of the principles of object-oriented (OO) design.

The container you'll use for your Student and Teacher objects is one from the Standard Template Library (STL), namely a deque. In this program you won't stretch its capabilities, because you're only adding, deleting, and searching for objects. The deque container is chosen because it's relatively easy to use, but you can also use a map or a multiset if you wish. You'll use the deque container to store objects of type Person*, because, with polymorphism, you're then able to store both Student and Teacher objects, both of which are derived from the Person class.

The main() function and the other functions contained in the MainProg.cpp file have few responsibilities. First and foremost, main() directs program execution. However, it also validates user selections from the available menu options, and it uses the container class. The main() function contains no object-specific code; instead it directs program execution.

The Person Class

The Person class contains the basic structure of both the Student- and Teacher-derived classes. It is the base class of the Student and Teacher classes, and it's here where most of the code associated with all the classes is found. It is structured to take full advantage of member variable data hiding:

- The member function setup() is declared private because it will be called only from within the constructor.

- The virtual function set_other_info() is also private because it is called from public member functions of the derived classes.

- All the member variables are private, again to take full advantage of data hiding and the security it gives you.

The Student- and Teacher-Derived Classes

The Student and Teacher classes are derived from the Person class. Each of these classes contains member variables and member functions specific to their type. Also, each class implements a unique version of the virtual function set_other_info().

The Container

The container class is created to store pointers to Person class objects in order to take full advantage of polymorphism. Because of this implementation, the container can contain elements of both the Teacher- and Student-derived classes. Maintenance is easy, as there is only one container to worry about. Anytime a record is required within the container; a simple for loop does the trick. The following functions are performed on this container:

- Adding elements

- Deleting elements

- Searching elements

Also, before the program exits, you need to empty the container, as you should always tidy up after yourself.

Saving and Restoring Data

When you exit from the program you'll lose all the data you've entered unless you take steps to save it to disk. Because you don't want to get too complicated, you'll adopt a very simple approach and allow the user to save the records in text form to a standard disk file. Not only is this simple to implement using the <iostream> classes, it also aids debugging because you can see what is being written into the file.

You can make up the record format to suit yourself, but I'd suggest that you make the first line of the file contain some sort of special token so that you can easily verify that you're trying to read a file of the right type.

There are a lot of ways in which this program can be improved, so you can use the program as a basis on which to build and extend its functionality (so that, for example, you could add a Principal class). Above all, remember that if you use C++ in a clean and simple way, code maintenance will be very much easier. Always assume that another developer will be looking over your code and will need to understand how it works—you'll be thankful you did so in the long run!

Index

forums.apress.com

FOR PROFESSIONALS BY PROFESSIONALS™

JOIN THE APRESS FORUMS AND BE PART OF OUR COMMUNITY. You'll find discussions that cover topics of interest to IT professionals, programmers, and enthusiasts just like you. If you post a query to one of our forums, you can expect that some of the best minds in the business—especially Apress authors, who all write with *The Expert's Voice™*—will chime in to help you. Why not aim to become one of our most valuable participants (MVPs) and win cool stuff? Here's a sampling of what you'll find:

DATABASES
Data drives everything.

Share information, exchange ideas, and discuss any database programming or administration issues.

INTERNET TECHNOLOGIES AND NETWORKING
Try living without plumbing (and eventually IPv6).

Talk about networking topics including protocols, design, administration, wireless, wired, storage, backup, certifications, trends, and new technologies.

JAVA
We've come a long way from the old Oak tree.

Hang out and discuss Java in whatever flavor you choose: J2SE, J2EE, J2ME, Jakarta, and so on.

MAC OS X
All about the Zen of OS X.

OS X is both the present and the future for Mac apps. Make suggestions, offer up ideas, or boast about your new hardware.

OPEN SOURCE
Source code is good; understanding (open) source is better.

Discuss open source technologies and related topics such as PHP, MySQL, Linux, Perl, Apache, Python, and more.

PROGRAMMING/BUSINESS
Unfortunately, it is.

Talk about the Apress line of books that cover software methodology, best practices, and how programmers interact with the "suits."

WEB DEVELOPMENT/DESIGN
Ugly doesn't cut it anymore, and CGI is absurd.

Help is in sight for your site. Find design solutions for your projects and get ideas for building an interactive Web site.

SECURITY
Lots of bad guys out there—the good guys need help.

Discuss computer and network security issues here. Just don't let anyone else know the answers!

TECHNOLOGY IN ACTION
Cool things. Fun things.

It's after hours. It's time to play. Whether you're into LEGO® MINDSTORMS™ or turning an old PC into a DVR, this is where technology turns into fun.

WINDOWS
No defenestration here.

Ask questions about all aspects of Windows programming, get help on Microsoft technologies covered in Apress books, or provide feedback on any Apress Windows book.

HOW TO PARTICIPATE:

Go to the Apress Forums site at **http://forums.apress.com/**.
Click the New User link.